CPA
PROBLEMS
and APPROACHES
to SOLUTIONS

Volume I

PROBLEMS AND APPROACHES

CPA PROBLEMS and APPROACHES to SOLUTIONS

Volume I
PROBLEMS AND APPROACHES

FOURTH EDITION

CHARLES T. HORNGREN, CPA
Stanford University

J. ARTHUR LEER, CPA
University of Wisconsin—Milwaukee

PRENTICE-HALL, Inc.   Englewood Cliffs, New Jersey

Library of Congress Cataloging in Publication Data

Horngren, Charles T
  CPA problems and approaches to solutions.

  Bibliography: v. 1, p.
  CONTENTS: v. 1. Problems and approaches.
  v. 2. Solutions.
    1. Accounting—Problems, exercises, etc. I. Leer,
J. Arthur, joint author. II. Title.
HF5661.H623   657   73-18410
ISBN 0-13-187872-7 (v. 1)

10   9   8   7   6   5   4

PRENTICE-HALL INTERNATIONAL, INC., *London*
PRENTICE-HALL OF AUSTRALIA PTY, LTD., *Sydney*
PRENTICE-HALL OF CANADA, LTD., *Toronto*
PRENTICE-HALL OF INDIA PRIVATE LIMITED, *New Delhi*
PRENTICE-HALL OF JAPAN, INC., *Tokyo*

Printed in the United States of America

TO OUR PARENTS

Contents

Section 1

CPA Examination in Accounting Practice

Each topical area I-XV includes a *General Approach,* problems
and a *Specific Approach* for each problem.

I Accounting Fundamentals: Financial Statements; Cash versus
Accrual Basis; Correction of Errors; Incomplete Records;
Financial Ratios

*Estimated time for completion of the problem. All problems and questions are taken
from AICPA examinations. The specific source for each problem is given in Volume II.
    †The page on which the problem appears is given in roman type; the page on which the
Specific Approach appears is given in italics.

XIII Taxation

XIV Miscellaneous Review Problems

XV Review Problems: A Complete Examination in Accounting Practice

The General Approach also contains an itemized listing of the review problems.

Section 2

CPA Examination in Accounting Theory (Theory of Accounts)

QUESTIONS

Section 3

CPA Examination in Auditing

QUESTIONS

Section 4

CPA Examination in Business (Commercial) Law

Preface

CPA Problems and Approaches to Solutions is a complete review of all four sections of the CPA examination. The book contains text and problems on all CPA topics, including income taxes. It is designed to aid candidates in developing approaches to solutions of problems and answers to questions in the CPA examination. The emphasis is on the most productive procedures in the preparation of solutions and on the reasoning underlying them rather than merely on the solutions themselves.

Working with only a problem and its final solution often is not the best available means of preparation. Too frequently, the candidate works in reverse. He scans the solution without conscientiously attempting to analyze or to solve the problem. This results in a haphazard, inadequate review.

Volume I, as explained in the Introduction, tries to span the gap between the awesome problem and the final solution. Evidence in *Information for CPA Candidates*, a booklet prepared by the American Institute of Certified Public Accountants, indicates that candidates often are heavily penalized because of inept approaches to solutions. A unique feature of this book is its emphasis on the approach.

The fourth edition is thoroughly revised. The major change is a pervasive updating of the problem material. The content of the CPA examination gradually changes through the years. A major objective of this edition is to capture the examination's current flavor by keeping abreast of changes in content. At the same time, there is a sprinkling of our favorite older problems—problems that are particularly effective in conveying important basic points. Of the 118 problems, 100 are new and have been taken from the most recent examinations. All the Auditing, Theory, and Business Law questions are new. Sources of all problem material will be found in Volume II.

To simulate actual examination conditions, candidates should always (1) try to solve a problem at one sitting and within the indicated time limits; and (2) work individually. The CPA examination tests individual, not group, performance.

When these volumes are used for CPA Review classes, it is strongly recommended that the instructor control the solutions. For example, each student should be required to turn over his solutions volume to the instructor. As problems are discussed, the solutions may be distributed. In this way, with the answers unavailable until the class meeting, the student is more likely to attempt his own solutions.

A General Approach is offered for Topics I-XIII inclusive. These summaries are intended to provide a brief, convenient, over-all presentation of the major issues and methods of attack in the topical area. Some topics lend themselves easily to summary treatment, whereas others do not. The General Approaches for Business Combinations (Topic XI) and Governmental Accounting (Topic XII) are not so exhaustive as those for Funds Statements (Topic II) and Process Costs (Topic V). In other words, the depth and breadth of the General Approaches vary between the topics because of the desire to keep the scope of the book within manageable limits. The General Approaches do not exclude the necessity for a thorough textbook review of a given topic.

A Specific Approach is offered for almost all problems with the exception of those problems in Topic XV. Specific Approaches have the following advantages:

(1) They raise questions or jog memories on particular points in each problem, and at the same time they do not give away the answers. They offer in a convenient fashion brief explanations of key difficulties in the problems.

(2) For the reasons in (1) above, they aid the candidate in preparing more adequately before class; consequently, class sessions are not bogged down by the instructor's spending undue time on issues which the candidate could have resolved for himself before class. In this way, more problems can be covered in a single session and a more thorough CPA Review is possible.

(3) If Specific Approaches (not Solutions) are available for each problem, candidates are likely to have more incentive for making honest efforts at solutions before class, rather than giving up when a difficult point arises and waiting to discover the best means of attack in the class meeting. The Specific Approaches may be supplemented, altered, or replaced where an instructor has developed his own approach on a particular problem. The format is flexible enough so that an instructor may use the book in a variety of ways to fit the needs of his class.

Sections are devoted to Theory, to Auditing, and to Business Law. These include approaches and questions in Volume I and answers in Volume II.

The topical organization is for convenience in using the book. Many educators, including the authors, feel that a review for the CPA examination should not concentrate upon one subject at a time. Thus, many users of the book may wish to vary assignments so that important topics always reappear as the review progresses. The number of problems under each topic reflects fairly closely the relative frequency of that topic in recent examinations. The Introduction contains a detailed discussion of topical frequency.

We are indebted to the American Institute of Certified Public Accountants for permission to use the AICPA materials that make these volumes possible. The Municipal Finance Officers Association of the United States and Canada has granted permission to reproduce material from its volume, *Governmental Accounting, Auditing, and Financial Reporting,* (1968), the eighteenth publication of the National Committee on Governmental Accounting. We are especially grateful to Professors Paul M. Fischer, University of Wisconsin-Milwaukee, and John Grant Rhode, University of Washington, for their assistance and suggestions. Our thanks extend to the following students for their aid: Robert Bowen, Martin Gregorich, Court Huber, and William Wagner. Our sincere appreciation also goes to Claire Bartels and Cristina Faragher, who typed parts of the manuscript. We also thank Margaret McAbee, Sally Lewis, and the people at Prentice-Hall. We welcome comments from users.

CHARLES T. HORNGREN
J. ARTHUR LEER

CPA
PROBLEMS
and APPROACHES
to SOLUTIONS

Volume I

PROBLEMS AND APPROACHES

Introduction

Nature and Purpose

The purpose of Volume I is to present *approaches* to the solutions of problems and answers to questions on topics most frequently covered in recent CPA examinations. Volume II presents solutions to problems and answers to questions.

The volumes are organized as follows:

Volume I

Section 1–CPA Examination in Accounting Practice
This section is organized by problem topics. Each major topic contains a *General Approach,* actual CPA problems, and a *Specific Approach* for each problem.

General Approach–This is a summary of the nature of the over-all accounting difficulties in each major topical area (for instance, consolidations or process costs).

Specific Approach–There is one for each problem. Each offers suggestions on how to attack the particular problem.

Section 2–CPA Examination in Accounting Theory

Section 3–CPA Examination in Auditing

Section 4–CPA Examination in Business Law (Commercial Law)

Sections 2, 3, and 4 each contain questions organized by topics and a *General Approach.*

1

Volume II

1. Detailed step-by-step solutions to the problems in Volume I, Section 1, are presented in loose-leaf form.
2. Answers to the Theory, Auditing, and Commercial Law questions are presented in loose-leaf form.

There is no painless method of preparing for the CPA examination. CPA problem situations are complex. The candidate can best prepare by dealing with these complex situations. He should solve *actual* examination problems, not condensed or similar problems.

Even when equipped with a technical background, the candidate often faces a dilemma in his review for the Accounting Practice section of the examination. Too often, at this stage, he has collected a group of nonrelated techniques used in specific cases, but he has not formulated any general policies of approach. As a result, when faced with a fairly complex situation, he does not know where or how to begin. Some candidates glance furtively at the solution, if one is available, without even attempting to solve the problem. Others, using the solution as a crutch, half-solve the problem. The danger of these procedures is that the individual lulls himself into thinking that he has prepared adequately for the given problem-topic. *The mere fact that he has to resort to the solution should be adequate warning of his deficiency.*

As a collection of problems, together with suggested approaches to solutions, this book is designed to aid the candidate in learning *how* to proceed in solving the problem. The following procedure is recommended:

1. Read the *General Approach* to obtain a summarized review of the topic at hand.

2. Study the problem until you fully understand the facts, the requirements, and where the most troublesome areas lie.

3. Keeping in mind the requirements of the problem, decide upon a method of attack. Attempt a solution without looking at the *Specific Approach.*

4. If difficulty is encountered, consult the *Specific Approach* for concrete suggestions on how to tackle the given problem.

5. After studying the suggestions, solve the problem as completely as possible. If you are still unable to continue, do not check with the final solution, but obtain additional background by reading and by working less difficult problems in this area. Then make a second attempt.

6. Only when you feel you have a satisfactory solution, consult the final solution in *Volume II.* Naturally, one is interested in knowing how correct his results are, and a step-by-step solution is provided as a basis for comparison.

It is beyond the scope of this book to supply a complete theoretical and technical background on all phases of accounting. The intent is to present problems in those phases considered important for candidates and to suggest techniques for their solutions. Whenever the reader believes that he has encountered an area in which he is deficient, he should locate a source from which he can secure an adequate background before attempting the problem. Recommended sources are indicated for each section of the examination.

General Suggestions

The Uniform CPA Examination is used in all the states and territories of the United States. It is aimed at measuring technical knowledge, skills in the application of such knowledge, and the exercise of good judgment. The Board of Examiners has stated that the examination "is directed to the level of competence required for general practice in a medium-sized community including the audit of a medium-sized organization."

General Preparation

A CPA candidate should carefully study *Information for CPA Candidates,* a valuable booklet published by the American Institute of Certified Public Accountants (hereafter abbreviated as *AICPA* or referred to as *the Institute*). This booklet discusses the general scope and coverage of the examination, offers suggestions as to preparation, and presents many aspects of taking the examination itself. Some highlights of the suggestions in *Information for CPA Candidates* (pp. 14-20) are the following:

1. *Don't delay.* An appropriately educated candidate should take the examination as soon as he is eligible. Although practical experience is likely to help performance on Auditing, it is of little, if any, help on the other sections. The statistics show clearly that candidates who have no experience or less than one year of experience are more likely to pass the entire examination at one sitting than are average candidates.

2. *Prepare for all sections simultaneously.* Candidates should not think that it is more efficient to aim for passing only one or two sections at a sitting. On the contrary, AICPA studies show that the best performance is achieved by candidates who prepare for all sections simultaneously. This is so probably because Auditing, Theory, and Practice are heavily interrelated. Thus, review for Theory helps in Practice and Auditing; review for Practice helps in Theory and Auditing.

3. *Don't prepare halfheartedly.* Candidates should take the examination only with the expectation of passing. Too often, candidates say they are taking the examination for "practice" or "experience." A person who wishes to practice should use the old CPA Examination questions and answers for that purpose.

4. *Have a definite review program.* A candidate should formulate a rigorous plan of study and review.

5. *Solve past CPA questions and problems.* A candidate should use these as his major study materials.

6. *Be aware of alternative terminology and solutions.* In his preparation for

likely accounting topics, the candidate must recognize two special characteristics of a national examination. First, accounting terminology is not uniform. Second, alternative solutions are possible for many accounting problems. As is pointed out on pp. 17-18 of *Information for CPA Candidates:*

> Variations in terminology will inevitably appear in a national examination which is drawn from many sources. Thus, the candidate should be familiar with the variety and interchangeability of many accounting terms. For example, *factory overhead* is usually interchangeable with the following terms: indirect manufacturing costs, manufacturing expenses, factory burden, and manufacturing overhead.
>
> Alternative solutions can arise because (a) there are slight variations in practical accounting procedures or techniques and (b) there are different schools of thought on certain accounting matters. Therefore, the candidate must anticipate problem situations that do not exactly coincide with either the text treatments which he knows or the situations in practice which he has encountered.

The American Institute of Certified Public Accountants takes elaborate steps to insure equitable grading of CPA Examinations. The examiners recognize and give full credit to all alternative solutions that are reasonable. Therefore, the CPA candidate should not be discouraged if, in the course of his review, he finds published CPA solutions that do not precisely agree with the approach he learned in his accounting courses. The Institute finds it impracticable to publish a number of alternative solutions, so it usually confines its "unofficial answers" to one widely accepted approach. These published answers are neither official nor necessarily the only acceptable solutions. Yet many candidates have the mistaken belief that the solutions published by the Institute are *the* only acceptable answers. . . .

In summary, while the candidate does not have to worry about the acceptability of alternate solutions to a given CPA problem, he should be aware of divergencies in accounting practice and terminology. Then he can tailor-make his solutions within bounds of reason and common sense. His terminology should coincide with that given in the problem. He should also know what areas of accounting tend to have alternative treatments. In these areas, especially, he should take particular pains with his answer so that it will be clear to the graders.[1]

Finally—and this cannot be overemphasized even though it may seem like preaching—the candidate should map a strict study program for at least three months prior to the examination. There is plenty of time in each day for preparation. One of the candidate's major challenges is allotting a minimum of, say, two hours daily to productive study. The task is to determine what hours are best suited to study, and then to *study*. Among other things, *study* means writing out complete answers to past CPA questions and problems without peeking at the solutions. The candidate with an adequate intelligence level and

---

[1] "General Preparation for the Examination," in *Information for CPA Candidates* (New York: AICPA, 1970), pp. 17-18.

education who *conscientiously* prepares will succeed. Self-discipline is the most difficult task of all.

CPA Examination
in
Accounting Practice
in Perspective

Contents of the Examination

Information for CPA Candidates, p. 25, has made the following important observations about the content of the entire CPA examination:

> Each examination should provide a broad coverage of the full body of technical knowledge required of CPAs. Carefully selected multiple-choice questions are an effective means for providing the needed broad coverage in a minimum amount of time.
>
> Another major factor is the balance of subjects making up an examination. No single subject should receive undue weight on the examination. If, upon review of the entire examination, it is found that substantial attention is given to a topic such as cost accounting, income taxes, managerial accounting, or any other topic, questions on the topic will be replaced with others to bring the subject coverage into balance. . . .
>
> Unsuccessful candidates have often overlooked the balance and comprehensiveness of the examination, and may have limited their preparation to those topics which they guessed would be included.

Exhibit 1 on the next page is a topical analysis that should give a candidate some familiarity with the over-all nature of the Practice examination. The subject matter of Theory, Auditing, and Business Law is discussed under the "General Approaches" in later sections of this book.

In May 1974, the use of optional alternative problems in Accounting Practice was discontinued. The Board of Examiners decided that topics previously used in alternative problems have become an integral part of the common body of knowledge in accounting and should be examined as required subjects with appropriate regularity.

In 1973, the Board of Examiners announced that coverage on new authoritative pronouncements (for example, pronouncements of the Financial Accounting Standards Board) would commence twelve to eighteen months after publication. The extent of such coverage is to be consistent with the importance of the pronouncement to a practitioner and the clarity of supporting rules or interpretations relating to each pronouncement.

What subject matter review for the examination in Accounting Practice will best prepare a candidate? The answer is necessarily a matter of opinion, but serious consideration should be given to the points that follow on page 7.

Exhibit 1

TOPICAL ANALYSIS OF TEN CPA EXAMINATIONS IN ACCOUNTING PRACTICE (1968-1972)*

Description	Frequency Number	Per Cent	Topic in Section 1 of this Book
Income taxes:			
In general	10		
Individuals	5		
Partnerships	1		
Corporations	4		
Total income taxes	20	18%	XIII
Cost accounting:			
In general	4		
Cost-volume-profit relationships....	3		
Standard costs	3		
Relevant costs for special decisions..	3		
Sub-total	13		IV
Process costs	4		
Joint costs....................	1		
Sub-total	5		V
Total cost accounting	18	16	
Quantitative methods:			
Multiple choice	5		
Other	6	11**	10	VI
Governmental and institutional			
accounting	10	9	XII
Current assets....................	9	8	III
General review, multiple choice			
questions mostly on financial			
accounting	8	7	XIV
Ownership equities:			
Corporations.................	4		
Partnerships	4	8	7	X
Accounting fundamentals: financial			
statements, cash vs. accrual basis,			
correction of errors, etc.	7	6	I
Consolidations	5	5	XI
Liabilities.......................	5	5	IX
Statements of funds flow, cash flow,			
and comprehensive budgets	4	4	II
Investments	4	4	VII
Fixed assets	1	1	VIII
	110	100%***	

*The May, 1973 Practice examination is wholly reproduced in Topic XV of this text.

**Most of the quantitative method problems could also be sub-classified as cost accounting problems.

***Percentages are rounded. These percentages are based on the total number of problems, although a few problems were optional. Interpretations of relative importance should be tempered accordingly. For example, if a candidate is strongly prepared in governmental accounting, he need not be concerned with its relative importance in the CPA examination. He simply can expect such a problem. Certain states require the candidate to solve the governmental problem; therefore, each uniform CPA examination contains such a problem.

Points are allocated approximately in proportion to the time required for each problem. Therefore, another way to analyze the relative importance of the questions is by the total time allowed to each topic. However, our analysis using time allowances showed about the same relative importance as above.

1. Priority should be given to those subjects that are most likely to be encountered and that are sharply defined as far as problem-solving techniques are concerned. A candidate should concentrate on accounting fundamentals (Topic I), income taxes, essentials of cost accounting (particularly process costs), governmental accounting, inventories, partnerships, consolidations, and statements of sources and applications of funds. The subjects named either appear regularly on the CPA examination or lend themselves to solution techniques that may be learned easily and that may be applied to a wide range of specific problem situations. For example, a knowledge of the general approaches to funds statements (Topic II), process costing (Topic V), and governmental accounting (Topic XII) can decidedly strengthen the candidate's confidence.

2. A conscientious candidate will never feel completely prepared. This is natural. The scope of the subject matter that may justifiably be included is vast and is increasing. Therefore, some calculated risks in preparation must be taken. Among the topics of low priority are the following: real estate, insurance, bank, brokerage, and contractor accounting; estates and trusts; receiverships; and statements of realization and liquidation.

3. Among the topics that have been getting more stress on recent examinations are the following: quantitative methods; relevant costs for special decisions; standard costs; cost-volume-profit relationships; multiple choice questions on financial accounting; current assets; and ownership equities. The increase in importance of cost accounting is largely concentrated in the uses of accounting for management decisions.

4. The candidate should be on the alert for topics that may be growing in importance and that, therefore, may be more likely to appear on future examinations. For example, the statement of changes in financial position is now a required financial statement. In particular, be on the alert for FASB pronouncements issued a year or two before the date of the CPA examination.

5. Because the content changes through the years, the candidate should not analyze topical frequency for a span longer than five to ten years prior to the most recent examination. Primary attention should be devoted to the most recent five-year span.

Basic Nature of Examination

Although the accounting phase of the CPA examination is divided into three main sections (Auditing, Theory, and Practice), the candidate must remember particularly that the Practice section cannot be handled successfully without an adequate background in theory. Accounting problems are such that theory is woven into almost every problem situation. The "why" and the "how to" are interrelated and may seldom be divorced. In essence, the Practice section tests an understanding of accounting principles and their application.

Successful writing of the Practice examination involves the following skills:

1. Adequate working knowledge of accounting principles and procedures;
2. Ability to distinguish the relevant from the irrelevant in a mass of data;

3. Adequate clerical ability and arithmetical knowledge;
4. Ability to organize and present data clearly;
5. Ability to do all the above within reasonable time limits.

Reading the Problem

The beginning of a good solution lies in a careful reading of the problem. Time spent in achieving understanding of the facts and the requirements of the problem is generally the most productive time of all. Too many candidates are overly anxious to make calculations or to write something; this is the inefficient, unproductive approach. The fellow candidate who appears to be far ahead is either a genius or a fool. It is unnecessary to compete with the former (the examination is not designed for him), and the latter is not in competition no matter how busy he appears to be.

Every problem should receive at least two careful readings. The first reading gives the feel of the over-all situation and orients the reader as to the relationship of the problem data and the requirements of the problem. The second reading should be coupled with some type of technique described below.

One technique might be termed the underlining approach. Underscore the problem itself as to dates, figures, important facts, and any other key information. Insert marginal notes or draw lines connecting related data.

Another technique may be used in certain problem situations that lend themselves to a fairly uniform approach to solution (for instance, process-cost, funds statements). This technique involves reviewing the uniform steps needed to solve the type of problem and linking the key problem data with the uniform steps.

Plan of Attack

After becoming familiar with the facts and the requirements of the problem, the candidate should ask himself, "What specifically do I have to do to satisfy the requirements?" He should outline the steps needed to achieve the solution. In outlining these steps, he should be doubly certain to omit unnecessary work. This procedure forces thorough anticipation of the entire job at hand and prevents overlooking essential features of the problem, which often occurs when the candidate rushes wildly into the solution itself.

An outline of the steps needed for a solution has the following advantages:

1. Perspective is retained.
2. Organized, efficient techniques are more likely to be used.
3. Overlooking of requirements is avoided.
4. Graders have some basis for evaluating unfinished sections in cases of incomplete solutions.

Problem Requirements

Obviously, a solution must be framed around its ultimate objective of satisfying the specific requirements of the problem. Candidates lose points because they:

1. Misinterpret a requirement;
2. Fail to answer the requirement with a direct, adequate reply;
3. Fail to complete a requirement;
4. Omit requirements.

Many of the above deficiencies could be eliminated by careful reading, by thorough outlining of solutions, and, finally, by reviewing the completed solution in light of the requirements.

1. *Misinterpretation of a requirement.* The Institute emphasizes that requirements have been pilot-tested to remove ambiguities. Problems are designed to be straightforward. Requirements should be taken at face value. *Special assumptions are rarely necessary.* Sometimes a candidate still feels that an assumption must be made. If so, the assumption should be stated, together with the reasons therefor. Such reasons should include a statement as to why a possible alternate assumption is being rejected.

2. *Failure to answer the requirement with a direct, adequate reply.* Requirements that are not answered directly usually center around theoretical aspects. For example: "Comment on any items which you feel require explanation." "Give the reasons for your conclusions."

3. *Failure to complete a requirement.* There are several basic reasons for failure to complete a requirement. They include lack of knowledge, poor budgeting of time, failure to *plan* a solution, and nonproductive solution methods. The latter is a major factor in contributing to this deficiency. The most common cause of lost time is the inappropriate use of work sheets.

A well-planned solution will involve the most direct route to the required answers. If the candidate has the basic knowledge, he can develop his techniques to the point where the time available for solution will almost always be adequate. One of the objectives of this volume is to develop such techniques.

Only required items should be prepared. If working papers are specifically called for, they must be prepared. In many cases a satisfactory solution may be achieved without complete working papers. Preparation of formal working papers requires time. If the candidate cannot proceed without the help of complete working papers, he should then prepare them; but he should realize that he will be penalized if he is incapable of submitting all items required.

4. *Omission of requirements.* Where requirements are overlooked or ignored, the grader can only assume that the candidate was either careless or incapable of presenting a solution to the section neglected. A planned solution will minimize this danger.

Pressure

1. *Time.* In actual practice, CPA's are forced to consider time—in setting fees, in meeting deadlines, in working during busy seasons, in determining the scope and detail of audits, and in judging performance. CPA examinations justifiably contain time limits. If a candidate has adequate knowledge and knows how to approach a series of problems, he will find the time allotment adequate. The time factor becomes oppressive to one without adequate knowledge or to one whose approach to problem-solving is so inefficient that he makes a number of false starts. One start—the right one—is all that is needed. Careful reading and solution-planning will minimize time pressures.

Suggested time estimates are given at the beginning of each problem on the examination. The candidate may use these as a guide in budgeting his own time, because the times are derived after careful pretesting of the examination by the Institute.

The wisdom of not devoting excessive time to a single problem is apparent from the above quotation. Further, if lack of time prevents the submission of a complete solution, a detailed outline of the remaining steps can salvage some credit. However, a word picture will not replace the solution itself. A grader would be unfavorably impressed if a step-by-step outline was so elaborate as to be a substitute for the real requirements of the problem. Prudence is necessary in these situations; bluffing should be avoided.

2. *Freezing.* The importance of self-confidence cannot be overestimated. Examination pressures can destroy self-confidence very quickly. The chances of "freezing" or "choking-up" will diminish if the candidate works problems in the inverse order of apparent difficulty. A miserable start, because problem number one may be the most difficult for the candidate, may destroy the confidence needed for success. Selecting the easiest problem as the first one to be solved promotes confidence. Its psychological value may measure the difference between passing and failing. A good start often sets the tone of success for the entire examination.

3. *Errors in computations.* Examination pressures sometimes result in erroneous arithmetical calculations. How do such errors influence the grading? Errors are not regarded as serious if they result from arithmetic mistakes that should not be detected by a glance at the figures. However, the failure to use cross-checks and other common accounting controls may be regarded as a serious defect. The senseless error may also be regarded as damaging; for example, a candidate who divides $20,000 by 200,000 units and arrives at a unit cost of $10.00 may be viewed as not using good judgment.

Institute Suggestions

The American Institute of Certified Public Accountants distributes the following suggestions to candidates. Candidates should profit greatly from an early study of these suggestions:

1. The estimated minimum time and the estimated maximum time that the candidate may need for giving adequate answers to each question or group of questions is given in the printed examinations. These estimates should be used as a guide to allotment of time. It is recommended that the candidate not spend more than the estimated maximum time on any one question until the others have been completed except to the extent that the maximum time has not been used on prior questions. No point values are shown for the individual questions. Points will be approximately proportionate to the time required. The following is an example of time estimates as they appear on the printed examination booklets:

	Estimated Minutes	
	Minimum	Maximum
Group I (All required):		
No. 1	25	30
No. 2	25	30
No. 3	20	25
No. 4	25	30
No. 5	25	30
No. 6	25	30
Total for Group I..............	145	175
Group II (One required)...............	30	35
Total for examination	175	210

2. If the candidate is unable to complete all the answers called for in the examination, a partial answer is better than none and will receive appropriate credit. When more questions are answered out of a group of optional questions than are required, *the excess answers will not be graded.*

3. The candidate should avoid explaining how to solve the problem instead of actually solving it in the best way he can. If time grows short, a brief statement to the point is permissible, but full credit cannot be obtained by this expedient.

4. Formal journal entries should not be prepared unless specifically required by the problem. Time may be saved by entering adjustments, reclassifications, etc., directly on the working papers. Elaborate working papers should not be prepared unless they are of assistance in solving the problem. If both working papers and formal statements are required and time is not adequate to complete both, the working papers should be completed.

5. In problems or questions which permit alternative treatment the credit given for the solution will depend on the knowledge and intelligence indicated by the candidate's presentation.

6. Due weight will be given to the arguments presented to support the candidate's answer even though the examiners may not agree with his conclusions.

7. All amounts given in a problem are considered material unless otherwise stated.

8. The CPA is continually confronted with the necessity of expressing his opinions and conclusions in written reports in clear, unequivocal language. Although the primary purpose of the examination is to test the candidate's knowledge and application of the subject matter, the ability to organize and present such knowledge in acceptable written language will be considered by the examiners.

The following directions extracted from the Institute's General Rules Covering Examination must be considered:

> 2. Identify your answers by using the proper question number. Begin your answer to each question on a separate page and number pages *in accordance with the instructions on the examination.* Arrange your answers in the order of the questions.
>
> 3. Answers may be written in pencil or ink. If pencil is used it should be soft enough to leave an easily visible impression. Credit cannot be given for solutions that are illegible. Use only one side of the working papers. . . . *Neatness and orderly presentation of work are important.*
>
> 4. Attach all computations to the papers containing your answers. Identify them as to the question to which they relate. The rough calculations and notes may assist the examiners in understanding your solutions.

Summary

In preparing for the CPA examination, the candidate should consider the following points:

1. Plan his over-all review on all sections of the examination. Budget his time for study. Several short study periods are more productive than a weekend marathon. Abide by his time budget. Self-discipline is the most difficult task of all.

2. Study the following: *Information for CPA Candidates* and the pertinent AICPA publications described subsequently.

3. Preparing for the Practice section is the most time-consuming phase of study. Actual examination conditions should be reproduced insofar as possible. Problems should be solved individually, not by joint action. Problems should be attempted within the suggested time limits and at one sitting.

4. Specific points to be remembered about writing the Practice section follow:

    (a) Read the problem at least twice. Underline or make marginal notes of important facts.

    (b) Relate the facts to the requirements.

    (c) Relate the requirements to their fulfillment by visualizing your presentation in final form.

    (d) Decide upon your approach to solution. Outline the most efficient step-by-step procedure needed to satisfy the requirements.

    (e) Do not prepare elaborate working papers unless absolutely necessary.

    (f) Budget your time.

    (g) Use common-sense checks on arithmetical calculations.

    (h) If you cannot complete a solution, be specific in outlining how you would continue.

    (i) Pressure will be lessened and self-confidence will be better maintained by first attacking what seems to be the easiest problem. However, spending too much time on the easiest problem will impinge upon the time needed for the more difficult problems.

(j) Study the AICPA suggestions to candidates presented above.

(k) Be aware of alternative terminology and solutions.

5. The Topics most frequently encountered are income taxes, cost accounting, quantitative methods, and governmental accounting.

6. Candidates should not take the CPA examination as a "dry-run." Half-hearted preparation will probably result in failure. A person who wishes to practice may use the old CPA examination questions and answers for that purpose.

References to Other Literature

Accounting Practice and Accounting Theory

Besides using his favorite *up-to-date* textbooks and *Information for CPA Candidates* as a basis for review, the candidate should consider the two-volume reference, *APB Accounting Principles* (hereafter often abbreviated as APBAP), as fundamental.

Volume 1 covers all currently effective Opinions and Statements of the Accounting Principles Board, Accounting Interpretations, and Accounting Research Bulletins still in effect. All changes have been recognized by amendments and deletions in the text and the contents are usefully arranged by subject and fully indexed.

Volume 2 is a companion reference that is arranged chronologically and includes all the pronouncements in their original exact form.

Throughout this book, references will frequently be made to the various original APB pronouncements as well as to APBAP, Volume 1. The latter is obviously the safer volume to use because it interweaves the amendments of the original pronouncements. However, practitioners and others habitually use the original numbers when they refer to these pronouncements.

College bookstores often have the *APB Accounting Principles* books available at special student prices. These volumes, as well as other Institute literature, may also be obtained by AICPA members through the mail from AICPA headquarters, 666 Fifth Avenue, New York 10019. Special discount prices are available for ordering both volumes of *APB Accounting Principles.* If you decide to order only one volume, buy Volume 1.

Nonmembers of the AICPA may usually obtain any Institute literature directly from the Institute. However, *APB Accounting Principles* is an exception; nonmembers must order those volumes from Commerce Clearing House, Inc., 4025 W. Peterson Avenue, Chicago 60646.

Of course, the candidate should also be abreast of all pronouncements of the Financial Accounting Standards Board.

The following textbooks are widely used sources for further review for Topics I-III, VII-XI, and Accounting Theory:

Bedford, Norton, Kenneth Perry, and Arthur Wyatt, *Advanced Accounting,* 3rd Ed. (New York: John Wiley & Sons, Inc., 1973).

Copeland, Ronald M., D. Larry Crumbley, and Joseph F. Wodjak, *Advanced Accounting* (New York: Holt, Rinehart and Winston, Inc., 1971).

Davidson, Sidney, editor, *Handbook of Modern Accounting* (New York, McGraw-Hill Book Company, 1970).

Gentry, James A., and Glenn L. Johnson, *Finney and Miller's Principles of Accounting, Intermediate,* 7th Ed. (Englewood Cliffs, N.J.: Prentice-Hall, Inc., 1974).

———, *Finney and Miller's Principles of Accounting, Advanced,* 6th Ed. (Englewood Cliffs, N.J.: Prentice-Hall, Inc., 1971).

Griffin, Charles H., Thomas H. Williams, and Kermit D. Larson, *Advanced Accounting,* Rev. Ed. (Homewood, Illinois: Richard D. Irwin, Inc., 1971).

Hendriksen, Eldon S., *Accounting Theory,* Rev. Ed. (Homewood, Illinois: Richard D. Irwin, Inc., 1970).

Meigs, Walter B., A. N. Mosich, and Charles E. Johnson, *Intermediate Accounting,* 3rd Ed. (New York: McGraw-Hill Book Company, Inc., 1973).

Meigs, Walter B., Charles E. Johnson, and Thomas F. Keller, *Advanced Accounting* (New York: McGraw-Hill Book Company, Inc., 1966).

Miller, Herbert E., and George C. Mead, editors, *CPA Review Manual,* 4th Ed., (Englewood Cliffs, N.J.: Prentice-Hall, Inc., 1972).

Simons, Harry, *Intermediate Accounting,* Comprehensive Volume, 5th Ed. (Cincinnati: South-Western Publishing Co., 1972).

———, *Advanced Accounting,* Comprehensive Volume, 4th Ed. (Cincinnati: South-Western Publishing Co., 1968).

Welsch, Glenn A., Charles T. Zlatkovich, and John Arch White, *Intermediate Accounting,* 3rd Ed. (Homewood, Illinois: Richard D. Irwin, Inc., 1972).

Wixon, Rufus, Walter G. Kell, and Norton M. Bedford, editors, *Accountants' Handbook,* 5th Ed. (New York: The Ronald Press Company, 1970).

References for Topics IV-VI, XII, XIII, Auditing, and Commercial Law will be found at the end of the General Approaches to those sections.

Section 1

CPA Examination
in
Accounting Practice

Accounting Fundamentals: Financial Statements; Cash versus Accrual Basis; Correction of Errors; Incomplete Records; Financial Ratios

GENERAL APPROACH

CPA examinations invariably contain one or more problems of a non-specialized nature. Such problems test a candidate's knowledge of accounting fundamentals and his judgment in applying this knowledge. The candidate is faced with a mass of disorganized and incomplete data, some of which may be irrelevant.

Success in dealing with problems of this type requires a working knowledge of accounting principles and procedures plus alertness and common sense. The candidate should have:

1. Adequate background in basic concepts and accounting principles;
2. An understanding of cash and accrual methods of accounting;
3. Knowledge of the techniques of determining key unknown figures by working from the known;
4. Proficiency in a methodology of making adjustments and corrections.

Many people who take the CPA examination are inadequately grounded in accounting theory. Much has been written about the theories or principles which are the bases for accounting procedures. As a start, those who have not kept abreast of current literature in these areas should review thoroughly the appropriate material in an up-to-date intermediate accounting text. Simultaneously, APB *Statement No. 4,* particularly Chapters 5 through 8, should be studied (or APBAP Vol. 1, Sect. 1021-1029). An efficient way to prepare for Accounting Practice and Theory is to become acquainted early with the official AICPA literature, especially APB *Opinions,* and with the pronouncements of the Financial Accounting Standards Board, the APB's successor that began operations in 1973.

The need to know the fundamental meaning and interrelationships of assets, equities, revenue, and expense is obvious. Yet a surprising number of candidates never take time to organize their thinking on these essential concepts. This lack of perspective is common. Because of a weak understanding of fundamental concepts they work with daily, some candidates are unable to grapple successfully with the unfamiliar situations presented on a CPA examination. The problems in Topic I require a strong grasp of the meaning of assets, equities, revenue, expenses, and their relationships, in addition to efficient problem-working techniques.

Basic Concepts and Accounting Principles

Generally accepted accounting principles (GAAP) is a technical term that encompasses the conventions, rules, and procedures necessary to define accepted accounting practice at a particular time. These principles are not influenced solely by formal logical analysis. Experience, reason, custom, usage, and practical necessity contribute to the set of principles. It might be better to call them *conventions,* because principles connotes that they are a product of airtight logic.

APB *Statement No. 4* divides principles into three broad categories: pervasive, broad operating, and detailed. The following discussion will give some highlights of each category, but it does not pretend to be exhaustive.

Pervasive principles are the basis for much of the accounting process; they include measurement principles (for example, realization) and modifying conventions (for example, conservatism).

Broad operating principles are general rules derived from the pervasive principles. The broad principles govern the application of the detailed principles. They include principles of selection (for example, exchanges are recorded but specific price level changes are not) and principles of financial statement presentation (for example, earnings per share should be disclosed on the face of the income statement).

Detailed accounting principles are the many rules and procedures that are based on the broad principles and specify the way that data are processed and presented in specific situations. For example, APB *Opinion No. 15* (or see APBAP Vol. 1, Sect. 2011) has profuse instructions regarding how to compute earnings per share.

Many familiar accounting terms are defined in APB *Statement No. 4,* including among others, assets, liabilities, revenue, expenses, and net income. All of the definitions include the qualifying phrase "in conformity with general accepted accounting principles." For example, principles are used to determine whether an obligation is or is not a liability. Some of these terms are briefly discussed below.

1. *Assets* are frequently defined as economic resources devoted to business purposes within a specific accounting entity. *Statement No. 4* highlights the fact that assets and economic resources, which are the scarce means available for conducting economic activities, are not interchangeable terms. That is, all items that may be regarded as assets in an economist's sense may not qualify as assets in an accountant's sense. Instead, assets are those economic resources selected and measured in conformity with GAAP. For example, an outlay for a huge research effort or an initial advertising campaign to launch a new product may be an asset in terms of economic analysis but an expense in accordance with GAAP.

Assets may be thought of as bundles of services awaiting *future* use or expiration. A useful point of view is to think of assets other than cash and receivables as prepaid costs or "stored" costs (for example, inventories or fixed assets) which are carried forward to future periods rather than charged immediately against revenue.

2. *Income determination* is the process of relating revenue and expenses for an accounting period. *Revenue* usually arises from sales of products and services to customers. A realization principle is used to determine when revenue is recorded. To be realized, revenue must usually meet the following two tests: First, the earning process must be complete or virtually complete in that the goods and services must be fully rendered. Second, an exchange must take place.

3. *Expenses* are the costs that are associated with ("matched" with) the revenue of the period, often based on a direct cause and effect relationship but frequently indirectly through a relationship with the given period. Expenses may be thought of as expired costs. In much accounting literature, losses are sometimes distinguished from expenses as being those expired costs that produce no revenue. *Statement No. 4* (footnote 54 or see APBAP Vol. 1, Sect. 1027.25, R-9C) makes no such distinction; therefore, flood losses or theft losses are regarded as a type of expense.

To summarize, expenses are "used-up" assets. Thus, most assets may be conveniently viewed as costs held back from the expense stream and carried on the balance sheet awaiting the release as expense in some future period. As inventories are used, their costs are released to cost of goods sold (expense). As delivery trucks are used, their original costs become expenses through depreciation charges.

4. *Value.* Caution should be employed in the use of this word. The use of precise, current terminology in an examination creates a favorable impression on graders. Whenever a candidate is tempted to use the word *value*, he should try to apply some other descriptive term. For example, one should generally refer to the *costs* of fixed assets and inventories rather than to their *values*. However, a

candidate may use the word *value* where it is accepted current usage. In such cases, *value* should be modified by another descriptive word (for example, *market value, net realizable value).* The term *fair value* is used frequently in the Institute literature. Fair value is the amount of money that would be involved if the assets or liabilities in question resulted from exchanges that involved money prices. In other words, fair value is used instead of the term *cash equivalent value.*

APB *Statement No. 4* is an imposing pronouncement, so the candidate should distinguish among the relative importance of its many ideas. Some of the concepts seem more concrete than others and are more likely to be covered on a CPA examination. In addition to those mentioned elsewhere in this General Approach, the following key topics deserve special study; they can be found easily in *Statement No. 4:* accounting entity, going concern, verifiability, consistency, deferred charges and credits, all the pervasive principles (including conservatism), and nonreciprocal transfers (e.g., cash dividends, acquistion of treasury stock). For additional discussion of terminology, see Chapter 1 of *Statement No. 4* (or see APBAP Vol. 1, Sect. 1021.08).

Cash versus Accrual Basis

The process of determining income and financial position is anchored to the accrual basis of accounting, as distinguished from the cash basis. In accrual accounting the impact of events (such as sales on credit) on assets and liabilities is recognized in the time periods when goods or services are utilized or rendered instead of when cash is paid or received. Therefore, income is affected by measurements of noncash resources and obligations. The accrual basis is the principal conceptual means of matching accomplishments (revenue) with efforts (expenses).

In contrast, the cash basis recognizes revenue when the cash is collected and most expenses when they are paid. Depreciation is an exception. It is usually recognized as an expense under either the accrual or the cash method.

Problems usually involve the ability to change from one basis to the other, often from the cash to the accural basis. In addition, problems on correction of errors or incomplete records will often involve some relationship of cash flow to revenue or expense recognition.

Two short questions are given below. The solutions and comments about technique follow. *Before* glancing at the solutions and comments, attempt to get the answers on scratch paper.

Question 1

From the following information calculate gross sales for May:

Accounts receivable, 5/1	$15,000	Cash discounts allowed on credit	
Accounts receivable, 5/31	14,600	sales	$100
Collections on account	8,050	Write-offs of accounts receivable	300
Cash sales	3,000	Allowances on sales	200

Question 2

From the following information calculate the cost of goods sold for the year. Assume that cash discounts are treated as offsets against purchases rather than as other income:

Accounts payable		Inventory, 12/31	$13,000
(for merchandise), 1/1	$20,000	Cash discounts taken on credit	
Accounts payable, 12/31	22,000	purchases	500
Cash payments on account	50,000	Purchase returns	2,000
Inventory, 1/1	11,000	Cash purchases..............	5,000

Similar questions used in class tests have resulted in a very high percentage of error. Likelihood of error may be minimized through the use of key T accounts as work sheets for cash versus accrual and incomplete record problems. The use of key T accounts offers the following advantages:

1. A candidate works with a familiar device,
2. T accounts are constructed so that built-in checks on accuracy exist.

Solution to Question 1

Step 1: Enter all known items into the key T account. Knowledge of the usual components of such an account is essential.

ACCOUNTS RECEIVABLE

Balance, 5/1	15,000	Write-offs	300
Gross credit sales	X	Allowance on sales	200
		Discounts allowed	⎰ 100*
		Collections	⎱ 8,050
Total Debits	(15,000 + X)	*Total Credits*	8,650
Balance, 5/31	14,600		

*The brace is used to highlight the analytical usefulness of subdividing the credit to Accounts Receivable arising from collections subject to cash discounts. For example, if a $1,000 debt subject to a 2 per cent cash discount were collected, the journal entry would be:

Cash	980	
Cash discounts allowed	20	
Accounts receivable		1,000

For analytical purposes, the $1,000 credit is subdivided into $980 and $20, even though the real-life posting would be a lump sum of $1,000.

Step 2: Find the unknown by solving for X. Simple arithmetic will yield the answer, but the following solution illustrates the algebraic nature of relationships in a debit balance account:

$$Total\ Debits\ -\ Total\ Credits = Balance$$
$$(15,000 + X) - 8,650 \qquad = 14,600$$
$$15,000 + X \qquad\qquad = 23,250$$
$$X = \ \ 8,250$$

Credit sales plus cash sales equals gross sales: $8,250 plus $3,000 equals *$11,250.*

Alternate Solution to Question 1

Working with *net change* in the beginning and ending balance of a particular account is less awkward in problems of this type. To show how this is done, let us rework the solution to Question 1.

The algebraic nature of relationships in the Accounts Receivable can be used to show the following:

Beginning Balances + Current Debits − Current Credits = Ending Balance (1)
or: Current Debits − Current Credits = Ending Balance− Beginning Balance (2)

Equation (2) can be used as a basic approach to cash versus accrual problems. The steps to be taken are:

Step 1: Insert the *net change* in the balances at the *top* of the account, drawing a single line below the net change as indicated.

ACCOUNTS RECEIVABLE

Increase	*Decrease*
	400

Step 2: Enter all other known items in the T account.

ACCOUNTS RECEIVABLE

		Net change	400
Gross credit sales	X	Write-offs	300
		Allowance on sales	200
		Discounts allowed	100
		Collections	8,050
Total Current Debits	X	*Total Current Credits*	8,650

If a correct analysis is made, the difference between the Total Current Debits and Total Current Credits should equal the Net Change at the top of the account.

Step 3: Find the unknown.

$$Current\ Debits - Current\ Credits = Ending\ Balance - Beginning\ Balance$$
$$X - \$8,650 = -\$400*$$
$$X = -\$400 + \$8,650$$
$$X = \$8,250$$
$$*\$14,600 - \$15,000 = -\$400$$

Solution to Question 2
Steps 1 and 2: Enter the net change at the proper side of the top of the T account, then enter all other known items.

ACCOUNTS PAYABLE

Decrease		*Increase*	2,000
Purchase returns	2,000	Credit purchases	X
Discounts taken	500		
Cash payments	50,000		
	52,500		X

Step 3: Obtain the unknown.

Current Credits − Current Debits = Net Change in Balance
$$X − \$52,500 \quad = \$ \ 2,000$$
$$X = \$54,500$$

Total Credit purchases plus cash purchases equals $54,500 plus $5,000, or $59,500.

Step 4: There is a tendency to overlook the necessity for getting cost of goods sold, not purchases. Candidates often stop after the third step. Never forget the requirements of the problem.

Inventory, 1/1			$11,000
Purchases.....................		$59,500	
Returns	$2,000		
Discounts	500	2,500	57,000
			$68,000
Inventory, 12/31			13,000
Cost of goods sold			$55,000

This key T-account technique may be used to advantage in many problem situations (for example, Problem I-6).

Statement of Cash Receipts and Disbursements

A statement of cash receipts and disbursements is merely a formal repro-
duction and analysis of the content of a cash account. The use of a cash T account together with other key T accounts as a work-sheet is often the most efficient means of solving problems that require such a statement.

Correction of Errors

Problems on correction of errors again test practical comprehension of the accrual basis of accounting. Many CPA problems contain erroneous entries or statements. Such problems are probably chosen by the examiners because the problems (a) present unfamiliar situations, (b) require more analytical thought than problems of a more stereotyped nature, and (c) require knowledge not only of correct methods, but in addition require ability to work from an incorrect to a correct method (usually through adjusting or correcting entries).

The most troublesome errors frequently are those that affect two or more fiscal periods. These errors may be divided into two major types:

1. Counterbalancing errors are omissions or misstatements in one fiscal period which are counterbalanced by offsetting errors in the ordinary bookkeeping process in the next period. Examples are errors affecting accruals,

prepayments, deferrals, and inventories. Such errors affect income by identical offsetting amounts in successive periods; they also affect the balance sheet of the first period but not the second.

For example, the omission of $1,000 of accrued salaries would (a) overstate income and understate year-end liabilities by $1,000 in the first year, and (b) understate income by $1,000 and have no effect on year-end liabilities in the second year. Note that the retained earnings balance at the end of the second year would be correct (ignoring income tax considerations). The total of the two incorrect net incomes would be identical with the total of the two correct net incomes.

2. Some errors are not counterbalanced in the ordinary bookkeeping process. Until specific correcting entries are made, all subsequent balance sheets will be in error. Such errors include erroneous depreciation estimates, charging original bond discounts directly to retained earnings, capitalizing repairs, and charging capital outlays to expense.

For example, excessive depreciation expense of $2,000 in *one year* (a) would understate income, assets, and retained earnings by $2,000 in that year and (b) would continue to understate assets and retained earnings on successive balance sheets for the life of the fixed asset. But observe that income for each subsequent year would not be affected unless the same error is committed again.

Where errors are apparent, correction usually involves one of three basic approaches:

1. Where many complex errors have been made, it is usually better to ignore temporarily what was done in the books and to reconstruct *correct* entries in T accounts from the beginning. Then, the differences between correct T-account balances and incorrect book balances will form the basis for a compound correcting journal entry(s). One word of caution—candidates should remember the problem requirements. Often, candidates offer *correct* entries when *correcting* entries are required.

2. Where corrections are many but relatively simple, it is not necessary to reconstruct all correct entries. The correcting entries may be drafted merely by comparing the incorrect figure(s) with the easily determined correct figure(s). Here a simple work sheet may be used to advantage. Use columns for the trial balance, adjustments and corrections, and either the income statement or the balance sheet or both. Correcting adjustments may then be entered directly on a work sheet, keyed, and explained below with descriptions or schedules.

3. When a series of errors affecting two or more years is encountered, a candidate should consider the effect of each error separately. A work sheet such as the following is often helpful:

	Net Income			Income Taxes Payable December 31,
	19x1	*19x2*	*19x3*	*19x3*
Corrections:				
Omission of accrued salaries, December 31, 19x1	$ (1,000)	$ 1,000		
Understatement of income taxes, 19x1 and 19x2 ...	(2,000)	2,000		$4,000
Total corrections	$ (3,000)	$(1,000)	...	$4,000
Book balances (given)	13,000	16,000	11,000	3,500
Corrected balances	$10,000	$15,000	$11,000	$7,500

NOTE: Negative amounts are in parentheses. Also, the understatement of income taxes is considered to be material in amount for each year.

Notice the effect on retained earnings. The three-year total increase per books was $40,000; corrected increase, $36,000. The only correcting entry as of the end of 19x3 would be:

Retained earnings (as of January 1, 19x3)......... 4,000
    Income taxes payable 4,000

This type of entry illustrates a *prior-period adjustment*, which, according to APB *Opinion No. 9*, should be reflected as an adjustment of the opening balance of Retained Earnings. Such an adjustment must be material and must relate directly to the operations of a specific prior period or periods.

Accounting Changes

The preceding entry illustrates a correction of an error as it is narrowly defined in APB *Opinion No. 20 - Accounting Changes* (or see APBAP Vol. 1, Sect. 1051.13). This Opinion was issued to achieve uniformity in reporting various types of accounting changes: (1) changes resulting from choosing one accepted accounting principle instead of the one used previously (e.g., Lifo to Fifo), (2) changes in accounting estimates (e.g., altering the previous predictions of the useful lives of equipment), (3) changes in the reporting entity (e.g., presenting consolidated statements in place of statements of individual companies), and (4) changes resulting from the correction of an error (e.g., see the preceding entry).

The required reporting of the various types of accounting changes has been immensely complicated by this four-fold distinction among changes. Ideally, a candidate should master all the nuances of these distinctions and their effects on financial reports. But obtaining that mastery is time-consuming and does not deserve high priority. As a minimum, however, a candidate should be aware that the distinctions exist and that changes in accounting estimates get "prospective" rather than "retroactive" treatment, as will now be explained.

Opinion No. 20 maintains that a correction of an error is distinguishable from a change in estimate. Examples of items (paragraph 10) "for which estimates are necessary include uncollectible receivables, inventory obsolescence, service lives and salvage values of depreciable assets, warranty costs, periods benefited by deferred cost, and recoverable mineral reserves." *Opinion No. 20* requires that such changes in "estimates" be spread "prospectively" instead of "retroactively" by altering, for instance, future depreciation schedules rather than by tampering with beginning balances of retained earnings or restating past financial statements. Some critics of this approach maintain that two wrongs are committed (past statements and future statements are incorrect) unless restatement is made or the beginning-of-the-year retained earnings balance is adjusted.

Extraordinary Items

Various concepts of net income have been advanced by accountants through the years. Every CPA candidate should be particularly familiar with APB *Opinion No. 9* (or see APBAP Vol. 1, Sect. 2010), which reviews many of the concepts and which leans heavily toward the "all-inclusive" concept. Paragraph 2010.16 states that

> net income should reflect all items of profit and loss recognized during the period with the sole exception of prior period adjustments described below. *Extraordinary items* should, however be segregated from the results of ordinary operations and shown separately in the income statement, with disclosure of the nature and amounts thereof.

As explained more fully in our discussion of the correction of errors, *prior-period adjustments* are rare. They will directly affect retained earnings and will not appear in the computation of current net income.

Extraordinary items would affect net income but would be segregated as follows:

Income before extraordinary items
Extraordinary items (less applicable income tax)
Net income

Paragraph 2010.27 points out that the following items should be excluded from the determination of net income under all circumstances:

(a) Adjustment or charges or credits resulting from transactions in the company's own capital stock;
(b) Transfers to and from accounts properly designated as appropriated retained earnings (such as general purpose contingency reserves or provisions for replacement costs of fixed assets);
(c) Adjustments made pursuant to a quasi-reorganization.

CPA examinations in the 1970s are likely to ask about extraordinary items on the income statement. Therefore, candidates should give high priority to studying APB *Opinion No. 30,* which narrowed the rules. In this, the Board concluded that an event or transaction should be presumed to be an ordinary and usual activity of the reporting entity, and hence includible in income before extraordinary items, unless the evidence clearly supports its classification as an extraordinary item as defined in the Opinion. Extraordinary items result from events that must have both an *unusual nature* and an *infrequency of occurrence.*

The environment in which an entity operates is a primary consideration in determining whether some specific event is abnormal and significantly different from the ordinary activities of the entity. Moreover, extraordinary events cannot reasonably be expected to recur in the foreseeable future. Therefore, writedowns of receivables, inventories, and deferred research costs are ordinary items, as are gains or losses on the sale or abandonment of fixed assets. The effects of a strike and foreign currency revaluations are also ordinary items. In short, the burden of proof is on the reporting company to demonstrate that a special item is extraordinary. The Opinion specifically states that casualties such as an earthquake or governmental expropriation or prohibition are examples of events that are likely to qualify as extraordinary items.

Financial Ratios

Candidates are expected to know the most popular financial ratios, among which are various ways of measuring return on investment. Special care is needed to be sure how "return" and how "investment" are defined in a particular problem. In some cases the numerator is net income and the denominator is average stockholders' equity. In other cases, the numerator is operating income and the denominator is the beginning balance of the net book value of total assets. Be on guard for the specific meaning of the ratio in question.

Return on total assets is frequently subdivided as follows:

$$\text{Return} = \frac{\text{Sales}}{\text{Average total assets}} \times \frac{\text{Net income}}{\text{Sales}}$$

or

$$\text{Return} = \text{Asset turnover} \times \text{Net profit percentage}$$

The computation of earnings per share of common stock is described in detail in the General Approach to Topic X. In its simplest form, earnings per share is:

$$\frac{\text{Net income} - \text{Preferred dividends}}{\text{Number of common shares outstanding}}$$

Computations related to stockholders' investments include:

$$\text{Price-earnings ratio} = \frac{\text{Current market price per share of common stock}}{\text{Earnings per share of common stock}}$$

$$\text{Dividend yield ratio} = \frac{\text{Common dividends per share of common stock}}{\text{Current market price per share of common stock}}$$

$$\text{Book value per share of common stock} = \frac{\text{Stockholders' equity at a given date} - \text{Liquidating value of preferred stock}}{\text{Number of common shares outstanding}}$$

Sometimes the average market price rather than the current market price is required when computing price-earnings ratio and dividend yield ratio. The current market price should be used however, if nothing is said to indicate otherwise.

Other ratios include:

$$\text{Times bond interest earned} = \frac{\text{Income before bond interest and taxes}}{\text{Bond interest expense}}$$

$$\text{Current ratio} = \frac{\text{Current assets}}{\text{Current liabilities}}$$

$$\text{Acid-test or quick ratio} = \frac{\text{Cash} + \text{Receivables} + \text{Short term investments}}{\text{Current liabilities}}$$

$$\text{Average collection period (or average number of days' sales uncollected)} = \frac{\text{Average gross accounts receivable}}{\text{Sales on account}} \times 365 \text{ (or 360) days}$$

$$\text{Accounts receivable turnover} = \frac{\text{Sales on account}}{\text{Average gross accounts receivable}}$$

$$\text{Inventory turnover} = \frac{\text{Cost of goods sold}}{\text{Average inventory}}$$

CPA PROBLEMS

Problem I-1: Worksheet, cash to accrual basis (50-60 min.)

On January 2, 1970 Nolan-Paszkowski, Inc. was organized with two stock-holders, Richard Nolan and Lynn Paszkowski. Richard Nolan purchased 500 shares of $100 par value common stock for $50,000 cash; Lynn Paszkowski received 500 shares of common stock in exchange for the assets and liabilities of a men's clothing shop that she had operated as a sole proprietorship. The trial balance immediately after incorporation appears on the accompanying worksheet.

No formal books have been kept during 1970. The following information has been gathered from the checkbooks, deposit slips and other sources:

1. Most balance sheet account balances at December 31, 1970 have been determined and recorded on the worksheet.

2. Cash receipts for the year are summarized as follows:

Advances from customers .... $	700
Cash sales and collections on accounts receivable (after sales discounts of $1,520 and sales returns and allowances of $1,940	126,540
Sale of equipment costing $5,000 on which $1,000 of depreciation had accumulated	4,500
	$131,740

3. Cash disbursements for the year are summarized as follows:

Insurance premiums .... $	825
Purchase of equipment	18,000
Addition to building	4,600
Cash purchases and payments on accounts payable (after purchase discounts of $1,150 and purchase returns and allowances of $1,800)	82,050
Remittance of payroll taxes (income tax of $3,200 and F.I.C.A. taxes of $1,250—divided equally between employee withholdings and employer)	4,450
Net salaries paid to employees	38,620
Utilities	1,850
Dividends paid	1,500
Total cash disbursements	$151,895

4. Dividends of $.75 per share were declared on June 30, September 30 and December 31.

5. For tax purposes the depreciation expense for 1970 was: building $800, equipment $3,350. For financial accounting purposes the depreciation expense was: building $400, equipment $1,750.

6. Bad debts are estimated to be 1.2% of total sales for the year. The ending accounts receivable balance of $18,700 has been reduced by $650 for specific accounts which were written off as uncollectible.

7. Annual income tax rates are: 22% of the first $25,000, 48% on all income over $25,000, a surcharge of 2½% for 1970 and no surcharge beyond 1970. Assume that advances from customers are not included in taxable income.

Required:

Complete the accompanying worksheet for the preparation of accrual basis financial statements. Formal financial statements and journal entries are not required.

Nolan–Paszkowski, Inc.
WORKSHEET FOR PREPARATION OF ACCRUAL BASIS
FINANCIAL STATEMENTS
For the Year 1970

	Balance Sheet January 2, 1970		Summary and Adjusting Entries		Income Statement 1970		Balance Sheet December 31, 1970	
	Debit	Credit	Debit	Credit	Debit	Credit	Debit	Credit
Cash.	$ 50,000						18,700	
Accounts receivable	12,400						24,500	
Merchandise inventory.	23,000							
Unexpired insurance	350						200	
Land	15,000						15,000	
Buildings	20,000							
Accumulated depreciation— buildings.		$ 7,000						
Equipment	8,000							
Accumulated depreciation— equipment		2,400						
Accounts payable.		17,300						8,679
Advances from customers		900						550
Salaries payable		600						1,595
Income taxes withheld		450						775
F.I.C.A. taxes payable		100						190
Capital stock		100,000						100,000
	$128,750	$128,750						

Problem I-2: Worksheet for estimated value basis (40-50 min.)

Z. D. Danberry, who practices dentistry as a sole proprietor, recently filed as a candidate for mayor of his city. He has requested your assistance in preparing combined personal financial statements for himself and his wife. The statements are to show both the cost and estimated value bases. Your firm rendered an unqualified opinion on similar statements last year in connection with an examination conducted to support Dr. Danberry's application for a bank loan which was not made.

Dr. Danberry's bookkeeper has provided you with a trial balance listing the Danberrys' assets and liabilities on the cost basis at April 30, 1971. Your examination disclosed the following additional information:

1. A summary of cash receipts and disbursements for the year ended April 30, 1971 follows:

Disbursements:

Personal expenditures, including personal life insurance premium	$16,000	
Purchase of Kindred Company 6% bonds at par	8,000	
Income taxes	4,100	
Interest on mortgage	1,400	
Mortgage principal amortization	1,300	
Real estate taxes	900	$31,700

Receipts:

Withdrawals from Danberry's dental practice	21,000	
Sale of Inco stock (purchased June 1, 1968 for $3,200; market value on April 30, 1970, $4,500)	6,100	
Dividends on stock	1,540	
Interest on bonds	240	28,880
Decrease in cash		$ 2,820

2. The bonds were purchased on July 31, 1970. Interest is payable semi-annually on January 31 and July 31.

3. In 1964 Danberry invested $10,000 to begin his dentistry practice and since has made additional investments. On April 2, 1971 Danberry was offered $31,000 for the net assets of his dental practice.

4. Danberry owns 25% of the outstanding stock of the closely held corporation, Dental Supply, Inc.

5. The April 30, 1971 statements of net assets of Danberry's dental practice and Dental Supply, Inc., both accompanied by unqualified opinions rendered by a CPA, were composed of the following assets and liabilities:

	Danberry's Dental Practice	Dental Supply, Inc.
Current assets	$ 6,000	$30,000
Noncurrent assets	36,000	70,000
Current liabilities	3,650	17,000
Long-term liabilities	16,350	35,000
Deferred credits	2,500	4,000

6. Investments in marketable securities on April 30, 1971 were composed of the following:

	April 30, 1971 Latest Prices	
	Bid	Asked
Stocks:		
Steele, Inc.	$15,100	$15,500
Gilliam Corp.	4,000	4,200
Bond:		
Kindred Company 6% bonds	7,800	7,900
	$26,900	$27,600

7. The valuation (at 100% of fair market value) of other property owned by the Danberrys on April 30, 1971 was as follows:

Residence	$60,000
Automobiles	4,300
Paintings	14,500
Household furnishings	7,600

There has been no appreciation during this or prior years in the value of automobiles or household furnishings.

8. The accounts payable as of April 30, 1970 and April 30, 1971 represent liabilities for personal living costs.

9. The Danberrys would have to pay a capital gains tax at an effective rate of 25% if the unrealized appreciation of the assets were realized. Decreases in asset values may be ignored in making this computation.

10. Accrued income taxes payable of $2,225 as of April 30, 1971 represents the Danberry's total tax liability.

Required:

Complete the worksheet on the page that follows to record the necessary summary and adjusting entries for the year ended April 30, 1971. After all extensions, your worksheet will provide the data necessary for the preparation of financial statements on April 30, 1971 on the estimated value basis and should identify the individual changes in the various accounts. Formal financial statements and journal entries are not required.

Problem I-3: Adjusting entries versus footnote disclosure (40-50 min.)

You have been engaged in an audit of the financial statements of the Hayhurst Company for the year ended March 31, 1971. Field work was completed on May 4, 1971, and you are now preparing a list of potential adjustments and disclosures for the financial statements. To do this, you must evaluate the following points raised in the course of the audit:

1. A review of accounts payable vouchers for April and May 1971 disclosed the following items which were not recorded until April or May and were listed for evaluation as possible unrecorded liabilities:

    a. Voucher 4-07 to Albion Supply Co. for saleable merchandise; FOB destination, shipped March 22, 1971, received March 28; merchandise was included in the physical inventory on March 31—$1,200.

Dr. and Mrs. Z. D. Danberry
WORKSHEET FOR ESTIMATED VALUE BASIS
FINANCIAL STATEMENTS
For The Year Ended April 30, 1971

| Assets and Liabilities | Cost Basis April 30, 1971 | Estimated Value Basis April 30, 1970 | Summary and Adjusting Entries | | Estimated Value Basis—April 30, 1971 | | |
| | | | | | Statement of Changes in Net Assets | | Statement of Net Assets |
			Debit	Credit	Debit	Credit	
Assets							
Cash	$ 3,300	$ 6,120					
Marketable securities	23,000	21,400					
Cash value of life insurance	4,250	3,900					
Net assets of Danberry's dental practice	19,500	27,000					
Interest in Dental Supply, Inc.	6,100	8,600					
Residence	50,000	55,600					
Automobiles	6,000	6,800					
Paintings	11,000	12,700					
Household furnishings	9,000	7,800					
	$132,150	$149,920					
Liabilities							
Accounts payable	$ 3,100	$ 2,850					
Accrued income taxes payable	2,225	1,900					
Accrued income taxes on unrealized asset appreciation		2,200					
Mortgage payable	34,000	35,300					
	$ 39,325	$ 42,250					

    b. Voucher 4-13 to Skyview Office Management; payment due April 1 for April rental of office space–$450.

    c. Voucher 4-28 to Albion Supply Co. for saleable merchandise; FOB destination, shipped March 26, received April 2; merchandise was not included in physical inventory on March 31–$650.

    d. Voucher 4-81 to Hoosier Equipment Co. for the final payment on a new machine which went into service in late March 1971–$3,450. (Two previous payments of $3,450 each were charged to the Property, Plant and Equipment account in March.)

    e. Voucher 5-01 to Acme Services for janitorial services in the months of March, April and May–$1,800.

    f. Voucher 5-06 to Phelps and Cox, Attorneys at Law, for invoice dated May 2 for retainer fee for March and April at $750 per month–$1,500.

2. Cash collections of $144,000 were made during the period April 1 to May 4, 1971 for accounts receivable outstanding as of March 31, 1971.

3. On April 15, 1971, a payment of $17,000 was made to retire currently maturing serial bonds. This amount was recorded on a March accounts payable voucher and included in the balance of accounts payable at March 31, 1971. Serial bonds of $20,000 will mature on April 15, 1972; these have been included among current liabilities for the March 31, 1971 balance sheet.

4. Emory Company, a debtor, filed for bankruptcy on April 5, 1971. Full provision had been made as of March 31, 1971 in estimated uncollectibles for the $2,000 account receivable.

5. As a result of the general economic recovery and a later Easter season, sales of the Company's products in April 1971 were $5,500 higher than in April 1970.

6. The Company has been informed by the Second National Bank that Gregory Supply Co. failed to pay a $30,000 note due May 1, 1971. Hayhurst had provided an accommodating endorsement for this note. As of May 4 Gregory's financial status was uncertain.

7. The Company owes $25,000 on a note payable on demand to the Second National Bank. The note is presented in the March 31, 1971 balance sheet as a current liability, but Company officials indicated the note probably would not be called or paid during the year ending March 31, 1972.

8. The Company began using an accelerated depreciation method for both income tax and financial reporting on all property additions after April 1, 1971 which meet Internal Revenue Service requirements. Prior to April 1, 1971 only the straight-line method was used.

9. At its April 5, 1971 meeting the board of directors authorized:

    a. The doubling of plant capacity to be financed by issuing bonds and additional common stock. (Contractual arrangements for a $300,000 building program were concluded on April 26, 1971 and the Company plans to expend an additional $400,000 on equipment during the next two years.)

    b. The extension from April 30, 1971 to April 30, 1972 of the maturity date of a $10,000 loan by the Company to its president. (The loan has been presented in the balance sheet as a current asset.)

    c. The extension of the Company's lease to its primary manufacturing site from its scheduled expiration in 1975 to 1985.

10. March raw materials issue slips of $14,000 were misplaced and not found until after the process costing entries for March had been completed. These slips were then included with the April issues. Raw materials inventory records are

maintained on a perpetual basis, and no physical inventory was taken at the end of March. Of the goods manufactured in March using these raw materials, 50% were still in work in process and finished goods inventory at March 31, 1971.

11. A $13,000 check for an interbank transfer of Company funds was listed in the March 31 bank reconciliations as a deposit in transit to one bank and as an outstanding check to another bank. This check cleared both banks during April.

12. A letter from Phelps and Cox, Company attorneys, disclosed the following:

   a. The Company is defending itself against a patent infringement suit in which a competitor is seeking $1,000,000 in compensatory damages and an injunction to stop Hayhurst's production and sale of the competing product. The attorneys state in writing that Hayhurst will prevail with no loss to the Company. (The $120,000 cost of developing the new product is being written off over a ten-year period ending in fiscal year 1980.)

   b. Legal fees of $6,500 accumulated to March 31, 1971 by Phelps and Cox for defending the patent infringement suit have not been billed to the Hayhurst Company.

   c. The Company has been sued for $76,000 by a former executive under an employment contract which had an expiration date of January 1, 1973. The executive's services were terminated on January 1, 1971. The Company has offered to settle for $15,000 and expects that this will be accepted by the former executive.

   d. The Company has been sued for $200,000 in connection with a personal injury from a February 1969 accident involving one of the Company's trucks. The Company is fully insured.

   e. An examination of the Company's federal income tax returns by revenue agents is in progress for fiscal years 1968, 1969 and 1970. It is believed that all potential deficiencies are fully provided for in the federal income tax liability account.

   f. At March 31, 1971 Phelps and Cox had not been paid the $750 due on the retainer for regular legal services for the month of March.

Unless otherwise noted, no provision has been made for any of the above items in the accounts of the Hayhurst Company to March 31, 1971.

Required:

The points discussed above have been listed in abbreviated form on the schedule shown on the accompanying page. Complete this schedule of proposed adjustments and disclosures as follows:

If an adjusting journal entry is appropriate, show the effects of this entry in the proper column(s).

If footnote disclosure is advisable, place a check mark in the appropriate column. You should indicate this only if you feel a footnote is necessary for adequate disclosure. Footnote disclosure may be used either as supplementary explanation of an adjustment to the financial statements or when no adjustment is required.

If the item requires no adjusting journal entry or footnote disclosure, place a check mark in the No Further Consideration column.

Formal footnote disclosures and journal entries are not required.

Hayhurst Company

SCHEDULE OF PROPOSED ADJUSTMENTS AND DISCLOSURES   March 31, 1971

Adjusting Journal Entries—Debit (Credit)

Item Number	Description	Current Assets	Other Assets	Current Liabilities	Other Liabilities	Stockholders' Equity	Income Statement	Footnote Disclosure	No Further Consideration
1.	Accounts payable vouchers								
a.	Vo. 4-07 Albion								
b.	Vo. 4-13 Skyview								
c.	Vo. 4-28 Albion								
d.	Vo. 4-81 Hoosier								
e.	Vo. 5-01 Acme								
f.	Vo. 5-06 Phelps and Cox								
2.	Collections of accounts receivable								
3.	Current maturities of serial bonds								
4.	Emory bankruptcy								
5.	Increase in April sales								
6.	Gregory note								
7.	Note payable to Second National Bank								
8.	Change in depreciation method								
9.	Actions by board of directors								
a.	Expansion plans								
b.	Loan to company president								
c.	Lease extension								
10.	March issue slips								
11.	Interbank transfer								
12.	Legal letter								
a.	Patent infringement suit								
b.	Legal fee on above suit								
c.	Suit on employment contract								
d.	Personal injury suit								
e.	Revenue agents' examination								
f.	March retainer fee due								

35

Problem I-4: Financial ratios and analysis of variation in gross profit (40-50 min.)

Derr Sales Corporation's management is concerned over the Corporation's current financial position and return on investment. They request your assistance in analyzing their financial statements and furnish the following statements:

Derr Sales Corporation
STATEMENT OF WORKING CAPITAL DEFICIT
December 31, 1968

Current liabilities		$223,050
Less current assets:		
Cash	$ 5,973	
Accounts receivable, net	70,952	
Inventory	113,125	190,050
Working capital deficit		$ 33,000

Derr Sales Corporation
INCOME STATEMENT
For the Year Ended December 31, 1968

Sales (90,500 units)	$760,200
Cost of goods sold	452,500
Gross profit	307,700
Selling and general expenses, including $22,980 depreciation	155,660
Income before taxes	152,040
Income taxes	76,020
Net income	$ 76,020

Additional data:
Assets other than current assets consist of land, building, and equipment with a book value of $352,950 on December 31, 1968.

Required:

a. Assuming Derr Sales Corporation operates 300 days per year compute the following (show your computations):
1. Number of days' sales uncollected.
2. Inventory turnover.
3. Number of days' operations to cover the working capital deficit.
4. Return on total assets as a product of asset turnover and the net income ratio (sometimes called profit margin).
b. Sales of 100,000 units are forecasted for 1969. Within this relevant range of activity costs are estimated as follows (excluding income taxes):

	Fixed Costs	Variable Costs Per Unit
Cost of goods sold		$4.90
Selling and general expenses, including $15,450 depreciation	$129,720	1.10
Totals	$129,720	$6.00

The income tax rate is expected to be 50 per cent. Past experience indicates that current assets vary in direct proportion to sales.

1. Management feels that in 1969 the market will support a sales price of $8.30 at a sales volume of 100,000 units. Compute the rate of return on book value of total assets after income taxes assuming management's expectations are realized.
2. Assuming sales of 100,000 units at a price of $8.30 per unit in 1969 prepare an analysis of the variation in gross profit between 1968 and 1969. Your analysis should show the effects of changes in 1969 in sales volume, sales prices and unit costs on gross profit.

Problem I-5: Reconstructing financial statements from given ratios (40-50 min.)

Ratio analysis is often applied to test the reasonableness of the relationships among current financial data against those of prior financial data. Given prior financial relationships and a few key amounts, a CPA could prepare estimates of current financial data to test the reasonableness of data furnished by his client.

Argo Sales Corporation has in recent prior years maintained the following relationships among the data on its financial statements:

1. Gross profit rate on net sales 40%
2. Net profit rate on net sales 10%
3. Rate of selling expenses to net sales 20%
4. Accounts receivable turnover .... 8 per year
5. Inventory turnover .... 6 per year
6. Acid-test ratio .... 2 to 1
7. Current ratio .... 3 to 1
8. Quick-asset composition: 8% cash, 32% marketable securities, 60% accounts receivable
9. Asset turnover .... 2 per year
10. Ratio of total assets to intangible assets .... 20 to 1
11. Ratio of accumulated depreciation to cost of fixed assets .... 1 to 3
12. Ratio of accounts receivable to accounts payable .... 1.5 to 1
13. Ratio of working capital to stockholders' equity .... 1 to 1.6
14. Ratio of total debt to stockholders' equity .... 1 to 2

The Corporation had a net income of $120,000 for 1968 which resulted in earnings of $5.20 per share of common stock. Additional information includes the following:

1. Capital stock authorized, issued (all in 1960), and outstanding:
   Common, $10 per share par value, issued at 10% premium
   Preferred, 6% nonparticipating, $100 per share par value, issued at a 10% premium
2. Market value per share of common at December 31, 1968: $78
3. Preferred dividends paid in 1968: $3,000
4. Times interest earned in 1968: 33
5. The amounts of the following were the same at December 31, 1968 as at January 1, 1968: inventory, accounts receivable, 5% bonds payable—due 1970, and total stockholders' equity
6. All purchases and sales were "on account."

Required:

a. Prepare in good form the condensed (1) balance sheet and (2) income statement for the year ending December 31, 1968 presenting the amounts you would expect to appear on Argo's financial statements (ignoring income taxes). Major captions appearing on Argo's balance sheet are: Current Assets, Fixed Assets, Intangible Assets, Current Liabilities, Long-term Liabilities, and Stockholders' Equity. In addition to the accounts divulged in the problem, you should include accounts for Prepaid Expenses, Accrued Expenses, and Administrative Expenses. Supporting computations should be in good form.

b. Compute the following for 1968 (show your computations):

1. Rate of return on stockholders' equity.
2. Price-earnings ratio for common stock.
3. Dividends paid per share of common stock.
4. Dividends paid per share of preferred stock.
5. Yield on common stock

Problem I-6: Incomplete records; preparation of income statement (50-60 min.)

Arthur Jacobs, a merchant, kept very limited records. Purchases of merchandise were paid for by check, but most other items of cost were paid out of cash receipts. Weekly the amount of cash on hand was deposited in a bank account. No record was kept of cash in bank nor was a record kept of sales. Accounts receivable were recorded only by keeping a copy of the charge ticket, and this copy was given to the customer when he paid his account.

Jacobs had started in business on January 1, 19X0 with $20,000 cash and a building which had cost $15,000, of which one-third was the value of the building site. The building depreciated 4% a year. An analysis of the bank statements showed total deposits, including the original cash investment, of $130,500. The balance in the bank per bank statement on December 31, 19X0 was $5,300, but there were checks amounting to $2,150 dated in December but not paid by the bank until January. Cash on hand December 31 was $334.

An inventory of merchandise taken on December 31, 19X0 showed $16,710 of merchandise on a cost basis. Tickets for accounts receivable totaled $1,270, but $123 of that amount is probably not collectible. Unpaid suppliers' invoices for merchandise amounted to $3,780. During the year Jacobs had borrowed $10,000 from his bank but repaid by check $5,000 principal and $100 interest. He had taken from the collections cash for personal expenses of $4,800. Expenses paid in cash were as follows:

Utilities	$554
Advertising	50
Sales help (part-time)	590
Supplies, stationery, etc.	100
Insurance	234
Real estate taxes	350

Store fixtures with a list price of $7,000 were purchased early in January on a one-year installment basis. During the year, checks for the down payment and all maturing installments totaled $5,600. At December 31, the final installment of $1,525 remains unpaid. The fixtures have an estimated useful life of ten years.

Based on the above information, you are to prepare a statement of income for 19X0, supported by all computations necessary to determine the sales and purchases for the year.

SPECIFIC APPROACH

Problem I-1

Many additional lines will be needed on the worksheet to provide for income statement items.

1. Prepare a compound entry for cash receipts.
2. Prepare a compound entry for cash disbursements.
3. Make the adjustments that are needed for insurance, advances from customers, salaries, dividends, depreciation, bad debts, and deferred income taxes.
4. Be especially careful with the adjustment for bad debts. Assume that Bad Debt Expense for the year is 1.2% of total sales. Assume that the $650 writeoff consists of accounts that arose from current sales.

Problem I-2

1. Many additional lines will be needed to provide for the identification of specific changes on net assets.
2. The focus is on all changes in value, regardless of whether exchanges of assets have occurred. For example, if the value of the paintings increased, an entry would be made as follows:

```
Paintings ................  xxxx
    Increase in value of paintings  ....  xxxx
```

Similarly, an opposite entry would be made if the value of household furnishings declined.

Problem I-3

1. Note that items 1(e) and 1(f) need recognition for March only.
2. Item (3) might be segregated as a special liability, but it is not necessary.

Problem I-4

1. To calculate the number of days' operations needed to cover the working capital deficit, divide the deficit by the funds generated by operations.
2. The sales price variation is the difference in the unit selling price times the number of units sold in 1969. The sales volume variation is the difference in units sold times the 1968 unit selling price. Similar computations apply to cost of sales; note that the cost of goods sold is variable.

Problem I-5

1. This is not an easy problem to solve in fifty minutes. In requirement (a), prepare skeleton financial statements and then start filling in the unknown items. One place to begin is with the income statement, using the ratios as clues to develop the needed numbers. Of course, you must know the composition of the various ratios. To illustrate how the relationships develop, you could begin with computations of sales, gross profit, cost of goods sold, and selling expenses. Then the accounts receivable turnover divided into sales would yield accounts receivable. In turn, the total quick assets would be accounts receivable divided by .60.

2. In requirement (b), notice that dividends were equal to current earnings because there was no change in beginning and ending stockholders' equity.

Problem I-6

1. As pointed out in the General Approach to Topic I, the use of skeleton T accounts as a working method for solution is a helpful device in problems of this type. T accounts for Cash in the Bank, Cash on Hand, Accounts Receivable, and Accounts Payable should be sufficient. A knowledge of the usual components of such accounts is helpful, not only in this specific problem, but in most problems involving cash versus accrual basis.

2. This problem entails an analysis of the cash accounts as a major step in solution. A reconciliation of the bank and book balances is essential and is the starting point for collecting the necessary details for sales and purchases.

Statement of Changes in Financial Position; Statement of Cash Flow; Comprehensive Budgeting

GENERAL APPROACH

APB *Opinion No. 19* (or see APBAP Vol. 1, Sect. 2021) requires that a statement of changes in financial position (often called the funds statement) be presented as a basic financial statement when a balance sheet and a statement of income and retained earnings are issued. This 1971 Opinion is a landmark pronouncement because it elevates the funds statement to the same status held by an income statement and a balance sheet. Before 1971, the statement was most widely known as a statement of sources and applications of funds. For brevity in the ensuing discussion, the statement will frequently be called a funds statement.

Because of its new esteem, the statement of changes in financial position will probably get increased coverage on the CPA examination. Therefore, candidates should be thoroughly acquainted with *Opinion No. 19*.

Concept and Format of Funds Statement

The funds statement summarizes the financial and investing activities of the enterprise. The statement shows directly information that can otherwise be obtained only by makeshift analysis and interpretation of balance sheets and statements of income and retained earnings.

There has been long-standing disagreement on the concept and format of the funds statement. The most popular approach had been to view the statement as an explanation of how net working capital has changed for a given period.

Therefore, most funds statements have displayed the sources and applications of net working capital.

Critics of the net working capital approach have stressed that it excludes the disclosure of some important financing and investing activities that do not entail the direct use of net working capital but that belong in any statement of changes in financial position. Consequently, *Opinion No. 19* requires disclosure of all the important aspects of financing and investing activities "regardless of whether cash or other elements of working capital are directly affected." For example, acquisitions of property by issuance of securities or in exchange for other property should be appropriately reflected on the statement.

The broader coverage of the funds statement required by *Opinion No. 19* has been accompanied by flexibility (some commentators might say fuzziness) in form, content, and terminology. The statement of changes in financial position may be in balanced form (i.e., total sources equal total uses) or in a form ending with the net change in financial position "in terms of cash, of cash and temporary investments combined, of all quick assets, or of working capital."

Opinion No. 19 has the following disclosure requirements:

Working capital provided from operations (or cash provided from operations, depending on the concept of funds used) should be separately identified. The effects of extraordinary items should not be mingled with these operating items.

If the format shows the flow of working capital, a tabulation of changes in the elements of working capital should be furnished. In addition, the following items should be identified:

Issuance, assumption, redemption, and reacquisition of long-term debt, preferred stock, and common stock.

Conversion of long-term debt or preferred stock to common stock.

Proceeds from sale of and outlays for long-term assets (identifying separately such items as investments, property, and intangibles).

Dividends in cash or in kind (except stock dividends and stock split-ups).

Using a Net Working Capital Concept

Many conventional presentations of the principles and procedures of funds statement preparation are unnecessarily complex. A candidate who is exposed to a strictly procedural approach involving formidable working papers will probably not be as well grounded as the candidate who understands the reasoning that underlies the statement.

The examiners specifically caution against the use of unnecessary working papers. A candidate who develops a good analytical flair for funds statement problems may save time and trouble because of his ability to prepare the statement without using working papers. Therefore, the following discussion will emphasize analytical techniques rather than the columnar working papers. A standard intermediate or advanced text will offer a detailed review of the use of working papers in funds statement preparation.

Given the flexibility of *Opinion No. 19,* how should the candidate prepare for problems on the statement of changes in financial position? We recommend obtaining a thorough knowledge of the most widely used concept of funds; funds are defined as net working capital. Then you can easily grasp variations in both concept and format.

Net working capital is the excess of current assets over current liabilities. In addition to the usual items, current assets include: prepaid current expenses, temporary investments, ordinary installment and deferred receivables, and receivables from officers, employees, affiliates, and so forth, if collectible within a year. The following items are excluded from current assets: cash not available for current operations, long-term investments, long-term deferred charges, and cash surrender value of life insurance.

Current liabilities include income taxes; miscellaneous debts payable within 12 months (serial note maturities; estimated liabilities, such as those provided for guaranteed servicing of products already sold); and collections received in advance for goods or services to be delivered in the near future. Current liabilities *exclude* long-term deferred credits: deferred income taxes: and currently maturing long-term debt, if payment is to be made by other than the use of current assets.

Nature of the Statement Based on Net Working Capital

In thinking about the nature of the funds statement, you may divide the balance sheet into two major divisions as in Exhibit 2-1.

Exhibit 2-1

A Company
COMPARATIVE BALANCE SHEETS
December 31, 19x1 and 19x2

WORKING CAPITAL SEGMENT

	19x1	*19x2*		*19x1*	*19x2*
Current assets......	$100,000	$150,000	Current liabilities ..	$ 50,000	$ 80,000
			Net working capital	50,000	70,000
				$100,000	$150,000

NONWORKING CAPITAL SEGMENT

	19x1	*19x2*		*19x1*	*19x2*
Investments	$ 20,000	$ 10,000	Long-term debt ...	$ 40,000	$ 55,000
Plant	110,000	125,000	Capital stock......	100,000	100,000
Investment in working capital segment (see above).	50,000	70,000	Retained income ..	40,000	50,000
	$180,000	$205,000		$180,000	$205,000

A frame of reference for this method is the natural division of the balance sheet into the working capital segment and the nonworking capital segment (all noncurrent items). The task then is to trace or reconstruct transactions "between" the two major segments of the balance-sheet accounts.

A funds statement attempts to show *causes* for the change in net working capital for a period. The funds statement is a report of additions and subtractions to the net working capital as reflected in (theoretical) transfers of capital into or out of the working capital segment. By analyzing the transactions recorded in the noncurrent accounts, you may isolate the items having an impact upon working capital, and hence upon the funds statement.

T-Account Method

The following paragraphs highlight a shortcut approach to solutions rather than the working-paper method. If you can develop your confidence in this area by reviewing a method that is already familiar to you, concentrate upon that method. The major objection to the working-paper approach is its time-consuming nature.

The T-account method (developed by Professor William Vatter) is the basic recommended approach. The complete methodology is illustrated, and a shortcut T-account version follows:

ILLUSTRATIVE PROBLEM

From the following trial balances of Sample Company prepare a statement of changes in net working capital position.

	Dec. 31 19x1	Dec. 31 19x2
Assets:		
Cash	$ 80,000	$ 40,000
Receivables	100,000	140,000
Inventories	250,000	351,000
Prepaid expenses	20,000	10,000
Fixed assets, net	1,000,000	1,566,000
Goodwill	650,000	360,000
Total assets	$2,100,000	$2,467,000

	Dec. 31 19x1	Dec. 31 19x2
Equities:		
Accounts payable	$ 120,000	$ 180,000
Wages payable	10,000	5,000
Miscellaneous current liabilities	70,000	65,000
Long-term bonds payable	100,000	250,000
Capital Stock, at par value	800,000	1,000,000
Paid-in capital in excess of par value of stock	300,000	500,000
Retained income	700,000	467,000
Total equities	$2,100,000	$2,467,000

On March 31, 19x2, $300,000 of goodwill was charged off as a special item.

In the first half of 19x2, the company bought the assets of another business—$100,000 worth of equipment and $50,000 worth of inventory and accounts receivable. The amount paid was $170,000, the excess of $20,000 being considered the cost of the goodwill acquired. Various other cash purchases of equipment totaled $550,000.

Old machinery was sold for $1,000; it originally cost $12,000 and $8,000 depreciation had been accumulated.

Early in 19x2, the company received $400,000 cash for a new issue of capital stock which had a par value of $200,000. Long-term bonds were also issued for $150,000 cash.

Net income was $17,000 after deductions of $80,000 for depreciation, $10,000 for amortization of goodwill, and deductions for the loss on the sale of machinery and the special write-down of goodwill.

Steps in Preparation

First, compute the change in net working capital, as Exhibit 2-2 shows.

Exhibit 2-2

TABULATION OF CHANGES IN ELEMENTS OF
NET WORKING CAPITAL

	Dec. 31		Increase
	19x1	*19x2*	*(Decrease)*
Current assets:			
Cash	$ 80,000	$ 40,000	$ (40,000)
Receivables	100,000	140,000	40,000
Inventories	250,000	351,000	101,000
Prepaid expenses	20,000	10,000	(10,000)
Total current assets	$450,000	$541,000	$ 91,000
Less: Current liabilities:			
Accounts payable	$120,000	$180,000	$ 60,000
Wages payable	10,000	5,000	(5,000)
Miscellaneous..........	70,000	65,000	(5,000)
Total current liabilities...........	$200,000	$250,000	$ 50,000
Net working capital	$250,000	$291,000	$ 41,000

This technique for solving the problem centers on the relationship between the net working capital T account and all nonworking capital accounts. The *net change* in the individual balances is entered at the top of each account, a single line being drawn below each entry as indicated. (This step is keyed by the letter *B* in the T accounts [Exhibit 2-3] that follow.)

This approach explains the change in net working capital by analyzing the influence of the changes in the nonworking capital accounts. Attention is concentrated upon the reconstruction of entries in the noncurrent accounts as they affect net working capital.

Let us examine the entries in Exhibit 2-3 step by step. The postings are keyed numerically.

Exhibit 2-3

T-ACCOUNT APPROACH TO SAMPLE PROBLEM

NET WORKING CAPITAL

Increases			Decreases	
	B. 41,000			
		Sources	Applications	
Operations:				
1. Net income	17,000		5. Purchase of equipment	100,000
2. Depreciation	80,000		5. Purchase of goodwill	20,000
3. Amortization	10,000		7. Various purchases of plant	
4. Extraordinary			and equipment	550,000
write-off of			9. Cash dividends paid	250,000
goodwill	300,000			
6. Loss of machinery	3,000	410,000		
Other Sources:				
6. Proceeds of machinery sale		1,000		
8. Issuance of capital stock		400,000		
8. Issuance of long-term bonds		150,000		

Fixed Assets (Net)			Goodwill		
B. 566,000				*B.* 290,000	
5. Purchase	2. Depreciation		5. Purchase	3. Amortization	
100,000	80,000		20,000	10,000	
7. Purchases	6. Sales			4. Write-off	
550,000	4,000			300,000	

Long-term Bonds Payable		Capital Stock	
	B. 150,000		*B.* 200,000
	8. Issuance		8. Issuance
	150,000		200,000

Paid-in Capital		Retained Income	
	B. 200,000	*B.* 233,000	
	8. Issuance of	9. Cash dividends	1. Net income
	stock 200,000	250,000	17,000

1. A good starting point is net income and its relationship to net working capital (i.e., funds) provided by operations. A summary of the net income effect is entered: debit Net Working Capital, credit Retained Income. But Net Income does not directly reflect the impact of operations on Net Working Capital. Net income is a residual figure, the difference between revenue and all expenses and losses—including some expenses and losses (e.g., depreciation, amortization, and losses on the disposal of long-term assets) which do not affect Net Working Capital.

Our purpose is to ascertain the net effect of operations on Net Working Capital. The most straightforward way to accomplish this is to begin with the total sales figure and then deduct all the operating expenses that drained working capital (e.g., cost of goods sold, selling and administrative expenses, etc.). This is a cumbersome way of arriving at funds provided by operations, so accountants use a shortcut. Instead of beginning with the Sales total on the income statement and working down ($A-B-C$ in Exhibit 2-4), accountants usually start with Net Income and work up ($E + D$ in Exhibit 2-4) toward the entry Net Funds Provided by Operations. That is, they add back all charges not requiring working capital.

This shortcut is used in the Net Working Capital T account (see Exhibit 2-3). Notice that Increases are divided into two major sections: Operations and Other Sources. Sufficient space should be allowed in the Operations section for short-cut adjustments to net income to obtain the funds provided by operations. The subtotal ($410,000 in Exhibit 2-4) will then be the funds provided by operations.

Exhibit 2-4

ANALYSIS OF INCOME STATEMENT
TO SHOW EFFECTS OF OPERATIONS ON WORKING CAPITAL

(A)	Sales		xxx,xxx
(B)	Less: Cost of goods sold (detailed)		xxx,xxx
	Gross profit		xxx,xxx
(C)	Less: Operating expenses requiring working capital (detailed)		xxx,xxx
(desired figure) →	Net funds provided by operations		$410,000
(D)	Less: Operating charges not requiring working capital:		
	Depreciation	$80,000	
	Amortization of goodwill	10,000	
	Loss on disposal on noncurrent assets	3,000	93,000
(E)	Net income		$317,000

2. Depreciation:

Net working capital (adjustment to net income) .	80,000	
Fixed assets (net)		80,000

3. Amortization:

Net working capital (adjustment to net income) . .	10,000	
Goodwill		10,000

4. Write-off of goodwill (no effect on working capital):

Net working capital (adjustment to net income) .	300,000	
Goodwill		300,000

5. Purchase of assets:

Fixed assets	100,000	
Goodwill	20,000	
Net working capital		120,000

Note that the purchase of inventory and receivables had no effect on net working capital. The purchase was merely an exchange of current assets for current assets.

6. Sale of old machinery:

Net working capital (cash received)	1,000	
Net working capital (adjustment to net income)	3,000	
Fixed assets (net)		4,000

7. Various purchases of fixed assets:

Fixed assets...........................	550,000	
Net working capital		550,000

8. Issuance of equities:

Net working capital.....................	400,000	
Capital stock		200,000
Paid-in capital		200,000
Net working capital 150,000		
Long-term bonds payable		150,000

9. Note that, at this point, all explicit information has been entered in the pertinent accounts. A preliminary addition of debits and credits below the line in each account will show that all changes in all accounts have been explained, except in the Net Working Capital account and the Retained Income account. Therefore, a hidden, implicit transaction is derived after all explicit, explained transactions have been posted. That transaction must be the payment of cash dividends:

Retained income	250,000	
Net working capital		250,000

Now all changes have been accounted for. All the ingredients of a funds statement are in the Net Working Capital T account of Exhibit 2-3. The difference between the debits and credits below the line in Net Working Capital is now equal to the $41,000 change that appears at the top of the account. From the Net Working Capital T account of Exhibit 2-3, a funds statement (Exhibit 2-5) may be prepared.

Exhibit 2-5 illustrates the "net change" format. An alternative statement could have a "balanced" format as in Exhibit 2-6.

Shortened T-Account Method

Close study of the previous example reveals that most of the transactions affecting working capital and noncurrent accounts may be posted directly to the Net Working Capital T account *without* formally completing entries in all noncurrent T accounts. *By wise use of additional information in the problem itself, plus scanning the changes in noncurrent items, you can produce most of the sources and applications directly.* T accounts for Fixed Assets and Retained Income will still be helpful in most instances, however.

Exhibit 2-5

Sample Company
STATEMENT OF CHANGES IN NET WORKING CAPITAL
For the Year Ending December 31, 19x2

Sources of net working capital:
  From operations:
    Net income .... $ 17,000
    Add charges not requiring working capital:
      Depreciation .... $ 80,000
      Amortization of goodwill 10,000
      Special write-off of goodwill 300,000
      Loss on sale of machinery 3,000   393,000

Net working capital provided by operations $410,000
From sale of machinery 1,000
From issuance of capital stock 400,000
From issuance of long-term bonds payable 150,000

    Total sources of net working capital $961,000
Application of net working capital:
  To purchase of business:
    Equipment $100,000
    Goodwill 20,000

Net funds applied to purchase $120,000
Various purchases of plant and equipment 550,000
Cash dividends paid 250,000

    Total applications of net working capital 920,000

Net increase in net working capital (see tabulation
  in Exhibit 2-2)... $ 41,000

Exhibit 2-6

Balanced Format

Sources:
  (Same as Exhibit 2-5)
    Total sources $961,000

Applications:
  To purchase of business:
    Equipment $100,000
    Goodwill 20,000 $120,000
  Various purchases of plant and equipment 550,000
  Cash dividends paid 250,000
  Increase in net working capital 41,000

    Total applications $961,000

An example of the shortened approach, using the same illustrative problem, is given in Exhibit 2-7.

Exhibit 2-7

SHORTENED T-ACCOUNT METHOD

NET WORKING CAPITAL

Increases			Decreases	
	B.	41,000		
		Sources	Applications	
Operations:				
1. Net income	17,000		5. Purchase of equipment	100,000
2. Depreciation	80,000		5. Purchase of goodwill	20,000
3. Amortization	10,000		7. Various purchases of plant	
4. Special			and equipment	550,000
write-off of			9. Cash dividends paid	250,000
goodwill	300,000			
6. Loss on machinery	3,000	410,000		
Other Sources:				
6. Proceeds of machinery sale		1,000		
8. Issuance of capital stock		400,000		
8. Issuance of long-term bonds		150,000		

Fixed Assets (Net)		Retained Income	
B. 566,000		B. 233,000	
5. Purchase	2. Depreciation	9. Cash dividends	1. Net income
100,000	80,000	250,000	17,000
7. Purchases	6. Sale		
550,000	4,000		

After net changes in T accounts for Net Working Capital, Fixed Assets, and Retained Income, have been entered, additional information is scanned. Fund flow effects are picked out, and all entries are labeled for later reference. Let us examine the entries which are, again, posted numerically.

1,2,3, and 4. Enter net income and adjustments thereto, to get net working capital provided by operations.

5. Purchase of assets: equipment and goodwill.

6. Sale of old machinery.

7. Various purchases of fixed assets.

8. Issuances of stock and bonds.

9. The balance in Retained Income is now $17,000, but the net change is a decrease of $233,000. The payment of cash dividends in the amount of $250,000 is therefore an implied transaction—the only apparent explanation for the $41,000 net increase in Net Working Capital and the $233,000 net decrease in Retained Income.

This method saves time and helps to isolate hidden transactions. But it must be remembered that it is merely a shortcut version of the complete T-account method illustrated previously.

Summary of Approach to Solutions
of Funds Statement Problems

Solution Steps

Funds statements may be derived by using T accounts rather than bulky working papers. The major features of the T-account approach are (1) time is saved and (2) working with familiar T accounts helps clarify thinking on the whole subject of funds statement preparation.

The frame of reference for this method is the natural division of the balance sheet into two major segments. Then the task is to trace or to reconstruct the transactions between the two divisions of the balance-sheet accounts.

A summary of the solution steps follows:

1. Determine net increase or decrease in working capital.
2. Enter the increase or decrease at the top of a Net Working Capital T account.
3. Enter net increases or decreases in noncurrent accounts at the top of individual T accounts. (It is not always necessary to use all noncurrent accounts. Often the relationship or nonrelationship between changes in many noncurrent accounts and net working capital is so obvious that the actual setting up of T accounts is unnecessary. All that needs to be done is to enter the source or application in the working capital T account. However, in most cases it is helpful to use T accounts for fixed assets and retained earnings.)
4. Reconstruct entries in noncurrent accounts that affect working capital. First, consult the additional information in the problem. Second, by scanning the noncurrent accounts for unexplained changes, reconstruct the hidden transactions.
5. Using the working capital T account, prepare the formal funds statement.

Pitfalls to Avoid

1. Be certain that there is an appropriate classification of current assets and current liabilities before computing changes in net working capital.
2. Use columnar working papers only when absolutely necessary.
3. In almost all situations where there is a net loss, there will still be funds provided by operations. Depreciation and other nonworking capital charges are deductions in the computation of a net loss. When these are added back to the final net loss figure, the result shows a positive amount of funds provided by Operations. The following hypothetical T account illustrates this point.

NET WORKING CAPITAL

			Dividends	25,000
		40,000		
Operations:				
Net loss	(10,000)			
Depreciation	25,000	15,000		
Other sources:				
Sale of bonds		50,000		

4. One major feature of problems on funds statements is the presence of transactions which are not explicitly stated and which must be derived from your analysis of the changes in noncurrent accounts. First, all explicit additional information is traced. Then the implicit, hidden transaction are reconstructed by a step-by-step consideration of all unexplained changes in noncurrent accounts accounts.

5. Your formal presentation of the funds statement should include a subtotal of funds provided by operations. The mere listing of net profit, depreciation, amortization, and so forth, as sources of funds would cause some graders to think there might be some misunderstanding of the relationship of depreciation to the flow of funds.

Alternative Concepts and Formats

A statement of the flow of funds supposedly portrays the financial management habits of a company. However, a strictly held definition of *funds* as "net working capital" often results in the exclusion of important financial transactions from a funds flow statement. For example, conversion of bonds into stock, the exchange of noncurrent assets for other noncurrent assets, and the acquisition of property for cash plus a substantial mortgage can all be ignored or only partially reported in a funds statement in which funds are equated with net working capital.

The disadvantages of defining funds as working capital have led to a variety of substitute definitions. Among them are "cash," "net liquid assets exclusive of inventories," and "all financial resources." All have various strengths and weaknesses.

"All financial resources" is a broader concept than net working capital and would incorporate nearly all relevant financial transactions, but it presents some difficulties. For example, some accountants support the notion that a stock dividend (common on common) should be reported as a source of funds and as a use of funds, since it is equivalent to paying a cash dividend that is immediately reinvested in the corporation by the stockholder. But *Opinion No. 19* specifically excludes such a transaction from the "all financial resources" concept.

When using an "all financial resources" concept of funds, always follow the balanced format. Moreover, even when a net working capital concept of funds is used, *Opinion No. 19* requires that we include major financing and investing transactions that solely affect the non-working capital segment of the balance sheet.

For instance, suppose the Sample Company acquired machinery in a direct exchange for a long-term note of $100,000. Working capital would be unaffected, but the Statement in Exhibit 2-6 would have a new line item, Issuance of long-term note, under Sources and a new line item, Purchase of machinery, under Applications. The total sources and the total applications would each be $1,061,000 instead of $961,000.

The inclusion of non-working capital items in a funds statement and the labeling of the report as a statement of changes in financial position will probably lead to the eventual disuse of "sources" and "applications" as names for the two major sections of the statement. Instead, the terms "increases in resources" and "decreases in resources" or perhaps simply "increases" and "decreases" may be adopted.

Statement of Cash Flow

A cash flow statement is similar to a statement of sources and applications of funds, but the two differ in scope. As we have just seen, the funds statement is often a summary explanation of transactions that have a direct impact upon *net working capital.* The cash flow statement is a summary explanation of transactions that have a direct impact upon *cash,* a narrower concept.

Essentially, this means that Cash, rather than Net Working Capital, is the master T account. Furthermore, it requires that we analyze changes in all balance-sheet items other than cash in order to determine the impact of such changes on cash. The solution technique calls for reconstructing cash transactions in the same manner in which funds transactions are reconstructed for a funds flow statement.

The basic format for the cash flow statement follows:

Cash was provided by:		
Operations (see schedule)		xxx
Issuance of capital stock		xxx
Issuance of bonds		xxx
Sale of investments		xxx
Total		xxx
Cash was applied to:		
Acquisition of plant and equipment	xxx	
Decrease of short-term bank loans	xxx	
Payment of long-term notes	xxx	
Payment of dividends	xxx	xxx
Increase (or decrease) in cash balance		xxx

The most difficult part of preparing a cash flow statement is a step-by-step analysis of all income statement items so that net income on an accrual basis may be converted to cash flow from operations. Probably the easiest way to begin is with the cash inflow from sales, then convert all expenses to a cash-outflow basis. This analysis may be conducted on the left side of the master Cash T account; it is similar to the analysis conducted on the left side of the master Net Working Capital account in order to compute funds provided by operations.

In converting income statement items to the cash basis, remember that declines in inventories and prepayments and increases in payables result in less outflow of cash for conducting current operations. Also, increases in receivables mean that all current sales are not being transformed immediately into cash inflows.

Problem II-4 illustrates some of these techniques.

Comprehensive Budgeting

The basic steps in preparing budgeted financial statements follow:

1. *The sales forecast is the starting point for budgeting* because inventory levels and production (hence, costs) generally are geared to the rate of sales activity.

2. After sales are budgeted, the production budget may be prepared. First, the units of budgeted production of finished products must be predetermined. This unit calculation may be expressed: Units to Be Produced equals Desired Ending Inventory of Finished Goods plus Planned Sales minus Beginning Inventory of Finished Goods.

3. When the level of production activity has been determined, the following budget schedules may be constructed:

   a. Material usage and purchases. Usage depends upon the level of production activity determined in step 2 above. Purchases are affected as follows: Purchases in units equals Desired Ending Material Inventory Quantities plus Usage minus Beginning Inventory Quantities.

   b. Direct labor costs. These depend upon the type of products produced and labor rates and methods that must be used to obtain desired production.

   c. Factory overhead costs. These depend upon the behavior of costs of individual overhead items in relation to the anticipated level of production.

   d. Inventory levels. These are the desired ending inventories. This information is required for the construction of budgeted financial statements.

4. Cost of Goods Sold budget. This budget depends upon information gathered in step 3.

5. Budget of selling, administrative, and other expenses.

6. Budgeted income statement.

7. Cash budget. Estimate effects of the above level of operations on cash position. Ordinarily, the cash budget (Budgeted Statement of Cash Receipts and Disbursements) has the following main sections:

   a. The beginning cash balance plus cash receipts yield total cash available for needs, before financing. Cash receipts depend on collections of accounts receivable, cash sales, and miscellaneous recurring sources such as rental or royalty receipts. Studies of the prospective collectibility of accounts receivable are needed for accurate predictions. Key factors include bad-debt experience and average time lag between sales and collections.

   b. Cash disbursements:

     (1) Material purchases—depend on credit terms extended by suppliers and bill-paying habits of the buyer.

     (2) Direct labor and other wage outlays—depend on payroll dates.

     (3) Other costs and expenses—depend on timing and credit terms. Note that depreciation does not entail a cash outlay.

     (4) Other disbursements—purchases of fixed assets, long-term investments.

   c. Financing requirements depend on how the total cash available compares with the total cash needed. Needs include disbursements plus the ending cash balance desired. Financing plans depend on the relationship of cash available to cash sought. If there is an excess, loans may be repaid or temporary investments made. Pertinent outlays for interest expenses are usually shown in this section of the cash budget.

   d. The ending cash balance.

  8. Budgeted balance sheet. Each item is projected in the light of the details of the business plan as expressed in the previous schedules. For example, the ending balance of Accounts Receivable would be computed by adding budgeted sales to the beginning balance, then subtracting cash receipts.

  9. Skill in presentation and layout of budget schedules is important. For example, sometimes a cash forecast may be presented in one master schedule without being unwieldy. Adequate cross-referencing is essential.

CPA PROBLEMS

Problem II-1: Statement of source and application of funds (50-60 min.)

The financial statements of Frank Manufacturing Corporation for 1964 and 1963 follow on pp. 56-57. The Corporation was formed on January 1, 1961.

The following information was given effect in the preparation of the foregoing financial statements:

1. The 10% stock dividend was distributed on August 1. The investment in land for a future plant site was obtained by the issuance of 10,000 shares of the Corporation's common stock on October 1. On December 1, 20,000 shares of common stock were sold to obtain additional working capital. There were no other 1964 transactions affecting contributed capital.

2. During 1964 depreciable assets with a total cost of $17,500 were retired and sold as scrap for a nominal amount. These assets were fully depreciated at December 31, 1963. The only depreciable asset acquired in 1964 was a new building which was completed in December; no depreciation was taken on its cost.

Frank Manufacturing Corporation
COMPARATIVE BALANCE SHEETS
December 31, 1964 and 1963

Assets	*1964*	*1963*	*Increase (Decrease)*
Current assets			
Cash	$ 33,500	$ 27,000	$ 6,500
Accounts receivable (net of allowance for			
bad debts of $1,900 and $2,000)........	89,900	79,700	10,200
Inventories (at lower of cost or market)	136,300	133,200	3,100
Prepaid expenses	4,600	12,900	(8,300)
Total	264,300	252,800	11,500
Investments			
Land held for future plant site	35,000	. . .	35,000
Fixed assets			
Land.............................	47,000	47,000	. . .
Buildings and equipment (net of accumulated			
depreciation of $155,600 and $117,000).	551,900	425,000	126,900
Total..........................	598,900	472,000	126,900
Other assets			
Organization expense	1,500	3,000	(1,500)
Total..........................	$899,700	$727,800	$171,900
Liabilities & Stockholders' Equity			
Current liabilities			
Accounts payable	$ 3,000	$ 7,800	$ (4,800)
Notes payable.......................	8,000	5,000	3,000
Mortgage payable	3,600	3,600	. . .
Accrued liabilities....................	6,200	4,800	1,400
Income taxes payable	87,500	77,900	9,600
Total..........................	108,300	99,100	9,200
Long-term liabilities			
Notes payable.......................	. . .	18,000	(18,000)
Mortgage payable	70,200	73,800	(3,600)
Total..........................	70,200	91,800	(21,600)
Deferred income—investment credit..........	16,800	18,900	(2,100)
Stockholders' equity			
Capital stock; $1 par value; shares author-			
ized, 300,000 in 1964 and 200,000 in			
1963; shares issued and outstanding,			
162,000 in 1964 and 120,000 in 1963 ..	162,000	120,000	42,000
Capital contributed in excess of par value...	306,900	197,900	109,000
Reserve for contingencies	25,000	. . .	25,000
Retained earnings	210,500	200,100	10,400
Total..........................	704,400	518,000	186,400
Total	$899,700	$727,800	$171,900

Frank Manufacturing Company
STATEMENT OF INCOME AND RETAINED EARNINGS
For the Years Ended December 31, 1964 and 1963

	1964	1963	Increase (Decrease)
Sales...............................	$980,000	$900,000	$ 80,000
Cost of goods sold	540,000	490,000	50,000
Gross profit	440,000	410,000	30,000
Selling and administrative expenses	262,000	248,500	13,500
Net income from operations.............	178,000	161,500	16,500
Other income and (deductions), (net)	(3,000)	(1,500)	1,500
Net income before income taxes	175,000	160,000	15,000
Provision for income taxes................	85,400	77,900	7,500
Net income after income taxes	89,600	82,100	7,500
Retained earnings, January 1	200,100	118,000	82,100
Ten per cent stock dividend distributed.......	(36,000)	...	(36,000)
Cash dividends paid	(18,200)	...	(18,200)
Appropriation for contingent loss	(25,000)	...	(25,000)
Retained earnings, December 31..........	$210,500	$200,100	$ 10,400

3. When new equipment, with an estimated life of 10 years, was purchased on January 2, 1963 for $300,000, the decision was made to record the resulting investment credit in a deferred income account with the benefit of the investment credit being allocated over the useful life of the machine by a reduction of the provision for income taxes. The income-tax rate for 1963 and 1964 was 50%.

4. In 1964 $10,000 was paid in advance on long-term notes payable. The balance of the long-term notes is due in 1965.

5. A reserve for a contingent loss of $25,000 arising from a law suit was established in 1964.

Required:

Prepare a formal statement of source and application of funds for the Frank Manufacturing Company for the year ended December 31, 1964. The formal statement should include the financial aspects of all significant transactions. Supplementary schedules, such as the schedule of changes in working capital accounts, should be presented in good form.

Problem II-2: Statement of source and application of funds (50-60 min.)

The president of Tuttle Specialties Company requests that you prepare a statement of source and application of funds for the benefit of the stockholders. Comparative balance sheets for the Company are presented on the next page.

Tuttle Specialties Company
GENERAL LEDGER POST-CLOSING TRIAL BALANCES
For the Years Ended December 31, 1966 and 1965

			Increase
Debits	*1966*	*1965*	*(Decrease)*
Cash..................................	$ 157,700	$ 100,400	$ 57,300
Certificates of deposit due March 31, 1967 ...	175,000		175,000
Marketable securities	100,100	262,100	(162,000)
Customers' notes and accounts receivable.....	390,000	327,300	62,700
Inventories...........................	155,400	181,200	(25,800)
Investment in wholly owned subsidiary at equity in net assets	140,000	190,400	(50,400)
Bond sinking fund		62,200	(62,200)
Advance to suppliers	137,500		137,500
Plant and equipment	2,138,600	1,952,600	186,000
Goodwill		150,000	(150,000)
Discount on bonds payable		10,200	(10,200)
Total debits.....................	$3,394,300	$3,236,400	$157,900

Credits			
Notes receivable discounted	$ 100,000		$100,000
Accounts payable......................	192,400	$ 147,600	44,800
Bank loans–current		70,000	(70,000)
Allowance for depreciation	510,000	359,700	150,300
Accrued payables......................	47,100	72,300	(25,200)
Income and other taxes payable...........	128,700	25,500	103,200
Deferred income taxes..................	58,500	65,000	(6,500)
5% mortgage bonds due 1974		320,000	(320,000)
4% serial bonds	100,000		100,000
Capital stock, $10 par value..............	1,110,000	900,000	210,000
Premium on capital stock................	152,100		152,100
Retained earnings appropriated for the retirement of 5% mortage bonds		62,200	(62,200)
Retained earnings unappropriated	995,500	1,214,100	(218,600)
Total credits	$3,394,300	$3,236,400	$157,900

Additional Information

1. An analysis of Retained Earnings Unappropriated account follows:

Retained earnings unappropriated, December 31, 1965	$1,214,100
Add: Net income for the year	112,200
Transfer from appropriation for retirement of 5% mortgage bonds	62,200
Total	1,388,500
Deduct: Write-off of goodwill $150,000	
Cash dividends 90,000	
10% stock dividend 153,000	393,000
Retained earnings unappropriated, December 31, 1966	$ 995,500

2. On January 2, 1966 marketable securities costing $162,000 were sold for $165,800. The proceeds from the sale of the securities, the funds in the Bond

Sinking Fund, and the amount received from the sale of the 4% serial bonds were used to retire the 5% mortgage bonds at 102½.

3. The Company paid a stock dividend of 10% on stock outstanding at February 1, 1966. The market value per share at that date was $17.00.

4. The Company advanced $137,500 to a supplier on August 15 for the purchase of special machinery which is to be delivered in June 1967.

5. Accounts receivable of $15,000 and $12,500 were considered uncollectible and written off against income in 1966 and 1965, respectively.

6. The stockholders approved a stock option plan on September 1, 1966. Under the plan 100,000 shares of capital stock are reserved for issuance to key employees at prices not less than market value at the dates of grant. The options will become exercisable in three equal installments starting one year after the date of grant and will expire five years after the date of grant. At December 31, 1966 options were granted for 20,000 shares at $16.00 per share. The options are carried on a memo basis and are not recorded in the accounts.

7. Extraordinary repairs of $12,500 to the equipment were charged to the Allowance for Depreciation account during the year. No assets were retired during 1966.

8. The wholly-owned subsidiary reported a loss for the year of $50,400. The loss was booked by the parent.

Required:

Prepare a statement of source and application of funds and a statement of changes in working capital for year ended December 31, 1966. Supporting schedules should be in good form.

Problem II-3: Statement of source and application of funds (50-60 min.)

Comparative balance sheets for the Plainview Corporation are shown on page 60.

Your workpapers and other sources disclose the following additional information relating to 1970 activities:

1.The Retained Earnings account was analyzed as follows:

Retained earnings, December 31, 1969		$758,200
Add net income after extraordinary items		236,580
		994,780
Deduct:		
Cash dividends	$130,000	
Loss on reissue of treasury stock	3,000	
10% stock dividend	100,200	233,200
Retained earnings, December 31, 1970		$761,580

You noted that the client's determination of net income complied with Opinion No. 9 of the Accounting Principles Board.

2. On January 2, 1970 marketable securities costing $110,000 were sold for $127,000. The proceeds from this sale, the funds in the bond sinking fund and the amount received from the issuance of the 8% debentures were used to retire the 6% mortgage bonds.

Plainview Corporation
COMPARATIVE BALANCE SHEETS
For The Years Ended December 31, 1969 and 1970

Assets	1970	1969	Increase (Decrease)
Cash..................................	$ 142,100	$ 165,300	$ (23,200)
Marketable securities (at cost)	122,800	129,200	(6,400)
Accounts receivable (net).................	312,000	371,200	(59,200)
Inventories...........................	255,200	124,100	131,100
Prepaid expenses	23,400	22,000	1,400
Bond sinking fund		63,000	(63,000)
Investment in subsidiary (at equity).........	134,080	152,000	(17,920)
Plant and equipment (net)	1,443,700	1,534,600	(90,900)
	$2,433,280	$2,561,400	$(128,120)

Equities			
Accounts payable......................	$ 238,100	$ 213,300	$ 24,800
Notes payable—current		145,000	(145,000)
Accrued payables......................	16,500	18,000	(1,500)
Income taxes payable...................	97,500	31,000	66,500
Deferred income taxes	53,900	43,400	10,500
6% mortgage bonds (due 1982)		300,000	(300,000)
Premium on mortgage bonds		10,000	(10,000)
8% debentures (due 1990)	125,000		125,000
Allowance for estimated casualty losses......	74,000	85,000	(11,000)
Common stock, $10 par value	1,033,500	950,000	83,500
Premium on common stock	67,700	51,000	16,700
Retained earnings	761,580	758,200	3,380
Treasury stock—at cost of $3 per share	(34,500)	(43,500)	9,000
	$2,433,280	$2,561,400	$(128,120)

3. The treasury stock was reissued on February 28, 1970.

4. The stock dividend was declared on October 31, 1970 when the market price of Plainview Corporation's stock was $12 per share.

5. On April 30, 1970 a fire destroyed a warehouse which cost $100,000 and upon which depreciation of $65,000 had accumulated. The deferred income tax credit relating to the difference between tax and book depreciation on the warehouse was $12,700. The loss was charged to the Allowance for Estimated Casualty Losses account.

6. Plant and equipment transactions consisted of the sale of a building at its book value of $4,000 and the purchase of machinery for $28,000.

7. In 1970 a $30,000 charge was made to accumulated depreciation for excessive depreciation taken in prior years but disallowed by the Internal Revenue Service. A tax deficiency of $16,000 was paid and charged against deferred income taxes.

8. Accounts receivable written off as uncollectible were $16,300 in 1969 and $18,500 in 1970. Expired insurance recorded in 1969 was $4,100 and $3,900 in 1970.

9. The subsidiary, which is 80% owned, reported a loss of $22,400 for 1970.

Required:

Prepare a formal statement of source and application of funds (working capital) for the year ended December 31, 1970, applying the "all financial resources" concept. Include supporting schedules in good form.

Problem II-4: Sources and uses of cash (50-60 min.)

The following financial data were furnished to you by the Relgne Corporation:

Relgne Corporation
COMPARATIVE TRIAL BALANCES
At Beginning and End of Fiscal Year Ended October 31, 1969

	October 31 1969	Increase	Decrease	November 1 1968
Cash.........................	$ 226,000	$176,000	$	$ 50,000
Accounts receivable..............	148,000	48,000		100,000
Inventories.....................	291,000		$ 9,000	300,000
Unexpired insurance..............	2,500	500		2,000
Long-term investments at cost.......	10,000		30,000	40,000
Sinking fund....................	90,000	10,000		80,000
Land and building	195,000			195,000
Equipment	215,000	125,000		90,000
Discount on bonds payable	8,500		500	9,000
Treasury stock at cost	5,000		5,000	10,000
Cost of goods sold	539,000			
Selling and general expenses	287,000			
Income tax	32,000			
Loss on sale of equipment	1,000			
Capital gains tax	3,000			
Total debits	$2,053,000			$876,000
Allowance for doubtful accounts.....	$ 8,000	$ 3,000		$ 5,000
Accumulated depreciation—building ..	26,250	3,750		22,500
Accumulated depreciation— equipment	39,750	12,250		27,500
Accounts payable................	55,000	.	5,000	60,000
Notes payable—current	70,000	50,000		20,000
Accrued expenses payable	18,000	3,000		15,000
Taxes payable	35,000	25,000		10,000
Unearned revenue................	1,000		8,000	9,000
Note payable—long-term	40,000		20,000	60,000
Bonds payable—long-term..........	250,000			250,000
Common stock..................	300,000	100,000		200,000
Appropriation for sinking fund	90,000	10,000		80,000
Unappropriated retained earnings	94,000		18,000	112,000
Paid-in capital in excess of par value	116,000	111,000		5,000
Sales........................	898,000			
Gain on sale of investments	12,000			
Total credits.................	$2,053,000			$876,000

The following information was also available:
1. All purchases and sales were on account.
2. The sinking fund will be used to retire the long-term bonds.
3. Equipment with an original cost of $15,000 was sold for $7,000.
4. Selling and General Expenses includes the following expenses:

Expired insurance	$ 2,000
Building depreciation............	3,750
Equipment depreciation..........	19,250
Bad debts expense	4,000
Interest expense................	18,000

5. A six-months note payable for $50,000 was issued towards the purchase of new equipment.

6. The long-term note payable requires the payment of $20,000 per year plus interest until paid.

7. Treasury stock was sold for $1,000 more than its cost.

8. All dividends were paid by cash.

Required:

    a. Prepare schedules computing
       1. Collections of accounts receivable.
       2. Payments of accounts payable.
    b. Prepare a Statement of Sources and Uses of Cash (sometimes called a Cash Flow Statement) for Relgne Corporation. Supporting computations should be in good form.

Problem II-5: Comprehensive budgeting for a college (40-50 min.)

DeMars College has asked your assistance in developing its budget for the coming 1971-72 academic year. You are supplied with the following data for the current year:

1.

	Lower Division (Freshman– Sophomore)	Upper Division (Junior– Senior)
Average number of students per class	25	20
Average salary of faculty member	$10,000	$10,000
Average number of credit hours carried each year per student	33	30
Enrollment including scholarship students..........	2,500	1,700
Average faculty teaching load in credit hours per year (10 classes of 3 credit hours).............	30	30

For 1971-72 lower division enrollment is expected to increase by 10%, while the upper division's enrollment is expected to remain stable. Faculty salaries will be increased by a standard 5%, and additional merit increases to be awarded to individual faculty members will be $90,750 for the lower division and $85,000 for the upper division.

2. The current budget is $210,000 for operation and maintenance of plant and equipment; this includes $90,000 for salaries and wages. Experience of the past three months suggests that the current budget is realistic, but that expected increases for 1971-72 are 5% in salaries and wages and $9,000 in other expenditures for operation and maintenance of plant and equipment.

3. The budget for the remaining expenditures for 1971-72 is as follows:

Administrative and general	$240,000
Library	160,000
Health and recreation	75,000
Athletics	120,000
Insurance and retirement	265,000
Interest	48,000
Capital outlay	300,000

4. The College expects to award 25 tuition-free scholarships to lower division students and 15 to upper division students. Tuition is $22 per credit hour and no other fees are charged.

5. Budgeted revenues for 1971-72 are as follows:

> Endowments $114,000
> Net income from auxiliary services 235,000
> Athletics 180,000

The College's remaining source of revenue is an annual support campaign held during the spring.

Required:

a. Prepare a schedule computing for 1971-72 by division (1) the expected enrollment, (2) the total credit hours to be carried and (3) the number of faculty members needed.

b. Prepare a schedule computing the budget for faculty salaries by division for 1971-72.

c. Prepare a schedule computing the tuition revenue budget by division for 1971-72.

d. Assuming that the faculty salaries budget computed in part "b" was $2,400,000 and that the tuition revenue budget computed in part "c" was $3,000,000, prepare a schedule computing the amount which must be raised during the annual support campaign in order to cover the 1971-72 expenditures budget.

Problem II-6: Comprehensive budgeting (45-55 min.)

Modern Products Corporation, a manufacturer of molded plastic containers, determined in October 1968 that it needed cash to continue operations. The Corporation began negotiating for a one-month bank loan of $100,000 which would be discounted at 6 per cent per annum on November 1. In considering the loan the bank requested a projected income statement and a cash budget for the month of November.

The following information is available:

1. Sales were budgeted at 120,000 units per month in October 1968, December 1968 and January 1969 and at 90,000 units in November 1968.

The selling price is $2 per unit. Sales are billed on the 15th and last day of each month on terms of 2/10 net 30. Past experience indicates sales are even throughout the month and 50 per cent of the customers pay the billed amount within the discount period. The remainder pay at the end of 30 days, except for bad debts which average ½ per cent of gross sales. On its income statement the Corporation deducts from sales the estimated amounts for cash discounts on sales and losses on bad debts.

2. The inventory of finished goods on October 1 was 24,000 units. The finished goods inventory at the end of each month is to be maintained at 20 per cent of sales anticipated for the following month. There is no work in process.

3. The inventory of raw materials on October 1 was 22,800 pounds. At the end of each month the raw materials inventory is to be maintained at not less than 40 per cent of production requirements for the following month. Materials are purchased as needed in minimum quantities of 25,000 pounds per shipment.

Raw material purchases of each month are paid in the next succeeding month on terms of net 30 days.

4. All salaries and wages are paid on the 15th and last day of each month for the period ending on the date of payment.

5. All manufacturing overhead and selling and administrative expenses are paid on the 10th of the month following the month in which incurred. Selling expenses are 10 per cent of gross sales. Administrative expenses, which include depreciation of $500 per month on office furniture and fixtures, total $33,000 per month.

6. The standard cost of a molded plastic container, based on "normal" production of 100,000 units per month, is as follows:

Materials—½ pound	$ .50
Labor	.40
Variable overhead	.20
Fixed overhead	.10
Total	$1.20

Fixed overhead includes depreciation on factory equipment of $4,000 per month. Over- or under-absorbed overhead is included in cost of sales.

7. The cash balance on November 1 is expected to be $10,000.

Required:

Prepare the following for Modern Products Corporation assuming the bank loan is granted. (Do not consider income taxes.)

  a. Schedules computing inventory budgets by months for
    1. Finished goods production in units for October, November and December.
    2. Raw material purchases in pounds for October and November.
  b. A projected income statement for the month of November.
  c. A cash forecast for the month of November showing the opening balance, receipts (itemized by dates of collection), disbursements and balance at end of month.

SPECIFIC APPROACH

Problem II-1

1. Use the method outlined in the General Approach. Set up the necessary T accounts. Although you will be tempted to use a single account for building and equipment (net), your analysis will be facilitated by using one account for original cost and one for accumulated depreciation.

2. Be alert for the amortization of investment credit and the reclassification of long-term liabilities.

Problem II-2

A shortcut solution would require at most accounts for Net Working Capital, Allowance for Depreciation, Capital Stock, Premium on Capital Stock, and Retained Earnings.

1. Deferred income tax is not a current liability.
2. The disposition of marketable securities was the sale of a current asset rather than a noncurrent asset; any resulting gain or loss would appear in the income statement and would not require an adjustment in the course of preparing a funds statement. In short, where current items are disposed of, the gains or losses appear as part of funds provided by operations and require no adjustment.
3. Bond retirement is a complicated transaction which is best divided into (a) the liquidation of the sinking fund, (b) the sale of the serial bonds, and (c) the retirement. The loss from retirement would include the unamortized discount as well as the retirement premium.
4. What are the implicit transactions?

Problem II-3

1. In this case, the "all financial resources" concept does not mean that your general approach should change. Set up a net working capital T account in the usual manner. However, the format of the formal statement will change so that one major section will be Total Funds Provided. The other major section, Total Funds Applied, will include a provision for funds applied to "increase in net working capital" as one of its line items.
2. Deferred income taxes are not current liabilities.
3. To obtain the net funds provided by operations, be especially alert for charges to expense or loss for retirement of bonds, deferral of income taxes, and casualty losses. In addition, the correction of prior year's profits for depreciation will need your consideration.

Problem II-4

1. When you compute the collections of accounts receivable, be on guard concerning the current Sales. Notice that the decrease in Unearned Revenue must have been transferred to current Sales because there is no other income item that accounts for this decrease. For computations regarding both Accounts Receivable and Accounts Payable, be careful about signs; that is, it is easy to add when you should subtract, and vice versa.
2. In requirement (2), an elaborate T-account approach is not really needed. The computations in requirement (1) provide a beginning. Obtain the increase in cash from operations by taking collections and deducting payments for operating expenses (including interest), insurance purchases, and income taxes. Then proceed through the other accounts in the trial balance to make sure no changes are overlooked.

3. Other than operations, sources of cash include sales of long-term investments, equipment, treasury stock, and new common stock. Cash payments include a sinking fund deposit, purchase of equipment, dividends, and the reduction of the long-term note payable.

Problem II-5

This is a straightforward budgeting problem that is self-explanatory. No special comments are needed on the approach to the solution.

Problem II-6

1. Sales is the cornerstone of both income budgeting and cash budgeting.
2. Production schedules are computed by adding desired ending inventories to budgeted sales and then deducting ending inventories. The same approach is applicable to raw material purchases.
3. Depreciation is included in an income statement, but it has no place in a cash forecast.
4. For the income statement, assume that over- or under-applied overhead is included in cost of sales.

Current Assets: Receivables; Inventories; Consignments; Installments; Retail Methods; Fire Losses; Insurance; Contractor Accounts

GENERAL APPROACH

The scope of this topic is extremely broad. The candidate should be familiar with bank reconciliations; receivables; uncollectible accounts; inventory shortages and fire losses; consignments; installments; contractor accounting; and a variety of inventory costing methods, especially first in, first out; last in, first out; retail method; and lower of cost or market.

It is impossible to offer a single general approach which will encompass the variety of problems in this topic. Comments on special areas may be found under the Specific Approaches to those specialized problems. The following discussion and review is confined to general areas of inventory accounting, including consignments, installments, and contractor accounting. An overwhelming majority of problems in the current asset area deal with some phase of inventory accounting.

Inventory Shortages, Fire Losses, Incomplete Records

Most problems involving inventory losses present a great amount of factual information. The candidate must pick and choose the relevant from the irrelevant in working toward the unknown inventory figure. Essentially, most of these problems require a recasting of the conventional cost-of-goods-sold section and working from given amounts to the unknown inventory amount.

One effective way to work these problems involves preparing a schedule of the conventional sales and cost-of-goods-sold section of the income statement:

67

Sales		$1,000	(100%)
Less cost of sales:			
Beginning inventory	$ 400		
Purchases	1,500		
Available for sale	$1,900		
Ending inventory	*X*		
Cost of sales		*Y*	
Gross profit		*Z*	(40%)

The facts in a problem will supply sufficient figures so that the candidate can fill in the conventional schedule with known figures and then obtain the unknown—working from the bottom (gross profit) up, or from the top (net sales) down.

Use of the gross profit relationship is usually an integral part of solving such problems. Unless otherwise stated, any gross profit percentage given is based upon *net sales,* not cost. In the example above, the gross profit percentage is 40%. Cost of goods sold must be 60% of sales, or $600. Therefore, the ending inventory must be $1,300.

Of course, the gross profit relationship may be stated algebraically. Candidates who have facility with algebra may prefer, wherever feasible, to use equations such as the following:

$$\text{Cost of sales} = \text{Net sales} - \text{Gross profit}$$
and
$$\text{Cost of sales} = \text{Beginning inventory} + \text{Net purchases} - \text{Ending inventory}$$

Inventory Methods

The choice of a specific method of inventory valuation has an important impact upon the measurement of income. Cost, determined in one of numerous ways, is the general basis for valuation of inventories. However, the estimation of cost as goods are purchased or manufactured is entwined in a web of difficulties. The definition of cost as applied to incoming materials or merchandise is an example. What is "cost" in these cases? Is it part or all of the following: Invoice price, freight charges, handling, insurance, storage, purchasing department costs, or any other indirect or direct charges?

Once "cost" is defined, the question arises as to how to allocate these product costs for a given year and how to divide them between goods sold and goods still on hand. There are many variations and combinations of valuation methods: first in, first out; last in, first out; a variety of average cost methods; base stock; specific identification; standard costs; retail method; and ultimate sales price less cost of disposition.

Lower of Cost or Market

When the concept of market price is superimposed upon a cost method, the combined method is often called the "lower of cost or market" method. That is, the current market price is compared to cost (derived by FIFO, weighted average or other method), and the lower of the two is selected as the basis for valuation of goods at a specific inventory date. "Market" *generally* means *replacement cost* or its equivalent. It does not mean the ultimate selling price to customers. APBAP Vol. 1, Sect. 5121.08 comments:

> As used in the phrase *lower of cost or market,* the term *market* means current replacement cost (by purchase or by reproduction, as the case may be) except that:
>
> (1) Market should not exceed the net realizable value (i.e., estimated selling price in the ordinary course of business, less reasonably predictable cost of completion and disposal) and
> (2) Market should not be less than net realizable value reduced by an allowance for an approximately normal profit margin.

Assume that an ending inventory totals $10,000 at cost and $7,000 at market. If the lower market is indicative of lower ultimate sales prices, an inventory write-down of $3,000 is in order. $3,000 of cost is considered to have expired during the current period because it cannot be justifiably carried forward to the future. Furthermore, the decision to purchase was probably made during the current period, and unfortunate fluctuations occurred in the replacement market during the period. The latter caused the inventory to lose some utility, some revenue-producing power. (On the other hand, if *selling prices* were not likely to fall, the revenue-producing power of the inventory would have been maintained; no write-down would be justified.)

The new $7,000 valuation is what is left of the original cost of the inventory. In other words, the market price may be thought of as the new cost of inventory for future accounting purposes.

The lower-of-cost-or-market method has been termed a conservative method. Compared to a strict cost method, it does result in less income in the current period; however, it also results in more net income in a future period. For example, assume no other sales in the second period except the disposal of the inventory in question.

	Cost		Lower of Cost or Market	
	Period 1	Period 2	Period 1	Period 2
Net sales	$100,000	$11,000	$100,000	$11,000
Cost of goods available	$ 80,000	$10,000	$ 80,000	$ 7,000
Ending inventory after write-down	10,000	...	7,000	...
Cost of sales	$ 70,000	$10,000	$ 73,000*	$ 7,000
Margin	$ 30,000	$ 1,000	$ 27,000	$ 4,000

*Cost of sales is increased by the $3,000 inventory write-down in this example. Many accountants favor isolating the write-down and deducting it separately after the ordinary gross margin.

Note that the total margin for the two periods is $31,000 under both methods.

Retail Method

Consider the following CPA problem:

The Blank Corporation, which uses the conventional retail inventory method, wishes to change to the last in, first out retail method beginning with the accounting year ending December 31, 19x0.

Amounts as shown by the firm's books are as follows:

	At Cost	At Retail
Inventory, January 1, 19x0	$ 5,210	$ 15,000
Purchases in 19x0	47,250	100,000
Markups in 19x0		7,000
Markdowns in 19x0		2,000
Sales in 19x0		95,000

You are to assume that all markups and markdowns apply to 19x0 purchases, and that it is appropriate to treat the entire inventory as a single department.

Required:

Compute the inventory at December 31, 19x0 under:

(a) Conventional retail method.
(b) Last in, first out retail method, effecting the change in method as of January 1, 19x0.

Solution

(a) Ending inventory for 19x0 under the conventional retail method:

	Cost	Retail
Inventory, January 1, 19x0	$ 5,210	$ 15,000
Purchases	47,250	100,000
Markups		7,000
Available for sale	$52,460	$122,000
Cost ratio	43%	100%
Sales		$ 95,000
Markdowns		2,000
		$ 97,000
Inventory, December 31, 19x0		$ 25,000
Inventory, December 31, 19x0, 43% of $25,000 $10,750		

Note that markdowns are excluded from computation of the cost ratio. This conventional approach provides a lower cost ratio than otherwise, hence it approximates a lower-of-cost-or-market method.

(b) Ending inventory for 19x0 under the last in, first out method:

	Cost	Retail
Cost-to-retail ratio:		
Purchases	$47,250	$100,000
Markups		7,000
Markdowns		(2,000)
	$47,250	$105,000
Cost ratio	45%	100%
Inventory, December 31, 19X0 at last in, first out cost:		
First layer (cost ratio is 35% rounded)	$ 5,210	$ 15,000
Incremental second layer (cost ratio is 45%) .	4,500	10,000
Total inventory	$ 9,710	$ 25,000

In the LIFO retail method, the bottom layer is usually the cost of the beginning inventory in the year when LIFO is adopted. The second layer is the increment purchased during that initial year, the third layer is the increment purchased during the subsequent year, and so on. Similarly, if the layers are depleted, the top layer is assumed to be used first.

Cost ratios are used to convert retail values to LIFO cost layers. As the preceding tabulation shows, the cost ratio recognizes markdowns as well as mark ups. Furthermore, a different cost ratio will be computed for each annual increment. Consequently, beginning inventories are excluded from the computation of the cost ratio applicable to a given year's increment.

Dollar-Value LIFO Method

A *dollar-value LIFO* method is a widely used variation of the *LIFO* inventory method. It has arisen to facilitate an approximation of the underlying physical change in the units of inventory. If unit prices change through the years, and unless recognition is given to unit price fluctuations, the size of the inventory may be miscalculated. For example, suppose there are 100 units in inventory on January 1 with a unit retail value of $10, or $1,000. Suppose the retail value of the inventory at the following December 31 is $1,050. Has the underlying physical inventory changed? If the price level has risen by 5 per cent, the physical size of the inventory is probably unchanged.

In dollar-value LIFO, the ending inventory at retail is restated in terms of the original retail prices by applying a price index, $1,050 ÷ 1.05, or $1,000. Then the cost ratio is applied to $1,000 rather than $1,050 to obtain the LIFO valuation at cost in terms of the layer-year price levels.

Any increase in inventory is priced at the current year's prices, ordinarily using the price index at the end of the year for simplicity.

Consider an illustration of dollar-value LIFO, given the following data:

	Cost Ratio	Price Index	Lifo Cost	Retail
Inventory on December 31, 19x0 when dollar-value LIFO is adopted	-	100	$9,710	$25,000
Inventory, December 31, 19x1	42%	104	?	31,200
Inventory, December 31, 19x2	40%	110	?	36,300

Computation of LIFO cost, December 31, 19X1:

1. Convert ending inventory to base year prices
   $31,200 ÷ 1.04 .... $30,000
2. Subtract the beginning inventory at base year prices
   to obtain increase or decrease in inventory.......... 25,000
   Increment in inventory in terms of December 31,
   19x0 prices .... $ 5,000
3. Express the increment in terms of current prices
   $5,000 x 1.04 .... $ 5,200
4. Convert the 19x1 increment to LIFO cost and
   summarize inventory
   $5,200 x .42 .... $ 2,184
   Base layer 9,710

   December 31, 19x1 inventory at LIFO cost $11,894

The computations look more imposing than they really are. The major characteristic of the dollar-value method is to convert the ending and beginning inventories to a common price level at retail ($30,000 and $25,000). The difference, $5,000, is the increase or decrease in the physical quantity of goods on hand expressed in common dollars. Then the LIFO layers are priced in accordance with the price index at the end of the year the layer was created.

Computation of LIFO cost, December 31, 19x2:

1. Convert ending inventory to base year prices
   $36,300 ÷ 1.10 .... $33,000
2. Subtract the beginning inventory at base year prices to
   obtain the increase or decrease in inventory......... 30,000
   Increment in inventory in terms of December 31,
   19x0 prices .... $ 3,000
3. Express the increment in terms of current prices
   $3,000 x 1.10 .... $ 3,300

4. Convert the 19x2 increment to LIFO cost and
   summarize inventory:
   $3,300 x .40 = 19x2 layer................... $ 1,320
   19x1 layer 2,184
   Base layer 9,710

   December 31, 19x2 inventory at LIFO cost $13,214

General Review

The following multiple-choice questions were selected from the Theory section of a CPA examination. The questions cover most of the fundamental points that a candidate should know about inventory methods. Before glancing

at the answers which follow, try to answer the questions completely. Then check
your answers.

Question (25 to 35 min.)

Write the numbers 1 through 20 on an answer sheet. For each question *insert*
on the answer sheet *the letter that identifies the answer* you select. Choose the
best answer to each of the following questions:

(1) An inventory method developed from consideration of the flow of
costs rather than the flow of goods is:
   (a) First in, first out
   (b) Last in, first out
   (c) specific identification
   (d) standard cost
   (e) Answer not given
(2) An inventory method designed to approximate inventory valuation at
the lower of cost or market is:
   (a) Last in, first out
   (b) First in, first out
   (c) base stock
   (d) retail
   (e) Answer not given
(3) An inventory method which is particularly useful in connection with
the valuation of the overhead element of work in process is:
   (a) physical count
   (b) specific identification
   (c) market price of product less cost of disposition
   (d) standard cost
   (e) Answer not given
(4) An inventory valuation procedure which is particularly adaptable to
accounting for by-products is:
   (a) First in, first out
   (b) Last in, first out
   (c) market price of product less cost of disposition
   (d) common costs
   (e) Answer not given
(5) An inventory method which cannot be used in conjunction with valuation at the lower of cost or market is:
   (a) First in, first out
   (b) weighted average cost
   (c) specific identification
   (d) unweighted average cost
   (e) Answer not given
(6) An inventory method which is not acceptable for Federal income-tax
purposes is:
   (a) base stock
   (b) lower of cost or market
   (c) Last in, first out
   (d) specific identification
   (e) Answer not given
(7) In situations where there is a rapid inventory turnover, an inventory

method which produces almost the same results as the first in, first out method is:
   (a) average cost
   (b) base stock
   (c) joint costs
   (d) prime cost
   (e) Answer not given
   (8) An inventory method which necessitates the keeping of a perpetual inventory record is:
   (a) First in, first out
   (b) retail
   (c) base stock
   (d) market price of product less cost of disposition
   (e) Answer not given
   (9) An inventory method which may be used for Federal income-tax purposes only if it is used for general accounting purposes is:
   (a) specific identification
   (b) Last in, first out
   (c) First in, first out
   (d) market price less cost of disposition
   (e) Answer not given
   (10) In a period of rising prices, the inventory on the balance sheet is valued nearest to current cost when the inventory method being used is:
   (a) base stock
   (b) Last in, first out
   (c) specific identification
   (d) retail
   (e) net realizable value

The Saunders Corporation uses raw material A in a manufacturing process. Information as to balances on hand, purchases, and requisitions of material A are given in the following table. You are to choose the best answer to each question based on this information. For each question *insert* on the answer sheet the *letter that identifies the answer* you select.

Raw Material A

Date		Received	Quantities Issued	Balance	Unit Price	Received	Dollars Issued	Balance
Jan.	1			100	$1.50			$150
Jan.	24	300		400	1.56	$468		
Feb.	8		80	320				
Mar.	16		140	180				
June	11	150		330	1.60	240		
Aug.	18		130	200				
Sept.	6		110	90				
Oct.	15	150		240	1.70	255		
Dec.	29		140	100				

   (11) If a perpetual inventory record of material A is operated on a Fifo basis, it will show a *closing inventory* of:
   (a) $150   (b) 152   (c) $159   (d) $162   (e) $170
   (f) Answer not given

(12) If a perpetual inventory record of material A is operated on a Lifo basis, it will show a *closing inventory* of:
(a) $150   (b) $152   (c) $156   (d) $160   (e) $170
(f) Answer not given

(13) If a perpetual inventory record of material A is operated on a moving average basis, it will show a *closing inventory* which is:
(a) lower than on the Lifo basis
(b) lower than on the Fifo basis
(c) higher than on the Fifo basis
(d) Answer not given

(14) Assume that no perpetual inventory is maintained for material A and that quantities are obtained by an annual physical count. The accounting records show information as to purchases but not as to issues. On this assumption, the *closing inventory* on a Fifo basis will be:
(a) $150   (b) $156   (c) $159   (d) $160   (e) $170

(15) Assume that no perpetual inventory is maintained for material A and that quantities are obtained by an annual physical count. The accounting records show information as to purchases but not as to issues. On this assumption, the *closing inventory* on a Lifo basis will be:
(a) $150   (b) $152   (c) $156   (d) $160   (e) $170
(f) Answer not given

The Berg Corporation *began business on January* 1, 19x4. Information about its inventories under different valuation methods is shown next. Using this information, you are to choose the phrase that best answers each of the following questions. For each question *insert* on the answer sheet the *letter which identifies the answer* you select.

Inventory

	Lifo Cost	Fifo Cost	Market	Lower of Cost or Market
Dec. 31, 19x4	$10,200	$10,000	$ 9,600	$ 8,900
Dec. 31, 19x5	9,100	9,000	8,800	8,500
Dec. 31, 19x6	10,300	11,000	12,000	10,900

(16) The inventory basis that would show the *highest net income for* 19x4 is:
(a) Lifo cost (b) Fifo cost (c) Market (d) Lower of cost or market

(17) The inventory basis that would show the *highest net income for* 19x5 is:
(a) Lifo cost (b) Fifo cost (c) Market (d) Lower of cost or market

(18) The inventory basis that would show the *lowest net income for the three years combined is:*
(a) Lifo cost (b) Fifo cost (c) Market (d) Lower of cost or market

(19) For the year 19x5, how much higher or lower would profits be on the *Fifo cost basis* than on the *lower-of-cost-or-market basis?*
(a) $400 higher   (e) $1,000 higher
(b) $400 lower   (f) $1,000 lower
(c) $600 higher   (g) $1,400 higher
(d) $600 lower   (h) $1,400 lower

(20) On the basis of the information given, it appears that *the movement of prices* for the items in the inventory was:
(a) Up in 19x4 and down in 19x6 (b) Up in both 19x4 and 19x6
(c) Down in 19x4 and up in 19x6 (d) Down in both 19x4 and 19x6

Answers and Comments

1. (b) The Lifo method releases the most recent (or last) inventory costs as costs of goods sold. It attempts to match the most current cost of obtaining inventory against sales for a period. As compared to Fifo, Lifo results in less income during periods of rising prices and more income in periods of falling prices.

2. (d) Markdowns are generally excluded in computing the ratio of cost to the retail value of goods available for sale. This results in an ending inventory amount which approximates the lower of cost or market.

3. (d) The standard cost method excludes the impact of variations in production activity from inventory costs. Costs are accumulated by operations so that valuation at any stage where work is inventoried can be readily determined.

4. (c) By-products yield small sales volume in relation to sales of major products. It is not expedient to assign costs accumulated before the split-off point (joint costs) to by-products. Therefore, estimated by-product revenue less the cost of disposition is usually deducted from major product cost or production.

5. (e) Last in, first out cannot be used for tax purposes if used in conjunction with lower of cost or market.

6. (a)

7. (a) If turnover is great, the effect of the latest unit prices yield an inventory valuation under average cost which is nearly the same as under Fifo.

8. (b) To apply the retail method, it is necessary to keep records of dollar amounts of purchases, markups, markdowns, and sales. Of course, these records are not ordinarily thought of as a perpetual inventory record. Yet (b) appears to deserve the nod over (e).

9. (b)

10. (d) The best answer is Fifo, but it is not included among the given alternatives. If special assumptions cannot be made, (d) would be the best choice. The retail method approximates the lower of cost or market, and the inventory should be closest to current costs. If one assumed that the calculation of net realizable value allowed for a normal margin, then he would probably pick (e).

11. (e) Under Fifo the ending inventory valuation may be obtained most easily by working back from the closing date until the number of units purchased equals the number of units in ending inventory. Then apply the appropriate unit purchase costs to obtain total dollar amount. In this example, 100 units @ $1.70 is $170.

12. (b) 90 units @ $1.50 plus 10 units @ $1.70 equals $152. Under Lifo generally the ending inventory valuation can be obtained by working forward from the beginning inventory until the total number of units equals the number of units in the ending inventory. Then apply the appropriate beginning inventory unit costs and the early purchase unit costs to obtain the total dollar amount.

However, under a perpetual Lifo method, a temporary reduction below the number of units in the beginning inventory calls for assignment of the base inventory price to the number of units released from the base inventory. Compare with answer to question 15.

13. (b) Fifo assigns earliest costs to cost of sales and latest costs to inventory. Unit prices have been rising during the period. Therefore, more of the

earlier and lower-cost units are contained in the ending inventory under the moving average than under Fifo. (See also answer 7.)

14. (e) 100 units @ $1.70 or $170. The answer is identical (see answer 11) under perpetual or periodic systems.

15. (a) 100 units @ $1.50 or $150. (See answer 12.) Under a periodic Lifo method, a temporary reduction below the number of units in the beginning inventory will have no effect upon the valuation of the ending inventory as long as the number of units in the ending inventory is at least equal to the beginning inventory.

16. (a) $10,200 is the largest closing inventory at December 31, 19x4. The initial inventory was zero.

17. (d) $8,900 − $8,500 is $400, which is the smallest decrease in inventory figures for 19x5.

18. (a) $10,300 is the smallest closing inventory as of December 31, 19x6.

19. (d) Decreases in inventories for 19x5:

```
Fifo:  . . . . . . . . . . $10,000 − $9,000 or $1,000
Cost or market . . . . . 8,900 −  8,500 or     400
                                            ─────────
                                      $   600 decrease
```

Thus Fifo released $600 more as cost of goods sold than the lower-of-cost-or-market method.

20. (c) December 31, 19x4: cost was higher than market; December 31, 19x6: cost was lower than market.

Consignments

To refresh the candidate's memory, the following typical entries on the consignor's books are presented. The method assumes that the consignor uses a perpetual inventory system and keeps consignment profits separate. Remember that the Consignment Out account serves basically as an inventory account for goods not on the premises of the consignor:

1. Shipments: 10 units @ $10.	Consignment out $100	
	Inventory	$100
2. Freight of consignor: 10 units @ $1.	Consignment out . . . . $ 10	
	Cash	$ 10
3. Cartage of consignee chargeable to consignor: 10 units @ $2.	None until account sales is rendered.	
4. Remittance of balance owed together with account sales. Sale of 7 units @ $20. 25% commission allowed.	Cash . . . . $ 85	
	Consignment out (expenses of consignee) 20	
	Commission expense on consignments 35	
	Consignment sales	$140
To remove cost of goods sold from consignment out.	Cost of consignment sales , . $ 70	
	Consignment out	$ 70
To assign applicable portion of miscellaneous outlays against units sold.	Shipping, freight expense on consignments . . . . $ 21	
	Consignment out	$ 21

The Consignment Out account would appear as follows:

CONSIGNMENT OUT

1.	100	4.	70
2.	10	4.	21
4.	20		

Balance, inventory on consignment plus prepaid expenses	39

Note that in the final entry the freight and cartage applicable to the units sold were "expensed," while that applicable to units unsold were "inventoried." Some accountants would probably show the latter $9 (freight out, $3; cartage, $6) amount as a prepaid consignment expense on a formal balance sheet; other accountants would merely add it to the inventory on consignment because of its lack of materiality.

In complex situations, where there are a variety of outlays pertinent to goods on consignment (freight, cartage, delivery, servicing), a working schedule such as the following will be helpful:

Description	Total Amount	Identified with Sale	Identified with Inventory
Consignor:			
Cost of merchandise..............	$100	$ 70	$30
Freight out....................	10	7	3
Consignee:			
Cartage.......................	20	14	6
Commissions	35	35	
Total accounted for...............	$165	$126	$39

Installments

Problems dealing with installment sales generally center about the timing of gross profit realization and about accounting for defaults and repossessions. In most cases, gross profit is recognized as earned in proportion to cash collections. That is, an installment is assumed to include a return of cost and gross profit in the ratio that each bears to the total sales price.

Installment problems usually raise questions concerning the proper valuations of the following accounts for two or more years: installment accounts receivable, deferred (unrealized) gross profit, inventory of repossessions, net gain or loss on repossessions, and realized gross profit for the current year. The most fruitful method of attack usually will involve the following factors:

Knowledge of how to obtain proper gross profit percentages.

Knowledge that an adjusted balance of a deferred gross profit account must have a precise relationship to the adjusted balance of the related installment accounts receivable account. Example: If, at December 31, 19x7, installment accounts receivable on 19x6 sales amounted to $100,000 and the applicable gross profit percentage was 40%, then the deferred gross profit on 19x6 installment sales must be $40,000.

Knowledge that the amount of installment gross profit realized for any given year is always based upon total cash collected upon installment contracts during the year (including down payments).

Knowledge that gains or losses on repossessions and resales are usually excluded from gross profit calculations.

The appropriate entry upon repossession of merchandise depends upon the underlying assumptions made concerning the proper amount to attach to the merchandise for inventory purposes. The basic entry is:

```
Inventory of repossessed merchandise ...............    ?
Deferred (unrealized) profit ......................   xxxx
    Installment contracts receivable  .......................   xxxx
    Gain (or loss would be a debit) on repossessions ...........    ?
```

As seen from that entry, gain or loss recognition is dependent upon the amount attached to inventory. Alternate methods include:

1. Carrying inventory at unrecovered cost (that is, uncollected balance minus unrealized gross profit). This means that no gain or loss is recognized upon repossession.

2. Carrying inventory at market (appropriate wholesale price for used merchandise). Market should not exceed net realizable value nor should it be less than net realizable value reduced by an allowance for an approximately normal profit margin. If the market prices can be determined objectively, this method is superior to the other two.

3. Not carrying the repossessed merchandise as an asset. Charge as a loss the whole excess of the balance of the receivable over the related unrealized gross profit. When the merchandise is resold, recognize the proceeds as income.

This method might be used where inventory and resale proceeds are minor or cannot be determined.

Fire Insurance

If the insured does not carry insurance equal to a required percentage of the insurable value, the insurance company will pay for only a fraction of the loss. Insurable value is equal to replacement value at the time of loss, not original cost.

For example, suppose that the total inventory had a historical cost of $140,000 and a replacement cost of $150,000. The coinsurance requirement was 80% and the total insurance carried was $108,000. A fire destroyed a portion of the inventory, which originally cost $52,000 and which has a current replacement cost of $55,000. The amount collectible would be $49,500, computed as follows:

$$\text{Amount collectible} = \frac{\text{Face amount of policy}}{\text{Insurance required by coinsurance clause}} \times \text{Amount of loss}$$

$$= \frac{\$108,000}{.80\,(\$150,000)} \times \$55,000 = \$49,500$$

Additional complications arise when the same property is insured with several insurance companies, each with a different coinsurance requirement. Each company whose policy contains a *contribution clause* assumes a liability for only a pro rata portion of the loss. Assume the same facts as above, except that the $108,000 of insurance was carried by the following insurance companies:

Company	Coinsurance Clause, %	Insurance Required	Carried	Coinsurance Requirement Met?*
X	70	$105,000	$ 27,000	Yes
Y	80	120,000	60,000	No
Z	None	...	21,000	Yes
			$108,000	

*Note that this question is answered by referring to the *total* amount carried under all pertinent insurance policies.

Contributions are computed as follows for each company:

$$\text{Amount collectible} = \frac{\text{Face amount of specific policy}}{\text{Face amount of all policies*}} \times \text{Amount of loss}$$

*Except that the coinsurance requirement is used where such a requirement is not met in *total*. See Co. Y below.

The detailed conditions of coinsurance requirements and contribution clauses described above are somewhat difficult to remember. The following general formula is very handy because it is applicable to all coinsurance situations whether one or more insurance companies are involved:

Recovery = Loss × Coinsurance factor

$$\frac{\text{Recovery from individual policy}}{} = \frac{\text{Amount of loss}}{} \times \frac{\text{Total face of all policies}}{\text{Individual policy requirement or total over-all insurance, whichever is greater}} \times \frac{\text{Individual policy face}}{\text{Total face of all policies}}$$

The first numerator and the second denominator cancel out, yielding the following general formula:

$$\frac{\text{Recovery from individual policy}}{} = \frac{\text{Amount of loss}}{} \times \frac{\text{Individual policy face}}{\text{Individual policy requirement or total over-all insurance, whichever is greater}}$$

Of course, recovery may never exceed the face of the policy.

If we apply this to our example, the amounts collectible from the various insurance companies would be:

$$\text{Co. } X = \$55,000 \times \frac{\$27,000}{.70\,(\$150,000)\text{ or }\$108,000,\text{ whichever is greater}}$$

$$= \$55,000 \times \frac{\$\ 27,000}{\$108,000} = \$13,750$$

$$\text{Co. } Y = \$55,000 \times \frac{\$60,000}{.80\,(\$150,000)\text{ or }\$108,000,\text{ whichever is greater}}$$

$$= \$55,000 \times \frac{\$\ 60,000}{\$120,000} = 27,500$$

$$\text{Co. } Z = \$55,000 \times \frac{\$21,000}{\text{zero or }\$108,000}$$

$$= \$55,000 \times \frac{\$\ 21,000}{\$108,000} = \underline{10,700}\ (\text{rounded})$$

$$\text{Total collectible} \qquad\qquad \underline{\underline{\$51,950}}$$

Accounting for Long-Term Construction Contracts

AICPA *Accounting Research* APBAP Vol. 1, Sect. 4031 summarizes the two generally accepted methods of contractor accounting.

1. *Completed contract method.* This parallels the method followed by businesses generally, where revenues are realized only upon substantial completion and delivery of the goods or services in question, where related expenses are matched against such revenue, and where provisions are made for expected losses (even though the contract is not fully completed).

The "costs of uncompleted contracts in excess of related billings" is usually classified as a current asset; the "billings on uncompleted contracts in excess of related costs" is usually classified as a current liability.

2. *Percentage of completion method.* This method spreads revenues, related costs, and resulting net income over the life of the contract in proportion to the work accomplished. Recognized net income is typically a percentage of estimated net income. This percentage is based on incurred costs to date divided by these known costs plus the estimated future costs to complete the contract. For example, suppose that a company had encountered the following:

Project	Total Contract Price	Contract Costs Accumulated to December 31 19x1	Estimated Additional Costs to Complete	Billings to December 31 19x1	Cash Collections to December 31 19x1
A	$500,000	$360,000	$ 90,000	$300,000	$250,000
B	400,000	396,000	44,000	350,000	325,000
C	300,000	80,000	160,000	120,000	110,000

The percentage of completion method would be applied as follows:
Compute applicable percentages or fractions:

$$\text{Percentage of completion} = \frac{\text{Costs incurred to date}}{\left(\begin{array}{c}\text{Costs incurred} \\ \text{to date}\end{array}\right) + \left(\begin{array}{c}\text{Estimated additional} \\ \text{costs to complete}\end{array}\right)}$$

$$\text{For Project A} = \frac{\$360,000}{\$360,000 + \$90,000} = 80\%$$

$$\text{For Project B} = \frac{\$396,000}{\$396,000 + \$44,000} = 90\%$$

$$\text{For Project C} = \frac{\$80,000}{\$80,000 + \$160,000} = 33.3\%$$

Compute net income:

Project	Revenue	Cost Incurred	Net Income
A	.80 X $500,000 = $400,000	$360,000	$40,000
B	.90 X $400,000 = $360,000	396,000	(36,000)*
C	.333 X $300,000 = $100,000	80,000	20,000

*If a loss is foreseen, provision should be made for the loss on the entire contract. Therefore, a $4,000 provision for loss would have to be made in addition to the $36,000 loss shown; the total effect of Project B on net income would be a negative $40,000.

Under this method, the balance-sheet accounts may be measured by the revenue computed above, which is sometimes called "costs and estimated earnings," minus related billings. If the computation is positive, the item is classified as a current asset such as Costs and Recognized Net Income in Excess of Billings, or Costs and Estimated Earnings in Excess of Billings. If the computation is negative, the item is classified as a current liability such as Billings in Excess of Costs and Recognized Net Income. Where loss is anticipated on the entire contract, the entire estimated loss, rather than a percentage of such loss, should be incorporated in these calculations:

Project	Revenue	Related Billings	Current Asset: Costs and Recognized Net Income in Excess of Billings	Current Liability: Billings in Excess of Costs and Recognized Net Income
A	$400,000	$300,000	$100,000	
B	356,000*	350,000	6,000	
C	100,000	120,000		$20,000

*$360,000 revenue reduced by the $4,000 provision for loss.

Advocates of the percentage of completion method maintain that spreading the net income better measures performance; otherwise, under the completed contract method, all net income appears in one chunk upon completion of a project, as if it were earned on a single day.

As each year transpires, the percentage of completion depends on the most current estimates of total costs. Of course, the total costs (*hence* total profit) used as bases for the computations may differ from year to year.

CPA PROBLEMS

Problem III-1: Examination of accounts receivable (40-50 min.)

You are engaged in the annual examination of The Mountainview Corporation, a wholesale office supply business, for the year ended September 30, 1970. A review of internal control has revealed substantial weaknesses. You have been assigned to examine the accounts receivable.

The following information is available at September 30, 1970:

1. The general ledger accounts for accounts receivable and the allowance for doubtful accounts have debit balances of $780,430 and $470, respectively. The total of accounts receivable in the subsidiary ledger is $768,594.

2. In preparing to confirm accounts receivable you find that the amounts vary greatly in size and decide upon a three-strata procedure. You will use (a) negative confirmation requests for accounts of less than $200; (b) positive confirmation requests, unrestricted random sampling and the technique of estimation sampling for variables for accounts of $200 to $2,000; and (c) positive confirmation requests for all accounts of $2,000 or more.

3. Your review of accounts receivable and discussions with the client disclose that the following items are included in the accounts receivable (of both the control and the subsidiary ledgers):
   a. Accounts with credit balances total $1,746.
   b. Receivables from officers total $8,500.
   c. Advances to employees total $1,411.
   d. Accounts that are definitely uncollectible total $1,187.

4. Uncollectible accounts are estimated to be ½% of the year's net credit sales of $15,750,000.

5. The confirmations and analysis of the subsidiary ledger provide the following information:
   a. The 1,270 subsidiary ledger accounts with balances of less than $200 total $120,004. Twenty-seven confirmations show a net overstatement of $970. The client agrees that these errors were made.
   b. The 625 subsidiary ledger accounts with balances of $200 to $2,000 total $559,875. The following errors were reported in the replies received from the random sample of 50 positive confirmation requests (the appropriateness of a sample of 50 items was determined statistically based upon desired levels of precision and reliability and investigation established that the customers were correct):

	Balance per Books	*Correct Balance*
Customer #714	$ 847	$ 827
Customer #107	500	400
Customer #101	1,900	2,100
Customer #514	206	196
Customer #909	1,400	1,250
Customer #445	400	–
Customer #399	1,700	1,300
Customer #184	557	597
	$7,510	$6,670

Subsidiary ledger balances of $37,280 were affirmed in the replies to all of the remaining 42 positive confirmation requests.

   c. The 28 accounts with balances of $2,000 and above comprise the remainder of the accounts receivable subsidiary ledger. Investigation established that errors existed in 5 of these accounts and that the net overstatement is $4,570.

Required:

   a. Prepare any journal entry (entries) required (1) to reclassify items which are not trade accounts receivable, (2) to write off uncollectible accounts and (3) to adjust the allowance for doubtful accounts.

   b. Using the arithmetic mean of the sample as a basis, prepare a schedule computing an estimate of the dollar amount of the middle stratum of accounts receivable at September 30, 1970. (Do not compute the standard deviation.)

   c. Assuming that the net adjustment of accounts receivable computed in part "a" was $10,000 and that the estimate of the middle stratum in part "b" was $600,000, prepare a schedule computing an estimate of total trade accounts receivable at September 30, 1970.

Problem III-2: Miscellaneous inventory methods (40-50 min.)

Several Incorporated, a conglomerate, has four subsidiary companies: Art, Bat, Cot and Dale. Each company is engaged in a separate business.

Art Company is in the commodity business dealing in a single commodity. Inventory at December 31, 1967 totaled $240,000. Quantities on hand were 800,000 and 1,000,000 on December 31, 1967 and 1968 respectively.

Following are purchases made during 1968:

	Quantity	*Cost*
January	600,000	$210,000
April	500,000	200,000
September	1,000,000	246,000
November	400,000	160,000

Bat Company buys and sells land. On January 1, 1968, a tract of land was bought for $100,000. Costs of leveling the land were $25,000. The lots were subdivided as follows:

25 Class A lots to sell for $4,000 each
30 Class B lots to sell for $3,000 each
10 Class C lots to sell for $1,000 each

On December 31, 1968, the unsold lots consisted of 15 Class A lots, 6 Class B lots and 3 Class C lots.

Cot Company sells beds. The perpetual inventory was stated as $19,600 on the books at December 31, 1968. At the close of the year a new approach for compiling inventory was used and apparently a satisfactory cutoff was not made. Some events that occurred follow:

1. Beds shipped to a customer January 2, 1969 costing $2,000 were included in inventory at December 31, 1968.

2. Beds costing $9,000 received December 30, 1968 were recorded as received on January 2, 1969.

3. Beds received costing $1,900 were recorded twice.

4. Beds shipped December 28, 1968 per date of shipping advice which cost $7,000 were not recorded as delivered until January 1969.

5. Beds on hand which cost $2,300 were not recorded on the books.

Dale Company is in the construction business. A long-term contract was entered into in 1966. The contract price was $700,000 and the Company expected to earn $80,000 before taxes. Following are data on experience to date:

Year Ended December 31	Cumulative Costs Incurred	Estimated Cost to Complete Contract
1966	$ 49,600	$570,400
1967	172,800	467,200
1968	378,000	252,000

Required:

a. Prepare a schedule computing the cost of the December 31, 1968 inventory of Art Company using the weighted average method.

b. Prepare a schedule computing the cost of unsold lots at December 31, 1968 of Bat Company.

c. Prepare a schedule showing the adjustments to year-end inventory of Cot Company to effect a proper cutoff.

d. Prepare a schedule computing the income earned in 1966, 1967 and 1968 by Dale Company under the percentage-of-completion method based on costs incurred.

Problem III-3: Examination of inventories (50-60 min.)

The president of Knight Coat Company has retained you to assist his accountant in analyzing the content and pricing of the Company's inventories at December 31, 1971. Below is the information collected.

1. Controlling accounts are maintained in the general ledger for manufacturing overhead, selling expenses, and general and administrative expenses. Detail ledgers support each controlling account and are balanced monthly. Analysis of detail charges revealed account classification errors resulting in a

need to decrease manufacturing overhead by $300,000 and increase selling expenses by $85,000 and general and administrative expenses by $215,000.

2. Overhead is charged to work-in-process monthly, crediting applied manufacturing overhead, based on direct labor cost at an expected rate of 47.5%. The balances before adjustment of manufacturing overhead and applied manufacturing overhead at December 31, 1971, were $1,000,000 and $950,000, respectively. Direct labor charges for 1971 were $2,000,000.

3. All inventory on hand at December 31, 1970, has been sold.

4. Inventories are priced on a first-in, first-out basis at the lower of cost or market. Complete physical inventories were taken on December 31, 1971, and priced on a first-in, first-out basis. The inventory accounts have been adjusted to the physical quantities and prices at December 31, 1971. No test has been made comparing inventory cost to market. Details of the inventory accounts as adjusted at December 31, 1971, follow:

	Material	Direct Labor	Applied Overhead	Total
Raw materials	$395,000	$ –	$ –	$395,000
Work-in-process......	425,000	80,000	38,000	543,000
Finished goods	315,000	60,000	28,500	403,500

5. While reviewing the inventory pricing the following was discovered:

   a. Knight received raw materials costing $12,000 on January 20, 1972. The goods had been shipped December 12, 1971, at which time title passed to Knight. The invoice was recorded in the December 1971 voucher register, but the goods were not included in the December 31, 1971, physical inventory.

   b. Invoices for $25,000 of raw materials physically counted at December 31, 1971, were recorded in the January 1972 voucher register.

6. A further review of the January 1972 voucher register revealed:

   a. Invoices for $15,000 of raw materials invoiced in December; the goods were received in January 1972. Further investigation revealed that title to the goods passed to Knight in 1971.

   b. Invoices for $30,000 of raw materials invoiced in December; the goods were received in January. Further investigation revealed that title passed to Knight in 1972.

7. A review of the January 1972 sales journal revealed December 30 and 31, 1971, invoices totaling $17,555. The goods were shipped December 30 and 31, and title passed immediately to the customer. Cost of the sales was $12,500. None of these goods were included in the physical count.

8. Review of correspondence files disclosed that Knight had shipped finished goods on consignment to King, Inc., on December 1, 1971. The goods (having equal unit costs) had a material and labor cost of $17,000 and $4,000, respectively. Knight paid shipping costs of $1,600 charged to selling expenses (not considered in the analysis described under 1 above). King notified Knight on January 18, 1972, that one-third of the inventory had been sold through December 31, 1971, for $9,500 net of commissions. Consigned goods were not included in the physical count.

9. A comparison of inventory cost with market revealed finished goods inventory with material and direct labor costs of $100,000 and $22,000, respectively, had a replacement cost of $122,000 at December 31, 1971. Sales value of this inventory is $150,000. Selling costs are 20% of the selling price, and the normal profit margin is 10% of the selling price.

Required:

The books have not been closed. Prepare necessary adjusting journal entries complete with explanations. Schedules supporting calculations should be in good form and either be included as part of the journal entry explanation or properly cross referenced to the appropriate journal entry.

Problem III-4: Consignments; corrections of errors (45-55 min.)

You are examining the December 31, 1963 financial statements of the Conol Sales Company, a new client. The Company was established on January 1, 1962 and is a distributor of air conditioning units. The Company's income statements for 1962 and 1963 were presented to you as follows:

The Conol Sales Company
STATEMENTS OF INCOME AND EXPENSE
For the Years Ended December 31, 1963 and 1962

	1963	*1962*
Sales	$1,287,500	$1,075,000
Cost of sales	669,500	559,000
Gross profit	618,000	516,000
Selling and administration expense	403,500	330,000
Net income before income taxes	214,500	186,000
Provision for income taxes @ 50%	107,250	93,000
Net income	$ 107,250	$ 93,000

Your examination disclosed the following:

1. Some sales were made on open account; other sales were made through dealers to whom units were shipped on a consignment basis. Both sales methods were in effect in 1962 and 1963. In both years, however, the Company treated all shipments as outright sales.
2. The sales price and cost of the units were the same in 1962 and 1963. Each unit had a cost of $130 and was uniformly invoiced at $250 to open account customers and to consignees.
3. During 1963 the amount of cash received from consignees in payment for units sold by them was $706,500. Consignees remit for the units as soon as they are sold. Confirmations received from consignees showed that they had a total of 23 unsold units on hand at December 31, 1963. Consignees were unable to confirm the unsold units on hand at December 31, 1962.
4. The cost of sales for 1963 was determined by the client as follows:

		Units
Inventory on hand in warehouse, December 31, 1962		1,510
Purchases		4,454
Available for sale		5,964
Inventory on hand in warehouse, December 31, 1963		814
Shipments to: open account customers	3,008	
consignee customers	2,142	5,150 @ $130 = $669,500

Required:

a. Compute the total amount of the Conol Sales Company's inventory at
   (1) December 31, 1963
   (2) December 31, 1962

b. Prepare the auditor's work-sheet journal entries to correct the financial statements for the year ended December 31, 1962.

c. Prepare the formal adjusting journal entries to correct the accounts at December 31, 1963. (The books have not been closed. Do not prepare the closing journal entries.)

Problem III-5: Installment method (50-60 min.)

Downtemp Company, on January 2, 1967, entered into a contract with a manufacturing company to purchase room-size air conditioners and to sell the units on an installment plan with collections over approximately 30 months with no carrying charge.

For income tax purposes Downtemp elected to report income from its sales of air conditioners according to the installment method.

Purchases and sales of new units were as follows:

	Units Purchased		Units Sold	
Year	*Quantity*	*Price Each*	*Quantity*	*Price Each*
1967	1,200	$100	1,000	$150
1968	1,800	90	2,000	140
1969	800	105	700	143

Collections on installment sales were as follows:

	Collections Received		
	1967	*1968*	*1969*
1967 sales	$30,000	$60,000	$ 60,000
1968 sales		70,000	115,000
1969 sales			21,000

In 1969, 40 units from the 1968 sales were repossessed and sold for $72.50 each on the installment plan. At the time of repossession $1,200 had been collected from the original purchasers and the units had a fair value of $2,520.

General and administrative expenses for 1969 were $50,000. No charge has been made against current income for the applicable insurance expense from a three-year policy expiring June 30, 1970 costing $3,000, and for an advance payment of $10,000 on a new contract to purchase air conditioners beginning January 2, 1970.

Required:

Assuming that the weighted-average method is used for determining the inventory cost, including repossessed merchandise, prepare schedules computing for 1967, 1968 and 1969:

a. (1) The cost of goods sold on installments.
   (2) The average unit cost of goods sold on installments for each year.

b. The gross profit percentages for 1967, 1968 and 1969.
c. The gain or loss on repossessions in 1969.
d. The taxable income from installment sales for 1969.

Problem III-6: Retail inventory method; last in, first out (50-60 min.)

Under your guidance as of January 1, 1965, the Little Corner Sporting Goods Store installed the retail method of accounting for its merchandise inventory.

When you undertook the preparation of the Store's financial statements at June 30, 1965, the following data were available:

	Cost	Selling Price
Inventory, January 1	$26,900	$ 40,000
Markdowns		10,500
Markups		19,500
Markdown cancellations		6,500
Markup cancellations		4,500
Purchases	86,200	111,800
Sales		122,000
Purchase returns and allowances	1,500	1,800
Sales returns and allowances		6,000

Required:

a. Prepare a schedule to compute the Little Corner Sporting Goods Store's June 30, 1965 inventory under the retail method of accounting for inventories. The inventory is to be valued at cost under the LIFO method.

b. Without prejudice to your solution to part "a," assume that you computed the June 30, 1965 inventory to be $44,100 at retail and the ratio of cost to retail to be 80%. The general price level has increased from 100 at January 1, 1965 to 105 at June 30, 1965.

Prepare a schedule to compute the June 30, 1965 inventory at the June 30 price level under the dollar-value LIFO method.

Problem III-7: Various retail methods (50-60 min.)

Lopez Department Store converted from the conventional retail method to the LIFO retail method on January 1, 1966 and is now considering converting to the dollar-value LIFO inventory method. Management requested during your examination of the financial statements for the year ended December 31, 1967 that you furnish a summary showing certain computations of inventory costs for the past three years.

Available information follows:

1. The inventory at January 1, 1965 had a retail value or $45,000 and a cost of $27,500 based on the conventional retail method.

2. Transactions during 1965 were as follows:

	Cost	Retail
Gross purchases	$282,000	$490,000
Purchase returns	6,500	10,000
Purchase discounts	5,000	
Gross sales		492,000
Sales returns		5,000
Employee discounts		3,000
Freight inward	26,500	
Net markups		25,000
Net markdowns		10,000

3. The retail value of the December 31, 1966 inventory was $56,100, the cost ratio for 1966 under the LIFO retail method was 62 per cent and the regional price index was 102 per cent of the January 1, 1966 price level.

4. The retail value of the December 31, 1967 inventory was $48,300, the cost ratio for 1967 under the LIFO retail method was 61 per cent and the regional price index was 105 per cent of the January 1, 1966 price level.

Required:

a. Prepare a schedule showing the computation of the cost of inventory on hand at December 31, 1965 based on the conventional retail method.

b. Prepare a schedule showing the computation of the cost of inventory on hand at the store on December 31, 1965 based on the LIFO retail method. Lopez Department Store does not consider beginning inventories in computing its LIFO retail cost ratio. Assume that the retail value of the December 31, 1965 inventory was $50,000.

c. Without prejudice to your solution to part "b," assume that you computed the December 31, 1965 inventory (retail value $50,000) under the LIFO retail method at a cost of $28,000. Prepare a schedule showing the computations of the cost of the store's 1966 and 1967 year-end inventories under the dollar-value LIFO method.

Problem III-8: Fire loss; coinsurance (50-60 min.)

On April 15, 1966 fire damaged the office and warehouse of King Wholesale Corporation. The only accounting record saved was the general ledger from which the trial balance on page 91 was prepared.

The following data and information have been gathered:

1. The fiscal year of the Corporation ends on December 31.

2. An examination of the April bank statement and cancelled checks revealed that checks written during the period April 1-15 totaled $11,600: $5,700 paid to accounts payable as of March 31, $2,000 for April merchandise shipments, and $3,900 paid for other expenses. Deposits during the same period amounted to $10,650, which consisted of receipts on account from customers with the exception of a $450 refund from a vendor for merchandise returned in April.

3. Correspondence with suppliers revealed unrecorded obligations at April 15 of $8,500 for April merchandise shipments, including $1,300 for shipments in transit on that date.

4. Customers acknowledged indebtedness of $26,400 at April 15, 1966. It was also estimated that customers owed another $5,000 which will never be

King Wholesale Corporation
TRIAL BALANCE
March 31, 1966

Cash	$ 7,000	
Accounts receivable	27,000	
Inventory, December 31, 1965	50,000	
Land	24,000	
Building and equipment	120,000	
Allowance for depreciation		$ 27,200
Other assets	3,600	
Accounts payable		23,700
Other expense accruals		7,200
Capital stock		100,000
Retained earnings		47,700
Sales		90,400
Merchandise	42,000	
Other expenses	22,600	
	$296,200	$296,200

acknowledged or recovered. Of the acknowledged indebtedness, $600 will probably be uncollectible.

5. The following insurance coverage was in effect at the date of the fire:

Insurance Company	Amount of Coverage	Property Covered	Coinsurance, %
A	$30,000	Inventory	80
B	20,000	Inventory	70
C	10,000	Inventory	None

6. The companies insuring the inventory agreed that the Corporation's fire loss claim should be based on the assumption that the over-all gross profit ratio for the past two years was in effect during the current year. The Corporation's audited financial statements disclosed the following:

	Year Ended December 31	
	1965	*1964*
Net sales	$400,000	$300,000
Net purchases	226,000	174,000
Beginning inventory	45,000	35,000
Ending inventory	50,000	45,000

7. Inventory with a cost of $6,500 was salvaged and sold for $3,000. The balance of the inventory was a total loss.

Required:

a. Prepare a schedule computing the amount of the inventory fire loss. The supporting schedule of the computation of the gross profit margin should be in good form.

b. Assume that the amount of inventory fire loss computed in part (a) is $48,000 and that the actual cash value of the inventory at the date of the fire loss was $80,000. Prepare a schedule computing the pro rata claims to be filed with each insurance company for the inventory fire loss.

Problem III-9: Percentage of completion (40-50 min.)

Weinstein Contractors, Inc. undertakes long-term, large-scale construction projects and began operations on October 15, 1968 with contract No. 1, its only job during 1968. A trial balance of the Company's general ledger at December 31, 1969 follows:

Weinstein Contractors, Inc.
TRIAL BALANCE
December 31, 1969

Cash	$ 68,090	
Accounts receivable	136,480	
Costs of contracts in progress	421,320	
Plant and equipment	35,500	
Accumulated depreciation		$ 8,000
Accounts payable		70,820
Deferred income taxes		1,908
Billings on contracts in progress		459,400
Capital stock		139,000
Retained earnings		2,862
Selling and administrative expenses	20,600	
	$681,990	$681,990

The following information is available:

1. The Company has the approval of the Internal Revenue Service to determine income on the completed contract basis for federal income tax reporting and on the percentage-of-completion basis for accounting and financial statements.

2. At December 31, 1969 there were three jobs in progress, the contract prices of which had been computed as follows:

	Contract 1	*Contract 2*	*Contract 3*
Labor and material costs	$169,000	$34,500	$265,700
Indirect costs	30,000	5,500	48,000
Total costs	$199,000	$40,000	$313,700
Add: Profit in contract	40,000	3,000	30,300
Total	$239,000	$43,000	$344,000

During the year, billings are credited to billings on contracts in progress; at year-end this account is charged for the amount of revenue to be recognized.

3. All job costs are charged to cost of contracts in progress. Cost estimates are carefully derived by engineers and architects and are considered reliable. Data on costs to December 31, 1969 follow:

| | | | Incurred to Date | |
Contract	Original Estimate	Total	Labor & Materials	Indirect
1	$199,000	$115,420	$ 92,620	$22,800
2	40,000	32,000	26,950	5,050
3	313,700	313,700	265,700	48,000
Totals	$552,700	$461,120	$385,270	$75,850

4. At December 31, 1968 accumulated costs on contract 1 were $39,800; no costs had accumulated on contracts 2 and 3.
5. Assume that the federal income tax rate is 40 percent.

Required:

a. Prepare a schedule computing the percentage of completion of contracts in progress at December 31, 1969.
b. Prepare a schedule computing the amounts of revenue, related costs, and net income to be recognized in 1969 from contracts in progress at December 31, 1969.
c. Prepare a schedule computing the provision for federal income taxes and the federal income tax liability at December 31, 1969.
d. Give the adjusting journal entries that are necessary at December 31, 1969 to recognize revenues, cost of recognized revenues, and federal income taxes.

SPECIFIC APPROACH

Problem III-1

1. In requirement (b), add the total of the accounts showing errors to the total of accounts showing no errors. Divide the correct total by 50, then multiply by 625 to obtain the required estimate.
2. In requirement (c), the third stratum would consist of the total in the subsidiary ledger less the first stratum, second stratum, net adjustments in part "a," and the discovered overstatement in the third stratum.

Problem III-2

1. In requirement (a), add the beginning inventory costs to the costs of purchases to obtain the cost of goods available for sale. Divide the latter cost by the number of units available to obtain average unit cost.
2. In requirement (b), see the General Approach to Topic V for discussion of the relative sales value method.

3. Requirement (c) calls for a routine inventory cut-off.

4. See the General Approach to Topic III for a summary of the percentage of completion method.

Problem III-3

1. The adjustment prompted by the information in item (2) is affected by adjustment (1) and the direct labor content in the inventories in item (4). Use special care, because many of the subsequent adjustments entail the use of the correct overhead rate.

2. Adjustments regarding the voucher register in items (5) and (6) result from the usual purchase cut-off tests made by auditors.

3. The shipping costs on consigned goods are part of the inventory costs. Use the correct overhead application rate.

4. The net realizable value in item (9) is less than the replacement cost. Therefore, the write-down should use net realizable value.

Problem III-4

Read the General Approach about accounting for consignments. This problem basically entails the correction of errors arising from regarding shipments on consignment as though such shipments were bona fide sales. This means that beginning and ending inventories are understated and also that Accounts Receivable, Sales, Cost of Goods Sold, and income-tax accounts would be affected for both years.

Problem III-5

1. In requirement a(2), when you compute the average unit cost for 1969, include the fair value of the repossessed units as part of the "purchased" units.

2. The gross profit percentage for 1969 would be the overall percentage based on sales of both new and repossessed units.

3. Loss on repossessions is the unpaid balance minus the sum of (1) the unrealized gross profit on that balance plus (2) the value of the repossessed merchandise.

4. Taxable income would be (1) collections multiplied by the pertinent gross profit percentages plus (2) gain or loss on repossessions minus (3) the correct amount of general and administrative expenses.

Problem III-6

1. Consult the General Approach to the retail method. The ending inventory can be regarded as consisting of two layers. The second layer is the increment purchased in 1965. A cost ratio must be computed to convert the second layer from a retail to a cost basis.

2. In part (b), express the June 30 inventory at retail at the January 1 price level; deduct the beginning inventory to obtain the inventory increment at retail. Convert the latter to the June 30 price level, then reduce this second layer from retail value to cost. The first layer will be the $26,900 cost.

Problem III-7

1. See the material on the retail method in the General Approach before undertaking this problem. In requirement (a), net markdowns and employee discounts are excluded in computation of the cost ratio.

2. In requirement (b), exclude the beginning inventory from the totals used in computing the cost ratio in requirement (a). Also, because LIFO is a strict cost method rather than a lower-of-cost-or-market method, deduct net markdowns from your retail computations. No price indexes are needed.

3. In requirement (c), note that the cost ratio for the January 1, 1966 inventory base is $28,000 ÷ $50,000, or 56%.

Problem III-8

1. Read the section on fire losses at the beginning of the General Approach.

2. Compute one over-all gross profit ratio for the two years ended December 31, 1965.

3. Read the section on coinsurance in the General Approach.

Problem III-9

1. The General Approach to Topic III contains a summary of the percentage of completion method.

2. When you compute the income taxes, do not overlook the selling and administrative expenses. Part of the current provision for income taxes (income tax expense) will be deferred income taxes.

Production Costs: Breakeven Analysis; Standard Costs; Analysis of Variances; Direct Costing; Relevant Costs; Discounted Cash Flow

GENERAL APPROACH

Cost accounting (Topics IV, V, and VI) and income taxes (Topic XIII) are the two most important topics in the Practice section of the CPA examination. The diverse demands of modern practice require that the CPA be strongly equipped in three major areas: auditing, taxes, and management services. The AICPA Council has proclaimed as an objective of the Institute that CPAs be encouraged to extend their services beyond those relating to audits and income-tax accounting to embrace the entire scope of management services which are consistent with professional competence, ethical standards, and responsibility. Therefore, a candidate can expect increased emphasis on the management decision-making purposes of cost accounting in the CPA examination rather than the inventory and income-determination purposes. Topics in the examination cover standard costs, flexible budgets, analysis of variances, cost-volume-profit analysis, direct costing, relevant costs for special decisions, and discounted cash-flow analysis. Each recent examination has also included quantitative methods and techniques, including mathematics, statistics, and probability analysis. Problems on product costing emphasize cost allocations, process costs including spoilage, and joint costs.

The subject of production costs includes several special areas. Process cost problems are found in Topic V. Quantitative methods problems are in Topic VI. Problems in Topic IV cover:

1. General manufacturing accounting, including computation of unit costs overhead rates, and cost allocations

96

2. Breakeven analysis and cost-volume relationships
3. Standard costs and analysis of variances
4. Direct costing
5. Relevant costs for special decisions (also in Topic VI)
6. Capital budgeting and discounted cash flow (also in Topic VI)

Meanings of Cost

Like the word *value,* the scope of the term *cost* is extremely broad and general. When used, the word *cost* usually is linked with some adjective in order to avoid ambiguity. *AICPA Terminology Bulletin No. 4* (p. 1) defines *cost* as follows:

> *Cost* is the amount, measured in money, of cash expended or other property expended or other property transferred, capital stock issued, services performed, or a liability incurred, in consideration of goods or services received or to be received. Costs can be classified as unexpired or expired. Unexpired costs (assets) are those which are applicable to the production of future revenues. Expired costs are those which are not applicable to the production of future revenues, and for that reason, are treated as deductions from current revenues or are charged against retained earnings.

The American Accounting Association Committee on Cost Concepts and Standards defined types of cost as follows[1] :

Historical cost is cost measured by actual cash payments or their equivalent at the time of outlay.

Standard costs are scientifically predetermined costs.

Estimated costs are predetermined costs.

Product cost is cost associated with units of output.

Period cost is that cost associated with the income of a time period. Narrowly applied, as a contrasting term to product cost, the concept refers to all costs except product costs that are charged against the revenue of a time period. Used broadly, period cost refers to all charges against the revenue of a time period including product costs.

Direct costs are those costs obviously traceable to a unit of output or a segment of business operations.

Indirect costs are those costs not obviously traceable to a unit of output or a segment of business operations.

Thus defined, the term *indirect costs* is synonymous with overhead costs. These costs are commonly associated with units of output by means of an overhead rate or rates. Prior to such association, various bases of allocation are

---

[1]Committee on Cost Concepts and Standards, American Accounting Association, "Report of the Committee on Cost Concepts and Standards," *Accounting Review*, Vol. XXVII, No. 2, pp. 174-180.

employed to allocate indirect costs to operations, processes, or departments. The relativity of the terms *direct* and *indirect* should be clearly understood. Whereas certain costs may be indirect relative to product, they may be direct to other objects, such as a machine, an operation, or a department.

Fixed costs are those costs which do not change in total as the rate of output of a concern or process varies.

The terms *fixed* and *variable* must be conceived as relative rather than as absolute terms. If a sufficiently large change occurs in the rate of output, practically all costs may vary.

Variable costs are those costs which do change in total with changes in the rate of output.

Imputed costs are costs that do not involve at any time actual cash outlay and which do not, as a consequence, appear in the financial records; nevertheless, such costs involve a foregoing on the part of the person or persons whose costs are being calculated.

Controllable costs are those costs subject to direct control at some level of managerial supervision.

Uncontrollable costs are those costs not subject to control at some (a given) level of managerial authority.

Joint costs exist when, from any one unit source, material, or process, there are produced units of goods or services which have different unit values.

These "units of goods or services" are termed *joint products.* The joint costs are the total costs incurred up to the point of separation. The relative proportions of joint products may vary considerably in different situations, ranging all the way from scrap to products of approximate equality. Usually, joint products of minor significance are classified as by-products.

Sunk costs are historical costs which are irrecoverable in a given situation.

Discretionary costs, often termed escapable or avoidable costs, are those costs which are not essential to the accomplishment of a managerial objective.

Postponable costs are those costs which may be shifted to the future with little or no effect on the efficiency of current operations.

Out-of-pocket costs are those costs which, with respect to a given decision of management, give rise to cash expenditures.

Differential costs are the increases or decreases in total cost, or the changes in specific elements of cost, that result from any variation in operations.

Product Costs (Inventoriable Costs) and Income Measurement

A major objective of accounting is income measurement. In their efforts to refine the measure of income, accountants have developed certain practical classification techniques for distinguishing between assets and expenses. This is accomplished to a large extent by viewing manufacturing costs as inventoriable costs.

If costs can be looked upon as "attaching" or "clinging" to units produced, they are classified as *inventoriable costs,* also commonly called *product costs.* These costs are assets until the goods to which they relate are sold; then the costs are released as expenses and matched against sales. Direct material, direct labor, and factory overhead items are inventoriable costs because they are costs of services utilized in forming the product. In general, the costs of factory operation—the manufacturing costs—are classified as product costs.

Two decisions must be made about costs with regard to income determination. Decision 1: Which costs apply to the current accounting period? Decision 2: Which of those under decision (1) are inventoriable? For example, a three-year $300 insurance premium may be charged originally to an asset account, *unexpired insurance.* Subsequent accounting for this cost will hinge on (1) the amount applicable to the current period—say, $100 for the first year—and (2) the purpose of the insurance coverage. Insurance on factory machinery is inventoriable and is therefore transferred from unexpired insurance to an inventory account. Insurance on a sales office is not inventoriable and is therefore transferred from unexpired insurance to an outright expense account.

Let us review the terminology. In manufacturing accounting many unexpired costs (assets) are transferred from one classification of unexpired costs to another before becoming expired costs (expense). Examples are factory insurance, depreciation on plant, and wages of production workers. These items are held back as product costs (inventory costs) by being charged to Work in Process; they are released later to expense as part of cost of goods sold (an expense). You need to distinguish sharply between merchandising accounting and manufacturing accounting for such costs as insurance, depreciation, and wages. In merchandising accounting, such items are generally treated as expired costs (expenses), whereas in manufacturing accounting most of such items are related to production activities and thus are inventoriable costs—costs which do not expire (become expense) until the goods to which they relate are sold. These relationships are depicted in Exhibit 4-1.

Troublesome Terminology

There are many terms that have very special meanings in accounting. The meanings often differ from company to company. Each organization seems to develop its own distinctive and extensive accounting language. This is why you will save much confusion and wasted time if you always find out the exact meanings of any strange jargon that you encounter.

For example, the term *manufacturing expenses,* which is often used to describe factory overhead, is a misnomer. Factory overhead is not an expense. It is a part of product cost and will funnel into the expense stream only when product costs are released as cost of goods sold.

Also, *cost of goods sold* is a widely used term that is somewhat misleading when trying to pin down the meaning of cost. Cost of goods sold is an *expense*

Exhibit 4-1

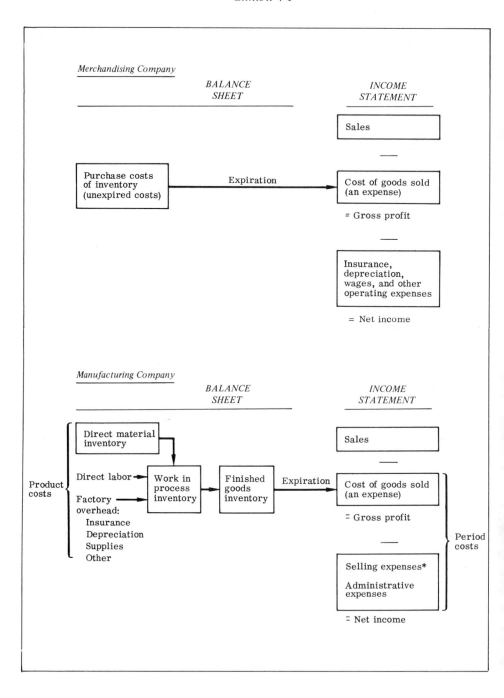

because it is an expired cost; cost of goods sold is every bit as much an expense as salesmen's commissions.

Two of the three major elements of manufacturing costs are sometimes combined in cost terminology as follows: *Prime cost* consists of direct material plus direct labor. *Conversion cost* consists of direct labor plus factory overhead.

Breakeven Analysis and Cost-Volume Relationships

Usually the cost behavior patterns in CPA problems divide conveniently into fixed and variable categories. Study the basic questions below. Obtain the answers on scratch paper before looking at the comments that follow.

Question 1

A person plans to sell a toy rocket at the state fair. He may purchase these rockets at 50 cents each with the privilege of returning all unsold rockets. The booth rental is $200, payable in advance. The rockets will be sold at 90 cents each. (a) How many rockets must be sold to break even? (b) How many rockets must be sold to yield a 20% operating margin?

Answer to Part (a)

The first approach to solution may be called the *equation technique*. Every income statement may be expressed in equation form as follows:

$$\text{Sales} = \text{Variable expenses} + \text{Fixed expenses} + \text{Net profit}$$

This equation may be adapted to any breakeven or profit estimate situation. For Question 1:

> Let X = number of units to be sold to break even
> $\$.90X = \$.50X + \$200 + 0$
> $\$.40X = \$200 + 0$
> $X = 500$ units

A second solution method is the *contribution margin* or *marginal income* technique. Contribution margin is the difference between sales and variable expenses. Sales and expenses are analyzed as follows:

Where breakeven point is desired:

	Unit sales price
minus	Unit variable expenses
equals	Unit contribution to coverage of fixed expenses

The unit contribution is divided into total fixed expenses to secure the number of units which must be sold to break even.

This technique may be applied in Question 1 as follows:

How many rockets must be sold to break even?

Unit sales price	$.90
Unit variable expenses	.50
Unit contribution margin	$.40

Fixed expenses, $200, divided by $.40 equals 500 units.

Stop a moment and relate this contribution margin technique to the equation technique. The key calculation was dividing $200 by $.40. Look at the third line in the equation solution. It reads:

$$\$.40X = \$200 + 0$$

$$X = \frac{\$200 + 0}{\$.40,} \quad \text{giving us a general formula:}$$

$$\text{Breakeven in units} = \frac{\text{Fixed expenses} + \text{Desired net profit}}{\text{Contribution margin per unit}}$$

The *contribution margin technique* is merely a restatement of the *equation* in different form. Use either technique; the choice is a matter of personal preference.

Answer to Part (b)

Part (b) introduces a profit element. The same basic approach may be used:

Let X = number of units to be sold to yield desired net profit
Sales = Variable expenses + Fixed expenses + Net profit
$\$.90X = \$.50X + \$200 + .20(\$.90X)$
$\$.90X = \$.50X + \$200 + \$.18X$
$\$.22X = \$200$
$X = 909.09$, which is rounded to 910 units

Proof:

Sales 910 × $.90	$819	100.00%
Variable expenses 910 × $.50	455	55.56%
Contribution margin	$364	44.44%
Fixed expenses	200	24.42%
Net income	$164	20.02%

The contribution margin approach follows:

$$X = \frac{\text{Fixed expenses} + \text{Desired net profit}}{\text{Unit contribution margin}}$$

$$X = \frac{\$200 + .20(\$.90X)}{\$.40}$$

$$\$.40X = \$200 + \$.18X$$

$$\$.22X = \$200$$

$$X = 910 \text{ units}$$

Question 2

Here is the income statement of C Company:

Net sales		$500,000
Less expenses:		
Variable	$350,000	
Fixed	250,000	600,000
Net loss		$100,000

Assume that variable expenses will always remain the same percentage of sales.

(a) If fixed expenses are increased by $100,000, what amount of sales will cause the firm to break even?

(b) With the proposed increase in fixed expenses, what amount of sales will yield a profit of $50,000?

This example differs from Question 1 because all data are expressed in dollars; no information on the number of units is given. Most firms have more than one product, and the over-all breakeven point is often expressed in sales dollars because of the variety of product lines. One of the most widely used measures of volume is the sales dollar. For example, while apples and oranges cannot be meaningfully added, their sales values provide an automatic common denominator.

Answers may be computed as follows:

(a) Let S = breakeven sales in dollars

S = Variable expenses + Fixed expenses

$$= \frac{\$350,000}{\$500,000}S + (\$250,000 + \$100,000)$$

S = .70S + $350,000

.30S = $350,000

S = $1,166,667

(b) Let S = sales needed to earn $50,000

S = .70S + $350,000 + $50,000

.30S = $400,000

S = $1,333,333

Note that 30% of each sales dollar is available for the coverage of fixed expenses and the making of a net profit. This *contribution margin ratio (variable income ratio* or *contribution percentage)* is computed by subtracting the variable expense percentage, 70%, from 100%. This relationship is the foundation for the following formulas, which are variations of the fundamental equation for the income statement:

Part (a)	*Part (b)*

Second from the last
step in equations:

.30S = $350,000   .30$S$ = $400,000

or

Same calculation:

$$S = \frac{\$350,000}{.30} \qquad\qquad S = \frac{\$400,000}{.30}$$

Formulas:

$$S = \frac{\text{Fixed expenses}}{\text{Contribution margin }\%} \qquad S = \frac{\text{Fixed expenses} + \text{Net profit}}{\text{Contribution margin }\%}$$

These examples demonstrate some very fundamental points about breakeven analysis. The most important point is the contribution margin notion, the idea that every dollar of sales contains a contribution toward the coverage of fixed costs and the earning of net income.

Standard Costs

Standard costs are carefully predetermined costs. Comparisons of actual costs with standard costs yield differences (variances). Analysis and investigation of variances help to find better ways of accomplishing managerial objectives.

Standard costs may be integrated into the general ledger in a number of ways, depending on the preferences of the person who is setting up the standard cost system. The candidate should be familiar with alternative methods because the specific general ledger procedure described in a given problem will influence a solution. No computations or entries should be prepared until the given general ledger procedure (and special types of variance analysis called for, if any) is fully comprehended. Problems on standard costs usually emphasize variance analysis.

Many systems of entries provide information which will facilitate analysis of variances. A key account, Work in Process, could appear as follows, depending upon the system employed:

(Alternative 1)   **WORK IN PROCESS**

Actual quantities X Actual prices	Standard quantities X Standard prices

(Alternative 2)   **WORK IN PROCESS**

Actual quantities X Standard prices	Standard quantities X Standard prices

(Alternative 3)   **WORK IN PROCESS**

Standard quantities X Standard prices	Standard quantities X Standard prices

Flexible Budget and Its Relation to Overhead

A *flexible budget* for factory overhead often is an important part of a standard cost system. Other terms used to denote the same kind of budget are *variable budget, sliding scale budget, performance budget, formula budget,* and *expense control budget.* In substance, the flexible budget is a set of different budgets which are keyed to different levels of operations. For example:

Condensed Flexible Budget
For the Month Beginning January 1, 19—

Standard direct labor hours allowed........	*1,200*	*1,400*	*1,600*
Factory overhead—variable..............	$1,200	$1,400	$1,600
Factory overhead—fixed	700	700	700
	$1,900	$2,100	$2,300

Often a budget formula is used to arrive at budget totals for any given rate of activity. The formula in this example would be: variable overhead, $1.00 per man-hour, plus fixed overhead, $700 at any anticipated activity level.

The flexible budget permits comparison of actual results with what should have been expected at a specific level of operations. The flexible budget approach says, "You tell me what your activity level was during the past month, and I'll go to my flexible budget tool bag and tailor a budget to the particular volume—after the fact." For instance, if operations were actually carried out at a 1,200 level of standard hours worked, results would be compared to the budget for the 1,200 level.

Condensed Cost Comparison—Budgeted vs. Actual
For the Month Ending January 31, 19—

	Budget	Actual	Variance
Standard direct labor hours allowed—1,200.......			
Factory overhead—variable	$1,200	$1,300	$ 100*
Factory overhead—fixed	700	710	10*
	$1,900	$2,010	$ 110*

    *Unfavorable.

Notice that, if a static budget based on a 1,400 level were in use, reports comparing actual results with the budget would be confusing and meaningless in themselves because one would be comparing results garnered at one level of activity with expected results at another level of activity. In other words, the variances may be due largely to costs based on different *volumes.* Hence, the flexible budget permits meaningful comparisons, because the level of activity underlying the comparison is the same.

Two important aspects of terminology deserve special attention. First, the flexible budget is not as flexible as its title implies. It really consists of two parts. The part representing variable costs may be accurately referred to as flexible.The part representing fixed costs is really a static budget, because the total amount of budgeted fixed costs is unaffected by fluctuations in the volume of activity. Second, the term *standard labor hours allowed* (sometimes called *standard hours earned* or *standrard hours worked*) is the amount of time that should have been taken to produce a given output. *Note that it is based on output rather than input.* For example, a lathe operation may have a standard of 10 pieces to be turned per hour. If the necessary operation is performed on 100 pieces in 11 hours, the actual hours worked would be 11, but the standard hours allowed would be 100 divided by 10, or only 10 hours.

A flexible budget allowance is typically based on volume measured by standard hours allowed for the good output produced, rather than by actual hours of input. Suppose in the example in the preceding paragraph that supply usage was budgeted at 40 cents per hour. The flexible budget allowance based on standard hours allowed would be 10 hours X 40¢, or $4.00, rather than 11 hours X 40¢, or $4.40. In general, then, the amounts allowed through the use of standards and budgets are based on outputs, whereas actual costs are based on inputs.

Review Problem

The McDermott Furniture Company has established standard costs for the cabinet department, in which one size of a single four-drawer style of dresser is produced. The standard costs are used in interpreting actual performance. The standard costs of producing one of these dressers are shown below:

Standard Cost Card
Dresser, Style AAA

Materials: Lumber—50 board feet @ $.20................ $10.00
Direct labor: 3 hours at $6.00 .... 18.00
Indirect costs:
    Variable charges—3 hours at $1.00 .... 3.00
    Fixed charges—3 hours at $.50 .... 1.50
        Total per dresser $32.50

The costs of operations to produce 400 of these dressers during January are stated below (there were no initial inventories):

Materials purchased: 25,000 board feet @ 21 .... $5,250.00
Materials used: 19,000 board feet ....
Direct labor: 1,100 hours at $5.90 .... 6,490.00
Indirect costs:
    Variable charges 1,300.00
    Fixed charges 710.00

The flexible budget for this department for normal monthly activity called for 1,400 direct labor hours of operation. At this level, the variable indirect cost was budgeted at $1,400, and the fixed indirect cost at $700. This volume level was used as a basis for computing a predetermined fixed indirect cost rate of 50 cents per hour.

Required:

All journal entries. Also compute the following variations from standard cost. Label your answers as *favorable* or *unfavorable* (F) or (U).

1. Materials purchase price.
2. Materials usage.
3. (a) Direct labor rate;
   (b) Direct labor efficiency.
4. Two-way overhead analysis, whereby overhead variances are classified as two basic kinds: budget variances and volume variances. (The volume variance exists solely because of the existence of fixed overhead; there is no volume variance for variable overhead.)
5. Three-way overhead analysis, whereby the budget variance computed in item 4 is subdivided into spending and efficiency variances. This means that three variances are computed: spending, efficiency, and volume. (The approach demonstrated here computes an efficiency variance for variable overhead only; there is no efficiency variance for fixed overhead because short-run performance ordinarily cannot affect the incurrence of fixed factory overhead.)

Try to prepare your own solution before referring to the suggested solution that follows.

Suggested Solution

Journal entries are supported by pertinent variance analysis.

Analysis of Variances

Material price variances

1. Stores control (25,000 board feet @ $.20) 5,000
   Material purchase price variance (25,000 board feet @ $.01) 250
      Accounts payable (25,000 board feet @ $.21) 5,250

Alternative (a). The material price variance is usually computed by multiplying the *difference in unit price* times the *actual quantity purchased.* Note that the method illustrated in this problem assumes that the price variance is isolated as materials are purchased. Therefore, materials in stores are carried at standard prices. The authors prefer this method because it isolates variances more quickly and is likely to be more useful for control purposes.

Alternative (b). Some companies prefer to carry materials in stores at actual prices. In these cases, the price variance is not isolated until the materials are issued to production. Therefore, the price variance would be computed by multiplying the *difference in unit price* by the *actual quantity issued to production.*

Material usage variance

2. Work in process control (400 units X 50 board feet X $.20)........ 4,000
   Material usage variance (1,000 board feet X $.20) 200
      Stores control (19,000 board feet X $.20)..................... 3,800

This variance is sometimes called a *quantity* variance. It is computed by multiplying the *difference in quantity used* times the *standard unit price.* Typically, usage is the major responsibility of one department head, while price may be the major responsibility of a different department head. Therefore, the quantity variance should not be influenced by changes in unit prices. Price is held constant at standard, and the resultant usage variance is attributable solely to off-standard usage. Note that, throughout this problem, Work in Process will be carried at standard quantities and standard prices. Note also that unfavorable variances have debit balances and that favorable variances have credit balances.

Direct labor variances

3. Work in process control (400 units X $18.00) 7,200
    Direct labor rate variance 110
    Direct labor efficiency variance 600
    Accrued payroll 6,490

The handling of direct labor costs in the general ledger varies considerably. The objective is to charge products at standard cost (standard usage X standard rate) but to recognize actual liabilities as incurred. The basic format for analysis of labor variances follows:

Incurred		*Applied*
Actual Hours	Actual Hours	Standard Hours Allowed
X Actual Rate	X Standard Rate	X Standard Rate
(1,100 X $5.90)	(1,100 X $6.00)	(400 units X 3 hours X $6.00)
$6,490	$6,600	$7,200

Rate variance, $110 F   Efficiency variance, $600F
(1,100 hours X $.10)   (100 hours X $6.00)
Total labor variance, $710F

The labor rate variance is the *difference in rate* times the *actual hours used.* The labor efficiency variance (also called *time variance, hours variance,* and *performance variance*) is the *difference in time* times the *standard rate.*

Overhead variances

4 and 5. Variable overhead control 1,300
    Accounts payable and other accounts 1,300
    Work in process control 1,200
    Variable overhead applied (400 X 3 X $1.00) 1,200
    Fixed overhead control 710
    Accounts payable and other accounts 710
    Work in process control 600
    Fixed overhead applied (400 X 3 X $.50) 600

Accountants disagree a great deal about the validity and usefulness of (a) overhead variance analysis in general, (b) the two-way versus the three-way analysis, and (c) the terminology to be applied to the variety of possible variances. The analysis that is demonstrated here is only one way of approaching overhead variances, but its methodology can be applied successfully to the usual CPA problem requirements.

The easiest way to account for overhead variance is probably to allow the overhead control and applied accounts to accumulate month-to-month postings until the end of the year. Monthly variances would not be isolated formally in the accounts (Note that overhead variances are not isolated in the above journal entries), although monthly variance reports would be prepared.

For analysis of all overhead variances, see Exhibit 4-2. The two-way analysis, in response to requirement (4) of the problem, is shown at the top of the exhibit. The three-way analysis, in response to requirement (5) of the problem, is shown at the bottom of the exhibit, along with the interrelationships of the three-way and two-way analyses. Because an overhead rate which combines both the fixed and variable elements is often used in applying overhead to products, the appropriate analysis in such a situation is also shown in Exhibit 4-2.

The exhibit is a convenient work sheet for attacking problems of overhead variance. Careful study of its contents should be rewarding, although it should be kept in mind that this subject can become intricate and space here does not permit an elaborate discussion.[2] Key points follow. Points (a) through (d) deal with the "Two-way Analysis" part of the exhibit:

(a) *Budget variance* (often called *controllable variance*) is the difference between incurred and budgeted amounts.

(b) When a flexible budget is used, the budgeted amount for *variable* overhead depends on production expressed as standard hours allowed.

(c) The total budget for *fixed* overhead will *be the same at any activity level.*

(d) The *volume variance* is also called the *capacity variance,* the *utilization variance,* and the *activity variance.* It is the difference between the fixed overhead applied and budgeted. For product costing purposes, it is necessary to apply fixed overhead by using a predetermined rate which is usually based on standard hours allowed at "normal" volume (sometimes called "standard" volume or "denominator" volume):

$$\text{Fixed overhead rate} = \frac{\text{Budgeted fixed overhead}}{\text{Normal volume}}$$

$$\text{Rate} = \frac{\$700}{1,400 \text{ hours}} = 50\text{¢ per hour}$$

This rate is used to cost production regardless of the activity levels encountered. A volume variance ($100 in this example) arises whenever production expressed in standard hours allowed deviates from the normal activity level (or any activity level selected as the denominator for computing the product-costing rate) used for setting the predetermined rate.

There is no volume variance for variable overhead. The concept of volume

---

[2]For an expanded discussion, see Charles T. Horngren, *Cost Accounting: Managerial Emphasis,* 3rd ed. (Englewood Cliffs, N.J.: Prentice-Hall, Inc., 1972), Chapters 8 and 9. Chapter 28 is entitled "Cost Accounting in the CPA Examination."

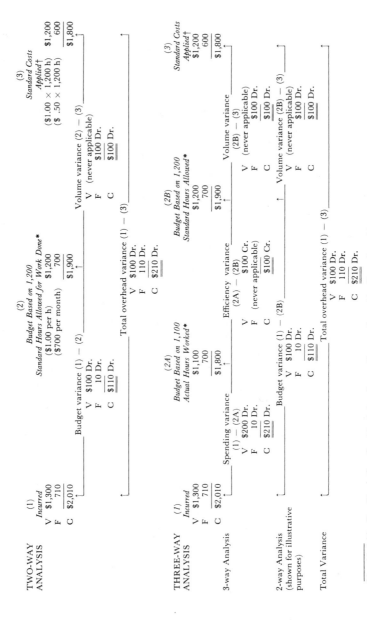

Exhibit 4-2

McDERMOTT FURNITURE COMPANY
Work sheets Analysis of Overhead Variances

TWO-WAY ANALYSIS

	(1) Incurred
V	$1,300
F	710
C	$2,010

(2) Budget Based on 1,200 Standard Hours Allowed for Work Done*
($1.00 per h) $1,200
($700 per month) 700
$1,900

(3) Standard Costs Applied†
($1.00 × 1,200 h) $1,200
($ .50 × 1,200 h) 600
$1,800

Budget variance (1) − (2)
V $100 Dr.
F 10 Dr.
C $110 Dr.

Volume variance (2) − (3)
V (never applicable)
F $100 Dr.
C $100 Dr.

Total overhead variance (1) − (3)
V $100 Dr.
F 110 Dr.
C $210 Dr.

THREE-WAY ANALYSIS

	(1) Incurred
V	$1,300
F	710
C	$2,010

(2A) Budget Based on 1,100 Actual Hours Worked*
$1,100
700
$1,800

(2B) Budget Based on 1,200 Standard Hours Allowed*
$1,200
700
$1,900

(3) Standard Costs Applied†
$1,200
600
$1,800

3-way Analysis

Spending variance (1) − (2A)
V $200 Dr.
F 10 Dr.
C $210 Dr.

Efficiency variance (2A) − (2B)
V $100 Cr.
F (never applicable)
C $100 Cr.

Volume variance (2B) − (3)
V (never applicable)
F $100 Dr.
C $100 Dr.

2-way Analysis (shown for illustrative purposes)

Budget variance (1) − (2B)
V $100 Dr.
F 10 Dr.
C $110 Dr.

Volume variance (2B) − (3)
V (never applicable)
F $100 Dr.
C $100 Dr.

Total Variance

Total overhead variance (1) − (3)
V $100 Dr.
F 110 Dr.
C $210 Dr.

V = Variable; F = Fixed; C = Combined; h = hours; Dr. = unfavorable; Cr. = favorable.
* Formula: $700 per month plus $1.00 per hour.
† Formula: Predetermined rates × standard hours allowed.

110

variance arises for fixed overhead because of the conflict between accounting for control (by budgets) and accounting for product costing (by application rates). See Exhibit 4-3. Note carefully that the budget for fixed overhead serves the control purpose whereas the computation of a fixed overhead rate results in the treatment of fixed overhead as if it were a variable cost. In other words, the applied line in Exhibit 4-3 is artificial in the sense that, for product-costing purposes, it seemingly transforms a fixed cost into a variable cost.

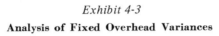

Exhibit 4-3

Analysis of Fixed Overhead Variances

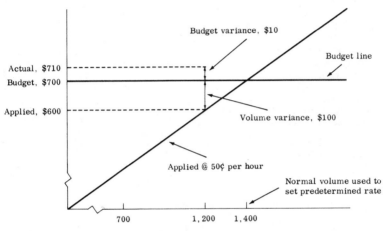

VOLUME IN STANDARD DIRECT HOURS ALLOWED

The volume variance can be computed by multiplying the predetermined rate times the difference between standard hours allowed and normal hours. In our example, this would be $.50 × (1,200 hours – 1,400 hours) = $100, unfavorable. The volume variance is favorable when actual volume exceeds normal volume, and vice versa.

(e) The only real difference between the two-way and three-way analyses is the breakdown of the variable overhead budget variance into two sub-variances—a *spending variance* and an *effieciency variance*—much as the direct labor variance is split into an efficiency variance and a rate variance. The efficiency variance is the variable overhead rate times the difference between actual hours worked and standard hours allowed. Note the similarity between the efficiency variances for direct labor and for variable overhead. Both are differences between actual hours and standard hours allowed multiplied by a standard rate. The *spending variance* is the difference between the amount incurred and the amount that would be specified in a budget based on *actual* hours worked.

(f) For fixed factory overhead, the amount of the budget variance under the two-way analysis will always be identical with spending variance under the three-way analysis. There is no efficiency variance for fixed factory overhead because short-run performance cannot affect incurrence of fixed factory overhead.

The following is a summary of variances:

1. Materials purchase price $250U*
2. Materials usage 200F
3. (a) Direct labor rate 110F
   (b) Direct labor efficiency 600F
4. Two-way analysis:
   (a) Budget variances
       Variable overhead 100U
       Fixed overhead 10U
   (b) Volume variance–Fixed overhead 100U
5. Three-way analysis:
   (a) Spending variances
       Variable overhead 200U
       Fixed overhead 10U
   (b) Efficiency variance–Variable overhead 100F
   (c) Volume variance–Fixed overhead 100U

*U=Unfavorable; F=Favorable

Direct Costing

Direct costing would be more accurately called *variable* or *marginal costing,* because in substance it is the inventory costing method which applies only variable production costs to product; fixed factory overhead is not assigned to product. Typically variable production costs are direct material costs, direct labor costs, and variable overhead costs. Direct costing differs from *absorption costing,* sometimes called *conventional costing,* because fixed factory overhead is treated as a period cost (charged against revenue immediately) rather than as a product cost (assigned to units produced).

Advocates of direct costing maintain that the fixed portion of factory overhead is more closely related to the capacity to produce than to the production of specific units. Opponents maintain that inventories should carry a fixed cost component because both variable and fixed costs are necessary to produce goods; both these costs should be inventoriable regardless of the differences in their behavior patterns.

The notion of direct costing is a formal recognition of the ideas underlying flexible budgets, breakeven analysis, and revenue-cost-volume relationships. It is an application of these relationships which involves a change in the conventional treatment of fixed overhead in relation to income determination. The comparative statements in Exhibit 4-4 should help clarify some fundamental ideas.

Exhibit 4-4

A Company

INCOME STATEMENTS

FOR THE YEAR ENDING DECEMBER 31, 19x1

(Assume no beginning inventory)

ABSORPTION COSTING

Sales, 1000 units @ $10.00			$10,000
Cost of sales:			
Variable manufacturing costs, 1,100 units @ $6.00	$6,600		
Fixed manufacturing costs	2,200		
	$8,800		
Less ending inventory, 100 units (1/11 X $8,800)	800*	8,000	
Gross margin		$ 2,000	
Less total selling and administrative expenses		900	
Net income		$ 1,100	

DIRECT COSTING

Sales			$10,000
Variable cost of sales:			
Variable manufacturing costs	$6,600		
Less ending inventory 1/11 X $6,600	600*	6,000	
Variable gross margin		$ 4,000	
Less variable selling and administrative expenses		400	
Operating contribution margin		$ 3,600	
Less period costs:			
Fixed manufacturing costs	$2,200		
Fixed selling and administrative expenses	500	2,700	
Net income		$ 900	

*The $200 difference in net income is caused by the $200 ($800 − $600) difference in ending inventories. Under absorption costing, $200 of the $2,200 fixed manufacturing costs is held back in inventory, while under direct costing the $200 is released immediately as a period charge.

Note the following points about the exhibit:

Under absorption costing, fixed production costs are assigned to product, to be subsequently released to expense as a part of cost of goods sold. On the other hand, under direct costing, fixed production cost are treated as period costs and are immediately released as expense.

Under direct costing, only the variable manufacturing costs are regarded as product costs. This approach emphasizes the interplay of revenue, cost, and profits, because the contribution margin is highlighted and is an integral part of the formal presentation of operating results. Variability with volume is the criterion for the classification of costs into product or period categories.

The term *direct* costing is misleading when compared with the use of the word "direct" as applied to absorption product costing (for example, direct material, direct labor). In direct costing, the variable factory overhead is considered a part of the direct costs of production; in absorption costing, the variable factory overhead is regarded as an indirect cost along with fixed factory overhead.

In direct costing, the *contribution margin*—the excess of sales over variable costs—is a highlight of the income statement. Other terms for *contribution margin* include *marginal income, marginal balance, profit contribution,* and *contribution to fixed costs.*

The absorption costing statement in Exhibit 4-4 differentiated between the variable and fixed costs for illustrative purposes only. The conventional absorption costing statement rarely classifies costs into fixed and variable categories.

Relevant Costs for Special Decisions

Modern CPA practice embraces three major areas: auditing, taxes, and management advisory services. The CPA needs a comprehensive knowledge of cost accounting in order to perform management advisory services.

Modern cost accounting provides information for three broad purposes:

(1) planning and controlling current operations,
(2) making special decisions and formulating long-range plans, and
(3) inventory valuation and income determination.

In short, the theme is "different costs for different purposes."

Recent CPA examinations have recognized the increasing importance of management advisory services by including problems on cost analysis for special decisions. This tendency is likely to continue.

The accountant's role in special decisions is basically that of a technical expert on cost analysis. His responsibility is to see that the manager uses relevant data in guiding his decisions.

To be relevant to a particular decision, a cost must meet two criteria:

(1) it must be an expected *future* cost; and

(2) it must be an element of *difference* between alternatives.

The key question is, "What difference does it make?" All *past (historical)* costs are irrelevant to any decision about the future.

The role that past costs play in decision making is an auxiliary one; the distinction here should be definitive, not fuzzy. Past (irrelevant) costs are useful because they provide empirical evidence that often helps sharpen predictions of future costs. But the expected future costs are the *only* cost ingredients in any analysis of alternatives.

In decisions about activity levels (the special order, make or buy, and adding or dropping a product line) there may be a temptation to say that variable costs are always relevant and that fixed costs are always irrelevant. This is a dangerous generalization, because fixed costs are often affected by a decision. For example, plans to buy a second car for family use should be most heavily influenced by the new set of fixed costs that would be encountered. Conceivably, if the total family mileage were unaffected, the variable costs could be wholly irrelevant.

For a given set of facilities or resources, the key to maximizing net income is to obtain the largest possible contribution per unit of constraining factor or scarce resource. Hours of available machine time or square feet of selling space are examples of scarce resources.

Make or buy decisions are, fundamentally, examples of obtaining the most profitable utilization of given facilities.

Generally, in cost analysis it is advisable to use total costs, not unit costs, because unitized fixed costs are often erroneously interpreted as if they behaved like variable costs. A common activity or volume level must underlie the comparison of equipment.

The book value of old equipment is always irrelevant in replacement decisions. Disposal value, however, is usually relevant. When income taxes are considered, the writing off of the book value may influence income-tax payments. But the difference in *future* income-tax flows is the relevant item—not the book value of the old fixed assets per se.

Incremental or differential costs are the differences in total costs under each alternative.

An opportunity cost is the maximum sacrifice in rejecting an alternative; it is the maximum contribution to earnings that might have been obtained if the productive good, service, or capacity had been put to some alternative use.[3]

---

[3]The concepts of relevant costs and proper cost analysis for special decisions are often subtle. Space does not permit thorough discussion here. For an expanded discussion, see Charles T. Horngren, *Cost Accounting,* 3rd ed. (Englewood Cliffs, N.J.: Prentice-Hall, Inc., 1972), Chapter 11.

Capital Budgeting and Discounted Cash Flow

What type of equipment should we buy? Should we add this product to our line? Managers must make these and similar decisions that have long-range implications; these decisions are commonly called capital budgeting decisions. Because the discounted cash flow method explicitly and automatically weighs the time-value of money, it is the best method to use for capital budgeting decisions.

An understanding of the fundamentals of compound interest[4] is absolutely essential to understanding discounted cash flow approaches to capital budgeting. The following example blends some relevant cost analysis with the discounted cash flow approach:

A company owns a packaging machine, which was purchased three years ago for $56,000. It has a remaining useful life of five years, but will require a major overhaul at the end of two more years of life, at a cost of $10,000. Its disposal value now is $20,000; in five years its disposal value is expected to be $8,000. The cash operating costs of this machine are expected to be $40,000 annually.

A salesman has offered a substitute machine for $51,000, or for $31,000 plus the old machine. The new machine will slash annual cash operating costs by $10,000, will not require any overhauls, will have a useful life of five years, and will have a disposal value of $3,000.

Required:

Assume that the minimum desired rate of return is 14%. Using the net present value technique, show whether the new machine should be purchased, using (1) a total project approach or (2) an incremental approach.

Solution

A difficult part of long-range decision making is the structuring of data. We want to see the effects of each alternative on future cash flows. The focus here is on bona fide *cash* transactions, not on opportunity costs. Using an opportunity cost approach may yield the same answers, but repeated classroom experimentation with various analytical methods has convinced the authors that the following steps are likely to be the clearest:

Step 1. Arrange the relevant cash flows by project, so that a sharp distinction is made between total project flows and incremental flows. The incremental flows are merely algebraic differences between two alternatives. (There are *always* at least two alternatives. One is the *status quo,* the alternative of doing nothing.) Exhibit 4-5 shows how the cash flows for *each* alternative are sketched.

Step 2. Discount the expected cash flows and choose the project with the least cost or the greatest benefit. Both the total project approach and the

---

[4]For a thorough discussion see Charles T. Horngren, *Cost Accounting: A Managerial Emphasis,* 3rd ed. (Englewood Cliffs, N.J.: Prentice-Hall, Inc., 1972), Chapters 13 and 14.

Exhibit 4-5

TOTAL PROJECT VERSUS INCREMENTAL APPROACH TO NET PRESENT VALUE
(Data from Example 2)

End of Year	Present Value Discount Factor, @14%	Total Present Value	Sketch of Cash Flows 0	1	2	3	4	5
TOTAL PROJECT APPROACH								
A. Replace								
Recurring cash operating costs, using an annuity table	3.433	$(102,990)		($30,000)	($30,000)	($30,000)	($30,000)	($30,000)
Disposal value, end of year 5	.519	1,557						3,000
Initial required investment	1.000	(31,000)	($31,000)					
Present value of net cash outflows		$(132,433)						
B. Keep								
Recurring cash operating costs, using an annuity table	3.433	$(137,320)		($40,000)	($40,000)	($40,000)	($40,000)	($40,000)
Overhaul, end of year 2	769	(7,690)			(10,000)			
Disposal value, end of year 5	.519	4,152						8,000
Present value of net cash outflows		$(140,858)						
Difference in favor of replacement		$ 8,425						
INCREMENTAL APPROACH								
(A) – (B) Analysis Confined to Differences								
Recurring cash operating savings, using an annuity table	3.433	$ 34,330		$10,000	$10,000	$$10,000	$10,000	$10,000
Overhaul avoided end of year 2	.769	7,690			$10,000			
Difference in disposal values, end of year 5	.519	(2,595)						(5,000)
Incremental initial investment	1.000	(31,000)	($31,000)					
Net present value of replacement		$ 8,425						

117

incremental approach are illustrated in Exhibit 4-5. Which approach you use is a matter of preference. In this example, the $8,425 net difference in favor of replacement is the ultimate result under either approach.

Analysis of Typical Items under Discounted Cash Flow

1. *Future disposal values.* The disposal value at the date of termination of a project is an increase in the cash inflow in the year of disposal. Errors in forecasting disposal value are usually not crucial because the present value is usually small.

2. *Current disposal values and required investment.* There are a number of correct ways to analyze this item, all of which will have the same ultimate effect on the decision. Probably the simplest way was illustrated in Exhibit 4-5, where the $20,000 was offset against the $51,000 purchase price and the actual *cash* outgo was shown. Generally, the required investment is most easily measured by offsetting the disposal value of the old assets against the gross cost of the new assets.

3. *Book value and depreciation.* Depreciation is a phenomenon of accrual accounting that entails an allocation of cost, not a specific cash outlay. Depreciation and book value are ignored in discounted cash flow approaches for the reasons mentioned earlier.

4. *Overhead analysis.* In relevant cost analysis, only the overhead that will differ between alternatives is pertinent. There is need for careful study of the fixed overhead under the available alternatives. In practice, this is an extremely difficult phase of cost analysis, because it is difficult to relate the individual costs to any single project.

5. *Unequal lives.* Where projects have unequal lives, comparisons may be made either over the useful life of the longer-lived project or over the useful life of the shorter-lived project. In general, estimate what the residual values will be at the end of the longer-lived project; also assume a reinvestment at the end of the shorter-lived project. This makes sense primarily because the decision maker should extend his time horizon as far as possible. If he is considering a longer-lived project, he should give serious consideration to what would be done in the time interval between the termination dates of the shorter-lived and longer-lived projects.

6. *A word of caution.* The foregoing material has been an *introduction* to the area of capital budgeting, which is, in practice, complicated by a variety of factors: unequal lives; major differences in the size of alternative investments; peculiarities in time-adjusted rate-of-return computations; various ways of allowing for uncertainty; changes, over time, in desired rates of return; the indivisibility of projects in relation to a fixed over-all capital budget appropriation; and more. These niceties are beyond the scope of this introduction to capital budgeting.

7. *The general guide to capital budgeting decisions.* The following decision

rule, subject to the cautionary words just stated, should guide the selection of projects: The net present value method should be used, and *any* project that has a positive net present value should be undertaken. When the projects are mutually exclusive, so that the acceptance of one automatically entails the rejection of the other (e.g., buying Dodge or Ford trucks), the project which maximizes wealth measured in net present value in dollars should be undertaken.

Income Taxes and Discounted Cash Flow

For simplicity, income-tax considerations were excluded from our example. They do play a major role in actual decisions and should be regarded as cash disbursements in discounted cash flow analyses.

Effects of Depreciation Deductions

Exhibit 4-6 shows the interrelationship of net income before taxes, income taxes, and depreciation. Assume that the company has a single fixed asset purchased for $100,000 cash, which has a four-year life and zero disposal value. The purchase cost, less the estimated disposal value, is tax-deductible in the form of yearly depreciation. This deduction has been called a *tax shield* aptly, because it protects that amount of income from taxation.

Exhibit 4-6

**Basic Analysis of Income Statement,
Income Taxes, and Cash Flows**

TRADITIONAL INCOME STATEMENT

(A)	Sales	$130,000
(B)	Less: Expenses, excluding depreciation	$ 70,000
(D)	Depreciation (straight line)	25,000
	Total expenses	$ 95,000
	Net income before taxes	$ 35,000
(E)	Income taxes @ 60%	21,000
(F)	Net income after taxes	$ 14,000

Net after-tax cash inflow from operations:
either $A - B - E = \$130,000 - \$70,000 - \$21,000 =$ $ 39,000
or $F + D = \$ 14,000 + \$25,000 = \$39,000$

ANALYSIS OF THE ABOVE FOR CAPITAL BUDGETING

(A − B)	Cash inflow from operations: $130,000 − $70,000 =	$ 60,000
	Income-tax effects, @ 60%	36,000
	After-tax effects of cash inflow from operations	$ 24,000
	Tax-Shield	
(D)	Straight line depreciation: $100,000 ÷ 4 = $25,000	
	Income-tax savings, @ 60%	15,000*
	Total cash provided by operations after consideration of tax shield	$ 39,000

*Net cash outflow for income taxes, $36,000 − $15,000 = $21,000.

The asset represents a valuable tax deduction of $100,000. The present value of this deduction directly depends on its specific yearly effects on future income-tax payments. Therefore, the present value is influenced by the depreciation method selected, the tax rates, and the discount rate. In almost all cases some form of accelerated depreciation is preferable to straight-line depreciation in order to maximize net present value.

REFERENCES

Crowningshield, Gerald R. *Cost Accounting: Principles and Managerial Applications,* 2nd ed. Boston: Houghton Mifflin, 1969.

Horngren, Charles T. *Cost Accounting: A Managerial Emphasis,* 3rd ed. Englewood Cliffs, N.J.: Prentice-Hall, Inc., 1972.

Matz, Adolph, and Othel J. Curry. *Cost Accounting,* 5th ed. Cincinnati: South-Western Publishing Company, 1972.

Shillinglaw, Gordon, *Cost Accounting,* 3rd ed. Homewood, Illinois: Richard·D. Irwin, Inc., 1972.

CPA PROBLEMS

Problem IV-1: Overhead absorption (40-50 min.)

Your client recently purchased an engineering consulting practice from James Dider who wishes to retire, and agreed to employ Mr. Dider and all of his employees for one year. You have been engaged to determine an estimate of the total cost of operations per chargeable man-hour, for each member of the professional staff, in order that suitable billing rates may be established.

Your estimates of the hours for which the professional staff will be paid, their annual salaries, and the proportions of their working hours which will not be directly chargeable to any specific client follow:

Employee	Total Hours	Annual Salary	Percentage of Time Devoted to Firm Overhead
Able	1,200	$ 2,400	40%
Briscol	2,400	12,000	10%
Case	2,000	8,000	20%
Dider	800	10,000	40%
Emel	2,400	7,200	5%

Mr. Dider's other costs of operating his firm, including clerical wages, have averaged about $39,100 per year for the last three years.

Required:

a. Prepare schedules computing the following with respect to the year following acquisition of Dider's engineering consulting practice:
    1. Total overhead cost.
    2. Total employees' salaries directly billable to clients.

3. An estimate of the total cost of operations per chargeable man-hour of each member of the professional staff assuming total overhead is to be allocated on the basis of total billable professional salaries.

b. Without regard to the effect on total overhead and assuming no factor changes unless specified, state whether each of the following unrelated situations will result in

— Over-absorption
— Estimated (standard) absorption
— Under-absorption

of overhead and state the reason for this result:

1. Able spends 50 percent of his time in overhead functions.
2. Briscol works 100 hours less than expected during the year and his salary is reduced accordingly.
3. Case works 100 hours more than expected during the year and his salary is increased accordingly.
4. Dider works 200 hours more than expected during the year and his annual salary is unchanged.
5. Emel receives a salary increase but his billing rate is not changed.

Problem IV-2: Overhead allocation (50-60 min.)

Thrift-Shops, Inc. operates a chain of three food stores in a state which recently enacted legislation permitting municipalities within the state to levy an income tax on corporations operating within their respective municipalities. The legislation establishes a uniform tax rate which the municipalities may levy, and regulations which provide that the tax is to be computed on income derived within the taxing municipality after a reasonable and consistent allocation of general overhead expenses. General overhead expenses have not been allocated to individual stores previously and include warehouse, general office, advertising and delivery expenses.

Each of the municipalities in which Thrift-Shops, Inc. operates a store has levied the corporate income tax as provided by state legislation and management is considering two plans for allocating general overhead expenses to the stores. The 1969 operating results before general overhead and taxes for each store were as shown below:

| | Store | | | |
	Ashville	*Burns*	*Clinton*	*Total*
Sales, net	$416,000	$353,600	$270,400	$1,040,000
Less cost of sales	215,700	183,300	140,200	539,200
Gross margin	200,300	170,300	130,200	500,800
Less local operating expenses:				
Fixed	60,800	48,750	50,200	159,750
Variable	54,700	64,220	27,448	146,368
Total	115,500	112,970	77,648	306,118
Income before general overhead and taxes	$ 84,800	$ 57,330	$ 52,552	$ 194,682

General overhead expenses in 1969 were as follows:

Warehousing and delivery expenses:		
Warehouse depreciation	$20,000	
Warehouse operations	30,000	
Delivery expenses	40,000	$ 90,000
Central office expenses:		
Advertising.................................	18,000	
Central office salaries.......................	37,000	
Other central office expenses..................	28,000	83,000
Total general overhead		$173,000

Additional information includes the following:

1. One-fifth of the warehouse space is used to house the central office and depreciation on this space is included in other central office expenses. Warehouse operating expenses vary with quantity of merchandise sold.

2. Delivery expenses vary with distance and number of deliveries. The distances from the warehouse to each store and the number of deliveries made in 1969 were as follows:

Store	Miles	Number of Deliveries
Ashville	120	140
Burns..........................	200	64
Clinton	100	104

3. All advertising is prepared by the central office and is distributed in the areas in which stores are located.

4. As each store was opened, the fixed portion of central office salaries increased $7,000 and other central office expenses increased $2,500. Basic fixed central office salaries amount to $10,000 and basic fixed other central office expenses amount to $12,000. The remainder of central office salaries and the remainder of other central office expenses vary with sales.

Required:

a. For each of the following plans for allocating general overhead expenses, compute the income of each store that would be subject to the municipal levy on corporation income:

Plan 1.   Allocate all general overhead expenses on the basis of sale volume.

Plan 2.   First, allocate central office salaries and other central office expenses evenly to warehouse operations and each store. Second, allocate the resulting warehouse operations expenses, warehouse depreciation and advertising to each store on the basis of sales volume. Third, allocate delivery expenses to each store on the basis of delivery miles times number of deliveries.

b. Management has decided to expand one of the three stores to increase sales by $50,000. The expansion will increase local fixed operating expenses by $7,500 and require ten additional deliveries from the warehouse. Determine which store management should select for expansion to maximize corporate profits.

Problem IV-3: Budgets and overhead allocation (40-50 min.)

In June 1960, after ten years with a large CPA firm, John B. Johnson, CPA, opened an office as a sole practitioner.

In 1962 Walter L. Smith, CPA, joined Johnson as a senior accountant. The partnership of Johnson and Smith was organized July 1, 1967 and a fiscal year ending June 30 was adopted and approved by the Internal Revenue Service.

Continued growth of the Firm has required additional personnel. The current complement, including approved salaries for the fiscal year ending June 30, 1973, is as follows:

	Annual Salary
Partners:	
John B. Johnson, CPA	$24,000
Walter L. Smith, CPA	18,000
Professional staff:	
Supervisor:	
Harold S. Vickers, CPA	17,500
Senior Accountant:	
Duane Lowe, CPA	12,500
Assistants:	
James M. Kennedy	10,500
Viola O. Quinn	10,500
Secretaries:	
Mary Lyons	7,800
Johnnie L. Hammond	6,864
Livia A. Garcia	6,864

A severe illness kept Johnson away from the office for over four months in late 1971. The Firm suffered during this period, mainly because other personnel lacked knowledge about the practice.

After Johnson's illness, a plan was developed for delegation of administrative authority and responsibility and for standardization of procedures.

The goals of the plan included (1) income objectives, (2) standardized billing procedures (with flexibility for adjustments by the partners) and (3) assignment schedules to eliminate overtime and to allow for nonchargeable time such as vacations and illness. The Firm plans a 52-week year with five-day, forty-hour weeks.

The partners have set an annual income target (after partners' salaries) of at least $55,000. The budget for fiscal year 1973 is 700 hours of chargeable time at $45 per hour for Johnson and 1,100 hours at $40 per hour for Smith. Johnson and Smith are to devote all other available time, except as specified below, to administration. The billing rates for all other employees including secretaries are to be set at a level to recover their salaries plus the following overhead items: fringe benefits of $15,230, other operating expenses of $49,380 and a contribution of $20,500 to target income.

The partners agree that salary levels are fair bases for allocating overhead in setting billing rates with the exception that salary costs of the secretaries' nonchargeable time are to be added to overhead to arrive at total overhead to be allocated. Thus the billing rate for each secretary will be based upon the salary costs of her chargeable time plus her share of the total overhead. No portion of total overhead is to be allocated to partners' salaries.

The following information is available for nonchargeable time:

1. Because of his recent illness, Johnson expects to be away an additional week. Smith expects no loss of time from illness. All other employees are to be allowed one illness day per month (12 days each).

2. Allowable vacations are as follows:

1 Month	Johnson
	Smith
3 Weeks	Vickers
	Lyons
2 Weeks	All other employees

3. The Firm observes seven holidays annually. If the holiday falls on a weekend, the office is closed the preceding Friday or following Monday.

4. Kennedy and Quinn should each be allotted three days to sit for the November 1972 CPA examination.

5. Hours are budgeted for other miscellaneous activities of the personnel as follows:

	Johnson	Smith	Vickers	Lowe	Kennedy	Quinn	Lyons	Hammond	Garcia
Firm projects		100	40	40	40		200		
Professional development . . .	80	80	56	40	40	50	24	16	24
Professional meetings	184	120	40	40	16	16	24	8	8
Firm meetings	48	48	48	24	24	24	48	8	8
Community activities	80	40	40	24	16	16	12		
Office time other than Firm administration			84	72			1,000	716	808
Total other miscellaneous . .	392	388	308	240	136	106	1,308	748	848

6. Unassigned time should be budgeted for Lowe, Kennedy and Quinn at 8, 38 and 78 hours respectively.

Required:

a. Prepare a time allocation budget for Johnson, Smith and each employee ending with budgeted chargeable time for the year ending June 30, 1973.

b. Independent of your solution to part a and assuming the following data as to budgeted chargeable hours, prepare a schedule computing billing rates by employee for the year ending June 30, 1973. The schedule should show the proper allocation of appropriate expenses and target income contribution to salaries applicable to chargeable time in accordance with the objective established by the partners. (Round allocation calculations to one decimal place. Round billing rate calculations to the nearest dollar.)

	Budgeted Chargeable Hours
Vickers	1,600
Lowe	1,650
Kennedy	1,550
Quinn	1,450
Lyons	500
Hammond	1,150
Garcia	1,200

c. Independent of your solutions to parts a and b, and assuming the following data as to budgeted chargeable hours and billing rates, prepare a condensed statement of budgeted income for the year ending June 30, 1973.

	Budgeted Chargeable Hours	Budgeted Hourly Billing Rate
Johnson	700	$45
Smith	1,100	40
Vickers	1,600	32
Lowe	1,650	25
Kennedy	1,550	15
Quinn	1,450	17
Lyons	500	5
Hammond	1,150	7
Garcia	1,200	7

Problem IV-4: Budgets and overhead allocation (50-60 min.)

The administrator of Wright Hospital has presented you with a number of service projections for the year ending June 30, 1972. Estimated room requirements for inpatients by type of service are:

Type of Patient	Total Patients Expected	Average Number of Days in Hospital		Percent of Regular Patients Selecting Types of Service		
		Regular	Medicare	Private	Semi-Private	Ward
Medical	2,100	7	17	10%	60%	30%
Surgical	2,400	10	15	15	75	10

Of the patients served by the hospital 10% are expected to be Medicare patients, all of whom are expected to select semi-private rooms. Both the number and proportion of Medicare patients have increased over the past five years. Daily rentals per patient are: $40 for a private room, $35 for a semi-private room and $25 for a ward.

Operating room charges are based on man-minutes (number of minutes the operating room is in use multiplied by the number of personnel assisting in the operation). The per man-minute charges are $.13 for inpatients and $.22 for outpatients. Studies for the current year show that operations on inpatients are divided as follows:

Type of Operation	Number of Operations	Average Number of Minutes Per Operation	Average Number of Personnel Required
A	800	30	4
B	700	45	5
C	300	90	6
D	200	120	8
	2,000		

The same proportion of inpatient operations is expected for the next fiscal year and 180 outpatients are expected to use the operating room. Outpatient operations average 20 minutes and require the assistance of three persons.

The budget for the year ending June 30, 1972, by departments, is:

General services:

Maintenance of plant	$ 50,000
Operation of plant	27,500
Administration	97,500
All others	192,000

Revenue producing services:

Operating room	68,440
All others	700,000
	$1,135,440

The following information is provided for cost allocation purposes:

General services:	Square Feet	Salaries
Maintenance of plant	12,000	$ 40,000
Operation of plant	28,000	25,000
Administration	10,000	55,000
All others	36,250	102,500
Revenue producing services:		
Operating room	17,500	15,000
All others	86,250	302,500
	190,000	$540,000

Basis of allocations:
Maintenance of plant—salaries
Operation of plant—square feet
Administration—salaries
All others—8% to operating room

Required:

Prepare schedules showing the computation of:

a. The number of patient days (number of patients multiplied by average stay in hospital) expected by type of patients and service.

b. The total number of man-minutes expected for operating room services for inpatients and outpatients. For inpatients show the breakdown of total operating room man-minutes by type of operation.

c. Expected gross revenue from routine services.

d. Expected gross revenue from operating room services.

e. Cost per man-minute for operating room services assuming that the total man-minutes computed in part "b" is 800,000 and that the step-down method of cost allocation is used (i.e., costs of the general services departments are allocated in sequence first to the general services departments that they serve and then finally to the revenue producing departments).

Problem IV-5: Unit costs and breakeven analysis (50-60 min.)

Metal Industries, Inc. operates its production department only when orders are received from one or both of its two products, two sizes of metal discs. The manufacturing process begins with the cutting of doughnut-shaped rings from rectangular strips of sheet metal; these rings are then pressed into discs. The sheets of metal, each 4 feet long and weighing 32 ounces, are purchased at $1.36 per running foot. The department has been operating at a loss for the past year:

Sales for the year	$172,000
Expenses	177,200
Net loss for the department	$ 5,200

The following information is available.

1. Ten thousand 4-foot pieces of metal yielded 40,000 large discs, each weighing 4 ounces and selling for $2.90, and 40,000 small discs, each weighing 2.4 ounces and selling for $1.40.

2. The Corporation has been producing at less than "normal capacity" and has had no spoilage in the cutting step of the process. The skeletons remaining after the rings have been cut are sold for scrap at $.80 per pound.

3. The variable conversion cost of each large disc is 80 percent of the disc's direct material cost and variable conversion cost of each small disc is 75 percent of the disc's direct material cost. Variable conversion costs are the sum of direct labor and variable overhead.

4. Fixed costs were $86,000.

Required:

a. For each of the parts manufactured, prepare a schedule computing:

    1. Unit material cost after deducting the value of salvage.

    2. Unit variable conversion cost.

    3. Unit contribution margin.

    4. Total contribution margin for all units sold.

b. Assuming you computed the material cost for large discs at $.85 each and for small discs at $.51 each, compute the number of units the Corporation must sell to break even based on a normal production capacity of 50,000 units. Assume no spoiled units and a product mix of one large disc to each small disc.

Problem IV-6: Cost-volume-profit analysis and discounted cash flow (40-50 min.)

Thorne Transit, Inc. has decided to inaugurate express bus service between its headquarters city and a nearby suburb (one-way fare $.50) and is considering the purchase of either 32- or 52-passenger buses, on which pertinent estimates are as follows:

	32-Passenger Bus	52-Passenger Bus
Number of each to be purchased	6	4
Useful life	8 years	8 years
Purchase price of each bus (Paid on delivery)	$80,000	$110,000
Mileage per gallon	10	7½
Salvage value per bus	$ 6,000	$ 8,000
Drivers' hourly wage	$ 3.50	4.20
Price per gallon of gasoline	$ .30	.30
Other annual cash expenses	$ 4,000	$ 3,000

During the four daily rush hours all buses would be in service and are expected to operate at full capacity (state law prohibits standees) in both directions of the route, each bus covering the route 12 times (6 round trips) during that period. During the remainder of the 16-hour day, 500 passengers would be carried and Thorne would operate only 4 buses on the route. Part-time drivers would be employed to drive the extra hours during the rush hours. A bus traveling the route all day would go 480 miles and one traveling only during rush hours would go 120 miles a day during the 260-day year.

Required:

a. Prepare a schedule showing the computation of estimated annual revenue of the new route for both alternatives.

b. Prepare a schedule showing the computation of estimated annual drivers' wages for both alternatives.

c. Prepare a schedule showing the computation of estimated annual cost of gasoline for both alternatives.

d. Assume that your computations in parts "a," "b" and "c" are as follows:

	32-Passenger Bus	52-Passenger Bus
Estimated revenues	$365,000	$390,000
Estimated drivers' wages	67,000	68,000
Estimated cost of gasoline	16,000	18,000

Assuming that a minimum rate of return of 12% before income taxes is desired and that all annual cash flows occur at the end of the year, prepare a schedule showing the computation of the present values of net cash flows for the eight-year period; include the cost of buses and the proceeds from their disposition under both alternatives, but disregard the effect of income taxes. The following data are relevant:

Year	Present Value of $1.00 Due at the End of the Indicated Year Discounted at 12%	Present Value of $1.00 Due Annually and the End of Each Year Discounted at 12%
1	.89	.89
2	.80	1.69
3	.71	2.40
4	.64	3.04
5	.57	3.61
6	.51	4.11
7	.45	4.56
8	.40	4.97

Problem IV-7: Standard costs and variance analysis (40-50 min.)

Ross Shirts, Inc., manufactures short- and long-sleeve men's shirts for large stores. Ross produces a single-quality shirt in lots to each customer's order and attaches the store's label to each. The standard costs for a dozen long-sleeve shirts are:

Direct materials	24 yards @ $ .55	$13.20
Direct labor	3 hours @ $2.45	7.35
Manufacturing overhead	3 hours @ $2.00	6.00
Standard cost per dozen		$26.55

During October 1969 Ross worked on three orders for long-sleeve shirts. Job cost records for the month disclose the following:

Lot	Unit in Lot	Material Used	Hours Worked
30	1,000 dozen	24,100 yards	2,980
31	1,700 dozen	40,440 yards	5,130
32	1,200 dozen	28,825 yards	2,890

The following information is also available:

1. Ross purchased 95,000 yards of material during the month at a cost of $53,200. The materials price variance is recorded when goods are purchased and all inventories are carried at standard cost.

2. Direct labor incurred amounted to $27,500 during October. According to payroll records, production employees were paid $2.50 per hour.

3. Overhead is applied on the basis of direct labor hours. Manufacturing overhead totaling $22,800 was incurred during October.

4. A total of $288,000 was budgeted for overhead for the year 1969 based on estimated production at the plant's normal capacity of 48,000 dozen shirts per year. Overhead is 40 percent fixed and 60 percent variable at this level of production.

5. There was no work in process at October 1. During October lots 30 and 31 were completed and all material was issued for lot 32 and it was 80 per cent completed as to labor.

Required:

a. Prepare a schedule computing the standard cost for October 1969 of lots 30, 31 and 32.

b. Prepare a schedule computing the materials price variance for October 1969 and indicate whether the variance is favorable or unfavorable.

c. Prepare schedules computing (and indicating whether the variances are favorable or unfavorable) for each lot produced during October 1969 the:

1. Materials quantity variance in yards.
2. Labor efficiency variance in hours.
3. Labor rate variance in dollars.

d. Prepare a schedule computing the total controllable and noncontrollable (capacity) manufacturing overhead variances for October 1969 and indicate whether the variances are favorable or unfavorable.

Problem IV-8: Analysis of variances (40-50 min.)

Conti Pharmaceutical Company processes a single compound-product known as NULAX and uses a standard cost accounting system. The process requires preparation and blending of three materials in large batches with a variation from the standard mixture sometimes necessary to maintain quality. Conti's cost accountant became ill at the end of October 1968 and you were engaged to determine standard costs of October production and explain any differences between actual and standard costs for the month. The following information is available for the Blending Department:

1. The standard cost card for a 500-pound batch shows the following standard costs:

	Quantity	Price	Total Cost	
Materials:				
Mucilloid	250 pounds	$.14	$35	
Dextrose	200 pounds	.09	18	
Ingredients	50 pounds	.08	4	
Total per batch	500 pounds			$ 57
Labor:				
Preparation and blending	10 hours	$3.00		30
Overhead:				
Variable	10 hours	$1.00	10	
Fixed	10 hours	.30	3	13
Total standard cost per 500-pound batch				$100

2. During October 410 batches of 500 pounds each of the finished compound were completed and transferred to the Packaging Department.

3. Blending Department inventories totaled 6,000 pounds at the beginning of the month and 9,000 pounds at the end of the month (assume both inventories were completely processed but not transferred and consisted of materials in their standard proportions).

Inventories are carried in the accounts at standard cost prices.

4. During the month of October the following materials were purchased and put into production:

	Pounds	Price	Total Cost
Mucilloid.....................	114,400	$.17	$19,448
Dextrose.....................	85,800	.11	9,438
Ingredients	19,800	.07	1,386
Totals	220,000		$30,272

5. Wages paid for 4,212 hours of direct labor at $3.25 per hour amounted to $13,689.

6. Actual overhead costs for the month totaled $5,519.

7. The standards were established for a normal production volume of 20,000 pounds (400 batches) of NULAX per month. At this level of production variable factory overhead was budgeted at $4,000 and fixed factory overhead was budgeted at $1,200.

Required:

a. Prepare a schedule presenting the computation for the Blending Department of:
1. October production in both pounds and batches.
2. The standard cost of October production itemized by components of materials, labor and overhead.

b. Prepare schedules computing the differences between actual and standard costs and analyzing the differences as:
1. Materials variances (for each material) caused by
   (a) Price differences.
   (b) Usage differences.
2. Labor variances caused by
   (a) Rate difference.
   (b) Efficiency difference.
3. Overhead variances caused by
   (a) Controllable factors.
   (b) Volume factors.

c. Explain how the materials variances arising from usage differences could be further analyzed (no computations are necessary).

Problem IV-9: Analysis of variances (40-50 min.)

The Bronson Company manufactures a fuel additive which has a stable selling price of $40 per drum. Since losing a government contract, the Company has been producing and selling 80,000 drums per month, 50% of normal capacity. Management expects to increase production to 140,000 drums in the coming fiscal year.

In connection with your examination of the financial statements of the Bronson Company for the year ended September 30, 1970, you have been asked to review some computations made by Bronson's cost accountant. Your working papers disclose the following about the Company's operations:

1. Standard costs per drum of product manufactured:

Materials:
8 gallons of miracle mix	$16
1 empty drum	1
	$17

Direct labor—1 hour	$ 5
Factory overhead	$ 6

2. Costs and expenses during September 1970:

Miracle mix:
500,000 gallons purchased at
cost of $950,000; 650,000
gallons used
Empty drums:
94,000 purchased at cost of
$94,000; 80,000 used
Direct labor:
82,000 hours worked at cost
of $414,100
Factory overhead:

Depreciation of building and machinery (fixed)	$210,000
Supervision and indirect labor (semi-variable)	460,000
Other factory overhead (variable)	98,000
	$768,000

3. Other factory overhead was the only actual overhead cost which varied from the overhead budget for the September level of production; actual other factory overhead was $98,000 and the budgeted amount was $90,000.

4. At normal capacity of 160,000 drums per month, supervision and indirect labor costs are expected to be $570,000. All cost functions are linear.

5. None of the September 1970 cost variances are expected to occur proportionally in future months. For the next fiscal year, the cost standards department expects the same standard usage of materials and direct labor hours. The average prices expected are: $2.10 per gallon of miracle mix, $1 per empty drum and $5.70 per direct labor hour. The current flexible budget of factory overhead costs is considered applicable to future periods without revision.

6. The Company uses the two-variance method of accounting for overhead.

Required:

a. Prepare a schedule computing the following variances for September 1970: (1) materials price variance, (2) materials usage variance, (3) labor rate variance, (4) labor usage (efficiency) variance, (5) controllable (budget) overhead variance, and (6) volume (capacity) overhead variance. Indicate whether variances were favorable or unfavorable.

b. Prepare a schedule of the actual manufacturing cost per drum of product expected at production of 140,000 drums per month—using the following cost categories: materials, direct labor, fixed factory overhead, and variable factory overhead.

Problem IV-10: Direct costing and cost-volume-profit relationships (40-60 min.)

Flear Company has a maximum productive capacity of 210,000 units per year. Normal capacity is regarded as 180,000 units per year. Standard variable manufacturing costs are $11 per unit. Fixed factory overhead is $360,000 per year. Variable selling expenses are $3 per unit and fixed selling expenses are $252,000 per year. The unit sales price is $20.

The operating results for 1961 are: sales, 150,000 units; production, 160,000 units; beginning inventory, 10,000 units; and net unfavorable variance for standard variable manufacturing costs, $40,000. All variances are written off as additions to (or deductions from) standard cost of sales.

Required:

For items a, b, and c, assume no variances from standards for manufacturing costs.
  a. What is the breakeven point expressed in dollar sales?
  b. How many units must be sold to earn a net income of $60,000 per year?
  c. How many units must be sold to earn a net income of 10% on sales?
  d. Prepare formal income statements for 1961 under:
    1. Conventional costing
    2. "Direct" costing
  e. Briefly account for the difference in net income between the two income statements.

Problem IV-11: Relevant costs and breakeven analysis (50-60 min.)

Ruidoso Ski Lodge operates a ski shop, restaurant and lodge during the 120-day ski season from November 15 to March 15. The proprietor is considering changing his operations and keeping the Lodge open all year.

Results of the operations for the year ended March 15, 1969 were as follows:

	Ski Shop Amount	Ski Shop Per Cent	Restaurant Amount	Restaurant Per Cent	Lodge Amount	Lodge Per Cent
Revenue	$27,000	100%	$40,000	100%	$108,000	100%
Costs:						
Costs of goods sold	14,850	55	24,000	60		
Supplies	1,350	5	4,000	10	7,560	7
Utilities........	270	1	1,200	3	2,160	2
Salaries........	1,620	6	12,000	30	32,400	30
Insurance	810	3	800	2	9,720	9
Property taxes on building ..	540	2	1,600	4	6,480	6
Depreciation....	1,080	4	2,000	5	28,080	26
Total costs ..	20,520	76	45,600	114	86,400	80
Net income or (loss).........	$ 6,480	24%	$ (5,600)	(14)%	$ 21,600	20%

1. The lodge has 100 rooms and the rate from November 15 to March 15 is $10 per day for one to two persons. The occupancy rate from November 15 to March 15 is 90 per cent.

2. Ski shop and restaurant sales vary in direct proportion to room occupancy.

3. For the ski shop and restaurant, cost of goods sold, supplies, and utilities vary in direct proportion to sales. For the lodge, supplies and utilities vary in direct proportion to room occupancy.

4. The ski shop, restaurant and lodge are located in the same building. Depreciation on the building is charged to the lodge. The ski shop and restaurant are charged with depreciation only on equipment. The full cost of the restaurant equipment became fully depreciated on March 15, 1969 but the equipment has a remaining useful life of 3 years. The equipment can be sold for $1,200, but will be worthless in 3 years. All depreciation is computed by the straight-line method.

5. Insurance premiums are for annual coverage for public liability and fire insurance on the building and equipment. All building insurance is charged to the lodge.

6. Salaries are the minimum necessary to keep each facility open and are for the ski season only except for the lodge security guard who is paid $5,400 per year.

Two alternatives are being considered for the future operation of Ruidoso Ski Lodge:

1. The proprietor believes that during the ski season the restaurant should be closed because "it does not have enough revenue to cover its out-of-pocket costs." It is estimated that lodge occupancy would drop to 80 per cent of capacity if the restaurant were closed during the ski season. The space utilized by the restaurant would be used as a lounge for lodge guests.

2. The proprietor is considering keeping the lodge open from March 15 to November 15. The ski shop would be converted into a gift shop if the lodge should be operated during this period with conversion costs of $1,000 in March and $1,000 in November each year. It is estimated that revenues from the gift shop would be the same per room occupied as revenues from the ski shop, that variable costs would be in the same ratio to revenues and that all other costs would be the same for the gift shop as for the ski shop. The occupancy rate of the lodge at a room rate of $7 per day is estimated at 50 per cent during the period from March 15 to November 15 whether or not the restaurant is operated.

Required:

(Ignore income taxes and use 30 days per month for computational purposes.)

a. Prepare a projected income statement for the ski shop and lodge from November 15, 1969 to March 15, 1970 assuming the restaurant is closed during this period and all facilities are closed during the remainder of the year.

b. Assume that all facilities will continue to be operated during the 4-month period of November 15 to March 15 of each year.

1. Assume that the lodge is operated during the 8 months from March 15 to November 15. Prepare an analysis which indicates the projected marginal income or loss of operating the gift shop and lodge during this 8-month period.
2. Compute the minimum room rate which should be charged to allow the lodge to break even during the 8 months from March 15 to November 15 assuming the gift shop and restaurant are not operated during this period.

Problem IV-12: Variety of objective questions (50-60 min.)

Instructions

Select the best answer for each of the following items relating to *a variety of managerial accounting problems.* In determining your answer to each item consider the information given in the preceding lettered statement of facts or data.

A. The Groomer Company manufactures two products, Florimene and Glyoxide, used in the plastics industry. The Company uses a flexible budget in its standard cost system to develop variances. Selected data follow:

	Florimene	*Glyoxide*
Data on standard costs:		
Raw material per unit	3 pounds at $1.00 per pound	4 pounds at $1.10 per pound
Direct labor per unit.	5 hours at $2.00 per hour	6 hours at $2.50 per hour
Variable factory overhead per unit . .	$3.20 per direct labor hour	$3.50 per direct labor hour
Fixed factory overhead per month . .	$20,700	$26,520
Normal activity per month	5,750 direct labor hours	7,800 direct labor hours
Units produced in September	1,000	1,200
Costs incurred for September:		
Raw material	3,100 pounds at $.90	4,700 pounds at $1.15
Direct labor.	4,900 hours at $1.95 per hour	7,400 hours at $2.55 per hour
Variable factory overhead.	$16,170	$25,234
Fixed factory overhead	$20,930	$26,400

16. The total variances to be explained for both products for September are
   a. Florimene, $255 favorable; Glyoxide, $909 unfavorable.
   b. Florimene, $7,050 favorable; Glyoxide, $6,080 favorable.
   c. Florimene, $4,605 favorable; Glyoxide, $3,131 favorable.
   d. Florimene, $2,445 unfavorable; Glyoxide, $2,949 unfavorable.
   e. None of the above.

17. The labor efficiency variances for both products for September are
   a. Florimene, $195 favorable; Glyoxide, $510 unfavorable.
   b. Florimene, $1,700 favorable; Glyoxide, $1,000 favorable.
   c. Florimene, $200 favorable; Glyoxide, $500 unfavorable

   d. Florimene, $195 unfavorable; Glyoxide, $510 favorable.
   e. None of the above.

18. The labor rate variances for both products for September are
   a. Florimene, $245 favorable; Glyoxide, $370 unfavorable.
   b. Florimene, $200 favorable; Glyoxide, $500 unfavorable
   c. Florimene, $1,945 favorable; Glyoxide, $630 favorable.
   d. Florimene, $245 favorable; Glyoxide, $370 favorable.
   e. None of the above.

19. The spending variances for variable overhead for both products for
September are
   a. Florimene, $490 unfavorable; Glyoxide, $666 favorable.
   b. Florimene, $167 unfavorable; Glyoxide, $35 unfavorable.
   c. Florimene, $170 unfavorable; Glyoxide, $34 unfavorable.
   d. Florimene, $1,900 favorable; Blyoxide, $1.960 favorable.
   e. None of the above.

B. The officers of Bradshaw Company are reviewing the profitability of the
Company's four products and the potential effect of several proposals for varying
the product mix. An excerpt from the income statement and other data follow:

	Totals	Product P	Product Q	Product R	Product S
Sales	$62,600	$10,000	$18,000	$12,600	$22,000
Cost of goods sold	44,274	4,750	7,056	13,968	18,500
Gross profit	18,326	5,250	10,944	(1,368)	3,500
Operating expenses	12,012	1,990	2,976	2,826	4,220
Income before income taxes	$ 6,314	$ 3,260	$ 7,968	$ (4,194)	$ (720)
Units sold		1,000	1,200	1,800	2,000
Sales price per unit		$ 10.00	$ 15.00	$ 7.00	$ 11.00
Variable cost of goods sold per unit		$ 2.50	$ 3.00	$ 6.50	$ 6.00
Variable operating expenses per unit		$ 1.17	$ 1.25	$ 1.00	$ 1.20

   Each of the following proposals is to be considered independently of the
other proposals. Consider only the product changes stated in each proposal; the
activity of other products remains stable. *Ignore income taxes.*
20. If product R is discontinued, the effect on income will be
   a. $900 increase.
   b. $4,194 increase.
   c. $12,600 decrease.
   d. $1,368 increase.
   e. None of the above.
21. If product R is discontinued and a consequent loss of customers causes a
decrease of 200 units in sales of Q, the total effect on income will be
   a. $15,600 decrease.
   b. $2,866 increase.
   c. $2,044 increase.
   d. $1,250 decrease.
   e. None of the above.

22. If the sales price of R is increased to $8 with a decrease in the number of units sold to 1,500 the effect on income will be
    a. $2,199 decrease.
    b. $600 decrease.
    c. $750 increase.
    d. $2,199 increase.
    e. None of the above.

23. The plant in which R is produced can be utilized to produce a new product, T. The total variable costs and expenses per unit of T are $8.05, and 1,600 units can be sold at $9.50 each. If T is introduced and R is discontinued, the total effect on income will be
    a. $2,600 increase.
    b. $2,320 increase.
    c. $3,220 increase.
    d. $1,420 increase.
    e. None of the above.

24. Part of the plant in which P is produced can easily be adapted to the production of S, but changes in quantities may make changes in sales prices advisable. If production of P is reduced to 500 units (to be sold at $12 each) and production of S is increased to 2,500 units (to be sold at $10.50 each), the total effect on income will be
    a. $1,765 decrease.
    b. $250 increase.
    c. $2,060 decrease.
    d. $1,515 decrease.
    e. None of the above.

25. Production of P can be doubled by adding a second shift, but higher wages must be paid, increasing variable cost of goods sold to $3.50 for each of the additional units. If the 1,000 additional units of P can be sold at $10 each, the total effect on income will be
    a. $10,000 increase.
    b. $5,330 increase.
    c. $6,500 increase.
    d. $2,260 increase.
    e. None of the above.

C. The Dilly Company marks up all merchandise at 25% of gross purchase price. All purchases are made on account with terms of 1/10, net/60. Purchase discounts, which are recorded as miscellaneous income, are always taken. Normally, 60% of each month's purchases are paid for in the month of purchase while the other 40% are paid during the first 10 days of the first month after purchase. Inventories of merchandise at the end of each month are kept at 30% of the next month's projected cost of goods sold.

Terms for sales on account are 2/10, net/30. Cash sales are not subject to discount. Fifty percent of each month's sales on account are collected during the month of sale, 45% are collected in the succeeding month, and the remainder are usually uncollectible. Seventy percent of the collections in the month of sale are subject to discount while 10% of the collections in the succeeding month are subject to discount.

Projected sales data for selected months follow:

	Sales on Account–Gross	Cash Sales
December	$1,900,000	$400,000
January	1,500,000	250,000
February	1,700,000	350,000
March.....................	1,600,000	300,000

26. Projected gross purchases for January are
    a. $1,400,000.
    b. $1,470,000.
    c. $1,472,000.
    d. $1,248,000.
    e. None of the above.

27. Projected inventory at the end of December is
    a. $420,000.
    b. $441,600.
    c. $552,000.
    d. $393,750.
    e. None of the above.

28. Projected payments to suppliers during February are
    a. $1,551,200.
    b. $1,535,688.
    c. $1,528,560.
    d. $1,509,552.
    e. None of the above.

29. Projected sales discounts to be taken by customers making remittances during February are
    a. $5,250.
    b. $15,925.
    c. $30,500.
    d. $11,900.
    e. None of the above.

30. Projected total collections from customers during February are
    a. $1,875,000.
    b. $1,861,750.
    c. $1,511,750.
    d. $1,188,100.
    e. None of the above.

SPECIFIC APPROACH

Problem IV-1

1. The first two parts of requirement (a) are unusually simple. In the third part, obtain total cost per hour by applying an overhead factor to the salary rate per hour. The overhead factor is the total overhead cost divided by total salaries billable to clients.

2. In requirement (b), the estimated (standard) absorption means the point where overhead is neither under- or over-absorbed.

Problem IV-2

1. Requirement (a) merely entails the careful following of explicit instructions.

2. Requirement (b) calls for an incremental (differential) approach. Management should choose the store that would necessitate the smallest increase in total expenses. For each store, compute the percent of local variable costs to sales. Apply this percentage to the increase in sales to obtain the predicted increase in local variable costs. Also, compute the increase in delivery expenses for each store.

Problem IV-3

In requirement (a), divide your answer into three major sections: total potential hours, planned or expected non-chargeable hours, and budgeted chargeable hours.

In requirement (b), compute the salaries applicable to chargeable time. The allocated expenses and income contribution consist of fringe benefits, operating expenses, income contribution, and some portion of secretarial salaries.

The budgeted income statement in requirement (c) is uncomplicated.

Problem IV-4

In part (a), remember to include a breakdown by type of service.

The schedules in (c) and (d) are dependent on the results in (a) and (b).

In part (e), note that general services is divided into four subcategories or departments. Maintenance ($50,000) should be allocated to the other three general service categories and revenue producing services first. Then operation of plant, whose cost will now be higher than the direct charges of $27,500, should be allocated to the remaining two general service categories and revenue producing services. Then, in turn, administration and "all others" should be allocated.

Problem IV-5

What happens to the 32 ounces of weight of each strip? Trace all of it, including the portion that results in scrap. Obtain a net cost of good material and divide it by the ounces of good material to obtain the material cost per ounce.

The breakeven computation in requirement (b) is not difficult if you regard the "unit" as being a package of one large disc and one small disc. Then you can compute revenue per package and variable cost per package.

Problem IV-6

In requirement (a), the 500 passengers represent 500 one-way fares.

In requirement (b), compile the total annual driver hours; then apply the hourly rate.

In requirement (c), compile the total annual mileage as the first step.

In requirement (d), compute the net annual cash inflow, which can be regarded as an annuity. Add the present salvage value and deduct the purchase price.

Problem IV-7

In requirement (a), a four-column list consisting of lots, quantity, unit standard cost, and total standard cost will suffice. Adjust the unit cost of Lot 32 because the lot is incomplete.

Computation of the material and labor variances is straightforward.

The overhead variances are those illustrated in the two-way analysis in Exhibit 4-2. Budget variance and "controllable" variance are synonymous terms. Controllable overhead variance is the difference between actual overhead and the flexible budget for the output achieved. The capacity variance is the difference between the latter and the total overhead applied to the units produced.

Problem IV-8

The key to this solution is the computation of equivalent production. Note that the number of batches completed and transferred is not necessarily the same as batches produced.

The overhead variances are akin to those shown in the two-way analysis in Exhibit 4-2. Controllable overhead variance (budget variance) is the actual overhead minus the flexible overhead budget for the batches produced. In turn, the volume variance would be the flexible budget minus the standard overhead applied.

Problem IV-9

The material price variance should be computed on the basis of materials purchased rather than materials used.

As usual, the overhead analysis is the most difficult. The actual overhead is given. The budgeted amount is also given, although you must think carefully to gather it together. Of course, the applied overhead is the application rate times the good output.

In requirement (b), take a high-low approach to split the semi-variable cost into its variable and fixed components. The variable rate for supervision and indirect labor is the change in semi-variable cost divided by the difference in units at two given levels of activity. When the variable rate is computed, it may be used to get the total variable cost component at any level of activity; therefore, the fixed component is the total semi-variable cost minus the variable component.

Problem IV-10

The first three parts of this problem deal with routine cost-volume-profit relationships. Apply the techniques described in the General Approach.

The direct costing income statement is easier to prepare than the conventional costing income statement. Make a sharp distinction between variable costs and fixed costs in your formal presentation. The major items, in descending order, should be: sales, variable costs and expenses, contribution margin, fixed expenses, and net income.

The most troublesome aspect of the conventional costing income statement is the danger of neglecting the *volume variance,* which is not mentioned explicitly in the problem. As explained in the General Approach, the volume variance arises when *actual production* differs from *normal production.*

A $20,000 difference in net income is traceable to the capitalization of $20,000 fixed factory overhead in inventory under conventional costing because of a 10,000-unit increase in inventory.

Problem IV-11

This is a routine problem in incremental (marginal) analysis. Notice that property taxes on the building are evidently fully allocated, but insurance and depreciation on the building are charged solely to the lodge.

Because the facilities will be open twice as long in requirement b(1), lodge supplies and utilities should be doubled; then apply the new occupancy factor to obtain the new costs of supplies and utilities. Omit the entire salary of the security guard.

To compute the breakeven room rate, set up an equation, letting the unknown to be the room rate. All are components, the unit volume, variable costs, and fixed costs were computed in b(1).

Problem IV-12

The time pressure here may be intense, because much is tested in a small amount of time. Plenty of pencil-pushing is needed.

Part A does not state whether an absorption costing method or a variable (direct) costing method is applicable; however, the presence of a normal activity level is the clue that absorption costing is used. The most troublesome question here is (16), because it necessitates several computations. The total variance is the difference between total costs incurred and total costs applied to product. The latter requires a calculation of the fixed factory overhead rate for product costing.

Part B is simple. Ignore fixed costs. Also be careful when you compute differences. It is easy to get algebraic signs confused.

Part C requires painstaking attention to detail. For example, do not overlook the cash sales or cash discounts. Purchases equal desired ending inventory plus the cost of goods sold less the beginning inventory.

Process Costs and Joint Costs

GENERAL APPROACH

Process Costs

Equivalent Units: The Key

Process costing is most often found in industries where there is mass production of like units, in contrast to production of tailor-made or unique goods. Where manufacturing is conducted by continuous operations, costs are accumulated by departments (sometimes called *operations* or *processes*). These departmental costs are applied to relatively great numbers of units which pass through the department. The center of attention is the total department costs for a given time period in relation to the units processed. In these cases, some type of averaging must be adopted to derive the costs to be attached to (a) goods completed and (b) goods in process.

EXAMPLE 1

Beginning inventory, in process	0
Units placed in process	40,000
Units finished	38,000
Units in process, end, ½ finished	2,000

Total costs to account for, $39,000. Assume that the flow of all costs is a continuous and constant stream.

In deriving average unit cost, it is evident that the units in process should not be weighted the same as finished units. The partially completed units have received only half the attention and effort that the finished units have received. Thus, the notion of "equivalent performance" or "equivalent units" is used as a technique for establishing the cost per unit. In substance, the notion of equivalent units is the expression of physical units in terms of *doses* or *charges* of work applied thereto. So a physical unit is viewed by an accountant as a bundle of work charges, as a collection of the factors of production (material and conversion costs). Equivalent units are calculated as follows:

Units finished, charged with full dose of cost	38,000
Units in process, end, each unit is ½ completed	
2,000 X ½	1,000
Total equivalent unit performance	39,000
Unit cost, per equivalent unit ($39,000/39,000)	$ 1.00
Costs to be attached to finished units:	
38,000 X $1.00	$38,000
To work in process:	
1,000 X $1.00	1,000
Total costs accounted for	$39,000

Note that unit cost is *not* calculated on the basis of physical units. It *is* calculated on the basis of equivalent unit performance—that is, on the basis of "charges" or "doses" of cost needed to finish a given unit. Therefore, a finished unit gets a full charge while a half-finished unit is assigned one-half charge.

Five Basic Steps to Solution

Many process cost situations contain complex production flows. It is essential to understand the production cycle itself before making any calculations; a sketch of the physical flow of units is often helpful. In making computations, you should concentrate on physical flow and equivalent units at the outset. *Disregard dollar amounts until equivalent units are computed.*

Building in self-checks in a step-by-step solution is an extremely helpful technique. Such self-checks are woven into the five-step uniform approach outlined below. Use caution as you study these steps. There is a real danger in clinging to the five steps as a mechanical technique without understanding *why* nearly all process cost problems can be solved with the five-step method. The reasoning will be explained as the discussion progresses. If the basic nature of accounting for process costs is understood, the five steps may be developed at any time. Memorization will not be necessary.

As can readily be seen in our examples, most process cost problems can be solved by a uniform approach as follows:

Step 1. Physical Flow. Trace the physical flow of production (Where did units come from? Where did they go?). In other words, (a) What are the units to account for? and (b) How are they accounted for? Draw flow charts as a preliminary step, if necessary.

Step 2. Equivalent Units. Convert the physical flow, as accounted for in step 1 (b) above, into equivalent units of production. Thus, if 6,000 physical units are 2/3 complete as to materials and 1/2 complete as to conversion costs, it means that 4,000 *doses* of material and 3,000 *doses* of conversion costs have been applied. (See Example 2 below.)

Step 3. Total Costs to Account For. Summarize, using material, labor, overhead, and so forth, the *total* costs to be accounted for.

Step 4. Cost Per Equivalent Whole Unit. Divide the data in step 3 by the equivalent units calculated in step 2. The result will be the cost per equivalent whole unit.

Step 5. Build the TOTAL *Cost of Production and Inventories.* Apply the unit costs obtained in step 4 to inventories and to goods transferred out. Be sure to *total* these figures to see that they agree with the *grand* total obtained in step 3.

Using the Five Steps

These five steps are noted parenthetically by number in the examples below.

In the actual presentation of a complete solution, steps 1 and 2 and steps 3 and 4 may be combined to make two schedules for the four steps.

It is not claimed that this five-step approach is the only or the fastest way to solve process cost problems. Nevertheless, it is logical and has self-checks. By applying the five-step approach, you will develop your confidence and comprehension. Armed with this approach, you should be able to handle adequately any process cost situation. Shortcuts should be applied wherever feasible. But it is difficult to generalize on shortcut methods, because they differ depending upon the specific problem and the candidate's ability to use them.

Beginning Inventories

Calculations become more complicated when beginning inventories exist. There are two commonly used methods of tracing beginning inventory costs: *weighted average* and *first in, first out* (Fifo).

The data in Example 2 will be used (a) to compare weighted-average and Fifo inventory methods and (b) to illustrate the handling of interdepartmental transfers. *For the time being, concentrate on data for Department A only.*

EXAMPLE 2

A company has two processes. Material is introduced at the *beginning* of the process in Department A, and additional material is added at the *end* of the process in Department B. Conversion costs are applied uniformly throughout both processes. As the process in Department A is completed, goods are immediately transferred to the next department; as goods are completed in Department B, they are transferred to Finished Goods.

Data for the month of March, 19x1, include the following:

	Department A	Department B
Work in process, beginning	10,000 units 2/5 completed, $7,500 (Materials, $6,000; conversion costs, $1,500)	12,000 units 2/3 completed, $21,000 (Transferred-in costs, $9,800; conversion costs, $11,200)
Units completed during March ..	48,000	44,000
Units started during March.....	40,000	?
Work in process, end	2,000, 1/2 complete	16,000, 3/8 complete
Materials costs added	$22,000	$13,200
Conversion costs added	$18,000	$63,000

Required:

Compute the cost of goods transferred out of each department. Also show journal entries for the transfers. Compute ending inventory costs for goods remaining in each department.

(a) Assume weighted-average costing.

(b) Assume first in, first out costing.

Whenever you want to review process costs, you will find it helpful to take the data in this example and try to obtain the requirements on your own. Then you can check your work against the solution, which is explained below.

Weighted-Average Method

The weighted-average method treats the beginning Work in Process as if it were begun and finished during the current period. The beginning work-in-process inventory is looked upon as being part and parcel of current production, regardless of the fact that it was begun prior to the current period. Therefore, beginning inventory costs are mingled with current costs. When equivalent units are calculated, work done in the past is regarded as if it were done currently.[1] As may be seen by comparing computations for Department A in Exhibits 5-1 and 5-2, the weighted-average method is far easier to use than Fifo for process costing.

First In, First Out

The solution for Department A in Exhibit 5-2 carries costs separately for (a) goods carried over in beginning Work in Process and for (b) goods started and finished in the current month. The unit costs differ for each portion (batch) of the total goods completed during the month. The Fifo method treats beginning inventory as if it were a batch of goods separate and distinct from goods started and finished within the same period.

---

[1] Professor William J. Vatter calls the weighted-average method the "roll-back" method because the averaging of cost doses is "rolled back" to include the work carried over from last month.

Exhibit 5-1

PRODUCTION COST REPORT
FOR THE MONTH ENDING MARCH 31, 19x1
Weighted-Average Method

Department A

Quantities	(STEP 1) Physical Flow	(STEP 2) Equivalent Units — Materials	(STEP 2) Equivalent Units — Conversion Costs
Work in process, beginning	10,000(2/5)*		
Units started (or transferred in)	40,000		
To account for	50,000		
Units completed	48,000	48,000	48,000
Work in process, end	2,000(1/2)*	2,000	1,000
	50,000	50,000	49,000

Costs	Totals	Details — Materials	Details — Conversion Costs	Equivalent Whole Unit
Work in process, beginning	$ 7,500	$ 6,000	$ 1,500	
Current costs	40,000	22,000	18,000	
(STEP 3) Total costs to account for	$47,500	$28,000	$19,500	
(STEP 4) Divide by equivalent units		÷50,000	÷49,000	
Cost per equivalent unit		$ .56	$ .398	$ .958
(STEP 5) Summary of costs				
Units completed (48,000)	$45,982†			48,000($.958)
Work in process, end (2,000):				
Transferred-in costs	$			
Materials	1,120	2,000($.56)		
Conversion costs	398		1,000($.398)	
Total cost of work in process	$ 1,518			
Total costs accounted for	$47,500			

Department B

Quantities	(STEP 1) Physical Flow	(STEP 2) Equivalent Units — Transferred-in Costs	(STEP 2) Equivalent Units — Materials	(STEP 2) Equivalent Units — Conversion Costs
Work in process, beginning	12,000(2/3)*			
Units started (or transferred in)	48,000			
To account for	60,000			
Units completed	44,000	44,000	44,000	44,000
Work in process, end	16,000(3/8)*	16,000	....	6,000
	60,000	60,000	44,000	50,000

Costs	Totals	Details — Transferred-in Costs	Details — Materials	Details — Conversion Costs	Equivalent Whole Unit
Work in process, beginning	$ 21,000	$ 9,800	$	$11,200	
Current costs	122,182	45,982	13,200	63,000	
(STEP 3) Total costs to account for	$143,182	$55,782	$13,200	$74,200	
(STEP 4) Divide by equivalent units		÷60,000	÷44,000	÷50,000	
Cost per equivalent unit		$ .9297	$ .30	$ 1.484	$2.7137
(STEP 5) Summary of costs					
Units completed (44,000)	$119,403				44,000($2.7137)
Work in process, end (16,000):					
Transferred-in costs	$ 14,875	16,000($.9297)			
Materials	....				
Conversion costs	8,904			6,000($1.484)	
Total cost of work in process	$ 23,779				
Total costs accounted for	$143,182				

*Degree of completion on converstion costs of this department.
†Rounded from 45,984 for decimal discrepancy.

147

Exhibit 5-2

PRODUCTION COST REPORT
FOR THE MONTH ENDING MARCH 31, 19x1

Quantities

	Department A (STEP 1) Physical Flow	Department A (STEP 2) Materials	Department A (STEP 2) Conversion Costs	Department B (STEP 1) Physical Flow	Department B (STEP 2) Transferred-in Costs	Department B (STEP 2) Materials	Department B (STEP 2) Conversion Costs
Work in process, beginning	10,000(2/5)*			12,000(2/3)*			
Units started (or transferred in)	40,000			48,000			
To account for	50,000			60,000			
Units completed:							
From beginning inventory	10,000	...	6,000	12,000	...	12,000	4,000
From current production	38,000	38,000	38,000	32,000	32,000	32,000	32,000
Work in process, end	2,000(1/2)	2,000	1,000	16,000(3/8)	16,000	...	6,000
Units accounted for	50,000	40,000	45,000	60,000	48,000	44,000	42,000

Costs — *Details*

	A Totals	A Materials	A Conversion Costs	A Equivalent Whole Unit	B Totals*	B Transferred-in Costs	B Materials	B Conversion Costs	B Equivalent Whole Unit
Work in process, beginning	$ 7,500				$ 21,000				
Current costs	40,000	$22,000	$18,000		122,200	$46,000	$13,200	$63,000	
(STEP 3) Total costs to account for	$47,500				$143,200				
(STEP 4) Divide by equivalent units		÷40,000	÷45,000			÷48,000	÷44,000	÷42,000	
Cost per equivalent unit		$ .55	$ .40	$ .95		$ .958333	$ .30	$ 1.50	$2.75833

(STEP 5) *Summary of costs*

	A Totals	A Materials	A Conversion Costs	A Equivalent Whole Unit	B Totals*	B Transferred-in Costs	B Materials	B Conversion Costs	B Equivalent Whole Unit
Units completed (48,000):									
From beginning inventory (10,000)	$ 7,500				$ 21,000				
Current costs added:									
Materials					3,600		12,000($.30)		
Conversion costs	2,400		6,000($.40)		6,000			4,000($1.50)	
Total from beginning inventory	$ 9,900				$ 30,600				
Started and completed (38,000)	36,100			38,000($.95)	88,267	32,000($2.75833)			
Total costs transferred out	$46,000				$118,867				
Work in process, end (2,000):									
Transferred-in costs					$ 15,333	16,000($.95833)			
Materials	$ 1,100	2,000($.55)							
Conversion costs	400		1,000($.40)		9,000			6,000($1.50)	
Total cost of work in process	$ 1,500				$ 24,333				
Total costs accounted for	$47,500				$143,200				

*Degree of completion on conversion costs of this department.

Interdepartmental Transfers

Now we return to Department B in Example 2. Most process cost situations have two or more departments in the production cycle. Ordinarily, as goods move from department to department, related costs are also transferred. Exhibits 5-1 and 5-2 show how such a transfer is handled under two inventory methods.

Transferred-in costs tend to give candidates much trouble, so special study is needed here. As far as Department B is concerned, units coming in from Department A may be viewed as if they were the raw material of Department B. Costs transferred from Department A to Department B are similar to the material costs brought into Department A, although they are called *transferred-in* or *previous department* costs, not material costs. That is, one might visualize the situation as if Department B bought the goods from an outside supplier. Thus, Department B's computations must provide for transferred-in costs, for any new material costs added in Department B, and for conversion costs added in Department B.

Production Cost Reports

If the five-step procedure is employed the mechanics of the solution are unchanged from our prior illustrations. However, as process cost situations become more complex, the details become more intricate and unwieldy in terms of jamming them into a work sheet that can also serve as a cost report. The format in Exhibits 5-1 and 5-2 is logical and easy to follow.

Journal Entries

Journal entries under both costing methods are the same except for the amounts. For detailed computations, see Exhibits 5-1 and 5-2.

	Weighted Average		Fifo	
Department B—Work in process control	45,982		46,000	
Department A—Work in process control . .		45,982		46,000
To transfer costs from Department A.				
Finished goods control	119,403		118,867	
Department B—Work in process control. . .		119,403		118,867
To transfer costs of goods finished.				

Sometimes a problem requires that the Work in Process account be split into Work in Process—Materials, Work in Process—Labor, and Work in Process—Overhead. In these cases, the journal entries would contain this greater detail, even though the underlying reasoning and techniques would be unaffected.

Transfers Effect: Modification of Fifo

In a series of interdepartmental transfers, each department is regarded as a distinct accounting entity. All transferred-in costs during a given period are carried at one unit cost, regardless of whether weighted-average or Fifo techniques were used by previous departments.

Thus, although the Fifo method as used by Department A may show batches of goods accumulated and transferred at different unit costs, these goods are typically costed by Department B at *one* average unit cost.

Spoilage

A main objective in accounting for spoilage is to obtain separate costs of spoiled units. Then, when the costs of the spoiled units are secured, such costs may be reallocated as the problem directs.

Abnormal spoilage is generally considered to be a "lost cost." Thus, costs of abnormal spoilage are charged off directly against revenue as a loss.

Normal spoilage is considered to be unavoidable and thus is included in the costs of *good* production.

As a general rule, then, in solving process cost problems, it is safest (although shortcut methods are available, especially where there are no work-in-process inventories to be considered) to trace and build the costs of spoilage separately. Then allocate the normal spoilage costs to Work in Process or Finished Goods, depending on where in the production cycle the spoilage takes place. Spoilage is typically assumed to occur at the stage of completion where inspection occurs, because spoilage is recognized at that point. Normal spoilage need not be allocated to units that have not yet reached this point in the production process, because spoiled units are related solely to units that have passed inspection.

Example 3 shows how spoilage is handled and reviews Fifo versus weighted-average calculations.

Illustration of Process Accounting for Spoilage

EXAMPLE 3–B COMPANY

The costs of producing one of the B Company's products are accumulated on a process cost basis. Materials for this product are put in at the beginning of the cycle of operations; labor and indirect costs are assumed to flow evenly over the cycle. Some units of this product are spoiled as a result of defects not ascertainable before inspection of finished units. Normally the spoiled units are 1/10 of the good output.

At January 1, the inventory of work in process on this product was $29,600, representing 2,000 pounds of material ($15,000) and conversion cost of $14,600, representing four-fifths completion. During January, 8,000 pounds of material ($61,000) were put into production. Direct labor of $40,200 was charged to the process. Indirect costs are assigned at the rate of 100% of direct labor cost. The inventory at January 31 consisted of 1,500 pounds, two-thirds finished. 7,200 pounds of good product were transferred to finished goods stock after inspection.

Required:

Show calculations of:

(a) The dollar and unit amount of the abnormal spoilage during January
(b) Total product costs transferred to finished stock
(c) The work-in-process inventory at January 31
(d) Journal entries for transfers out of work-in-process inventory

Exhibit 5-3

B Company
PRODUCTION COST REPORT
For the Month Ending January 31, 19x1
Weighted-Average Method

Quantities	(STEP 1) Physical Flow	(STEP 2) Equivalent Units Materials	Conversion Costs	Equivalent Whole Unit
Work in process, beginning	2,000(4/5)			
Units started	8,000			
To account for	10,000			
Abnormal spoilage	580	580	580	
Normal spoilage	720	720	720	
Good units completed	7,200	7,200	7,200	
Work in process, end	1,500(2/3)	1,500	1,000	
	10,000	10,000	9,500	

Costs	Totals	Materials	Conversion Costs	Details Conversion Costs	Equivalent Whole Unit
Work in process, beginning	$ 29,600	$15,000	$14,600		
Current costs	141,400	61,000	80,400		
(STEP 3) Total costs to account for	$171,000	$76,000	$95,000		
(STEP 4) Divide by equivalent units		÷10,000	÷ 9,500		
Cost per equivalent unit		$ 7.60	$ 10.00		$17.60
(STEP 5) *Summary of costs*					
Abnormal spoilage (580)	$ 10,208				580($17.60)
Units completed (7,200):					
Costs before adding spoilage	$126,720				7,200($17.60)
Normal spoilage	12,672				720($17.60)
Total cost transferred out	$139,392				
Work in process, end (1,500):					
Materials	$ 11,400			1,500($7.60)	
Conversion costs	10,000			1,000($10.00)	
Total cost of work in process	$ 21,400				
	$171,000				

151

Exhibit 5-4

B Company

PRODUCTION COST REPORT

For the Month Ending January 31, 19x1

Fifo Method

	(STEP 1) Physical Flow	(STEP 2) Equivalent Units	
		Materials	Conversion Costs
Quantities			
Work in process, beginning	2,000(4/5)		
Units started	8,000		
To account for	10,000		
Abnormal spoilage	580	580	580
Normal spoilage	720	720	720
Good units completed:			
From beginning inventory	2,000	. . .	400
Started and completed	5,200	5,200	5,200
Work in process, end	1,500(2/3)	1,500	1,000
Account for	10,000	8,000	7,900

Costs	*Totals*	*Materials*	*Conversion Costs*	*Equivalent Whole Unit*
Work in process, beginning	$ 29,600			
Current costs	141,400	$61,000	$80,400	
(STEP 3) Total costs to account for	$171,000			
Divide by equivalent units		÷ 8,000	÷ 7,900	
(STEP 4) Cost per equivalent unit		$ 7.625	$10.1772	$17.8022

(Continued on next page.)

Exhibit 5-4 (Continued)

		Details		
	Totals	*Materials*	*Conversion Costs*	*Equivalent Whole Unit*
(STEP 5) *Summary of Costs*				
(A) Abnormal spoilage (580)	$ 10,325.28			580($17.8022)
Units completed (7,200):				
From beginning inventory (2,000)...	$ 29,600.00			
Current costs added	$ 4,070.88		400($10.1772)	
Total cost from beginning inventory before spoilage	$ 33,670.88			
Started and completed before spoilage (5,200)	92,571.56			5,200($17.8022)
Normal spoilage	12,817.58			720($17.8022)
(B) Total costs transferred out	$139,060.02			
Work in process, end (1,500):				
Materials	$ 11,437.50	1,500($7.625)		
Conversion costs	10,177.20		1,000($10.1772)	
(C) Total cost of work in process	$ 21,614.70			
(A) + (B) + (C) Total costs accounted for	$171,000.00			

Example 3 illustrates a spoilage situation in process cost accounting.[2] Exhibits 5-3 and 5-4 employ weighted-average and Fifo techniques, respectively. The requested journal entries follow:

	Weighted Average		Fifo	
Finished goods	139,392		139,060.02	
Processing department—Work in process		139,392		139,060.02
To transfer good units completed in January.				
Loss from abnormal spoilage............	10,208		10,325.28	
Processing department—Work in process		10,208		10,325.28
To recognize abnormal spoilage in January.				

Pitfalls to Avoid in Working Problems

1. Remember to include transferred-in costs from previous departments in your calculations. Such costs should be treated as if they were another kind of material cost, because each department is treated as a separate entity. In other words, when successive departments are involved, transferred goods from one department become all or a part of the raw material of the next department, although they are called *transferred-in costs,* not raw material.

2. Material and conversion costs (labor and overhead) are often not applied at the same rates. Special care should be used, therefore, in expressing work in process in terms of equivalent units. For material doses, the degree of completion may be 100% for some material (if all material is added at the beginning of the production cycle) and 0% for material which will not be added until the end of the process. At the same time, conversion doses may be 50% or 75%.

3. In calculating costs to be transferred on a first in, first out basis, do not overlook the costs attached at the beginning of the period to goods that were in process but are now included in the goods transferred.

4. Unit costs may fluctuate between periods. Therefore, transferred goods may contain batches accumulated at different unit costs (see point 3). These goods, when transferred to the next department, are typically valued by that next department at *one* average unit cost.

5. Units may be expressed in terms of pounds in one department and gallons in the next. Consider each department separately. Unit costs would be based on pound measures in the first department and gallons in the second. As goods are received by the second department, they may be converted to the gallon unit of measure.

6. If the problem calls for first in, first out calculations, do not use the weighted-average approach, and vice versa.

---

[2] This illustration assumes inspection upon completion. In contrast, inspection may take place at some other stage, say, at the halfway point in the production cycle. In such a case, normal spoilage costs would be reallocated to completed goods and to the units in process that are more than half completed.

Accounting for Joint Costs and By-Product Costs

Definitions and Assumptions

Joint cost is the term most often applied to the cost of two or more distinct products that are produced or otherwise acquired by a single process, and that are not identifiable as different individual products up to a certain stage of production or acquisition known as the *split-off point.* Joint costs are total costs incurred up to the point of separation of the different products.

The accountant has two basic methods for splitting the joint cost between the joint products so that ending inventories may be costed and income determined: (1) relative sales values and (2) physical measures. Of course, there are many variations of both commonly used approaches. The relative sales value method is the most popular because it assumes that all end products should show some profit margin under typical marketing conditions. However, physical measures often yield satisfactory approximations and are therefore used by many companies.

Example of Allocation Methods

(1) *Relative sales value method*—Note that the example assumes that the joint products are not sold at their stage of completion at the split-off point. Further separate costs are needed to put them into salable form. The conventional approach is shown below; it takes the ultimate sales value at the point of sale and works backward to approximate (computed) relative sales value at the split-off point:

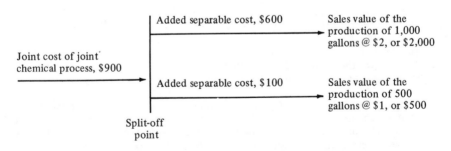

	Production in Terms of Sales Values	Less Costs Beyond Split-off Point	Approximate Relative Sales Value at Split-off Point	Weighting	Joint Costs Assigned
A (1,000 gallons @ $2.00)	$2,000	$600	$1,400	1,400/1,800 × $900	$700
B (500 gallons @ $1.00)	500	100	400	400/1,800 × $900	$200
	$2,500	$700	$1,800		$900

(2) *Physical weighting*—This method is basically simple. The $900 cost produced 1,500 gallons of product; therefore, the unit cost is 60 cents. Costs are assigned as follows: $600 to A, $300 to B. This example reveals no dramatic difference between the two methods. However, note that physical measures may easily bear no relationship to the sales-generating power of the individual products. Thus, if the joint cost of a hog were assigned to its various products on the basis of weight, center-cut pork chops would have the same unit cost as pigs' feet, lard, bacon, ham, and so forth. Fabulous profits would be shown for some cuts while losses would consistently be shown for other cuts.

By-Product Accounting

By-products are joint products that have minor sales value as compared with that of the major product(s). There is a wide variety of methods of accounting for by-products. Generally, the term *by-product accounting* implies that no joint processing costs are allocated to the by-product. Conceptually, the best method entails computing the net realizable value (sales value less estimated costs of disposal) of the by-products produced and deducting it from the total costs of producing the main product.

REFERENCES

See the references for Topic IV.

CPA PROBLEMS

Problem V-1: Fifo process costs, one department, lost units (40-50 min.)

In the course of your examination of the financial statements of the Zeus Company for the year ended December 31, 1971, you have ascertained the following concerning its manufacturing operations:

- Zeus has two production departments (fabricating and finishing) and a service department. In the fabricating department polyplast is prepared from miracle mix and bypro. In the finishing department each unit of polyplast is converted into six tetraplexes and three uniplexes. The service department provides services to both production departments.
- The fabricating and finishing departments use process cost accounting systems. Actual production costs, including overhead, are allocated monthly.
- Service department expenses are allocated to production departments as follows:

Expense	*Allocation Base*
Building maintenance	Space occupied
Timekeeping and personnel	Number of employees
Other	½ to fabricating, ½ to finishing

• Raw materials inventory and work in process are priced on a FIFO basis.
• The following data were taken from the fabricating department's records for December 1971:

Quantities (units of polyplast):

In process, December 1	3,000
Started in process during month	25,000
Total units to be accounted for	28,000
Transferred to finishing department	19,000
In process, December 31	6,000
Lost in process	3,000
Total units accounted for	28,000

Cost of work in process, December 1:

Materials	$ 13,000
Labor	17,500
Overhead	21,500
	$ 52,000
Direct labor costs, December	$154,000
Departmental overhead, December	$132,000

• Polyplast work in process at the beginning and end of the month was partially completed as follows:

	Materials	Labor and Overhead
December 1	66 2/3%	50%
December 31	100 %	75%

• The following data were taken from raw materials inventory records for December:

	Miracle Mix		Bypro	
	Quantity	Amount	Quantity	Amount
Balance, December 1	62,000	$62,000	265,000	$18,550
Purchases:				
December 12	39,500	49,375		
December 20	28,500	34,200		
Fabricating department usage ...	83,200		50,000	

• Service department expenses for December (not included in departmental overhead above) were:

Building maintenance	$ 45,000
Timekeeping and personnel	27,500
Other	39,000
	$111,500

Other information for December 1971 is presented below:

	Square Feet of Space Occupied	Number of Employees
Fabricating	75,000	180
Finishing................	37,500	120
	112,500	300

Required:

a. Compute the equivalent number of units of polyplast, with separate calculations for materials and conversion cost (direct labor plus overhead), manufactured during December.

b. Compute the following items to be included in the fabricating department's production report for December 1971, with separate calculations for materials, direct labor and overhead. Prepare supporting schedules.

    1. Total costs to be accounted for.

    2. Unit costs for equivalent units manufactured.

    3. Transfers to finishing department during December and work in process at December 31. Reconcile to your answer to part b. 1.

Problem V-2: Weighted average process costs (40-50 min.)

Ballinger Paper Products manufactures a high quality paper box. The box department applies two separate operations—cutting and folding. The paper is first cut and trimmed to the dimensions of a box form by one machine group. One square foot of paper is equivalent to four box forms. The trimmings from this process have no scrap value. Box forms are then creased and folded (i.e., completed) by a second machine group. Any partially processed boxes in the department are cut box forms that are ready for creasing and folding. These partly processed boxes are considered 50% complete as to labor and overhead. The materials department maintains an inventory of paper in sufficient quantities to permit continuous processing, and transfers to the box department are made as needed. Immediately after folding, all good boxes are transferred to the finished goods department.

During June 1971 the material department purchased 1,210,000 square feet of unprocessed paper for $244,000. Conversion costs for the month were $226,000. A quantity equal to 30,000 boxes was spoiled during paper cutting and 70,000 boxes were spoiled during folding. All spoilage has a zero salvage value, is considered normal and cannot be reprocessed. All spoilage loss is allocated between the completed units and partially processed boxes. Ballinger applies the weighted average cost method to all inventories. Inventory data for June are given below.

Inventory	Physical Unit	June 30, 1971 Units on Hand	June 1, 1971 Units on Hand	Cost
Materials Department: paper...............	square feet	200,000	390,000	$76,000
Box Department boxes cut, not folded....	number	300,000	800,000	55,000*
Finished Goods Department: completed boxes on hand	number	50,000	250,000	18,000

*Materials...............	$35,000
Conversion cost	20,000
	$55,000

Required:

Prepare the following for the month of June 1971:

a. A report of cost of paper used for the Materials Department.

b. A schedule showing the physical flow of units (including beginning and ending inventories) in the Materials Department, in the Box Department and in the Finished Goods Department.

c. A schedule showing the computation of equivalent units produced for materials and conversion costs in the Box Department.

d. A schedule showing the computation of unit costs for the Box Department.

e. A report of inventory valuation and cost of completed units for the Box Department.

f. A schedule showing the computation of unit costs for the Finished Goods Department.

g. A report of inventory valuation and cost of units sold for the Finished Goods Department.

Problem V-3: Process costs; weighted average (50-60 min.)

The Mantis Manufacturing Company manufactures a single product that passes through two departments: extruding and finishing-packing. The product is shipped at the end of the day in which it is packed. The production in the extruding and finishing-packing departments does not increase the number of units started.

The cost and production data for the month of January are as follows:

Cost Data	Extruding Department	Finishing-Packing Department
Work in process, January 1:		
Cost from preceding department	...	$60,200
Material	$ 5,900	...
Labor	1,900	1,500
Overhead	1,400	2,000
Costs added during January:		
Material	20,100	4,400
Labor	10,700	7,720
Overhead	8,680	11,830
Percentage of completion of work in process:		
January 1:		
Material.................................	70%	0%
Labor....................................	50	30
Overhead	50	30
January 31:		
Material.................................	50	0
Labor....................................	40	35
Overhead.................................	40	35
January Production Statistics		
Units in process, January 1......................	10,000	29,000
Units in process, January 31	8,000	6,000
Units started or received from preceding department ..	20,000	22,000
Units completed and transferred or shipped	22,000	44,000

In the extruding department materials are added at various phases of the process. All lost units occur at the end of the process when the inspection operation takes place.

In the finishing-packing department the materials added consist only of packing supplies. These materials are added at the midpoint of the process when the packing operation begins. Cost studies have disclosed that one-half of the labor and overhead costs apply to the finishing operation and one-half to the packing operation. All lost units occur at the end of the finishing operation when the product is inspected. All the work in process in this department at January 1 and 31 was in the finishing operation phase of the manufacturing process.

Required:

The Company uses the average costing method in its accounting system.

a. Compute the units lost, if any, for each department during January.

b. Compute the output divisor for the calculation of unit costs for each department for January. ("Output divisor" is used in the average costing method as "equivalent production" is used in the first in, first out costing method.)

c. Prepare a cost of production report for both departments for January. The report should disclose the departmental total cost and cost per unit (for material, labor, and overhead) of the units (1) transferred to the finishing-packing department and (2) shipped. Assume that January production and costs were normal. (Submit all supporting computations in good form.)

Problem V-4: Standard process costs; direct costing and absorption costing (40-50 min.)

Norwood Corporation is considering changing its method of inventory valuation from absorption costing to direct costing and engaged you to determine the effect of the proposed change on the 1968 financial statements.

The Corporation manufactures Gink which is sold for $20 per unit. Marsh is added before processing starts and labor and overhead are added evenly during the manufacturing process. Production capacity is budgeted at 110,000 units of Gink annually. The standard costs per unit of Gink are:

Marsh, 2 pounds	$3.00
Labor	6.00
Variable manufacturing overhead	1.00
Fixed manufacturing overhead	1.10

A process cost system is used employing standard costs. Variances from standard costs are now charged or credited to cost of goods sold. If direct costing were adopted only variances resulting from variable costs would be charged or credited to cost of goods sold.

Inventory data for 1968 follow:

	Units	
	January 1	*December 31*
Marsh (pounds).................	50,000	40,000
Work in process		
2/5 processed.................	10,000	
1/3 processed.................		15,000
Finished goods	20,000	12,000

During 1968 220,000 pounds of Marsh were purchased and 230,000 pounds were transferred to work in process. Also, 110,000 units of Gink were transferred to finished goods. Actual fixed manufacturing overhead during the year was $121,000. There were no variances between standard variable costs and actual variable costs during the year.

Required:

a. Prepare schedules which present the computation of:
   1. Equivalent units of production for material, labor, and overhead.
   2. Number of units sold.
   3. Standard unit costs under direct costing and absorption costing.
   4. Amount, if any, of over- or under-applied fixed manufacturing overhead.

b. Prepare a comparative statement of cost of goods sold using standard direct costing and standard absorption costing.

Problem V-5: Joint products and by-products (40-50 min.)

In its three departments Amaco Chemical Company manufactures several products:

- In Department 1 the raw materials amanic acid and bonyl hydroxide are used to produce Amanyl, Bonanyl, and Am-Salt. Amanyl is sold to others who use it as a raw material in the manufacture of stimulants. Bonanyl is not salable without further processing. Although Am-Salt is a commercial product for which there is a ready market, Amaco does not sell this product, preferring to submit it to further processing.
- In Department 2 Bonanyl is processed into the marketable product, Bonanyl-X. The relationship between Bonanyl used and Bonanyl-X produced has remained constant for several months.
- In Department 3 Am-Salt and the raw material Colb are used to produce Colbanyl, a liquid propellant which is in great demand. As an inevitable part of this process Demanyl is also produced. Demanyl was discarded as scrap until discovery of its usefulness as a catalyst in the manufacture of glue; for two years Amaco has been able to sell all of its production of Demanyl.

In its financial statements Amaco states inventory at the lower of cost (on the first-in, first-out basis) or market. Unit costs of the items most recently produced must therefore be computed. Costs allocated to Demanyl are computed so that after allowing for packaging and selling costs of $.04 per pound no profit or loss will be recognized on sales of this product.

Certain data for October 1972 follow:

Raw Materials	Pounds Used	Total Cost
Amanic acid	6,300	$5,670
Bonyl hydroxide	9,100	6,370
Colb	5,600	2,240

Conversion Costs (labor and overhead)	Total Cost
Department 1	$33,600
Department 2	3,306
Department 3	22,400

	Pounds Produced	Inventories, Pounds		Sales Price per pound
		September 30	October 31	
Amanyl	3,600			$ 6.65
Bonanyl..............	2,800	210	110	
Am-Salt	7,600	400	600	6.30
Bonanyl-X	2,755			4.20
Colbanyl.	1,400			43.00
Demanyl	9,800			.54

Required:

Prepare for October 1972 the schedules listed below. Supporting computations should be prepared in good form. Round answers to the nearest cent.

a. Cost per pound of Amanyl, Bonanyl, and Am-Salt produced—relative sales value method.

b. Cost per pound of Amanyl, Bonanyl, and Am-Salt produced—average unit cost method.

c. Cost per pound of Colbanyl produced. Assume that the cost per pound of Am-Salt produced was $3.40 in September 1972 and $3.50 in October 1972.

SPECIFIC APPROACH

Problem V-1

This is a straightforward process cost problem. Note that some irrelevant information about the finishing department is included. Ignore the lost units when you compute the equivalent units of polyplast.

Problem V-2

1. In requirement (b), note that spoilage occurs at two stages in the box department. No spoilage occurs elsewhere.

2. In requirement (c), under the weighted-average method, the beginning work-in-process inventory is regarded as part of current production even though it was begun prior to the current period. (Note that this is an assumption for product costing purposes; for control purposes, current performance should be judged solely on the basis of current equivalent output and current costs incurred.)

3. Requirements (d) through (g) are routine applications of the weighted-average method to inventory costing.

Problem V-3

Apply the five steps described in the General Approach. When your solution is completed, identify and label via footnote those parts that respond to the specific requirements. In this way your work can be followed easily.

Sixty minutes is not a very generous time allotment.

Problem V-4

1. When you compute the units started, divide the units of Marsh by two because two pounds are needed to begin a unit of Gink.
2. In part (b), no variances would be shown except for the over-applied fixed manufacturing overhead under absorption costing. Divide your presentation to show beginning inventory, cost of goods manufactured, and ending inventory. Of course, a condensed statement showing only the cost of goods sold would be an acceptable alternative, particularly because you could cite schedule b(2) as a supporting tabulation.

Problem V-5

The following sketch may be useful:

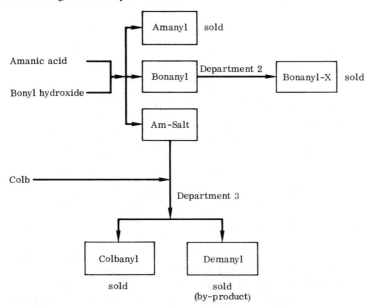

1. In requirement (a), note that a yield factor must be used to compute the pounds of Bonanyl-X that can be produced from Bonanyl. See the General Approach for a description of the relative sales value method.
2. Requirement (b) necessitates a simple computation whereby the total production costs in Department 1 are divided by the pounds produced in Department 1.
3. In requirement (c), the total costs incurred by Department 3 should be reduced by the net sales value of Demanyl, which is being accounted for as a by-product.

Quantitative Methods

GENERAL APPROACH

Since May, 1968, each CPA examination has included questions and problems on quantitative methods and techniques as they apply to accounting. The range of coverage has been wide, as the problems in this section demonstrate.

Many problems have made some use of QM, particularly elementary decision theory and probabilites, as a component of a main problem that concentrates on some major accounting topic such as relevant cost analysis. *Information for CPA Candidates,* p. 7, warns: "The testing will be progressively more extensive to the point where candidates are tested for their knowledge of the application of modern algebra (linear and nonlinear), calculus (differential and integral), probability and statistics, and other mathematical techniques developed for business applications."

The range of coverage in the QM applications is imposing. Consider the topics matrix algebra, conditional and marginal probabilities, elementary decision theory entailing construction of a probability distribution and payoff table, transportation problem, least-squares regression, learning curve, differential calculus, queuing theory, linear programming, PERT network analysis, economic order quantities, interpretation of linear programming analysis with sensitivity analysis, and statistical sampling. (Discounted cash flow analysis is covered in Topic IV and is not viewed here as part of QM although obviously it could be so classified.)

Given this range, what should a candidate do to prepare for any QM problem that he encounters? The level of difficulty of the QM problems is likely to be elementary, but the variety of topics is staggering. In our view, two alternatives seem attractive. First, those candidates who have strong backgrounds should review their QM textbooks and plan on solving any of the QM problems on the CPA examination. Second, those candidates with weak backgrounds should do minimal preparation and not invest the considerable time needed to become adequately prepared.

In short, a weak QM background is unlikely to be strengthened enough by extra study during CPA preparation, particularly when you envision the enormous variety of potential QM topics that warrant review. However, as a minimum each candidate should know the elementary ideas in the next section on decision theory, probabilities, and expected values (payoffs). These ideas appear frequently, and they are often a sub-part of some ordinary accounting problem that would not deserve an over-all QM label.

Decision Theory, Probabilities, and Payoffs

The basic approach of decision theory[1] has the following characteristics:

1. An organizational objective that can be quantified. This objective can take many forms. Most often, it is expressed as a maximization (or minimization) of some form of profit (or cost). This quantification is often called a *choice criterion* or an *objective function*. This objective function is used to evaluate the courses of action and to provide a basis for choosing the best alternative.

2. A set of the alternative courses of action under explicit consideration. This set of *actions* should be collectively exhaustive and mutually exclusive.

3. A set of all the relevant events or *states,* or states of nature, that can occur. This set should also be collectively exhaustive and mutually exclusive. Therefore, only one of the states will actually occur.

4. A set of *probabilities* that describes the possibilities of the various states' occurrence.

5. A set of *payoffs* or *expected values* that describes the consequences of the various possible outcomes evaluated in terms of the objective function. These are conditionally dependent on a specific course of action and a specific state.

An example may clarify the essential ingredients of a formal model. Suppose a decision maker has two mutually exclusive and exhaustive alternative courses of action regarding the quality-control aspects of his project: accept or reject. He also predicts that two mutually exclusive and exhaustive states of nature will affect his payoffs. Either the product conforms to the quality standards, or it does not. The combinations of actions and states and their conditional payoffs can be presented in a *payoff table:*

---

[1]Much of the material in this General Approach is adapted from Charles T. Horngren, *Cost Accounting,* 3rd ed. (Englewood Cliffs, N.J.: Prentice-Hall, Inc., 1972), Chapters 15, 23, and 27.

Alternative	Alternative States of Nature	
Action	Conform	Nonconform
Accept	$12[1]	$2[2]
Reject	$ 7[3]	$7[4]

Note: The superior figures in the table above relate to corresponding numbers in the list which follows.

The conditional payoffs are assumed to take the pattern shown because:

1. Acceptance and conformance should bring the normal "contribution" to profit.
2. Acceptance and nonconformance eventually results in expensive rework after the product is processed through later stages.
3. Rejection and conformance results in unnecessary rework that reduces the normal contribution.
4. Rejection and nonconformance results in immediate necessary rework.

The payoff table includes three of the five ingredients of the formal model: actions, states, and payoffs. The other two ingredients are the probabilities and the choice criterion. Assume that the probability of conform is 0.6 and that of nonconform is 0.4. Assume also that the choice criterion is to maximize the expected value of the dollar payoff. Given this model, the decision maker would always accept the product, because the expected payoff A for each action is

$$\text{If Accept}, \overline{A} = \$12\,(0.6) + \$2\,(0.4) = \$8$$
$$\text{If Reject}, \overline{A} = \$7\,(0.6) + \$7\,(0.4) = \$7$$

An expected value is an arithmetic mean, a weighted average using the probabilities as weights. The formula is

$$\overline{A} = \sum_{x=1}^{n} A_x P_x$$

An example of the general approach to dealing with uncertainty may clarify some of the preceding ideas.

Problem

Once a day, a retailer stocks bunches of fresh-cut flowers, each of which costs 40¢ and sells for $1. The retailer never cuts his price; leftovers are given to a nearby church. He estimates demand characteristics as follows:

Demand	Probability
0	0.05
1	0.20
2	0.40
3	0.25
4	0.10
5 or more	0.00
	1.00

He wants to know how many units he should stock in order to maximize profits. Try to solve before consulting the solution that follows:

Solution

The profit, per unit sold, is 60¢ ; the loss, per unit unsold, is 40¢ . All the alternatives may be assessed in the following *payoff table.*

State of nature: Demand of	0	1	2	3	4	Expected Value (Payoff)
Probability of state:	0.05	0.20	0.40	0.25	0.10	
Actions, units purchased;						
0	$ 0	$ 00	$0	$0	$0	$0
1	− .40	.60	.60	.60	.60	.55
2	− .80	.20	1.20	1.20	1.20	.90
3	−1.20	−.20	.80	1.80	1.80	.85
4	−1.60	−.60	.40*	1.40	2.40	.55

*Example of computation (2 × $1.00) − (4 × $.40) = $.40

As was shown in an earlier section, the computation of expected value (A) for each action is affected by the probability weights and the conditional payoff associated with each combination of actions and states.

$\overline{A}$ (Stock 1) = 0.05 (−.40)+0.20(.60)+0.40(.60)+0.25(.60) + 0.10(.60) = $.55

$\overline{A}$ (Stock 2)= 0.05(−.80) + 0.20(.20) + 0.40(1.20) + 0.25 (1.20) + 0.10(1.20)
= $.90

and so on.

To maximize expected payoff, the retailer should stock two units $(A = \$.90)$.

Inventory Control Systems

There are two central questions that must be faced in designing an inventory control system: How much should we buy (or manufacture) at a time? When should we buy (or manufacture)? Now we turn to the first of these questions.

1. *How much to order?* A key factor in inventory policy is computing the optimum size of either a normal purchase order for raw materials or a shop order for a production run. This optimum size is called the *economic order quantity,* the size that will result in minimum total annual costs of the item in question.

Example 1

A refrigerator manufacturer buys certain steel shelving in sets from outside suppliers at $4.00 per set. Total annual needs are 5,000 sets at a rate of 20 sets per working day.

The following cost data are available:

> Desired annual return on inventory investment,
>   10% X $4.00. . . . . $.40
> Rent, insurance, taxes, per unit per year 10
>   Carrying costs per unit per year . . . . $ .50
> Costs per purchase order:
>   Clerical costs, stationery, postage, telephone, etc. $10.00
> What is the economic order quantity?

A tabulation of total annual costs could be made under various alternatives. The column with the least cost would indicate the economic order quantity.

Alternatively, an order-size formula could be used. The formula is a result of applying differential calculus to the problem. The total annual cost (for any case, not just this example) is differentiated with respect to order size. Where this derivative is zero, the minimum annual cost is attained. The widely used formula approach to the order-size problem may be expressed in a variety of ways, one of which follows:[6]

$$E = \sqrt{\frac{2AP}{S}}$$

where E = order size; A = annual quantity used in units; P = cost of placing an order; and S = annual cost of carrying one unit in stock for one year. Substituting:

$$E = \sqrt{\frac{2(5,000)\,(\$10)}{\$.50}} = \sqrt{\frac{\$100,000}{\$.50}} = \sqrt{200,000}$$

E = 448, the economic order quantity

As we may expect, the order size gets larger as A or P gets bigger or as S gets smaller.

2. *When to order?* Although we have seen how to compute economic order quantity, we have not yet answered another key question: When to order? This

[6]The formula may be derived as follows:

(1) $C = \dfrac{AP}{E} + \dfrac{ES}{2}$ (4) $SE^2 = 2AP$

(2) $\dfrac{dC}{dE} = \dfrac{-AP}{E^2} + \dfrac{S}{2}$ (5) $E^2 = \dfrac{2AP}{S}$

(3) Set $\dfrac{dC}{dE} = 0; \dfrac{S}{2} - \dfrac{AP}{E^2} = 0$ (6) $E = \sqrt{\dfrac{2AP}{S}}$

question is easy to answer only if we know the *lead time,* the time interval between placing an order and receiving delivery, know the economic order quantity, and are *certain* of demand during lead time. The graph in Exhibit 6-1 clarifies the relationships between:

Economic order quantity	448 sets of steel shelving
Lead time	2 weeks
Average usage	100 sets per week

Exhibit 6-1, Part A, shows that the *reorder point*—the quantity level that automatically triggers a new order—is dependent on expected usage during lead time; that is, if shelving is being used at a rate of 100 sets per week and the lead time is two weeks, a new order would be placed when the inventory level reaches 200 sets.

Exhibit 6-1

DEMAND IN RELATION TO INVENTORY LEVELS

PART A: Demand Known With Certainty

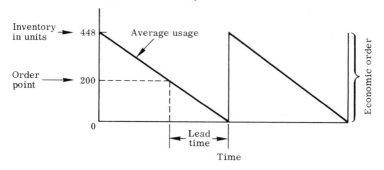

PART B: Demand Not Known With Certainty: Role of Safety Stock

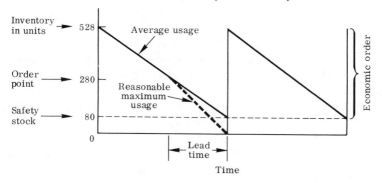

Minimum Inventory: Safety Allowance for Fluctuations in Demand

Our previous example assumed that 100 sets would be used per week—a demand pattern that was known with certainty. Businesses are seldom blessed with such accurate forecasting. Instead, demand may fluctuate from day to day, from week to week, or from month to month. Thus, the company will run out of stock if there are sudden spurts in usage beyond 100 per week, delays in processing orders, or delivery delays. Obviously, then, nearly all companies must provide for some safety stock—some minimum or buffer inventory as a cushion against reasonable expected maximum usage. Part B of Exhibit 6-1 is based on the same facts as Part A, except that reasonable expected maximum usage is 140 sets per week. The safety stock would be 80 sets (excess usage of 40 sets per week X 2 weeks). The reorder point is commonly computed as safety stock plus the average usage during the lead time.

Linear Programming

Linear programming (LP) is an application of linear algebra to a problem of optimization where constraints are present. The following example explains the approach.

Consider a company that has two departments, machining and finishing. This plant makes two products, each of which requires processing in each of the two departments. Relevant data are summarized as follows:

Products	Capacities (per day) in Units		Contribution Margin Per Unit
	Dept. 1 Machining	Dept. 2 Finishing	
A	200	120	$2.00
or			
B	100	200	$2.50

Severe material shortages for Product B will limit its production to a maximum of 90 per day. How many units of each product should be produced to obtain the maximum profit?

Two underlying assumptions are necessary for using linear-programming techniques. First, all relationships between capacity and the amounts produced are linear; that is, these relationships can be demonstrated graphically by straight lines rather than by curves. Second, all factors and relationships are stated with certainty; in other words, all ingredients of the situation are assumed to be certain rather than uncertain or probable.[3]

The linear-programming approach has the following basic pattern, although variations and short cuts are available in unique situations:

---

[3]However, probabilities may be used to forecast the specific data used in the construction of the linear-programming model.

1. Determine objectives. Usually this takes some form of either maximization of profit or minimization of cost. Technically, this objective is called an *objective function*, a figure of merit, or a measure of effectiveness.
2. Determine basic relationships in the situation, especially the constraints.
3. Determine available *feasible* alternatives.
4. Compute the optimum solution. Techniques may vary here. In uncomplicated situations, the graphic approach is easiest to see. However, algebraic approaches are more widely used in practice.

Using our example, let's apply these steps.

1. *Determine objectives.* The objective here will be to find the product combination that maximizes *total* contribution margin. This can be expressed in equation form as $2.00A + $2.50B = Total contribution margin. We want to maximize this objective function.
2. *Determine basic relationships.* The relationships here can be depicted by inequalities as follows:

Department 1:	$A + 2B \leq 200$
Department 2:	$A + .6B \leq 120$
Material shortage for Product B:	$B \leq 90$
Because negative production is impossible,	$B \geq 0$ and $A \geq 0$

The three solid lines on the graph in Exhibit 6-2 will aid visualization of the existing constraints for Departments 1 and 2 and of the material shortage.
3. *Determine available feasiable alternatives.* The feasible alternatives are those that are technically possible. We do not want to bother with useless computations for impossible alternatives. The shaded area in Exhibit 6-2 shows the boundaries of those product combinations that are feasible.
4. *Compute optimum solution.* In steps 2 and 3 we have concentrated on physical relationships alone. Now we return to the economic relationships expressed as the objective in step 1. We test various feasible product combinations to see which one maximizes the total contribution margin.

In the graphic solution, we are fortunate because the optimum solution must lie on one of the corners of the "Area of feasible product combinations." Methods exist for moving from one corner to another to see if the total contribution is improved. This procedure is continued until the optimum solution is found. In this case, the optimum corner shows that the best combination is 86 units of A plus 57 units of B.

The same result can be accomplished algebraically, usually by working with the corners of the polygon. The steps are simple:
a. Start with a possible combination.
b. Compute the profit.
c. Move to another possible combination to see if the result in *b* will be improved. Keep moving from corner to corner until no further improvement is possible.

Exhibit 6-2

LINEAR PROGRAMMING–GRAPHIC SOLUTION

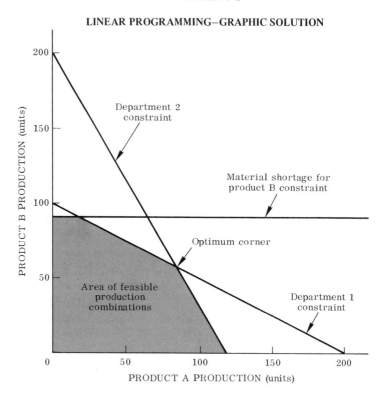

These computations, corner by corner, are summarized as follows:

Trial	Corner	Combination Product A	Combination Product B	Total Contribution Margin
1	0,0	0	0	$2.00 (0) + $2.50 (0) = $ 0
2	0,90	0	90	2.00 (0) + 2.50 (90) = 225.00
3	20,90	20	90	2.00 (20) + 2.50 (90) = 265.00
4	86,57	86	57	2.00 (86) + 2.50 (57) = 314.50*
5	120,0	120	0	2.00 (120) + 2.50 (0) = 240.00

*Optimum.

Why must the best solution lie on a corner? Consider all possible combinations that will produce a total contribution margin of $1 ($2.00 A + $2.50 B = $1). This is a straight line through (.5,0) and (0,.4). Other total contribution margins are represented by lines parallel to this one. Their associated total contribution margins increase as the lines get further from the origin. The optimum line is the one furthest from the origin that has a feasible point on it; intuitively, we know that this happens at a corner (86,57). Furthermore, if you put a ruler on the graph and move it parallel with the $1 line, the optimum corner will become apparent.

At the outset of this example, you may have jumped to the conclusion that production of Product B, which promises the most margin *per unit,* should be maximized. Then any remaining productive capacity should be devoted to Product A. This is fallacious reasoning, because the scarce factor is productive capacity. The key to the optimum solution rests in the relative rates of substitution and profitability per unit (hour or day) of *productive capacity.* This point becomes clearer if we examine the graph. Moving from corner (20,90) to corner (86,57) implies that the company is transferring the scarce resource (productive capacity) between the products. In Department 1, each productive hour devoted to one unit of Product B may be given (sacrificed or traded) for two units of Product A. Will this exchange add to profitability? Yes, as shown below:

```
Total contribution margin at corner (20,90)  . . . . . . . . . . . . . $265.00
Added contribution margin from Product A:
   66 units @ $2.00 . . . . . . . . . . . . . . . . . . . . . . . . $132.00
Lost contribution margin Product B;
   33 units @ $2.50 . . . . . . . . . . . . . . . . . . . . . .    82.50
Net additional contribution . . . . . . . . . . . . . . . . . . . . . . . .    49.50

Total contribution margin at corner (86,57)  . . . . . . . . . . . . $314.50
```

As we move from corner (86,57) to corner (120,0), we face the Department 2 constraint rather than the Department 1 constraint. The rate of substitution may be stated as follows: Each productive hour devoted to one unit of Product B may be devoted to .6 of a unit of Product A. This would entail giving up $2.50 contribution margin in exchange for .6($2.00) or $1.20 contribution margin, a decrease of the total contribution margin of $1.30 for each unit of Product B given up. Therefore, corner (86,57) is the optimum solution.

Note that the heart of these substitutions is a matter of swapping a given contribution margin per unit of scarce resource for some other contribution margin per unit of scarce resource; it is not simply a matter of comparing margins per unit of *product.*

Simplex Method

The fundamental problem of linear programming is to discover the specific set of variables that satisfies all constraints and maximizes (or minimizes) the objective sought. Although graphical methods aid visualization and are useful for two or possibly three variables, they are impractical where many variables exist. The *simplex method,* a general technique for solving any linear-programming problem, is an iterative, step-by-step process that is very effective, especially when a digital computer performs the calculations. Although it is much too detailed to be described here, the simplex method essentially starts with a specific feasible alternative and algebraically tests it by substitution to see if the solution can be improved. These substitutions continue until no further improvement is possible, and thus the optimum solution is produced.

REFERENCES

Bierman, Harold, Charles P. Bonini, and Warren H. Hausman, *Quantitative Analysis for Business Decisions,* 4th Ed. (Homewood, Illinois: Richard D. Irwin, Inc., 1973).

Bierman, Harold, and Thomas R. Dyckman, *Managerial Cost Accounting* (New York: The Macmillan Company, 1971).

Corcoran, A. Wayne, *Mathematical Applications in Accounting* (New York: Harcourt Brace Jovanovich, Inc., 1968).

Dopuch, Nicholas, and Jacob Birnberg, *Cost Accounting,* 2nd Ed. (New York: Harcourt Brace Jovanovich, Inc., 1974).

Horngren, Charles T., *Cost Accounting,* 3rd Ed. (Englewood Cliffs, N.J.: Prentice-Hall, Inc., 1972), Chapters 23-27.

Levin, Richard I., and Charles A. Kilpatrick, *Quantitative Approaches to Management,* 2nd Ed. (New York: McGraw-Hill Book Company, 1971).

CPA PROBLEMS

Problem VI-1: Probabilities, discounted cash flow (40-50 min.)

During your examination of the financial statements of Benjamin Industries, the president requested your assistance in the evaluation of several financial management problems in his home appliances division which he summarized for you as follows:

1. Management wants to determine the best sales price for a new appliance which has a variable cost of $4 per unit. The sales manager has estimated probabilities of achieving annual sales levels for various selling prices as shown in the following chart:

Sales Level	Selling Price			
(Units)	$ 4	$ 5	$ 6	$ 7
20,000	–	–	20%	80%
30,000	–	10%	40%	20%
40,000	50%	50%	20%	–
50,000	50%	40%	20%	–

2. The division's current profit rate is 5% on annual sales of $1,200,000; an investment of $400,000 is needed to finance these sales. The Company's basis for measuring divisional success is return on investment.

3. Management is also considering the following two alternative plans submitted by employees for improving operations in the home appliances division:

> Green believes that sales volume can be doubled by greater promotional effort, but his method would lower the profit rate to 4% of sales and require an additional investment of $100,000.

Gold favors eliminating some unprofitable appliances and improving efficiency by adding $200,000 in capital equipment. His methods would decrease sales volume by 10% but improve the profit rate to 7%.

4. Black, White, and Gray, three franchised home appliance dealers, have requested short-term financing from the Company. The dealers have agreed to repay the loans within three years and to pay Benjamin Industries 5% of net income for the three-year period for the use of the funds. The following table summarizes by dealer the financing requested and the total remittances (principal plus 5% of net income) expected at the end of each year:

	Black	White	Gray
Financing requested	$ 80,000	$ 40,000	$ 30,000
Remittances expected at end of—			
Year 1	$ 10,000	$ 25,000	$ 10,000
Year 2	40,000	30,000	15,000
Year 3	70,000	5,000	15,000
	$120,000	$ 60,000	$ 40,000

Management believes these financing requests should be granted only if the annual pre-tax return to the Company exceeds the target internal rate of 20% on investment. Discount factors (rounded) which would provide this 20% rate of return are:

Year 1	.8
Year 2	.7
Year 3	.6

Required:

a. Prepare a schedule computing the expected incremental income for each of the sales prices proposed for the new product. The schedule should include the expected sales levels in units (weighted according to the sales manager's estimated probabilities), the expected total monetary sales, expected variable costs and the expected incremental income.

b. Prepare schedules computing (1) the Company's current rate of return on investment in the home appliances division, and the anticipated rates of return under the alternative suggestions made by (2) Green and (3) Gold.

c. Prepare a schedule to compute the net present value of the investment opportunities of financing Black, White and Gray. The schedule should determine if the discounted cash flows expected from (1) Black, (2) White and (3) Gray would be more or less than the amounts of Benjamin Industries' investment in loans to each of the three dealers.

Problem VI-2: Probabilities and discounted cash flow (40-50 min.)

Vernon Enterprises designs and manufactures toys. Past experience indicates that the product life cycle of a toy is three years. Promotional advertising produces large sales in the early years, but there is a substantial sales decline in the final year of a toy's life.

Consumer demand for new toys placed on the market tends to fall into three classes. About 30 percent of the new toys sell well above expectations, 60 percent sell as anticipated and 10 percent have poor consumer acceptance.

A new toy has been developed. The following sales projections were made by carefully evaluating consumer demand for the new toy:

Consumer Demand for New Toy	Chance of Occurring	Estimated Sales in Year 1	Year 2	Year 3
Above average	30%	$1,200,000	$2,500,000	$600,000
Average	60	700,000	1,700,000	400,000
Below average	10	200,000	900,000	150,000

Variable costs are estimated at 30 percent of the selling price. Special machinery must be purchased at a cost of $860,000 and will be installed in an unused portion of the factory which Vernon has unsuccessfully been trying to rent to someone for several years at $50,000 per year and has no prospects for future utilization. Fixed expenses (excluding depreciation) of a cash-flow nature are estimated at $50,000 per year on the new toy. The new machinery will be depreciated by the sum-of-the-years' digits method with an estimated salvage value of $110,000 and will be sold at the beginning of the fourth year. Advertising and promotional expenses will be incurred uniformly and will total $100,000 the first year, $150,000 the second year, and $50,000 the third year. These expenses will be deducted as incurred for income tax reporting.

Vernon believes that state and federal income taxes will total 60 percent of income in the foreseeable future and may be assumed to be paid uniformly over the year income is earned.

Required:

a. Prepare a schedule computing the probable sales of this new toy in each of the three years, taking into account the probability of above average, average and below average sales occurring.

b. Assume that the probable sales computed in "a" are $900,000 in the first year, $1,800,000 in the second year, and $410,000 in the third year. Prepare a schedule computing the probable net income for the new toy in each of the three years of its life.

c. Prepare a schedule of net cash flows from sales of the new toy for each of the years involved and from disposition of the machinery purchased. Use the sales data given in part "b."

d. Assuming a minimum desired rate of return of 10 percent, prepare a schedule of the present value of the net cash flows calculated in "c." The following data are relevant:

Year	Present Value of $1.00 Due at the End of Each Year Discounted at 10 percent	Present Value of $1.00 Earned Uniformly Throughout the Year Discounted at 10 percent
1	.91	.95
2	.83	.86
3	.75	.78

Problem VI-3: Probabilities and payoff table (50-60 min.)

Commercial Products Corporation, an audit client, requested your assistance in determining the potential loss on a binding purchase contract which will be in effect at the end of the Corporation's fiscal year. The Corporation produces a chemical compound which deteriorates and must be discarded if it is not sold by the end of the month during which it is produced.

The total variable cost of the manufactured compound is $25 per unit and it is sold for $40 per unit. The compound can be purchased from a vertically integrated competitor at $40 per unit plus $5 freight per unit. It is estimated that failure to fill orders would result in the complete loss of 8 out of 10 customers placing orders for the compound.

The Corporation has sold the compound for the past 30 months. Demand has been irregular and there is no sales trend. During this period sales per month have been:

Units Sold per Month	Number of Months*
4,000	6
5,000	15
6,000	9

*Occurred in random sequence.

Required:

a. For each of the following, prepare a schedule (with supporting computations in good form) of the
   1. Probability of sales of 4,000, 5,000 or 6,000 units in any month.
   2. Marginal income if sales of 4,000, 5,000 or 6,000 units are made in one month and 4,000, 5,000 or 6,000 units are manufactured for sale in the same month. Assume all sales orders are filled. (Such a schedule is sometimes called a "payoff table.")
   3. Average monthly marginal income the Corporation should expect over the long run if 5,000 units are manufactured every month and all sales orders are filled.

b. The cost of the primary ingredient used to manufacture the compound is $12 per unit of compound. It is estimated that there is a 60 per cent chance that the primary ingredient supplier's plant may be shut down by a strike for an indefinite period. A substitute ingredient is available at $18 per unit of compound but the Corporation must contract immediately to purchase the substitute or it will be unavailable when needed. A firm purchase contract for either the primary or the substitute ingredient must now be made with one of the suppliers for production next month. If an order were placed for the primary ingredient and a strike should occur, the Corporation would be released from the contract and management would purchase the compound from the competitor.

Assume that 5,000 units are to be manufactured and all sales orders are to be filled.

   1. Compute the monthly marginal income from sales of 4,000, 5,000 and 6,000 units if the substitute ingredient is ordered.

2. Prepare a schedule computing the average monthly marginal income the Corporation should expect if the primary ingredient is ordered with the existing probability of a strike at the supplier's plant. Assume that the expected average monthly marginal income from manufacturing will be $65,000 using the primary ingredient or $35,000 using the substitute and the expected average monthly loss from purchasing from the competitor will be $25,000.

3. Should management order the primary or substitute ingredient during the anticipated strike period (under the assumptions stated in "b.2" above)? Why?

4. Should management purchase the compound from the competitor to fill sales orders when the orders cannot be otherwise filled? Why?

Problem VI-4: Probabilities and expected values (50-60 min.)

Food Products, Inc., an audit client, posed the following problem to your CPA firm and requested guidelines which can be applied in the future to obtain the largest net income.

A Food Products plant on the coast produces a food product and ships its production of 10,000 units per day by air in an airplane owned by Food Products. The area is sometimes fogbound and shipment can then be made only by rail. The plant does not operate unless shipments are made. Extra costs of preparation for rail shipment reduce the marginal contribution of this product from $.40 per unit to $.18 per unit and there is an additional fixed cost of $3,100 for modification of packaging facilities to convert to rail shipment (incurred only once per conversion).

The fog may last for several days and Food Products normally starts shipping by rail only after rail shipments become necessary to meet commitments to customers.

A meteorological report reveals that during the past 10 years the area has been fogbound 250 times for 1 day and that fog continued 100 times for a second consecutive day, 40 times for a third consecutive day, 20 times for a fourth consecutive day and 10 times for a fifth consecutive day. Occasions and length of fog were both random. Fog never continued more than 5 days and there were never 2 separate occurrences of fog in any 6-day period.

Required:

a. Prepare a schedule presenting the computation of the daily marginal contribution (ignore fixed conversion cost)
  1. When there is no fog and shipment is made by air.
  2. When there is fog and shipment is made by rail.
b. Prepare a schedule presenting the computation of the probabilities of the possible combinations of foggy and clear weather on the days following a fogbound day. Your schedule should show the probability that, if fog first occurs on a particular day,
  1. The next 4 days will be foggy.
  2. The next 3 days will be foggy and day 5 will be clear.
  3. The next 2 days will be foggy and days 4 and 5 will be clear.
  4. The next day will be foggy and days 3, 4 and 5 will be clear.
  5. The next 4 days will be clear.

c. Assume you determine it is probable that it would be unprofitable to start shipping by rail on either the fourth or fifth consecutive foggy day. Prepare a schedule presenting the computation of the probable (expected) marginal income or loss that should be expected from rail shipments if rail shipments were started on the third consecutive foggy day and the probability that the next 2 days will be foggy is .25, the probability that the next day will be foggy and day 5 will be clear is .25, and the probability that the next 2 days will be clear is .50.

d. In this engagement the CPA should consider the reliability of the data upon which he bases his conclusions. What questions should he consider regarding

1. Financial data reliability?
2. Meteorological data reliability?

Problem VI-5: Minimizing transportation costs (50-60 min.)

Delaney, Inc. manufactures dictating machines in its three factories and ships them to warehouses in three cities. Shipping costs were uniform throughout the fiscal year ending June 30, 1969. A schedule of shipping costs follows:

COST OF SHIPPING ONE FINISHED UNIT
Fiscal Year Ended June 30, 1969

To Warehouses in	From Factories in		
	Red City	Bluefield	Green Valley
Blacktown	$3	$8	$5
Orange	5	4	2
Indigo	4	7	3

Sales of the Delaney machine have been excellent and the Company has had to operate its three plants at full capacity to fill orders. During the year the following shipments were made:

UNITS SHIPPED TO WAREHOUSES
Fiscal Year Ended June 30, 1969

To Warehouses in	From Factories in			
	Red City	Bluefield	Green Valley	Total
Blacktown	5,000	7,000		12,000
Orange		3,000	13,000	16,000
Indigo		7,000	2,000	9,000
Total shipments	5,000	17,000	15,000	37,000

Management is aware that the above allocation of production probably did not result in the lowest possible total cost of freight and is concerned about the impact of this on the valuation of the June 30, 1969 finished goods inventory. The Company wishes to value inventories at the cost of manufacturing plus the freight charges applicable under an allocation of production scheme which would result in the lowest total cost of freight.

At June 30, 1969, Delaney had the following finished goods inventories:

In Blacktown warehouse .... 3,000 units (all from Red City)
In Orange warehouse .... 1,000 units (all from Green Valley)
In Indigo warehouse .... 2,000 units (all from Bluefield)

Total finished goods .... 6,000 units

The cost of manufacturing a dictating machine is $78 at Red City and $80 at both Bluefield and Green Valley.

Required:

a. Prepare a schedule computing the actual cost of finished goods inventory in warehouses, including freight, at June 30, 1969. The Company uses the first-in, first-out method.

b. Prepare a schedule showing the manner in which production during fiscal 1969 should have been shipped to warehouses to minimize total freight costs. A format similar to the schedule, "Units Shipped to Warehouses," above is recommended.

c. Prepare a schedule computing the cost of finished inventory at June 30, 1969, including the cost of freight which would have been applicable if the Company had followed the lowest-cost allocation in "b," assuming for any warehouse receiving shipments from more than one factory that the units on hand pertain to the production of the factory from which the freight cost is minimal.

d. Assume that the 1,000 units in the Orange warehouse were shipped there from the Blacktown warehouse at a shipping cost of $7 per unit and that the units had originally been shipped to Blacktown from the factory in Bluefield. At what amount should these 1,000 units be valued in inventory? Why?

Problem VI-6: Statistical sampling and auditing (40-50 min.)

Levelland, Inc., a client of your firm for several years, uses a voucher system for processing all cash disbursements which number about 500 each month. After carefully reviewing the company's internal controls, your firm decided to statistically sample the vouchers for eleven specific characteristics to test operating compliance of the voucher system against the client's representations as to the system's operation. Nine of these characteristics are non-critical; two are critical. The characteristics to be evaluated are listed on the worksheet on page 183.

Pertinent client representations about the system follow:

• Purchase orders are issued for all goods and services except for recurring services such as utilities, taxes, etc. The controller issues a check request for the latter authorizing payment. Receiving reports are prepared for all goods received. Department heads prepare a services-rendered report for services covered by purchase orders. (Services-rendered reports are subsequently considered receiving reports.)

•Copies of purchase orders, receiving reports, check requests, and original invoices are forwarded to accounting. Invoices are assigned a consecutive voucher number immediately upon receipt by accounting. Each voucher is rubber-stamped to provide spaces for accounting personnel to initial when (a) agreeing invoice with purchase order or check request, (b) agreeing invoice with receiving report and (c) verifying mathematical accuracy of the invoice.

•In processing each voucher for payment, accounting personnel match each invoice with the related purchase order and receiving report or check request. Invoice extensions and footings are verified. Debit distribution is recorded on the face of each invoice.

•Each voucher is recorded in the voucher register in numerical sequence after which a check is prepared. The voucher packets and checks are forwarded to the treasurer for signing and mailing the checks and canceling each voucher packet.

•Canceled packets are returned to accounting. Payment is recorded in the voucher register, and the voucher packets are filed numerically.

Following are characteristics of the voucher population already determined by preliminary statistical testing. Assume that each characteristic is randomly distributed throughout the voucher population.

•Eighty percent of vouchers are for purchase orders; 20% are for check requests.
•The average number of lines per invoice is four.
•The average number of accounts debited per invoice is two.

Appropriate statistical sampling tables are on page 182. For values not provided in the tables, use the next value in the table which will yield the most conservative result.

Required:

a. Year one:
An unrestricted random sample of 300 vouchers is to be drawn for year one. Enter in column A of the worksheet the sample size of each characteristic to be evaluated in the sample.

b. Year two:
1. Given the estimated error rates, specified upper precision limits, and required reliability (confidence level) in columns B, C, and D respectively, enter in column E the required sample size to evaluate each characteristic.
2. Disregarding your answers in column E and considering the assumed sample size and numbers of errors found in each sample as listed for each characteristic in columns F and G respectively, enter in column H the upper precision limit for each characteristic.
3. On a separate sheet, identify each characteristic for which the sampling objective was not met and explain what steps the auditor might take to meet his sampling or auditing objectives.

Table 1

DETERMINATION OF SAMPLE SIZE
Reliability (Confidence Level): 95%

Sample Size	Precision (Upper Limit) Percentage					
	1	2	3	4	5	6
90				0	0	
120			0	.8	.8	1.7
160		0	.6	1.2	1.9	2.5
240		.4	.8	1.7	2.5	3.3
340	0	.6	1.2	2.1	2.9	3.5
460	0	.9	1.5	2.4	3.3	3.9
1,000	.4	1.2	2.0	2.9	3.8	4.7

Table 2

PROBABILITY IN PERCENT OF INCLUDING AT
LEAST ONE OCCURRENCE IN A SAMPLE
For Populations Between 5,000 and 10,000

Sample Size	.1%	.2%	.3%	.4%	.5%	.75%
	The Probability of Including at Least One Occurrence in the Sampling is:					
240	22	39	52	62	70	84
300	26	46	60	70	78	90
340	29	50	65	75	82	93
400	34	56	71	81	87	95
460	38	61	76	85	91	97
500	40	64	79	87	92	98
600	46	71	84	92	96	99
700	52	77	89	95	97	99+
800	57	81	92	96	98	99+
900	61	85	94	98	99	99+
1,000	65	88	96	99	99	99+

Note: 99+ indicates a probability of 99.5% or greater.

Table 3

EVALUATION OF RESULTS
NUMBER OF OCCURRENCES IN SAMPLE
Reliability (Confidence Level): 95%

Sample Size	Precision (Upper Limit) Percentage					
	1	2	3	4	5	6
90				0		1
120			0	1		2
160		0	1	2	3	4
240		1	2	4	6	8
340	0	2	4	7	10	12
460	0	4	7	11	15	18
1,000	4	12	20	29	38	47

Levelland, Inc.
VOUCHER TEST WORKSHEET
Years Ended December 31

CHARACTERISTICS	YEAR 1	YEAR 2						
	Column A	Column B	Column C	Column D	Column E	Column F	Column G	Column H
	Sample Size	Estimated Error Rate	Specified Upper Precision Limit	Reliability (Confidence Level)	Required Sample Size	Assumed Sample Size	Number of Errors Found	Upper Precision Limit
Non-Critical								
1. Invoice in agreement with purchase order or check request.		1.1%	3	95%		460	4	
2. Invoice in agreement with receiving report.		.4%	2	95%		340	2	
3. Invoice mathematically accurate.								
a. Extension		1.4%	3	95%		1,000	22	
b. Footings		1.0%	3	95%		460	10	
4. Account distributions correct.		.3%	2	95%		340	2	
5. Voucher correctly entered in voucher register.		.5%	2	95%		340	1	
6. Evidence of Accounting Department checks.								
a. Comparison of invoice with purchase order or check request.		2.0%	4	95%		240	2	
b. Comparison of invoice with receiving report.		1.3%	4	95%		160	2	
c. Proving mathematical accuracy of invoice.		1.5%	3	95%		340	10	
Critical								
7. Voucher and related documents cancelled.		At or near 0	.75%	95%		600	5	
8. Vendor and amount on invoice in agreement with payee and amount on check.		At or near 0	.4%	95%		800	0	

183

Problem VI-7: PERT, economic order quantities, linear programming (50-60 min.)

Select the best answer choice for each of the following items which relate to the application of quantitative methods to accounting. Your grade will be determined from your total of correct answers.

Items to be Answered

A construction company has contracted to complete a new building and has asked for assistance in analyzing the project. Using the Program Evaluation Review Technique (PERT), the following network has been developed:

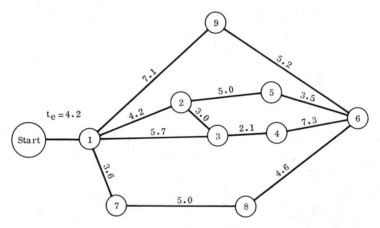

All paths from the start point to the finish point, event 6, represent activities or processes that must be completed before the entire project, the building, will be completed. The numbers above the paths or line segments represent expected completion times for the activities or processes. The expected time is based upon the commonly used, 1-4-1, three-estimate method. For example, the three-estimate method gives an estimated time of 4.2 to complete event 1.

19. The critical path (the path requiring the greatest amount of time) is
    a. 1-2-5-6.
    b. 1-2-3-4-6.
    c. 1-3-4-6.
    d. 1-7-8-6.
    e. 1-9-6.
20. Slack time on path 1-9-6 equals
    a. 4.3
    b. 2.8
    c. .9
    d. .4
    e. 0

21. The latest time for reaching event 6 via path 1-2-5-6 is
    a. 20.8
    b. 19.3
    c. 17.4
    d. 16.5
    e. 12.7

22. The earliest time for reaching event 6 via path 1-2-5-6 is
    a. 20.8
    b. 16.9
    c. 16.5
    d. 12.7
    e. 3.5

23. If all other paths are operating on schedule but path segment 7-8 has an unfavorable time variance of 1.9,
    a. The critical path will be shortened.
    b. The critical path will be eliminated.
    c. The critical path will be unaffected.
    d. Another path will become the critical path.
    e. The critical path will have an increased time of 1.9.

A manufacturer expects to produce 200,000 widgets during the year ending June 30, 1972 to supply a demand which is uniform throughout the year. The setup cost for each production run of widgets is $144 and the variable cost of producing each widget is $5. The cost of carrying one widget in inventory is $.20 per year. After a batch of widgets is produced and placed in inventory, it is sold at a uniform rate, and inventory is exhausted when the next batch of widgets is completed.

Management wishes an equation to describe the above situation and determine the optimal quantity of widgets to produce in each run in order to minimize total production and inventory carrying costs.

Let c = Total annual cost of producing and carrying widgets in inventory.
X = Number of widgets to be produced in each production run.

24. The number of production runs to be made in fiscal year 1972 could be expressed as
    a. $200,000 + 144 X$
    b. $200,000 + X$
    c. $200,000$
    d. $\dfrac{200,000}{X}$
    e. $\dfrac{X}{200,000}$

25. Total setup costs for fiscal year 1972 could be expressed as
    a. $\$144 \left(\dfrac{200,000}{X} \right)$
    b. $\dfrac{\$200,000}{X}$

    c. $\$144X$

    d. $\dfrac{\$144X}{200,000}$

    e. $\dfrac{\$144}{200,000} + \$X$

26. Total cost of carrying inventory during fiscal year 1972 could be expressed as

    a. $\$.20\,(\$144X)$

    b. $\$.20X$

    c. $\$.20\ \left(\dfrac{200,000}{X}\right)$

    d. $\$.20\ \left(\dfrac{X}{2}\right)$

    e. $\$.20\ \left(\dfrac{\$144X}{200,000}\right)$

27. The derivative *"dc/dx, of the"* equation to determine the optimal quantity of widgets which should be produced during each production run in fiscal year 1972 is

    a. $-28,800,000X^{-2} + \dfrac{.20}{2}$

    b. $-144(200,000)X^{-1} + \dfrac{.20}{2}$

    c. $-28,800,000X^{2} + 1,000,000 + \dfrac{.20}{2}$

    d. $-28,800,000X + \dfrac{.20}{2}$

    e. $-28,800,000X$

28. The quantity of widgets (to the nearest whole number) which should be produced in each run in fiscal year 1972 to minimize total costs is

    a. 19,000.

    b. 17,000.

    c. 16,000.

    d. 12,480.

    e. 12,000.

A company markets two products, Alpha and Gamma. The marginal contributions per gallon are $5 for Alpha and $4 for Gamma. Both products consist of two ingredients, D and K. Alpha contains 80% D and 20% K, while the proportions of the same ingredients in Gamma are 40% and 60% respectively. The current inventory is 16,000 gallons of D and 6,000 gallons of K. The only company producing D and K is on strike and will neither deliver nor produce them in the foreseeable future. The company wishes to know the numbers of gallons of Alpha and Gamma that it should produce with its present stock of raw materials in order to maximize its total revenue.

29. The objective function for this problem could be expressed as

    a. $f_{max} = 0X_1 + 0X_2 + 5X_3 + 5X_4$

    b. $f_{min} = 5X_1 + 4X_2 + 0X_3 + 0X_4$

    c. $f_{max} = 5X_1 + 4X_2 + 0X_3 + 0X_4$

    d. $f_{max} = X_1 + X_2 + 5X_3 + 4X_4$

    e. $f_{max} = 4X_1 + 5X_2 + X_3 + X_4$

30. The constraint imposed by the quantity of D on hand could be expressed as

    a. $X_1 + X_2 \geqslant 16,000.$

    b. $X_1 + X_2 \leqslant 16,000.$

    c. $.4X_1 + .6X_2 \leqslant 16,000.$

    d. $.8X_1 + .4X_2 \geqslant 16,000.$

    e. $.8X_1 + .4X_2 \leqslant 16,000.$

31. The constraint imposed by the quantity of K on hand could be expressed as

    a. $X_1 + X_2 \geqslant 6,000.$

    b. $X_1 + X_2 \leqslant 6,000.$

    c. $.8X_1 + .2X_2 \leqslant 6,000.$

    d. $.8X_1 + .2X_2 \geqslant 6,000.$

    e. $.2X_1 + .6X_2 \leqslant 6,000.$

32. To maximize total revenue the company should produce and market
    a. 106,000 gallons of Alpha only.
    b. 90,000 gallons of Alpha and 16,000 gallons of Gamma.
    c. 16,000 gallons of Alpha and 90,000 gallons of Gamma.
    d. 18,000 gallons of Alpha and 4,000 gallons of Gamma.
    e. 4,000 gallons of Alpha and 18,000 gallons of Gamma.

33. Assuming that the marginal contributions per gallon are $7 for Alpha and $9 for Gamma, the company should produce and market
    a. 106,000 gallons of Alpha only.
    b. 90,000 gallons of Alpha and 16,000 gallons of Gamma.
    c. 16,000 gallons of Alpha and 90,000 gallons of Gamma.
    d. 18,000 gallons of Alpha and 4,000 gallons of Gamma.
    e. 4,000 gallons of Alpha and 18,000 gallons of Gamma.

Problem VI-8: Simplex method; matrix algebra and overhead allocation; break-even analysis for two products. (50-60 min.)

Select the best answer choice for each of the following items, which relate to applications of quantitative methods to accounting.

Beekley, Inc., manufactures widgets, gadgets, and trinkets and has asked for advice in determining the best production mix for its three products. Demand for the company's products is excellent, and management finds that it is unable to meet potential sales with existing plant capacity.

Each product goes through three operations: milling, grinding, and painting. The effective weekly departmental capacities in minutes are: milling, 10,000; grinding, 14,000; and painting, 10,000.

The following data are available on the three products:

	Selling Price Per Unit	Variable Cost Per Unit	Per-Unit Production Time (in Minutes)		
			Milling	Grinding	Painting
Widgets	$5.25	$4.45	4	8	4
Gadgets	5.00	3.90	10	4	2
Trinkets	4.50	3.30	4	8	2

1. The quantitative technique most useful in determining the best product mix would be
   a. Least-squares analysis
   b. Queuing theory
   c. Linear regression
   d. Linear programming
2. The objective function for this problem using the simplex method might be expressed
   a. $f_{min} = 4.45X_1 + 3.90X_2 + 3.30X_3 + 0X_4 + 0X_5 + 0X_6$
   b. $f_{max} = 5.25X_1 + 5.00X_2 + 4.50X_3 + X_4 + X_5 + X_6$
   c. $f_{max} = .80X_1 + 1.10X_2 + 1.20X_3 + X_4 + X_5 + X_6$
   d. $f_{max} = .80X_1 + 1.10X_2 + 1.20X_3 + 0X_4 + 0X_5 + 0X_6$
3. The requirement that total production time in the painting department may not exceed 10,000 minutes per week might be expressed
   a. $4X_1 + 2X_2 + 2X_3 \geqslant 10,000$
   b. $4X_1 + 2X_2 + 2X_3 > 10,000$
   c. $4X_1 + 2X_2 + 2X_3 \leqslant 10,000$
   d. $4X_1 + 2X_2 + 2X_3 < 10,000$
4. The variables X_4, X_5, and X_6 included in the answers to item 2 are referred to as
   a. Artificial variables
   b. Primary variables
   c. Stochastic variables
   d. Slack variables
5. The variables X_1, X_2, and X_3 included in the answers to item 2 are referred to as
   a. Artificial variables
   b. Primary variables
   c. Stochastic variables
   d. Slack variables
6. The coefficients for X_1, X_2, and X_3 included in the answers to item 2 are
   a. The coefficients of the objective function in the problem
   b. The coefficients of the artificial variables in the problem
   c. The coefficients of the constraints in the problem and represent the contribution margin for each project
   d. The shadow prices of the stochastic variables in the problem
7. If Beekley were willing to pay $.12 for every minute of additional grinding time that might be made available, this may be called
   a. A primal restraint
   b. A slack variable
   c. A shadow price
   d. An artificial variable

8. A significant advantage of applying the simplex method to certain problems having four or more variables of a single class is that solutions may be arrived at quickly using
    a. Graphic analysis
    b. Electronic computer routines
    c. Simple algebraic methods
    d. Set theory

A manufacturer's plant has two service departments (designated below as S_1 and S_2) and three production departments (designated below as P_1, P_2, and P_3) and wishes to allocate all factory overhead to production departments. A primary distribution of overhead to all departments has already been made and is indicated below. The company makes the secondary distribution of overhead from service departments to production departments on a reciprocal basis, recognizing the fact that services of one service department are utilized by another. Data regarding costs and allocation percentages are as follows:

SERVICE-DEPARTMENT OVERHEAD COST ALLOCATION

Service Department	Percentage to be Allocated to Departments				
	S_1	S_2	P_1	P_2	P_3
S_1	0%	10%	20%	40%	30%
S_2	20	0	50	10	20

Primary Overhead to be Allocated

$98,000	$117,600	$1,400,000	$2,100,000	$640,000

Matrix algebra is to be used in the secondary allocation process. The amount of overhead to be allocated to the service departments you express in two simultaneous equations as:

$$S_1 = 98,000 + .20S_2 \text{ or } S_1 - .20S_2 = \$ 98,000$$
$$S_2 = 117,600 + .10S_1 \text{ or } S_2 - .10S_1 = \$117,600$$

9. The system of simultaneous equations above may be stated in matrix form as

a.
$$\begin{array}{ccc} A & S & b \end{array}$$
$$\begin{bmatrix} 1 & -.20 \\ -.10 & 1 \end{bmatrix} \begin{bmatrix} S_1 \\ S_2 \end{bmatrix} = \begin{bmatrix} \$ 98,000 \\ \$117,600 \end{bmatrix}$$

b.
$$\begin{array}{ccc} A & S & b \end{array}$$
$$\begin{bmatrix} 1 & \$ 98,000 & 1 \\ -.20 & \$117,600 & -.10 \end{bmatrix} \begin{bmatrix} S_1 \\ S_2 \end{bmatrix} = \begin{bmatrix} \$ 98,000 \\ \$117,600 \end{bmatrix}$$

c.
$$\begin{array}{ccc} A & S & b \end{array}$$
$$\begin{bmatrix} 1 & S_1 & 1 \\ -.20 & S_2 & -.10 \end{bmatrix} \begin{bmatrix} S_1 \\ S_2 \end{bmatrix} = \begin{bmatrix} \$ 98,000 \\ \$117,600 \end{bmatrix}$$

d.
$$\begin{array}{ccc} A & S & b \end{array}$$
$$\begin{bmatrix} 1 & 1\,S_1 \\ -.20 & -.10\,S_2 \end{bmatrix} \begin{bmatrix} S_1 \\ S_2 \end{bmatrix} = \begin{bmatrix} \$ 98,000 \\ \$117,600 \end{bmatrix}$$

10. For the correct matrix A in item 9, there exists a unique inverse matrix A^{-1}. Multiplication of the matrix A^{-1} by the matrix A will produce
   a. The matrix A
   b. Another inverse matrix
   c. The correct solution to the system
   d. An identity matrix

11. Without prejudice to your previous answers, assume that the correct matrix form in item 9 was

$$\overset{A}{\begin{bmatrix} 1 & -.20 \\ -.10 & 1 \end{bmatrix}} \overset{S}{\begin{bmatrix} S_1 \\ S_2 \end{bmatrix}} = \overset{b}{\begin{bmatrix} \$\ 98,000 \\ \$117,600 \end{bmatrix}}$$

Then the correct inverse matrix A^{-1} is

a. $\begin{bmatrix} \dfrac{1}{.98} & \dfrac{.20}{.98} \\[2mm] \dfrac{.10}{.98} & \dfrac{1}{.98} \end{bmatrix}$ c. $\begin{bmatrix} \dfrac{1}{.30} & \dfrac{.20}{.30} \\[2mm] \dfrac{.10}{.30} & \dfrac{1}{.30} \end{bmatrix}$

b. $\begin{bmatrix} \dfrac{1}{.98} & \dfrac{1}{.98} \\[2mm] \dfrac{.20}{.98} & \dfrac{.10}{.98} \end{bmatrix}$ d. $\begin{bmatrix} \dfrac{1}{.98} & -\dfrac{1}{.98} \\[2mm] -\dfrac{.20}{.98} & \dfrac{.10}{.98} \end{bmatrix}$

12. The total amount of overhead allocated to department S_1 after receiving the allocation from department S_2 is
   a. $141,779; b. $124,000; c. $121,520; d. $117,600.

13. The total amount of overhead allocated to department S_2 after receiving the allocation from department S_1 is
   a. $392,000; b. $220,000; c. $130,000; d. $127,400.

14. Without prejudice to your previous answers, assume that the answer to item 12 is $100,000 and to item 13 is $150,000; then the total amount of overhead allocated to production department P_1 would be
   a. $1,508,104; b. $1,495,000; c. $1,489,800; d. $108,104.

The Dooley Co. manufactures two products, baubles and trinkets. The following are projections for the coming year:

	Baubles		Trinkets		
	Units	Amout	Units	Amount	Totals
Sales	10,000	$10,000	7,500	$10,000	$20,000
Costs:					
Fixed		$ 2,000		$ 5,600	$ 7,600
Variable		6,000		3,000	9,000
		$ 8,000		$ 8,600	$16,600
Income before taxes		$ 2,000		$ 1,400	$ 3,400

15. Assuming that the facilities are not jointly used, the breakeven output (in units) for baubles would be
a. 8,000; b. 7,000; c. 6,000; d. 5,000.
16. The breakeven volume (dollars) for trinkets would be
a. $8,000; b. $7,000; c. $6,000; d. $5,000.
17. Assuming that consumers purchase composite units of four baubles and three trinkets, the composite unit contribution margin would be
a. $4.40; b. $4.00; c. $1.33; d. $1.10.
18. If consumers purchase composite units of four baubles and three trinkets, the breakeven output for the two products would be
a. 6,909 baubles; 6,909 trinkets
b. 6,909 baubles; 5,182 trinkets
c. 5,000 baubles; 8,000 trinkets
d. 5,000 baubles; 6,000 trinkets
19. If baubles and trinkets become one-to-one complements and there is no change in the Dooley Co.'s cost function, the breakeven volume would be
a. $22,500; b. $15,750; c. $13,300; d. $10,858.
20. If a composite unit is defined as one bauble and one trinket, the composite contribution margin ratio would be
a. 7/10; b. 4/7; c. 2/5; d. 19/50.

Problem VI-9: Linear programming, matrix algebra, functions and derivatives (50-60 min.)

Select the best answer for each of the following items which relate to applications of quantitative methods to accounting. Your grade will be determined from your total of correct answers.

Items to be Answered

16. In a linear programming maximization problem for business problem solving, the coefficients of the objective function usually are
a. Marginal contributions per unit.
b. Variable costs.
c. Profit based upon allocations of overhead and all indirect costs.
d. Usage rates for scarce resources.
e. None of the above.
17. The constraints in a linear programming problem usually model
a. Profits.
b. Restrictions.
c. Dependent variables.
d. Goals.
e. None of the above.
18. If there are four activity variables and two constraints in a linear programming problem, the most products that would be included in the optimal solution would be
a. 6.
b. 4.
c. 2.
d. 0.
e. None of the above.

19. Linear programming is used most commonly to determine
    a. That mix of variables which will result in the largest quantity.
    b. The best use of scarce resources.
    c. The most advantageous prices.
    d. The fastest timing.
    e. None of the above.

20. Assume the following data for the two products produced by Wagner Company:

	Product A	Product B
Raw material requirements (units)		
X	3	4
Y	7	2
Contribution margin per unit	$10	$4

If 300 units of raw material X and 400 units of raw material Y are available, the set of relationships appropriate for maximization of revenue using linear programming would be

a. $3A + 4B \geqslant 300$
    $7A + 2B \geqslant 400$
    $10A + 4B$ MAX

b. $3A + 7B \geqslant 300$
    $4A + 2B \geqslant 400$
    $10A + 4B$ MAX

c. $3A + 7B \leqslant 300$
    $4A + 2B \leqslant 400$
    $10A + 4B$ MAX

d. $3A + 4B \leqslant 300$
    $7A + 2B \leqslant 400$
    $10A + 4B$ MAX

e. None of the above.

21. A final tableau for a linear programming profit maximization problem is shown below:

	X_1	X_2	X_3	S_1	S_2	
X_1	1	0	4	3	−7	50
X_2	0	1	−2	−6	2	60
	0	0	5	1	9	1,200

If X_1, X_2 and X_3 represent products, S_1 refers to square feet (in thousands) of warehouse capacity and S_2 refers to labor hours (in hundreds); the number of X_1 that should be produced to maximize profit would be
    a. 60.
    b. 50.
    c. 1.
    d. 0.
    e. None of the above.

22. Assuming the same facts as in item 21, the contribution to profit of an additional 200 hours of labor would be

    a. 9.
    b. 2.
    c. 1.
    d. −7.
    e. None of the above.

23. Assuming the same facts as in item 21, an additional 1,000 square feet of warehouse space would

    a. Increase X_1 by 3 units and decrease X_2 by 6 units.
    b. Decrease X_2 by 6 units and increase X_1 by 2 units.
    c. Decrease X_1 by 7 units and increase X_2 by 2 units.
    d. Increase X_1 by 3 units and decrease X_2 by 7 units.
    e. Do none of the above.

24. The following is the final tableau of a linear programming profit maximization problem:

	X_1	X_2	S_1	S_2	
X_1	1	0	−5	3	125
X_2	0	1	1	−1	70
	0	0	5	7	500

The marginal contribution to profit of 5 for each added resource unit S_1 can be maintained if the added resource units do not exceed

    a. 125.
    b. 100.
    c. 70.
    d. 25.
    e. None of the above.

25. Assume the following per unit raw material and labor requirements for the production of products A and B.

	Product A	Product B
Pounds of lead	5	7
Hours of labor	3	4

Assuming that 13,400 pounds of lead and 7,800 hours of labor are available, the production of products A and B required to use all of the available lead and labor hours is shown in the following final Gaussian tableau.

1	0	−4	7	1,000
0	1	3	−5	1,200

If the available amounts were increased to 15,000 pounds of lead and 8,800 hours of labor, the matrix operation to perform to determine the production schedule which would fully utilize these resources is

    a. $\begin{pmatrix} 5 & 7 \\ 3 & 4 \end{pmatrix} \begin{pmatrix} 15,000 \\ 8,800 \end{pmatrix}$

b. $\begin{pmatrix} 15,000 \\ 8,800 \end{pmatrix} \begin{pmatrix} -4 & 7 \\ 3 & -5 \end{pmatrix}$

c. $\begin{pmatrix} -4 & 7 \\ 3 & -5 \end{pmatrix} \begin{pmatrix} 1,000 \\ 1,200 \end{pmatrix}$

d. $\begin{pmatrix} -4 & 7 \\ 3 & -5 \end{pmatrix} \begin{pmatrix} 15,000 \\ 8,800 \end{pmatrix}$

e. None of the above.

26. The following schedule provides data for product A, which is processed through processes 1 and 2, and product B, which is processed through process 1 only:

	Product A	*Product B*
Raw material cost per gallon	$ 4	$ 9
Process 1 (500 gallon input capacity per hour):		
Processing cost per hour.........................	$60	$60
Loss in processing.............................	30%	20%
Process 2 (300 gallon input capacity per hour):		
Processing cost per hour.........................	$50	
Loss in processing.............................	10%	
Selling price per gallon.............................	$20	$40

If the objective is to maximize profit per eight-hour day, the objective function of a profit-maximizing linear programming problem would be

   a. $20A + 40B - 4A - 4B$.

   b. $20A + 40B - 4A - 4B - 60(A + B) - 50A$.

   c. $20(.63A) + 40(.80B) - 4(.63A) - 9(.8B)$

$$- 60 \left(\frac{A + B}{500} \right) - 50 \left(\frac{.7A}{300} \right).$$

   d. $20(.63A) + 40(.80B) - 4A - 9B$

$$- 60 \left(\frac{A}{500} + \frac{B}{500} \right) - 50 \left(\frac{.7A}{300} \right).$$

   e. None of the above.

27. Assuming the same facts as in item 26, a constraint of the problem would be

   a. $.63A \leqslant 2,400$.

   b. $.8A \leqslant 2,400$.

   c. $.7A + .8B \leqslant 4,000$.

   d. $.9A \leqslant 4,000$.

   e. None of the above.

28. The following graph shows engineering estimates of costs of various volumes:

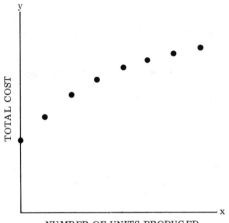

NUMBER OF UNITS PRODUCED

In developing the firm's cost function, the point at x = 0 would be
  a. An estimate of variable cost.
  b. An estimate of fixed cost.
  c. The total cost of the first unit.
  d. The slope of the curve
  e. None of the above.

29. Dancy, Inc. is going to begin producing a new chemical cleaner. It will be produced by combining alcohol, peroxide and enzyme. Each quart of the new cleaner will require ½ quart of alcohol, one quart of peroxide and 1/3 quart of enzyme. The costs per quart are 40¢ for alcohol, 60¢ for peroxide and 20¢ for for enzyme. The matrix operation to determine the cost of producing one quart of cleaner is

a. $(1/2, 1, 1/3) \begin{pmatrix} .40 \\ .60 \\ .20 \end{pmatrix}$

b. $\begin{pmatrix} 1/2 \\ 1 \\ 1/3 \end{pmatrix} \begin{pmatrix} .40 \\ .60 \\ .20 \end{pmatrix}$

c. $(1/2, 1, 1/3) \, (.40, .60, .20)$

d. $\begin{pmatrix} .40 \\ .60 \\ .20 \end{pmatrix} (1/2, 1, 1/3)$

e. None of the above.

30. A linear programming model is being used to determine for two products having different profitabilities per unit the quantities of each to produce to maximize profit over a one-year period. One component of cost is raw materials. If both products use the same amount of the same raw material,

    a. This cost may be ignored because it is the same for each product.
    b. This cost must be ignored because it is the same for each product.
    c. This cost must be included in the objective function since it varies with the independent variables in the model.
    d. More information about the products and the other components of the objective function is needed to determine whether to include this cost.
    e. None of the above.

31. The integral of a marginal cost function is a function for
    a. Average cost.
    b. Marginal cost.
    c. Total cost.
    d. Fixed cost.
    e. None of the above.

32. The following graphs represent profit relationships:

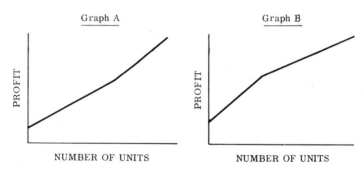

The graph(s) showing the profit relationships that can be included in one linear programming tableau by using two variables is(are)
    a. A.
    b. B.
    c. Both A and B.
    d. Neither A nor B.
    e. Not determinable from graphs.

33. A second derivative that is positive and large at a critical point indicates
    a. An important maximum.
    b. An unimportant maximum.
    c. An important minimum.
    d. An unimportant minimum.
    e. None of the above.

Problem VI-10: Least squares, learning curves, calculus, queuing theory (50-60 min.)

This problem deals with the application of various quantitative methods to accounting. Your grade will be determined from your total score of correct answers.

Statement of Facts

During your examination of the 1969 financial statements of MacKenzie Park Co., which manufactures and sells trivets, you wish to analyze selected aspects of the Company's operations.

Labor hours and production costs for the last four months of 1969, which you believe are representative for the year, were as follows:

Month	Labor Hours	Total Production Costs
September	2,500	$ 20,000
October	3,500	25,000
November	4,500	30,000
December	3,500	25,000
	14,000	$100,000

Based upon the above information and using the least-squares method of computation with the letters listed below, select the best answer for each of questions 1 through 5.

Let a = Fixed production costs per month
  b = Variable production costs per labor hour
  n = Number of months
  x = Labor hours per month
  y = Total monthly production costs
  Σ = Summation

1. The equation(s) required for applying the least-squares method of computation of fixed and variable production costs could be expressed
   a. $\Sigma xy = a\Sigma x + b\Sigma x^2$
   b. $\Sigma y = na + b\Sigma x$
   c. $y = a + bx^2$
     $\Sigma y = na + b\Sigma x$
   d. $\Sigma xy = a\Sigma x + b\Sigma x^2$
     $\Sigma y = na + b\Sigma x$
2. The cost function derived by the least-squares method
   a. Would be linear.
   b. Must be tested for minima and maxima.
   c. Would be parabolic.
   d. Would indicate maximum costs at the point of the function's point of inflection.
3. Monthly production costs could be expressed
   a. $y = ax + b$
   b. $y = a + bx$
   c. $y = b + ax$
   d. $y = \Sigma a + bx$
4. Using the least-squares method of computation, the fixed monthly production cost of trivets is approximately
   a. $10,000.
   b. $9,500.
   c. $7,500
   d. $5,000.
5. Using the least-squares method of computation, the variable production cost per labor hour is

a. $6.00
b. $5.00
c. $3.00
d. $2.00

The average number of minutes required to assemble trivets is predictable based upon an 80 percent learning curve. That is, whenever cumulative production doubles, cumulative average time per unit becomes 80 percent of what it was at the previous doubling point. The trivets are produced in lots of 300 units and 60 minutes of labor are required to assemble each first lot.

Using the concept of the learning curve and the letters listed below, select the best answer for each of questions 6 through 10.

Let MT = Marginal time for the xth lot
M = Marginal time for the first lot
X = Lots produced
b = Exponent expressing the improvement; b has the range $-1 < b \leqslant 0$

6. A normal graph, i.e., not a log or a log-log graph, of average minutes per lot of production where cumulative lots are represented by the x-axis and average minutes per lot are represented by the y-axis, would produce a
   a. Linear function sloping downward to the right.
   b. Linear function sloping upward to the right.
   c. Curvilinear function sloping upward to the right at an increasing rate.
   d. Curvilinear function sloping downward to the right at a decreasing rate.

7. A log-log graph of average minutes per lot of production, where cumulative lots are represented by the x-axis and average minutes per lot are represented by the y-axis, would produce a
   a. Linear function sloping downward to the right.
   b. Linear function sloping upward to the right.
   c. Curvilinear function sloping upward to the right at a decreasing rate.
   d. Curvilinear function sloping downward to the right at a decreasing rate.

8. The average number of minutes required per lot to complete four lots is approximately
   a. 60.0
   b. 48.5
   c. 38.4
   d. 30.7

9. Average time to produce X lots of trivets could be expressed
   a. MX^{b+1}
   b. MX^{b}
   c. MT^{b+1}
   d. MX^{b-1}

10. Assuming that b = $-.322$, the average number of minutes required to produce X lots of trivets could be expressed
    a. $40.08X^{.678}$
    b. $40.08X$
    c. $60X^{-.322}$
    d. $60X^{1.322}$

MacKenzie Park sells its trivets for $.25 per unit and during 1969 reported net sales of $500,000 and net income of $35,000. Production capacity is limited to 15,000 trivets per day and trivets are produced 300 days each year. Variable costs are $.10 per trivet.

The Company does not maintain an inspection system but has an agreement to reimburse the wholesaler $.50 for each defective unit the wholesaler finds. The wholesaler uses a method of inspection which detects all defective units. The number of defective units in each lot of 300 units is equal to the daily unit production rate divided by 200.

Letting X = daily production in units, select the best answer for each of questions 11 through 15.

11. The number of defective units per day could be expressed

a. $\dfrac{X}{60,000}$

b. $\left(\dfrac{200}{X}\right)\left(\dfrac{X}{300}\right)$

c. $\dfrac{X}{500}$

d. $\dfrac{X^2}{60,000}$

12. The equation to compute the maximum daily contribution to profit, including the reimbursement to the wholesaler for defective units, could be expressed

a. $.25X - .10X - .50\left(\dfrac{X}{60,000}\right)$

b. $.25X - .10X - .50\left(\dfrac{X^2}{60,000}\right)$

c. $.25X - .10X - \dfrac{X^2}{60,000} - \dfrac{125,000}{300}$

d. $.25X - .10X - \dfrac{X}{60,000} - 125,000$

13. The first derivative of the equation to determine the number of units to maximize daily profits could be expressed

a. $.25 - .10 - \dfrac{X}{60,000}$

b. $.10 - .25 - \dfrac{X^2}{60,000}$

c. $\dfrac{X^2}{60,000}$

d. $\dfrac{X}{(200)\,(300)}$

14. The second derivative of the equation to determine the number of units to be produced daily to maximize profits would be

a. $\dfrac{1}{(200)\ (300)}$

b. $\$.25 - \$.10 - \dfrac{1}{60,000} - \$125,000$

c. $\dfrac{\$125,000}{60,000}$

d. $-\dfrac{1}{60,000}$

15. To maximize profits, the results of the equation to determine the daily contribution margin of MacKenzie Park Co. should yield a
 a. Negative first derivative and a positive second derivative.
 b. Positive first derivative and a negative second derivative.
 c. Negative first and second derivatives.
 d. Positive first and second derivatives.

MacKenzie Park has recently experienced costly production slowdowns due to maintenance problems in its assembly department. There are four machines in the department and one repairman to service them. Experience indicates that the repairman can service ten machines in one eight-hour day if necessary, and that two machines generally require his services during any one day.

Management is considering the employment of a second repairman for the department and has asked for your advice. It has been decided that the Company will hire the second repairman if it is found that the average time a machine lies idle waiting to be serviced exceeds one hour.

Use the letters and formulas below and select the best answer for each of questions 16 through 20.

Let: A = Average number of machines needing repairs during a day.

S = Average number of machines that can be repaired in a unit of time, assuming machines are available for repair.

m = Total number of machines.

k = Number of machines operating.

p_m = Probability of all machines being down and either waiting or being serviced.

p_o = Probability of no machines being down.

$E(t)$ = Average time a machine spends waiting.

And $p_m = \left\{ 1 + \dfrac{1}{1!}\left(\dfrac{S}{A}\right)^1 + \ldots + \dfrac{1}{m!}\left(\dfrac{S}{A}\right)^m \right\}^{-1}$

$p_{m-k} = \dfrac{1}{k!}\left(\dfrac{S}{A}\right)^k p_m$

$E(t) = \dfrac{1}{S}\left(\dfrac{m}{1-p_o} - \dfrac{1+A/S}{A/S}\right)$

16. As evidenced by the formulas shown above, the quantitative technique being used here is known as
    a. Linear programming.
    b. Game theory.
    c. The transportation model.
    d. Queueing theory.

17. The probability of all machines being down and either waiting or being serviced (after rounding the denominator to the nearest whole number) is

    a. $\dfrac{1}{5}$

    b. $\dfrac{1}{13}$

    c. $\dfrac{1}{39}$

    d. $\dfrac{1}{65}$

18. The probability of no machines being down (after rounding the denominator to the nearest whole number) is

    a. $\dfrac{4}{5}$

    b. $\dfrac{125}{312}$

    c. $\dfrac{25}{78}$

    d. $\dfrac{1}{65}$

19. The average portion of a day that a machine spends waiting (after rounding) is
    a. .47
    b. .25
    c. .15
    d. .07

20. On the basis of your computations and the criterion specified by management, you should advise MacKenzie Park
    a. That the decision is a borderline one because there is a difference of only $\pm$ 2 minutes between the average time a machine spends waiting and management's one-hour limitation.
    b. Not to hire the additional repairman.
    c. To hire the additional repairman.
    d. To eliminate the existing repairman position.

Problem VI-11: Linear programming (40-50 min.)

The Fiske Corporation manufactures and sells two products, A and B. The demand for both products exceeds current production capacity. The Corporation has been unable to maintain an inventory of either product or of product

B's primary raw material which presently is in short supply. Labor also is in short supply, but the existing force can be used for production of either of the two products. Data are available on the number of units of each product sold (net of returns) and on the number of direct labor hours expended on each product. Machinery life is directly related to the number of units of each of the products manufactured.

The Company utilizes a standard costing system and has determined that the standard unit cost of these products is as shown below:

	Product A	Product B
Direct materials	$1.000	$1.953
Direct labor	.375	.781
Factory overhead	.975	1.344
	$2.350	$4.078

Overhead shown on the standard cost sheets is obtained from the flexible budget on the accompanying table. This budget is based upon an assumption that 8,000 units of product A and 6,400 units of product B are being produced.

Outside consultants have been engaged to determine an optimal product mix, and they currently are developing a linear programming model to determine how many units of each product to manufacture in order to maximize profit.

The following pro forma statement (in thousands of dollars) has been prepared for the month of April 1972:

	Product A	Product B
Sales:		
A-8,000 units	$30.5	
B-6,400 units		$40.8
Gross sales	30.5	40.8
Less: Returns and allowances	.3	1.0
Discounts	.5	.8
Net sales	29.7	39.0
Cost of sales:		
Direct materials	8.0	12.5
Direct labor	3.0	5.0
Factory overhead	7.8	8.6
Total	18.8	26.1
Gross margin	10.9	12.9
Operating expense:		
General and administrative	2.9	4.6
Selling	4.3	6.1
Total	7.2	10.7
Income from operations	3.7	2.2
Other:		
Interest revenue	.8	.5
Interest expense	(1.0)	(.8)
Total	(.2)	(.3)
Income before taxes	3.5	1.9
Income taxes	1.0	.6
Net income	$ 2.5	$ 1.3

Fiske Corporation
OVERHEAD BUDGET
For April 1972

	Fixed	Variable*	Total	Allocation to Product A	Allocation to Product B	Basis for Allocation to Product
Factory overhead:						
Indirect labor	$ 500		$ 500	$ 200	$ 300	Direct labor hours
Depreciation:						
Machinery	5,000		5,000	2,000	3,000	Direct labor hours
Building	7,200		7,200	4,000	3,200	Estimated number of units sold
Insurance—property and plant	800		800	300	500	Per unit sales price
Payroll taxes	95	$ 1,505	1,600	600	1,000	Per unit sales price
Utilities	500		500	200	300	Direct labor hours
Supplies	800		800	500	300	Traced to product
Total	14,895	1,505	16,400	7,800	8,600	
General and administrative:						
Product A	429	2,500	2,929	2,929		
Product B	571	4,000	4,571		4,571	
Total	1,000	6,500	7,500	2,929	4,571	
Selling:						
Commissions		8,820	8,820	2,970	5,850	
Advertising	1,000		1,000	1,000		
Bad debts	500		500	300	200	
Total	1,500	8,820	10,320	4,270	6,050	
Total overhead	$17,395	$16,825	$34,220	$14,999	$19,221	

*Based upon a projected production and sales volume of 8,000 units of product A and 6,400 units of product B.

For each of the numbered items below select the lettered answer that best indicates in what way the preceding financial data should be used in the determination of the optimal product mix. Assume that variable revenues and expenses are completely variable.

Your grade will be determined from your total of correct answers.

Answer Choices

a. This aggregate dollar amount for the month divided by the aggregate number of units sold during the month should be used.
b. This aggregate dollar amount should be used.
c. This cost or revenue item should not be used.
d. This cost or revenue item should be included but amounts inappropriate for financial accounting purposes should be used.
e. The information given is insufficient to determine whether or not the item should be used.

Items to be Answered

19. Sales.
20. Sales returns and allowances.
21. Sales discounts.
22. Direct materials.
23. Direct labor.
24. Standard overhead per unit.
25. Indirect labor.
26. Depreciation—machinery.
27. Depreciation—building.
28. Insurance.
29. Variable payroll taxes.
30. Utilities.
31. Supplies.
32. General and administrative expenses—variable.
33. General and administrative expenses—fixed.
34. Commissions.
35. Advertising.
36. Bad debts.
37. Interest income.
38. Interest expense.
39. Income tax.

(*Authors' note:* Many of the answers are difficult to defend because of ambiguity regarding what is "marginal" or "incremental" cost.)

SPECIFIC APPROACH

Problem VI-1

1. In requirement (a), for each sales price compute the expected monetary sales by weighting each unit sales level by the assigned probability and multiplying by the selling price. For example, expected monetary sales at the $4 price would be .50(40,000) ($4) + .50(50,000) ($4) = $180,000.

2. In requirement (b), apply the discount factor to each cash flow and then sum to obtain the total present value for each person. Then deduct the financing requested. The result will be the net present value of each investment.

Problem VI-2

1. See the section in the General Approach on probabilities and expected values.

2. When you compute the probable net income in requirement (b), ignore any income tax deferrals. Parts (c) and (d) could be combined in one schedule. Select the discount factors carefully.

Problem VI-3

The General Approach discusses probabilities, payoff tables, and expected values (average monthly marginal income in this problem).

In part (b) 2, the computation should be based on ordering the primary ingredient and relying on the competitor if the supplier strikes. Is the substitute ingredient irrelevant in this part? In part (b) 3?

Problem VI-4

1. Requirement (a) is so simple that you may think that you are overlooking something.

2. In requirement (b), the total probabilities of the five alternatives must sum to 1.00. The computation of the probability of alternative (1) is straightforward. The other computations are a bit tricky. For example, if fog persists 20 times for four consecutive days, then those 20 times include the 10 times that fog will persist for a fifth day. Similarly, if fog persists 40 times for three consecutive days, then those times include the times that fog will persist for a fourth day or a fifth day.

3. Requirement (c) has probabilities that are not dependent on your answers to (b). The probable or expected marginal income would be the weighted average computed by multiplying the probability of each of the three possible events by the net additional contribution. The total contribution is the number of days by rail multiplied by the daily marginal contribution. The $3,100 fixed cost is then deducted to obtain the net additional contribution for each event.

Problem VI-5

Requirements (a), (c), and (d) are not difficult. Requirement (b) can be solved in one of two ways, by trial and error or by the so-called "transportation method." The latter is discussed in any basic textbook on quantitative methods or linear programming.

Problem VI-6

1. This is the first auditing problem on statistical sampling that is included in a Practice examination instead of an Auditing examination. References include *An Auditor's Approach to Statistical Sampling*, Volumes 2 and 4, published by the AICPA.

2. All answers in requirement (a) are either 300 or some multiple of 300. For example, characteristic (2) would be 80% of 300.

3. Table 1 is useful for requirement b(1) through characteristic (6). Table 2 is useful for characteristics (6) and (7).

4. Table 3 is useful for requirement b(2) through characteristic (6). The answers for characteristics (7) and (8) have to be approximated via interpolation in Table 3.

Problem VI-7 through VI-11

It is infeasible to offer specific approaches for these objective questions; however, the answers in Volume 2 include explanatory material.

Investments and Branch Accounting

GENERAL APPROACH

Topic VII includes problems on investments in stocks of uncontrolled companies and investments in unconsolidated subsidiaries. CPA problems involving bonds have usually emphasized bonds as liabilities rather than as investments. Discussion of bonds payable will be found in Topic IX. Also see Topic XI for a discussion of how to account for investments in entities subject to consolidation.

Investments in General

Balance Sheet Classification

Investments are classified according to *purpose.* An investment is carried as a current asset if it is a temporary holding of otherwise idle cash; it is part of a separate "investments" classification if it is long-term in nature. The "investments" classification usually appears on the balance sheet between current and fixed assets.

Carrying Value

Bonds held as long-term investments are carried at acquisition cost adjusted for amortization of premiums or discounts. (The process of amortization of discounts on investments sometimes is referred to more accurately as "accumulation" of discounts.) Premiums or discounts on bonds are rarely accounted for in separate ledger accounts. Instead, amortization is directly entered in the Investment in Bonds account.

Stocks held as temporary investments are generally carried at acquisition cost. Stocks held as long-term investments are generally accounted for under the equity method if the investment represents 20% or more of the voting stock; if less than 20%, the investment is generally carried at cost.

Lower of Cost or Market

Accountants generally favor applying the lower-of-cost-or-market rule to the total portfolio of temporary investments. Some authors favor writing down to market whenever market prices are below cost at a given balance sheet date. However, APBAP Vol. 1, Sect. 1027.09, S-5B grants more latitude because a loss must be recorded only if the decline is "not due to a temporary condition." Moreover, APB *Opinion No. 18* (Paragraph 19h) states that a decline in the quoted market price below the carrying amount is not necessarily indicative of a loss in value that is other than temporary. In short, professional judgment is still the dominant force in deciding whether a loss is "not due to a temporary condition." A valuation account is often used when write-downs are made; this preserves the record of cost or cost adjusted for amortization.

The most informative presentation of either temporary or long-term investments would reveal both carrying amounts and market values. The latter may appear parenthetically or in footnote form.

Exchange and Conversions

Stocks and bonds may be acquired by means other than with cash, for example purchases made with other assets or with different types of securities (with other investments or by issuance of the acquiring company's own stocks or bonds). Such exchanges raise the question of (a) the proper amount to be debited for the newly acquired securities and (b) the recognition of gain or loss on the exchange.

In exchanges, the proper amount to be debited for acquisition is the "fair value" of either the outgoing or incoming item(s), whichever is more objectively determinable. If "fair values" are unavailable or indeterminate, the cost or book value of the item parted with may be regarded as the cost of acquisition. This procedure results in recognition of gain or loss amounting to the difference between the cost of the new securities and the carrying amount of the item(s) exchanged.

When securities are exchanged pursuant to a conversion privilege, no gain or loss is recognized for tax purposes. Opinion is unsettled regarding whether gain or loss should be recognized for financial accounting purposes. Market quotations, when available, are an objective basis for computing gain or loss on a conversion; however, many accountants maintain that there is no actual realization of gain or loss—that a mere cost transfer has taken place. The form of the investment has been changed in accordance with a "deferred common stock" privilege which was obtained upon the purchase of the old asset. In this sense, all investments in convertible securities are made with the intention and expectation of their being eventually transformed into common stock. Therefore, the conversion itself is a transaction of form rather than substance; no realization test has been met.

Sales

When holdings of the same security consist of purchases made at different unit prices, what cost should be released if a portion of the holdings are sold? Conventional methods of determining the cost to be assigned to securities sold include: specific identification; first in, first out; and average cost. Average costs are not recognized for income tax purposes.

Investments in Bonds

EXAMPLE 1

Prepare journal entries on scratch paper for the transactions below. Assume straight-line amortization of premiums or discounts. Compare your entries with the solution and comments which follow:

5/1/x1	Purchased for cash a 6%, $1,000 bond (interest dates, January 1 and July 1, maturing in 140 months) at 93 and accrued interest.
7/1/x1	Interest is collected
12/31/x1	Prepare appropriate entries for interest.
11/1/x5	Sold bond at 98 and accrued interest.

Solution and Comments

```
5/1/x1    Investment in bond .................................   930
          Accrued interest receivable (or interest income) ...........    20
              Cash ..........................................                    950
              Note that accrued interest on bond(s) at date of purchase
              (or sale) should be isolated and accounted for separately.
7/1/x1    Cash ........................................           30
              Accrued interest receivable (or interest income) .........           20
              Interest income ...................................                  10
              To record collection of interest.
12/31/x1  Accrued interest receivable ...........................   30
          Investment in bond .................................    4
              Interest income ...................................        34
              Discounts (and premiums) are considered to be
              adjustments of nominal interest. The amortization entry
              is usually made annually, although monthly or semi-
              annual adjustments could be made. The total discount of
              $70 must be spread over 140 months (50¢ per month)
              so that the investment will accumulate to par at maturity
              date. In this entry, 8 months' discount has been accu-
              mulated.
11/1/x5   Investment in bond ................................    5
              Interest income ..................................         5
              To accumulate discount for 19x5 up to date of sale.
          Cash .........................................        1,000
              Investment in bond (cost plus discount accumulation) ......        957
              Interest income (4 months) ..........................              20
              Gain on sale of bond ($980 − $957) ...................             23
              To record sale. Note that discount accumulation must be
              brought up to date before gain is computed.
```

Difficulties in accounting for investments in bonds usually center around failure:

(a) to record cost properly,

(b) to amortize premiums or discounts,

(c) to accrue interest,

(d) upon sale, to adjust the investment account for amortization of the current period prior to calculating gain or loss on disposition.

Premiums and discounts should really be amortized by using compound interest methods rather than straight-line methods. In this way, the accounting would be in better accordance with how bonds are actually valued and how bond yields are actually computed in the bond markets. However, hand calculations of these amortization schedules are cumbersome, so this is the major reason why the simpler straight-line method is seen so widely in textbooks. See any intermediate text for an explanation of the compound interest method of amortization.

Investments in Stocks

EXAMPLE 2

What adjustments should be made to the following accounts? Answer the question on scratch paper before referring to the solution and comments which follow.

Investment in Baker Common Stock ($20 par)

2/1/x7	Cost of 50 shares	7,500	9/10/x7	Sales of 120 rights	
4/1/x7	Receipt of 10 shares as			@ $3.00	360
	a stock dividend ...	500	10/1/x7	Sale of 60 shares	2,700
7/1/x7	Receipt of 60 shares			To balance	6,680
	upon a 2-for-1 split.	1,500			
9/1/x7	Receipt of 120 rights				
	(see note)	240			
12/31/x7	Balance............	6,680			

Income Summary

			4/1/x7	Stock dividend........	500
			7/1/x7	Stock split	1,500
			9/1/x7	Stock rights	240
	To balance	2,330	12/1/x7	Cash dividend.........	90
			12/31/x7	Balance	2,330

NOTE: Each right entitled the holder to subscribe for ¼ share at $40 per share. On the date of issuance of rights, market quotations were: shares, ex-rights, $48; rights, $2.

Solution and Comments

The correcting journal entry would be:

Income Summary	3,080	
Investment in Baker common stock...............		3,080
To correct accounts per accompanying schedule.		

Schedule of Corrections

		Investment in Baker Stock		Investment in Rights				
	Description	#Shares	Cost	#Rights	Cost	Income Summary		
2/1/x7	Cost	50	$7,500					
4/1/x7	Stock dividend . . .	10	. . .					
7/1/x7	Stock split	60	. . .					
9/1/x7	Stock rights*		(300)	120	$300			
9/10/x7	Sale of rights @ $3			(120)	(300)	Gain	$ 60	Cr.
10/1/x7	Sale of 60 shares @ $45 or $2,700	(60)	(3,600)			Loss	(900)	Dr.
12/1/x7	Cash dividend					Dividend	90	Cr.
12/31/x7	Correct balances	60	$3,600	. . .	. . .		$ 750	Dr.
12/31/x7	Per books	60	6,680	. . .	. . .		2,330	Cr.
	Corrections	. .	$3,080 Cr.	. . .	. . .		$3,080	Dr.

*Cost of share ($7,500 ÷ 120) is $62.50, which must be apportioned between rights and shares. Market value on date of issuance of rights: right, $2; share, $48. Apportionment: 2/50 x $62.50 = $2.50 to rights, 48/50 x $62.50 = $60.00 to shares.

From the investor's standpoint, ordinary stock dividends and stock splits are treated exactly alike. Only the number of shares is adjusted. Total original cost is spread over the new number of shares, resulting in less cost per share but the same total cost.

Note that stock dividends, stock splits, or stock rights do not of themselves result in any income recognition by the investor. Corporate assets have not been distributed. The shareholder's total equity has not changed.

When stock rights are received, the total investment may be clearly divided between rights and shares. This apportionment of *cost* is made as shown above on the basis of the relative market value of the stock ex-rights and the rights at date of issuance.

Right, $2.50

Original cost, $62.50

Share, $60.00

Apportionment may be made in the memorandum form or by formal apportionment. If rights are exercised, their cost is added to the cost of new shares purchased. If rights are sold, the gain or loss is the difference between sales proceeds and cost. If rights are allowed to expire, the cost is written off as a loss.

Difficulties in accounting for investments in stocks usually involve failure to (a) treat stock dividends, stock rights, and stock splits properly and (b) distinguish between separate lots of stock acquired or sold.

The Equity Method

APB *Opinion No. 18,* which applies to fiscal periods beginning after December 31, 1971, will probably get attention in the CPA examination. The Opinion has extended the equity method as a replacement for the cost method.

The equity method requires an investor to record his initial investment at cost; however, the carrying amount is then adjusted to recognize the investor's share of the earnings of the investee after the date of acquisition. Dividends received reduce the carrying amount of the investment. See the General Approach to Topic XI for additional discussion.

Opinion No. 18 requires that the equity method be used for (a) investments in the common stock of all unconsolidated domestic and foreign subsidiaries (with some rare exceptions regarding foreign exchange restrictions), (b) corporate joint ventures, and (c) investments in voting stock that give the investor the ability to exercise significant influence over operating and financial policies of an investee even though the investor holds 50% or less of the voting stock. Ability to exercise the latter influence may be indicated in several ways, including representation on the board of directors, participation in policy making, significant intercompany transactions, interchange of management, or technology dependence.

To achieve some uniformity in application, the APB concluded that an investment of 20% or more in the voting stock of an investee is a presumption that the investor can exercise significant influence. Detailed procedures for applying the equity method are enumerated in APBAP Vol. 1 Sect. 5131.19. Among them are requirements for the elimination of intercompany profits and for the amortization of goodwill.

Branch Accounting

An investment by a home office in a branch factory, warehouse, or sales office is usually accounted for by using reciprocal accounts. On home office books, the account is akin to an investment account and is often called Branch Office or Branch Office Current Account. Its reciprocal on the branch office books is akin to an equity account and is often called Home Office or Home Office Current Account. Theoretically, these accounts should have identical balances. Practically, these balances rarely agree because of a variety of lags or errors in the recording process.

Each reciprocal account is usually analyzed separately to obtain a reconciling balance as of a cutoff date. Common causes of discrepancies are in-transit cash and inventories. Suppose that December 31 is the cutoff date. For each account this means adjusting to be certain that all December shipments and cash transfers are recorded; furthermore, it means adjusting to exclude transactions which qualify as January entries.

Where shipments to a branch office are recorded at some amount higher than cost, it is necessary to eliminate the overstatement of the pertinent accounts for sales, purchases, and inventories.

CPA PROBLEMS

Problem VII-1: General coverage of investments (40-50 min.)

In connection with your examination of the financial statements of the Acme Investing Company for the year ended September 30, 1971 you have been furnished analyses of the Investments and Investment Revenue accounts. Additional information concerning these two accounts is given below:

1. Syntechnique Corporation common stock was split two for one on April 15, 1971. The quarterly dividend rate was $1.25 per share prior to the split and $.75 per share after the split. Quarterly dividends during 1970 and 1971 were paid on January 15, April 15, July 15 and October 15 to stockholders of record on the 26th of the month preceding payment. Acme prefers to accrue dividends receivable at the date of record. Syntechnique Corporation is listed on a regional stock exchange. The last exchange price for the stock on September 30, 1971 was $40 per share. The investment in Syntechnique was made originally for the purpose of seeking control. This objective now has been abandoned, and the Company plans to sell its remaining shares during the coming year.

2. Good Systems common stock was issued originally at a discount. On May 21, 1971 Acme paid an $8,200 assessment that had been levied against Good Systems stockholders.

3. The dividend notice from Sure-Hit Mines, Inc. indicated that 40% of the June 15 cash distribution represented costs recovered from assets subject to depletion.

4. On August 1, 1971 Acme acquired $600,000 of Cass County 7% revenue bonds for $588,000 including accrued interest. The bonds mature April 1, 1980 and interest is payable semiannually on April 1 and October 1. The bonds had been issued originally at face value on April 1, 1960. The Company prefers to amortize the bond discount using the straight-line method.

5. The Good Systems and Sure-Hit Mines common stock and the Cass County 7% revenue bonds are traded over-the-counter. Their estimated market values at September 30, 1971 are:

Good Systems	$ 51,000
Sure-Hit Mines	41,000
Cass County Bonds	560,000
	$652,000

The investment in Good Systems, a supplier, was made as an accommodation. Sure-Hit Mines is expected to be liquidated over the next five years with a full recovery of cost. Acme plans to hold the Cass County bonds to maturity.

Acme Investing Company
ANALYSES OF INVESTMENTS AND INVESTMENT REVENUE
For The Year Ended September 30, 1971

Date	Description	Balance Oct. 1, 1970	Recorded Transactions Debit	Recorded Transactions Credit	Balances, Sept. 30, 1971 Investments Debit	Balances, Sept. 30, 1971 Investment Revenue Credit	Adjusting and Reclassifying Entries Debit	Adjusting and Reclassifying Entries Credit	Adjusted Balances, Sept. 30, 1971 Investments Debit	Adjusted Balances, Sept. 30, 1971 Investment Revenue Credit
	Investments Account									
Oct. 1, 1970	Syntechnique—2,000 shares, at cost	$ 120,000								
Jan. 1, 1971	Syntechnique—purchased 2,000 shares.		$ 160,000							
July 3, 1971	Syntechnique—sold 2,000 shares			$ 100,000	$ 180,000					
Oct. 1, 1970	Good Systems—10,000 shares, at cost	38,000			38,000					
Oct. 1, 1970	Sure-Hit Mines—1,000 shares, at cost	21,500			21,500					
Aug. 1, 1971	Purchase of 7% Cass County bonds		588,000		588,000					
Oct. 1, 1970	Raiborn Corp., at equity	607,000	15,000		622,000					
Oct. 1, 1970	Mercan Ltd.—400 shares, at cost	900,000								
Oct. 1, 1970	Mercan Ltd.—serial loan maturing 1988	750,000		50,000	1,600,000					
Oct. 1, 1970	Undeveloped real estate, at cost	6,000,000								
Apr. 15, 1971	Proceeds from sale of one-half of undeveloped real estate			4,700,000	1,300,000					
		$8,436,500	$ 763,000	$4,850,000	$4,349,500					

Acme Investing Company
ANALYSES OF INVESTMENTS AND
INVESTMENT REVENUE
For The Year Ended September 30, 1971 (cont'd)

| Date | Investment Revenue Account | Recorded Transactions | | Investment Revenue |
		Debit	Credit	Credit
	Various Syntechnique cash dividends.....		$ 13,500	$13,500
May 21, 1971	Good Systems—stock assessment........	$ 8,200		(8,200)
June 15, 1971	Sure-Hit Mines—cash distribution........		15,500	15,500
July 15, 1971	Raiborn Corp.—cash dividend		20,000	20,000
Oct. 1, 1970	Mercan Ltd.—interest accrual reversing entry............	9,375		(9,375)
Aug. 1, 1971	Mercan Ltd.—interest · received.........		56,250	56,250
		$ 17,575	$ 105,250	$87,615

6. Acme owns 70% of the outstanding common stock of Raiborn Corporation, a domestic subsidiary. The recorded balance for the investment in Raiborn represents equity in underlying net assets at October 1, 1970 plus $15,000 advanced to Raiborn in September 1971 on a three-month loan. Raiborn's net income for the year ended September 30, 1971 was $60,000.

7. Acme owns 30% of the outstanding common stock of Mercan Ltd., a foreign corporation. In addition, Acme made a $1,000,000, 7½% serial loan to Mercan which is being repaid in equal annual installments over 20 years. Payment must be made in U.S. dollars. The sixth installment and the annual interest were received on August 1, 1971.

Mercan's host country devalued its currency in 1971. Acme's 30% share of the loss on exchange was $35,000.

8. Acme uses the FIFO flow assumption to determine the cost of security sales.

9. The Investments account is classified as a long-term asset in the balance sheet.

Required:

Complete the worksheet on the accompanying page. Supporting computations should be in good form. Entries should be numbered. Formal adjusting and reclassifying entries are not required.

Problem VII-2 Investments; corrections of errors (40-50 min.)

Smitters Corp. has various long-term investments and maintains its books on the accrual basis. The books for the year ended December 31, 1965 have not been closed. An analysis of the Investment account for the year follows:

Smitters Corp.
ANALYSIS OF INVESTMENT ACCOUNT
Year Ended December 31, 1965

			Account Per Books	
1965	*Transactions*	*Fol.*	*Debit*	*Credit*
Jan. 1	5,000 shares Backand Oil Co.		$ 5,000	
	1,000 shares General Corp.		33,500	
	50 shares, 6% Pfd. Grey Steel		6,000	
	$10,000 4% bonds, Martin Co.		10,225	
Feb. 10	Purchased 5,000 shares, Wash Motors	CD	15,000	
Mar. 1	Cash dividend, Grey Steel	CR		$ 300
April 1	Interest, Martin Co. bonds	CR		200
May 15	Sold 800 rights, General Corp.	CR		1,200
May 16	Exercised 200 rights, General Corp. to purchase 50 shares, General Corp.	CD	2,250	
Aug. 5	Sold 200 shares, Wash Motors	CR		2,500
Sept. 18	Sold 100 shares, General Corp.	CR		3,350
Oct. 1	Interest, Martin Co. bonds	CR		200
			$71,975	$7,750

AUTHORS' NOTE: A work sheet was furnished containing the above analysis of transactions recorded in the Investment account during 1965. The analysis occupied the left half of the work sheet.

Your work papers for the year ended December 31, 1964 show the following securities in the Investment account:

Date of Acquisiton	Number of Shares or Face Value of Bonds	Type of Security	Name of Issuer	Amount
Jan. 2, 1957	5,000	Common stock, no par value	Backand Oil Co.	$ 5,000
April 1, 1958	1,000	Common stock, $100 par value	General Corp.	33,500
Nov. 15, 1958	50	6% preferred stock par value $100	Grey Steel	6,000
Oct. 1,1963	$10,000	4% bonds	Martin Co.	10,225
				$54,725

After inquiry the following additional data were obtained:

1. The General Corp. on May 12 issued warrants representing the right to purchase, at $45 per share, one share for every four shares held. On May 12 the market value of the stock rights-on was $50 and ex-rights was $49. Smitters Corp. sold 800 rights on May 15 when the market price of the stock was $51. On May 16, 200 rights were exercised.

2. On June 30 Wash Motors declared a reverse stock split of 1 for 5. One share of new $.50 par value common was exchanged for 5 shares of old $.10 par value common.

3. Smitters Corp. acquired the Martin Co. bonds, which are due September 30, 1968, for $10,300. Interest is payable April 1 and October 1.

4. The sale of 100 shares of General Corp. stock was part of the 1,000 shares purchased on April 1, 1958. The stock was sold for $65 per share.

5. The government of Backand in early 1965 confiscated the assets of the Backand Oil Co. and nationalized the Company. Despite the protest of the United States government, the Backand government has refused to recognize any claims of the stockholders or management of the Backand Oil Co.

Required:

Prepare a work sheet showing the adjustments to arrive at the correct balance at December 31, 1965 in the Investment account. The work sheet should include the names of other accounts affected by the adjustments or reclassifications. (Formal journal entries are not required. Supporting computations should be in good form.)

Problem VII-3: Equity method of investments (40-50 min.)

Sterling, Inc., a domestic corporation having a fiscal year ending June 30, has purchased common stock in several other domestic corporations. As of June 30, 1972, the balance in Sterling's Investments account was $870,600, the total cost

of stock purchased less the cost of stock sold. Sterling wishes to restate the Investments account to reflect the provisions of APB Opinion No. 18, "The Equity Method of Accounting for Investments in Common Stock."
Data concerning the investments follow:

		Turner, Inc.	*Grotex, Inc.*	*Scott, Inc.*
Shares of common stock outstanding...............		3,000	32,000	100,000
Shares purchased by Sterling	(a)	300	8,000	30,000
	(b)	810		
Date of purchase	(a)	July 1, 1969	June 30, 1970	June 30, 1971
	(b)	July 1, 1971		
Cost of shares purchased	(a)	$ 49,400	$ 46,000	$ 670,000
	(b)	$ 142,000		
Balance sheet at date indicated:				

Assets	*July 1, 1971*	*June 30, 1970*	*June 30, 1971*
Current assets................	$ 362,000	$ 39,600	$ 994,500
Fixed assets, net of depreciation .	1,638,000	716,400	3,300,000
Patent, net of amortization			148,500
	$2,000,000	$756,000	$4.443,000

Liabilities and Capital	*July 1, 1971*	*June 30, 1970*	*June 30, 1971*
Liabilities..................	$1,500,000	$572,000	$2,494,500
Common stock...............	260,000	80,000	1,400,000
Retained earnings.............	240,000	104,000	548,500
	$2,000,000	$756,000	$4,443,000

	Turner	*Grotex*	*Scott*
Changes in common stock since July 1, 1969	None	None	None
Average remaining life of fixed assets at date of balance sheet (above)	12 years	9 years	22 years
Analysis of retained earnings:			
Balance, July 1, 1969	$234,000		
Net income, July 1, 1969 to June 30, 1970	53,400		
Dividend paid—April 1, 1970	(51,000)		
Balance, June 30, 1970	236,400	$104,000	
Net income (loss), July 1, 1970 to June 30, 1971........	55,600	(2,000)	
Dividend paid—April 1, 1971 .	(52,000)		
Balance, June 30, 1971	240,000	102,000	$548,500
Net income, July 1, 1971 to June 30, 1972........	25,000	18,000	330,000
Dividends paid:			
December 28, 1971......			(150,000)
June 1, 1972..........		(5,600)	
Balance, June 30, 1972	$265,000	$114,400	$728,500

Sterling's first purchase of Turner's stock was made because of the high rate of return expected on the investment. All later purchases of stock have been made to gain substantial influence over the operations of the various companies.

In December 1971, changing market conditions caused Sterling to reevaluate its relation to Grotex. On December 31, 1971, Sterling sold 6,400 shares of Grotex for $54,400.

For Turner and Grotex, the fair values of the net assets did not differ materially from the book values as shown in the above balance sheets. For Scott, fair values exceeded book values only with respect to the patent which had a fair value of $300,000 and a remaining life of 15 years as of June 30, 1971.

At June 30, 1972, Sterling's inventory included $48,600 of items purchased from Scott during May and June at a 20% markup over Scott's cost.

Required:

Prepare a workpaper to restate Sterling's Investments account as of June 30, 1972, and its investment income by year for the three years then ended. Transactions should be listed in chronological order and supporting computations should be in good form. *Ignore income taxes.* Amortization of goodwill, if any, is to be over a forty-year period. Use the following columnar headings for your workpaper:

| | | Investments | | | Investment Income, Year Ended June 30 | | | Other Accounts | |
		Turner	Grotex	Scott	1970	1971	1972	Amount	Name
Date	Description	Dr. (Cr.)	Dr. (Cr.)	Dr. (Cr.)	Cr. (Dr.)	Cr. (Dr.)	Cr. (Dr.)	Dr. (Cr.)	

Problem VII-4: Worksheet, branch, consignments (40-50 min.)

You are examining the financial statements of Conrad Sales Company for the year ended December 31, 1967. Conrad has not had an audit before. Sales are made from Conrad's Home Office, a newly opened Branch Office and through consignees. Shipments to consignees are recorded at Conrad's cost by charging a consignment account and crediting the Home Office Inventory account. Conrad bears the cost of shipping to consignees.

A general ledger trial balance as of December 31, 1967 appears on page 220. The following information was also available:

1. An inventory taken at the Home Office on December 31, 1967 had a cost of $196,200 and a fair market value of $198,300. A perpetual inventory system is maintained.

2. Merchandise costing $149,000 was consigned to Nelson on September 1, 1967 and was shipped to Nelson directly from the supplier's factory. On December 31, 1967 Nelson reported sales totaling $50,000 since September 1 and claimed $10,000 for his commission of 20 per cent of sales. Nelson also claimed reimbursement of $5,000 for freight paid September 1 and $500 for advertising expense to be borne by Conrad. Nelson applied the $34,500 balance due to Conrad against $40,000 owed by Conrad for merchandise purchased from Nelson (the $40,000 was included in Conrad's accounts payable at December 31, 1967). Nelson's inventory of consigned merchandise amounted to $119,200 at original cost as determined by Conrad at December 31, 1967.

Conrad Sales Company
GENERAL LEDGER TRIAL BALANCE
Year Ended December 31, 1967

Accounts	General Ledger Trial Balance	
	Debit	Credit
Cash	$ 65,400	
Accounts receivable–home office	311,500	
Allowance for bad debts		$ 9,000
Merchandise inventory–home office	200,600	
Merchandise inventory–branch	100,000	
Consignment to Nelson	149,000	
Investments	165,000	
Prepaid incentive bonus	20,000	
Prepaid expenses	32,100	
Other assets	164,000	
Accounts payable		205,600
Accrued incentive bonus		35,000
Capital stock, $1 par value		500,000
Retained earnings at beginning of year		366,600
Sales–home office		1,022,500
Sales–consignment		21,300
Cost of sales–home office	738,600	
Cost of sales–consignment	8,200	
Selling expenses–home office	92,400	
Selling expenses–branch	9,600	
Selling expenses–consignment	5,600	
General and administrative expenses–home office	91,000	
General and administrative expenses–branch	4,100	
General and administrative expenses–consignment	2,900	
Totals	$2,160,000	$2,160,000

3. On November 10, 1967 Conrad signed an agreement with Towers who agreed to become a consignee on January 31, 1968. In November 1967 Conrad prepaid expenses of $1,200 related to the Towers agreement and charged General and Administrative Expenses–Consignment for the disbursement.

4. The Investments account balance at December 31, 1967 in the general ledger was composed of the following:

Cost of 40,000 shares of Conrad treasury stock purchased in 1965	68,000
Marketable securities at cost (market value December 31, 1967, $82,000)	80,000
Cost of exclusive distribution franchises with unlimited lives	17,000
Total	$165,000

5. Conrad paid $20,000 for incentive bonus on December 22, 1967 before the bonus was due. The entire bonus of $35,000 was accrued at December 31, 1967 and the balance of $15,000 was paid on January 15, 1968.

6. Other Assets included $10,000 of market survey costs for a sales project undertaken and abandoned in 1967, $1,000 of deposits held by utility companies and $153,000 of net fixed assets. Examination of fixed asset records revealed that Conrad deducted the correct amount of depreciation each year from the recorded cost of fixed assets. The $153,000 was comprised of original

costs of $53,000 for land, $100,000 for a building and $28,000 for furniture and equipment less accumulated depreciation of $22,000 on the building and $6,000 on the furniture and equipment.

7. On September 15, 1967 Conrad established a Branch Office and shipped to it merchandise having a retail value of $140,000 (140 per cent of Conrad's cost). At December 31, 1967 the Branch Office inventory was $56,000 priced at retail value. The Branch Office reported 1967 sales of $84,000, of which $50,400 had been collected by the branch and represented cash in transit to Conrad at December 31 and $33,600 was receivable from branch customers. The Branch Office considered all its accounts collectible at December 31, 1967. Branch Office administrative expenses totaling $4,100 were paid by Conrad in 1967 and charged to the General and Administrative Expenses—Branch account.

8. The Home Office Accounts Receivable consisted of the following:

Various small 1966 balances in dispute	$ 2,000
Account balances of bankrupt customers from whom no additional amounts will be collected	9,500
Remaining accounts for which it is estimated 3 per cent will prove uncollectable	300,000
Total	$311,500

Bad Debts Expense of $4,000 was included in the General and Administrative Expenses-Home Office account at December 31, 1967.

Required:

Prepare a worksheet to adjust the accounts of Conrad Sales Company for the year ended December 31, 1967. Formal adjusting journal entries and financial statements are not required. Supporting computations should be in good form. Ignore income taxes.

SPECIFIC APPROACH

Problem VII-1

1. Provide ample space for additional accounts that you will need for adjustments and reclassifications.

2. Although an argument could be made on behalf of reclassifying some or a portion of the investment in Sure-Hit Mines as a current asset, this solution does not do so because there is no definite plan to sell the stock within the ensuing year.

3. Be sure to account for accrued interest correctly throughout the solution.

Problem VII-2

Your work sheet should reproduce the given Analysis of Investment Account at the left: to the right, provide columns as follows:

		Adjustments			
Investment Account		*Other Accounts*			*Adjusted Investment Account*
Debit	*Credit*	*Account*	*Debit*	*Credit*	*Balance*

Problem VII-3

APBAP Vol. 1, Sect. 5131.19 provides guidance regarding the application of the equity method.

1. Either reconstruct the transactions (a) for all investments simultaneously and chronologically or (b) for Grotex first, because it is the easiest investment to analyze. Be sure not to overlook any data.

2. The carrying amount for 300 shares of Turner acquired on July 1, 1969 must be adjusted on July 1, 1971 from the cost basis to the equity basis. This adjustment will affect investment income for 1970 and 1971.

3. Goodwill must be amortized for Turner and Scott. Goodwill is often the excess of cost over the underlying equity in the net assets of the investee. However, this difference may also be explained by differences between fair values and book values of investee assets. For example, the Scott investment requires amortizations related to patents and goodwill.

4. Sterling should eliminate 30% of intercompany profit.

Problem VII-4

Although the entries are voluminous, most of them are routine adjustments. See the General Approach for comments about typical adjustments and eliminations needed in branch accounting.

1. Freight for placing goods on consignment is usually an addition to the consignment out account, which is fundamentally an inventory account. In contrast, advertising is an expense.

2. Under A.P.B. *Opinion No. 17,* the franchises should be subject to amortization. However, there is no basis for amortization, so none is used here because we are unsure of the original cost. Alternatively, one-fortieth of $17,000 might be charged to income, because 40 years is the maximum useful life permitted for all intangible assets even though their lives are unlimited.

Fixed Assets: Valuation; Disposal;
Depreciation; Appraisals

GENERAL APPROACH

Assets are the embodiment of future services available for or beneficial to future operations. Fixed assets consist of relatively long-lived forms of property used in the operations of a business, not held primarily for resale. By nature they are divided into two groups—tangible (sometimes referred to as "Plant and Equipment") and intangible.

In general the measure of usefulness of a fixed asset at time of acquisition is cost, which is the invoice amount plus freight and installation outlays, less discounts. If the asset is constructed, cost will include not only material and direct labor, but also all other costs necessary to achieve completion (for example, architects fees to design a building) and possibly overhead. The last item has been the subject of much discussion—what portion of overhead shall be allocated to the capitalizable cost? One of two positions is usually taken: (1) capitalize only that portion of overhead which can be specifically identified with construction; (2) capitalize overhead on the same basis that overhead is apportioned to manufactured goods. With recent emphasis on more accurate allocation of costs, the second technique is gaining support. The construction-period theory approves capitalization of expenditures related to the asset while construction is in progress. Adherents to this theory would capitalize insurance premiums expired during the construction period or the portion of property taxes allocable to the construction period. The alternative is to treat these items as expenses.

The following Institute problem, adapted, indicates some of the questions which arise when a fixed asset is purchased or constructed.

The following property control account is shown on the books of the X Company:

Balance, Dec. 31, 19x0			$586,000
Additions—			
Feb. 28	Transfer from construction work in progress—building completed	$100,000	
28	Removal of old building (formerly used in operations) to make room for new structure ..	15,000	
June 30	19x1 taxes on real estate. Valuations: land, $50,000; building, $100,000; rate $3 per $100	4,500	
July 31	Legal and out-of-pocket expenses for title search of property not acquired	200	
Oct. 31	Purchase of two machines, including $78.00 freight and $100.00 installation	1,078	
31	Cost of removing used machines replaced by above purchase	45	
Nov. 30	Cost of moving the two machines to 3rd floor to effect more economical operation	72	120,895
			$706,895
Credits, Mar. 31 Sale of old building materials			200
Balance, Dec. 31, 19x1			$706,695

What adjustments would you suggest, and why?

(AICPA, adapted)

Before reading the suggested solution, the candidate is encouraged to prepare his own.

Suggested Solution

Feb. 28   The net cost of removing the old building ($15,000 - $200) should not be capitalized but should be written off as an expense, since it had been used in operations.

June 30   Under the construction-period theory, that portion of the tax applicable to the construction period may be capitalized. Only the taxes for January and February (1/6 of $4,500 or $750) are capitalizable. The balance would be written off as an expense. An alternative solution would treat the entire amount of $4,500 as expense, since capitalization of property taxes during the construction period is optional.

July 31   Legal and out-of-pocket costs for title search where property was not acquired should be treated as an expense.

Oct. 31   Cost of removing used machines replaced by new ones should be charged as an expense.

Nov. 30   Cost of moving the two machines to effect more economical operation may be capitalized only if the undepreciated remainder of the original installation cost has been removed from the accounts. In all other cases, especially if the amount is relatively small, the item would be charged off as expense.

In his solution the candidate might explain that he is assuming supporting records for fixed assets are maintained for proper presentation of data on the balance sheet.

Depreciation

Depreciation is the estimated allocation of cost of fixed asset facilities charged to an accounting period. If the asset is wasting, the term *depletion* is used; if the asset is intangible, the term *amortization* is used. In each case, the charge represents the portion of the long-term prepayment for service allocated to a period of time. Note that depreciation accounting is primarily concerned with allocation, not with valuation. The candidate is urged to be precise in his terminology.

The amount to be allocated is the difference between the total capitalized cost and the salvage value. The allocation may be made on a basis of time or on the basis of service. On the basis of time, the charge may be computed in a number of ways. The formula for each method is given, using the following symbols:

Let C = total capitalized cost
S = scrap or salvage value
n = estimated life
D = amount of depreciation per unit of n
r = rate of depreciation

Straight-Line Depreciation

In pro rata or straight-line depreciation, the capitalized cost minus scrap value is allocated over the estimated life to produce the amount charged as expense.

$$D = \frac{C - S}{n}$$

If none of the factors changes, D remains constant.

The rate of write-off per unit of n is found by dividing D by C. Therefore,

$$r = \frac{D}{C}$$

This rate is called the straight-line rate adjusted for salvage and is always multiplied by total capitalized cost to arrive at the amount of depreciation.

A company purchased equipment with an estimated useful life of 10 years for $5,000, the estimated scrap value being $500.

$$D = \frac{\$5,000 - \$500}{10} = \$450 \text{ depreciation per year}$$

$$r(\text{adjusted}) = \frac{\$450}{\$5,000} = 9\% \text{ per year}$$

D would, therefore, also equal rC or 9% of $5,000. Unless there is a statement to the contrary, problems use the adjusted rate.

The rate unadjusted for salvage is found by dividing 100% by the units of useful life. In this same example, r unadjusted for salvage would equal 100% ÷ 10 or 10%. If a rate unadjusted for salvage is used, the amount of depreciation is computed by multiplying the rate by $(C - S)$.

If depreciation is computed on the basis of service, the straight-line formula is used, except that n is now an expression of life in terms of output or in terms of working hours.

A truck is purchased at a cost of $4,000, with estimated scrap value of $1,000 after performing for 100,000 miles. On a mileage basis, the amount of depreciation per mile is computed thus:

$$D \text{ per mile} = \frac{\$4,000 - \$1,000}{100,000} = \$0.03$$

The total cost of a fixed asset allocated to a period is the sum of depreciation plus repairs. Normal costs of upkeep are charged to expense. Since detailed unit records on a particular fixed asset are not usually available in examination problems, major repairs which extend the useful life of the asset or improve its productivity are debited to the Allowance for Depreciation account. Depreciation is then recomputed, based on the new estimated life, with the revised book value minus scrap value charged to expense over the remaining periods. With complete data available on major repairs, one would remove the cost of the item replaced, along with its accumulated depreciation from the proper accounts. The asset would be debited for the cost of the replacing unit.

Accelerated Depreciation

During the last few years, and especially since the passage of the Internal Revenue Code of 1954 (hereinafter referred to as the Code), various forms of accelerated depreciation have gained popularity. The most common methods are

(1) the application of a fixed percentage to a diminishing base, and (2) the application of a diminishing percentage or fraction to a constant base.

An illustration of the first is the declining-balance method approved by the Code. For property built or rebuilt after 1953, with a useful life of at least three years, the declining-balance method, at not more than twice the straight-line rate unadjusted for salvage, may be used. New or used depreciable real property acquired after July 24, 1969, except *new* residential rental housing acquired after that date, does not qualify for this method for tax purposes. In the first example, the maximum rate for the declining-balance method would be 2 X 10% or 20%. For tax purposes, the rate is applied to the book value (capitalized cost minus allowance for depreciation). In the first year, the amount of depreciation would be 20% X $5,000 or $1,000. For the second year, it should be 20% of ($5,000 − $1,000) or $800, and so on. In discussing the declining-balance method, APBAP Vol. 1, Sect. 4074.02 says:

> The declining balance method is one of those which meets the requirements of being "systematic and rational" (*Accounting Terminology Bulletin No. 1*, paragraph 56). In those cases where the expected productivity or revenue-earning power of the asset is relatively greater during the earlier years of its life, or where maintenance charges tend to increase during the later years, the declining balance method may well provide the most satisfactory allocation of cost. The conclusions of this bulletin also apply to other methods, including the "sum-of-the-years digits" method, which produce substantially similar results.

A second illustration of a fixed percentage applied to a diminishing balance is the rate produced by the formula:

$$r = 1 - \sqrt[n]{S/C}$$

Once calculated, the rate is applied to the book value. If there is no scrap value, a nominal scrap value of $1 is used to produce a useful rate.

The Code specifically mentions another method—the sum-of-the-years digits. This is an example of the application of a diminishing percentage or fraction to a constant base. The annual amount of depreciation is found by multiplying total capitalized cost minus scrap value by a fraction, the numerator of which is the number of remaining years of life of the asset, and the denominator of which is the total of the numbers representing the years of life. With the same example as previously used, wherein C is $5,000, S is $500, and n is 10, depreciation would be calculated as follows:

$$\text{1st year: } D = \frac{10}{1 + 2 + 3 \ldots + 10} (\$5,000 - \$500)$$

$$D = \frac{10}{55} (\$4,500) = \$818.18$$

$$\text{2nd year: } D = \frac{9}{55} (\$4,500) = \$736.36$$

The following chart compares the amounts of annual depreciation produced by the four techniques for an asset whose cost is $1,050, estimated scrap value is $50, and estimated life is 5 years. Results are rounded off to the nearest dollar. The amount for the declining balance at twice the straight-line rate method is computed in accordance with the Code.

Annual Depreciation

Year	Straight-Line*	Declining Balance at Twice Straight-line Rate†	Sum-of-Years Digits‡	Formula–Fixed Percentage¶
1	$ 200	$420	$ 333	$ 479
2	200	252	267	260
3	200	151	200	142
4	200	91	133	77
5	200	54	67	42
Total	$1,000	$968	$1,000	$1,000

* (Using rate unadjusted for salvage) 20% ($1,050 – $50).
† 40% × $1,050; 40% ($1,050 – $420); etc.
‡ 5/15 ($1,050 – $50); 4/15 ($1,050 – $50); etc.
¶ $r = 1 - \sqrt[n]{S/C} = 1 - \sqrt[5]{\$50/\$1,050} = 45.6\%$.
45.6% × $1,050; 45.6% ($1,050 – $479); etc.

An inspection of the totals shows that all methods have allocated the same total amount of depreciation to the five-year period (an amount equal to cost minus scrap), except the declining-balance method, which uses twice the straight-line rate unadjusted for scrap. The latter method will never fully depreciate the base, a fact foreseen by Congress when it passed the 1954 Code. It therefore allowed the taxpayer to change to the straight-line method at any time without first receiving permission. The taxpayer could, at the beginning of the fifth year, for example, switch to the straight-line technique. The total allowance for depreciation for the first four years, using the data in the preceding chart, is $914. Since the maximum depreciation allowed for this asset over its five-year life is $1,000, the taxpayer would deduct $86 in the fifth year, thus deriving full benefit of the total depreciation deduction allowable.

The Internal Revenue Service permits companies to use accelerated methods of depreciation when computing taxable income even though straight-line methods of depreciation are used in annual reports to stockholders. Therefore, income tax payments are lower in the early years of the useful life of the asset and higher in the later years than they would be if straight-line depreciation were used for both tax and stockholder reporting purposes. These differences in the timing of cash payments for income tax purposes have generated the use of income tax allocation procedures, which are discussed in Topic IX.

Change in Depreciation Estimates

The majority of elements that affect computation of depreciation are estimates—scrap value, service life, even cost, in some cases. The future may prove that an earlier appraisement was inaccurate. How should a change in estimate be handled? In *Opinion No. 20*, the APB concluded:

> that the effect of a change in accounting estimate should be accounted for in (a) the period of change if the change affects that period only or (b) the period of change and future periods if the change affects both. A change in an estimate should not be accounted for by restating amounts reported in financial statements of prior periods or by reporting pro forma amounts for future periods. (See APBAP Vol. 1, Sect. 1051.31.)

Depreciation and Changing Price Level

Management has come to the accounting profession with this problem: Depreciation expense on our assets is not sufficient to cover the cost of replacement. Should one record depreciation based on current prices or replacement prices?

The Institute answers:

> ... business management has the responsibility of providing for replacement of plant and machinery ... in reporting profits today, the cost of material and labor is reflected in terms of "inflated" dollars while the cost of productive facilities in which capital was invested at a lower price level is reflected in terms of dollars whose purchasing power was much greater. There is no doubt that in considering depreciation in connection with product costs, prices, and business policies, management must take into consideration the probability that plant and machinery will have to be replaced at costs much greater than those of the facilities now in use.
>
> When there are gross discrepancies between the cost and current values of productive facilities, ... it is entirely proper for management to make annual appropriations of net income or surplus in contemplation of replacement of such facilities at higher price levels.
>
> It has been suggested in some quarters that the problem be met by increasing depreciation charges against current income. The committee does not believe that this is a satisfactory solution at this time. It believes that accounting and financial reporting for general use will best serve their purposes by adhering to the generally accepted concept of depreciation on cost, at least until the dollar is stabilized at some level. An attempt to recognize current prices in providing depreciation, to be consistent, would require the serious step of formally recording appraised current values for all properties, and continuous and consistent depreciation charges based on the new values. Without such formal steps, there would be no objective standard by which to judge the propriety of the amount of depreciation charges against current income, and the significance of recorded amounts of profit might be seriously impaired. (See APBAP Vol. 1, Sect. 4071.05-.07.)

If fixed assets have been reappraised, such information may be presented either parenthetically or by a footnote to the balance sheet, thus conforming to the principle that the accounting for fixed assets should normally be based on cost. If, however, reappraisal is to be recorded, separate accounts should be maintained to prevent an account from having a hybrid balance—being in part cost and in part reappraisal increment.

Depletion

In the extractive industries (coal, minerals, oil, gas, and so forth), as units of the natural resource are consumed, there is a physical shrinkage of the quantity still available. These assets are spoken of as wasting assets. The cost allocable to the periods in which the units are made available for use is termed *depletion* and is generally computed on the basis of the number of units estimated to be commercially available. The formula to determine depletion per extracted unit would be:

$$\text{Depletion expense per extracted unit} = \frac{\text{Total cost to be written off less salvage value}}{\text{Total number of units commercially available}}$$

The numerator of the fraction should include the original outlay for the resource, and also the development costs necessary to bring it to a producing stage, if such development costs have a usefulness during the entire period of exploitation.

EXAMPLE

Property containing an estimated 1,000,000 tons of coal is acquired for $750,000. Development costs total $60,000. Land, after operations are completed, will have a value of $10,000.

$$\text{Depletion per ton of coal} = \frac{\$750,000 + \$60,000 - \$10,000}{1,000,000}$$

$$= \$0.80 \text{ per ton}$$

If there is a substantial change in any of the factors used in the computation of depletion, an adjustment to the Allowance for Depletion account may be desirable, although in many cases only the future depletion charge is revised.

Leases

To date, three opinions have been issued by the Board relating to the subject of leases: *Opinion No. 5* tackling the problems of the lessee, and *Opinions No. 7* and *27,* dealing with those of the lessor. With the tremendous expansion of leasing arrangements, the future will present more leasehold problems for authoritative bodies to solve.

Different treatments have been used in the past by lessees to record similar leasing arrangements. Some made no formal entry and no footnote disclosure; some made no formal entry but revealed the existence of leases; some made formal entries, indicating both leased assets and lease liability. In the hope of resolving some of the issues, the Board issued *Opinion No. 5.* Basically it said that unless the lease was essentially equivalent to an installment purchase of property, "the right to use property and a related obligation to pay specific rents over a definite future period are not considered . . . to be assets and liabilities under present accounting concepts." It stipulated the conditions under which a lease was "essentially equivalent" to an installment purchase, and did require disclosure by the lessee of minimum annual rentals, the period over which payments would be made under the lease, and disclosure of the current year's payments if it differed significantly from the minimum. Unfortunately, terms used were sometimes vague and resulted in varying interpretations. One of the problems the successor body to the APB will undoubtedly consider is the topic of the lessee's reporting of leases on financial statements.

If conditions exist which permit the lessee to record the asset and the liability under the lease agreement, the amount to be used should be the present value (discounted value) of the series of required payments. Thereafter, journal entries should record interest expense on the unpaid balance, the periodic reduction of the liability resulting from payments, and the charge to expense for leased assets. To illustrate:

> Wagner Corporation has signed a long-term equipment lease effective January 1, 19x0. Ten annual payments of $10,000 are required at the end of each year. The management of the company requests information about the effects of a policy of capitalization of the lease and asks you to prepare entries under the conventional method and under the capitalization method. (The present value of an annuity of $1 for 10 periods at the going rate of 8% is $6.71.) Entries are shown on the following page.

Under conventional recording the total expense is an operating one, while under the capitalization technique the expense is divided between operating and financial, often the financial expense being the larger as is the case with early payments on a mortgage. Although total expense is identical under both methods, the expense definition seems more precise if conditions permit the lease to be capitalized.

Opinion No. 7 dictated that under certain conditions a lessor must treat a lease as a sale, yet *No. 5* said the lessee could treat it as other than a purchase. This inconsistency appears unwarranted, and the subject of leases is still receiving attention. In November, 1972, the Board issued *Opinion No. 27,* which stipulates in paragraph 4 that a manufacturer or dealer lessor should treat a lease transaction as a sale if:

LEASES—Conventional versus Capitalized Treatment

Event	Conventional treatment	Lease capitalized

Signing of equipment lease	no entry	Leased equipment 67,100
		Liability under lease
		  contract—current 4,632
		  —long-term 62,468
		(See lease amortization table below.)

Annual lease payment	Rent expense on leased
	  equipment 10,000
	  Cash 10,000
		Interest expense (8% x $67,100) 5,368
		Liability under lease
		  contract—current 4,632
		  Cash........................ 10,000
		
		Rent on leased equipment............ 4,632
		  Accumulated amortization
		  of leased equipment 4,632
		
		Liability under lease
		  contract—long-term 5,003
		Liability under lease
		  contract—current 5,003

Partial Lease Amortization Table

Date	Book value of liability	Total payment	Interest at 8% on beginning book value	Amortization of lease
1-1-x0	$67,100	$10,000	$5,368	$4,632
1-1-x1	62,468	10,000	4,997	5,003
1-1-x2	57,465	10,000	4,597	5,403

(a) collectibility of the payments required from the lessee is reasonably assured;

(b) no important uncertainties ... surround the amount of costs yet to be incurred under the lease; and

(c) any one of the following conditions is present:

    (i) the lease transfers title to the property to the lessee by the end of its fixed, noncancelable term; or

    (ii) the lease gives the lessee the option to obtain title to the property without cost or at a nominal cost by the end of the fixed, noncancelable term of the lease; or

    (iii) the lease property, or like property, is available for sale and the sum of (1) the present value of required rental payments ... and (2) any related investment tax credit retained by the lessor ... is equal to or greater than the normal selling price; or

    (iv) the fixed, noncancelable term of the lease ... is substantially equal to the remaining economic life of the property.

Thus the Board has attempted to refine conditions whereunder the lease should be treated as a sale by a manufacturer or dealer lessor. One may expect the future to produce additional pronouncements on leases by the successor Financial Accounting Standards Board.

Intangibles

Prior to the issuance of **APB** *Opinion No. 17* there was much variation in the intangible asset amortization process, especially where useful life was indefinite. To paraphrase a famous line, "to amortize or not to amortize—that is the question." The Board answers:

> ... the value of intangible assets at any one date eventually disappears and ... the recorded costs of intangible assets should be amortized by systematic charges to income over the periods estimated to be benefited. (See APBAP Vol. 1, Sect. 5141.27.)

If the life of the intangible is limited, either by law, or by agreement, or by economic factors, the process is simplified. Not only is the life known, but the Board has specified that the straight-line method of amortization must be used for all intangibles, except where it can be proved that another method is more appropriate. The process is similar to straight-line depreciation for tangibles.

There are intangibles which, at the time of acquisition, do not have a definite life, such as goodwill. Here the Board indicates that "a reasonable estimate of the useful life may often be based on upper and lower limits even though a fixed existence is not determinable," but this period shall not exceed 40 years.

CPA PROBLEMS

Problem VIII-1: Depletion allowance; conversion from cash to accrual basis; deferred income taxes (50-60 min.)

Calor Drilling Company applied for a bank loan to finance the purchase of a new drilling rig. The bank required Calor to submit financial statements audited by a CPA and Calor engaged you. A trial balance as of December 31, 1967 taken from Calor's general ledger, which is maintained on the cash basis, appears below:

Calor Drilling Company
TRIAL BALANCE (CASH BASIS)
December 31, 1967

Accounts	Debit	Credit
Cash	$ 145,000	
Productive oil leases	100,000	
Allowance for depletion		$ 137,500
Land, building and equipment	1,800,000	
Allowance for depreciation		800,000
Employees' withholding taxes		5,500
Notes payable (due 1968)		250,000
Common stock ($10 par value)		300,000
Retained earnings		252,000
Drilling revenue		1,200,000
Salaries and wages	381,000	
Payroll taxes	24,000	
Pipe and supplies	245,000	
Insurance	44,000	
Depreciation	300,000	
Interest	1,000	
Other expenses	50,000	
Oil royalties		200,000
Depletion	55,000	
Total	$3,145,000	$3,145,000

The following information had not been recorded at the dates indicated:

	December 31	
	1966	1967
Accounts receivable from drilling contracts (1)	$150,000	$192,000
Drilling contracts included in accounts receivable for the cost of unproductive oil leases (1)	25,000	22,000
Estimated uncollectible accounts (1)	6,000	8,000
Prepaid insurance (2)	12,000	70,000
Accounts payable (3)	28,000	67,000
Insurance note payable (2)		40,000
Accrued expenses payable:		
Salaries and wages	11,000	4,000
Payroll taxes (4)	1,200	500
Interest (4)	900	2,200

1. Accounts receivable include all unpaid drilling contracts. Occasionally an interest in a lease being drilled is taken as the fee on a drilling contract and the fee is included in accounts receivable. Productive leases are recorded by journal entry at cost to charge off the fractional working interest of intangible drilling costs to expense and capitalize the balance of tangible and intangible drilling costs as assets and the fee as drilling revenue. The $25,000 of unproductive leases and $6,000 of uncollectible accounts from 1966 were removed from accounts receivable during 1967. Leases are abandoned when they are drilled and found to be unproductive.

2. All insurance policies were renewed as 3-year policies on July 1, 1967 with premiums aggregating $84,000. A payment of $44,000 was made and a $40,000 note payable July 1, 1968 was signed for the balance.

3. Accounts payable were for pipe and supplies which were purchased as needed for use. No inventory was maintained.

4. Accrued expenses included the employer's portion of all payroll taxes and accrued interest payable on all notes.

Additional information includes the following:

5. On December 29, 1967 Calor issued 1,000 shares of common stock in exchange for a productive oil lease with a fair market value of $15,000 and made no entry to record the transaction.

6. Depletion on oil leases owned was recorded under the statutory depletion method at 27½ per cent of the oil royalties received from the leases. It was estimated that 75 per cent of the oil reserves were still recoverable at December 31, 1967 and 84 per cent were recoverable at December 31, 1966 from the $100,000 of leases owned during 1966 and 1967.

7. Accelerated depreciation was recorded in conformity with income tax reporting. For its financial statements Calor would like to compute depreciation under the straight-line method. Accumulated depreciation under the straight-line method would have been $370,000 at December 31, 1966 and $560,000 at December 31, 1967.

8. Income tax returns had been examined through 1966 and accepted as filed. Income tax expense for 1966 amounted to $7,500 and was paid in 1967 and charged to Other Expenses. Payments totaling $36,000 on 1967 estimated income taxes were also charged to Other Expenses. Income tax expense for 1967 on the accrual basis amounted to $235,000. Deferred income taxes payable amounted to $99,000 at December 31, 1966 and $133,000 at December 31, 1967 (assume the amounts stated for income taxes are correct).

Required:

Prepare a worksheet for the preparation of Calor Drilling Company's financial statements at December 31, 1967 on the accrual basis. Number your adjustments on the worksheet to correspond with the numbers for the information given. Supporting computations should be in good form. Formal adjusting journal entries and financial statements are not required.

Problem VIII-2: Price-level accounting; price-level gain or loss (40-50 min.)

Skadden, Inc., a retailer, was organized during 1966. Skadden's management has decided to supplement its December 31, 1969 historical dollar financial statements with general price-level financial statements. The following general ledger trial balance (historical dollar) and additional information have been furnished:

Skadden, Inc.
TRIAL BALANCE
December 31, 1969

	Debit	Credit
Cash and receivables (net)	$ 540,000	$
Marketable securities (common stock)	400,000	
Inventory	440,000	
Equipment	650,000	
Equipment–Accumulated depreciation		164,000
Accounts payable		300,000
6% First mortgage bonds, due 1987		500,000
Common stock, $10 par		1,000,000
Retained earnings, December 31, 1968	46,000	
Sales		1,900,000
Cost of Sales....................................	1,508,000	
Depreciation.....................................	65,000	
Other operating expenses and interest	215,000	
	$3,864,000	$3,864,000

1. Monetary assets (cash and receivables) exceeded monetary liabilities (accounts payable and bonds payable) by $445,000 at December 31, 1968. The amounts of monetary items are fixed in terms of numbers of dollars regardless of changes in specific prices or in the general price level.

2. Purchases ($1,840,000 in 1969) and sales are made uniformly throughout the year.

3. Depreciation is computed on a straight-line basis, with a full year's depreciation being taken in the year of acquisition and none in the year of retirement. The depreciation rate is 10 percent and no salvage value is anticipated. Acquisitions and retirements have been made fairly evenly over each year and the retirements in 1969 consisted of assets purchased during 1967 which were scrapped. An analysis of the equipment account reveals the following:

Year	Beginning Balance	Additions	Retirements	Ending Balance
1967	–	$550,000	–	$550,000
1968	$550,000	10,000	–	560,000
1969	560,000	150,000	$60,000	650,000

4. The bonds were issued in 1967 and the marketable securities were purchased fairly evenly over 1969. Other operating expenses and interest are assumed to be incurred evenly throughout the year.

5. Assume that Gross National Product Implicit Price Deflators (1958 = 100) were as follows:

Annual Averages	Index	Conversion Factors (1969 4th Qtr. = 1.000)
1966	113.9	1.128
1967	116.8	1.100
1968	121.8	1.055
1969	126.7	1.014

Quarterly Average			
1968	4th	123.5	1.040
1969	1st	124.9	1.029
	2nd	126.1	1.019
	3rd	127.3	1.009
	4th	128.5	1.000

Required:

a. Prepare a schedule to convert the Equipment account balance at December 31, 1969 from historical cost to general price-level adjusted dollars.

b. Prepare a schedule to analyze in historical dollars the Equipment—Accumulated Depreciation account for the year 1969.

c. Prepare a schedule to analyze in general price-level dollars the Equipment—Accumulated Depreciation account for the year 1969.

d. Prepare a schedule to compute Skadden, Inc.'s general price-level gain or loss on its net holdings of monetary assets for 1969 (ignore income tax implications). The schedule should give consideration to appropriate items on or related to the balance sheet and the income statement.

Problem VIII-3: Discounted present value of leased terminal facilities (40-50 min.)

In 1969 the Archibald Freight Company negotiated and closed a long-term lease contract for newly constructed truck terminals and freight storage facilities. The buildings were erected to the Company's specifications on land owned by the Company. On January 1, 1970 Archibald Freight Company took possession of the leased properties. On January 1, 1970 and 1971 the Company made cash payments of $1,200,000 which were recorded as rental expenses.

Although the terminals have a composite useful life of 40 years, the non-cancelable lease runs for 20 years from January 1, 1970 with a favorable purchase option available upon expiration of the lease. You have determined that the leased properties and related obligation should be accounted for as an installment purchase. Internal Revenue Service agents have indicated that purchase accounting will be required for tax purposes and that an assessment will be made for deficiencies in 1970 income taxes.

The 20-year lease is effective for the period January 1, 1970 through December 31, 1989. Advance rental payments of $1,000,000 are payable to the lessor on January 1 of each of the first 10 years of the lease term. Advance rental payments of $300,000 are due on January 1 for each of the last 10 years of the lease. The Company has an option to purchase all of these leased facilities for $1 on December 31, 1989. It also must make annual payments to the lessor of $75,000 for property taxes and $125,000 for insurance. The lease was negotiated to assure the lessor a 6% rate of return.

Required (round all computations to the nearest dollar):

a. Prepare a schedule to compute for Archibald Freight Company the discounted present value of the terminal facilities and related obligation at January 1, 1970.

b. Prepare a schedule to compute an estimate of Archibald Freight Company's deficiency in federal income taxes for 1970. Assume the following:

The discounted present value of the terminal facilities and related obligation at January 1, 1970 was $10,000,000.

The cost of the leased properties is to be amortized by the straight-line method with an estimate of zero salvage value.

The effective tax rate is 40%.

c. Assuming again that the discounted present value of terminal facilities and related obligation at January 1, 1970 was $10,000,000, prepare journal entries for Archibald Freight Company to record the:

(1) Cash payment to the lessor on January 1, 1972.
(2) Amortization of the cost of the leased properties for 1972 using the straight-line method and assuming a zero salvage value.
(3) Accrual of interest expense at December 31, 1972 using the effective-interest method.

Selected present value factors are as follows:

Periods	For an Ordinary Annuity of $1 at 6%	For $1 at 6%
1	.943396	.943396
2	1.833393	.889996
8	6.209794	.627412
9	6.801692	.591898
10	7.360087	.558395
19	11.158117	.330513
20	11.469921	.311805

Problem VIII-4: Full cost versus incremental cost of self-constructed equipment (30-40 min.)

Ellford Corporation received a $400,000 low bid from a reputable manufacturer for the construction of special production equipment needed by Ellford in an expansion program. Because the Company's own plant was not operating at capacity, Ellford decided to construct the equipment there and recorded the following production costs related to the construction:

Services of consulting engineer	$ 10,000
Work subcontracted	20,000
Materials	200,000
Plant labor normally assigned to production	65,000
Plant labor normally assigned to maintenance	100,000
Total	$395,000

Management prefers to record the cost of the equipment under the incremental cost method. Approximately 40% of the Corporation's production is devoted to government supply contracts which are all based in some way on cost. The contracts require that any self-constructed equipment be allocated its full share of all costs related to the construction.

The following information is also available:

1. The above production labor was for partial fabrication of the equipment in the plant. Skilled personnel were required and were assigned from other projects. The maintenance labor would have been idle time of nonproduction plant employees who would have been retained on the payroll whether or not their services were utilized.

2. Payroll taxes and employee fringe benefits are approximately 30% of labor cost and are included in manufacturing overhead cost. Total manufacturing overhead for the year was $5,630,000.

3. Manufacturing overhead is approximately 50% variable and is applied on the basis of production labor cost. Production labor cost for the year for the Corporation's normal products totaled $6,810,000.

4. General and administrative expenses include $22,500 of executive salary cost and $10,500 of postage, telephone, supplies, and miscellaneous expenses identifiable with this equipment construction.

Required:

a. Prepare a schedule computing the amount which should be reported as the full cost of the constructed equipment to meet the requirements of the government contracts. Any supporting computations should be in good form.

b. Prepare a schedule computing the incremental cost of the constructed equipment.

c. What is the greatest amount that should be capitalized as the cost of the equipment? Why?

SPECIFIC APPROACH

Problem VIII-1

1. For item (1), set up a gross Accounts Receivable account and an Allowance for Bad Debts. Remove all costs associated with leases from Accounts Receivable. What is drilling revenue for the year? Drilling revenue for the previous year should be credited to Retained Earnings, not to current revenue. In fact, when you switch from the cash to the accrual basis, all adjustments that relate to the previous year should affect Retained Earnings.

2. Depletion should be recorded on the cost basis, since use of the statutory percentage method would not produce financial statements on a pure accrual basis.

3. To produce the adjusting entry for item (8), follow this procedure:

a. Determine what entries should have been made at the end of 1966 and 1967.

b. What entries were actually made?

c. Compare the two and derive the adjustment.

Problem VIII-2

1. What are "conversion factors" shown in the problem? Conversion factors are a one-step approach to price-level alteration through direct multiplication, rather than the usual two-step process. Conversion factors are the result of dividing the price level index for the time point to which costs are to be adjusted by the price level index existing when the item was incurred or acquired. Thus, in the problem, the conversion factor for 1967 of 1.100 is 128.5/116.8. Items for 1967 may be converted to the 1969 price level by directly multiplying by 1.100.

2. Although the problem asks for two separate schedules in requirements (b) and (c), the data are more understandable if presented thus:

Shadden Inc.
SCHEDULE OF ANALYSIS OF EQUIPMENT–ACCUMULATED DEPRECIATION
In Historical and Price-Level Dollars

		Depreciation			Accumulated Depreciation		
Year	Asset	1967	1968	1969	Historical Dollars	Conversion Factor	Price-Level Dollars
1967	$550,000	$55,000	$55,000	$49,000	$159,000 X	1.100	= $174,900
1968	10,000		1,000	1,000	2,000 X	1.055	= 2,110
1969	150,000			15,000	15,000 X	1.014	= 15,210
1969	(60,000)				(12,000) X	1.100	= (13,200)
	$650,000	$55,000	$56,000	$65,000	$164,000		$179,020

3. Requirement (d) is asking: if all monetary flows in 1969 could immediately reflect changes in price levels, what would net monetary total be on December 31, 1969? Then compare that to actual net monetary total on December 31, 1969 to determine general price-level gain or loss.

What are net monetary assets? Monetary assets are those assets with a fixed dollar flow established—cash and receivables. If a customer owes you $500, regardless of price-level changes, he pays $500. Investments are excluded because they adjust to changes in price-levels, although not always immediately nor in positive correlation. Monetary liabilities are defined the same way—those with a fixed dollar flow, which embraces almost all liabilities, including long-term. Net holdings of monetary assets equal monetary assets minus monetary liabilities.

Problem VIII-3

1. Often a pictorial approach to present value determinations increases the odds for success. All amounts in a series of payments must be reflected at one point of time—in this problem, January 1, 1970. The diagram might be:

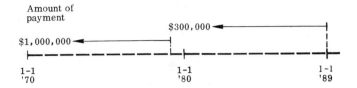

The discounted present value of the series of payments will equal: $1,000,000 (the immediate payment January 1, 1970), plus the present value of an ordinary annuity of the next nine $1,000,000 payments, plus the present value of the last ten $300,000 payments as of January 1, 1980 (computed in the same manner as the $1,000,000 series) discounted to January 1, 1970.

2. To determine the tax deficiency for 1970, subtract the total expenses allowable under tax law from the rental deduction claimed of $1,200,000 and apply the 40% rate. Remember to include interest on the unpaid balance as one of the allowable expenses.

3. Accrual of interest expense on December 31 is based on the amount of leasehold debt outstanding for the year. The immediate payment of $1,000,000 on the leasehold obligation reduces outstanding debt for 1970 to $9,000,000 on which interest is accrued at the end of 1970. Each year that portion of the $1,000,000 payment not applicable to interest reduces the leasehold obligation. A simple schedule could pay unusual rewards:

Year	Principal reduction from Jan. 1 payment	Assumed present value of debt outstanding	Annual interest at 6% on debt outstanding
		$10,000,000	
1970	$1,000,000	9,000,000	$540,000
1971	460,000[a]	8,540,000	512,400
etc.			

[a]$1,000,000 − 540,000 interest payment

Problem VIII-4

1. Calculation of the full cost of the constructed equipment may differ, depending on the assumptions. It would seem most logical to conclude that all maintenance labor is included in manufacturing overhead. Therefore, in determining the ratio of total manufacturing overhead to production labor, adjustment should be made for the respective items involved in the self-constructed equipment.

2. For your own benefit, define "incremental cost" of self-constructed items.

3. What limit must be considered when implementing the recommendation of most accounting authorities that self-constructed assets should be allocated overhead on the same basis as other production when a plant is not operating at full capacity?

Liabilities: Current and Long-Term

GENERAL APPROACH

What is a liability?

In its *Accounting Terminology Bulletin No. 1* (pp. 13-14), the Institute defines it as:

> Something represented by a credit balance that is or would be properly carried forward upon a closing of books of account according to the rules or principles of accounting, provided such credit balance is not in effect a negative balance applicable to an asset. Thus the word is used broadly to comprise not only items which constitute liabilities in the popular sense of debts or obligations (including provision for those that are unascertained), but also credit balances to be accounted for which do not involve the debtor and creditor relation. For example, capital stock and related or similar elements of proprietorship are balance sheet liabilities in that they represent balances to be accounted for, though these are not liabilities in the ordinary sense of debts owed to legal creditors.

In this topic, however, only obligations to creditors—both current and long-term—will be discussed.

In the balance sheet the liabilities are grouped according to the time of payment. The Institute points out:

> The term "current liabilities" is used principally to designate obligations whose liquidation is reasonably expected to require the use of existing resources properly classifiable as current assets, or the creation of other current liabilities. As a balance-sheet category, the classification is intended to include obligations for items which have entered into the operating cycle, such as payables incurred in the acquisition of

materials and supplies to be used in the production of goods . . . and debts which arise from operations directly related to the operating cycle, such as accruals for wages, . . . rentals, royalties, and income and other taxes. Other liabilities whose regular and ordinary liquidation is expected to occur within a relatively short period of time, usually twelve months, are also intended for inclusion. (APBAP Vol. 1, Sect. 2031.07.)

Liabilities that will not become due within the operating cycle or within one year, whichever is longer, are long-term. The proceeds obtained from long-term commitments are usually employed for the acquisition of plant and equipment. Repayment is dependent upon the accumulation of resources over the relatively longer period of time during which management employs the borrowed funds.

Examination problems concentrating on liabilities generally involve adherence to a contractual agreement. Subject areas would be escrow statements, profit-sharing trusts, pension plans, warranty or royalty agreements, and bond recitals. Under these conditions, careful reading of the problem is particularly essential to successful solution.

Bond Premium and Discount

The rate that a bond stipulates it will pay is the nominal or contract rate. The rate of interest that similar bonds will pay on the bond investment market is the effective or market rate. If the two rates are identical, at the time of issuance, a bond will sell for its face value. If the nominal rate is higher than the market rate, the bonds will command a premium. If it is lower than the market rate, they will be offered at a discount.

Accounting recognizes that premium or discount on bonds is an interest adjustment factor. Periodically, the portion of the premium amortized will be credited to the Bond Interest Expense account, producing as a balance in that account an amount that approximates the effective interest. The entries may be compounded:

> Bond interest expense (for effective interest) xx
> Premium on bonds payable (for premium amortized) .   xx
>   Cash (for nominal interest payment) xx

The accumulation of discount will be debited to the Interest Expense account along with the nominal interest:

> Bond interest expense (for effective interest) xx
>   Discount on bonds payable (for discount accumulated) xx
>   Cash (for nominal interest payment) xx

Amortization of premium or accumulation of discount on issued bonds is conducted in one of two ways—pro rata method or compound interest method. Under the pro rata technique, an equal amount is written off per period over the life of the issue for a given face value.

EXAMPLE

On January 1, 19x0 a 5% $1,000 ten-year bond, paying interest semiannually July 1 and January 1, is issued at 102. The entry to record the interest payment and pro rata amortization of the premium on July 1, 19x0, is:

```
Bond interest expense  .....................    24.00
Premium on bonds payable  .................     1.00
    Cash  ..........................................          25.00
```

For each successive six-month period, the amount of the premium written off will be the same.

Although the pro rata method of amortization allocates a constant amount to each period, it does not allocate a constant percentage of the book value (face plus unamortized premium or minus unaccumulated discount).

The compound interest technique of amortization of premium or accumulation of discount on bonds payable was developed to assign to each period an amount of interest expense computed at a fixed rate. Each interest period is charged with an amount of interest expense on bonds issued equal to the effective rate per period multiplied by the book value of the bonds at the *beginning* of that interest period. The product is the effective interest. The difference between the effective interest amount and the nominal interest amount (for which the checks are actually issued) is the amount amortized or accumulated. A table will be of assistance in working problems of this type.

EXAMPLE

On January 1, 19x0 a 6% bond is sold for $1018.81 to yield 5%. Interest is payable July 1 and January 1.

Amortization Table

For Six Months Ended	Nominal Interest–3%	Effective Interest–2½%	Premium Amortized	Book Value
Jan. 1, 19x0	-0-	-0-	-0-	$1018.81
July 1, 19x0	$30.00	$25.47*	$4.53	1014.28
Jan. 1, 19x1	30.00	25.36†	4.64	1009.64
July 1, 19x1	30.00	25.24	4.76	1004.88
Jan. 1, 19x2	30.00	25.12	4.88	1000.00

*2½% of $1018.81.
†2½% of $1014.28, etc.

The entry to record the interest payment on July 1, 19x0 would be:

```
Bond interest expense (for the effective interest) ... 25.47
Premium on bonds payable (for premium amortized)  4.53
    Cash (for nominal interest)  .........................30.00
```

In a serial bond issue, a portion of the bonds is retired periodically. Amortization is calculated by the bonds-outstanding method. The amount of premium or discount to be allocated to a period is found by multiplying the total premium or discount by a fraction, the numerator of which is the face value of the bonds outstanding during that period and the denominator of which is the total of the face values of bonds outstanding for all periods.

EXAMPLE

On January 1, 19x0 a $100,000 3% bond issue is sold for 96. At the end of the second year and of each year thereafter, one-fifth of the bonds will be retired. Computation of the discount to be written off each year follows:

**Bonds-Outstanding Method
of Calculating Accumulation of Bond Discount**

Year	Bonds Outstanding	Fractional Allocation	Accumulation
19x0	$100,000	10/40	$1,000.00
19x1	100,000	10/40	1,000.00
19x2	80,000	8/40	800.00
19x3	60,000	6/40	600.00
19x4	40,000	4/40	400.00
19x5	20,000	2/40	200.00
Totals	$400,000	40/40	$4,000.00

Unaccumulated bond discount and unamortized bond premium should be shown as a deduction from, or as an addition to, the face amount of the bond issue in the long-term liability section.

Sinking Fund

Bond indentures will frequently require that a sinking fund for bond retirement be accumulated. Contributions to the fund are usually made at the end of each period. One of two methods—the pro rata or the compound interest—is followed in determining the amount of the periodic contribution.

Under the pro rata technique, the amount desired in the fund is divided by the number of periods the bonds will be outstanding. From this quotient the net earnings of the fund for the current period are subtracted, resulting in the amount that must be contributed.

EXAMPLE

On January 1, 19x0 a $100,000 ten-year 5% bond issue is sold at 101. A contribution to the retirement fund must be made at the end of each year on a pro rata basis. The amount of the first contribution is:

$$\frac{\$100,000}{10} = \$10,000$$

Assuming that the fund will earn a net of 3% per annum, one would subtract the earnings of $300 from the base amount of $10,000, resulting in $9,700 as the contribution at the end of the second year. Since earnings are kept in the fund, the total growth per annum (combined contribution and interest) is a constant.

Under the compound interest method of accumulating a sinking fund, the contribution is computed by dividing the sum required in the fund by the amount of an ordinary annuity of $1 for a given number of periods at the interest rate to be earned by the fund. For example, the amount of an ordinary annuity of $1.00 for 10 periods at 3% compound interest is $11.46 ($11.463879).

EXAMPLE

Assume the same facts as in the previous example, except that the contribution to the sinking fund is to be accumulated using the compound interest technique. The annual contribution may be found by dividing $100,000 by $11.463879, which equals $8,723.05. At the end of each year, the entry to record cash contributed to the fund would be:

```
Bond sinking fund ......................  8,723.05
   Cash  .........................................          8,723.05
```

In addition, an entry would be made to record the net earnings of the fund during the period just ended:

```
Bond sinking fund ...........................  xx
   Sinking fund earnings  ................................          xx
```

Note that the periodic cash contribution to the fund under the compound interest method is a constant, whereas under the pro rata technique, it decreases.

Refunding

The procedure of floating a bond issue whose proceeds will be used to redeem an existing bond issue is known as refunding. If a bond issue is refunded, and a difference exists between the cost of reacquisition and the net carrying value of those bonds, the Accounting Principles Board in par. 20 of *Opinion No. 26* stipulates that the difference

> should be recognized currently in income of the period of extinguishment as losses or gains and identified as a separate item.

Pension Costs

Three terms must be defined if pension costs are to be understood:

Normal cost: the annual cost applicable to years subsequent to inception of a pension plan;

Past service cost: total pension cost applicable to years prior to the inception of a pension plan;

Prior service cost: total pension cost applicable to years prior to the date of a particular actuarial valuation. Thus, prior service cost includes any remaining past service cost.

Since the benefits to be received under a pension plan are normally affected by the employees' length of service, there exists a past service cost at the inception of the pension plan. It is possible for an actuary to approximate the present value of the cost of future benefits resulting from the past service factor. Although there was little argument as to the existence of past service cost, there was widespread disagreement as to its proper accounting. In Accounting Research Study No. 8 Mr. Hicks summarizes four possible treatments of accounting for past service costs:

1. Charge the total cost to prior years through retained earnings at the inception of the plan;

2. Charge the total cost against earnings of the year of inception of the plan as an extraordinary item;

3. Charge as expense to present and future periods, but only to the extent of the actual amount funded plus interest on the unfunded past service cost;

4. Charge as expense to present and future periods the amortization of past service costs plus interest.

There is little justification for a direct charge to past periods' retained earnings, resulting from management's adoption of a plan to pay benefits in the future. The Board has specifically stated that neither past service cost nor current cost may be charged against retained earnings but must be expensed against income.

The accounting for pension costs has exhibited unbelievable variations, many of which ignore the principle of matching expenses and revenues. Rather than enforce a narrow interpretation, the Board adopted a minimum and maximum limit. As long as the annual provision for pension costs (that amount charged as expense for the period) was based on an acceptable actuarial cost method and fell within the limits expressed in APB *Opinion No. 8* it was acceptable. The limits were stated as follows:

a. Minimum: The annual provision for pension cost should not be less than the total of (1) normal cost, (2) an amount equivalent to interest on any unfunded prior service cost and (3) a provision for vested benefits where the funded portion appears inadequate.

b. Maximum: The annual provision for pension cost should not be greater than the total of (1) normal cost, (2) 10 per cent of past service cost (until fully amortized), (3) 10 per cent of the amounts of any increases or decreases in prior service cost arising on amendments of the plan (until fully amortized) and (4) interest ... on the difference between provisions and amounts funded. (APBAP Vol. 1, Sect. 4063.17.)

Keep in mind that "provision for pension cost" refers to the estimated expense charged against income, whether funding has or has not occurred. The difference between the provision and the amount funded should be shown as an accrued pension cost or as a prepaid pension cost. Legal obligation for pension payments is determined by the nature of the plan adopted. Any amount by which the legal obligation exceeds the amount funded or accrued must be shown on the balance sheet both as a liability and as a deferred charge.

The fact that pension plans, once begun, would be difficult to terminate without serious, adverse effects has led the Board to conclude that accounting for pension costs should not be discretionary, but should be treated in accordance with *Opinion No. 8.*

Income Tax Allocation

If the taxable income of a corporation on its tax return and the pretax accounting income on its income statement were identical, and if no nominal items were accorded special tax treatment, the provision for income taxes would be:

```
Income tax expense ........................ xxxx
    Income tax payable ................................ xxxx
```

But the taxable income and the pretax accounting income are rarely identical, for the objective of the two bodies which govern their determination is not identical. The Treasury Department must raise money for government operation and must use the taxing system to influence public policy in whatever manner it deems advisable. The objective of professional accountants is to determine the net results of operation in accordance with generally accepted accounting principles. Income tax allocation procedures have been developed to account for the difference between the two income figures. In addition to reflecting the correct tax liability, income tax allocation procedures indicate what the income tax expense would be if net income on the income statement were also the taxable income. A deferred income tax expense or a deferred income tax payable account is used to account for the tax prepaid or tax postponed.

The difference between taxable income and pretax accounting income may be a timing difference, in which case future activities will counteract it, or it may be a permanent difference. According to APB *Opinion No. 11* timing differences are:

differences between the periods in which transactions affect taxable income and the periods in which they enter into the determination of pretax accounting income. Timing differences originate in one period and reverse or "turn around" in one or more subsequent periods. (APBAP Vol. 1, Sect. 4091.12e.)

Illustrations of timing differences include variation in revenue recognition on long-term contracts and installment sales, variation in depreciation methods for tax and internal purposes, and variation in recognition of expense resulting from estimating future obligations, as in warranties.

Assume that X Corporation has a contract that will take more than one year to complete. The estimated net profit earned on the contract in the first year is $200,000. The contract is finished in the second year with an additional net profit of $80,000. Financial statements are prepared using percentage of completion method, while tax returns are prepared on the completed contract basis. Compare the final portion of the income statements for the two years, with and without tax allocation procedure:

	With tax allocation		Without tax allocation	
	Year 1	*Year 2*	*Year 1*	*Year 2*
Income before taxes	$200,000	$80,000	$200,000	$ 80,000
Income tax expense (assume a 45% rate)..............	90,000	36,000	-0-	126,000
Net income (or net loss)........	$110,000	$44,000	$200,000	$ (46,000)

Unless tax allocation procedures are employed, how could one expect a rational interpretation of the accounting data? Journal entries with tax allocation would show:

```
End of year 1:  Income tax expense .............     90,000
                  Deferred income tax payable ....                90,000

End of year 2:  Income tax expense .............     36,000
                  Deferred income tax payable .......  90,000
                      Income tax payable...........                126,000
```

Permanent Differences

According to APB *Opinion No. 11* permanent differences are:

differences between taxable income and pretax accounting income arising from transactions that ... will not be offset by corresponding differences or "turn around" in other periods. (APBAP Vol. 1, Sect. 4091.12f.)

An item may be recognized as expense in accounting, but it is not permitted as a deduction in the calculation of taxable income. For example, life insurance premiums paid by a corporation on its officers are not deductible if the corporation is the beneficiary.

Tax law may permit the deduction of an expense that good accounting procedure would not recognize. The percentage depletion provision in the Code permits a depletion deduction even though the total cost of the property has been recovered through prior depletion charges. (Currently, any depletion in excess of cost basis is a tax preference item subject to a minimum tax.)

Some accounting revenue items are tax exempt. Generally, interest received on obligations of a state or political subdivision are excludible in determining taxable income.

Since permanent differences are not washed out or counteracted, they are not subject to interperiod tax allocation procedures. If material in amount, such permanent differences should be revealed in the narrative of the financial statement proper or in footnotes. For example, a corporation that has paid a premium of $100,000 on the life insurance policy of an officer, with the corporation as beneficiary, might disclose the information within the income statement thus:

Income before income taxes		$1,000,000
Less: Income tax expense (45%)	$450,000	
Plus additional tax from non-deductibility of insurance premium of $100,000 at 45%	45,000	495,000
Net income		$ 505,000

This technique of reporting would also be useful where there is an extraordinary gain or loss, now required to be revealed in the income statement, according to APB *Opinion No. 9.* The extraordinary item should be shown net of tax, thus:

Income from operations		$3,000,000
Income tax expense at 45% (excluding tax relief from extraordinary loss)		1,350,000
Income before extraordinary items		$1,650,000
Extraordinary flood loss	$200,000	
Less: Resulting reduction in income tax at 45%	90,000	110,000
Net income		$1,540,000

In recent Opinions, where a Board position might lead to unnecessary variation in interpretation, it has specified the approved treatment. Witness its statement in APB *Opinion No. 17:*

> Amortization of acquired goodwill and of other acquired intangible assets not deductible in computing income taxes payable does not create a timing difference, and allocation of income taxes is inappropriate. (APBAP Vol. 1, Sect. 5141.30.)

Special Tax Provisions—The Carryback

Although some may think of them as a subdivision of permanent differences, special relief procedures permitted by tax law introduce a possible third category affecting income tax provision and liability. Such tax procedures permit claim for refund of previously paid taxes or reduction of taxes to be paid in the future.

At the time of this writing, a net operating loss may be carried back to each of the three preceding years and carried forward to each of the five following years. Let us examine the case of the net operating loss carryback.

EXAMPLE

H Corporation has the following taxable incomes for the years indicated: 19x0, $30,000; 19x1, $5,000; 19x2, $7,000. In 19x3, it suffers a net operating loss of $23,000. The carryback provisions permit the company to apply for a refund of taxes paid on taxable income of 19x0, which could be recorded thus:

Income tax refund receivable	10,350	
Tax benefit derived from net		
operating loss deduction		10,350
(Assumed rate of 45% on $23,000)		

Possible presentation on the income statement for 19x3:

Loss from operations	($23,000)
Less: Tax benefit derived from net	
operating loss deduction	10,350
Net loss	($12,650)

SPECIAL TAX PROVISIONS—THE CARRYFORWARD

One cannot deny the benefit resulting from the net operating loss deduction which results in a refund. The case for the carryforward is not quite so strong. If a newly formed corporation has net operating losses in its first few years of operation, with no positive signs of the dawning of profit periods, of what value are the carryforward provisions? With a high degree of uncertainty, it would be wise to reflect the full operating loss in the income statement of each year, with no suggestion of the potential benefits from available carryforward provisions, except by footnote. Should future years ultimately prove profitable, the reductions in tax liability resulting from the carryforward procedure are available as corrections to the losses of prior periods.

Where a firmly entrenched and successful organization suffers an extraordinary operating loss, but reason would leave little doubt of the potential benefit from an operating loss carryforward, one should recognize the tax benefit as an adjustment to net loss from operations, similar to the technique shown in the previous income statement illustration.

CPA PROBLEMS

Problem IX-1: Calculation of deferred income taxes and timing differences (40-50 min.)

Your firm has been appointed to examine the financial statements of Clark Engineering, Inc. (CEI) for the two years ended December 31, 1971 in conjunction with an application for a bank loan. CEI was formed on January 2, 1960 by the nontaxable incorporation of the Clark family partnership.

Early in the engagement you learned that the controller was unfamiliar with income tax accounting and that no tax allocations have been recorded.

During the examination considerable information was gathered from the accounting records and client employees regarding interperiod tax allocation. This information has been audited and is as follows (with dollar amounts rounded to the nearest $100):

1. CEI uses a bad debt write-off method for tax purposes and a full accrual method for book purposes. The balance of the Allowance for Doubtful Receivables account at December 31, 1969 was $62,000. Following is a schedule of accounts written off and the corresponding year(s) in which the related sales were made.

Year(s) in Which Sales Were Made	Year in Which Accounts Written Off	
	1971	*1970*
1969 and prior	$19,800	$29,000
1970	7,200	
1971		
	$27,000	$29,000

The following is a schedule of changes in the Allowance for Doubtful Receivables account for the two years ended December 31, 1971:

	Year Ended December 31	
	1971	*1970*
Balance at beginning of year......................	$66,000	$62,000
Accounts written off during the year	(27,000)	(29,000)
Bad debt expense for the year....................	38,000	33,000
Balance at end of year	$77,000	$66,000

2. Following is a reconciliation between net income per books and taxable income:

	Year Ended December 31	
	1971	1970
Net income per books	$333,100	$262,800
Federal income tax payable during year............	182,300	236,800
Taxable income not recorded on the books this year:		
Deferred sales commissions	10,000	
Expenses recorded on the books this year not deducted on the tax return:		
(a) Allowance for doubtful receivables	11,000	4,000
(b) Amortization of goodwill	8,000	8,000
Total	544,400	511,600
Income recorded on the books this year not included on the tax return:		
Tax exempt interest—Watertown 5% Municipal Bonds	5,000	
Deductions on the tax return not charged against book income this year:		
Depreciation	83,700	38,000
Total	88,700	38,000
Taxable income	$455,700	$473,600

3. Assume that the effective tax rates are as follows:

1969 and prior years: 60%
1970: 50%
1971: 40%

4. In December 1971 CEI entered into a contract to serve as distributor for Brown Manufacturer, Inc.'s engineering products. The contract became effective December 31, 1971, and $10,000 of advance commissions on the contract were received and deposited on December 31, 1971. Since the commissions had not been earned, they were accounted for as a deferred credit to income on the balance sheet at December 31, 1971.

5. Goodwill represents the excess of cost over fair value of the net tangible assets of a retiring competitor that were acquired for cash on January 2, 1966. The original balance was $80,000.

6. Depreciation on plant assets transferred at incorporation and acquisitions through December 31, 1969 have been accounted for on a straight-line basis for both financial and tax reporting. Beginning in 1970 all additions of machinery and equipment have been depreciated using the declining-balance method for tax reporting but the straight-line method for financial reporting. Company policy is to take a full year's depreciation in the year of acquisition and none in the year of retirement. There have been no sales, trade-ins or retirements since incorporation. Following is a schedule disclosing significant information about depreciable property and related depreciation:

DEPRECIATION SCHEDULE

Asset	Cost	Life	Annual Straight-line Amount*	Declining-balance Depreciation 1971	Declining-balance Depreciation 1970	Depreciation Taken Through December 31, 1969
Buildings	$1,190,000	20 & 50 yrs.	$31,000			$380,000
Machinery and equipment:						
Transferred at incorporation or acquired through December 31, 1969	834,000	Various	45,900			495,800
Acquisitions since December 31, 1969:						
1970	267,000	6 yrs.	38,000	$ 63,700	$ 76,000	
1971	395,000	6 yrs.	58,000	116,000		
Total asset cost	$2,686,000					

Total Depreciation Expense

	1971	1970	Through December 31, 1969
For book purposes	$172,900	$114,900	$875,800
For tax purposes	$256,600	$152,900	$875,800

*After giving appropriate consideration to salvage value.

Required:

a. Prepare a schedule calculating (1) the balance of deferred income taxes at December 31, 1970 and 1971, and (2) the amount of the timing differences between actual income tax payable and financial income tax expense for 1970 and 1971. Round all calculations to the nearest $100.

b. Independent of your solution to part a and assuming the following data, prepare the section of the income statement beginning with pretax accounting income to disclose properly income tax expense for the years ended December 31, 1971 and 1970.

	1971	1970
Pretax accounting income	$480,400	$465,600
Taxes payable currently	182,300	236,800
Year's net timing difference—Dr. (Cr.)	28,100	(24,500)
Balance of deferred tax at end of year—Dr. (Cr.).........	(44,200)	(16,100)

Problem IX-2: Taxable wages and payroll tax returns (40-50 min.)

In January 1969 you were examining the financial statements of Lang Manufacturing Company for the year ended December 31, 1968. Lang filed the necessary payroll tax returns for the first three quarters of 1968 and had prepared drafts of the returns scheduled to be filed by January 31, 1969.

The following information was available from the general ledger, copies and drafts of payroll tax returns and other sources:

Lang Manufacturing Company

General Ledger:

Account	Balance December 31, 1968	Composition of Balance
Wages (various expense accounts)	$121,800	12 monthly entries from payroll summaries.
Payroll Taxes Expense	6,963	F.I.C.A. (4.4% of $102,500) $4,510; state unemployment tax (2.7% of $59,000) $1,593; federal unemployment tax (.4% of $102,500) $410; amounts withheld from employees for F.I.C.A. tax in October and November and paid to depositary $450.
Employees' Payroll Taxes Withheld	2,145	December income tax $1,530; October thru December F.I.C.A. $615.
Employer's Payroll Taxes Payable	774	December F.I.C.A. $165; October thru December state unemployment tax $199; 1968 federal unemployment tax $410.

Copies of 1968 Tax Returns:

	Totals for Year	First Three Quarters (Duplicate Copies of Returns)	Last Quarter (Pencil Draft)
Gross wages	$121,800	$95,870	$25,930
Wages taxable for F.I.C.A.	102,500	88,520	13,980
F.I.C.A. tax	9,020	7,790	1,230
Income tax withheld	15,740	11,490	4,250
Wages taxable for state unemployment tax	59,000	51,640	7,360
Total state unemployment tax (employer only)	1,593	1,394	199
Total federal unemployment tax—employer only (pencil draft of return for full year) ...	410		

Information from other sources:

1. In August 1968 six laborers were hired to tear down an old warehouse building located on the site where a new warehouse would soon be constructed. The laborers' 1968 wages totaling $1,000 were charged to the Land and Buildings account. Payroll taxes were not withheld.

2. Included in a 1968 Wages Expense account is one month's salary of $1,400 paid to the president on December 30, 1968 for his 1967 vacation allowance.

3. A gross factory payroll of $1,200 through December 31, 1968 and the related F.I.C.A. taxes (employer and employee) were accrued on the general ledger at the year end for a portion of the week ending January 4, 1969. Each of the employees included in this payroll earned between $4,000 and $6,000 as a Lang employee in 1968.

4. In December 1968 a contractor was paid $2,300 for making repairs to machinery usually made by Company employees and the amount was charged to Wages Expense. No payroll taxes were withheld.

Required:

a. Prepare a schedule presenting the computation of total taxable wages to be reported on the 1968 payroll tax returns for F.I.C.A. and for state unemployment taxes.

b. Prepare a schedule presenting the computation of the amounts (to the nearest dollar) which should be paid with each of the year-end payroll tax returns to be filed in January 1969 for (1) F.I.C.A. taxes and income tax withheld, (2) state unemployment tax and (3) federal unemployment tax.

c. Prepare a schedule to reconcile the differences between the amounts which should be paid with payroll tax returns to be filed in January 1969 (as computed for "b") and the balances shown at December 31, 1968 in the related general ledger liability accounts.

Problem IX-3: Interperiod tax allocation and deferred credits (40-50 min.)

In January 1968 you began the examination of the financial statements for the year ended December 31, 1967 of Hines Corporation, a new audit client.

During your examination the following information was disclosed:

1. Federal tax liabilities reported on tax returns were:

Year	Amount Due Per Tax Return
1965	$33,850
1966	77,020
1967	51,966

2. On January 2, 1965 packaging equipment was purchased at a cost of $225,000. The equipment had an estimated useful life of five years and a salvage value of $15,000. The Corporation was entitled to and claimed an investment credit of $5,250 on its 1965 income tax return. For financial reporting purposes, the investment credit was treated as an offset against the cost of the equipment. The sum-of-the-years' digits method of depreciation was used for income tax reporting and the straight-line method was used on the financial statements.

3. On January 8, 1966 $60,000 was collected in advance rental of a building for a three-year period. The $60,000 was reported as taxable income in 1966, but $40,000 was reported as deferred revenue in 1966 in the financial statements. The building will continue to be rented for the foreseeable future.

4. On January 5, 1967 office equipment was purchased for $10,000. The office equipment has an estimated life of 10 years and no salvage value. Straight-line depreciation was used for both financial and income tax reporting purposes. Management, however, elected to take the allowable additional first year depreciation of $2,000 for income tax reporting. As a result, the depreciation reported on the income tax return for this equipment was $2,800 in 1967. (Ignore the investment credit for simplicity.)

5. On February 12, 1967 the Corporation sold land with a book and tax basis of $150,000 for $200,000. The gain, reported in full in 1967 on the financial statements, was reported by the installment method on the income tax return equally over a period of 10 years and is taxable at capital gains rate.

6. On March 15, 1967 a patent developed at a cost of $34,000 was granted. The Corporation is amortizing the patent over a period of four years on the financial statements and over 17 years on its income tax return. The Corporation elected to record a full year's amortization in 1967 on both its financial statements and income tax return.

7. The income tax rates for 1965, 1966 and 1967 were:

	Rate
Ordinary income:	
First $25,000	22%
Excess over $25,000	48%
Long-term capital gains	25%

Required:

a. Prepare a schedule computing the amount of the total net deferred tax debits or credits for each year ended December 31 for 1965, 1966 and 1967.

b. Prepare a schedule computing the total amount of income tax expense for financial reporting purposes for each year ended December 31 for 1965, 1966 and 1967.

Problem IX-4: Income tax allocation for unaudited corporation with errors in records (40-50 min.)

You have been engaged to examine the financial statements of Helen Corporation for the year 1970. The bookkeeper who maintains the financial records has prepared all of the unaudited financial statements for the Corporation since its organization on January 2, 1968. You discover numerous errors that have been made in these statements. The client has asked you to compute the correct income for the three years 1968 through 1970 and to prepare a corrected balance sheet as of December 31, 1970.

In the course of your examination you discover the following:

1. The Corporation includes sales taxes collected from customers in the Sales account. When sales tax collections for a month are remitted to the taxing authority on the 15th of the following month, the Sales Tax Expense account is charged. All sales are subject to a 3% sales tax. Total sales plus sales taxes for 1968 through 1970 were $495,430, $762,200 and $924,940, respectively. The totals of the Sales Tax Expense account for the three years were $12,300, $21,780 and $26,640.

2. Furniture and fixtures were purchased on January 2, 1968 for $12,000 but no portion of the cost has been charged to depreciation. The Corporation wishes to use the straight-line method for these assets which have been estimated to have a life of ten years and no salvage value.

3. In January 1968 installation costs of $5,700 on new machinery were charged to Repairs Expense. Other costs of this machinery of $30,000 were correctly recorded and have been depreciated using the straight-line method with an estimated life of ten years and no salvage value. Current estimates are that the machinery has a life of 20 years, a salvage value of $4,200 and that the sum-of-the-years-digits depreciation method would be most appropriate.

4. An account payable of $8,000 for merchandise purchased on December 23, 1968 was recorded in January 1969. This merchandise was not included in inventory at December 31, 1968.

5. Merchandise having a cost of $6,550 was stored in a separate warehouse and was not included in the December 31, 1969 inventory, and merchandise having a cost of $2,180 was included twice in the December 31, 1970 inventory. The Corporation uses a periodic inventory method.

6. The year-end salary accrual of $1,925 on December 31, 1970 has not been recorded.

7. A check for $1,895 from a customer to apply to his account was received on December 30, 1968 but was not recorded until January 2, 1969.

8. Quarterly dividends of $2,500 have been declared near the end of each calendar quarter since the Corporation was organized. The bookkeeper has consistently followed the practice of recording all dividends at the date of payment which is the 15th of the month following the month of declaration.

9. At December 31, 1968 sales catalogues advertising a special January 1969 white sale were on hand but their cost of $1,360 was included in Advertising Expense for 1968.

10. At December 31, 1970 there was an unexplained cash shortage of $48.

11. When the 500 shares of outstanding stock having a par value of $100 were initially issued on January 2, 1968, the $55,000 cash received for them was credited to the Common Stock account.

12. The Corporation has used the direct writeoff method of accounting for bad debts. Accounts written off during each of the three years amount to $1,745, $2,200 and $5,625, respectively. The Corporation has decided that the allowance method would be more appropriate. The estimated balances for the Allowance for Doubtful Accounts at the end of each of the three years are: $6,100, $8,350 and $9,150.

13. On January 2, 1969, $100,000 of 6% 20-year bonds were issued for $98,000. The $2,000 discount was charged to Interest Expense. The bookkeeper records interest only on the interest payment dates of January 2 and July 1.

14. A pension plan adopted on January 2, 1970 includes a provision for a pension fund to be administered by a trustee. The employees who joined the Corporation in 1968 and 1969 were given credit for their past service. A payment of $25,000 for the full amount of these past service costs was paid into the fund immediately. A second payment of $15,000 was made into the fund near the end of 1970. However, actuarial computations indicate that pension costs attributable to 1970 employee services are $16,600. The only entries applicable to the pension fund made during 1970 were debits to Pension Expense and credits to Cash. The Corporation wishes to make the maximum annual provision for pension cost in accordance with generally accepted accounting principles.

15. Property tax assessments of $15,600, $16,080 and $15,900 were made on January 1 of 1968, 1969 and 1970, respectively. The assessments are billed each year following the assessment on July 1, the beginning of the fiscal year of the taxing authority, and taxes are payable in two equal installments on September 10 and December 10. The bookkeeper has always charged Property Tax Expense on the dates the cash payments are made. The Corporation wishes to charge the tax expense against revenue during the fiscal year of the taxing authority.

Required:

a. Prepare a working paper showing the computation of the effects of the errors upon income for 1968, 1969 and 1970 and upon the balance sheet as of December 31, 1970. The worksheet analysis should be presented in the same order as the facts are given with corresponding numbers, 1 through 15. (Formal journal entries or financial statements are not required.) Use the following columnar headings for your working paper:

	Income 1968		Income 1969		Income 1970		Balance Sheet Corrections at December 31, 1970		
Explanation	Debit	Credit	Debit	Credit	Debit	Credit	Amount Debit	Credit	Account

b. Prepare a schedule showing the computation of the income tax expense and liability for each of the years 1968, 1969 and 1970. Assume that the net income computed after all adjustments and corrections in part "a" was $180,000 for 1968, $212,000 for 1969 and $252,000 for 1970 and that the income tax rate was 40% in each of the three years. Without prejudice to your answer in part "a" assume that depreciation expense and rent and interest revenue have been included in accounting income and taxable income for 1968 through 1970 as follows:

	Accounting Income	Taxable Income
Depreciation expense:		
1968	$50,000	$70,000
1969	54,000	71,000
1970	58,000	68,000
Rent revenue:		
1968	9,000	9,750
1969	9,000	8,250
Interest revenue (on		
municipal bonds):		
1968	3,000	–
1969	3,000	–
1970	3,000	–

Problem IX-5: Corporate pension plan; contribution and vested interests (40-50 min.)

Jarman Corporation adopted a pension plan for its employees on January 1, 1971. A trial balance of the records of the plan at December 31, 1972 follows:

	Debit	Credit
Cash	$ 400	
Investments (at cost)	3,400	
Bone, equity		$1,590
Cohan, equity		1,060
Dohler, equity		850
Income from investments received in 1972		300
	$3,800	$3,800

The following data pertain to the corporation's employees for 1972:

	Date Employed	Date Terminated	Salary Paid in 1972
Bone	12/ 8/67	. . .	$17,900
Cohan	2/ 1/69	. . .	14,100
Dohler	12/ 8/69	4/ 9/72	3,500
Kolman	9/15/70	. . .	8,000
Jones	9/21/72	12/22/72	3,000
Lohman	5/ 6/72	. . .	5,500
			$52,000

Provisions of the plan include the following:

1. The corporation shall contribute 10% of its net income before deducting income taxes and the contribution, but not in excess of 15% of the total salaries paid to the participants in the plan who are in the employ of the corporation at year end. The employees make no contributions to the plan.

2. An employee shall be eligible to participate in the plan on January 1 following the completion of one full year of employment.

3. The corporation's contribution shall be allocated to the participants' equities on the following point system:

a. For each full year of employment—2 points
b. For each $100 of salary paid in the current year—1 point
4. A participant shall have a vested interest of 10% of his total equity for each full year of employment. Forfeitures shall be distributed to the remaining participants in proportion to their equities in the plan at the beginning of the year. Terminated employees shall receive their vested interests at year end.
5. Income from the plan's investments shall be allocated to the equities of the remaining participants in proportion to their equities at the beginning of the year.

The Jarman Corporation's net income in 1972 before income taxes and contribution to the plan was $73,250.

Required:

a. Prepare a schedule computing the corporation's contribution to the plan for 1972.
b. Prepare a schedule computing the vested interests of the participants terminating their employment during 1972.
c. Prepare a schedule showing the allocation of the corporation's 1972 contribution to each participant.
d. Prepare a schedule showing the allocation of the plan's 1972 income on investments and forfeitures by terminated participants.

Problem IX-6: Bonds: issuance, amortization, conversion (50-60 min.)

The board of directors of the Nelson Company authorized a $1,000,000 issue of 5% convertible 20-year bonds, dated March 1, 1968. Interest is payable on March 1 and September 1 of each year. The conversion agreement provides that until March 1, 1973 each $1,000 of bonds may be converted into 6 shares of $100 par value common stock, and that interest accrued to date of conversion will be paid in cash. After March 1, 1973 the bonds are convertible into 5 shares of common for each $1,000 of bonds.
The company sold the entire issue on June 30, 1968 at 98 and accrued interest. Deferrable costs incurred in making the sale amounted to $8,320. The company adjusts its books at the end of each month and closes them on December 31 of each year. Interest is paid as due. On February 1, 1970 a holder of $20,000 of bonds converts them into common stock.

Required:

Prepare entries in journal form to reflect the transactions arising out of the existence of these bonds on each of the following dates:

a. June 30, 1968
b. September 1, 1968
c. December 31, 1969, including closing entries
d. February 1, 1970
e. December 31, 1970, including closing entries

In support of the above entries, prepare a summary analysis of the un-amortized bond discount and expense account for the period to December 31, 1970.

SPECIFIC APPROACH

Problem IX-1

Although the first requirement was to "prepare a schedule," the suggested Institute solution was a series of five schedules. Not only does this fail to meet the requirement strictly, but multiple, fragmented schedules weaken a solution. It is recommended that you concentrate on the structure of a single schedule which will meet both parts of requirement (a). Only four amount columns would be required: Amount, Tax Rate, Deferred Tax 1970, Deferred Tax 1971.

Treat each subject completely (depreciation, doubtful receivables, commissions) before tackling the next. This permits concentration and is likely to yield better results.

In the treatment of doubtful receivables, the turn-about effect must be handled at the same tax rate used in initial consideration of the elements and their influence on deferred income taxes.

Problem IX-2

1. As is true with most accounting schedules, proper columnar construction aids a candidate in reaching a better solution. All three requirements of this problem begin, "Prepare a schedule." Time invested in careful design yields excellent dividends.

2. Wages under F.I.C.A. are taxable when paid.

3. Since no state is given nor are any specific requirements of state laws, do not introduce variations of *your* state in regard to state and federal unemployment taxes. Do not concern yourself with individual maximum taxable wage bases.

4. In requirement (b), the balance to be paid in January of 1969 is the difference between the liability applicable to the fourth quarter and the amounts paid to the depository for October and November.

5. The schedule in requirement (c) will reflect changes in the F.I.C.A., and unemployment taxes necessitated by the net corrections to wages as shown in the schedule for requirement (a).

What correction is necessary because amounts withheld from employees for F.I.C.A. tax in October and November and paid to depository were charged to Payroll Taxes Expense?

6. Candidate should verify that the grand total of columnar totals in final schedule equal "the balances shown at December 31, 1968 in the related general ledger liability accounts," as the requirement specifies.

Problem IX-3

1. Four items are treated differently for tax reporting purposes than for financial statement purposes and result in interperiod tax allocation taxed at ordinary income tax rates: depreciation on packaging equipment, depreciation on office equipment, patent amortizaton, and rental income. Determine in one sub-schedule the annual net deduction for income tax reporting attributable to these items. In a separate sub-schedule, determine the annual net deductions for financial statements.

2. By using final totals from the two sub-schedules, the candidate will show in the schedule for requirement (a), tax deductions in excess of financial statement deductions taxed at ordinary rates. Addition of the deferred tax credit on the sale of land at capital gains rate would yield the total annual net deferred tax credits or debits, which should be cumulated to comply strictly with the wording of the requirement.

3. The schedule for computation of income tax expense for financial reporting is simple, if one recalls that the income tax expense and liability differ by the amount of the deferred tax credit or debit.

Problem IX-4

1. In completing the worksheet analysis, remember the requirements to show "the effects of the errors upon income for 1968, 1969, and 1970 and upon the balance sheet as of December 31, 1970." Some items may not affect either income or the balance sheet.

2. For the schedule showing computation of income tax expense and liability, begin with the accounting income for each of the three years, itemizing additions and deductions which will produce taxable income. The annual income tax expense base will exclude the nontaxable interest on municipal bonds.

3. APB *Opinion No. 8* does not provide a definite technique for assignment of past service costs, but does establish minimum and maximum levels, the latter equal to 10% of past and prior service costs plus any interest on the unfunded past and prior service costs. Refer to the General Approach for this Topic.

Problem IX-5

1. To decide whether the contribution shall be based on a percentage of net income or of salaries paid, compute the salaries paid to eligible participants.

2. Since allocation of the 1972 contribution is based on points, calculate the

total points for each eligible participant. Convert the points to dollars, employing a percentage approach.

3. The allocation of 1972 income and forfeitures may also be accomplished by the per cent approach, using equities as the base.

Problem IX-6

The problem tests the candidate's grasp of fundamental entries for bonds payable.

1. The final sentence of the problem reads, in part, "prepare a summary analysis of the unamortized bond discount and expense account." The candidate should react by combining the unamortized bond discount and the deferrable costs of bond sale, thereby permitting a single computation per period for the amortization.

2. To prepare proper entries, it is crucial to remember that "The company adjusts its books at the end of each month and closes them on December 31 of each year."

TOPIC X

Ownership Equities: Corporations
and Partnerships

GENERAL APPROACH

The interests or equities of owners represent residual claims to assets. This discussion will consist of two major parts, corporations and partnerships.

Corporations

Stockholders' equity arises from two main sources: contributed capital and retained earnings. Balance-sheet presentation often tries to distinguish between these two sources, for example,

Stockholders' equity:
Common stock, authorized, 1,000,000 shares; issued and outstanding,
  500,000 shares; $5 par—stated or legal capital $2,500,000
Additional contributions in excess of legal requirements (Paid-in
  surplus) 1,000,000
    Total contributed capital $3,500,000
Retained earnings 6,000,000
    Total stockholders' equity $9,500,000

Note that contributed capital is subdivided above to show legal capital and capital in excess of legal capital.

The task of clear presentation is often complicated by state corporation laws. For example, an ordinary stock dividend (common on common) frequently results in a transfer of an amount from retained earnings to contributed capital.

If this is done, the distinction between contributed capital and retained earnings is blurred.

Another example involves treasury stock. In essence, the purchase of treasury stock is a contraction of stockholders' equity; there is no basic difference between unissued and treasury stock. But legal requirements again affect the accounting. There has been a tendency in accounting practice to deduct treasury stock from the gross stockholders' equity to arrive at a net equity figure. Again, although such treatment is generally accepted, it fails to draw a line of demarcation between contributed capital and retained earnings.

Terminology

AICPA *Terminology Bulletin No. 1* (paragraph 69) emphasizes:

(1) The use of the term *surplus* . . . be discontinued.
(2) The contributed portion of proprietary capital be shown as:
 (a) Capital contributed for, or assigned to, shares, to the extent of the par or stated value of each class of shares presently outstanding.
 (b) (i) Capital contributed for, or assigned to, shares in excess of such par or stated value (whether as a result of original issue of shares at amounts in excess of their then par or stated value, or of a reduction in par or stated value of shares after issuance, or of transactions by the corporation in its own shares); and
 (ii) Capital received other than for shares, whether from shareholders or from others.
(3) The term *earned surplus* be replaced by terms which will indicate source, such as *retained income, retained earnings.* . . . In the case of a deficit, the amount should be shown as a deduction from contributed capital with appropriate description.
(4) In connection with 2(b) and 3 there should, so far as practicable, be an indication of the extent to which the amounts have been appropriated or are restricted as to withdrawal. Retained income appropriated to some specific purpose nevertheless remains part of retained income. . . .
(5) Where there has been a quasi-reorganization, retained income should be "dated" for a reasonable time thereafter; and where the amount of retained income has been reduced as a result of a stock dividend or a transfer by resolution of the board of directors from unrestricted to restricted capital, the presentation should, until the fact loses significance, indicate the amount shown as retained income is the remainder after such transfers.
(6) Any appreciation included . . . other than as a result of a quasi-reorganization should be designated by such terms as *excess of appraised or fair value of fixed assets over cost* or *appreciation of fixed assets.*

Considering the above, a presentation of a stockholders' equity section is shown in the accompanying exhibit. Older terminology is in parentheses.

Sample Corporation,
STOCKHOLDERS' EQUITY (NET WORTH)
December 31, 19x1

5% preferred stock, $100 par value, authorized 10,000 shares; issued and outstanding 6,000 shares	$ 600,000	
Excess received over par value of preferred shares issued (Premium on preferred stock)	50,000	$ 650,000
Common stock, no par, stated value $10 per share, authorized 100,000 shares; issued 80,000 shares, of which 5,000 shares are held in the treasury	$ 800,000	
Excess received over stated value of common shares issued (Paid-in surplus)	1,000,000	
Excess received over cost of common treasury stock (Paid-in surplus on treasury stock)	10,000	1,810,000
Total legal capital*		$2,460,000
Donated capital—plant site received from City of Champion (Donated surplus)		200,000
Total		$2,660,000
Retained earnings (Earned surplus):		
Appropriated† (Reserve):		
For possible future price declines in inventory	$ 100,000	
For treasury stock	20,000	
For sinking fund................................	200,000	
For expansion	200,000	
For replacement of fixed assets	300,000	
For retirement of preferred stock	400,000	
For general contingencies	50,000	
For investment in working capital	200,000	
Total appropriated	$1,470,000	
Unappropriated	790,000	
Total retained earnings		2,260,000
Excess of appraised value of plant assets over cost (Appraisal surplus)		500,000
Sub-total		$5,420,000
Less: Cost of 5,000 shares of common stock reacquired and held in treasury (Treasury stock)		20,000
Stockholders' equity		$5,400,000

*Definitions of legal capital vary among states. Many states define legal capital as only the par or stated value of issued stock; see the prior example for the format under these conditions. The example here would be changed to show preferred stock at par plus common stock at stated value. All "paid-in surplus" accounts would then follow.

†The term "restricted" may be used in place of "appropriated."

Reserves

A candidate should be thoroughly familiar with the three broad types of reserves in accounting:

1. *Asset Valuation*—an offset to an asset. Examples: reserves for depreciation, depletion, bad debts, reduction of inventory or investments to market, deferred maintenance. "Allowance for. . ." is better terminology.

2. *Liability*—an estimate of a liability of indefinite or uncertain amount. Examples: reserves for income taxes, warranties, vacation pay. "Estimated liability for. . ." is better terminology.

3. *Retained Earnings Reserve*—a restriction of dividend-paying power denoted by a specific subdivision of retained earnings. Examples: reserves for contingencies, possible price declines or increases, sinking fund, expansion, treasury stock, retirement of preferred stock. AICPA *Terminology Bulletin No. 1* maintains that the term "reserve" should be confined *solely* to this category.

Retained earnings reserves (a) should be created by charging retained earnings, not income, (b) should never be used to relieve income of charges for expenses or losses, (c) should never influence the determination of net income for any year, and (d) should be restored to retained earnings directly when no longer needed.

To summarize:

Type of Reserve	*Creation*	*Disposition*
Asset valuation	Bad debts expense . . . . xxx 　Allowance for bad debts.　xxx	Allowance for bad debts . xxx 　Accounts receivable . . 　xxx
Liability	Income-tax expense . . . . xxx 　Estimated income taxes . 　payable . . . . 　xxx	Estimated income taxes . . 　payable . . . . xxx Cash . . . . 　xxx
Retained earnings	Retained earnings. . . . . xxx 　Reserve for contingencies　xxx	Reserve for contingencies. xxx 　Retained earnings . . . . 　xxx

Treasury Stock and Retired Stock

Paragraph 12 of APB *Opinion No. 6* (or see APBAP Vol. 1, Sect. 5542.136) gives much latitude toward accounting for retired or treasury stock. The following practices are favored:

When a corporation's stock is retired, or purchased for constructive retirement:

　　1. "*An excess of purchase price over par or stated value* may be allocated between capital surplus and retained earnings. The portion of the excess allocated to capital surplus should be limited to the sum of (a) all capital surplus arising from previous retirements and net 'gains' on sales of treasury stock of the same issue and (b) the pro rata portion of capital surplus paid in, voluntary transfers of retained earnings, capitalization of stock dividends, etc., on the same issue. . . . Alternatively, the excess may be charged entirely to retained earnings in recognition of the fact that a corporation can always capitalize or allocate retained earnings for such purposes."

　　2. "*An excess of par or stated value over purchase price* should be credited to capital surplus."

The cost of treasury stock can be shown separately as a deduction from total stockholders' equity, or may be accorded the same accounting treatment appropriate for retired stock, or in some circumstances may be shown as an asset. (The last conflicts with the position taken in many intermediate and advanced textbooks that treasury stock is not an asset.)

Suppose, as is often the case, that treasury stock is charged with cost upon acquisition. "Gains" upon resale (difference between proceeds and cost) should be credited to capital surplus. "Losses" should be charged to capital surplus to the extent that previous net "gains" from sales or retirements of the same class of stock are included therein—otherwise, to retained earnings.

Stock Dividends and Stock Split-Ups

APBAP Vol. 1, Sect. 5561.15 states:

> ... a stock split-up is defined as being confined to transactions involving the issuance of shares, without consideration moving to the corporation, for the purpose of effecting a reduction in the unit market price of shares of the class issued and, thus, of obtaining wider distribution and improved marketability of the shares. Where there is clearly the intent, no transfer from earned surplus to capital surplus or capital stock account is called for, other than to the extent occasioned by legal requirements. It is believed, however, that few cases will arise where the aforementioned purpose can be accomplished through an issuance of shares which is less than, say, 20% or 25% of the previously outstanding shares.

Ordinary stock dividends are issuances of additional shares (usually less than 20-25%) of stock which may not reasonably be expected to have the effect of reducing the share market value.

The recommended handling of stock dividends in *Bulletin No. 43* illustrates again the need for candidates to be familiar with Institute literature. The Institute favors debiting retained earnings and crediting capital stock and "paid-in" surplus at the "fair value of the additional shares issued." The latter is usually the market price as of the date of declaration or some approximation of an "average market price" just prior to declaration.

State statutes, on the other hand, generally provide for transferring only a designated legal value per share. When writing the CPA examination, a candidate would be wise to demonstrate his familiarity with the position of the AICPA publications.

Earnings Per Share

APB *Opinion No. 15* (or see APBAP Vol. 1, Sect. 2011) requires that earnings per share (EPS) data be presented on the face of the income statement. When the capital structure is relatively simple, computations of EPS are straightforward. For example, consider the following calculation (figures assumed):

$$\text{Earnings per share of common stock} = \frac{\text{Net income - Preferred dividends}}{\text{Weighted average number of shares outstanding during the period}}$$

$$= \frac{\$1,000,000 - \$200,000}{800,000} = \$1.00$$

EPS should be shown for (a) income before extraordinary items, (b) extraordinary items if any (less applicable income tax), and (c) net income, the total of items (a) and (b).

When preferred stock exists, the number of times that preferred dividends have been earned ("earnings coverage") may be revealed. Such a statistic should not be called earnings per share.

Dividends on cumulative preferred stock for the period, whether or not earned or paid, should be deducted in calculating earnings applicable to common stock.

Historical summaries of EPS must be made comparable by adjusting for (a) changes in capitalization structure (for example, stock splits and stock dividends) and (b) restatements of net income as a result of a prior-period adjustment during the current period.

Opinion No. 15 stresses that the foregoing simple computations are inadequate when companies have complex capital structures. Until the 1960's, there was a sharp traditional distinction between common shares and senior securities (that is, bonds and preferred stock), but the decade of the '60's was marked by the popularity of convertible securities—bonds and stock that could be transformed into common shares at the option of the holder. Consider the following example (figures assumed):

	Outstanding
5% Convertible preferred stock, $100 par, each share convertible into 2 common shares	100,000 shares
Common stock	1,000,000 shares
Computation of earnings per share:	
Net income	$10,500,000
Preferred dividends	500,000
Net income to common stock	$10,000,000
Earnings per share of common stock ($10,000,000 ÷ 1,000,000 shares)	$ 10.00
But if all shares were converted:	
Net income	$10,500,000
Preferred dividends	0
Net income to common stock	$10,500,000
Earnings per share of common stock— assuming full dilution ($10,500,000 ÷ 1,200,000 shares) . . . . $	8.75

Where there is potential material dilution of EPS, a supplementary "pro forma" EPS must be reported along with the "primary" EPS, shown at the bottom of the income statement with an additional footnote, as follows:

Earnings per common share (Note A)	$10.00
Earnings per common share assuming full dilution (Note B)	$ 8.75

> *Note A:* Per share data are based on the average number of common shares outstanding during each year, after recognition of the dividend requirements on the 5% preferred stock.
>
> *Note B:* Per share data based on the assumption that the outstanding preferred stock as converted into common shares at the beginning of the year, reflecting the 200,000 shares issuable on conversion and eliminating the preferred dividend requirements.

Common Stock Equivalents

Opinion No. 15 (paragraph 25) also took a position that drastically affects the denominator for computing the basic or primary EPS figure. The denominator now provides for any convertible security that is, in substance, equivalent to common stock:

> The holders of these securities can expect to participate in the appreciation of the value of the common stock resulting principally from the earnings and earnings potential of the issuing corporation. This participation is essentially the same as that of a common stockholder except that the security may carry a specified dividend or interest rate yielding a return different from that received by a common stockholder. The attractiveness of this type of security to investors is often based principally on this potential right to share in increases in the earnings potential of the issuing corporation rather than on its fixed return or other senior security characteristics.
>
> As a practical matter, the APB defined convertible securities as having common stock equivalence if the cash yield to the holder at time of issuance is significantly below what would be a comparable rate for a similar security of the issuer without the conversion option. Where it is impossible to ascertain such comparable rates, the Board concluded, as a practical approximation, that a convertible security should be considered a common stock equivalent upon issuance if, based on its market price, it has a cash yield of less than 66 2/3 percent of the then current bank prime interest rate.

To illustrate, suppose Green Company has the following capital structure:

5% Convertible bonds payable	$16,000,000
Preferred stock, non-convertible, 6%, $100 par value, $100 liquidating value	1,600,000
Common stock $10 par value, issued and outstanding, 200,000 shares	2,000,000
Additional paid-in capital	10,000,000
Retained earnings	11,000,000

Also suppose that the income statement ends as follows:

Operating income	$3,100,000
Interest expense	800,000
Income before income taxes	$2,300,000
Income taxes	1,150,000
Net income	$1,150,000
Dividends on preferred stock	96,000
Net income for holders of common stock	$1,054,000

If no common stock equivalents were present, EPS would be $1,054,000 ÷ 200,000 = $5.27.

Suppose in our Green Co. illustration that upon issuance the bonds payable were convertible into 200,000 shares of common stock and had a cash yield of 5 percent. Comparable bonds without the conversion feature were selling for an 8 percent yield. Such a convertible security clearly is a common stock equivalent. EPS for the Green Co. must be computed as follows:

Operating income	$3,100,000
Interest expense	0
Income before income taxes	$3,100,000
Income taxes @ 50%	1,550,000
Net income	$1,550,000
Dividends on preferred stock	96,000
Net income for common shares and common equivalent shares	$1,454,000*
Divide by 400,000 shares instead of 200,000 shares	
Earnings per common share and common equivalent share	$3.64

*Alternatively, this may be computed by adding back the $800,000 interest, less the $400,000 applicable income tax effect or $400,000, to the $1,054,000 of net income for holders of common stock shown in the preceding tabulation: $1,054,000 + $400,000 = $1,454,000.

Note particularly that the above analysis is the computation of a financial statistic; it is not a different form of income statement. That is, the basic income statement is unaffected except for the bottom line, which would become: Earnings per common share and common equivalent share (Note a) $3.64.

Note (a) would contain the following:

Earnings per share is based on the earnings applicable to the total of outstanding shares of common shares plus shares of common stock that would be issuable upon the conversion of the convertible bonds, which are regarded as common stock equivalents. In this computation, the interest (less applicable income tax effect) has been added back to the earnings applicable to common stock.

In this computation, any interest (or preferred dividends) on convertible bonds (or convertible preferred stocks) that are regarded as common stock equivalents are added back (less any applicable income tax effects) because the EPS figure is really an "as if" computation. That is, these securities are viewed as if they were common stock, not as bonds (or preferred stock). If so, the EPS figure should be predictive of what will occur when no interest (or preferred dividends) must be paid. In this example, only the convertible bonds qualified as common stock equivalents; preferred stock did not so qualify.

Note that $3.64 is $1.63 less than the $5.27 reported on the legalistic basis. In effect, this common stock equivalence approach broadens the notion of a common stock to include all convertible securities that upon issuance have "valuable" conversion rights. The mere existence of such rights upon issuance makes the convertible security a common stock equivalent by definition.

Options and Warrants (and Their Equivalents)

Options, warrants, and similar arrangements are common stock equivalents at all times (unless their effects do not dilute earnings per share). Their impact on primary EPS is computed by application of the "treasury stock" method. Under this method, options and warrants are assumed to have been exercised at the beginning of the period (or at time of issuance, if later), and the funds obtained therefrom are assumed to have been used to purchase common shares at the average market price during the period.

For example, if Green Co. had 30,000 warrants outstanding, exercisable at $50, and the average market price of the common stock during the period were $60, the $1,500,000 received upon exercise of the warrants and issuance of 30,000 shares would be sufficient to acquire 25,000 shares ($1,500,000 ÷ $60). Thus 5,000 shares would be added to the outstanding shares in computing primary EPS for the period. In our Green Co. illustration, primary EPS would be $1,454,000 divided by 405,000 instead of 400,000 shares, or $3.59.

The foregoing assumption of exercise need not be reflected in EPS until the market price of common stock obtainable has exceeded the exercise price for substantially all of three consecutive months, ending with the last month of the period to which EPS data relate. Moreover, the rules become more complex if the number of shares of common stock obtainable upon exercise exceeds 20% of the common shares outstanding at the end of the period. For elaboration, see *Opinion No. 15.*

The same methods used to compute primary earnings per share should also be used to compute fully diluted EPS. However, to reflect maximum potential dilution, the market price at the close of the period should be used under the treasury stock method if such market price exceeds the average price used to compute primary EPS.

The CPA candidate must take some risks in preparing. An understanding of the foregoing description of the major features of *Opinion No. 15* or APBAP Vol. 1, Sect. 2011) should be adequate preparation for most questions on earnings per share.

Employee Stock Compensation

APB *Opinion No. 25,* "Accounting for Stock Issued to Employees," distinguishes between two types of compensatory plans. The first type measures total compensation cost as the difference between quoted market price of stock *at the date of grant or award* and the price, if any, to be paid by an employee. Frequently, this means that compensation cost is zero, because the market price at the date of grant of the stock may equal the price to be paid by an employee when he exercises his award. Thus, if a stock option is granted for 1,000 shares at $10 per share (the current market price), the compensation cost is zero; if the exercise price is $8 per share, the compensation cost is $2,000.

The second type of plan measures total compensation cost at *other* than the date of grant or award. For plans in which either the number of shares of stock or the purchase price depends on future events, compensation cost must be determined at the time when both the number of shares and the purchase price are known.

In sum, the valuation model in paragraph 10(b) of *Opinion No. 25* (1) frequently provides a measurement of zero for a fixed option at date of grant and (2) for some other option and award plans, provides a measurement of compensation that is dependent on changes in market values subsequent to date of grant or award.

Under both types of employee stock compensation plans, the compensation cost is recognized as an expense over the period or periods when the employee performs the related services.

Partnerships

Most CPA problems on partnerships involve one or more of the following aspects: division of profits or losses, admission of new partner, liquidation.

Division of Profits or Losses

Profits should always be divided equally unless the partnership agreement provides otherwise. A common mistake is to neglect this fundamental rule by dividing profits or losses in the ratio of capital balances. Although not all accountants agree, the net income of the partnership is generally considered to be that income *before* consideration of apportionment, whether the latter is in the form of salaries, interest, or a fractional allocation.

Many accountants maintain that reasonable partners' salaries should be deducted in the computation of partnership net income. But suggested solutions to CPA examinations have held to the view that partners' salaries are apportionments (distributions) of net income rather than expense.

When partnership net income is apportioned, the steps should be applied fully—even though there is not sufficient net income to cover all the early steps.

Question

A and B are partners. The partnership agreement provides that profits shall be divided as follows:

1. A's annual salary is $7,000.
2. Interest is to be allowed at the rate of 6% per annum on average capital balances.
3. Any remaining profits or losses shall be divided equally.

There were no changes in the capital accounts during the year. The ending capital balances before consideration of any salaries, interest, and profit distribution were: A, $10,000; and B, $20,000. What is A's final capital balance after closing if the net income before apportionment was $7,800?

Solution

	Capital Balance	Salaries	Interest	Remainder	Ending Capital Balance
A	$10,000	$7,000	$ 600	$(500)	$17,100
B	20,000	. . .	1,200	(500)	20,700

The T account for Profit and Loss could appear as follows:

PROFIT AND LOSS

A's salary $7,000	Net income $7,800
A's interest. 600	
B's interest. 1,200	
	Remaining balance—
	divided equally 1,000

In summary, solutions should always apply fully the provisions of the partnership agreement as to the division of profits. If the apportionment of salaries or interest exceeds the net income, the resultant debit balance should be distributed in accordance with the profit and loss ratio.

Admission of New Partner

1. Admissions of new partners nearly always involve a revision of net assets *prior* to recording the admission.

2. Recognition may be given to a new partner for his special profit-making ability in the form of goodwill (debit Goodwill) or of bonus (transfer of portion of old capital accounts to the new capital account).

3. Recognition may be given to old partners for special profit-making ability in the form of goodwill (debit Goodwill, credit old partners' capitals) or of bonus (debit new partner's capital, credit old partners' capitals).

4. Any adjustments affecting the old partners' capitals should be made in their profit and loss ratio, whether because of appraisals, bonuses, or goodwill.

5. After admission the new partner's *capital* account balance must be equal to the agreed percentage interest of *total capital.* Candidates should check their calculations accordingly.

CPA problems will supply enough facts to indicate whether the bonus or goodwill method should be used; either the total capital of the new firm or the new partner's capital balance will be indicated.

EXAMPLES

A and B are partners. A's capital is $15,000; B's is $25,000. Profits and losses are shared equally. C is to be admitted. Tangible assets are appraised upward by $10,000 prior to admission.

Tangible assets	10,000	
A, capital		5,000
B, capital		5,000

The new capital balances are now: A, $20,000; B, $30,000. Study the following five alternative assumptions:

Assumption 1. C purchases A's interest. The price paid is irrelevant. This is a private transaction.

A, capital	20,000	
C, capital		20,000

Assumption 2. C invests $22,000 for a one-third interest. Total capital is to be $75,000. *Goodwill of C is recognized.*

Cash	22,000	
Goodwill	3,000	
C,capital		25,000

New capitals: A	$20,000	
B	30,000	
C	25,000	
	$75,000	

Assumption 3. C invests $22,000 for a one-third interest. Total capital is to be $72,000. *Bonus is allowed C.*

Cash	22,000	
A, capital	1,000	
B, capital	1,000	
C, capital		24,000

New capitals: A	$19,000	
B	29,000	
C	24,000	
	$72,000	

Assumption 4. C invests and is credited with $28,000 for a one-third interest. Total capital is to be $84,000. *Old partners' goodwill is recognized.*

```
Goodwill  ..............................   6,000
    A, capital ............................         3,000
    B, capital ............................         3,000
Cash  .................................  28,000
    C, capital ............................        28,000
```

```
New capitals: A  ..............  $23,000
              B  ..............   33,000
              C  ..............   28,000
                                 ───────
                                 $84,000
```

Assumption 5. C invests $28,000 for a one-third interest. Total capital is to be $78,000. *Bonus is allowed old partners.*

```
Cash  .................................  28,000
    A, capital ............................         1,000
    B, capital ............................         1,000
    C, capital ............................        26,000
```

```
New capitals: A  ..............  $21,000
              B  ..............   31,000
              C  ..............   26,000
                                 ───────
                                 $78,000
```

Liquidation

Lump-Sum Liquidations

1. In all liquidations, known gains or losses should be divided among partners in the profit and loss ratio before *any* cash is distributed to partners. This includes the division of the net profit or loss for the final period of operation.

2. Cash should be distributed in the following order of priority: (a) outside creditors, (b) partners' loans, (c) partners' capitals. The right of offset should be applied before making a cash distribution; that is, an amount due a partner because of his loan to the partnership might be offset against a debit balance in his capital account after apportioning all losses. Thus it would be possible to withhold payment on a loan even though payments are being made on other partners' capitals.

3. In cases involving personal insolvency, the rule of *marshalling of assets* must be applied. Under the Uniform Partnership Act, the concept of marshalling of assets dictates that partnership assets are first applied against partnership debts and that personal assets are first applied against personal debts. If the partnership creditors cannot be paid in full from partnership assets, they have a right to pursue payment from the personal assets of any solvent partner, provided that payments of his personal debts have been arranged. If a partner-

ship is solvent but a partner is insolvent, his personal creditors have a claim against his partnership interest.

Installment Liquidations

1. The basic rule to follow in installment liquidations is always to consider all possible losses before disbursing cash to the partners. Possible losses include: (a) potential loss on realization of all assets remaining after the disbursement under consideration and (b) potential loss on any deficient or conceivably deficient partners' interests. In other words, the total maximum possible loss at any time is the difference between net noncash assets and the cash to be disbursed in this particular installment. (See Schedule 1 below.) In this way, a partner will be entitled to receive cash only if he is able to bear his share of the maximum loss. The procedure will preclude overpayment to any partner.

2. Use of two schedules simplifies solution. The master schedule includes the balances in each partner's capital and loan account (if any), as well as showing the cash, other assets, and liabilities. One column is devoted to each item; total debits equal total credits.

3. A supporting or auxiliary schedule(s) is used to show the calculation of each of the cash disbursements to partners. Only one column, consolidating the loan and capital amount, is needed for each partner. Supporting schedules are used until the combined loan and capital totals for *every* partner are in proportion to the partners' profit and loss ratios. After this point is reached, future divisions of cash are made directly in the profit and loss ratio, without the necessity of resorting to the supporting schedule.

A careful study of the example on the following page concerning installment liquidations should clarify the above generalizations.

Problem

A, B, and C are partners. They share profits and losses 50%, 30% and 20%, respectively. They decide to liquidate the business. The balance sheet as of January 31, 19x8 follows:

Cash	$ 30,000	Accounts payable	$ 60,000
Accounts receivable	70,000	A, loan	10,000
Inventories	150,000	A, capital	90,000
Fixed assets	250,000	B, capital	180,000
		C, capital	160,000
	$500,000		$500,000

During February, some of the receivables, amounting to $34,000, were collected. Some inventory which had cost $66,000 was sold for $76,000 cash. All liabilities were paid. At the end of the month, the balance of the cash was paid to the partners.

During March, cash amounting to $140,000 was collected for assets which had been carried at $160,000. At the end of March, this cash was distributed to the partners.

During April, all remaining assets of the business were disposed of for $150,000 in cash. At the end of April, the final distribution of cash was made.

Required:

Prepare a liquidation statement together with supporting schedules for the above period.

Solution and Comments

See Statement of Liquidation on p. 280.

A, B, and C Schedule 1
FIRST CASH INSTALLMENT TO PARTNERS
February 28, 19x8

	A (50%)*	B (30%)*	C (20%)*
Balances before payments:			
Capitals	$ 95,000	$ 183,000	$ 162,000
Loans.	10,000		
Total	$ 105,000	$ 183,000	$ 162,000
Possible losses:			
Noncash assets, $370,000	−185,000	−111,000	−74,000
Balance	$ −80,000	$ 72,000	$ 88,000
Additional possible loss† :			
A's debit balance	80,000	−48,000	−32,000
First cash installment	$ . . .	$ 24,000	$ 56,000

*Profit and loss ratio.

†Note that this calculation depends upon the preceding computation. The $80,000 possible loss is apportioned to other partners in their profit and loss ratio (3:2).

A, B, and C Schedule 2
SECOND CASH INSTALLMENT TO PARTNERS
March 31, 19x8

	A (50%)*	B (30%)*	C (20%)*
Balances before payments:			
Capitals	$ 85,000	$ 153,000	$ 102,000
Loan.	10,000		
Total	$ 95,000	$ 153,000	$ 102,000
Possible losses:			
Noncash assets, $210,000	−105,000	−63,000	−42,000
Balance	$ −10,000	$ 90,000	$ 60,000
Additional possible loss:			
A's debit balance	10,000	−6,000	−4,000
Second cash installment	$ . . .	$ 84,000	$ 56,000

*Profit and loss ratio.

A, B, and C
STATEMENT OF LIQUIDATION
January 31 to April 30, 19x8

	Cash	Noncash Assets	Accounts Payable	A (50%)* Loan	A (50%)* Capital	B (30%)* Capital	C (20%)* Capital
Balance, 1/31/x8	30,000	470,000	60,000	10,000	90,000	180,000	160,000
February realization and gain	110,000	−100,000			5,000	3,000	2,000
Payments to creditors	−60,000		−60,000				
Balance, 2/28/x8	80,000	370,000		10,000	95,000	183,000	162,000
February cash distribution to partners (Schedule 1)	−80,000					−24,000	−56,000
Balance, 3/1/x8		370,000		10,000	95,000	159,000	106,000
March realization and loss	140,000	−160,000			−10,000	−6,000	−4,000
Balance, 3/31/x8	140,000	210,000		10,000	85,000	153,000	102,000
March cash distribution to partners (Schedule 2)	−140,000					−84,000	−56,000
Balance, 4/1/x8		210,000		10,000	85,000	69,000	46,000
April realization and loss	150,000	−210,000			−30,000	−18,000	−12,000
Balance, 4/30/x8	150,000			10,000	55,000	51,000	34,000
Final cash distribution	−150,000			−10,000	−55,000	−51,000	−34,000

*Profit and loss ratio.

Note that this statement shows (a) realization of assets and division of gain or loss thereon, (b) payment of liabilities, and (c) installment cash distributions to partners.

In CPA problems on installment liquidations, sometimes no actual amounts to be disbursed are furnished. A schedule is required which will indicate the manner of distribution no matter what amount is available. Consider the following illustration:

The partnership of March and Gans is to be liquidated. You are to prepare a schedule showing how any cash which may become available should be distributed. Their balance sheet is as follows:

March and Gans
BALANCE SHEET
December 31, 19xx

ASSETS		LIABILITIES AND CAPITAL	
Cash	$ 1,000	Accounts payable	$ 3,000
Noncash assets	35,000	Gans, loan	2,000
		Gans, capital	10,000
		March, capital	21,000
	$36,000		$36,000

Profits and losses are shared by March and Gans in the ratio of 70% and 30%, respectively.

To assist in preparing a schedule of cash payments, set up a schedule to determine the sequence of elimination, using the following columns: Partner, Loans, Capital, Total Equity, Profit and Loss Ratio, Quotient, and Sequence. Combine the original investment, the current account balance, and the loans to yield the total equity. Loans are given a priority in payment, but the liquidator has the right of offset. For each partner, determine the amount of the loss which will eliminate his equity and thus preclude a cash distribution to him. This is accomplished by dividing each partner's equity by his profit-and-loss percentage. The partner with the smallest quotient will be the first in the sequence of elimination:

Schedule 1
SCHEDULE DETERMINING SEQUENCE OF ELIMINATION

Partner	Loan	Capital	Total Equity	Profit and Loss Ratio	Quotient	Sequence
March..		$21,000	$21,000	70%	$21,000 ÷ 70% = $30,000	1
Gans...	$2,000	10,000	12,000	30	12,000 ÷ 30% = 40,000	2
	2,000	$31,000	$33,000	100%		

In a second schedule showing each partner's equity, determine the balance remaining after charging losses which will eliminate partners' accounts in the sequence previously determined:

* Schedule 2

SCHEDULE OF ELIMINATION OF PARTNER'S EQUITY

	March (70%)*	Gans (30%)*
Equity balances	$21,000	$12,000
Loss which would eliminate March		
(Quotient of $30,000 from Schedule 1).....	21,000	9,000
Balances	–0–	$ 3,000

*Profit-and-loss ratio.

This key Schedule 2 would be continued in a similar fashion where there are more than two partners. That is, if there were a third partner in the sequence, the *additional* loss which would eliminate Gans would be computed next, and the balance remaining would be the third partner's priority claim to an early cash distribution.

Remembering to provide for creditor payment, prepare a schedule of cash payments to be made as assets are realized, starting with the final amount determined in the second schedule and working backward. Amounts to be distributed in excess of this amount up to the total needed to eliminate the second partner would be allocated as the *additional* loss was split. This procedure would be followed until the point is reached where cash is distributed in accordance with the partners' profit-and-loss ratio:

Schedule 3

SCHEDULE OF DISTRIBUTION AS CASH BECOMES AVAILABLE

	Cash	Liabilities	Partners' Equity March	Gans
First.......................	$2,000	$2,000		
Next.......................	3,000			$3,000
Any additional cash			70%	30%

CPA PROBLEMS

Problem X-1: Miscellaneous stockholders' equity transactions (40-50 min.)

Superior Products, Inc. for the first time is including a five-year summary of earnings and dividends per share in its 1969 annual report to stockholders. At January 1, 1965 the Corporation had issued 7,000 shares of 4 percent cumulative, nonparticipating, $100 par value preferred stock and 40,000 shares of $10 par value common stock of which 108 shares of preferred and 4,000 shares of common stock were held in the treasury.

Dividends were declared and paid semiannually on the last day of June and December. Cash dividends paid per share of common stock and net income for each year were:

	1965	1966	1967	1968	1969
Net income (loss).......	$126,568	$(11,812)	$47,148	$115,824	$193,210
Dividend on Common:....					
June 30	.40	.11	.10	.40	.60
December 31........	.48	.11	.30	.40	.40

In addition, a 10 percent stock dividend was declared and distributed on all common stock (including treasury shares) on April 1, 1967 and common was split 5 for 1 on October 1, 1969. The Corporation has met a sinking-fund requirement to purchase and retire 140 shares of its preferred stock on October 1 of each year, beginning in 1968, using any available treasury stock. On July 1, 1966 the Corporation purchased 400 shares of its common stock and placed them in the treasury and on April 1, 1968 issued 5,000 shares of common stock to officers, using treasury stock to the extent available.

Required:

a. Prepare a schedule showing the computation of preferred stock dividends paid semiannually and annually for the five years. Use the following columnar headings:

		Number of Shares		Dividends Paid	
Year	Half (1st or 2nd)	Purchased & Retired	Outstanding	Semiannually	Annually

b. Prepare a schedule which shows for each of the five years the cash dividends paid to common stockholders and the average number of shares of common stock outstanding after adjustment for the stock dividend and split. Use the following format:

					Common Stock Adjusted for:	
Dividend Date	Shares of Common Stock In Treasury	Outstanding	Dividends Paid Per Share	Total	10% Stock Dividend	5 for 1 Stock Split
6/30/65						
12/31/65						
		Total for year				
		Average for year				

(Continue this format for remaining 4 years)

c. Prepare a five-year financial summary presenting for each year:
  1. Net income and dividends paid and
  2. Earnings and dividends per share for common stock.

Problem X-2: Common stock equivalents; earnings per share (40-50 min.)

The stockholders' equity section of Lowe Company's balance sheet as of December 31, 1970 contains the following:

$1.00 cumulative convertible preferred stock (par value $25 a share; authorized 1,600,000 shares, issued 1,400,000, converted to common 750,000 and outstanding 650,000 shares; involuntary liquidation value, $30 a share, aggregating $19,500,000)	$16,250,000
Common stock (par value $.25 a share; authorized 15,000,000 shares, issued and outstanding 8,800,000 shares)	2,200,000
Additional paid-in capital	32,750,000
Retained earnings	40,595,000
Total stockholders' equity	$91,795,000

On April 1, 1970 Lowe Company acquired the business and assets and assumed the liabilities of Diane Corporation in a transaction accounted for as a pooling of interests. For each of Diane Corporation's 2,400,000 shares of $.25 par value common stock outstanding, the owner received one share of common stock of the Lowe Company.

Included in the liabilities of Lowe Company are 5½% convertible subordinated debentures issued at their face value of $20,000,000 in 1969. The debentures are due in 1989 and until then are convertible into the common stock of Lowe Company at the rate of five shares of common stock for each $100 debenture. To date none of these have been converted.

On April 2, 1970 Lowe Company issued 1,400,000 shares of convertible preferred stock at $40 per share. Quarterly dividends to December 31, 1970 have been paid on these shares. The preferred stock is convertible into common stock at the rate of two shares of common for each share of preferred. On October 1, 1970, 150,000 shares and on November 1, 1970, 600,000 shares of the preferred stock were converted into common stock.

During July 1969 Lowe Company granted options to its officers and key employees to purchase 500,000 shares of the Company's common stock at a price of $20 a share. The options do not become exercisable until 1971.

During 1970 dividend payments and average market prices of the Lowe common stock have been as follows:

	Dividend Per Share	Average Market Price Per Share
First quarter.	$.10	$20
Second quarter	.15	25
Third quarter	.10	30
Fourth quarter	.15	25
Average for the year		25

The December 31, 1970 closing price of the common stock was $25 a share.

Assume that the bank prime interest rate was 7% throughout 1969 and 1970. Lowe Company's consolidated net income for the year ended December 31, 1970 was $9,200,000. The provision for income taxes was computed at a rate of 48%.

Required:

a. Prepare a schedule which shows the evaluation of the common stock equivalency status of the (1) convertible debentures, (2) convertible preferred stock and (3) employee stock options.

b. Prepare a schedule which shows for 1970 the computation of:
  1. The weighted average number of shares for computing primary earnings per share.
  2. The weighted average number of shares for computing fully diluted earnings per share.

c. Prepare a schedule which shows for 1970 the computation to the nearest cent of:
  1. Primary earnings per share.
  2. Fully diluted earnings per share.

Problem X-3: Common stock equivalents; earnings per share (40-50 min.)

The controller of Lafayette Corporation has requested assistance in determining income, primary earnings per share and fully diluted earnings per share for presentation in the Company's income statement for the year ended September 30, 1970. As currently calculated, the Company's net income is $400,000 for fiscal year 1969-1970. The controller has indicated that the income figure might be adjusted for the following transactions which were recorded by charges or credits directly to retained earnings (the amounts are net of applicable income taxes):

1. The sum of $375,000, applicable to a breached 1966 contract, was received as a result of a lawsuit. Prior to the award, legal counsel was uncertain about the outcome of the suit.
2. A gain of $300,000 was realized on the sale of a subsidiary.
3. A gain of $80,000 was realized on the sale of treasury stock.
4. A special inventory write-off of $150,000 was made, of which $125,000 applied to goods manufactured prior to October 1, 1969.

Your working papers disclose the following opening balances and transactions in the Company's capital stock accounts during the year:

1. Common stock (at October 1, 1969, stated value $10, authorized 300,000 shares; effective December 1, 1969, stated value $5, authorized 600,000 shares):
    Balance, October 1, 1969—issued and outstanding 60,000 shares.
    December 1, 1969—60,000 shares issued in a 2 for 1 stock split.
    December 1, 1969—280,000 shares (stated value $5) issued at $39 per share.
2. Treasury stock—common:
    March 1, 1970—purchased 40,000 shares at $38 per share.
    April 1, 1970—sold 40,000 shares at $40 per share.
3. Stock purchase warrants, Series A (initially, each warrant was exchangeable with $60 for one common share; effective December 1, 1969, each warrant became exchangeable for two common shares at $30 per share):
    October 1, 1969—25,000 warrants issued at $6 each.
4. Stock purchase warrants, Series B (each warrant is exchangeable with $40 for one common share):
    April 1, 1970—20,000 warrants authorized and issued at $10 each.
5. First mortgage bond, 5½%, due 1985 (nonconvertible; priced to yield 5% when issued):

Balance October 1, 1969—authorized, issued and outstanding—the face value of $1,400,000.

6. Convertible debentures, 7%, due 1989 (initially each $1,000 bond was convertible at any time until maturity into 12½ common shares; effective December 1, 1969 the conversion rate became 25 shares for each bond):

October 1, 1969—authorized and issued at their face value (no premium or discount) of $2,400,000.

The following table shows market prices for the Company's securities and the assumed bank prime interest rate during 1969-1970:

	Price (or Rate) at			Average for Year Ended September 30, 1970
	October 1, 1969	April 1, 1970	Spetember 30, 1970	
Common stock	66	40	36¼	37½*
First mortgage bonds........	88½	87	86	87
Convertible debentures	100	120	119	115
Series A Warrants	6	22	19½	15
Series B Warrants...........	–	10	9	9½
Bank prime interest rate	8%	7¾%	7½%	7¾%

*Adjusted for stock split

Required:

a. Prepare a schedule computing net income as it should be presented in the Company's income statement for the year ended September 30, 1970.

b. Assuming that net income after income taxes for the year was $540,000 and that there were no extraordinary items, prepare a schedule computing (1) the primary earnings per share and (2) the fully diluted earnings per share which should be presented in the Company's income statement for the year ended September 30, 1970. A supporting schedule computing the numbers of shares to be used in these computations should also be prepared. (Because of the relative stability of the market price for its common shares, the annual average market price may be used where appropriate in your calculations. Assume an income tax rate of 48% with no surcharge.)

Problem X-4: Admission of new partners, division of profits (40-50 min.)

You have been engaged to prepare financial statements for the partnership of Alexander, Randolph, and Ware as of June 30, 1972. You have obtained the following information from the partnership agreement as amended and from the accounting records.

1. The partnership was formed originally by Alexander and Barnes on July 1, 1971. At that date:
• Barnes contributed $400,000 cash.
• Alexander contributed land, building, and equipment with fair-market values of $110,000, $520,000, and $185,000, respectively. The land and building were subject to a mortgage securing an 8% per annum note (interest rate of similar notes at July 1, 1971). The note is due in quarterly payments of $5,000 plus interest on January 1, April 1, July 1, and October 1 of each year. Alexander made the July 1, 1971, principal and interest payment

personally. The partnership then assumed the obligation for the remaining $300,000 balance.

• The agreement further provided that Alexander had contributed a certain intangible benefit to the partnership due to his many years of business activity in the area to be serviced by the new partnership. The assigned value of this intangible asset plus the net tangible assets he contributed gave Alexander a 60% initial capital interest in the partnership.

• Alexander was designated the only active partner at an annual salary of $24,000 plus an annual bonus of 4% of net income after deducting his salary but before deducting interest on partners' capital investments (see below). Both the salary and the bonus are operating expenses of the partnership.

• Each partner is to receive a 6% return on his average capital investment, such interest to be an expense of the partnership.

• All remaining profits or losses are to be shared equally.

2. On October 1, 1971, Barnes sold his partnership interest and rights as of July 1, 1971, to Ware for $370,000. Alexander agreed to accept Ware as a partner if he would contribute sufficient cash to meet the October 1, 1971, principal and interest payment on the mortgage note. Ware made the payment from personal funds.

3. On January 1, 1972, Alexander and Ware admitted a new partner, Randolph. Randolph invested $150,000 cash for a 10% capital interest based on the initial investments at July 1, 1971, of Alexander and Barnes. At January 1, 1972, the book value of the partnership's assets and liabilities approximated their fair-market values. Randolph contributed no intangible benefit to the partnership.

Similar to the other partners, Randolph is to receive a 6% return on his average capital investment. His investment also entitled him to 20% of the partnership's profits or losses as defined above. However, for the year ended June 30, 1972, Randolph would receive one-half of his pro rata share of the profits or losses.

4. The accounting records show that on February 1, 1972, Other Miscellaneous Expenses had been charged $3,600 in payment of hospital expenses incurred by Alexander's eight year-old daughter.

5. All salary payments to Alexander have been charged to his personal account. On June 1, 1972, Ware made a $33,000 withdrawal. These are the only transactions recorded in the partners' personal accounts.

6. Presented below is a trial balance which summarizes the partnership's general-ledger balances at June 30, 1972. The general ledger has not been closed.

	Dr. (Cr.)
Current assets	$ 307,100
Fixed assets, net	1,285,800
Current liabilities	(157,000)
8% mortgage note payable	(290,000)
Alexander, capital	(515,000)
Randolph, capital	(150,000)
Ware, capital	(400,000)
Alexander, personal	24,000
Randolph, personal	—
Ware, personal	33,000
Sales	(827,600)
Cost of sales	695,000
Administrative expenses	16,900
Other miscellaneous expenses	11,100
Interest expense	11,700

Required:

Prepare a workpaper to adjust the net income (loss) and partners' capital accounts for the year ended June 30, 1972, and to close the net income (loss) to the partner's capital accounts at June 30, 1972. Supporting schedules should be in good form. Amortization of goodwill, if any, is to be over a ten-year period. (Ignore all tax considerations.) Use the following column headings and begin with balances per books as shown:

Description	Net Income (Loss)		Partners' Capital						Other Accounts		
			Alexander		Randolph		Ware		Amount		
	Cr.	(Dr.)	Cr.	(Dr.)	Cr.	(Dr.)	Cr.	(Dr.)	Dr. (Cr.)	Name
Book balances at June 30, 1972	$137,900		$515,000		$150,000		$400,000			

Problem X-5: Miscellaneous adjustments of capital balances; admission of new partner (40-50 min.)

Wells and Williams formed a partnership on January 1, 1966. They have agreed to admit Meyer as a partner on January 1, 1969. The books for the year ending December 31, 1968 are closed. The following additional information is available:

1. Wells and Williams shared profits equally until January 1, 1968 when they agreed to share profits 40 per cent and 60 per cent respectively. The profit-sharing ratio after Meyer is admitted will be 32 per cent to Wells, 48 per cent to Williams, and 20 per cent to Meyer.

2. Meyer will invest $25,000 cash for a one-fifth interest in the capital of the partnership.

3. Wells and Williams reported earnings of $22,000 in 1966, $35,000 in 1967, and $32,000 in 1968.

4. The partnership of Wells and Williams did not use accrual accounting for some items. It was agreed that before Meyer's admission is recorded adjustments should be made in the accounts retroactively to report properly the following items on the accrual method of accounting:

a. The collections on installment sales were regarded as representing first the realization of the gross profit on the contract. After recognition of the full gross profit on each installment sale all further collections were regarded as a recovery of cost. A minimum down payment equal to the gross profit was required on all installment sales. The full collection of the sales price on installment sales is not reasonably assured at the time of the sale and there is no reasonable basis for determining the degree of uncollectibility. Data pertaining to installment sales are summarized below:

	1966	1967	1968
Installment contracts receivable per books on December 31 for sales made in:			
1966	$18,000	$10,000	
1967		24,000	$11,000
1968			19,000
Collections on installment sales	51,000	55,000	60,000
Gross profit per cent on installment sales	30%	32%	33%

b. Bad debts on trade accounts receivable were recorded when accounts were deemed uncollectible. It was agreed that an allowance for bad debts should be established and should include $250 from 1967 sales and $950 from 1968 sales. Bad debts previously recorded and years of sale were:

Bad Debts Recorded		Bad Debts Recorded for Sales Made in		
Year	Amount	1966	1967	1968
1966	$ 800	$ 800		
1967	1,390	900	$ 490	
1968	1,575		750	$825
Totals	$3,765	$1,700	$1,240	$825

c. Salaries and insurance were recorded as expense when paid. The amounts of accrued salaries and prepaid insurance at the end of each year were:

	December 31		
	1966	1967	1968
Accrued salaries	$600	$650	$820
Prepaid insurance	330	420	580

Required:

a. Prepare schedules presenting the computation of the overstatement or understatement of net income each year for each of the following items because they were not recorded by the accrual method of accounting:
 1. Gross profit on installment sales contracts.
 2. Bad debts expense on trade accounts receivable.
 3. Salaries expense.
 4. Insurance expense.

b. Assume that your computations in part "a" resulted in net overstatements of net income of $7,000 in 1966 and $6,000 in 1967 and a net understatement of net income of $1,000 in 1968. Prepare a schedule presenting a computation of the adjustments necessary to properly report Wells' and Williams' capital account balances at December 31, 1966, 1967, and 1968.

c. Assume that the adjusted capital balances on January 1, 1969 were $60,000 for Wells and $76,000 for Williams. Prepare a schedule presenting (1) the computation of Meyer's capital balance if he is admitted under the goodwill method and (2) the amount of goodwill to be recognized.

Problem X-6: Conversion of partnership to corporation; goodwill (40-50 min.)

White Brothers Manufacturing Company was dissolved as a partnership on October 31, 1970. In order to obtain additional capital a new company called the White Manufacturing Corporation was incorporated in October and commenced business on November 1, 1970.

The trial balance of White Manufacturing Company at October 31, 1970, the close of its fiscal year, is as follows:

White Manufacturing Company
TRIAL BALANCE
October 31, 1970

	Debit	*Credit*
Cash	$ 50,000	
Notes receivable	10,000	
Installment contracts receivable	58,000	
Accounts receivable	80,000	
Allowance for doubtful accounts		$ 6,000
Inventories	60,000	
Marketable securities	30,000	
Plant, property and equipment	190,000	
Allowance for depreciation–plant, property		
and equipment		70,000
Accounts payable		105,000
Deferred gross profit on installment sales		22,000
Ed White, Capital		62,000
Ed White, Drawing	15,000	
Fred White, Capital		70,000
Fred White, Drawing	16,000	
Greg White, Capital		72,000
Greg White, Drawing	18,000	
Revenue		870,000
Cost of sales	500,000	
Operating expenses	250,000	
	$1,277,000	$1,277,000

The following information was available and unrecorded at October 31, 1970:

1. Approximately one-fourth of total sales are on the installment basis with payment periods of two to five years. In the past the partnership used the installment method of recognizing gross profit in proportion to cash collections. The three partners, Ed White, Fred White and Greg White, agreed that it would be more appropriate to recognize the full gross profit at the time of making an installment sale. All deferred gross profits on installment sales prior to incorporation are to be recognized in the year ending October 31, 1970. It is estimated that the collection and repossession expense to be incurred in connection with the installment contracts receivable at that date will be $8,000.

2. A customer, Wise Company, was in bankruptcy. Under a settlement approved by the court, $4,500 of the account receivable from Wise Company will be uncollectible.

3. The doubtful accounts among notes receivable, installment contracts receivable and accounts receivable excluding that of Wise Company were estimated to be $11,000.

4. Accrued interest on notes receivable was $300.

5. The net realizable value of the inventory was $63,000.

6. Marketable securities had a net current value of $21,900.

7. The current value of plant, property and equipment was $147,000.

8. Profits and losses were divided equally among the three partners.

9. Fifty thousand shares of common stock with a par value of $10 per share were authorized and 10,000 shares were issued to the public for cash at $12 per share on October 31, 1970.

10. Cash distributions were made to the partners as follows: Ed White, $5,900; Fred White, $12,900; and Greg White, $12,900. Each partner received 10,000 shares of stock in exchange for his share of the partnership's net assets including goodwill.

Required:

a. Complete a worksheet to adjust the trial balance of White Brothers Manufacturing Company at October 31, 1970 to the opening balances for White Manufacturing Corporation by giving effect to the above information. Formal journal entries are not required. Do not consider income taxes.

b. Prepare a schedule to present your computations of the goodwill which is to be recorded.

Problem X-7: Partnership dissolution by installments (30-40 min.)

On August 25, 1965 Norton, Olson and Parker entered into a partnership agreement to acquire a speculative second mortgage on undeveloped real estate. They invested $55,500, $32,000 and $12,500 respectively. They agreed on a profit-and-loss ratio of 4:2:1, respectively.

On September 1, 1965 they purchased for $100,000 a mortgage note with an unpaid balance of $120,000. The amount paid included interest accrued from June 30, 1965. The note principal matures at the rate of $2,000 each quarter. Interest at the annual rate of 8% computed on the unpaid balance is also due quarterly.

Regular interest and principal payments were received on September 30 and December 31, 1965. A working capital imprest fund of $150 was established, and collection expenses of $70 were paid in December.

In addition to the regular September payment on September 30 the mortgagor made a lump-sum principal reduction payment of $10,000 plus a penalty of 2% for prepayment.

Because of the speculative nature of the note, the partners agree to defer recognition of the discount until their cost has been fully recovered.

Required:

a. Assuming that no cash distributions were made to the partners, prepare a schedule computing the cash balance available for distribution to the partners on December 31, 1965.

b. After payment of collection expenses the partners expect to have cash in the total amount of $170,000 available for distribution to themselves for interest and return of principal. They plan to distribute the cash as soon as possible so that they can individually reinvest the cash.

Prepare a schedule showing how the total cash of $170,000 should be distributed to the individual partners by installments as it becomes available.

Problem X-8: Partnership dissolution; schedule of cash distribution (35-45 min.)

Part a

The partnership of Adams, Baker and Crane have called upon you to assist them in winding up the affairs of their partnership.

You are able to gather the following information:

1. The trial balance of the partnership at June 30, 1962 is as follows:

	Debit	Credit
Cash	$ 6,000	
Accounts receivable	22,000	
Inventory	14,000	
Plant and equipment (net)	99,000	
Adams, Loan	12,000	
Crane, Loan	7,500	
Accounts payable		$ 17,000
Adams, Capital		67,000
Baker, Capital		45,000
Crane, Capital		31,500
	$160,500	$160,500

2. The partners share profits and losses as follows: Adams, 50%; Baker, 30%; and Crane, 20%.

3. The partners are considering an offer of $100,000 for the accounts receivable, inventory, and plant and equipment as of June 30. The $100,000 would be paid to the partners in installments, the number and amounts of which are to be negotiated.

Required:

Prepare a cash distribution schedule as of June 30, 1962, showing how the $100,000 would be distributed as it becomes available.

Part b

Assume the same facts as in part a except that the partners have decided to liquidate their partnership instead of accepting the offer of $100,000. Cash is distributed to the partners at the end of each month.

A summary of the liquidation transactions follows:

July:
  $16,500—collected accounts receivable, balance is uncollectible
  $10,000—received for the entire inventory
  $ 1,000—liquidation expenses paid
  $ 8,000—cash retained in the business at end of the month
August:
  $ 1,500—liquidation expenses paid
    As part payment of his capital, Crane accepted a piece of special equipment that he developed which had a book value of $4,000. The partners agreed that a value of $10,000 should be placed on the machine for liquidation purposes.
  $ 2,500—cash retained in the business at end of the month
September:
  $75,000—received on sale of remaining plant and equipment
  $ 1,000—liquidation expenses paid
    No cash retained in the business

Required:

Prepare a schedule of cash payments as of September 30, 1962 showing how the cash was actually distributed.

SPECIFIC APPROACH

Problem X-1

1. In requirement (a), do not overlook the number of preferred shares in the treasury.

2. In requirement (b), carry the column on the stock split retroactively to June 30, 1965.

3. The financial summary is based on the computations in requirements (a) and (b).

Problem X-2

See the General Approach for guidance concerning common stock equivalents, earnings per share, and related matters.

1. In accounting for pooling of interests, remember that the issued stock is regarded as having been outstanding for the entire year regardless of its actual date of issuance.

2. The computations are straightforward applications of the principal provisions of APB *Opinion No. 15.*

Problem X-3

1. In requirement (a), which items do not belong in an income statement? Also distinguish between ordinary and extraordinary items. Assume that the lawsuit is a prior-period adjustment and that the gain on sale of the subsidiary is sufficiently unusual and infrequent to be regarded as extraordinary.

2. See the General Approach for guidance on common stock equivalents, earnings per share, and related matters. The key computation in requirement (b) is the weighted average shares outstanding during the fiscal year; include the impact of Series A warrants. Should Series B warrants affect the computation of earnings per share?

Problem X-4

1. Record the goodwill contributed by Alexander.

2. Ware's payment of principal and interest is an addition to his capital investment.

3. Randolph's investment is based on the bonus method; the adjustment to the old partners' capitals should be made in their profit and loss ratio.

4. The payment of hospital expenses is a withdrawal.

5. Alexander's bonus will be affected by the amortization of goodwill.

6. The interest expense for return on partners' capital depends on a computation of return on partners' average capital investment. Prepare a schedule of the partners' capital balance, month by month. Divide the total by 12 to obtain the average capital balance.

7. The final step is to compute the distribution of the remaining net income.

Problem X-5

1. The body of the problem (item 4a) contains some data about bad debts on trade accounts receivable. Ignore these data when computing the gross profit on installment sales contracts. In requirement a(1), recompute the total sales for each year; apply the gross profit percentage to obtain the gross profit recognized per books. Compare this gross profit with the gross profit that would be realized under the installment method of accounting; the general approach is explained in Topic III.

2. Understatement of bad debts expense for each year would be the excess of (a) the total bad debts expense computed on an estimated basis in the year of sale (the allowance method) minus (b) the bad debts recorded. For example, in 1967 the allowance method would provide $1,240 (written off in 1967 and 1968) plus $250 (which will be added now). The understatement of bad debts expense would be (a) $1,240 plus $250 minus (b) the $1,390 already recorded.

3. Computations of understatements of salaries expense and overstatements of insurance expense are routine applications of accrual accounting.

4. In requirement (b), merely indicate how each capital balance would be changed for each year, using the applicable profit-sharing ratio.

5. In requirement (c), the combined capital of Wells and Williams represents four-fifths of the new total capital.

Problem X-6

This problem is easy, but it will be hard to complete the solution within the 55 minute time limit. After adjusting the capital accounts, subtract their final balances from the market value of the stock shares to obtain the goodwill.

Problem X-7

1. The first requirement is straightforward. Cash receipts include interest, principal, and a repayment penalty. Cash availability would be decreased by the establishment of the imprest fund plus any reimbursements to the fund.

2. See the March and Gans illustration in the General Approach for guidance regarding the second requirement.

Problem X-8

1. In part a, a variation in partnership dissolution problems is introduced. A schedule must be prepared which will indicate the manner of distribution of cash as it becomes available. See the March and Gans illustration in the General Approach for a way of attacking this problem.

2. In part b, the cash is distributed without knowing what the eventual total payout will be. The same schedule of distribution as in a applies. Because Crane received the equipment in advance of the proper installment, he will owe Adams and Baker for the excessive amount he received in August. This amount should be offset against Crane in future distributions.

Business Combinations

GENERAL APPROACH

The broad topic of business combinations has been the focal point of much recent business activity and divergent accounting methods. From 1970 through 1972, the Accounting Principles Board issued four opinions that significantly affected the area of business combinations—numbers 16, 17, 18, and 24.

The attempt to expand markets and increase profits is a natural economic phenomenon. The most popular growth method is the acquisition of the earning capacity of an existing company through a business combination, which is defined as:

> any transaction whereby one economic unit obtains control over the assets and properties of another economic unit, regardless of the legal avenue by which such control is obtained and regardless of the resultant form of the economic unit emerging from the combination transaction.[1]

Control over assets may take two forms—direct or indirect. Direct control is the actual ownership of the assets, obtained by purchasing the properties and having title transferred. It usually results in the legal death of the company whose net assets were acquired, a single successor corporation being the resultant economic unit. Two types of direct acquisition exist—merger and consolidation.

Merger is synonymous with absorption by a pre-existing company. One or more constituent corporations merge into another constituent corporation, known as the survivor, with the result that the former cease to exist and the

---

[1]Arthur R. Wyatt, *A Critical Study of Accounting for Business Combinations,* (New York: AICPA, 1963), p. 12.

latter's corporate existence continues. For example, A corporation acquires title to B Corporation's assets, assumes B's liabilities, pays cash and/or A's securities to B, which distributes them and dissolves. To illustrate:

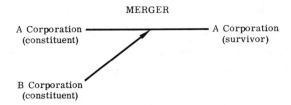

MERGER

A Corporation (constituent) ——————→ A Corporation (survivor)

B Corporation (constituent)

Consolidation, by *legal* definition, requires the formation of a new corporation. Two or more constituent corporations cease to exist and a new consolidated corporation results. For example, C Corporation acquires title to A's and B's assets, assumes their liabilities, and pays to A and B Corporation cash and/or its securities which are distributed to A and B stockholders, after which both A and B are dissolved. To illustrate:

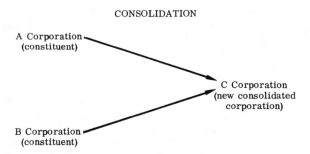

CONSOLIDATION

A Corporation (constituent)

B Corporation (constituent)

C Corporation (new consolidated corporation)

Indirect control is produced by purchasing sufficient voting stock to exercise control, with legal continuation of all corporate entities involved. In both accounting and finance, the term, "consolidation," is often used, to refer to the indirect control by a parent company which results from stock ownership in a subsidiary. In this Topic, we shall concentrate on accounting problems of indirect control and we shall use the term "consolidation" in its typical, accounting interpretation.

In business combinations resulting from indirect control, three areas must be understood for the candidate to feel confident: the initial recording, accounting for activities after date of acquisition, and preparation of working papers as a basis for formal financial statements.

Initial Recording

The initial entry for a major investment in another company might be recorded in one of two ways:

a. Summary recording—which uses an "Investment" account;
b. Detailed recording—which uses detailed accounts for investment in net assets, debiting specific assets (Cash, Accounts Receivable, Inventory, etc.) and crediting specific liabilities (Accounts and Notes Payable, etc.) for the proportionate interest in each, represented by the investment.

Without special procedures, the detailed approach does not yield results for either organization alone, but produces only combined results. Detailed recording is seldom employed, and we shall restrict ourselves to the more prevalent treatment—summary recording.

Purchase versus Pooling Methods

In *Opinion No. 16* the two acceptable methods of accounting for business combinations resulting from indirect control are referred to as the "purchase method" and the "pooling of interests method." (See APBAP Vol. 1, Sect. 1091.11 and 1091.12.)

> The purchase method accounts for a business combination as the acquisition of one company by another. The acquiring corporation records at its cost the acquired assets less liabilities assumed. A difference between the cost of an acquired company and the sum of the fair values of tangible and identifiable intangible assets less liabilities is recorded as goodwill. The reported income of an acquiring corporation includes the operations of the acquired company after acquisition, based on the cost to the acquiring corporation.
>
> The pooling of interests method accounts for a business combination as the uniting of the ownership interests of two or more companies by exchange of equity securities. No acquisition is recognized because the combination is accomplished without disbursing resources of the constituents. Ownership interests continue and the former bases of accounting are retained. The recorded assets and liabilities of the constituents are carried forward to the combined corporation at their recorded amounts. Income of the combined corporation includes income of the constituents for the entire fiscal period in which the combination occurs. The reported income of the constituents for prior periods is combined and restated as income of the combined corporation.

In a given set of conditions, only one set of the two acceptable methods of accounting for a business combination is appropriate. Unless circumstances permit use of the pooling of interests method, the combination must be recorded using the purchase method. As stipulated in APB *Opinion No. 16,* the requirements to qualify for use of the pooling of interests method are stringent. Some of the conditions for pooling as listed in APBAP Vol. 1, Sect. 1091.46-.47 are the following:

1. Each of the combining companies is autonomous and has not been a subsidiary or division of another corporation within two years before the plan of combination is initiated.

2. Each of the combining companies is independent of the other combining companies, holding as intercorporate investments no more than 10 percent in total of the outstanding voting common stock of any combining company.
3. The combination is effected in a single transaction or is completed in accordance with a specific plan within one year after the plan is initiated.
4. A corporation offers and issues only common stock with rights identical to those of the majority of its outstanding voting common stock in exchange for substantially all (90% or more) of the voting common stock interest of another company at the date the plan of combination is consummated.
5. None of the combining companies changes the equity interest of the voting common stock in contemplation of effecting the combination either within two years before the plan of combination is initiated or between the dates the combination is initiated and consummated.
6. The ratio of the interest of an individual common stockholder to those of other common stockholders in a combining company remains the same as a result of the exchange of stock to effect the combination.
7. The voting rights to which the common stock ownership interests in the resulting combined corporation are entitled are exercisable by the stockholders.

As you review the above requirements, note how they perpetuate corporate shareholders' rights and responsibilities, the essence of pooling. If the preceding requirements are not met, the combination must be treated as a purchase.

The Purchase Method

To record a business combination under the purchase method, one follows the usual rule for the acquisition of any asset—record it at cost to the buyer. Where issuance of stock is the method of acquisition, cost is equivalent to the present, fair market value of the net assets acquired. To account properly for the acquisition, the total cost must be allocated to each identified asset obtained and each liability assumed, since total cost is a combination of three factors:

1. the book value of the net assets on seller's books;
2. plus or minus an amount to adjust for the difference between book values and current, fair market values;
3. plus or minus the estimated value of unidentified factors.

The excess of total cost over the assigned value of identifiable total net assets is interpreted as goodwill, which is to be amortized over the periods to be benefited, but not to exceed 40 years. In practice, a complication arises because the investment in net assets is not achieved through direct, face-to-face negotiation, but rather indirectly through acquisition of voting stock on the open market. Frequently, the fair market value of the stock issued is accepted as "cost."

EXAMPLE

In exchange for $7,000 par value of its own stock, having a market value of $62,000, Company P acquires 70% of the common stock of Company S on January 2, 19x0, when the condensed balance sheet of Company S shows:

Company S
CONDENSED BALANCE SHEET
January 2, 19x0

Current assets	$30,000	Liabilities	$20,000
Other assets	50,000	Common stock–par	20,000
		Retained earnings	40,000
	$80,000		$80,000

The entry to record the acquisition on Company P's books under the purchase method would be:

Investment in Company S	62,000	
Common stock		7,000
Paid-in capital–excess over par		55,000

Cost is the basis for recording the acquisition under the purchase method, the cash-equivalent value of the stock establishing cost.

You might ask, "Why is Company P willing to pay $62,000 for 70% of total owners' equity of $60,000?" The answer must be either that there is a variance between book and current market values of net assets or that a goodwill factor is involved. In any case, the original entry to record the acquisition would be the investment cost. Later worksheet procedures will result in identification of the components.

Under the purchase method of recording the acquisition, what if the cost is *less* than the assigned value of identifiable assets acquired minus the liabilities assumed? APBAP Vol. 1 Sect. 1091.87 says that if this situation exists:

> . . . the values otherwise assignable to noncurrent assets acquired (except long-term investments in marketable securities) should be reduced by a proportionate part of the excess to determine the assigned values. A deferred credit for an excess of assigned value of identifiable assets over cost of an acquired company . . . should not be recorded unless those assets are reduced to zero value.

The Pooling Method

The very designation, "pooling of interests," suggests a blending of existing book values. In recording the acquisition of the subsidiary, the market value of the parent company's stock issued to consummate the transaction is ignored. Instead, the Investment in Subsidiary account is debited for the parent's acquired equity in total book value of the subsidiary's net assets. A corresponding amount is credited to various elements of the parent's owners equity, beginning with the credit to the parent's common stock account for the par or stated value of the stock issued. If the par or stated value of parent shares issued is less than the parent's portion of subsidiary total paid-in capital, retained earnings is credited for an amount up to the parent's share of the subsidiary's retained earnings, with paid-in capital credited for any excess.

EXAMPLE

Under conditions which permit recording under the pooling of interests method, Company P acquired 90% of the common stock of Company S. At the time, the condensed balance sheet of Company S shows:

Assets	$400,000	Liabilities		$ 50,000
		Common stock	$100,000	
		Other paid-in capital	50,000	
		Total paid-in capital	$150,000	
		Retained earnings	200,000	350,000
	$400,000			$400,000

What is the entry to record the acquisition, if the parent issued $110,000 par value common with a market value of $347,000? Since this is to be accorded "pooling of interest" treatment, the market value of $347,000 is ignored, and the entry becomes:

```
Investment in Company S (90% of $350,000). .   315,000
    Common stock (issued by Company P) .................   110,000
    Retained earnings (90% of $200,000) .................   180,000
    Paid-in capital ......................................    25,000
```

If the par or stated value of parent shares issued is equal to the parent's portion of total paid-in capital of the subsidiary, there is no credit to paid-in capital in the entry to record the acquisition. Assume that Company P acquired 90% interest by issuing $135,000 par value common. The entry would be:

```
Investment in Company S (90% of $350,000) ..   315,000
    Common stock (issued by Company P) ................   135,000
    Retained earnings (90% of $200,000) ................   180,000
```

If the par or stated value of parent shares issued is greater than its share of total subsidiary paid-in capital, a debit is made to the parent's paid-in capital, if any is available. Continuing with the same example, assume that $150,000 of par value common is issued by the parent whose books show ample paid-in capital. The entry would be:

Investment in Company S (90% of $350,000) . . 315,000
Paid-in capital   15,000
   Common stock (issued by Company P)   150,000
   Retained earnings (90% of $200,000)   180,000

If there is no paid-in capital on the parent's books, the credit to retained earnings is reduced. Under this situation, the entry for the previous illustration would be:

Investment in Company S (90% of $350,000) .   315,000
   Common stock (issued by Company P)   150,000
   Retained earnings   165,000

In each case, note that the increase in the parent's assets resulting from the recording of the Investment in Company S is matched by an increase in the parent owners' equity of an identical total amount, again depicting the blending of asset and equity elements.

Interim Acquisition

In CPA examinations and also in practice, an interest in a subsidiary is not always acquired at the beginning of a fiscal period. An interim acquisition presents the problem of determining the book value of the subsidiary's stockholders' equity at date of acquisition. In past examinations, consolidation problems have had interim acquisitions that were incorrectly recorded because the retained earnings balance at the beginning of the year was used to establish book value. The candidate would be required to make a correction to the original entry before proceeding. If no specific indication is given in the problem as to the allocation of subsidiary earnings in the year of acquisition, one should prorate annual earnings, thereby establishing the retained earnings balance as of the date of acquisition.

If a consolidated income statement is required for the year of acquisition, consolidated net income under the purchase method must not include the earnings of the subsidiary prior to date of acquisition. To insure removal of these "purchased profits," the eliminating entry could be:

Retained earnings (for parent's share of
   subsidiary earnings as of the
     beginning of the year of acquisition).   xxxx
Paid-in capital (if involved)   xxxx
Purchased income (parent's share to date
   of acquisition)   xxxx
   Investment in subsidiary   xxxx

The total consolidated income for the complete year is reduced by the minority interest and by the Purchased Income, leaving the amount that is truly consolidated net income.

Where the pooling of interests method is used to record a combination, the consolidated income statement for the year of acquisition reports operational results as though acquisition had occurred at the beginning of that period. (See APBAP Vol. 1, Sect. 1091.56.)

Accounting for Activities after Date of Acquisition

Upon the establishment of more than a 50% ownership of common stock, a parent-subsidiary relationship is established. Accounting for activities after the date of acquisition may be conducted under one of two methods—the cost or the equity method. The cost method is dominated by the law, perpetuating the aura of two, separate legal entities. As a result, the parent normally maintains its Investment in Subsidiary account at the original amount and records as income only the asset dividend declarations that are based on the subsidiary's earnings since the relationship was established.

In keeping with the idea that the parent and subsidiary are a single economic entity, the equity method records the Investment in Subsidiary at the original amount but recognizes the parent's share of subsidiary net income earned after date of acquisition by debiting Investment in Subsidiary and crediting an income account. If the subsidiary incurs a net loss, a loss account is debited and the Investment in Subsidiary is reduced by the corresponding credit. Asset dividends declared by the subsidiary are debited by the parent to a receivable account and credited to the Investment in Subsidiary account, which represents a partial liquidation of the investment.

The table on page 304 summarizes the two methods.

If Company P sells part or all of its investment in Company S, different results are recorded under the two methods. For example, if Company P sells all of its holdings in Company S for $110,000 on 1-1-x2, the following entries result:

Cost Method

Cash............................	110,000	
Investment in S.....................		100,000
Gain on sale of investments		10,000

Equity Method

Cash............................	110,000	
Loss on sale of investments	2,800	
Investment in S.....................		112,800

The $12,800 difference is explained by the fact that under the equity method the basis includes undistributed earnings of the subsidiary since date of acquisition.

Manner of Recording on Book of Parent Company

Data	Cost Method		Equity Method	

1-1-x0 P acquires 80% interest in S for $100,000 cash	Investment in S
	    Cash
		100,000
		100,000
			Investment in S
			    Cash
				100,000
				100,000

12-31-x0 S reports a net profit of $30,000 for the year	No entry		Investment in S Net income from S	24,000 24,000

12-31-x0 S declares a cash dividend of $10,000	Dividends receivable
	    Dividend income from S
		8,000
		8,000
			Dividends receivable
			    Investment in S
				8,000
				8,000

12-31-x1 S reports a net loss of $4,000	No entry (but if the loss were major, one might consider an adjustment)		Net loss of S Investment in S	3,200 3,200

The Consolidation Process

Legal boundaries between parent and subsidiary are erased in the consolidation process. The completed, consolidated statements constitute the fused statements of a group of related corporations where control is evidenced by intercompany stockholdings.

The conditions that are prerequisite to generation of consolidated financial statements should be reviewed. When two conditions are satisfied, consolidated financial statements would be prepared:

1. Objective criterion—majority ownership, evidenced by more than 50% ownership of common stock;
2. Subjective criterion—policy reasons. Consolidated statements would be prepared where that form of presentation would be most meaningful under the circumstances. All companies in the group must have interrelated activities.

The philosophy behind the preparation of consolidated financial statements is basically simple. It is as if an accountant said, "Here we have two (or more) companies. Let us pretend that they are one. We want to show the balance sheet, income statement, and the statement of changes in financial position which result from transactions with outsiders by this one economic unit, eliminating all intercompany activities."

The worksheet provides an organized framework for accomplishing the required eliminations and adjustments. Whether we start with trial balances or the finished financial statements of individual affiliates, the worksheet simply transforms them into one set of aggregate balances by means of an "Adjustment and Elimination" section. Adjustment and elimination entries appear only on the working papers. They never become actual book entries, except for the correction of errors existing in the books. CPA problems typically require preparation of working papers rather than requiring formal financial statements.

As with all accounting problems, the first step is to become thoroughly familiar with the given fact situation. Thereafter, answering a logical series of questions increases the probability of success in handling a consolidation situation.

> Question: Did the parent record the original acquisition of the subsidiary under the purchase method or pooling of interests method?

It is essential to be able to distinguish between the two methods, because a key eliminating entry will be affected. In past examinations, the method was either specifically stated in the problems or sufficient data were provided to conclude which method should be used.

> Question: Since date of acquisition, has the parent employed the cost or equity method to account for the investment?

Although final consolidated balances are not affected by the method adopted by the parent to account for its investment in a subsidiary after date of acquisition, the equity method is generally recognized as more accurately reflecting income. The issuance of *Opinion No. 18* decreases the likelihood of the cost method being used in actual practice or appearing on the examination. However, if the cost method is encountered, a simple conversion is available. One may switch from cost to equity by using the following procedure:

DEBIT the parent's investment account,
CREDIT the parent's retained earnings account for the parent's share of net increase in the subsidiary's retained earnings balance between the date of acquisition and the beginning of the current year.

To illustrate the application of the above rule, if entries from the table on page 304 were posted into the Investment in S account under the cost and equity methods, they would appear as follows:

Cost Method		Equity Method	
Investment in S		Investment in S	
100,000		100,000	8,000
		24,000	3,200
		Bal. 112,800	

An examination of the Retained Earnings account of Company S would indicate that since date of acquisition the balance has increased by the $30,000 profit earned in 19x0. The balance has decreased by the $10,000 dividend declared in 19x0 and by the net loss of $4,000 incurred in 19x1. The result was a net increase in retained earnings since date of acquisition of $16,000, 80% of which is $12,800. If it is desired to switch from the cost to the equity method, the entry would be:

Investment in S 12,800
    Retained earnings (of parent) 12,800

Question: Are there any adjustments required to correct accounts on the books of the individual companies involved?

Original data must be correct; therefore, one should adjust account balances for any of the following:
a. errors on the individual books of an affiliate, such as an incorrect or omitted recording of interest receivable;
b. items in transit not recorded by one of the affiliates, such as payment of an intercompany loan recorded by the debtor but not by the payee. Follow the rule that accounts should reflect balances that would exist if all events were carried forward to their logical conclusion and recorded;

c. if financial statements are to be consolidated for a period other than the year during which control was acquired, ascertain that the carrying amount of the investment is correct as of the beginning of the year. Any corrections to that balance would be in the nature of prior period adjustments which, on the worksheet, will affect retained earnings.

Question: What entry is necessary on the working papers to eliminate intercompany stockholdings?

The correct entries for eliminating intercompany stockholdings will depend on whether the original investment was recorded as a purchase or as a pooling, and thereafter, whether the cost or equity technique was invoked to record subsequent activities. To facilitate discussion, these possible groupings will be referred to as purchase-cost method, purchase-equity method, and pooling-equity method. Pooling-cost combination would produce an apparent incompatibility and will be ignored.

Where the Investment account is maintained under the purchase-cost method, no change is made in that account balance except for additional investment or for liquidation of investment. In the consolidating process, the eliminating entry would remove the parent's share of subsidiary equity accounts, always using amounts as of the date of acquisition:

Capital stock (of Co. S)	xxxx	
Retained earnings (of Co. S)	xxxx	
Investment in subsidiary (by Co. P)		xxxx

If after the entry, a debit balance remains in the Investment in Subsidiary account, it should be isolated. To the extent attributable to tangible and specific intangible assets, or to liabilities assumed, the difference should be allocated to them. The basis of allocation is fair market value, determined by the parent when controlling interest was acquired. Adjustments to subsidiary asset valuations appear only on consolidated working papers and statements; book values in the subsidiary's actual records are not changed. Fair value adjustments to long-lived assets require that depreciation and/or amortization thereon be considered in subsequent consolidations. If an excess of total investment over fair value still exists, it should be labeled "Goodwill" to be amortized over the period estimated to be benefited, but not to exceed 40 years. The minority interest in each element of subsidiary's owners' equity must be determined and extended to the proper column. Any balance remaining in the subsidiary's retained earnings now constitutes part of consolidated retained earnings.

EXAMPLE

Company P acquires an 80% interest in Company S for $75,000 cash, at a time when Company S ownership equity consists of $50,000 common stock and

$30,000 retained earnings. Company P uses the purchase-cost method to account for the investment. The eliminating entry on subsequent consolidations would be:

Common stock (Co. S)	40,000	
Retained earnings (Co. S)	24,000	
Investment in subsidiary (Co. P)		64,000

Whether the investment is recorded under the purchase or pooling method and whether subsequently, the Investment account is treated under cost or equity techniques, the eliminating entries must remove completely the Investment account balance. It might be convenient to think of the Investment as a reciprocal account, for which the net assets of the subsidiary will be substituted in the consolidating process. In this example, it is obvious that some additional adjustment is required. Assume that the remaining $11,000 balance in the Investment account is attributable to excess of market value over book value of land owned by the subsidiary. The additional adjustment on the working papers would be:

Land (Co. S)	11,000	
Investment in subsidiary (Co. P)		11,000

If the $11,000 were assignable to a building, a similar entry would be made, the debit to Buildings requiring consideration on the working papers for alteration of the subsidiary's building depreciation charge.

If the Investment account is maintained on the equity basis, whether purchase-equity or pooling-equity, the eliminating process would be basically similar. While the pooling-equity method requires only the elimination of intercompany stockholdings, the purchase-equity method must, in addition, consider possible subsidiary asset revaluations, including the goodwill factor. Nevertheless, equity treatment of the investment requires that the eliminating entry remove the parent's share of subsidiary equity elements based on balances as of the date of consolidation. If you are preparing only consolidated balance sheet working papers from either the post-closing trial balances of the affiliates or from their individual balance sheets, the procedure is straightforward.

EXAMPLE

For $70,000 cash Company P acquires a 70% interest in Company S, whose owners' equity at the time consists of $80,000 in common stock and $20,000 retained earnings. During the following year Company S earns $10,000, declaring a $4,000 dividend, resulting in a final balance in its retained earnings of $26,000. Company P uses the equity method and has made all necessary entries, producing a balance of $74,200 in the Investment account.

At the end of the year, the eliminating entry would be:

Common stock (Co. S)	56,000	
Retained earnings (Co. S)	21,000	
Investment in subsidiary (Co. P)		74,200
Dividends declared		2,800

Where a consolidated income statement, a retained earnings statement, and a balance sheet are desired, and where the starting data on the working papers are the pre-closing trial balances, the Earnings from Company S account would be eliminated, as well as the parent's share of subsidiary owners' equity items, thus:

Earnings from Company S (Co. P)	7,000	
Common stock (Co. S)	56,000	
Retained earnings (Co. S)	14,000	
Investment in subsidiary (Co. P)		74,200
Dividends declared		2,800

The only difference between the two previous entries is the segregation of the parent's share of subsidiary earnings of the current period from retained earnings.

On the partial working papers shown on pages 310 and 311, which show only accounts of immediate concern, note the treatment of the above entry (marked "a") and the method of forwarding data from one financial statement to the next.

If a problem begins with trial balances rather than with the financial statements of the affiliates, a variation in the design of the working papers permits more rapid results. With basically the same data as in the previous working paper, the alternate form is presented on page 311. Notice how easily elements flow from one section to another.

Intercompany Profits

Unless a subsidiary is wholly owned, a minority interest in the consolidated enterprise will exist. Generally, consolidated statements are prepared for the benefit of stockholders of the parent company to give them information that cannot be gleaned from statements of the parent company alone. The minority will look primarily to the financial statements of the individual company in which it holds an interest.

The similarity between affiliates in a consolidation and departments in a company becomes evident when an intercompany sale of assets occurs. If a subsidiary sells inventory to a parent at a profit, and the parent sells that inventory to an outsider, intercompany profit is realized and must be recognized. If, at the time of consolidation, the units remaining with the parent are still unsold, the profit of the subsidiary is unrealized and must be eliminated. When one speaks of the elimination of intercompany profit, it is the unrealized intercompany profit being discussed. Both the American Institute of Certified Public Accountants and the American Accounting Association recommend complete elimination of unrealized intercompany profit or loss in consolidation, regardless of the existence of a minority interest. *ARB No. 51* states:

CONSOLIDATED WORKING PAPERS
End of Period

	Individual financial statements of Companies		Adjustments & Eliminations		Minority Interest	Consolidated
	P	S				
Income Statement:						
Net income from operations	67,000	10,000			3,000	74,000
Earnings from S (70%)	7,000		a 7,000			
Total net income-forward	74,000	10,000	7,000		3,000	74,000
Statement of Retained Earnings:						
Balance-opening of Co. P	216,000					216,000
-opening of Co. S		20,000	a14,000		6,000	
Net income brought forward	74,000	10,000	7,000		3,000	74,000
Totals	290,000	30,000	21,000		9,000	290,000
Dividends declared	50,000*	4,000*		2,800a	1,200*	50,000*
Final balance forward	240,000	26,000	21,000	2,800	7,800	240,000
Balance Sheet:						
Assets-other	465,800	116,000				581,800
Investment in Co. S	74,200			74,200a		
Totals	540,000	116,000		74,200		581,800
Equities: Payables	110,000	10,000				120,000
Common stock-Co. P	190,000					190,000
-Co. S		80,000	a56,000		24,000	
Retained earnings—brought forward	240,000	26,000	21,000	2,800	7,800	240,000
Totals	540,000	116,000	77,000	77,000		550,000
Minority interest total					31,800	31,800
Total					31,800	581,800

*deduction

CONSOLIDATED WORKING PAPERS (Variation)
End of Period

	Trial Balances Co. P	Co. S	Adjustments and Eliminations	Consolidated Income	Minority Interest	Consolidated Retained Earnings	Consolidated Balance Sheet
Debits:							
Assets—other	465,800	116,000					581,000
Investment in Co. S	74,200		74,200 a				
Cost of goods sold	300,000	40,000		(340,000)			
Expenses	100,000	18,000		(118,000)			
Dividends	50,000	4,000	2,800 a		(1,200)	(50,000)	
	990,000	178,000					581,800
Credits:							
Payables	110,000	10,000					120,000
Common stock—Co. P	190,000						190,000
—Co. S		80,000	a 56,000		24,000		
Retained earnings at beginning							
—Co. P	216,000					216,000	
—Co. S		20,000	a 14,000		6,000		
Sales	467,000	68,000		535,000			
Earnings from S	7,000		a 7,000				
	990,000	178,000		77,000			
Minority interest in net profit of Co. S (30% x $10,000)				(3,000)	3,000		
Consolidated net income ($67,000 + 70% x $10,000)				74,000		74,000	
Total minority interest					31,800		31,800
Total consolidated retained earnings						240,000	240,000
							581,800

... The complete elimination of the unrealized intercompany profit or loss is consistent with the underlying assumption that consolidated statements represent the financial position and operating results of a single business enterprise. The elimination of the unrealized intercompany profit or loss may be allocated proportionately between the majority and minority interests. (See APBAP Vol. 1, Sect. 2051.13.)

However, note that in the case of an investor-investee relationship (where 50% or less of the voting stock is held), it is the relationship between the parties that determines whether all or a proportionate part of the intercompany profit or loss shall be eliminated. (See APBAP Vol. 1, Sect. U5131.003-.007.)

> Question: What entries are necessary to adjust for unrealized intercompany profits in inventory?

If a sale at a profit is made between affiliates during the current period, and the units have then been sold to outsiders, profit has been realized. The only elimination necessary is to counteract the entries for the original intercompany movement of inventory units.

EXAMPLE

Company P owns 90% of Company S. The latter records sales to the parent for $45,000, including a profit of $10,000. Company P sells the units to its customers for $60,000. The eliminating entry would be:

```
Sales (Co. S) ............................  45,000
    Cost of sales (Co. P)  ..............................      45,000
```

Cost to the group was $35,000, ultimately realizing $60,000 for a total profit of $25,000, of which $10,000 appears on Company S's books and $15,000 on Company P's.

If a sale at a profit is made between affiliates during the current period and these units remain unsold to outsiders, two adjustments are necessary. In addition to the example entry just shown, an adjustment must remedy the overvaluation of Company P's final inventory for the unrealized profit:

```
Cost of sales (Co. P) ......................  10,000
    Inventory (Co. P)  ..............................      10,000
```

A word of caution—since there has not been a sale to an outsider, no profit has been realized. Allocation of net profits to the minority interest of Company S must be reduced by the minority's share of unrealized intercompany profits in accordance with procedures recommended by accounting authorities.

One might ask, "If the parent maintains the Investment account under the equity procedure and has reflected its portion of the subsidiary's current profit, are not both the Investment and the Earnings of Subsidiary accounts also overstated because of unrealized intercompany profits reported by the subsidiary as realized?" The answer is, "Yes, but since both account balances will be eliminated in the consolidating process, no special treatment is required."

Now consider this situation:

EXAMPLE

Company P owns 90% of Company S. In 19X0, the latter records sales to the parent for $45,000 which includes a profit of $10,000. The next year, 19x1, Company P sells the units to its customers for $60,000.

At the end of 19x0, the adjustments previously described would have been made on the consolidating working papers, but none of the adjustments would have been made in the formal records. Therefore, the retained earnings of the subsidiary, which recognized the intercompany profit in 19x0, and the cost of sales to outsiders by the parent in the year of sale are overstated on the formal records. To correct the situation the entry on the consolidating working papers for 19x1 would shift the recognition of realized profit from 19x0 to 19x1, thus:

Retained earnings (Co. P)	8,000	
Retained earnings (Minority interest of Co. S) ...	2,000	
Consolidated net income		8,000
Minority net income		2,000

This procedure demonstrates that the profit on sale of inventory units should be recognized in the period in which sales were made to outsiders, not in the period when transfer of units between affiliates occurred.

Question: What entries are necessary to adjust for intercompany profits on the sale of non-inventory assets between affiliates?

From the viewpoint of a single business enterprise, intercompany balances and transactions must be eliminated to avoid double counting and premature recognition of income. Intercompany profits on long-lived assets remaining with the group are treated as follows:

a) Non-depreciable assets:

DEBIT—the gain account in the year of sale, to eliminate the gain from the income statement of the seller. Every year thereafter, eliminate the gain from the beginning balance of retained earnings of the seller.

CREDIT—the asset account of the buyer to eliminate the intercompany profit.

b) Depreciable assets—in the year of sale, the first eliminating entry is the same as for a non-depreciable asset. Every year thereafter, an additional entry is required:

DEBIT—accumulated depreciation for the total depreciation on intercompany gain to date.

CREDIT—depreciation expense on the consolidated income statement for the current year's depreciation attributable to the gain and also credit Retained Earnings for the overstatement of depreciation expense on intercompany profit for all prior periods.

Late in 19x0 Company P sells a machine to its 80% owned subsidiary, Company S, for $25,000 which includes a $5,000 profit. The machine has an estimated life of 5 years and is operational at the beginning of 19x1. The eliminating entries needed for the consolidating working papers at the end of each of the first three years are:

Year 19x0:	Gain on sale of machinery (Co. P)	5,000	
	Machinery (Co. S)		5,000
Year 19x1:	Retained earnings (Co. P)	5,000	
	Machinery (Co. S)		5,000
	Accumulated depreciation on Machinery (Co. S)	1,000	
	Depreciation expense (Co. S)		1,000
Year 19x2:	Retained earnings (Co. P)	5,000	
	Machinery (Co. S)		5,000
	Accumulated depreciation on Machinery (Co. S)	2,000	
	Depreciation expense (Co. S)		1,000
	Retained earnings (Co. P)		1,000

Question: What problems do intercompany bond holdings create?

Intercompany bonds purchased by an affiliate are treated on consolidated statements as if those bonds were prematurely retired. A liability is assumed to be extinguished by the purchaser's cost. The difference between carrying value of the debt and the investment in the bonds constitutes gain or loss on acquisition of intercompany bonds in the year of acquisition. Keep in mind that each affiliate affected by the bonds will be conducting amortization or accumulation procedures. In consolidated statement working papers in fiscal periods following the acquisition, the gain or loss should be reflected in consolidated retained earnings. Therefore, the net adjustment to the beginning of the year retained earnings' balance will be equal to the gain or loss on acquisition of intercompany bonds adjusted for prior periods' amortization or accumulation of premium or discount.

Company P issues $100,000 of bonds at face. At the end of 19x0, when the bonds are five years from maturity, its subsidiary, Company S, acquires 10% of the outstanding bonds for $9,500. What would the eliminating entries on consolidating working papers be for the next three years? (Recall that Company

S will accumulate the discount on repurchase of the intercompany bonds over the remaining five years, increasing its Investment in Company P Bonds account thereby.)

Year 19x0:	Investment in Company P bonds (Co. S)	500	
	Gain on acquisition of intercompany bonds (Co. P) .		500
	(From a practical point of view, the gain is generally granted to the issuer, since it could retire the bonds at market value, if it so desired.)		
	Bonds payable (Co. P)	10,000	
	Investment in Company P bonds (Co. S)		10,000
	(The above entry is made each year thereafter.)		
Year 19x1:	Investment in Company P bonds (Co. S)	400	
	Interest earned (Co. S—for annual accumulation of re-purchase discount).	100	
	Retained earnings (Co. P)		500
Year 19x2:	Investment in Company P bonds (Co. S)	300	
	Interest earned (Co. S).	100	
	Retained earnings (Co. P)		400

When one considers that the original bonds could have been issued by the parent or by the subsidiary at face, at a premium, or at a discount, and that the later intercompany reacquisition could also be made at face, at a premium, or at a discount, one realizes the many variations that are possible.

Accounting for Income Taxes on Undistributed Earnings of Subsidiaries

There have been occasions in the past when the Opinions of the Accounting Principles Board were applied so inconsistently that further investigation became essential. Such was the case in the adoption of pooling versus the purchase method of recording a business combination, and such was also the case for income taxes on undistributed earnings of a subsidiary. The result was the issuance by the Board of *Opinion No. 23,* wherein they specified:

> The Board believes it should be presumed that all undistributed earnings of a subsidiary will be transferred to the parent company. Accordingly, the undistributed earnings of a subsidiary included in consolidated income (or in income of the parent company) should be accounted for as a timing difference. . . . Income taxes attributable to a timing difference in reporting undistributed earnings of a subsidiary should be accounted for in accordance with the provisions . . . for interperiod allocation of taxes. (See APBAP Vol. 1, Sect. 4095.10)

An exception to this procedure is mentioned in Section 4095.12:

> . . . no income taxes should be accrued by the parent company, if sufficient evidence shows that the subsidiary has invested or will invest the undistributed earnings indefinitely or that the earnings will be remitted in a tax-free liquidation.

Multi-Tiered Structure

If a company, P, buys a controlling interest in another company, I, which is itself a parent of a third company, S, a multi-tiered structure is born. The intermediate company (I) functions simultaneously as parent and subsidiary. It is important to realize that P has bought a part of the combined interest of I and S. The equity purchased would be its share of I's capital stock plus its share of I and S consolidated retained earnings and such other items of ownership equity which might exist (for example, paid-in capital). A recommended procedure in this situation is to consolidate the directly related companies, beginning at the bottom, thus:

Step 1—Consolidate Companies I and S, thereby determining all consolidated values for this relationship.

Step 2—Consolidate Company P with the consolidated amounts resulting from Step 1.

Reciprocal Holdings

Situations exist wherein a subsidiary holds a stock interest in the parent—thus the term, "reciprocal holdings." Formerly, it was thought necessary to establish the interest of each in the other by use of simultaneous equations. *ARB 51* now advises that on the consolidated balance sheet, it is preferable to treat stock of the parent held by the subsidiary as if it were treasury stock. If any dividend has been declared by the parent, the amount applicable to the subsidiary would be eliminated as an unrealized intercompany profit, with a corresponding reduction in Dividends Declared (or increase in Retained Earnings) of the parent.

Summary of Technique of Solution

In solving a consolidation problem, a summary of the approach should be useful to the candidate, although all of the following steps may not be necessary for each problem.

1. After becoming thoroughly familiar with the facts of the problem, prepare a diagram showing the relationship of the units to be consolidated, including the percentage of stock owned between various affiliates and the dates such owner-

ship was acquired. Where a simple, direct relationship exists, this step is unnecessary.

2. Decide whether working papers are required. If specifically requested, they must be submitted. If they are not stipulated as a necessary part of the solution, decide whether they will materially assist in meeting the requirements. If you conclude that they must be prepared, your Step 1 diagram will assist in the design of the working papers.

3. Was the original investment recorded as a purchase or as a pooling?

4. Since date of acquisition, has the parent employed the cost or equity technique to account for the investment?

5. Are any adjustments to the balances of the constituents necessary? Failure to record an item or an error in recording will result in situations requiring adjustment.

6. Eliminate reciprocal elements, intercompany profits, and intercompany stockholdings.

7. Allocate to the minority interest its share of each item of subsidiary equity, including its share of the subsidiary's net income.

8. Combine remaining amounts in similar accounts to produce the results for presentation in consolidated statements.

9. Comment on any items which you feel require explanation. Whenever there is more than one method available, discuss the reasons or theory supporting your choice.

CPA PROBLEMS

Problem XI-1: Combination involving both pooling of interest and purchase; comparative consolidated income statement and stockholders' equity (50-60 min.)

Nickles, Inc., a manufacturer of restaurant and kitchen equipment, was incorporated in 1940. Its stock is closely held. You have been assigned to analyze certain transactions affecting a portion of the income statement and the stockholders' equity section of Nickles, Inc., and its subsidiaries. In accomplishing this assignment income taxes and earnings per share calculations are to be ignored.

The stockholders' equity section of the balance sheet at September 30, 1971, and the income statement for the year then ended follow. At that time, Nickles held no investments in other corporations.

Stockholders' Equity

$1 cumulative preferred stock, par value $15 per share, shares authorized 500,000; issued and outstanding 4,000 ...	$ 60,000
Common stock, $10 par value per share, shares authorized 1,000,000; issued and outstanding 110,000	1,100,000
Retained earnings	622,000
Total stockholders' equity	$1,782,000

Income Statement

Sales	$1,050,000
Cost of goods sold	725,000
Gross operating income	325,000
Selling, general, and administrative expenses	135,000
Net income	$ 190,000

Additional information:

1. On May 1, 1971, an empty warehouse with a book and fair-market value of $145,000 was completely destroyed by fire. Though the building was insured, the insurance company refused to pay for the loss. Nickles, Inc., immediately instigated litigation, and management was confident of winning; hence, no provision was made for a possible loss in fiscal 1971. The trial was completed October 5, 1972, finding for the insurance company.

2. The 4,000 shares of preferred stock were issued for cash at incorporation, and no other preferred shares have been issued prior to fiscal 1972. No dividends have been declared on the common stock prior to fiscal 1972.

3. Nickles' capital stock transactions during fiscal 1972 were:
   a. Preferred stock: On September 30, 1972, 8,000 shares were issued to the stockholders of Wixon, Inc., to acquire 100% of the outstanding common stock of the corporation which has a year end of September 30. The fair value of Wixon at acquisition was $140,000.
   b. Common stock:
      January 17, 1972—Sold 4,500 shares for cash to Horace Edwards at $25 per share.
      May 5, 1972—Sold 5,500 shares for cash to James Morgan at $25 per share.
      September 14, 1972—Purchased dissident stockholder Edwards' 4,500 shares at $27 per share. The shares are to be held as treasury shares and accounted for at cost. (Edwards violently opposed Nickles' expansion program. It was necessary to pay a $2 premium to eliminate his interest.)
      September 28, 1972—Contracted with Charles Trenton for the sale of 10,000 previously unissued shares at $25 per share to be issued when purchase price fully paid. At September 30, only $195,000 had been paid. Trenton agreed to pay the balance on or before November 3, 1972.
      September 30, 1972—Issued 51,000 previously unissued shares to the stockholders of Acme, Inc. in exchange for 100% of the outstanding common stock of the corporation which has a year end of September 30.

4. Dividends declared by Nickles during fiscal 1972 were:
   a. Preferred stock—A cash dividend of $1 per share was declared on May 15, 1972, for shares of record on May 27, 1972, and paid on June 12, 1972. There were no dividends in arrears on preferred stock at September 30, 1972.
   b. Common stock—A cash dividend of $1.25 per share and a 2% common stock dividend were declared on September 15, 1972, for shares of record on September 27, 1972, and payable October 10, 1972.

5. Data on Acme and Wixon:
    a. Both corporations are authorized to issue only no-par-value common stock. Data applicable at September 30, 1970 and 1972, (no change) follow:

	Acme	Wixon
Shares authorized	50,000	25,000
Shares issued and outstanding	34,000	2,500
Dollar balance in the common stock account...	$631,000	$105,000

    b. An analysis of retained earnings (deficit) for the two years ended September 30, 1972, follows:

	Acme	Wixon
Balance September 30, 1970	$(147,000)	$32,000
Net income [loss] (also net operating income [loss]) for the year ended Sep. 30, 1971	112,000	(15,000)
September 30, 1972	125,000	(6,000)
Balance September 30, 1972	$ 90,000	$11,000

    c. Prior to September 30, 1972, Acme and Wixon have never had any intercompany transactions with Nickles or between each other.
6. Nickles' unconsolidated net income (also net operating income) was $215,000 for the year ended September 30, 1972.
7. You have previously determined that the acquisitions of Acme and Wixon must be accounted for as a pooling of interests and a purchase respectively.

Required:

    a. Prepare a comparative consolidated statement of income beginning with net operating income and arriving at net income for the years ended September 30, 1972 and 1971. This statement should be supported by a schedule calculating consolidated net operating income.
    b. Assuming a consolidated net income of $405,000 and $240,000 for the years ended September 30, 1972 and 1971, respectively, prepare a comparative stockholders' equity section of the consolidated balance sheet for the years ended September 30, 1972 and 1971. This statement should be supported by the following schedules presented in the order given:

    •Changes in preferred stock account.
    •Changes in common stock account.
    •Calculation of number of shares to be issued for common stock dividend.
    •Calculation of paid-in-capital in excess of par.
    •Changes in retained earnings.

Problem XI-2: Consolidated balance sheet worksheet involving multiple acquisitions and intercompany bonds (50-60 min.)

Williard, Inc. acquired 10% of the 100,000 shares of $2.50 par value common stock outstanding of Thorne Corporation on December 31, 1969 for $38,000.

An additional 70,000 shares were acquired for $331,600 on June 30, 1971 (at which time there was no material difference between the fair and book values of Thorne's assets and liabilities). Williard uses the equity method of accounting for its investment in Thorne.

Enclosed are the balance sheets for both companies for the year ended December 31, 1971. The following information is also available:

1. An analysis of Investment in Thorne Corporation:

Date	Description	Amount
December 31, 1969	Investment	$ 38,000
June 30, 1971	Investment	331,600
December 31, 1971	80% of net increase in retained earnings of Thorne Corporation during 1971	36,000
		$405,600

2. An analysis of the companies' Retained Earnings accounts:

	Williard, Inc.	Thorne Corporation
Balance, December 31, 1969	$540,000	$101,000
Net income for 1970	55,000	40,000
Cash dividends in 1970		(5,000)
Balance, December 31, 1970	595,000	136,000
Net income:		
January 1-June 30, 1971	31,000	23,000
June 30-December 31, 1971	40,800	33,000
Dividends declared,		
December 15, 1971	(20,000)	(11,000)
80% of net increase in retained earnings of Thorne Corporation during 1971	36,000	
Balance, December 31, 1971	$682,800	$181,000

3. Thorne's other equity accounts have not changed since 1965.
4. Data on 1971 intercompany sales and ending inventories were as follows:

	Williard, Inc.	Thorne Corporation
Intercompany sales:		
January 1–June 30	$39,000	$24,000
June 30–December 31	$41,600	$41,000
Gross profit on sales	30%	25%
Intercompany payable at year end	$12,000	$ 7,000
Year-end inventory of intercompany purchases at FIFO cost	$26,000	$22,000

5. Williard, Inc. acquired $30,000 of the Thorne Corporation 6% bonds on August 31, 1971 for $30,580 plus accrued interest. Thorne Corporation issued

WORKSHEET TO PREPARE CONSOLIDATED BALANCE SHEET
December 31, 1971

	Williard, Inc.	Thorne Corporation	Adjustments and Eliminations Debit	Credit	Consolidated Balance Sheet Debit	Credit
Debits						
Cash...............................	$ 130,000	$ 60,000				
Accounts receivable...............	160,000	75,000				
Notes receivable..................	15,000	12,200				
Interest receivable...............	2,100	1,600				
Dividends receivable..............	8,800					
Marketable securities.............	31,220	9,700				
Inventories.......................	180,000	96,000				
Plant and equipment...............	781,500	510,000				
Investment in Thorne Corporation stock....	405,600					
Investment in Thorne Corporation bonds	30,580					
Advance to Thorne Corporation.....	32,000					
Unamortized bond discount		7,500				
	$1,776,800	$772,000				
Credits						
Allowance for depreciation	$ 87,000	$ 85,000				
Accounts payable	34,500	16,000				
Notes payable	5,500	3,800				
Dividends payable	20,000	11,000				
Interest payable	18,000	13,000				
Other accrued liabilities.........	15,000	1,200				
Advance from Williard, Inc........		32,000				
Bonds payable.....................	400,000	150,000				
Capital stock	500,000	250,000				
Capital in excess of par value ...	14,000	29,000				
Retained earnings.................	682,800	181,000				
	$1,776,800	$772,000				

the 20-year bonds on January 1, 1962 at 90 and has been paying the interest on each January 1 and July 1 due date.

6. On September 1, 1971 Williard, Inc. sold equipment with a cost of $40,000 and accumulated depreciation of $9,300 to Thorne Corporation for $20,200. Thorne Corporation recorded the equipment as having a cost of $29,500 with accumulated depreciation of $9,300. At that date the equipment had an estimated salvage value of $500 and an estimated life of ten years.

7. Included in Williard, Inc.'s Notes Receivable are $2,000 in noninterest bearing notes of Thorne Corporation.

Required:

Complete the worksheet on page 321 for the preparation of a consolidated balance sheet for Williard, Inc. and its subsidiary, Thorne Corporation, as of December 31, 1971. Formal statements and journal entries are not required. Assume that both companies made all of the adjusting entries required for separate financial statements unless an obvious discrepancy exists. Income taxes should not be considered in your solution. Any amortization required by APB *Opinion No. 17*, "Intangible Assets," is to be computed by the straight-line method over a 40-year period.

Problem XI-3: Consolidated balance sheet worksheet involving mid-year acquisition and intercompany profits (50-60 min.)

Brighton Corporation acquired 80 percent of the 1,250 shares of $100 par value common stock outstanding of Solvo Corporation on July 1, 1969 for $158,600. Brighton uses the equity method of accounting for its investment in Solvo.

The December 31, 1969 trial balances for both companies appear below:

Brighton Corporation and Subsidiary
TRIAL BALANCES
December 31, 1969

Assets	Brighton Corporation	Solvo Corporation
Cash	$ 200,000	$ 20,000
Accounts receivable	205,000	55,000
Notes receivable	180,000	11,000
Notes receivable discounted	(4,000)	
Accrued interest receivable	1,600	400
Dividends receivable	6,400	
Inventories	300,000	75,000
Plant and equipment	794,000	280,600
Allowance for depreciation	(260,000)	(30,000)
Investment in Solvo Corporation stock	167,400	
Investment in Solvo Corporation bonds	40,000	
Advance to Solvo Corporation	35,000	
Totals	$1,665,400	$412,000

Liabilities and Stockholders' Equity

Accounts payable	$ 220,400	$ 54,800
Notes payable	142,000	24,200
Dividends payable		8,000
Accrued interest payable	22,100	3,900
Other accrued liabilities	7,900	3,100
Advance from Brighton Corporation		35,000
Bonds payable	600,000	85,000
Capital stock	360,000	125,000
Capital in excess of par value	49,000	12,000
Retained earnings	264,000	61,000
Totals	$1,665,400	$412,000

The following information is also available:

1. Solvo Corporation reported net income and dividends for 1969 as follows:
Net income for six months ending:

June 30	$10,000
December 31	20,000

Dividends declared:

March 31	4,000
June 30	4,000
September 30	1,000
December 31	8,000

2. Data pertaining to 1969 intercompany sales and ending inventories were as follows:

	Brighton Corporation	Solvo Corporation
Intercompany sales:		
January 1 to June 30	$40,000	$ 95,000
July 1 to December 31	$60,000	$105,000
Markup on cost	20%	25%
Intercompany payable at year-end	$13,000	$ 5,500
Year-end inventory of intercompany purchases at FIFO cost	$25,000	$ 18,000

3. Sales of equipment by Brighton Corporation to Solvo Corporation during 1969 were as follows:

Date	Book Value on Brighton's Records	Price Paid by Solvo	Depreciation Method	Estimated Life
February 1	$11,000	$13,500	Double-declining balance	10 years
October 1	14,000	12,000	Straight-line	5 years

For depreciation purposes Solvo Corporation estimates salvage at 10 percent of the equipment's cost.

4. Brighton Corporation acquired $40,000 of the 6 percent Solvo Corporation bonds at par value on July 1, 1969. Interest is paid each July 1 and January 1 by Solvo Corporation.

5. On December 1, 1969, Brighton Corporation discounted $4,000 of noninterest bearing notes payable at Solvo Corporation.

Required:

Complete a worksheet for the preparation of a consolidated balance sheet for Brighton Corporation and its subsidiary, Solvo, Inc., as of December 31, 1969. Formal statements and journal entries are not required. You may assume that both companies made all of the adjusting entries required for separate financial statements unless an obvious discrepancy exists. Income taxes should not be considered in your solution.

Problem XI-4: Intermingling of fiduciary and business combination accounting (50-60 min.)

Fred Stone, one of three trustees appointed under the terms of a testamentary trust established by the will of Jac Allen, a bachelor, engaged you to prepare a consolidated balance sheet of the various interests in properties controlled and managed by the trustees as of September 30, 1969. These properties consist of estate assets, undistributed income, and a 90 per cent stock interest in the Bass Corporation purchased when the Corporation was formed. Bass Corporation in turn owns 80 per cent of the stock of the Crane Investment, Inc. All assets were valued for federal estate tax purposes as of the date of Allen's death.

Allen died on June 30, 1963 leaving his entire estate in trust for the benefit of his sister to pass on to her children. Under the terms of the will, the three appointed trustees are authorized to (1) act as directors of the two corporations and may, at their discretion, combine or dissolve them, (2) pay a minimum of $4,000 monthly as the sister's maintenance allowance from interest and dividend income remaining after payment of expenses of the Trust, and (3) buy or sell trust investments, reinvest estate assets and/or undistributed income. Gains or losses from the sale of trust assets are to be allocated to corpus.

The September 30, 1969 trial balances for the Allen Estate, Bass Corporation, and Crane Investments, Inc. appear on page 325.

Stone requested that you use, in lieu of cost for balance sheet valuation purposes, the fair market value of the securities at the date of Allen's death in order that the accountability of the trustees for subsequent events may be properly disclosed.

The following information was available:

1. Investments in bonds are reported at cost and represent their present market value. Interest of $9,000 had accrued on the bonds held by the Allen Estate but was not recorded on September 30, 1969.

2. Marketable securities held by Bass Corporation costing $794,000 and having a market value of $800,000 on Allen's death were still on hand at September 30, 1969. The market value of marketable securities purchased after Allen's death and held by Bass Corporation on September 30, 1969 was $2,200,000.

3. The market value of the securities held by Crane Investments, Inc. on June 30, 1963, as determined for federal estate tax purposes, was $250,000. These securities cost $240,000 on January 2, 1963 and were sold in 1965 for $295,000. The securities on hand at September 30, 1969 were purchased on

Allen Estate, Bass Corporation, and Crane Investments, Inc.
TRIAL BALANCES
September 30, 1969

Debits	*Allen Estates*	*Bass Corporation*	*Crane Investments, Inc.*
Cash in bank	$ 45,000	$ 195,000	$ 45,000
Due from Crane Investments, Inc.		4,500	
Investments at cost:			
Corporate bonds...................	300,000	500,000	
Marketable securities:			
Purchased prior to June 30, 1963 ...		794,000	
Purchased after June 30, 1963......		2,000,000	439,000
Stock of Bass Corporation—			
90% interest at cost	2,250,000		
Stock of Crane Investments, Inc.—			
80% interest at cost................		156,000	
Accrued interest receivable.............		21,000	
Trustees' expenses, taxes, etc. paid	218,000		
Distributions to sister.................	296,000		
	$3,109,000	$3,670,500	$484,000

Credits			
Sundry liabilities		$ 373,500	$ 38,250
Due to Bass Corporation			4,500
Income from dividends	$ 460,000		
Interest income	72,000		
Gain on sale of bonds................	2,000		
Equity of Jac Allen:			
Estate corpus	2,575,000		
Estate income....................			
Capital stock:			
Bass Corporation:			
Allen Estate		2,250,000	
Minority interest		250,000	
Crane Investments, Inc.:			
Bass Corporation...............			160,000
Minority interest			40,000
Retained earnings:			
Bass Corporation:			
Allen Estate...................		717,300	
Minority interest		79,700	
Crane Investments, Inc.:			
Bass Corporation...............			193,000
Minority interest			48,250
	$3,109,000	$3,670,500	$484,000

May 10, 1969 at a cost of $439,000 and had a market value of $441,000 on September 30, 1969.

4. The investment in Bass Corporation is reported on the trial balance at cost. The value of the investment reported for federal estate tax purposes was $2,700,000 which the trustees believe to be fair and represents the original cost plus appreciation of securities to June 30, 1963.

5. Bass Corporation's investment in Crane Investments, Inc. is reported on the trial balance at cost. On June 30, 1963 total owners' equity of Crane Investments, Inc. consisted of $200,000 in capital stock at par value and $20,000 in retained earnings. No dividends have been paid to Crane Investments, Inc.

Required:

Prepare a worksheet for the preparation of a consolidated balance sheet. Supporting computations should be in good form. Worksheet adjusting and eliminating entries should be numbered. Formal adjusting and eliminating entries and financial statements are not required.

Problem XI-5: Consolidated balance sheet worksheet for parent and two subsidiaries accounted for as a purchase (40-50 min.)

The December 31, 1968 balance sheets of the Major Corporation and its two subsidiaries appear below:

Major Corporation and Subsidiaries
BALANCE SHEETS
December 31, 1968

Assets	Major Corporation	Minor Corporation	Mode Corporation
Cash...............................	$ 100,000	$ 75,000	$ 95,000
Accounts receivable	158,200	210,000	105,000
Inventories.........................	290,000	90,000	115,000
Advance to Minor Corporation............	17,000		
Dividends receivable....................	24,000		
Property, plant and equipment............	777,600	325,000	470,000
Allowance for depreciation	(180,000)	(55,000)	(160,000)
Investment in Minor Corporation:			
6% bonds	23,800		
Common stock	308,600		
Investment in Mode Corporation:			
Preferred stock....................	7,000		
Common stock	196,000		
Totals	$1,722,200	$645,000	$625,000

Liabilities and Capital			
Accounts payable......................	$ 170,000	$ 96,000	$ 86,000
Notes payable	45,000	14,000	44,000
Bonds payable	285,000	150,000	125,000
Discounts on bonds payable..............	(8,000)	(12,000)	
Dividends payable	22,000	30,000	
Preferred stock, $20 par................	400,000		
Mode Corporation....................			50,000
Common stock, $10 par................	600,000		
Minor Corporation		250,000	
Mode Corporation			200,000
Retained Earnings	208,200		
Minor Corporation		117,000	
Mode Corporation			120,000
Totals	$1,722,200	$645,000	$625,000

Additional information available includes the following:

1. The investment in Minor Corporation stock by the Major Corporation is composed of the following items:

Date	Description	Amount
4/ 1/67	Cost of 5,000 shares of Minor Corporation stock..............	$ 71,400
12/31/67	20% of the dividends declared in December 1967 by the Minor Corporation	(9,000)
12/31/67	20% of the 1967 net income of the Minor Corporation.........	12,000
7/ 1/68	Cost of 15,000 shares of Minor Corporation stock	226,200
12/31/68	80% of the dividends declared in December 1968 by Minor Corporation	(24,000)
12/31/68	80% of the 1968 net income of the Minor Corporation.........	32,000
12/31/68	Total	$308,600

2. Major Corporation acquired 250 shares of fully participating preferred stock for $7,000 and 14,000 shares of common stock for $196,000 of the Mode Corporation on January 2, 1968. Mode Corporation had a net income of $20,000 in 1968 and did not declare any dividends.

3. Mode Corporation's inventory includes $22,400 of merchandise acquired from Minor Corporation for which no payment had been made. Minor Corporation marked-up the merchandise 40 per cent on cost.

4. Major Corporation acquired in the open market 25 $1,000 face-value 6% bonds of Minor Corporation for $21,400 on January 5, 1965. The Minor Corporation bonds mature December 31, 1970. Interest is paid each June 30 and December 31.

5. The 3 corporations are all in the same industry and their operations are homogeneous. Major Corporation exercises control over the boards of directors of both Minor Corporation and Mode Corporation and has installed new principal officers in both.

Required:

Prepare a worksheet for the preparation of a consolidated balance sheet as of December 31, 1968 for Major Corporation and its subsidiaries. Consolidated retained earnings should be allocated to Major Corporation and minority interests should be shown separately. The consolidation is to be accounted for as a purchase. Formal financial statements and journal entries are not required. Supporting computations should be in good form.

SPECIFIC APPROACH

Problem XI-1

1. Where applicable, structure schedules and statements in comparative form, 1972 versus 1971.

2. Should the acquisition of 100% of the outstanding common stock of Wixon be recorded as a pooling of interests?

3. In the Schedule of Changes in Common Stock Account, include a retroactive adjustment for pooling of interests. This retroactive adjustment for

pooling will also affect the calculation of paid-in capital in excess of par. In the case of the Wixon acquisition, the excess of the fair value of Wixon over the par value of preferred shares issued will constitute paid-in capital.

4. The Schedule of Changes in Retained Earnings should begin with the balance as of September 30, 1970. Remember to use the assumed consolidated net income amounts shown in requirement (b) rather than your computed amounts.

Problem XI-2

1. An error was made in applying the equity method of accounting to the investment in Thorne. The simplest approach would be to reverse the incorrect entry for $36,000 and record the correct amount of the parent's share of increase in Thorne Corporation's retained earnings.

2. The elimination of the Investment in Thorne Corporation Stock account and 100% elimination of all Thorne Corporation owners' equity balances permits you to create the minority interest in Thorne, as well as the excess of cost over book value.

3. Unless caution is exercised, you may select the wrong gross profit percentage in eliminating intercompany profit in inventories. If Thorne sells to Willard, what is the intercompany profit percentage to be applied to the $26,000 year-end inventory?

4. The most direct approach to eliminate intercompany bond elements is to compare the $30,000 face value of intercompany bonds with the sum of the unamortized bond discount and investment applicable thereto, charging minority interest with 20% of the difference.

5. At what amount should the intercompany equipment be carried? Both the asset and related depreciation must be corrected.

6. Should the amortization of the excess of cost over book value be for six months or a year? It is possible to determine whether any portion of the excess was attributable to the December 31, 1969 purchase by comparing 10% of Thorne's owners' equity total on that date with the $38,000 cost.

Problem XI-3

1. Although the more common approach is to eliminate parent's share of all owners' equity items, revealing minority interest in each element, one could proceed by eliminating completely the balance in each equity item, producing one amount for the total minority interest.

2. How should one treat purchases of fixed assets from a company prior to the time majority interest is acquired?

3. Problem holds nothing novel, with typical situations of intercompany activities that must be eliminated.

Problem XI-4

1. Determine what adjusting entries are necessary before proceeding to the eliminating entries.

2. Has the $4000 monthly payment for September been made to the sister?

3. In the entry to close nominal accounts, is the gain on the sale of a corpus asset considered corpus or income?

4. In writing up the cost to market value on date of death, separate the credits to retained earnings to show estate and minority interests.

5. Under the circumstances found in the problem, elimination of the 80% interest in Crane will be as of what date?

6. Before eliminating the 90% estate interest in Bass Corporation, segregate and transfer the 80% majority interest in Crane's retained earnings that belong to Bass.

Problem XI-5

1. During the years of stock acquisition, Major Corporation included its share of earnings in Minor Corporation for each entire year, rather than from date of acquisition. In such situations, one should assume that earnings may be spread equally throughout the year. In the entry to eliminate reciprocal elements in investment and equity accounts, adjust for the excess net income of Minor Corporation recorded in error by Major Corporation.

2. In the entry to eliminate reciprocal elements in Mode Corporation investment and equity accounts, what allocation process should be adopted to determine the retained earnings identified with the investments in preferred and common stock of Mode Corporation?

3. The entry to eliminate reciprocal elements in bond and bond discount accounts must take into consideration the difference between the unaccumulated discount on Minor's and Major's books for the intercompany bond holdings.

4. The procedure to transfer to Major its share of 1968 earnings of Mode, which are allocable to preferred and common, will be similar to that of Step 2 above.

Governmental and Institutional Accounting

GENERAL APPROACH

Governmental accounting embodies principles and techniques adopted by a unit of government to promote economy and efficiency in accounting for public funds in compliance with requirements stipulated by law.

In 1968, under the title, Governmental Accounting, Auditing, and Financial Reporting, the National Committee on Governmental Accounting (hereinafter, referred to as the "Committee") revised and combined two of its earlier publications: *Municipal Accounting and Auditing* (1951) and *A Standard Classification of Municipal Accounts* (1953). In the revision, the Committee recognized changes that had occurred which enhanced understanding of governmental accounting reports by promoting uniform terminology for items similar to those used in commercial accounting. For example, the Committee eliminated "Surplus," substituting "Retained Earnings" in enterprise funds or funds of a commercial nature, and "Fund Balance" for all other funds. "Reserve for Bad Debts" was replaced by its commercial accounting counterpart, "Allowance for Doubtful Accounts." Where terminology is unique to governmental activities, it was retained, but the Committee is to be applauded for eliminating differences in terminology where there were no differences in concepts.

Within certain spheres of governmental accounting, basic differences from commercial accounting continue. Except for self-supporting governmental activities, depreciation on general fixed assets should not be recognized. In the profit-motivated concern, depreciation is recognized as a measure of consumption of service potential. Governmental units are generally not profit-

330

oriented, nor do their general fixed assets determine borrowing power. To record depreciation would imply that there is a relationship between the expense and revenue, when no such causative association exists.

Recognizing that the accrual method of accounting is superior in its ability to match expenses and revenues, the Committee has encouraged its adoption for governmental accounting except where it would be inappropriate because of the nature of activities. In this latter case, the modified accrual basis is recommended. The Committee states in its 1968 publication (page 11):

> The accrual basis of accounting is recommended for Enterprise, Trust, Capital Projects, Special Assessment, and Intragovernmental Service Funds. For the General, Special Revenue, and Debt Service Funds, the modified accrual basis of accounting is recommended. The modified accrual basis of accounting is defined as that method of accounting in which expenditures other than accrued interest on general long-term debt are recorded at the time liabilities are incurred and revenues are recorded when received in cash, except for material or available revenues which should be accrued to reflect properly the taxes levied and the revenues earned.

One characteristic of governmental accounting is the segregation of financial activity by funds and groups. In commercial accounting, a fund is an accumulation of cash, investments, and other liquid assets to be used for a stipulated purpose. In governmental accounting, a fund is a group of accounts necessary to record activities specified by law. The fund may include asset, liability, revenue, and expenditure accounts that constitute an accounting entity having its own self-balancing set of accounts from which its reports are derived. Not all of the various funds available may be necessary or desirable for different governmental units because of their limited financial activity or size. The various funds recommended by the Committee to assist in attainment of sound financial administration are:

1. The General Fund to account for all financial transactions not properly accounted for in another fund;

2. Special Revenue Funds to account for the proceeds of specific revenue sources (other than special assessments) or to finance specified activities required by law or administrative regulation;

3. Debt Service Funds to account for payment of interest and principal on long-term debt other than special assessment and revenue bonds;

4. Capital Projects Funds to account for the receipt and disbursement of moneys used for the acquisition of capital facilities other than those financed by special assessment and enterprise funds;

5. Enterprise Funds to account for the financing of services to the general public where all or most of the costs involved are paid in the form of charges by users of such services;

6. Trust and Agency Funds to account for assets held by a governmental unit

as trustee or agent for individuals, private organizations, and other governmental units;

7. Intragovernmental Service Funds to account for the financing of special activities and services performed by a designated organization unit within a governmental jurisdiction for other organization units within the same governmental jurisdiction;

8. Special Assessment Funds to account for special assessments levied to finance public improvements or services deemed to benefit the properties against which the assessments are levied.

In addition to funds, the following self-balancing groups are frequently used:

1. General Fixed Assets Group to account for fixed assets not used exclusively by any one fund;

2. General Long-term Debt Group to account for long-term liabilities not presently the responsibility of any one fund.

General Fund

Most important of all funds is the General Fund, whose responsibility it is to account for all expenditures and revenues not specifically the domain of other funds. If a governmental unit has no other funds, it will have at least a general fund to record activities and to demonstrate its compliance with the law. In most cases the General Fund provides for the financing of general administration. Its major sources of revenue are taxes (property, income, gasoline, etc.), licenses and permits, fines and penalties. Frequently, there are activities between the General Fund and other funds established for a governmental unit. Should an unappropriated balance exist in a fund at the termination of a fiscal period, it is often transferred to the General Fund.

Another characteristic of governmental accounting is the use of budgets and budgetary accounts. Even if the law does not require budgetary procedures, they should be adopted to promote sound fiscal policy. When a budget is approved by the proper body, the following entry is made in the General Fund:

```
Estimated revenues ........................  xxx
    Appropriations ...................................  xxx
```

If budgeted revenues are estimated to exceed appropriations, the difference is reflected in the Fund Balance account, thus:

```
Estimated revenues .........................  xxx
    Appropriations ...................................  xxx
    Fund balance .....................................  xxx
```

Both Estimated Revenues and Appropriations are controlling budgetary accounts for which details are recorded in subsidiary ledgers or records to show sources of estimated revenues and authorized items of expenditures. It should be noted that the Estimated Revenues account is created as a debit balance account, while Appropriations is created as a credit balance account. This procedure permits closing the actual and estimated revenue controlling accounts at the end of each fiscal period, isolating and thus emphasizing whether the budgeted or the actual figure was the larger. For example, where actual revenues exceeded estimated revenues, the entry would be:

```
Revenues ...............................   xxx
    Estimated revenues .................................   xxx
    Fund balance ......................................   xxx
```

Taxes are a principal source of revenue. If a property tax is levied, a part of which is deemed uncollectible, it is recorded in the following manner:

```
Taxes receivable-current .....................   xxx
    Revenues .........................................   xxx
    Estimated uncollectible current taxes ...................   xxx
```

The Taxes Receivable-Current account functions as a controlling account for the detail presented in the subsidiary property tax records. Collection of property taxes is treated as is any collection of a receivable. Where taxes are not collected, the law provides procedures for the posting of a lien against the property for delinquent taxes, interest, and penalties. The entries would first reflect conversion of a current tax receivable to a delinquent tax:

```
Taxes receivable-delinquent ..................   xxx
Estimated uncollectible current taxes ...........   xxx
    Taxes receivable-current ...........................   xxx
    Estimated uncollectible delinquent taxes ...............   xxx
```

In accordance with procedures outlined under the law, if taxes were not paid, the exercise of the tax lien against the property would be entered:

```
Tax liens receivable .......................   xxx
Estimated uncollectible delinquent taxes ........   xxx
    Taxes receivable-delinquent ..........................   xxx
    Estimated uncollectible tax liens .....................   xxx
```

The final step in the procedure would reflect the sale of the foreclosed property:

```
Cash ....................................   xxx
Estimated uncollectible tax liens
    (for any loss on the sale) .................   xxx
    Tax liens receivable ...............................   xxx
```

As far as property taxes are concerned, an accrual basis is used, with recognition of revenue entered at the time taxes are originally levied. Not all activities of the General Fund are capable of such treatment—fines, for example, are treated on a cash basis, with the revenue accorded recognition only when the fine is paid. Thus, within a single fund, more than one basis of accounting is functioning simultaneously.

The General Fund operates within the framework of a budgeted amount approved for expenditure over an indicated period of time. It is important, therefore, to record activities which at some future time will result in an actual liability in order to insure against overexpenditure of the budgeted appropriation. This is accomplished by an encumbrance system, wherein an entry is made for each approved purchase order:

```
Encumbrances ...........................    xxx
    Reserve for encumbrances ..........................        xxx
```

When the material is received or the service has been performed and invoices are actually received, the above is reversed and an entry is made to record the actual liability, which may or may not agree in amount with the original encumbrance:

```
Reserve for encumbrances ...................    xxx
    Encumbrances ......................................        xxx

Expenditures ............................    xxx
    Vouchers payable .................................        xxx
```

Both the Encumbrances and Expenditures accounts are controlling accounts with details in supporting subsidiary records.

The amount available for commitment at any time is the Appropriations amount minus the Expenditures and Encumbrances. If total Appropriations from the budget were $100,000 and Encumbrances not vouchered totaled $30,000 with Expenditures of $25,000, the unencumbered appropriation would be $45,000 ($100,000 – $30,000 – $25,000).

At the end of the fiscal period, the closing entry relative to these accounts, assuming that appropriations exceeded expenditures and encumbrances, would be:

```
Appropriations ...........................    xxx
    Expenditures ......................................        xxx
    Encumbrances ......................................        xxx
    Fund balance ......................................        xxx
```

One should note that the Reserve for Encumbrances account is *not* closed by the entry above. Any balance in that account would be carried forward to be charged for encumbrances of the current period whose liability was not formally incurred until the succeeding period.

Financial Reports

Financial reports may be prepared at any point during a fiscal period or at the close of a period. Interim statements furnish the basis for analyzing a fund's ability to carry out its activities for the remaining portion of the fiscal period, providing the basis for remedial action where necessary. Illustrations of a General Fund balance sheet at year-end, an analysis of changes in the fund balance for the year, the statement of revenue—estimated versus actual, and the statement of expenditures and encumbrances compared with authorizations, are presented now in the form recommended by the Committee.

THE GENERAL FUND
Illustration 1
Name of Governmental Unit
GENERAL FUND
BALANCE SHEET
December 31, 19x2

ASSETS

Cash		$258,500
Investments		65,000
Interest receivable on investments		50
Accounts receivable	$10,300	
Less: Estimated uncollectible accounts receivable	2,000	
		8,300
Taxes receivable-delinquent	49,300	
Less: Estimated uncollectible delinquent taxes	8,800	
		40,500
Interest and penalties receivable on taxes	3,600	
Less: Estimated uncollectible interest and penalties	600	
		3,000
Tax liens receivable	20,100	
Less: Estimated uncollectible tax liens	5,300	
		14,800
Advance to Central Garage Fund		65,000
Due from Parks Fund		2,000
Due from State Government		30,000
Inventory of supplies		7,200
Total Assets		$494,350

LIABILITIES, RESERVES, AND FUND BALANCE

Vouchers payable	$107,861
Accounts payable	10,400
Contracts payable	57,600
Due to Water and Sewer Fund	2,000
Due to Employees' Retirement System Fund	10,189
Due to Central Garage Fund	12,000
Taxes collected in advance	15,000
Total liabilities	$215,050
Reserve for encumbrances	38,000
Reserve for inventory of supplies	7,200
Reserve for advance to Central Garage Fund	65,000
Fund balance (Illustration 2)	169,100
Total Liabilities, Reserves, and Fund Balance	$494,350

Illustration 2
Name of Governmental Unit
GENERAL FUND
ANALYSIS OF CHANGES IN FUND BALANCE
For the Fiscal Year Ended December 31, 19x2

Fund balance, January 1, 19x2		$ 84,300
Add:		
Excess of revenues over expenditures:		
Revenues (Illustration 3)	$1,314,500	
Expenditures (Illustration 4)	1,201,500	
		113,000
Reserve for encumbrances from 19x1 cancelled......................		1,300
Decrease in reserve for advance to Central Garage Fund		10,000
Total balances and additions		$208,600
Deduct:		
Reserve for encumbrances, December 31, 19x2...............	$38,000	
Increase in reserve for inventory of supplies	1,500	
		39,500
Fund balance, December 31, 19x2 (Illustration 2)		$169,100

Illustration 3
Name of Governmental Unit
GENERAL FUND
STATEMENT OF REVENUE – ESTIMATED AND ACTUAL
For the Fiscal Year Ended December 31, 19x2

	Estimated Revenue	Actual Revenue	Actual Over (Under) Estimated
Taxes:			
General property taxes – current	$ 880,000	$ 878,500	$ (1,500)
Penalties and interest on delinquent			
taxes – general property	2,500	2,800	300
Total taxes	882,500	881,300	(1,200)
Licenses and permits:			
Business licenses and permits	105,500	82,000	(23,500)
Non-business licenses and permits.......	20,000	21,000	1,000
Total licenses and permits	125,500	103,000	(22,500)
Intergovernmental revenue:			
Federal grants.....................	55,000	58,500	3,500
State grants.......................	145,000	128,000	(17,000)
Total intergovernmental revenue ..	200,000	186,500	(13,500)
Charges for services:			
General government	40,000	45,000	5,000
Public safety......................	10,000	11,000	1,000
Highways and streets	8,000	8,500	500
Sanitation........................	12,000	11,000	(1,000)
Culture – recreation	20,000	15,500	(4,500)
Total charges for services	90,000	91,000	1,000
Fines and forfeits:			
Fines............................	27,500	27,700	200
Forfeits	5,000	5,500	500
Total fines and forfeits..........	32,500	33,200	700
Miscellaneous revenue:			
Interest earnings...................	1,500	2,000	500
Rents and royalties.................	18,000	17,500	(500)
Total miscellaneous revenue......	19,500	19,500	–
Total Revenue	$1,350,000	$1,314,500	$(35,500)

Illustration 4
Name of Governmental Unit
GENERAL FUND
STATEMENT OF EXPENDITURES AND ENCUMBRANCES COMPARED WITH AUTHORIZATIONS
For the Fiscal Year Ended December 31, 19x2

Function/Activity/Object	Reserve for Encumbrances 19x1(1)	Expenditures 19x1(1)	Credit (Charge) to fund Balance	19x2 Appropriations Revised(2)	19x2 Expenditures(3)	19x2 Encumbrances (3)	19x2 Unencumbered Balance
General Government:							
Legislative							
Personal services	$ –	$ –	$ –	$ 15,000	$ 14,500	$ 500	$ –
Supplies	–	–	–	1,000	1,100	(100)	–
Other services and charges ..	–	–	–	3,000	3,000	–	–
Capital outlays	–	–	–	1,000	900	100	–
Total Legislative	–	–	–	20,000	19,500	500	300
Judicial (Itemize by Object).	500	250	250	17,000	15,700	1,000	300
Executive (Itemize by Object)	1,600	1,250	350	92,000	85,105	2,700	4,195
Total general government	2,100	1,500	600	129,000	120,305	4,200	4,495
Public Safety (4)	5,500	5,600	(100)	277,300	252,795	6,550	17,955
Highways and Streets(4)	10,000	9,400	600	94,500	86,000	5,500	3,000
Sanitation(4)	9,500	9,350	150	50,000	46,900	3,000	100
Health(4)	3,600	3,650	(50)	47,750	40,850	4,600	2,300
Welfare(4)	800	800	–	51,000	46,000	2,100	2,900
Culture-Recreation(4)	2,000	2,000	–	59,000	53,400	3,850	1,750
Education(4)	4,000	3,900	100	591,450	555,250	8,200	28,000
TOTAL	$37,500	$36,200	$1,300	$1,300,000	$1,201,500	$38,000	$60,500

(1) Where the Reserve for Encumbrances includes amounts encumbered prior to the year immediately preceding (19x1 in this illustration), the first two money columns in this statement should read, respectively, "Reserve for Encumbrances Prior Years" and "Expenditures–Prior Years,"

(2) In lieu of this single column, three headings may be used as follows: *Appropriations, Revisions, Final Appropriations.*

(3) Under appropriate circumstances where the number and amounts of encumbrances are not material, the "Expenditure" and "Encumbrances" columns may be combined into one column. Where this is done, there must be a proper notation that the column contains year-end encumbrances as well as actual expenditures.

(4) For illustrative purposes only, functional totals are shown here. In actual practice, each function should include detailed breakdowns on the basis of subfunctions (if any), activity, and. object of expenditure.

Comments

The design of the Statement of Revenue, displaying both estimated and actual revenues, permits a judgment of the reliability of original estimates, as well as review of elements that demonstrate the greatest variance. It is assumed that accounts are kept on an accrual basis, except for such items as fines, which are normally treated on a cash basis.

Comments

The design of the Statement of Expenditures and Encumbrances is interesting. Not only does it demonstrate how well a governmental unit has stayed within bounds of the authorized objectives, but also it provides the unexpended and unencumbered balances of authorizations useful in future budgetary planning.

Fixed Assets

The absence of fixed assets is perhaps the most striking difference between the balance sheet of a governmental unit General Fund and that of a commercial enterprise. As the Committee points out (page 9):

The primary purpose of an operating fund such as the General Fund is to account for revenues and expenditures on a current basis and to present fairly the status of current assets and liabilities so that net assets available for further appropriation can be accurately determined. These objectives can most readily be achieved by the exclusion of fixed assets from the operating fund accounts and by placing them in a single, separate, self-balancing group of accounts.

The recommended form for the Statement of General Fixed Assets follows:

Name of Governmental Unit
STATEMENT OF GENERAL FIXED ASSETS
December 31, 19x2

General Fixed Assets:

Land	$1,259,500
Buildings	2,855,500
Improvements other than buildings	1,036,750
Equipment	452,500
Construction work in progress	1,722,250
Total general fixed assets	$7,326,500

Investment in General Fixed Assets from:
Capital projects funds:

General obligation bonds	$3,954,100
Federal grants	1,000,000
State grants	300,000
County grants	625,000
General fund revenues	562,400
Special revenue fund revenues	309,500
Gifts	175,000
Special assessments	400,000
Total investment in general fixed assets	$7,326,500

Comments

The Statement of General Fixed Assets consists of only two parts: first, a list of the general fixed assets by nature, excluding those fixed assets specifically related to a particular function, such as the assets of a utility maintained in the Enterprise Fund; second, accounts showing the source of the assets. The assets are shown at cost. If any have been acquired through grants, their basis is cost to the grantor, or, if such amount is not known, at their appraised value at the time the grant was made. Assets acquired by gift are carried at their appraised value. No recognition is given depreciation.

Although special assessment improvements are financed only in part by the governmental unit, the entire cost is capitalized, including the amount financed from special assessments. The reason for such procedure is that the improvement belongs to the government, and the latter is responsible for maintaining and repairing it. If practicable, however, the accounts should be kept to show the extent to which the improvement was financed from special assessments levied against private property and from governmental funds.

On the Statement of General Fixed Assets, the assets are not offset or counterbalanced by a reflection of bonds payable, even if the assets were acquired by expenditure of proceeds of a bond issue. Fixed assets may have been acquired in ways other than through bond issues; bonds payable may have been issued for purposes other than the acquisition of general fixed assets. Except in the case of enterprise activities, rarely is the bonded debt secured by mortgages against specific property.

Bonds

It is the function of debt service funds to account for the payment of principal and interest on long-term bonds, except for those bonds which are the direct responsibility of enterprise or general assessment funds. Note that it is the *payment* of principal and interest on general obligations bonds which is accounted for by the bond service fund. Liability for bonds is accounted for in the general long-term debt group of accounts, and is reflected in the statement of General Long-Term Debt shown below, as recommended by the Committee:

Name of Governmental Unit
STATEMENT OF GENERAL LONG-TERM DEBT
December 31, 19x2

AMOUNT AVAILABLE AND TO BE PROVIDED
FOR PAYMENT OF GENERAL LONG-TERM DEBT

Term Bonds:		
Amount available in debt service funds	$ 196,205	
Amount to be provided	203,795	
Total—term bonds		$ 400,000
Serial Bonds:		
Amount Available in debt service funds	14,005	
Amount to be provided	2,385,995	
Total—Serial bonds		2,400,000
Total Available and to be Provided		$2,800,000

GENERAL LONG-TERM DEBT PAYABLE

Term bonds payable	400,000
Serial bonds payable	2,400,000*
Total General Long-Term Debt Payable	$2,800,000

*Includes $700,000 of outstanding 19x0 Waterworks General Obligation Bonds which are serviced by the Water and Sewer Fund.

Accounting for bonds of a governmental unit is often confusing to a candidate, since it may involve five or more funds and groups. The chart on pages 342 and 343 furnishes the entries for events relating to a bond issue.

Interfund Transactions

In governmental accounting, a transaction must often be recorded in more than one fund. Unless such activity is handled properly in all funds involved, incomplete and erroneous records will result. In the examination, the candidate may be asked to display familiarity with the more frequently occurring interfund transactions. To discuss the activities of all funds even in summary form is beyond the scope of this book, but an excellent review of the interfund material is given in *Governmental Accounting, Auditing, and Financial Reporting* issued by the National Committee on Governmental Accounting in 1968. The Chart of Selected Transactions given on p. 341 indicates the funds or groups in which designated events are normally recorded and should assist the CPA candidate in reviewing the handling of interfund activities.

Nonprofit Organizations

In the past the body of techniques employed for the accounting of nonprofit organizations has been referred to as "institutional accounting." The term is not sufficiently descriptive, for the intent was to convey the idea of a nonprofit organization whose primary purpose is to provide some form of service to the community. Not only are these organizations nonprofit, but to varying degrees they depend on generous contributors to break even. In this category, we find religious, educational, community health, and welfare organizations.

With service, rather than profit, the point of primary concern, accounting procedures and reports are more closely analogous to those of governmental units than to those of a typical business enterprise. Nonprofit organizations are granted limited resources for which they must account, demonstrating compliance with prescribed operational procedures and budgetary allocations.

Chart of Selected Transactions
Indicating Funds and Groups in Which Events are Recorded

Events	General	Special Revenue	Special Assessment	Capital Projects	Debt Service	Intragovernmental Service	Enterprise	Trust and Agency	General Fixed Asset	General Long-Term Debt
(a) Approval of budgeted revenue	X	X								
(b) Approval of budgeted appropriations	X	X								
(c) Levy of taxes for general revenue	X									
(d) Authorization of general bond issue				X						
(e) Sale of bonds in (d) for cash at par				X						X
(f) Building constructed and contractors paid from proceeds of general bond issue above				X					X	
(g) Purchase orders entered into	X	X								
(h) Items ordered in (g) received and vouchers approved	X	X								
(i) Equipment for police department purchased and voucher approved	X								X	
(j) Current taxes collected	X									
(k) Taxes written off as uncollectible were collected	X									
(l) Vouchers were approved for payment of salaries (usually no encumbrances are recorded for salaries) after deduction of amount for pension fund	X	X				X	X	X		
(m) Construction of streets approved—to be financed by levy on adjacent property			X							
(n) A payment is made by the general fund for eventual redemption of general bond issue	X				X					X
(o) Serial bonds matured and were retired—provision was made in the appropriation for this retirement	X				X					X
(p) Equipment retired and sold	X								X	
(q) Supplies requisitioned from the stores department	X					X				
(r) Depreciation of utility fixed assets recorded							X			
(s) Utility presents a bill to general fund for service rendered	X						X			

Chart of Entries Related to a Bond Issue

Events:	General Fund	Capital Projects Fund
(1) Legislature authorizes bond issue.		(1) Bonds authorized– unissued Fund balance
(2) Bonds are sold. (Premium, if any, is transferred to fund that will pay interest, usually Debt Service Fund.)		(2) Cash Bonds authorized– unissued

(3) Proceeds are used to purchase a building.		(3a) Expenditures
		    Vouchers payable
		(3b) Vouchers payable
		    Cash

(4) Required contributions and earnings for the period are recorded.		

(5) Cash contribution is made by General Fund to Debt Service Fund.	(5a) Expenditures
	    Vouchers payable
	(5b) Vouchers payable
	    Cash	

(6) Earnings on investments made by Debt Service Fund recorded, and its books closed periodically.		
(7) Increase in Debt Service Fund available to meet principal.		
(8) Interest is paid by Debt Service Fund.		
(9) Bonds are retired by Debt Service Fund.		

Debt Service Fund	Long-Term Debt Group	Fixed Asset Group
	(2) Amounts to be provided for payment of bond principals Bonds payable	
		(3) Buildings Investment in general fixed assets
(4) Required additions Required earnings Fund balance		
(5) Cash Required additions		
(6) Cash Revenues Revenues Required additions Fund balance		
	(7) Amount available in Debt Service Funds-Bonds principal Amount to be provided for payment of bond principal	
(8a) Expenditures Vouchers payable (8b) Vouchers payable Cash		
(9) Fund balance Cash	(9) Bonds payable Amount available in Debt Service Funds-Bonds principal	

Nonprofit organizations have adopted fund accounting procedures, where "fund" has the same meaning as in governmental accounting—a self-balancing group of accounts employed to record a segment of activity and capable of generating reports to demonstrate compliance with delegated authority. The use of budgetary accounts and an encumbrance system prove valuable to nonprofit organizations, another facet resembling governmental accounting procedure.

For those wishing a review of the accounting for nonprofit entities, a short but excellent presentation is found in *Advanced Accounting,* by Ronald Copeland, D. Larry Crumbley, and Joseph F. Wojdak, published by Holt, Rinehart and Winston, Incorporated (1971).

Summary

The following points may be helpful in the solution of governmental accounting problems:

1. Requirements of problems in governmental and nonprofit entity (institutional) accounting are generally limited to either or both of the following:
   a. Journal entries for a series of transactions in various funds, testing the ability of a candidate to work with accounts peculiar to this phase of accounting;
   b. Financial statements and reports requiring a demonstration of familiarity with the relationships and position of account balances.
2. If specifically requested, journal entries must be presented in the customary manner. Unless excused from presenting explanations, one should submit concise statements about each entry.
3. If only specific financial statements are required, but a series of transactions must be considered to arrive at the solution, there are two approaches commonly employed. If only one or two funds are involved, a worksheet permits concentration of data without becoming so involved as to defeat its purpose. It also permits proof of the balance existing in the opening trial balance, if one is present in the problem. Some accounts are used more often than others, for example, Cash or Accounts Payable. Provide ample spaces for these accounts. This technique becomes less desirable if a substantial number of funds is involved. In this case, the use of T accounts, classified by funds, becomes a more fruitful channel of action. When journal entries are entered either on a worksheet or in T accounts, elements of each entry should be similarly identified to assist in subsequent verification should such action become necessary. Thus, all elements of the first entry might be marked "a" or "1."

The most unusual characteristic of governmental accounting is the use of funds. Since accounting for nonprofit organizations requires the use of funds, the topics are frequently discussed as variations of a common system. Both usually employ budgetary systems. Both must be capable of demonstrating adherence to limitations and restrictions. Although account titles and specifics may differ, the principles of accounting discussed in this section as applicable to governmental units are equally pertinent to nonprofit organizations.

CPA PROBLEMS

Problem XII-1: Municipal worksheet with adjustments and reclassification to proper groups and funds (40-50 min.)

The City of Happy Hollow has engaged you to examine its financial statements for the year ended Decemer 31, 1971. The City was incorporated as a municipality and began operations on January 1, 1971. You find that a budget was approved by the City Council and was recorded, but that all transactions have been recorded on the cash basis. The bookkeeper has provided an Operating Fund trial balance. Additional information is given below:

1. Examination of the appropriation-expenditure ledger revealed the following information:

	Budgeted	Actual
Personal services	$ 45,000	$38,500
Supplies	19,000	11,000
Equipment	38,000	23,000
Totals	$102,000	$72,500

2. Supplies and equipment in the amounts of $4,000 and $10,000, respectively, had been received, but the vouchers had not been paid at December 31.
3. At Decemer 31, outstanding purchase orders for supplies and equipment not yet received were $1,200 and $3,800, respectively.
4. The inventory of supplies on December 31 was $1,700 by physical count. The decision was made to record the inventory of supplies. A city ordinance requires that expenditures are to be based on purchases, not on the basis of usage.
5. Examination of the revenue subsidiary ledger revealed the following information:

	Budgeted	Actual
Property taxes	$102,600	$ 96,000
Licenses	7,400	7,900
Fines	4,100	4,500
Totals	$114,100	$108,400

It was estimated that 5% of the property taxes would not be collected. Accordingly, property taxes were levied in an amount so that collections would yield the budgeted amount of $102,600.

City of Happy Hollow
WORKSHEET TO CORRECT TRIAL BALANCE
December 31, 1971

	Operating Fund Trial Balance	Adjustments Debit	Adjustments Credit	General Fund	Debt Service Fund	Capital Projects Fund	General Fixed Assets	General Long-Term Debt
Debits								
Cash	$238,900							
Expenditures	72,500							
Estimated revenues	114,100							
	$425,500							
Credits								
Appropriations	$102,000							
Revenues	108,400							
Bonds payable	200,000							
Premium on bonds payable	3,000							
Fund balance	12,100							
	$425,500							

6. On November 1, 1971, Happy Hollow issued 8% General Obligation Term Bonds with $200,000 face value for a premium of $3,000. Interest is payable each May 1 and November 1 until the maturity date of November 1, 1985. The city council ordered that the cash from the bond premium be set aside and restricted for the eventual retirement of the debt principal. The bonds were issued to finance the construction of a city hall, but no contracts had been let as of December 31.

Required:

a. Complete the worksheet on page 346, showing adjustments and distributions to the proper funds or groups of accounts in conformity with generally accepted accounting principles applicable to governmental entities. (Formal adjusting entries are not required.)

b. Identify the financial statements that should be prepared for the General Fund. (You are not required to prepare these statements.)

c. Draft formal closing entries for the General Fund.

Problem XII-2: Multiple choice questions on proper activities of various governmental funds (40-50 min.)

INSTRUCTIONS

Select the best answer for each of the following items relating to fund Mark only one answer for each item. Your grade will be determined from your total of correct answers.

Items to be Answered

40. The operations of a public library receiving the majority of its support from property taxes levied for that purpose should be accounted for in
   a. The general fund.
   b. A special revenue fund.
   c. An enterprise fund.
   d. An intragovernmental service fund.
   e. None of the above.

41. The liability for general obligation bonds issued for the benefit of a municipal electric company and serviced by its earnings should be recorded in
   a. An enterprise fund.
   b. The general fund.
   c. An enterprise fund and the general long-term debt group.
   d. An enterprise fund and disclosed in a footnote in the statement of general long-term debt.
   e. None of the above.

42. The liability for special assessment bonds which carry a secondary pledge of a municipality's general credit should be recorded in
   a. An enterprise fund.
   b. A special revenue fund and general long-term debt group.
   c. A special assessment fund and the general long-term debt group.
   d. A special assessment fund and disclosed in a footnote in the statement of general long-term debt.
   e. None of the above.

43. The proceeds of a federal grant made to assist in financing the future construction of an adult training center should be recorded in
    a. The general fund.
    b. A special revenue fund.
    c. A capital projects fund.
    d. A special assessment fund.
    e. None of the above.

44. The receipts from a special tax levy to retire and pay interest on general obligation bonds issued to finance the construction of a new city hall should be recorded in a
    a. Debt service fund.
    b. Capital projects fund.
    c. Revolving interest fund.
    d. Special revenue fund.
    e. None of the above.

45. The operations of a municipal swimming pool receiving the majority of its support from charges to users should be accounted for in
    a. A special revenue fund.
    b. The general fund.
    c. An intragovernmental service fund.
    d. An enterprise fund.
    e. None of the above.

46. The fixed assets of a central purchasing and stores department organized to serve all municipal departments should be recorded in
    a. An enterprise fund and the general fixed assets group.
    b. An enterprise fund.
    c. The general fixed assets group.
    d. The general fund.
    e. None of the above.

47. The monthly remittance to an insurance company of the lump sum of hospital-surgical insurance premiums collected as payroll deductions from employees should be recorded in
    a. The general fund.
    b. An agency fund.
    c. A special revenue fund.
    d. An intragovernmental service fund.
    e. None of the above.

48. Several years ago a city provided for the establishment of a sinking fund to retire an issue of general obligation bonds. This year the city made a $50,000 contribution to the sinking fund from general revenues and realized $15,000 in revenue from securities in the sinking fund. The bonds due this year were retired. These transactions require accounting recognition in
    a. The general fund.
    b. A debt service fund and the general long-term debt group of accounts.
    c. A debt service fund, the general fund and the general long-term debt group of accounts.
    d. A capital projects fund, a debt service fund, the general fund and the general long-term debt group of accounts.
    e. None of the above.

49. A city realized large capital gains and losses on securities in its library endowment fund. In the absence of specific instructions from the donor or state statutory requirements, the general rule of law holds that these amounts should be charged or credited to

a. General fund income.
b. General fund principal.
c. Trust fund income.
d. Trust fund principal.
e. None of the above.

50. The activities of a central motor pool which provides and services vehicles for the use of municipal employees on official business should be accounted for in

a. An agency fund.
b. The general fund.
c. An intragovernmental service fund.
d. A special revenue fund.
e. None of the above.

51. A transaction in which a municipal electric utility paid $150,000 out of its earnings for new equipment requires accounting recognition in

a. An enterprise fund.
b. The general fund.
c. The general fund and the general fixed assets group of accounts.
d. An enterprise fund and the general fixed assets group of accounts.
e. None of the above.

52. In order to provide for the retirement of general obligation bonds, a city invests a portion of its general revenue receipts in marketable securities. This investment activity should be accounted for in

a. A trust fund.
b. The enterprise fund.
c. A special assessment fund.
d. A special revenue fund.
e. None of the above.

53. The activities of a municipal employee retirement plan which is financed by equal employer and employee contributions should be accounted for in

a. An agency fund.
b. An intragovernmental service fund.
c. A special assessment fund.
d. A trust fund.
e. None of the above.

54. A city collects property taxes for the benefit of the local sanitary, park and school districts and periodically remits collections to these units. This activity should be accounted for in

a. An agency fund.
b. The general fund.
c. An intragovernmental service fund.
d. A special assessment fund.
e. None of the above.

55. A transaction in which a municipal electric utility issues bonds (to be repaid from its own operations) requires accounting recognition in

a. The general fund.
b. A debt service fund.
c. Enterprise and debt service funds.
d. An enterprise fund, a debt service fund and the general long-term debt group of accounts.
e. None of the above.

56. A transaction in which a municipality issued general obligation serial bonds to finance the construction of a fire station requires accounting recognition in the

a. General fund.
b. Capital projects and general funds.
c. Capital projects fund and the general long-term debt group of accounts.
d. General fund and the general long-term debt group of accounts.
e. None of the above.
57. Expenditures of $200,000 were made during the year on the fire station in item 56. This transaction requires accounting recognition in the
a. General fund.
b. Capital projects fund and the general fixed assets group of accounts.
c. Capital projects fund and the general long-term debt group of accounts.
d. General fund and the general fixed assets group of accounts.
e. None of the above.

Problem XII-3: Journal entries to reclassify activities recorded only in a municipal General Fund (50-60 min.)

Your examination of the accounts of your new client, the City of Delmas, as of June 30, 1971 revealed the following:

1. On December 31, 1970 the City paid $115,000 out of General Fund revenues for a central garage to service its vehicles, with $67,500 being applicable to the building which has an estimated life of 25 years, $14,500 to land and $33,000 to machinery and equipment which has an estimated life of 15 years. A $12,200 cash contribution was received by the garage from the General Fund on the same date.
2. The garage maintains no records, but a review of deposit slips and cancelled checks revealed the following:

Collections for services to City departments financed from
    the General Fund $30,000
Office salaries 6,000
Utilities 700
Mechanics' wages 11,000
Materials and supplies 9,000

3. The garage had uncollected billings of $2,000, accounts payable for materials and supplies of $500 and an inventory of materials and supplies of $1,500 at June 30, 1971.
4. On June 30, 1971 the City issued $200,000 in special assessment bonds at par to finance a street improvement project estimated to cost $225,000. The project is to be paid by a $15,000 levy against the City (payable in fiscal year 1971-72) and $210,000 against property owners (payable in five equal annual installments beginning October 1, 1971). The levy was made on June 30. A $215,000 contract was let for the project on July 2, 1971, but work has not begun.
5. On July 1, 1969 the City issued $400,000 in 30-year, 6% general obligation term bonds of the same date at par to finance the construction of a public health center. Construction was completed and the contractors fully paid a total of $397,500 in fiscal year 1970-71.
6. For the health center bonds the City sets aside General Fund revenues sufficient to cover interest (payable semiannually on July 1 and January 1 of

each year) and $5,060 to provide for the retirement of bond principal, the latter transfer being made at the end of each fiscal year and invested at the beginning of the next. Your investigation reveals that such investments earned $304 during fiscal year 1970-71, the exact amount budgeted. This $304 was received in cash and will be invested at the beginning of the next year.

Required:

The above information disclosed by your examination was recorded only in the General Fund. Prepare the formal entries as of June 30, 1971 to adjust the funds other than the General Fund. Entries should be classified into clearly labeled groups for each fund, and fund titles should be selected from the following list:

Special revenue fund
Capital projects fund (bond fund)
Debt service fund (sinking fund)
Trust fund (endowment fund)
Agency fund
Intragovernmental service fund (working capital fund)
Special assessment fund
Enterprise fund (utility fund)
General fixed assets group of accounts (general fixed assets)
General long-term debt group of accounts (general bonded debt and interest)

Problem XII-4: Municipal General Fund worksheet for distribution to proper funds or groups (50-60 min.)

At the start of your examination of the accounts of the City of Waterford, you discovered that the bookkeeper failed to keep the accounts by funds. The following trial balance of the General Fund for the year ended December 31, 1969 was available.

City of Waterford
GENERAL FUND TRIAL BALANCE
December 31, 1969

	Debit	Credit
Cash	$ 207,500	
Taxes receivable–current	148,500	
Allowance for uncollectible taxes–current		$ 6,000
Appropriation expenditures	760,000	
Revenues		992,500
Donated land	190,000	
River Bridge bonds authorized–unissued	100,000	
Work in process–River Bridge	130,000	
River Bridge bonds payable		200,000
Contracts payable–River Bridge		25,000
Retained percentage–River Bridge contracts		5,000
Vouchers payable		7,500
Surplus		300,000
Total	$1,536,000	$1,536,000

Your examination disclosed the following:

1. The budget for the year 1969, not recorded on the books, estimated revenues and expenditures as follows: revenues $815,000; expenditures $775,000.
2. Outstanding purchase orders at December 31, 1969 for operating expenses not recorded on the books totaled $2,500.
3. Included in the Revenues account is a credit of $190,000 representing the value of land donated by the state as a grant-in-aid for construction of the River Bridge.
4. Interest payable in future years totals $60,000 on River Bridge bonds sold at par for $200,000.
5. Examination of the subledger containing the details of the Appropriation Expenditures account revealed the following items included therein:

Current operating expenses	$472,000
Additions to structures and improvements	210,000
Equipment purchases	10,000
General obligation bonds paid	50,000
Interest paid on general obligation bonds	18,000

Required:

Prepare a worksheet showing the given General Fund trial balance, adjusting entries, and distributions to the proper funds or groups of accounts. The following column headings are recommended:

General Fund Trial Balance–Debit
General Fund Trial Balance–Credit
Adjustments–Debit
Adjustments–Credit
General Fund–Debit
General Fund–Credit
Bond Fund
General Fixed Assets
General Bonded Debt and Interest

Number all adjusting and transaction entries. Formal journal entries are not required.

Problem XII-5: Reclassification of General Fund activities with emphasis on Special Assessment Fund (50-60 min.)

You were engaged to examine the financial statements of the City of Homer for the year ended June 30, 1969 and found that the bookkeeper had recorded all transactions in the General Fund. You were furnished the General Fund Trial Balance, which appears on page 353.

Your audit disclosed the following:

1. Years ago the City Council authorized the recording of inventories, and a physical inventory taken on June 30, 1969 showed that materials and supplies with a cost of $37,750 were on hand at that date. The inventory is recorded on a perpetual basis.

City of Homer
GENERAL FUND TRIAL BALANCE
June 30, 1969

Debits

Cash	$ 125,180
Cash for construction	174,000
Taxes receivable–current	8,000
Assessments receivable–deferred	300,000
Inventory of materials and supplies	38,000
Improvements authorized	15,000
Estimated revenues	4,135,000
Interest expense	18,000
Encumbrances	360,000
Appropriation expenditures	4,310,000
Total Debits	$9,483,180

Credits

Allowance for uncollectible current taxes	$ 7,000
Vouchers payable	62,090
Interest payable	18,000
Liability under street improvement project	10,000
Bonds payable	300,000
Premium on bonds	3,000
Reserve for inventory	36,000
Reserve for encumbrances	360,000
Appropriations	4,450,000
Interest revenue	21,000
Unappropriated surplus	106,090
Revenues	4,110,000
Total Credits	$9,483,180

2. Current taxes are now considered delinquent and it is estimated that $5,500 of such taxes will be uncollectible.

3. Discounts of $32,000 were taken on property taxes. An appropriation is not required for discounts, but an allowance for them was not made at the time the tax levy was recorded. Discounts taken were charged to Appropriation Expenditures.

4. On June 25, 1969, the State Revenue Department informed the city that its share of a state-collected, locally-shared tax would be $75,000.

5. New equipment for the Police Department was acquired at a cost of $90,000 and was properly recorded in the General Fund.

6. During the year 100 acres of land were donated to the city for use as an industrial park. The land had a value of $250,000. No recording has been made.

7. The City Council authorized the paving and widening of certain streets at an estimated cost of $365,000, which included an estimated $5,000 cost for planning and engineering to be paid from the General Fund. The remaining $360,000 was to be financed by a $10,000 contribution from the city and $350,000 by assessments against property owners payable in seven equal annual installments. A $15,000 appropriation was made for the city's share at the time the annual budget was recorded, and the total $365,000 was also recorded as an appropriation. The following information is also relevant to the street improvement project:

    (a) Property owners paid their annual installment plus a $21,000 interest charge in full.

    (b) Special assessment bonds of $300,000 were authorized and sold at a premium of $3,000. An $18,000 liability for interest was properly recorded. The city does not amortize bond premium or discount.

    (c) The city's $15,000 share was recorded as an expenditure during the year. The $5,000 for planning and engineering fees was paid. Construction began July 5, 1968, and the contractor has been paid $200,000 under the contract for construction which calls for performance of the work at a total cost of $360,000. This $360,000 makes up the balance in the Reserve for Encumbrances.

    (d) The Cash for Construction account was used for all receipts and disbursements relative to the project. It is made up of the proceeds of the bond issue and collection of assessment installments and interest minus payments to the contractor.

Required:

Prepare a 14-column worksheet to adjust the account balances at June 30, 1969 and to distribute them to the appropriate funds or groups of accounts. It is recommended that the worksheet be in the order of the General Fund Trial Balance and have the following column headings:

    1. Balance per books.
    2. Adjustments—debit.
    3. Adjustments—credit.
    4. General Fund.
    5. Special Assessment Fund.
    6. General fixed assets.

(Number all adjusting entries. Formal journal entries or financial statements are not required. Supporting computations should be in good form.)

Problem XII-6: Vocational school worksheet involving an Annuity Fund (50-60 min.)

The bookkeeper for the Jacob Vocational School resigned on March 1, 1968 after he prepared the following general ledger trial balance and analysis of cash as of February 29, 1968:

Jacob Vocational School
GENERAL LEDGER TRIAL BALANCE
February 29, 1968

Debits

Cash for general current operations	$258,000
Cash for restricted current uses	30,900
Stock donated by D. E. Marcy	11,000
Bonds donated by E. T. Pearce	150,000
Building	33,000
Land	22,000
General current operating expenses	38,000
Faculty recruitment expenses	4,100
Total	$547,000

Credit

Mortgage payable on fixed assets	$ 30,000
Income from gifts for general operations	210,000
Income from gifts for restricted uses	196,000
Student fees	31,000
Unappropriated surplus	80,000
Total	$547,000

Jacob Vocational School
ANALYSIS OF CASH
For the Six Months Ended February 29, 1968

Cash for general current operations:			
Balance, September 1, 1967		$ 80,000	
Add: Student fees	$ 31,000		
Gift of W. L. Jacob	210,000	241,000	
		321,000	
Deduct: General current operation expenses. . .	38,000		
Payment on land and building.	25,000	63,000	$258,000
Cash for restricted uses:			
Gift of W. L. Jacob for faculty recruitment.		35,000	
Less faculty recruitment expenses		4,100	30,900
Checking account balance, February 29, 1968			$288,900

You were engaged to determine the proper balances for the school as of August 31, 1968, the close of the school's fiscal year. Your examination disclosed the following information:

1. D. E. Marcy donated 100 shares of Trans, Inc. stock in September 1967 with a market value of $110 per share at the date of donation. The terms of the gift provide that the stock and any income thereon are to be retained intact. At any date designated by the board of directors the assets are to be liquidated and the proceeds used to assist the school's director in acquiring a personal residence. The school will not retain any financial interest in the residence.

2. E. T. Pearce donated 6 per cent bonds in September 1967 with par and market values of $150,000 at the date of donation. Annual payments of $3,500 are to be made to the donor during his lifetime. Earnings in excess of these payments are to be used for current operations in the following fiscal year. Upon the donor's death the fund is to be used to construct a school cafeteria.

3. No transactions have been recorded on the school's books since February 29, 1968. An employee of the school prepared the following analysis of the checking account for the period from March 1 through August 31, 1968:

Balance, March 1, 1968.			$288,900
Deduct: General current operating expenses	$ 14,000		
Purchase of equipment	47,000	$ 61,000	
Less student fees		8,000	
Net expenses.		53,000	
Payment for director's residence	11,200		
Less sale of 100 shares of Trans, Inc. stock.	10,600	600	53,600
Total			235,300
Add: Interest on 6% bonds.		9,000	
Less payments to E. T. Pearce		3,500	5,500
Balance, August 31, 1968			$240,800

Required:

Prepare a worksheet presenting the trial balance at February 29, 1968, adjusting entries, transaction entries from March 1 through August 31, 1968, and distributions to the proper funds or groups of accounts. The following column headings are recommended for your worksheet:

1. Trial Balance, February 29, 1968.
2. Adjustments and Transactions—Debit.
3. Adjustments and Transactions—Credit.
4. General Current Fund.
5. Restricted Current Funds.
6. Plant Funds—Invested in Plant.
7. E. T. Pearce Annuity Fund.

Number all adjusting and transaction entries. Formal journal entries and statements are not required. Supporting computations should be in good form.

Problem XII-7: Government reimbursement for hospital inpatient services (50-60 min.)

Good Hope Hospital completed its first year of operation as a qualified institutional provider under the health insurance (HI) program for the aged and wishes to receive maximum reimbursement for its allowable costs from the government. The Hospital engaged you to assist in determining the amount of reimbursement due and furnished the following financial, statistical and other information:

1. The Hospital's charges and allowable costs for departmental inpatient services were:

Departments	Charges for HI Program Beneficiaries	Total Charges	Total Allowable Costs
Inpatient routine services (room, board, nursing)........................	$425,000	$1,275,000	$1,350,000
Inpatient ancillary service departments:			
X-ray...........................	56,000	200,000	150,000
Operating room..................	57,000	190,000	220,000
Laboratory.....................	59,000	236,000	96,000
Pharmacy	98,000	294,000	207,000
Other	10,000	80,000	88,000
Total ancillary...............	280,000	1,000,000	761,000
Totals	$705,000	$2,275,000	$2,111,000

2. For the first year the Reimbursement Settlement for Inpatient Services may be calculated at the option of the provider under either of the following apportionment methods:

(a) *The Departmental RCC (ratio of cost centers) Method* provides for listing on a departmental basis the ratios of beneficiary inpatient charges to total inpatient charges with each departmental beneficiary inpatient charge ratio applied to the allowable total cost of the respective department.

(b) *The Combination Method (with cost finding)* provides that the cost of routine services be apportioned on the basis of the average allowable cost per day for all inpatients applied to total inpatient days of beneficiaries. The residual part of the provider's total allowable cost attributable to ancillary (nonroutine) services is to be apportioned in the ratio of the beneficiaries' share of charges for ancillary services to the total charges for all patients for such services.

3. Statistical and other information:
   (a) Total inpatient days for all patients   40,000
   (b) Total inpatient days applicable to HI beneficiaries (1,200 aged patients whose average length of stay was 12.5 days)   15,000
   (c) A fiscal intermediary acting on behalf of the government's medicare program negotiated a fixed "allowance rate" of $45 per inpatient day subject to retroactive adjustment as a reasonable cost basis for reimbursement of covered services to the hospital under the HI program. Interim payments based on an estimated 1,000 inpatient-days per month were received during the 12-month period subject to an adjustment for the provider's actual cost experience.

Required:

a. Prepare schedules computing the total allowable cost of inpatient services for which the provider should receive payment under the HI program and the remaining balance due for reimbursement under each of the following methods:

1. Departmental RCC method.
2. Combination method (with cost finding).

b. Under which method should Good Hope Hospital elect to be reimbursed for its first year under the HI program assuming the election can be changed for the following year with the approval of the fiscal intermediary? Why?

c. Good Hope Hospital wishes to compare its charges to HI program beneficiaries with published information on national averages for charges for hospital services.

Compute the following (show your computations):

1. The average total hospital charge for an HI inpatient.
2. The average charge per inpatient day for HI inpatients.

Problem XII-8: Worksheet for nonprofit hospital establishing an Endowment Fund and Plant Fund (50-60 min.)

A newly elected board of directors of Central Hospital, a nonprofit corporation, decided that effective January 1, 1968

(a) the existing general ledger balances are to be properly adjusted and allocated to three separate funds (General Fund, John Central Endowment Fund and Plant Fund),

(b) the totals of the John Central Endowment Fund and the Allowance For Accumulated Depreciation are to be fully invested in securities, and

(c) all accounts are to be maintained in accordance with the principles of fund accounting. The board engaged you to determine the proper account balances for each of the funds.

The balances in the general ledger at January 1, 1968 were:

	Debit	Credit
Cash	$ 50,000	
Investment in U. S. Treasury bills	105,000	
Investment in common stock	417,000	
Interest receivable	4,000	
Accounts receivable	40,000	
Inventory	25,000	
Land	407,000	
Building	245,000	
Equipment	283,000	
Allowance for depreciation		$ 376,000
Accounts payable		70,000
Bank loan		150,000
John Central Endowment Fund		119,500
Surplus		860,500
Totals	$1,576,000	$1,576,000

The following additional information is available:

1. Under the terms of the will of John Central, founder of the hospital, "the principal of the bequest is to be fully invested in trust forevermore in mortgages secured by productive real estate in Central City and/or in U.S. Government securities ... and the income therefrom is to be used to defray current expenses."

2. The John Central Endowment Fund account balance consists of the following:

Cash received in 1871 by bequest from John Central	$ 81,500
Net gains realized from 1926 through 1959 from the sale of real estate acquired in mortgage foreclosures	23,500
Income received from 1960 through 1967 from 90-day U.S. Treasury Bill investments	14,500
Balance per general ledger on January 1, 1968	$119,500

3. The Land account balance was composed of:

1890 appraisal of land at $10,000 and building at $5,000 received by donation at that time. (The building was demolished in 1910.)	$ 15,000
Appraisal increase based on insured value in land title policies issued in 1927	380,000
Landscaping costs for trees planted	12,000
Balance per general ledger on January 1, 1968	$407,000

4. The Building account balance was composed of:

Cost of present hospital building completed in January 1927 when the hospital commenced operations	$300,000
Adjustment to record appraised value of building in 1937 .	(100,000)
Cost of elevator installed in hospital building in January 1953	45,000
Balance per general ledger on January 1, 1968	$245,000

The estimated useful lives of the hospital building and the elevator when new were 50 years and 20 years, respectively.

5. The hospital's equipment was inventoried on January 1, 1968. The cost of the inventory agreed with the Equipment account balance in the general ledger. The Allowance For Accumulated Depreciation account at January 1, 1968 included $158,250 applicable to equipment and that amount was approved by the board of directors as being accurate. All depreciation is computed on a straight-line basis.

6. A bank loan was obtained to finance the cost of new operating room equipment purchased in 1964. Interest on the loan was paid to December 31, 1967.

Required:

Prepare a worksheet to present the adjustments necessary to restate the general ledger account balances properly and to distribute the adjusted balances to establish the required fund accounts. Formal journal entries are not required. Computations should be in good form and should be referenced to the worksheet adjustments which they support. In addition to trial balance columns, the following columnar headings are recommended for your worksheet:

Adjustments		General Fund		John Central Endowment Fund		Plant Fund	
Debit	Credit	Debit	Credit	Debit	Credit	Debit	Credit

SPECIFIC APPROACH

Problem XII-1

1. Among the worksheet adjustments required will be entries to record the purchase of equipment, the December 31 inventory, the reclassification of bond issue proceeds, and the correct handling of the bond issue.

2. Read requirement (b) carefully before answering.

3. Only two entries are necessary to close the General Fund—one to close actual and estimated revenues and one to close appropriations, expenditures and encumbrances.

Problem XII-2

The problem consists of 18 multiple choice questions, testing the familiarity of the candidate with the scope of governmental funds. A thorough review of the "Chart of Selected Transactions Indicating Funds and Groups in Which Events are Recorded" found in the General Approach for Topic XII would have rewarded the candidate with a high score on this problem.

Problem XII-3

The examiners were kind to include the former, as well as the revised terminology. Be sure that you are familiar with both, for one must not rely on such generosity. Review also the function of each of the named funds or groups.

1. The Intragovernmental Service Fund should have entries to record the acquisition of the garage and cash, the revenues of the garage, and its inventory, expenses, and unrecorded liabilities. Should depreciation be recorded?

2. Although the liability for bonds payable is usually reflected in the long-term debt group of accounts, this is not true where special assessment bonds are issued to finance a project. In the latter case, the liability is reflected in the fund responsible for redemption.

3. In the entry to record the debt service fund for the Health Center bonds, why is the amount of the credit to the Fund Balance account identical with the amount entered in the General Long-term Debt group debiting Amount Available in Debt Service Fund?

Problem XII-4

It is unfortunate that two years after the recommendations of the National Committee on Governmental Accounting for revised terminology, problems continue to appear using the old. Perhaps this is a result of the time it takes to get new terms into textbooks and the time it takes for governmental units to adopt changes. Candidates must be familiar with both the traditional and the revised terminology (the latter is shown in parentheses in the suggested solution, whenever it differs).

Rather than skip from one fund activity to the other, a more logical approach would be to prepare entries by funds, facilitating the extension of amounts to proper funds and groups:

General Fund:
    1. Record 1969 budget and close the portion of the Surplus account applicable to the General Fund.

2. Record the encumbrance for outstanding purchase orders.

3. Remove accounts belonging to other funds.

Bond Fund (Capital Projects Fund): Segregate the River Bridge Bond transactions, but remember that bonds payable are not reflected in this
fund.

General Fixed Assets (General Fixed Assets Group of Accounts):

1. Record the donation of land.

2. Record the investment in fixed assets financed from issuance of bonds
and from current revenues.

General Bonded Debt and Interest (General Long-Term Group of Accounts):
Record the projected liability of the bonds.

Problem XII-5

This is a good illustration of a problem where only a basic knowledge of
governmental accounting will produce satisfactory results. It should encourage
the candidate to devote some time to review the area.

1. Not only must the inventory of materials and supplies be reduced, but the
Reserve for Inventory must be increased. What is the function of the Reserve for
Inventory account?

2. In converting the Allowance for Uncollectible Current Taxes to the Allowance for Uncollectible Delinquent Taxes, what account should be credited with
the difference?

3. Entries are necessary to establish the Investment in Fixed Assets for
equipment purchased. Should the same procedure be followed for donated fixed
assets?

4. Four entries will adjust all items relating to point 7:

    a. record city's share of street improvement project to be reflected in
Special Assessments Fund,

    b. reclassify the bond premium and interest collected on assessments,

    c. cancel encumbrances for contractor's progress billings paid,

    d. establish the investment in fixed assets for the construction work in
progress. Should planning and engineering fees be capitalized?

Problem XII-6

1. Construct interim transaction and adjusting entries to facilitate allocation
to the various funds and group. The destination of each new account created
should be known.

2. Transfer the gift of bonds to the Annuity Fund and apportion fixed assets
to the Plant Fund balance.

3. Record interim transactions. Should the loss in sale of Trans Inc. stock be charged against the general current fund or the restricted current fund.

4. Entries must be made to record the earnings of the Annuity Fund which will be available to the General Fund in the following fiscal year.

5. Extend amounts in the worksheet to proper columns.

Problem XII-7

1. Successful solution of this problem demands careful reading. When you begin work with item 1 of requirement (a), concentrate on the paragraph describing the Departmental RCC Method, foresaking all other data. It will become obvious that the hospital's charges and allowable costs data are convertible into the solution schedule requested merely by adding two columns, "Percentage of HI Program Charges to Total Charges" and "Portion of Allowable Costs Allocable to Beneficiary Service."

Then tackle the Combination Method and requirement (c) using the same approach.

2. The answer to requirement (b) is so simple, it may confuse you.

Problem XII-8

1. Adjusting entries must be designed to permit extension of adjusted balances into one of the three funds desired by the board.

2. Read carefully the terms of the will; they will suggest which investments shown in the trial balance comprise the Endowment Fund, and whether or not all items listed in item 2 should remain as components of the Endowment Fund.

3. The Land and Building accounts should reflect cost basis produced by normal accounting procedure.

4. In correcting accumulated depreciation, compare the total which should exist for building, elevator, and equipment to the present balance in Allowance for Depreciation. What additional adjustment will be necessary because of decision (b) of the board of directors?

5. Sub-totals of columns in the General Fund and Plant Fund sections of the worksheet will provide the basis for splitting the Surplus account balance as it is eliminated.

Taxation

GENERAL APPROACH

The relative importance of the area of taxation is apparent from the fact that it may constitute almost 20% of the examination. Certainly such emphasis is justified when one considers that no major decision in business should be made without considering tax consequences. Public accounting firms are frequently called upon to prepare state and Federal income tax returns. If an organization has its own tax department which prepares the returns, the public accounting firm performing the audit usually reviews the returns. A candidate must, therefore, expect to be tested on the adequacy of his knowledge of tax accounting.

Not only should one possess a knowledge of Federal tax law, but he should also be able to recognize the problems and know how to present the data in a completed income tax return. In taking the examination, the practicing accountant who has spent one or more seasons preparing tax returns will have a definite advantage. In some examinations, actual blank returns supplied by the Institute had to be completed. Thorough familiarity with the latest forms for individual, partnership, and corporation returns will strengthen a candidate's preparations, although it is difficult to predict when actual forms may be used.

The basic law of Federal taxation is the Internal Revenue Code. Official interpretation of the Code by the Treasury Department is found in Title 26 of the Code of Federal Regulations. Additional data may be found in the Administrative Rulings issued by the Treasury Department and the Internal Revenue Service. In recent years most comprehensive tax reform was accomplished by the Tax Reform Act of 1969. It affected capital planning, established minimum tax on tax preference items, altered depreciation policies, revised charitable deductions, provided for a maximum tax on earned income, and eliminated the tax on low-income taxpayers. Although there have been more recent revenue acts, not since the Internal Revenue Code of 1954 has there been such a thorough revision.

To attempt to prepare for the area of taxation by a detailed study of the Code, the Regulations, and the Rulings would be both time-consuming and possibly confusing. Instead, one should use the following material, which, if carefully studied, will provide an adequate basic knowledge to pass the portion of the examination devoted to taxation:

1. A current text providing a comprehensive explanation of Federal tax structure and training in the application of tax principles to specific cases. The latest Prentice-Hall *Federal Tax Course* is recommended because of the clarity of style and liberal use of problems illustrating application of the data in specific cases.

2. Instruction pamphlets issued by the Treasury Department. Copies are available from the nearest office of the Internal Revenue Service.

3. Specimen returns with forms for individual, partnership, and corporation returns completely worked out for a given case, equal in difficulty to the average examination problem. These two pamphlets are published by Prentice-Hall, Inc., under the title "Federal Income Tax—Specimen Returns."

The latest tax provisions should be familiar to the candidate who has just recently completed a tax course. For the person whose tax background was acquired one or more years ago, a useful procedure to update knowledge is to review recent major tax changes. For proper filing of returns in 1973, one should consider the Tax Reform Act of 1969 (some of whose provisions were delayed) and the Revenue Act of 1971, which produced the following major changes:

1. an increase in personal and dependency exemptions;
2. an increase in the standard deduction;
3. an increase in income levels before one is required to file a return;
4. introduction of a credit or deduction for contributions to political organizations;
5. enactment of the Class Life ADR (Asset Depreciation Range) system;
6. restoration of the investment credit for the full year;
7. recognition of a new corporation, the Domestic International Sales Corporation (DISC);
8. decrease in the top marginal tax rate on earned taxable income from 60% to 50%.

With limited time available for review, maximum advantage is derived by concentrating your study on recent major tax changes.

During their days at the university, many students of taxation were given "open book" examinations, where access to the text was permitted. Courses in taxation attempt to stress principles and philosophy, rather than details. The CPA examination is not open book. Thus a candidate is concerned about remembering even essentials. Two suggestions are offered. One, is to prepare a chart to organize data. For example, to gather information on the basis for determining gain or loss where cost is generally inappropriate, the following table would be useful:

BASIS FOR DETERMINING GAIN OR LOSS

Basis to be used in case of	*For determining Gain*	*For determining Loss*
Gift after 12/31/20**	Same as in hands of donor or last preceding owner by whom not acquired by gift	Same as in hands of donor or last preceding owner by whom not acquired by gift or fair market value, whichever is lower
Gift before 1/1/21	Fair market value at time of gift	Fair market value at time of gift
Property acquired from a decedent.	Fair market value at acquisition (date of death); or value 6 months after death or at distribution within 6 months of death, if executor uses such optional valuation date for estate tax purposes	Fair market value at acquisition (date of death); or value 6 months after death, or at distribution within 6 months of death, if executor uses such optional value date for estate tax purposes
Property acquired before 3/1/13	Cost or 3/1/13 value whichever is greater (cost of depreciable property must be adjusted to 3/1/13)	Cost
New residence replacing old residence when no gain or only part of the gain is recognized.	Cost less gain not recognized on sale of old residence.	Cost less gain not recognized on sale of old residence.

**The basis of gifts is increased by the amount of any gift tax paid on the transfer of the property. In no case is basis increased above the fair market value on transfer.

The variety of acceptable depreciation methods makes it difficult to remember which may be used with different types of property to produce the largest depreciation deduction. Organize the material in the form of a table:

SUMMARY OF AVAILABLE DEPRECIATION METHODS

Property	*Most Liberal Method Available*
Personal tangible property:	
Used—useful life of more than 1 year but less than 3 years	Straight line
New—useful life of more than 1 year but less than 3 years	Straight line
Used—useful life of more than 3 years but less than 6 years	Limited declining balance
New—useful life of more than 3 years but less than 6 years	Declining balance or sum of the years-digits
New or used—useful life of at least 6 years	Additional first-year allowance plus declining balance or sum of the years-digits
Real property:	
Used residential rental or commercial— acquired before 7-25-69—useful life of less than 3 years	Straight line
Used residential rental or commercial acquired before 7-25-69—useful life of more than 3 years but less than 20 years	Straight line
Used residential rental or commercial acquired during suspension period (10-10-66 to 3-9-67)	Limited declining balance (special rules apply)
Used residential rental acquired after 7-24-69—useful life of 20 years or more	Declining balance at 1¼ times the straight line rate
Used commercial acquired after 7-24-69	Straight line
New residential rental or commercial acquired before 7-25-69—useful life of at least 3 years	Declining balance or sum of the years-digits
New residential rental acquired after 7-24-69—useful life of at least 3 years	Declining balance or sum of the years-digits
New commercial acquired after 7-24-69— useful life of at least 3 years	Limited declining balance

The second suggestion to aid memory involves tax topics which do not lend themselves to charting, but for which an outline is invaluable. For example, you are studying the investment credit, reinstated by the Revenue Act of 1971. To nail down its principal provisions, you might prepare this summary:

1. Credit is 7% of investment, not to exceed $25,000 of the tax plus 1/2 of excess.
2. Qualified property: Depreciable tangible personal property and some depreciable realty (except buildings). Only $50,000 of cost of used property eligible.
3. Asset with useful life of 3-5 years: 1/3 of investment qualifies. 5-7 years: 2/3 of investment qualifies. 7 or more: total of investment qualifies.
4. Unused credit may be carried back 3 years and forward 7.
5. Credit recaptured on disposing of asset prematurely.

The latest edition of the Prentice-Hall *Federal Tax Course* provides these short summaries at the end of each chapter in their "Highlights." Time saved in preparing outlines means more time available for study.

In the Report of the American Accounting Association Committee on the CPA Examination, the following paragraph appears (*Accounting Review,* Vol. XXXVII, No. 2, p. 323):

> The tax questions should be of such a nature as to test general knowledge and understanding of basic concepts rather than memory of detailed technical tax facts and forms. There should be more questions on tax planning. To date nearly all tax questions have concentrated on tax determination. Questions in the area of tax planning would involve situations in which the candidate would have to recognize and explain the tax implications, giving consideration to available alternatives.

It is to be expected that future examinations will present more problems dealing with tax planning.

In reviewing solutions to tax questions and problems presented in this book, one must be aware that tax laws may have changed. Solutions indicate tax treatment in accordance with the Code and Regulations in effect for the period indicated in the problem.

CPA PROBLEMS

Problem XIII-1: Individual joint return taxable income for shareholders of Subchapter S corporation (50-60 min.)

You have been assigned to prepare selected schedules to be used in preparing the joint federal income tax return of Mr. and Mrs. Taxpayer for the year ended December 31, 1971. Your firm has prepared federal corporation tax returns for Family Growth, Inc. (FGI), incorporated April 1, 1965, by Mr. Taxpayer and Mr. Father-in-law.

You have collected the following information from the firm's files, corporate records, and information supplied to you by Mr. and Mrs. Taxpayer.

1. Mr. Taxpayer was 67 and Mrs. Taxpayer was 55 at December 31, 1971.
2. On April 4, 1971, Mr. Taxpayer sold 600 shares and Mrs. Taxpayer sold 100 shares (their total holdings) of FGI to Mr. Outsider for $200,000. Of the sales amount, $100,000 was received on the date of sale. The balance is payable in five, equal, annual installments plus interest at 8% on the unpaid balance commencing January 15, 1972. Background on these corporate holdings follow:

   a. At incorporation, Mr. Taxpayer transferred $60,000 cash to the corporation solely in exchange for 600 shares of its voting common stock.
   b. At incorporation, Mr. Father-in-law, formerly in business as a sole proprietor, transferred land, machinery, and equipment of his sole proprietorship to the corporation solely in exchange for 400 shares of its voting common stock. At transfer these assets had a fair-market

value of $40,000 and an adjusted tax basis of $21,500. The machinery and equipment had been purchased January 1, 1962, for $15,000. On April 1, 1965, the date of incorporation, it had an adjusted tax basis of $8,000 and a fair-market value of $13,000.

c. At incorporation, Mr. Taxpayer and Mr. Father-in-law owned all of the outstanding voting common stock of FGI, the only stock outstanding.

d. Proper consents were filed for FGI to elect to be taxed under Subchapter S beginning with the taxable year ending March 31, 1967.

e. On April 10, 1968, Mr. Father-in-law sold 300 shares of his FGI stock ex-dividend to Mr. Outsider for $62,000. Mr. Outsider did not consent to the Corporation's Subchapter S election.

f. On July 17, 1968, Mr. Father-in-law transferred his remaining 100 shares of FGI stock to Mrs. Taxpayer. The gift had a fair-market value of $22,000. Mr. Father-in-law paid $2,650 federal gift taxes with respect to the gift.

g. The table below provides data regarding FGI's taxable income and cash dividend payments.

Taxable Year Ended March 31	Taxable Income (Loss)	Cash Dividends Paid	
		Amount	Date
1966	$(6,000)	$ —	—
1967	50,000	16,000	March 28, 1967
1968	44,000	24,500	April 12, 1968
1969	25,000	12,000	April 10, 1969
1970	33,500	17,000	April 6, 1970
1971	61,000	32,000	March 19, 1971

3. Until March 31, 1971, Mr. Taxpayer was president of FGI and received a salary of $2,500 per month. The corporation also paid 50% of Mr. Taxpayer's medical insurance premiums pursuant to an Employee Group Medical Insurance Plan. The total monthly premium was $40. All salary and fringe benefits ceased after March 31, 1971.

4. Social security benefits received by Mr. Taxpayer during 1971 subsequent to his employment termination totaled $1,790.

5. Mr. Taxpayer received $1,950 interest in 1971 on a $17,500 loan to his brother, a resident of Peru. The loan was used by the brother to purchase equipment in Peru for use in his business there.

6. Form 1099s received by Mr. and Mrs. Taxpayer for 1971 revealed the following:

Payer	Description	Amount
American Buyers, Inc. (Mr.)	Dividend	$ 900
Western Manufacturing, Inc. (Mrs.).	Dividend	350
Central Savings and Loan (Joint)	Dividend	1,200
Growth Mutual Fund (Joint)	Dividend	250
Growth Mutual Fund (Joint)	Long-term capital gain	150

7. Effective January 1, 1952, Mr. Taxpayer executed a land lease with Clint, Inc. The land was vacant at the inception of the lease. The lease provided for an

annual rental of $9,500 payable on January 1 of each year. The lease term was to end December 31, 1971. During 1954, Clint, Inc., asked for and received permission to erect a building on the leased land for its use during the term of the lease and to be abandoned upon termination. The building cost $105,000 and had a useful life of 40 years with no salvage value. The lease terms were complied with and Mr. Taxpayer reassumed possession December 31, 1971. At that date the building erected by Clint, Inc., had a fair-market value of $45,000.

8. On August 16, 1971, Mr. Taxpayer granted an option for $7,000 to Ace Rental Co. to purchase the land and building then subject to the lease by Clint, Inc., for $150,000. The option was exercisable on or before November 15, 1971, with the sale closing to take place on January 3, 1972. The option was not exercised.

9. On December 1, 1971, Mr. Taxpayer borrowed $35,000 from City Bank and Trust Co., pledging the land and improvements (described in 7 and 8 above) as security for the loan. On December 31, 1971, Mr. Taxpayer exchanged the land and improvements subject to the mortgage owing to City Bank and Trust Co. to Bullock Engineering, Inc., for a piece of vacant land having a fair-market value of $125,000. Mr. Taxpayer had purchased the land in 1935 for $37,500.

Required:

Prepare schedules in good form for Mr. and Mrs. Taxpayer as follows:

    a. Taxable income (before personal exemptions and deductions) other than capital gains and losses.
    b. Capital gains and losses.

Problem XIII-2: Tax planning advice for an investment counseling corporation (50-60 min.)

DeStefano Corporation, a local investment counseling firm (incorporated on August 1, 1971), has engaged your firm to compute income subject to federal income tax for the nine months ended April 30, 1972 and to give income tax planning advice. The income statement for the nine months ended April 30, 1972 is supplied by DeStefano's bookkeeper as follows:

Revenues:		
Client counseling fees		$293,000
Interest income:		
Municipal bonds	$ 1,750	
Corporate bonds	2,200	3,950
Dividends from domestic corporations:		
Capital gains distribution	1,725	
Ordinary	2,275	4,000
Ordinary dividends from foreign corporation		
(no foreign tax withheld)		325
Rental on sublease of premises		900
Gain on sale of Elechue County bonds		2,475
Loss on sale of Surefire Corp. stock		(5,500)
Total Revenues forwarded		$299,150

Total revenues brought forward....................		$299,150
Expenses:		
Counselor salaries	91,000	
Clerical salaries	12,500	
Depreciation on office and quotation		
equipment (9 months)	7,000	
Provision for federal income tax	69,500	
Contributions	11,700	
State, local and other taxes	6,900	
Supplies...............................	2,300	
Advertising	3,100	
Utilities	1,800	
Rent (August 1 to April 30)	2,700	
Insurance (9 months)	925	
Repairs	475	
Interest expense	80	
Miscellaneous	60	210,040
Net income....................................		$ 89,110

The following additional information also is available:

1. The 36,000 shares of DeStefano capital stock outstanding (par $15) are held equally by the nine counselors of the firm who were also the promoters. None of the owners are related and only one class of stock is outstanding.

2. On October 1, 1971 the Corporation purchased 100 shares of Surefire Corp. common stock at par of $100 for the Corporation's own investment account. On December 31, 1971 the 100 shares of Surefire stock were sold at $45 per share after commissions.

3. $10,000 of Elechue County school district bonds purchased at par on October 29, 1971 were sold for 124¾, net of commissions and accrued interest, on April 30, 1972.

4. With the exception of two stockholder-counselors who actively serve as managers and received a salary of $14,000 each for the period, all stockholder-counselors received equal salaries.

5. The cost of incorporation totaled $2,400. Assume that the Corporation takes the maximum allowable deduction.

6. Contributions for the period were:

Financial Counselors' Institute	
(College Scholarship Fund)	$ 3,000
United Fund of Elechue County	1,825
Elechue County Republican Party	1,700
Science and Education Foundation	
of America	635
Henry Joseph Memorial Hospital	2,675
Home Haven Orphanage............................	500
Southern River Boy Scout Council	765
Miscellaneous churches and charitable	
campaigns	600
	$11,700

7. A dividend of $2 per share is planned upon completion of the tax work.

8. The office and quotation equipment was purchased on August 1, 1971 for $120,000. The equipment has an estimated useful life of 10 years and no salvage value. Straight-line depreciation is to be used.

Required:

a. Compute DeStefano's taxable income for the nine-month period ended April 30, 1972.

b. Discuss the tax planning advice that should be given at a meeting of the board of directors of DeStefano Corporation upon the completion of your work regarding each of the following:

1. Making an election to be taxed as a Subchapter S corporation. Include a discussion of the passive income limitation and show calculations for the nine-month period ended April 30, 1972.
2. The possibility of the Corporation being taxed as a personal holding company.

Problem XIII-3: Maximum reduction of corporate taxable income (50-60 min.)

Instructions

All of the following parts pertain to federal income taxation problems of the Mercury Corporation (1) which adopts for its assets the depreciation method that gives the largest first-year deduction and (2) which wishes to use every election available to reduce taxable income on the accrual basis in accordance with the current Internal Revenue Code and Tax Regulations.

Parts to be Answered

Part a. On January 2, 1970 the Mercury Corporation purchased a used factory building for $3,000,000, a new factory building for $6,000,000 and new machinery for $398,000. No other building or machinery expenditures were made by Mercury in 1970. It is estimated that the used building will have a useful life of 30 years and no salvage value, that the new building will have a useful life of 40 years and no salvage value and that the machinery will have a useful life of ten years and a salvage value of $18,000.

Required:
Prepare a schedule showing the computation of Mercury's 1970 depreciation expense deduction for the buildings and new machinery.

Part b. On January 2, 1967, Mercury Corporation purchased a new factory building for $1,000,000 and chose the double-declining-balance method of depreciation with an estimated life of 40 years and no salvage value. On December 31, 1970 Mercury sold this building and realized a gain of $92,000.

Required:
Prepare a schedule showing the computation of the effect(s) of this transaction upon Mercury's 1970 taxable income.

Part c. Mercury Corporation uses the allowance method of accounting for uncollectible accounts. Accounts receivable at December 31, 1970 were $1,200,000. Experience indicates that 2% of end-of-the-period receivables ultimately become uncollectible. The allowance on January 1, 1970 was $16,000 and accounts receivable of $13,500 became worthless and were written off during 1970.

Required:
Prepare a schedule showing the computation for 1970 of the bad debts expense deduction and the amount to be added to the Allowance for Uncollectible Accounts at December 31, 1970.

Part d. Mercury Corporation incurred organization expenses of $90,000 in 1964 and began doing business on July 1, 1965. In June 1970 the township where Mercury is located contributed to the Corporation land having a fair market value of $100,000 in appreciation for Mercury's involvement with environmental control projects. On August 31, 1970 Mercury sold one-half of this land for $45,000 and leased the remainder to the Ajax Parking Lot Company for $12,000 annually, payable in advance. Mercury believed that its stockholders should benefit directly from this rental fee and issued checks on a prorata basis to its stockholders for the entire amount.

Required:
Prepare a schedule showing the computation of the effect(s) of these transactions upon Mercury's 1970 taxable income.

Part e. On January 1, 1969 Mercury Corporation paid $800,000 for a computer-based information system. This was the only equipment expenditure made by Mercury in 1969. Of the $800,000, $625,000 was the invoice price of the computer; $160,000 was the separately stated costs of computer software and $15,000 was for fees paid to an accounting firm to establish a control system over the utilization of the computer-based information system. Mercury estimates that $75,000 of the computer billed price of $625,000 was for included costs of computer software. It is estimated that the system will have a maximum useful life of eight years and no salvage value, but that the software has a life that cannot be determined and will have no salvage value when it becomes obsolete.

Required:
Prepare a schedule showing the effect on income of computer-based information system costs for 1969 and 1970.

Problem XIII-4: Resolving effects of corporate items treated differently for book and tax purposes (40-50 min.)

The controller of Cazy Corporation requested the office manager to prepare a worksheet to be used in computing the Corporation's taxable income on an accrual basis for the calendar year 1970. He instructed him to extend all items that he knew would be the same for book and tax purposes to the income statement and balance sheet columns and all items which he thought might be handled differently to either a debit or credit suspense column. He asked that these questionable amounts be listed on a separate sheet with all pertinent information. The suspense analysis requested by the controller plus the related worksheet information for 1970 appear on the following pages.

	Suspense	
	Debit	Credit
Office typewriters	$ 5,000	
Machines	10,000	
Building–Oldsville	52,000	
Automobile	5,400	
Building–Newville	50,000	
Investment–Del Corporation	22,500	
Investment–Rab Corporation	29,600	
Investment–municipal obligations	33,000	
Cash surrender value of life insurance	14,000	
Accumulated depreciation on office typewriters		$ 2,600
Accumulated depreciation on machines		6,900
Accumulated depreciation on Oldsville building		21,000
Accumulated depreciation on Newville building		500
Note payable to stockholder		3,500
Accrued contribution		2,500
Mortgage payable on Oldsville building		34,000
Notes payable on machines		5,300
Proceeds from term life insurance policy		40,000
Proceeds from sale of office typewriters		3,200
Distribution from Rab Corporation		5,400
Interest on municipal obligations....................		1,300
Contributed building–Newville		50,000
Profit on sale of stock		8,300
Bad debt recovery		550
Depreciation on building–Newville	500	
Capital loss	2,000	
Charitable contribution	2,500	
Life insurance premium	2,900	

The following additional information was discovered for these transactions; all items are for 1970 unless otherwise indicated:

1. *Proceeds from sale of office typewriters*–Typewriters (purchased in 1966 for $5,000) with accumulated depreciation of $2,600 were sold to a qualified charitable organization for $3,200. Their actual fair market value was $4,000 on the date of sale.

2. *Notes payable on machines*–On December 30, the indebtedness on these notes was forgiven by the vendor in an arm's-length transaction. The machines were purchased for $10,000, and depreciation expense during 1970 was $2,200.

3. *Oldsville Building*–On December 20, 1970 title to the building along with the existing mortgage was transferred to Bob Barnes, a 25% stockholder. The building was purchased in 1955. This transfer did not relate to either a re-demption or a liquidation.

4. *Automobile*–On December 31 a limousine was received from Rab, a domestic corporation, representing a distribution of its earnings to Cazy Corporation, a 25% stockholder. Immediately prior to the distribution, the auto had an adjusted basis to Rab of $4,200 and a fair market value of $5,400.

5. *Contributed building–Newville*–This building, having a fair market value

of $50,000, was contributed to Cazy Corporation by a civic group solely to induce it to locate in the town of Newville.

6. *Investment in Del Corporation*—Cazy Corporation's holdings of all the stock of Del, a domestic corporation, became worthless in 1970. Del Corporation has received no personal holding company income.

7. *Life insurance premium*—Of the $2,900 premium $1,200 represents an increase in the cash surrender value of a policy on the life of an officer with the Corporation as beneficiary.

8. *Note payable—stockholder*—Jim Jarvis, a 25% stockholder, forgave the Corporation's $3,500 noninterest-bearing note payable to him.

9. *Charitable contribution*—The contribution was authorized by the Corporation's board of directors on December 15, 1970 and was paid by check on March 10, 1971.

10. *Profit on sale of stock*—This represents a premium on the Cazy Corporation common stock which was issued July 1.

11. *Bad debt recovery*—The Corporation writes off specific accounts when they are deemed to be uncollectible; a check of $550 was received on an account receivable that was written off in 1963. The bad debt deduction produced no tax benefit.

12. *Capital loss*—The Corporation realized a net short-term capital gain of $4,500 and a net long-term capital loss of $6,400 on marketable security transactions in 1970. In addition, there was an unused capital loss carryover from 1964 of $1,500.

13. The Corporation has a net operating loss carryover of $67,000 from 1969 operations.

Required:

a. Assuming that its net income before suspense items is $98,400, prepare a schedule showing the computation of the Cazy Corporation's unconsolidated taxable income for 1970 using every election available to reduce income (other than Subchapter S tax option status) in accordance with the current Internal Revenue Code and Tax Regulations. Include supporting schedules in good form.

b. Assume that accumulated earnings and profits as of January 1, 1970 were properly computed to be $8,340. Prepare a schedule showing the Cazy Corporation's computation of accumulated earnings and profits as of December 31, 1970 in accordance with the current Internal Revenue Code and Tax Regulations (disregard income tax for the current year).

Problem XIII-5: Joint taxable income involving family owned business (50-60 min.)

Mr. James Doe, age 66, and his wife, Myra, age 55, have engaged you to determine their joint federal taxable income for the year ended December 31, 1969. Both are employed and their dependents are: their son George, a full-time college student age 20, and Mrs. Doe's mother, Mrs. Alfred age 76.

Mr. Doe, self-employed, owns and operates The Doe Company which manufactures and sells sprays and other supplies to retail nurserymen. The following is a summarized income statement that has been prepared for The Doe Company for 1969:

```
Sales (net of state sales taxes) ............... $203,800
Gain on sale of equipment .................        380
Gain from condemnation of land ............      6,700
Warehouse rental income .................      4,600   $215,480

Less: Cost of goods sold ...................   102,110
      Sales, payroll and other business taxes  ...    5,100
      Salaries ..........................     38,080
      Insurance ........................      2,860
      Advertising ......................      1,540
      Depreciation .....................      4,700
      Miscellaneous ....................     16,420    170,810

Net income .......................................  $ 44,670
```

The following information for 1969 relating to the above statement was found in Company records:

1. The equipment which was purchased in 1965 for $6,000 was sold during the year for $2,180 when its book value (and adjusted basis) was $1,800.

2. The land was a three-acre tract bought in 1967 for $3,300 to be used for future factory expansion; it was condemned by the township in 1969 and Mr. Doe was awarded $10,000; Mr. Doe purchased a three-acre replacement tract for $8,400.

3. The warehouse rental income includes a penalty of $1,000 paid by Tenant A for a lease cancellation and an advance of $400 paid by Tenant B without restriction as to use to cover the last month of his lease expiring in 1970.

4. Cost of goods sold includes a $1,400 write-down for price reductions anticipated in early 1970 on the inventory of chemicals.

5. Sales, payroll and other business taxes includes federal self-employment tax of $538 and state consumer sales taxes of $857 which were collected by the Company and remitted to the state.

6. Salaries include $12,000 paid to Mr. Doe and $800 paid to his son George for two months of full-time work during the summer.

7. Insurance includes health insurance premiums of $800 ($640 paid for key employees and $160 paid for Mr. Doe) and fire and other insurance premiums of $180 paid on Mr. Doe's personal residence.

8. Advertising includes Mr. Doe's travel expense of $160 to volunteer testimony at state hearings on legislation affecting the wholesale nursery business and a contribution of $200 to the Midwest Political Association's lobbying fund.

The following information relating to 1969 was taken from personal records:

1. Mrs. Doe has been employed for many years as an executive secretary in The Jay Company. Her 1969 salary was $9,600 plus fringe benefits which included a fully-paid group health insurance premium of $130.

2. Mrs. Doe also exercised stock options under a qualified plan which she was granted in 1965 when the market price was $30 per share. She purchased 300 shares of Jay Company capital stock at the option price of $30 in July 1969 when the market price was $52; this price increased to $64 on December 31.

3. Interest credited to savings accounts but not withdrawn amounted to $2,236 for Mr. and Mrs. Doe, $2,230 for George, and $460 for Mrs. Alfred.

4. Mr. and Mrs. Doe's jointly-owned stock produced cash dividends of $4,310 out of earnings from taxable domestic corporations and $1,560, net of taxes, from foreign corporations.

5. Mr. and Mrs. Doe had long-term capital gains of $31,800 and short-term capital gains of $720 on sales of investments.

6. Medical expenses included qualified medicines and drugs of $970; unreimbursed doctor and dentist bills of $356 (including $116 that was unpaid at December 31) for Mr. Doe, $610 for Mrs. Doe, $880 for George and $524 for Mrs. Alfred; unreimbursed hospital bills of $720 for Mrs. Alfred; and health insurance premiums paid for George of $120.

7. In addition, Mr. Doe paid $2,400 (of which $900 was for meals and lodging) to a nursing home where Mrs. Alfred stayed during the period January-May primarily because of the availability of medical care and $2,600 during June-December for a housekeeper in the Doe residence who devoted 50% of her time to the nursing care of Mrs. Alfred. The family doctor recommended the use of domestic help because Mrs. Alfred was unable to perform her regular household duties.

8. Mrs. Doe received a reimbursement from her medical insurance for medical costs of $169 which had been paid and deducted in 1968 to reduce income taxes.

9. In December Mrs. Doe terminated her Jay Company employment so as to devote full time to the care of her mother and on December 31, 1969 received a check for $30,000 in settlement of her share in the Jay Company's qualified noncontributory profit-sharing plan. This amount consisted of Company contributions of $23,090 made through 1968 and $910 made in 1969 and an incremental accumulation of $6,000.

10. State income taxes paid or withheld amounted to $1,200.

11. Miscellaneous deductible personal payments not listed elsewhere amounted to $9,385.

12. The foreign tax credit on dividends received amounted to $170.

13. Mr. and Mrs. Doe made estimated tax payments of $36,000 and withholdings from Mrs. Doe's salary were $2,200 for federal income tax and $374 for social security tax.

Required:

Recognizing that all amounts above have been rounded to the nearest dollar, prepare the following for Mr. and Mrs. Doe for the year ended December 31, 1969:

a. A schedule adjusting the Doe Company income statement to taxable net profit.

b. A schedule computing capital gains.

c. A schedule computing joint taxable income.

Problem XIII-6: Corporate taxable income under accrual basis derived from cash records (40-50 min.)

The following information was prepared by the bookkeeper for Bledsoe Corporation for the calendar year ended December 31, 1969.

Cash receipts:

Collections on accounts receivable $756,500
  Less cash discounts taken 6,500 $750,000
Cash sales of merchandise 80,000
Sale of warehouse equipment 6,000
Insurance proceeds from boiler explosion 21,000
Sale of land on November 3 10,000

  Total $867,000

Cash disbursements:

Payments to trade creditors....................... $603,000
General and administrative expenses 102,000
Cash purchases of merchandise 60,000
Replacement of boiler 17,250
Repairs made on warranty contracts 3,200
Purchase of land on May 1 11,500
Purchase on November 10 of 100 shares of Rushing Co. stock 12,000

  Total $808,950

Supplementary information:

1. The following account balances were taken from the general ledger:

	December 31, 1968	December 31, 1969
Accounts receivable	$ 62,000	$ 73,000
Inventory	93,000	95,000
Prepaid expenses	4,800	4,200
Accrued expenses	3,500	4,500
Accounts payable	191,000	205,000

2. The direct write-off method of accounting for uncollectible accounts is used for tax reporting purposes. All accounts receivable were considered collectible at December 31, 1969 and no accounts were written off during 1969.

3. Depreciation for 1969 was $42,000.

4. The warehouse equipment sold during 1969 was acquired in 1964 at a cost of $12,500. The double-declining-balance method of depreciation was used and accumulated charges were $8,000 at date of sale. If the straight-line method had been used the accumulated depreciation at date of sale would have been $5,000.

5. An explosion occurred on January 15, 1969 in which a boiler, not the structural component of a building, was completely destroyed. It was purchased in January 1962 at a cost of $24,000; depreciation was recorded by the straight-line method and $10,000 had accumulated at the date of the explosion.

6. Land was purchased on May 1, 1969 and was used as a storage facility. It was found to be unsuitable for this purpose and was sold on November 3, 1969.

7. The company wishes to defer the recognition of all gains to the extent allowable.

Required:

Prepare a schedule computing the amount of income that Bledsoe Corporation should report for federal income tax purposes under the accrual method as subject to ordinary income rates for 1969. Include schedules showing your computations of sales, purchases, general and administrative expenses and other gains or losses.

Problem XIII-7: Determination of reasonableness of federal income tax liability (50-60 min.)

You were engaged to examine the financial statements for the year ended December 31, 1968 of Tyme Motor Freight, Inc. and must determine the reasonableness of the recorded federal income tax liability. The Corporation is an accrual basis taxpayer. The outstanding stock of the Corporation is constructively owned 55 per cent by Steve Brin and 45 per cent by non-related persons.

You are satisfied that the income per books before federal taxes of $70,100 is fairly stated. Your examination disclosed the following items which were included in the determination of income per books:

1. Entries in the Investment in Stock account were made to record the following:

Name of Stock	Number of Shares	Date Purchased	Cost	Date Sold	Sales Price	Loss Per Books
Vans, Inc.	250	3/15/66	$6,300			$4,200
Imke, Inc.	200	7/6/68	4,900			
Imke, Inc.	200	7/20/68	5,200	8/3/68	$4,500	700

Two thirds of the cost of the Vans, Inc. stock was written off as worthless during 1968 because of a decline in the market value of the stock resulting from the filing by Vans, Inc. of a petition in bankruptcy in federal court.

2. In 1968 the Corporation began to estimate and accrue on a monthly basis freight claim losses. During the year $12,000 in estimated losses were accrued of which $2,200 were paid.

3. Interest totaling $360 on a loan from Brin was accrued and deducted on the books in 1968. Because of a temporary shortage of cash the Corporation could not pay the loan or interest until April 1, 1969. Brin files his personal tax return on the cash basis and will include the interest on his 1969 return.

4. Fines and attorney's fees included the following:

Overloading fines $2,500
Attorney's fees for
  Unsuccessfully defending overloading charges 400
  Testifying before State Senate hearings on highway use taxes . 500
  Filings with Interstate Commerce Commission to extend
    routes (application denied in 1968) 1,400

5. Advertising expenses recorded in 1968 included:

Advertisement (with no business relationship established)
  in the program for a political convention $1,200
Advertisement in *The Truckers Journal* 1,100
One sixth of a T.V. advertising campaign 900
  (All of the advertising was telecast in December 1968 and the total cost of $5,400 was paid in advance. Management believes the advertising program will produce business for a total of 6 months.)

6. Data for fixed assets which were sold during 1968 are summarized below:

	Warehouse No. 15	2 Truck Tractors	Warehouse No. 19	Land
Date purchased	12/30/57	12/31/60	1/8/62	1/3/64
Cost	$100,000	$20,000	$110,000	$25,500
Accumulated depreciation:				
12/31/63	29,400	6,000	19,500	
12/31/67	49,000	14,000	59,500	
Depreciation method	S L	S L	SYD	
Life	20 years	8 years	20 years	
Estimated salvage value at acquisition .	$ 2,000	$ 4,000	$ 5,000	
Sales price	58,000	7,500	65,000	$31,000
Date Sold	1/5/68	1/5/68	1/11/68	1/5/68

7. On January 4, 1968 10 truck tractors were purchased for a total of $121,000. Salvage value is estimated at $900 each at the end of a 7-year useful life. The straight-line method is used for computing depreciation and the Corporation elects for tax purposes to deduct the additional 20 per cent first-year depreciation and to reduce salvage value to the minimum allowable for assets acquired in 1968. Depreciation per books was computed without regard to these elections.

Required:

Prepare a schedule for Tyme Motor Freight, Inc. computing the amount of income taxable as ordinary income. The first item on your schedule should be "Income per books before taxes—$70,100." Supporting schedules should identify gains taxable under Sections 1231, 1245 and 1250 and depreciation on assets acquired in 1968.

Problem XIII-8: Partnership ordinary income and partners' distributable share of separately reported items (40-50 min.)

Adair, Blinker, and Coe formed a partnership on January 2, 1967 under the name of Abcoe Engineering Services. Adair contributed $10,000 in cash, Blinker contributed $5,000 in cash and securities worth $5,000 (which he had purchased for $3,000 on September 30, 1966) and Coe contributed office furniture and equipment worth $10,000. Coe had purchased the office furniture and equipment for $20,000 during 1962, depreciated it under the double-declining balance method for a 10-year life and it had an adjusted basis to him of $5,240 at the date of contribution. Each partner's capital account was credited $10,000.

The partnership agreement stipulated the three partners would receive salaries, interest would be paid on their capital accounts and any remaining net income or loss would be divided equally. The agreement also provided that for purposes of income tax reporting the first $2,000 of taxable gain from the sale of securities would be allocated to Blinker, that all depreciation on the contributed office furniture and equipment would be allocated to Adair and Blinker, and the first $4,760 of taxable gain from the sale of the office furniture and equipment would be allocated to Coe.

The following information is also available:

1. Net income from all sources on the partnership income statement was $75,000 before allocations to the partners for salaries and interest. Salaries and interest for 1967 determined in accordance with the partnership agreement were:

	Salary	Interest
Adair	$18,000	$1,000
Blinker.......................	15,000	1,100
Coe	12,000	900

2. The securities contributed by Blinker were sold March 31, 1967 for $5,900. Dividends received on these securities before they were sold amounted to $60.

3. On June 30, 1967 Abcoe sold for its book value of $9,500 the office furniture and equipment contributed by Coe. The same day Abcoe moved to a new building constructed at a cost of $40,000 and furnished with new furniture and equipment which cost $30,000. In the financial statements 1967 depreciation of the building was $400 (10 per cent salvage, 45-year life) and 1967 depreciation of the new furniture and equipment was $1,350 (10 per cent salvage, 10-year life). The partners wish to deduct the maximum depreciation allowable, including additional first-year depreciation, for income tax purposes.

Required:

a. Prepare a schedule computing the ordinary income (or loss) which should be reported by Abcoe Engineering Services in its partnership income tax return for 1967. Start your schedule with the 1967 net income for financial statement purposes of $75,000 and itemize differences which must be considered to arrive at ordinary income to be shown in the partnership income tax return. Supporting computations should be in good form.

b. Prepare a schedule presenting each partner's distributable share of items to be reported for income tax purposes separately by each partner as a result of partnership transactions during 1967.

Problem XIII-9: *Multiple choice questions on taxation of corporations and partnerships (50-60 min.)*

Instructions

Select the best answer for each of the following items relating to the federal income taxation of corporations and partnerships. The answers should be selected in accordance with the current Internal Revenue Code and Tax Regulations. Mark only one answer for each item. Your grade will be determined from your total of correct answers.

Items to be Answered

1. The Allen, Smith, & Jones partnership's fiscal year ends on June 30. The partners are on a calendar-year tax basis. During the fiscal year ended June 30, 1971, Allen was paid a salary of $850 per month because he devoted all of his time to the partnership; during fiscal 1972 his salary was $1,000 per month. The

other two partners were not paid a salary in either of these years, but in accordance with the partnership's agreement the net income after deducting Allen's salary was divided among the three partners.

The net income after Allen's salary for fiscal 1971 was $27,000; for fiscal 1972 it was $36,000.

For the calendar year 1971, Allen should have reported taxable income from the partnership of
  a. $9,000.
  b. $19,200.
  c. $20,600.
  d. $22,100.
  e. None of the above.
2. The Sunra Corporation had the following data available:

Gross profit on sales $40,000
Dividend income from non-affiliated domestic corporations .. $ 2,000
Operating expenses (exclusive of charitable contributions). ... $28,000
Charitable contributions .... $ 900

Sunra's taxable income was
  a. $11,100.
  b. $11,685.
  c. $11,600.
  d. $13,100.
  e. None of the above.
3. Rambo Corporation owns 10% of the stock of Duntulum Corporation with a basis of $8,000 and a market value of $50,000. Rambo uses the Duntulum stock to redeem approximately 1%, or $10,000 par value, of its own outstanding stock. As a result of this transaction, Rambo must report
  a. $42,000 gain.
  b. No gain or loss.
  c. $2,000 gain.
  d. $50,000 gain.
  e. None of the above.
4. The Blalock Corporation was organized on January 2 of the current year under a charter that places no limitation on the corporate life. Blalock adopted a calendar year. The organization costs incurred were $6,000. The maximum amount of organization cost that may be written off this year is
  a. $0.
  b. $300.
  c. $1,200.
  d. $6,000.
  e. None of the above.
5. Able Corporation and Baker Corporation file a consolidated return on a calendar-year basis. In 1971, Able sold land to Baker for its fair-market value of $50,000. At the date of sale, Able had an adjusted basis in the land of $35,000 and had held the land for several years as an investment. Baker held the land primarily for sale to its customers in the ordinary course of its business and sold it to a customer in early 1972 for $60,000.

As a result of the sale of the land in 1972, the corporation should report on their consolidated return

    a. $10,000 ordinary gain.
    b. $25,000 ordinary gain.
    c. $25,000 long-term capital gain.
    d. $15,000 long-term capital gain and $10,000 ordinary gain.
    e. None of the above.

6. Will Benton owned all of the stock of a corporation that has been determined to be collapsible. The basis of the stock to Benton was $25,000, and the corporation had accumulated earnings and profits of $1,000. Benton sold his stock for $40,000. As a result of the sale Benton must report
    a. $15,000 ordinary gain.
    b. $1,000 ordinary income and $14,000 capital gain.
    c. $14,000 capital gain.
    d. $15,000 capital gain.
    e. None of the above.

7. Arnold Money invested $20,000 for a one-third interest in capital and profits of a partnership. Subsequent to his investment, the partnership had total taxable income of $30,000 and nontaxable income of $6,000, and Money withdrew $9,000. After these series of events, the tax basis of Money's interest in the partnership is
    a. $11,000.
    b. $20,000.
    c. $21,000.
    d. $23,000.
    e. None of the above.

8. Jim Cash, one of two partners, contributed business property with a basis to him of $15,000 and a fair-market value of $10,000 to the partnership of which he was a member His capital account was credited for $10,000. The property was later sold for $12,000. As a result of this transaction, Cash must report on his personal income tax return
    a. $1,000 gain.
    b. $1,500 loss.
    c. $2,000 gain.
    d. $3,000 loss.
    e. None of the above.

9. The Choate, Hamm, & Sloan partnership's balance sheet on a cash basis at September 30 of the current year was as follows:

Assets	Basis	Fair Market Value
Cash	$12,000	$ 12,000
Accounts receivable	-0-	48,000
Land	63,000	90,000
	$75,000	$150,000

Equities	Basis	Fair Market Value
Notes payable	$30,000	$ 30,000
Choate, capital	15,000	40,000
Hamm, capital	15,000	40,000
Sloan, capital	15,000	40,000
	$75,000	$150,000

If Choate withdraws under an agreement whereby he takes one-third of each of the three assets and assumes $10,000 of the notes payable, he should report
   a. $9,000 capital gain.
   b. $9,000 ordinary gain.
   c. $16,000 ordinary gain and $9,000 capital gain.
   d. No gain or loss.
   e. None of the above.
10. A net capital loss of a corporation may be carried
   a. Forward indefinitely.
   b. Forward for five years only.
   c. Back three years and forward five.
   d. Back five years and forward five.
   e. None of the above.
11. During the current year, a corporation retired obsolete equipment having an adjusted basis of $30,000 and sold it as scrap for $1,000. The only other transactions affecting taxable income resulted in $50,000 net income from operations. The taxable income of the corporation was
   a. $21,000.
   b. $35,000.
   c. $49,000 with a capital loss carryover of $27,000.
   d. $50,000 with a capital loss carryover of $14,500.
   e. None of the above.
12. Jesse Jenkins in a bona fide transaction transferred land worth $50,000 to his controlled corporation for stock of the corporation worth $20,000 and cash of $20,000. The basis of the property to him was $15,000, and it was subject to a $10,000 mortgage which the corporation assumed.
   Jenkins must report a gain of
   a. $10,000.
   b. $20,000.
   c. $30,000.
   d. $35,000.
   e. None of the above.
13. The Franklin Corporation with stock owned 20% by corporations and 80% by individuals had accumulated earnings of $65,000 at the beginning of the current year. The net after-tax earnings for the current year were $20,000. On October 1 of the current year, the corporation distributed securities worth $14,000 as a dividend to its shareholders. The securities had cost $8,000.
   As a result of the distribution, Franklin Corporation had to
   a. Leave accumulated earnings intact.
   b. Increase accumulated earnings by $6,000.
   c. Decrease accumulated earnings by $8,000.
   d. Decrease accumulated earnings by $14,000.
   e. None of the above.
14. The Glenraff Company, a three-man partnership, received dividends of $1,000 from domestic corporations. As a result of the receipt of the dividends, the ordinary income to be reported on the partnership return is increased by
   a. $0.
   b. $150.
   c. $700.
   d. $1,000.
   e. None of the above.

15. The Troika Partnership had an ordinary operating loss of $48,000 for the current year. The partnership had assets of $58,500 and liabilities of $15,000 at the end of the year. Before allocation of the loss, partner Ashford's one-third interest had an adjusted basis of $10,000 at the end of the current year. Ashford may deduct on his income tax return as his share of the loss
   a. $14,500.
   b. $10,000.
   c. $16,000.
   d. $15,000.
   e. None of the above.

Problem XIII-10: Multiple choice questions on taxation of individuals (50-60 min.)

Instructions

Select the best answer for each of the following items relating to the federal income taxation of individuals. The answers should be selected in accordance with the current Internal Revenue Code and Tax Regulations. Mark only one answer for each item. Your grade will be determined from your total of correct answers.

Items to be Answered

1. On January 1, 1971, when his life expectancy was 10 years, Bill Reeves began receiving monthly payments on an annuity. Under the annuity plan he received $2,000 during 1971 and will receive $2,000 per year for life. The annuity was purchased through Mr. Reeves' employer at a total cost of $16,000 under a qualified plan in which the employer and employee each paid one half of the cost. The annuity payments would increase Mr. Reeves' 1971 adjusted gross income by
   a. $2,000.
   b. $1,200.
   c. $400.
   d. $0.
   e. None of the above.
2. Blaine Bogg, age 67, no dependents and single, is computing his medical expense deduction for 1971 from the following data:

Adjusted gross income $6,000
Medicine and drugs 50
Hospitalization insurance premiums 200
Other medical expenses 60

Mr. Bogg's medical expense deduction would be
   a. $130.
   b. $100.
   c. $80.
   d. $0.
   e. None of the above.
3. Bill Nolen's personal automobile, which had a basis of $2,100, was completely demolished in an automobile accident during 1971. Its fair market value was $1,700 immediately before the accident. With the aid of an attorney,

Mr. Nolen recovered $1,200 from an insurance company but had to pay the attorney a fee of $300. Mr. Nolen's casualty loss deduction as a result of the accident would be
    a. $1,100.
    b. $800.
    c. $600.
    d. $500.
    e. None of the above.

[handwritten: F.M.VAL BEF LOSS − RECOVERIES −F.M.VAL AFT LOSS LOSS − 100 (LOSS DEDUCT) FLOOR | VAL BEF LOSS / VAL AFT LOSS / DECLINE IN FMV " " BASIS]

4. Ben Green operates a parking lot that yielded net income of $13,000 during 1971. The only other transactions that Mr. Green had during the year were a gain of $16,000 on the sale of some Westinghouse Corporation stock that he bought two years ago, a loss of $10,000 on the sale of one acre of the land used in his parking lot business and a gain of $4,000 on the sale of one-half acre of the land used in his parking lot business. All of the land used in his parking lot operations was purchased seven years ago. Mr. Green's net gain from sale or exchange of capital assets for 1971 would be
    a. $10,000.
    b. $8,000.
    c. $6,000.
    d. $5,000.
    e. None of the above.

[handwritten: SALARY IS BIZ INC. NON BIZ EXP MATCHES TO NON BIZ INC.]

5. Alex Gibson, single and no dependents, entered a new business venture during 1971 and incurred a $12,000 loss from it. In addition to the business loss his income was as follows: salary $6,000, interest on bank savings $500 and dividends from domestic corporations $700 in excess of the $100 exclusion. His itemized deductions for interest and taxes were $1,800. Mr. Gibson's net operating loss for 1971 would be
    a. $12,000.
    b. $6,600.
    c. $6,000.
    d. $4,800.
    e. None of the above.

6. During 1971 Fred Good traded a tractor used solely in his construction business for another tractor for the same use. On the date of the trade, the old tractor had an adjusted basis of $3,000 and a fair market value of $3,300. He received in exchange $500 in cash and a smaller tractor with a fair market value of $2,800. Mr. Good should report a gain on the exchange of
    a. $800.
    b. $500.
    c. $300.
    d. $0.
    e. None of the above.

7. Assuming the same facts as in item 6, the basis of the new tractor to Mr. Good would be
    a. $3,300.
    b. $3,000.
    c. $2,800.
    d. $2,300.
    e. None of the above.

8. A taxpayer is not required to obtain the permission of the Commissioner of Internal Revenue to change from the

    a. LIFO method to the FIFO method of valuing inventories.

    b. Units-of-production method to the straight-line method of computing depreciation.

    c. Cash basis to the accrual basis of reporting income.

    d. Accrual method to the installment method of reporting income.

    e. None of the above.

9. Joe Daily's house was destroyed by fire during the year. The uninsured loss was greater than his entire income for the year. The net loss (above the $100 floor for casualty losses) may be

    a. Carried forward indefinitely with $1,000 being deducted from income each year until the loss is exhausted.

    b. Carried back three years and forward five years with $1,000 being deducted each year.

    c. Neither carried forward nor carried backward, being simply a non-deductible loss.

    d. Carried forward only for five years with income in those years the only limiting factor on the amount that may be deducted.

    e. None of the above.

10. Jack Sims sold some common stock to his brother, Don, for $6,000—the current market price. He paid $7,500 for the stock two years ago. Jack Sims should report

    a. Neither a gain nor a loss.

    b. A long-term capital loss of $1,500.

    c. An ordinary loss of $1,500.

    d. A short-term capital loss of $1,500.

    e. None of the above.

11. Assume the same facts as in item 10. The stock market recovered rapidly and three months later Don Sims sold the stock to a business acquaintance for $8,000. He should report

    a. A long-term capital gain of $2,000.

    b. An ordinary gain of $2,000.

    c. A short-term capital gain of $2,000.

    d. Neither a gain nor a loss.

    e. None of the above.

12. Jeff Wills and Reid Bart formed a corporation during 1971 to which Mr. Wills contributed a building (current fair market value $20,000 and adjusted basis to Mr. Wills $12,000) and Mr. Bart contributed $20,000 in cash. Mr. Wills and Mr. Bart each received 200 shares of the corporation's common stock. As a result of this transaction, Mr. Wills should report

    a. An ordinary gain of $8,000.

    b. A Section 1231 gain of $8,000.

    c. A capital gain of $8,000.

    d. Neither a gain nor a loss.

    e. None of the above.

13. A Subchapter S (or tax option) corporation may lose its status as a Subchapter S corporation

    a. Only at the option of the Internal Revenue Service.

    b. If any one of the shareholders transfers some of his stock to a trust.

    c. If any one of the shareholders dies and his estate owns his stock.

    d. If the corporation has a net operating loss during the year.

    e. None of the above.

14. Greg North purchased for $3,600 an automobile to be used two-thirds for business and one-third for pleasure. Depreciation is computed on a straight-line basis using an estimated life of four years with no salvage value. If the car is sold at the end of the third year for $1,200, Mr. North would have
    a. A recognized gain of $200.
    b. A recognized gain of $100.
    c. No recognized gain or loss.
    d. A deductible loss of $600.
    e. None of the above.

15. Clay Brooks inherited some land from his father in 1905 when its fair market value was $10,000. His father had purchased it for $2,000 ten years earlier. The fair market value of the land on March 1, 1913 was $15,000. If Mr. Brooks sold the land for $35,000 during 1971, he should report
    a. A gain of $33,000.
    b. A gain of $25,000.
    c. A gain of $20,000.
    d. Neither a gain nor a loss.
    e. None of the above.

16. Assume the same facts as in item 15. If Mr. Brooks sold the land for $7,500, he should report
    a. A gain of $5,500.
    b. Neither a gain nor a loss.
    c. A loss of $2,500.
    d. A loss of $7,500.
    e. None of the above.

17. On January 15, 1971 Gene Bolin bought a vacant lot for $75,000 as a parking lot for his customers. The parking lot had been in use five months when the town began providing free parking facilities nearby. Mr. Bolin sold the lot on June 20, 1971 for $100,000 ($20,000 cash and four $20,000, 6% notes due on June 20 of each of the next four years). If Mr. Bolin elects to report the gain on this sale on the installment basis, the gain to be reported in the year of sale would be
    a. $25,000.
    b. $20,000.
    c. $6,250.
    d. $5,000.
    e. None of the above.

18. Assuming the same facts as in item 17 the gain on the sale of the parking lot would be
    a. An ordinary gain.
    b. A short-term capital gain.
    c. A long-term capital gain.
    d. A Section 1231 gain.
    e. None of the above.

Problem XIII-11: Multiple choice questions on taxation of individuals (50-60 min.)

Instructions

Select the best answer for each of the following items which relate to the federal income taxation of individuals. The answers should be selected in

Answers & CCH Reference paragraphs on Looseleaf Sheet In Book

accordance with the current Internal Revenue Code and Tax Regulations. Mark only one answer for each item. Your grade will be determined from your total correct answers.

Items to be Answered

1. Mrs. Parker, age 59, transferred securities to her son in exchange for his promise to pay her $600 per month ($7,200 per year) for life. The securities had an adjusted basis to Mrs. Parker of $30,000 and a market value at the date of transfer of $54,000. If Mrs. Parker had a life expectancy of 20 years at the date of transfer, the amount that she may exclude from income during each of the next 20 years of her life would be
   a. $4,000.
   b. $2,700.
   c. $1,800.
   d. $1,500.
   e. None of the above.

2. Assume the same facts as in item 1 with the added information that the present value of the annuity is $84,200; the amount to be reported as a capital gain in each of the next 20 years of Mrs. Parker's life would be
   a. $5,720.
   b. $4,500.
   c. $4,210.
   d. $2,710.
   e. None of the above.

3. Assume the same facts as in items 1 and 2. If Mrs. Parker continues in good health and is still receiving payments from her son at age 82, the tax effects of the payments received in her 82nd year would be
   a. Ordinary income of $3,200; capital gain of $4,000.
   b. Ordinary income of $2,700; capital gain of $4,500.
   c. Ordinary income of $0; capital gain of $7,200.
   d. Ordinary income of $0; capital gain of $0.
   e. None of the above.

4. Mr. Long had the following security transactions during 1970:

Number of Shares and Security

Date	Purchases	Total
January 2	100 – Xtra Corp.	$21,000
January 24	200 – Dowager Corp.	4,000
January 31	50 – Zeb Corp.	6,000
February 1	300 – Faith Corp.	2,500

Date	Sales	Total
April 20	50–Xtra Corp.	13,400
March 2	200–Dowager Corp.	1,000
August 18	50–Zeb Corp.	1,900
October 20	300–Faith Corp.	4,200

Assuming that Mr. Long's taxable income for 1970 was $10,000, he will have a long-term capital loss carryover to 1971 of
   a. $1,500.
   b. $750.
   c. $600.

d. $300.

e. None of the above.

5. The Tax Reform Act of 1969 imposes a 10% tax (in addition to other taxes) on certain tax preference items. An item that is not considered to be a tax preference item for 1970 is

   a. Operating loss carryover.

   b. Capital gain.

   c. Depletion.

   d. Excess investment interest.

   e. None of the above.

6. Mr. Jamison, who is self-employed, purchased items of depreciable property during 1970. An item that would not qualify for the additional first-year 20% depreciation bonus is

   a. A new building with a 50-year life.

   b. New office furniture with a 20-year life.

   c. A new car with an 8-year life.

   d. A used car with a 6-year life.

   e. None of the above.

7. For 1970 Miss Cheryle had taxable income of $180,000 consisting of $110,000 in salary as president of Lucky Corporation and $70,000 which was 50% of her net Section 1201 long-term capital gain. Assuming that her federal income tax (before considering minimum tax) was $101,540 for 1970, the income subject to the 10% minimum tax would be

   a. $140,000.

   b. $50,000.

   c. $40,000.

   d. $20,000.

   e. None of the above.

8. Assume the same facts as in item 7 with the added information that Miss Cheryle had excess investment interest of $80,000. The amount now subject to the 10% minimum tax would be

   a. $48,460.

   b. $38,460.

   c. $18,460.

   d. $0.

   e. None of the above.

9. Mr. Jackson is single and worked for five months during 1970. He earned gross wages of $3,005, had no exclusions from adjusted gross income and is not able to itemize deductions. If the amount considered to be the tax-free poverty level is $1,725, Mr. Jackson's taxable income for 1970 would be

   a. $2,125.

   b. $2,100.

   c. $1,725.

   d. $1,280.

   e. None of the above

10. During 1970 Mr. Dockey, age 63, and his wife, age 51, incurred and paid the following medical expenses for which they received no reimbursement:

Hospitalization insurance premiums	$360
Hospital	500
Doctors	340
Drugs and medicines	150

The Dockeys also paid $200 for prescription drugs for Mr. Dockey's dependent brother, age 77. Assuming that the Dockeys' adjusted gross income for 1970 was $15,000, the amount that they may claim as a medical deduction on a joint return would be

    a. $950.
    b. $740.
    c. $650.
    d. $540.
    e. None of the above.

11. On October 31, 1970 Miss Viola received $40,000 in a lump-sum distribution from the Flower Company's qualified profit-sharing plan. The plan is on a calendar year basis. Miss Viola and her employer each contributed $4,800 to the plan prior to December 31, 1969 and $200 after December 31, 1969. The tax effect of this distribution for calendar year 1970 would be

    a. Ordinary income of $5,000; long-term capital gain of $30,000.
    b. Ordinary income of $200; long-term capital gain of $35,000.
    c. Ordinary income of $200; long-term capital gain of $34,800.
    d. Ordinary income of $0; long-term capital gain of $35,000.
    e. None of the above.

12. On January 1, 1970 Mr. Peter took occupancy of his new building and began his practice as a CPA. On September 1, 1969 he signed a contract for the building that cost $40,000 and had an estimated useful life of 40 years and no salvage value. Mr. Peter wants to depreciate the building as rapidly as possible and decides to use the accelerated depreciation method that will give him the maximum allowable depreciation expense in the initial years of the building's life. For calendar year 1970 Mr. Peter's maximum depreciation expense deduction would be

    a. $3,900.
    b. $2,000.
    c. $1,951.
    d. $1,500.
    e. None of the above.

13. On February 3, 1969 Mr. Overton bought bonds for $10,000; on February 4, 1970, when their fair market value was $8,500, he gave them to his sister. If Miss Overton sold the bonds on August 4, 1970 for $7,700, the 1970 tax effect of these transactions would be

    a. Short-term capital loss of $800.
    b. Short term capital gain of $700.
    c. Long-term capital loss of $800.
    d. Long-term capital gain of $700.
    e. None of the above.

14. Assume the same facts as in item 13 except that Miss Overton sold the bonds on August 4, 1970 for $10,500. The 1970 tax effect of these transactions would be

    a. Long-term capital gain of $2,000.
    b. Long-term capital gain of $500.
    c. Short-term capital gain of $2,000.
    d. Short-term capital gain of $500.
    e. None of the above.

15. Mr. Korn purchased bonds for $20,000 on March 30, 1968. He died on January 5, 1970 and left to his sister the bonds, which then had a fair market value of $12,000; this valuation was used in the estate tax return. Miss Korn did

not actually receive the bonds until April 20, 1970 when their fair market value was $13,000. If Miss Korn sold the bonds for $14,000 on July 18, 1970, the 1970 tax effect of these transactions would be
- a. Long-term capital loss of $6,000.
- b. Long-term capital gain of $2,000.
- c. Short-term capital gain of $1,000.
- d. Short-term capital loss of $7,000.
- e. None of the above.

Problem XIII-12: Multiple choice questions on taxation of individuals (50-60 min.)

Instructions

Select the best answer choice for each of the following items which relate to the federal income taxation of individuals. The answers should be selected in accordance with the *current* Internal Revenue Code and Tax Regulations. Choose only one answer for each item. Your grade will be determined from your total of correct answers.

Items to be Answered

1. During January 1970 John Smith sold stock with a cost basis of $15,000 to his brother, Bob, for $14,500, the fair market value on the date of sale. Four months later Bob sold the same stock for $16,000 to a friend on a bona fide transaction. The 1970 tax effect of these transactions to John and Bob would be
- a. Gain to John of $1,500; transaction need not be reported by Bob.
- b. Gain to John of $1,000; transaction need not be reported by Bob.
- c. Nondeductible loss to John of $500; gain to Bob of $1,500.
- d. Nondeductible loss to John of $500; gain to Bob of $1,000.
- e. None of the above.

2. On January 2, 1970 Dennis Harrison began operations of his own Harrison Furniture Store. All furniture is sold on installment contracts and he computes taxable income on the installment method. The gross margin for 1970 was 60% and accounts receivable as of December 31 were $70,000. It is estimated that 20% of this amount will become uncollectible. Mr. Harrison desires to establish a reserve for uncollectible accounts at December 31. The bad debt deduction allowable for 1970 under the reserve method of computing taxable income would be
- a. $14,000.
- b. $8,400.
- c. $5,600.
- d. $0.
- e. None of the above.

3. Charles Carson owns and operates Carson Grocery as a self-employed individual. For the calendar year 1970 opening inventory was $15,000, purchases $40,000 and closing inventory $12,000. The following information for 1970 is also available:

Stock in trade which was included in the opening inventory and had a basis of $3,500 (fair market value $4,300) was donated to qualified charitable organizations.

Included in purchases is merchandise having a basis of $2,200 (fair market value of $2,900) used personally by Mr. Carson and his family.

Excluded from both ending inventory and purchases was $1,600 for merchandise on hand that was consigned from a new manufacturer of diet foods and $5,400 for purchased goods which were in transit on December 31; title to the latter had passed to the Carson Grocery at year's end. It is estimated that the value of the closing inventory will decline 20% early in 1971.

The cost of goods sold to be used in computing 1970 taxable income would be

    a. $42,700.
    b. $37,300.
    c. $35,800.
    d. $32,640.
    e. None of the above.

4. In January 1960 William Walker built a personal residence which cost $24,000 including the land. In 1966 he correctly claimed a $4,000 casualty loss deduction for fire damage in the basement and in 1968 he expended $4,000 for capital improvements to the house. He converted the property to rental use in 1970 when the fair market value of the land was $6,000 and the building $18,000. The basis for depreciation of the rental property is

    a. $28,000.
    b. $22,000.
    c. $18,000.
    d. $14,000.
    e. None of the above or not determinable from the above facts.

5. The following information is available with respect to an option granted to William Doe by his employer pursuant to a qualified stock option plan:

	Per Share
Fair market value and the option price on the date of grant, October 30, 1968	$50
Fair market value on date of exercise, June 5, 1969	60
Selling price on November 15, 1970	75
Number of shares acquired by exercise	200
Number of shares sold November 15, 1970	100

The effect of the November 15 sale on Mr. Doe's 1970 taxable income would be

    a. Long-term capital gain of $2,500.
    b. Long-term capital gain of $1,500.
    c. Long-term capital gain of $1,500; ordinary income of $1,000.
    d. Long-term capital gain of $1,000; ordinary income of $1,500.
    e. None of the above.

6. On the advice of Mrs. Sloan's physician, Mr. and Mrs. Sloan made the following expenditures during 1970 for treatment of her severe heart condition:

- Installation of a home elevator (which increased the value of the residence by $950) $1,260
- Trip to Arizona made by Mrs. Sloan consisting of the following items:

Special diet foods (as a substitute for food normally consumed)	$300
Two ounces of liquor twice a day for relief of angina pain from heart condition	75
Lodging	350
Transportation expense between home and Arizona	175
	$900

Before consideration of the 1% and 3% limitations, Mr. and Mrs. Sloan's joint medical expense deduction for 1970 would be
- a. $1,435.
- b. $900.
- c. $560.
- d. $485.
- e. None of the above.

7. On December 28, 1970 Bob Roe, a cash basis taxpayer, signed a note for $12,000 payable in 24 installments of $500 each starting January 31, 1971. Interest of $720 was deducted from the face value of the note and he received the net proceeds of $11,280. Although he had no legal obligation to do so, Mr. Roe made a $500 interest payment during 1970 on behalf of his sister. As the owner of a condominium apartment he paid interest of $1,850 on his share of the mortgage indebtedness on the property. Mr. Roe's interest deduction in computing 1970 taxable income would be
- a. $3,070.
- b. $2,570.
- c. $2,350.
- d. $1,220.
- e. None of the above.

8. On December 31, 1969 Harvey Goodwin assigned to his wife the right to receive all of the future income that he might earn from practicing law. During the calendar year 1970 he realized the following income and losses:

Income from law practice	$25,000
Total gambling winnings	15,000
Total gambling losses	2,000
Profit from stamp hobby	1,500
Loss from farming hobby	6,500

Assuming that Mr. Goodwin itemizes his deductions and files separately for 1970, his adjusted gross income would be
- a. $41,500.
- b. $39,500.
- c. $16,500.
- d. $8,000.
- e. None of the above.

9. On June 30, 1970 Jerry Anders, age 68, received $20,000 under a life

insurance contract and a $4,000 payment from his wife's employer, both paid to him as beneficiary upon the death of his wife. On November 10, 1970 Mr. Anders sold the personal residence in which he had lived for the past ten years. The adjusted sales price was $19,000 and the realized gain was $6,500. During 1970 he also received a bequest of municipal bonds valued at $100,000 upon which he received interest payments of $2,000. Mr. Anders' gross income for 1970 is

    a. $32,500.
    b. $12,500.
    c. $6,000.
    d. $0.
    e. None of the above.

10. David Jones was injured on June 1, 1970, the first day of his one-month fully paid vacation. He was hospitalized from June 1 to June 15. As he was preparing to return to work on the morning of July 1, his wife became ill and he was unable to return to work until July 16. During his absence in July he received $200 per week which was 50% of his regular pay. The amount of sick pay that Mr. Jones may exclude from his 1970 gross income would be

    a. $100 per week for the period June 1-June 15.
    b. $100 per week for the period July 1-July 15.
    c. $100 per week for the period June 1-June 15 and July 1-July 15.
    d. None of the wages received for the period June 1-July 15.
    e. None of the above.

11. On Decemer 31, 1968 Richard Able and Steven Baker formed a partnership agreeing to share all profits and losses equally. Mr. Able contributed $250,000 cash and Mr. Baker contributed a building having a fair market value of that amount. The following data are also available:

	1970	1969
•Ordinary taxable income (or loss)	$16,000	($200,000)
Cash distributions shared equally by partners . . .	32,000	—
Partnership liabilities (to third parties)	60,000	—

•There are no other relevant partnership agreements or elections; neither partner has loaned any money to the partnership.

•The building cost Mr. Baker $160,000 and had an adjusted basis of $90,000 to the partnership at the time of contribution. The partnership income (or loss) that Mr. Baker can claim in computing his 1969 taxable income would be

    a. $0.
    b. ($45,000).
    c. ($90,000).
    d. ($100,000).
    e. None of the above.

12. Assume that on Decemer 31, 1968 Able and Baker incorporated their business and elected to be treated as a Subchapter S (tax-option) corporation. All other facts are as indicated in item 11 except that there were no distributions to partners during 1970. Mr. Baker would report as his pro rata share of corporate profit (or loss) in computing his 1970 taxable income the amount of

a. $8,000.
b. $0.
c. ($2,000).
d. ($18,000).
e. None of the above.

13. Hoping to obtain employment in New York City, Bob Barnes and his wife drove there from Boston in April 1970 to search for a new house. While on the trip they purchased a home. Back in Boston on May 1, 1970 Mr. Barnes was interviewed and accepted an offer of employment at an office located five miles from the site of his new house. Mr. and Mrs. Barnes immediately gathered together their household goods and personal effects and left for New York where they stayed in a hotel for one week while awaiting the final alterations on their home. In computing their 1970 joint taxable income, Mr. and Mrs. Barnes may claim as moving expenses

a. Transportation expenses for the April trip only.
b. Transportation expenses for the May trip only.
c. Transportation expenses for the April and May trips plus costs of food and lodging in May for the temporary quarters.
d. $0.
e. None of the above.

14. On December 31, 1970 Jim Jones received a lump-sum distribution from a qualified profit sharing plan upon the termination of his employment. A letter received with the check provided the following information:

Total amount of distribution $45,000
Employer's pre-1970 contribution 26,000
Employer's post-1969 contribution 4,000
Employee's contribution 5,000

In the computation of his 1970 taxable income Mr. Jones would include the receipt of the $45,000 as

a. Long-term capital gain of $40,000.
b. Long-term gain of $36,000; ordinary income of $4,000.
c. Long-term capital gain of $30,000; ordinary income of $10,000.
d. Long-term capital gain of $10,000; ordinary income of $30,000.
e. None of the above.

15. On May 15, 1970 Panor Corporation paid $27,500 for a tax based on the unreasonable accumulation of corporate earnings and profits for the year ended December 31, 1968. The effect of this on the personal taxable income of a 90% stockholder of the Corporation for 1970 would be

a. Ordinary income of $90,000.
b. Ordinary income of $65,250.
c. Ordinary income of $20,250.
d. No effect.
e. None of the above.

Problem XIII-13: Multiple choice questions on taxation of corporations and partnerships (50-60 min.)

Instructions

Select the best answer for each of the following items which relate to federal income taxation. The answers should be selected in accordance with the *current*

Internal Revenue Code and Tax Regulations. Select only one answer for each item. Your grade will be determined from your total of correct answers.

Items to be Answered

1. During 1969 three employees of ARX Corporation exercised options which they were granted in 1966 according to a qualified stock option plan. When granted, the option price was slightly more than the market price of the stock; when the employees exercised their options, they obtained ARX stock with a market value of $37,000 for a payment of $12,000. The effect of the exercise of these options on ARX Corporation's taxable income would be
    a. A long-term capital loss.
    b. An additional compensation expense deductible in 1969.
    c. An additional compensation expense deductible pro rata in the period extending from date of grant to date of exercise.
    d. A carryforward of the deduction for the additional compensation until used up over five years.
    e. None of the above.

2. A Corporation had taxable income in 1969 of $130,000 which included a long-term capital gain of $8,000 from depreciation recapture under Sec. 1250. Its tax liability for the year (assuming a normal tax rate of 22%, a surtax rate of 26% on income in excess of $25,000 and a surcharge of 10%) would be
    a. $62,400.
    b. $55,900.
    c. $49,180.
    d. $47,260.
    e. None of the above.

3. During 1969 a strike halted manufacturing operations of Carpets, Inc. for four months. Depreciation of its spinning and weaving machines per books for 1969 using the straight-line method amounted to $216,000 (about 70% of the total depreciation of plant and equipment for the year); its operations for 1969 resulted in a loss of $132,000 (after deducting depreciation). Due to the curtailment of volume, the depreciation deduction for this equipment may be reduced by
    a. $92,400.
    b. $72,000.
    c. $44,000.
    d. $0.
    e. None of the above.

4. The books of Z-D Company, a partnership, show net income for 1969 of $51,000 which included the following:

Short-term capital loss	$(3,300)
Long-term capital gain (sale of securities)	4,000
Gain from involuntary conversion	
Long-term capital gain	1,400
Ordinary income (1245 Recapture Provision)	800
Dividends subject to $100 exclusion	300

Assuming profits and losses are shared equally by Z and D, each partner's share of partnership income (excluding all partnership items which must be taken into account separately) to be reported as taxable in 1969 would be

a. $25,500.
b. $24,450.
c. $24,300.
d. $23,900.
e. None of the above.

5. In April 1969 RD contributed to a partnership $5,000 in cash and three pieces of equipment which had a basis to him of $8,000 and a fair market value of $10,000. He acquired the equipment in 1964 at a cost of $15,000. His capital account was credited for $25,000, which constituted 1/3 of total partnership capital, and goodwill was recorded for the difference. The tax effects to RD of this transaction would be

a. Long-term capital gain of $2,000; short-term capital gain of $10,000.
b. Long-term capital gain of $2,000; ordinary income of $10,000.
c. Long-term capital gain of $12,000.
d. Long-term capital gain of $2,000.
e. None of the above.

6. X Corporation has incurred research and development costs for the first time. For financial reporting it wishes to defer the costs by project and write them off over the future years benefited; for tax purposes it wishes to write the costs off in the year incurred. X must

a. Write off the costs over 5 years or more.
b. Write off the costs over 3 years or more.
c. Write off the costs in the years of benefit or when loss can be determined.
d. Write off the costs according to prior written agreement with the Internal Revenue Service.
e. Do none of the above.

7. Y Corporation charged the following payments to advertising expense in 1969: (1) Travel expense of $78 for president to offer voluntary testimony at the state capital against proposed legislation regarded as unfavorable to its business; (2) Christmas gifts to 10 major customers at $50 each; (3) Contribution of $1,000 to an ad hoc committee of the Corporation's industry association to help cover costs of circulars, TV and newspaper advertisements, etc., ... to defeat proposed legislation; the maximum deduction Y can take for these is

a. $1,578.
b. $1,078.
c. $578.
d. $328.
e. None of the above.

8. For 4 years S Corporation has been using the straight-line method and an estimated life of 8 years with no salvage value in computing depreciation for item 8S. Changed conditions justify a revision of the estimated useful life of the item to 10 years with no salvage value. The tax effect of this revision will be annual depreciation charges over the remaining useful life of this item of

a. 16 2/3% of the original basis.
b. 16 2/3% of the adjusted basis.
c. 12 1/2% of the original basis.
d. 10% of the original basis.
e. None of the above.

9. The stockholders of L Corporation adopted a plan of liquidation pursuant to Sec. 337 on January 31, 1969. Within 12 months the Corporation sold its

property (including $220,000 of inventory) to an unrelated third party in one transaction and immediately distributed cash of $900,000 to stockholders in complete liquidation. Corporation retained earnings immediately prior to the distribution were $170,000. The aggregate stockholders' adjusted bases in the stock was $660,000. The tax effects of the liquidation to stockholders would be
    a. Ordinary income of $220,000; capital gain of $20,000.
    b. Ordinary income of $170,000; capital gain of $70,000.
    c. Ordinary income of $170,000; capital gain of $240,000.
    d. No ordinary income; capital gain of $240,000.
    e. None of the above.
    10. Assume the same facts as in item 9 with the added information that the L Corporation sold its assets for $250,000 more than their adjusted basis, that no part of the sale's proceeds represents amounts previously deducted for the cost of the items sold and that the proceeds do not relate to any recapture provisions; the recognized gain to the L Corporation would be
    a. $250,000.
    b. $125,000.
    c. $80,000.
    d. $0.
    e. None of the above.
    11. AX Corporation has adopted the Internal Revenue Service procedure of grouping its assets into guideline classes. The group, office furniture, fixtures, machines and equipment, has a total basis of $100,000 and is assigned a useful life of 10 years. Salvage value is a 20% factor and the Corporation computes its deduction under the double-declining-balance method. The class life being used is
    a. 12 1/2 years.
    b. 10 years.
    c. 8 years.
    d. 5 years.
    e. None of the above.
    12. Assume as in item 11 that AX Corporation has adopted the guideline procedure and that it has applied the reserve ratio test to prove that the depreciation reserve for assets in one guideline class bears a reasonable relationship to the basis of those assets. The result of this test is that the actual reserve ratio for the guideline class is 60% while 63.8% is the upper limit of the appropriate reserve ratio range. From this it would be reasonable to conclude that
    a. Corporate retirement and replacement practices are consistent with the class life used.
    b. The taxpayer is not using a proper class life.
    c. The Corporation will be required to justify the useful life with additional facts and circumstances.
    d. It will be necessary for the Corporation to apply the transitional allowance rule.
    e. None of the above are true.
    13. RX Corporation, not a Subchapter S (tax option) corporation, had a deficit of $50,000 at the end of 1968. Its net income after taxes in 1969 was $20,000 (including a long-term capital gain of $5,000). It made distributions to stockholders of $10,000 in 1969. RX Corporation should describe these payments as

a. Ordinary dividends, 100%.

b. Ordinary dividends, 75%; long-term capital gain, 25%.

c. Ordinary dividends, 50%; long-term capital gain, 50%.

d. Ordinary dividends, 50%; return of capital, 50%.

e. None of the above.

14. On September 12, 1969 R Corporation purchased special production equipment by giving a note having a face amount of $22,800 which covered the invoice price of $21,790, freight of $210 and interest of $800. In addition, installation costs were $400. The maximum basis of this equipment that would be acceptable for tax purposes is

a. $24,210.

b. $23,200.

c. $22,800.

d. $22,400.

e. None of the above.

15. The Internal Revenue Service has disallowed a portion of the compensation paid to stockholder-officers of a closely-held corporation. The excessive amounts were not in proportion to stockholdings. The corporation loses deduction of the excess payments in the current year and

a. Must regard the excess payments as a return of capital and so report them to the recipients.

b. May capitalize the excess payments as goodwill and amortize this amount over five years.

c. May carry the excess payments forward five years until used up.

d. May apply this excess against capital gains in current and future years.

e. None of the above.

16. The books of RA Corporation for 1969 show a net income of $550,000 after deducting a charitable contribution of $50,000. The contribution was authorized by the board of directors on December 25, 1969 and was actually paid January 31, 1970. Assuming RA Corporation to be on an accrual basis, it may

a. File a proper election, claim a deduction of $30,000 and carry the remainder over five succeeding tax years.

b. File a proper election and claim a 1969 deduction in the amount of $50,000.

c. File a proper election, claim a 1969 deduction of $27,500 and carry the remainder over five succeeding tax years.

d. Not gain a contribution deduction for 1969 under any circumstances.

e. Do none of the above.

17. On July 10, 1969 XB Corporation purchased factory equipment installed for $14,600. Salvage value was estimated at $1,000. By agreement with the Internal Revenue Service, the equipment will be depreciated over eight years using the double-declining-balance method. XB also elected to take the full first-year bonus depreciation. Counting the year of acquisition as one-half year, XB would deduct 1969 depreciation on this equipment of

a. $3,925.

b. $3,575.

c. $3,450.

d. $2,925.

e. $2,575.

400 Taxation

18. On October 1, 1965 XC Corporation purchased ten electric typewriters for $3,500. On October 1, 1969 these ten typewriters were donated to a qualified charitable organization. At the date of the contribution, accumulated depreciation on a straight-line basis was $1,400 and the fair market value was $2,700. Corporate income before any deduction for charitable contributions was $50,000. The Corporation may deduct
   a. $2,700.
   b. $2,500.
   c. $2,365.
   d. $2,100.
   e. None of the above.

19. On August 1, 1968 the XA Company acquired a factory building and land for $1,250,000 of which $50,000 represented the cost of the land. The Company expanded operations rapidly and moved to a larger factory selling this land and building on August 1, 1969 for $1,315,000 of which $50,000 was for the land. Accumulated depreciation was recorded to the date of sale using the double-declining-balance method with estimates of no salvage value and a 40-year life. The tax effects of the sale would be
   a. Ordinary income of $125,000.
   b. Capital gain of $125,000.
   c. Ordinary income of $30,000; capital gain of $95,000.
   d. Ordinary income of $24,000; capital gain of $101,000.
   e. None of the above.

20. Assume the same facts as in item 19 above except that XA Company sells the land and building on August 1, 1980 for $900,000 (of which $50,000 was for the land) and double-declining-balance depreciation recorded for tax purposes to that date is $520,000. The tax effects of its sale of the plant would be
   a. Ordinary income of $170,000.
   b. Capital gain of $170,000.
   c. Ordinary income of $112,000; capital gain of $58,000.
   d. Ordinary income of $160,000; capital gain of $10,000.
   e. None of the above.

Problem XIII-14: Multiple choice questions on taxation of individuals, partnerships, and corporations (40-50 min.)

Instructions

The following questions pertain to federal income taxation. Consider the information given in the lettered statement of facts preceding each set of questions in determining your answer for each question.

Write on a separate sheet your answer for each of the following questions. The answers should be selected in accordance with the current *Internal Revenue Code* and *Tax Regulations*. Select only one answer for each question.

An example of the manner in which the answer sheet should be marked is shown in the following illustration:

Lettered Statement of Facts

Z. Dobbs Corporation's 1969 financial statements reported $25,000 of depreciation expense. The Corporation computes depreciation by the straight-line method on its financial statements and by the declining-balance method for income tax reporting. Depreciation under the declining-balance method totaled $37,000.

Question
1. Dobbs Corporation should report 1969 depreciation of
   a. $62,000.
   b. $37,000.
   c. $25,000.
   d. $12,000.
   e. None of the above.

Answer Sheet
1. b.

Items to be Answered

A. Mattson is the plant manager for Eichberg Corporation. His salary for 1969 was $18,000. The Corporation uses the calendar year and the accrual basis for income tax reporting and Mattson reports on the cash basis. During 1969 Eichberg Corporation did not have funds available and Mattson was required to wait until April 1, 1970 for his November and December 1969 salary checks. Neither Mattson nor his family owns or has owned any shares of stock in the Corporation.
   1. The Eichberg Corporation may claim a 1969 deduction for Mattson's salary in the amount of
      a. $18,000.
      b. $15,000.
      c. $3,000.
      d. $0.
      e. None of the above.
   2. Mattson must include the amounts of his November and December 1969 salary checks, both received April 1, 1970, in his taxable income for
      a. Calendar year 1969.
      b. Calendar year 1970.
      c. Fiscal year 1969.
      d. Fiscal year 1970.
      e. None of the above.
   3. If Mattson's wife and his brother each owned 26 percent of Eichberg Corporation stocks as of Decemer 31, 1969, the Corporation may claim a 1969 deduction for Mattson's salary in the amount of
      a. $18,000.
      b. $15,000.
      c. $3,000.
      d. $0.
      e. None of the above.
   4. Assuming the same stock ownership as in "A.3" above, Eichberg Corporation may claim a 1970 deduction for Mattson's 1969 salary paid on April 1, 1970 in the amount of
      a. $18,000.
      b. $15,000.
      c. $3,000.
      d. $0.
      e. None of the above.

B. Compton sold real property that he owned with an adjusted basis of $76,000 and encumbered by a mortgage for $28,000 to Nelson in 1968. The terms of the sale required Nelson to pay $6,000 cash, assume the $28,000 mortgage, and give to Compton eleven notes for $6,000 each (plus interest at 7 percent). The first note was payable two years from date and each succeeding note became due at two-year intervals. Market value of the notes was equal to 80 percent of face value. Compton elected the installment basis for reporting the transaction.

5. The "selling price" was
    a. $104,000.
    b. $86,800.
    c. $72,000.
    d. $58,800.
    e. None of the above.
6. The contract price was
    a. $100,000.
    b. $72,000.
    c. $66,000.
    d. $58,800.
    e. None of the above.
7. Payments in the year of sale were
    a. $92,800.
    b. $34,000.
    c. $6,000.
    d. $4,800.
    e. None of the above.
8. If Nelson pays the 1970 note as promised, the recognized gain to Compton in 1970 (exclusive of interest) would be
    a. $4,363.
    b. $2,000.
    c. $1,440.
    d. $0.
    e. None of the above.

C. Betcode Partnership discontinued a segment of its business activity during the current tax year and sold a milling machine with an adjusted basis to the Partnership of $20,000 to Bettsehen (who has a 1/3 interest in capital and profits) for $29,900. In addition, the firm sold a drill press with an adjusted basis to the Partnership also of $20,000 to Cohn (who has a 1/3 interest in capital and profits) for $16,700. The third partner, DeFoe, sold land to the Partnership for $40,000 when it had an adjusted basis to him of $10,000. The three unrelated partners engaged in these transactions with their partnership other than in their capacity as partners.

9. Upon completion of the sale to Bettsehen, the Partnership had a gain to be shared by all three partners of
    a. $39,900.
    b. $6,600.
    c. $3,300.
    d. $0.
    e. None of the above.

10. Upon completion of the sale to Cohn, the Partnership had a loss to be shared by all three partners of
    a. $9,900.
    b. $6,600.
    c. $3,300.
    d. $0.
    e. None of the above.

11. Upon completion of the purchase from DeFoe, the Partnership had a basis in the newly acquired land of
    a. $40,000.
    b. $30,000.
    c. $10,000.
    d. $0.
    e. None of the above.

12. If the milling machine and drill press had been given to DeFoe in exchange for the land, the basis of the land to the Partnership would have been
    a. $46,600.
    b. $40,000.
    c. $36,700.
    d. $20,000.
    e. None of the above.

D. X-Cel Company, a calendar-year company, has operated as a Subchapter S ("tax option") corporation for four years (1964-1967). At December 31, 1967, it had accumulated earnings from years prior to 1964 of $112,000 and shareholders' undistributed taxable income of $145,000. Taxable income of X-Cel Company for 1968 including net long-term capital gains of $14,000 amounted to $60,000. The Company distributed dividends to its stockholders X, Y, and Z on February 20, 1969 as follows:
    X: $10,000,   Y: $10,000,   Z: $5,000.

13. The basis of Stockholder X's stock as of January 1, 1968 was $110,000. The basis of his stock as of February 20, 1969 would be:
    a. $134,000.
    b. $121,200.
    c. $118,400.
    d. $110,000.
    e. None of the above.

14. Income that would be taxable to the X-Cel Company as a Subchapter S corporation for 1968 would be:
    a. $60,000.
    b. $49,500.
    c. $35,000.
    d. $0.
    e. None of the above.

E. Kole, Inc., doing business in the U.S., is a domestic corporation with only one class of stock. All the stock was owned by Albert Kole, who sold his stock to John Redman on April 1, 1968 for $100,000, after properly electing 1120-S status for the year 1968. Redman continued the election for 1968 and 1969. During 1968 the Corporation earned $7,000 during each quarter of the year. In

1969 the firm had a loss of $12,000. No distributions were made to either Kole or Redman by the Corporation.

15. Albert Kole must include in his 1968 taxable income
   a. All of the $28,000 income for 1968.
   b. 25 percent of the $28,000 income for 1968.
   c. None of the $28,000 income for 1968.
   d. Any amount Redman tells Kole to report.
   e. None of the above.
16. Redman must include in his 1968 taxable income
   a. All of the $28,000 income for 1968.
   b. 75 percent of the $28,000 income for 1968.
   c. None of the $28,000 income for 1968.
   d. Any amount Kole tells Redman to report.
   e. None of the above.
17. Redman must include in his 1969 taxable income
   a. All of the $12,000 loss.
   b. 75 percent of the $12,000 loss.
   c. None of the $12,000 loss.
   d. The difference between his 1968 income from Kole, Inc. and the $12,000 loss.
   e. None of the above.
18. If Redman had Kole, Inc. make a $12,000 cash distribution to him on June 30, 1969, he must include in his 1969 taxable income
   a. All of the $12,000 loss.
   b. None of the $12,000 loss.
   c. A $12,000 income amount and a $12,000 loss.
   d. The difference between his 1968 income from Kole, Inc. and the $12,000 loss.
   e. None of the above.

F. On July 1, 1964, the Raaf Company bought new manufacturing equipment with an estimated life of eight years for $540,000. Salvage value was estimated at $20,000. First year "bonus" depreciation was taken and the double-declining-balance method of computing depreciation was used. Raaf Company's federal income tax liability for 1964 before application of the investment tax credit amounted to $40,000. On October 20, 1969, the equipment was sold for $125,000.

19. Depreciation on this equipment to be charged in 1964 would be:
   a. $108,000.
   b. $69,500.
   c. $69,250.
   d. $67,500.
   e. None of the above.
20. Assuming the adjusted tax basis of the equipment at October 20, 1969 amounts to $112,000, the effect of the sale of the equipment on the taxable income to be reported by Raaf Company for 1969 would be:
   a. Long-term capital gain equal to $13,000 plus the excess of declining-balance depreciation over applicable straight-line depreciation.
   b. Long-term capital gain of $13,000.
   c. Ordinary income of $13,000.
   d. Net gain of $6,500.
   e. None of the above.

Problem XIII-15: Multiple choice decisions on treatment of items in determining individual's taxable income (50-60 min.)

Instructions

Each of the numbered items to be answered is accorded only one of the following lettered treatments by an individual in determining his taxable income under the provisions of the *Internal Revenue Code* and *Income Tax Regulations* as they existed August 31, 1969 (assume the standard or minimum standard deductions are not taken):

    a. Fully excluded from gross income.
    b. Fully included in gross income.
    c. Partially included in gross income.
    d. Fully deductible from gross income.
    e. Partially deductible from gross income.
    f. Fully deductible only from adjusted gross income.
    g. Partially deductible only from adjusted gross income.
    h. Not deductible at any time.
    i. Must be capitalized and must not be amortized or depreciated.
    j. Must be capitalized and subsequently amortized or depreciated.

Select the best answer choice from the above lettered treatments for each of the following numbered items. Write on a separate answer sheet your answer choice. Select only one answer for each item.

An example of the manner in which the items should be answered is shown in the following illustration:

Example Items

X. Salary received for personal services.
Y. Cost of telephone service for business use.
Z. Cost of commuting to and from work.

Answer Sheet

    X. b.
    Y. d.
    Z. h.

Items to be Answered

    1. Embezzlement proceeds.
    2. A personal casualty loss of $300.
    3. Loss on the sale of personal residence.
    4. Compensatory damages received in personal libel suit.
    5. Rental paid for hotel sample room by outside salesman.
    6. Gift purchased costing $125 by taxpayer for customer.
    7. Interest at 7 per cent paid on personal automobile loan.
    8. Delinquent property tax on land purchased.
    9. Author's cost to secure copyright for manuscript published.
    10. Cost of race horse (not a hobby) to enter in races at county fairs.
    11. Fair market value of painting (equal to 10 per cent of taxpayer's adjusted income) donated to Kings College, Cambridge, England.

12. Receipt of alimony by divorced husband from former wife.

13. Payment of alimony by former wife to divorced husband.

14. Payment by divorced husband of child support to former wife.

15. Allowances received by dependents of U.S. Army personnel.

16. Rental of an automobile used 75 per cent for business and 25 per cent for personal use.

17. Death benefit of $12,000 received by daughter from deceased father's employer.

18. Commission paid to stock broker for securities purchased.

19. Unreimbursed cost of attending teachers' convention by high school teacher not required to attend.

20. Cost of a one-year subscription to *The Wall Street Journal* by a security investor for investment information.

21. Cost of three-year subscription to a tax service paid by a cash-basis CPA proprietor.

22. Gift of $8,000 cash received by son from father.

23. Unreimbursed cost of taxi paid by employee to deliver employer's product to customer; the employer's policy was not to reimburse for such expenditures.

24. Payment of $3,000 compensation by an individual proprietor-taxpayer to a minor son whose services were worth $500.

25. The first $600 earned by a taxpayer during the year.

26. Cost of a personal automobile not subject to state sales tax.

27. Purchase of a personal automobile subject to state sales tax.

28. Taxability to employee-taxpayer of premiums paid by employer for $100,000 group-term life insurance policy.

29. Rental allowance received by a minister of the gospel as part of his compensation and used to pay mortgage payments on his residence.

30. Cost of improvements to personal residence.

31. Sick pay of $80 per week received for six weeks by an employee whose regular salary is $100 per week.

32. Percentage depletion which exceeds both cost depletion and "net" income from the property before the deduction for depletion.

33. A $50,000 charitable contribution to his private tax exempt foundation by a taxpayer whose adjusted gross income is $100,000.

34. Short term capital gain realized from the sale of a municipal bond.

35. Fee paid to obtain new employment.

36. Travel expense incurred in searching for new employment.

37. Allowable depreciation on business property even though in excess of the decline in fair market value of the property.

38. Attorney's fees incurred in the purchase of a machine for business use.

39. Oil royalties received by a land owner.

40. Interest received on municipal bonds owned (not industrial development bonds).

SPECIFIC APPROACH

Problem XIII-1

1. The Schedule of Taxable Income offers little challenge. Remember to pick up the proportionate dividends of FGI, Inc.

2. For Subchapter S corporations, the basis of a shareholder's stock is increased for any corporate earnings taxed to him but not distributed. When the previously taxed income is distributed, the basis is reduced. Calculate the adjusted basis of FGI, Inc. stock separately for Mr. and Mrs. Taxpayer. In the computation of adjusted basis for the stock of Mrs. Taxpayer, determine it for 400 shares and merely take 1/4 of the final total.

3. In the exchange of land, to what extent is gain recognized?

Problem XIII-2

1. Computation of the corporation's taxable income involves no serious difficulties if one is familiar with the fundamentals of corporate taxation, including net capital loss treatment, contributions limitation, and dividend received deduction.

2. The real test of your abilities comes in the tax planning advice you are to provide. The opportunity is afforded to display the depth or limitation of your knowledge about the seven basic requirements a small business corporation must meet to qualify as a Subchapter S corporation and the two tests for a personal holding company.

3. Discuss both advantages and disadvantages.

Problem XIII-3

1. In the determination of the depreciation deduction for Part (a), the maximum allowable differs for each of the three assets acquired—the used building, the new building, and the new machinery. One must know the applicability of the limited declining balance technique to new realty acquired after July 24, 1969. For the machinery, in addition to first-year depreciation, what method gives the largest depreciation deduction in the first year of use?

2. For Part (b), compute pre-1970 excess depreciation deducted over straight-line, applying the proper percentage to determine the pre-1970 recapture. This amount added to the post-1969 excess depreciation produces the Sec. 1250 recapture accorded ordinary income treatment.

3. What amortization procedures applicable to the organization costs in Part (d) will minimize taxable income? What is the basis of a donated asset?

4. For Part (e), prepare a schedule to show the deductible computer based information system expense for both 1969 and 1970, recalling that the corporation wants the largest first-year (1969) deduction possible. What provision does the Code make for amortization of software costs, having "a life that cannot be determined?"

Problem XIII-4

1. Beginning with net income before suspense items, one must arrive at taxable income before contributions and special deductions.

2. Among the items to be added will be income from the sale of office typewriters. Whenever a sale results in a charitable deduction, the property's basis must be apportioned between the part sold and the part contributed. The portion of the basis (book value, in this case) allocated to the part sold is the percentage that the amount realized bears to the property's fair market value. The remainder of the basis represents the charitable contribution.

3. Will a deduction for depreciation expense be allowed on the machines where the indebtedness was forgiven?

4. Normally, loss on worthless stock is a capital loss on the last day of the tax year it becomes worthless. What special provisions come into play if the taxpayer is a domestic corporation and sustains the loss on stock of an affiliated corporation?

Problem XIII-5

1. A useful form for the first requested schedule would be to have three amount columns: one each for the income statement, adjustments, and taxable business profit.

2. Schedule C (Form 1040) does not provide for any type of revenue other than gross receipts or sales. The warehouse rental income is best reported in Part II of Schedules E & R (Form 1040). Exclude it in determining taxable business profit, as well as any other items which receive special treatment on the individual tax return. Exclude items which, under the Code, are not deductible.

3. In the schedule of capital gains, the gain on the sale of the condemned land should be included. The capital gain deduction should also appear. Why would the gain on sale of the equipment not appear in that schedule?

4. In filing a joint return, may the medical expenses for George and Mrs. Alfred be deducted?

Problem XIII-6

1. An excellent method to determine the amount of sales on account is to sketch a T account for Accounts Receivable, inserting the known items, as was discussed in Topic I:

ACCOUNTS RECEIVABLE

| Opening balance | $62,000 | Collections (gross) | $756,500 |
| Sales on account | X | Closing balance | $ 73,000 |

The data should be reorganized to meet the requirement of a requested "schedule."

2. The warehouse equipment sale produces a Section 1245 gain. Of what

significance is the statement that the boiler was "not a structural component of the building?"

3. Is any special treatment accorded the loss on the sale of land?

Problem XIII-7

Before attempting a solution, review Sections 1231, 1245, and 1250 of the Code. Watch particularly dates of acquisition and type of property acquired. To reach a satisfactory solution, one must know those sections and in addition be able to answer these questions:

1. Is a deduction allowed for partial worthlessness of an investment in stock?

2. What is a loss on a wash sale?

3. To be deductible, an expense must be paid or incurred during the tax year. How does this provision affect the freight claim losses?

4. What three conditions disallow the deduction for an unpaid expense?

5. Although fines are generally not deductible, what about legal fees in defense of the charge?

6. Although the benefits of advertising may extend into future years, may the cost be capitalized and prorated?

Problem XIII-8

1. Follow instructions in designing the schedule computing ordinary income to be reported on the partnership tax return:

a. In computing the depreciation adjustment for tax purposes on the old furniture and equipment sold, contributed property is treated as if the partnership bought it at a cost equal to contributing partner's adjusted basis.

b. In computing the depreciation adjustment for tax purposes on the new building, does that asset qualify for additional first-year depreciation allowance?

c. In computing the depreciation adjustment for tax purposes on the new furniture and equipment, when determining the amount of additional first-year depreciation, recall that each partner is considered to have bought his share of the asset. Is proration required for additional first-year depreciation?

d. In computing ordinary income for tax purposes, partnership may deduct salaries and interest to partners, providing the amounts are reasonable, and would exclude items afforded special treatment on the personal returns of the individual partners, such as capital gains and losses, charitable contributions and dividends from domestic corporations.

2. In the schedule of distributable shares, begin with the ordinary income determined in requirement (a), removing those items not subject to equal distribution. A list of items to be reported separately by each partner should then follow, including the investment credit on qualifying assets purchased.

Problems XIII-9 through XIII-15

No specific approach is offered for this series of multiple choice questions, which are in sequence, beginning with questions from the latest examinations first. In the past four years, examinations have included an average of two sets of multiple choice questions on taxation, since they permit broad coverage without excessive consumption of time. On the average, examinations allow approximately three minutes per item. The grade is usually determined from the total number of correct answers.

Miscellaneous Review Problems

GENERAL APPROACH

Multiple choice questions on the practice portion of the examination were formerly restricted to taxation. With a mushrooming of topics to be covered within a limited time span and with the desire to make the examination a deciding factor to establish technical competence, the Institute is resorting to multiple choice problem construction in many topic areas. From November of 1970 through November of 1972, examinations have averaged two such problems per examination, excluding those on taxation.

To give you some idea of the diversity of subject matter covered, a partial list would include: partnership admission and dissolution, retail inventory, cost of goods sold and gross margin analysis, business combinations, statement of changes in financial position, compound interest formulas, revenue recognition, direct versus absorption costing, lease or buy decisions, APB *Opinions 15, 16, 17, 18,* and *19.* It would seem that every accounting area is fertile ground for a crop of multiple choice questions.

When reading the instructions, be sure to note how your grade for the multiple choice questions will be determined. If it reads, "Your grade will be determined from your total of correct answers," it is wise to answer all questions, taking an educated guess where one is not sure of the answer. But should the instruction read, "Your grade will be determined from your total net score obtained by deducting your total of incorrect answers from your total of correct answers; an omitted answer will not be considered an incorrect answer," one should not guess. With a poor performance, it is possible under these conditions to receive a negative score.

One cannot prepare specifically for this topic area, since it has no finite dimension. Only thorough preparation will provide adequate background. To assist candidates in their preparation, specific approaches will highlight difficult or troublesome points more generously, where the number of questions in one area is sufficient to warrant discussion. Solutions given in Volume II provide logic or evidence to substantiate the answers selected, thereby enabling a candidate to discover the error in his thought process, should there be one.

CPA PROBLEMS

Problem XIV-1: Multiple choice questions on a variety of financial accounting problems (40-50 min.)

Instructions

Select the best answer for each of the following items relating to a variety of financial accounting problems. Use space on the separate printed answer sheet to indicate your answer. Mark only one answer for each item. Your grade will be determined from your total of correct answers.

Items to be Answered

1. The June bank statement of Lucas Company showed an ending balance of $187,387. During June the bank charged back NSF checks totaling $3,056, of which $1,856 had been redeposited by June 30. Deposits in transit on June 30 were $20,400. Outstanding checks on June 30 were $60,645, including a $10,000 check which the bank had certified on June 28. On June 14, the bank charged Lucas' account for a $2,300 item which should have been charged against the account of Luby Company; the bank did not detect the error. During June, the bank collected foreign items for Lucas; the proceeds were $8,684 and bank charges for this service were $19. On June 30, the adjusted cash in bank of Lucas Company is
   a. $149,442.
   b. $159,442.
   c. $147,142.
   d. $158,242.
   e. None of the above.

2. In 1964, Miss Jones purchased land for $6,000. In 1969, she died, leaving the land to her nephew, Mr. Smith. The land was appraised at $8,000 as of the date of death and that value was accepted for estate and inheritance tax purposes. In December 1971, the land was appraised at $9,000. In Mr. Smith's statement of assets and liabilities as of December 31, 1971, the land should be included at
   a. Appraised value of $9,000, no disclosure of cost data being necessary.
   b. Cost of $0 and appraised value of $9,000.
   c. Cost of $6,000 and appraised value of $9,000.
   d. Cost of $8,000 and appraised value of $9,000.
   e. None of the above.

3. The bookkeeper of Latsch Company, which has an accounting year ending December 31, made the following errors:

A $1,000 collection from a customer was received on December 29, 1970, but not recorded until the date of its deposit in the bank, January 4, 1971.

A supplier's $1,600 invoice for inventory items received in December 1970 was not recorded until January 1971. (Inventories at December 31, 1970 and 1971, were stated correctly, based on physical count.)

Depreciation for 1970 was understated by $900.

In September 1970 a $200 invoice for office supplies was charged to the Utilities Expense account. Office supplies are expensed as purchased.

December 31, 1970, sales on account of $3,000 were recorded in January 1971.

Assume that no other errors have occurred and that no correcting entries have been made. Ignore income taxes.

Net income for 1970 was
- a. Understated by $500.
- b. Understated by $2,100.
- c. Overstated by $2,500.
- d. Neither understated nor overstated.
- e. None of the above.

4. Assume the same facts as in item 3. Working capital at December 31, 1970 was
- a. Understated by $3,000.
- b. Understated by $500.
- c. Understated by $1,400.
- d. Neither understated nor overstated.
- e. None of the above.

5. Assume the same facts as in item 3. Total assets at December 31, 1971, were
- a. Overstated by $2,500.
- b. Overstated by $2,100.
- c. Understated by $2,500.
- d. Neither understated nor overstated.
- e. None of the above.

6. On January 1, 1972, Hage Corporation granted options to purchase 9,000 of its common shares at $7 each. The market price of common was $10.50 per share on March 31, 1972, and averaged $9 per share during the quarter then ended. There was no change in the 50,000 shares of outstanding common stock during the quarter ended March 31, 1972. Net income for the quarter was $8,268. The number of shares to be used in computing primary earnings per share for the quarter is
- a. 59,000.
- b. 50,000.
- c. 53,000.
- d. 52,000.
- e. None of the above.

7. Assume the same facts as in item 6. The number of shares to be used in computing fully diluted earnings per share for the quarter is
- a. 53,000.
- b. 50,000.
- c. 52,000.
- d. 59,000.
- e. None of the above.

8. During all of 1971, Littlefield, Inc., had outstanding 100,000 shares of common stock and 5,000 shares of noncumulative, $7 preferred stock. Each share of the latter, which is classified as a common stock equivalent, is convertible into 3 shares of common. For 1971, Littlefield had $230,000 income from operations and $575,000 extraordinary losses; no dividends were paid or declared. Littlefield should report 1971 primary earnings (loss) per share for income (loss) before extraordinary items and for net income (loss), respectively, of
   a. $2.30 and ($3.45).
   b. $2.00 and ($3.00).
   c. $2.19 and ($3.29).
   d. $2.26 and ($3.39).
   e. None of the above.
9. Odell Corporation quarries limestone at two locations, crushes it, and sells it to be used in road building. The Internal Revenue Code provides for 5% depletion on such limestone. *Quarry* #1 is leased, the Company paying a royalty of $.01 per ton of limestone quarried. *Quarry* #2 is owned, the Company having paid $100,000 for the site; the Company estimates that the property can be sold for $30,000 after production ceases. Other data follow:

	Quarry #1	Quarry #2
Estimated total reserves, tons	30,000,000	100,000,000
Tons quarried through December 31, 1970	2,000,000	40,000,000
Tons quarried, 1971	800,000	1,380,000
Sales, 1971	$600,000	$1,000,000

A 1971 depletion of Quarry #1 for financial reporting purposes is
   a. $3,000.
   b. $8,000.
   c. $30,000.
   d. $29,600.
   e. None of the above.
10. Assume the same facts as in item 9. 1971 depletion of Quarry #2 for financial reporting purposes is
   a. $0.
   b. $1,380.
   c. $966.
   d. $50,000.
   e. None of the above.
11. Assume the same facts as in item 9 except that a new engineering study performed early in 1971 indicated that as of January 1, 1971, 75,000,000 tons of limestone were available in Quarry #2. 1971 depletion of Quarry #2 for financial reporting purposes is
   a. $772.80.
   b. $840.
   c. $0.
   d. $50,000.
   e. None of the above.
12. Simon Construction Company uses the percentage-of-completion method of accounting. In 1970, Simon began work under contract #1348, which provided for a contract price of $2,000,000. Other details follow:

	1970	1971
Costs incurred during the year	$ 300,000	$1,575,000
Estimated costs to complete, as of December 31	1,200,000	0
Billings during the year	360,000	1,540,000
Collections during the year	250,000	1,550,000

The portion of the total contract price to be recognized as revenue in 1970 is
   a. $320,000.
   b. $360,000.
   c. $250,000.
   d. $400,000.
   e. None of the above.

13. Assume the same facts as in item 12 except that Simon uses the completed-contract method of accounting. The portion of the total contract price to be recognized as revenue in 1971 is
   a. $1,540,000.
   b. $2,000,000.
   c. $1,900,000.
   d. $1,800,000.
   e. None of the above.

14. On July 1, 1966, Wilkerson, Inc., issued at face value $100,000 in serial bonds with 5% interest payable January 1 and July 1 of each year and principal payable $10,000 on July 1 of each year from 1970 through 1979. Transactions related to this issue decreased working capital during 1971 by
   a. $14,250.
   b. $14,500.
   c. $4,250.
   d. $4,500.
   e. None of the above.

15. With certain of its products, Hite Foods, Inc., includes coupons having no expiration date which are redeemable in merchandise. In the Company's ·experience, 40% of such coupons are redeemed. The liability for unredeemed coupons at December 31, 1970, was $9,000. During 1971, coupons worth $18,000 were issued and merchandise worth $8,000 was distributed in exchange for coupons redeemed. The December 31, 1971, balance sheet should include a liability of
   a. $9,800.
   b. $13,000.
   c. $8,200.
   d. $7,600.
   e. None of the above.

Problem XIV-2: Multiple choice questions on ratios and other financial problems (40-50 min.)

Instructions

Select the best answer for each of the following items relating to a variety of financial accounting problems. Mark only one answer for each item. Your grade will be determined from your total of correct answers.

Items to be Answered

The following balance sheet, income statement and related information of the Brief Company pertain to items 1 through 8.

Brief Company
BALANCE SHEET
December 31, 1971

Assets

Cash ....$ 106,000
Accounts receivable 566,000
Inventories 320,000
Plant and equipment, net of depreciation 740,000
Patents 26,000
Other intangible assets 14,000
$1,772,000

Equities

Accounts payable ....$ 170,000
Federal income tax payable 32,000
Miscellaneous accrued payables 38,000
Bonds payable (4% due 1992) 300,000
Preferred stock ($100 par, 7% cumulative
  nonparticipating and callable at $110) 200,000
Common stock (No par, 20,000 shares authorized,
  issued and outstanding) 400,000
Retained earnings 720,000
Treasury stock –800 shares of preferred .... (88,000)
$1,772,000

Brief Company
INCOME STATEMENT
Year Ended December 31, 1971

Net sales $1,500,000
Cost of goods sold 900,000

Gross margin on sales 600,000
Operating expenses (including
  bond interest expense) 498,000

Income before federal income taxes 102,000
Income tax expense 37,000

Net income ....$ 65,000

Additional information: There are no preferred dividends in arrears and the balances in the Accounts Receivable and Inventory accounts are unchanged from January 1, 1971 and there were no changes in the Bonds Payable, Preferred Stock or Common Stock accounts during 1971.

1. At December 31, 1971 the current ratio was

a. $\dfrac{992}{170}$ to 1.

b. $\dfrac{992}{208}$ to 1.

c. $\dfrac{992}{240}$ to 1.

d. $\dfrac{672}{208}$ to 1.

e. None of the above.

2. The number of times bond interest was earned during 1971 using the theoretically preferable method was

a. $\dfrac{1,500}{12}$

b. $\dfrac{1\,14}{12}$

c. $\dfrac{102}{12}$

d. $\dfrac{650}{120}$

e. None of the above.

3. During 1971 the number of times bond interest and preferred dividends were earned was

a. $\dfrac{1,140}{204}$

b. $\dfrac{1,020}{204}$

c. $\dfrac{114}{27}$

d. $\dfrac{650}{260}$

e. None of the above.

4. During 1971 the average number of days' sales in ending inventories was

a. $365\left(\dfrac{150}{32}\right)$

b. $365\left(\dfrac{90}{32}\right)$

c. $365\left(\dfrac{1,500}{566}\right)$

d. $365\left(\dfrac{32}{150}\right)$

e. None of the above.

5. During 1971 the average number of days in the operating cycle was approximately

a. $365\left(\dfrac{150}{32}+\dfrac{1,500}{566}\right)$

b. $365\left(\dfrac{90}{32}+\dfrac{1,500}{566}\right)$

c. $365\left(\dfrac{32}{90}+\dfrac{566}{1,500}\right)$

d. $365\left(\dfrac{320+566}{1,500}\right)$

e. None of the above .

6. At December 31, 1971 the book value per share of common stock was
   a. $66.
   b. $61.60.
   c. $56.
   d. $51.60.
   e. None of the above.

7. The rate of return for 1971 based on the year-end common stockholders' equity was

a. $\dfrac{650}{11,120}$

b. $\dfrac{566}{10,320}$

c. $\dfrac{650}{12,320}$

d. $\dfrac{566}{11,120}$

e. None of the above.

8. At December 31, 1971, the debt-equity ratio with debt defined as total liabilities would be

a. $\dfrac{540}{1,112}$

b. $\dfrac{540}{1,120}$

c. $\dfrac{540}{1,232}$

d. $\dfrac{540}{1,772}$

e. None of the above

9. The Apex Company has been using the LIFO cost method of inventory valuation for 10 years. Its 1971 ending inventory was $12,000 but it would have been $18,000 if FIFO had been used. Thus, if FIFO had been used, Apex's net income before income taxes would have been
a. $6,000 greater over the 10-year period.
b. $6,000 less over the 10-year period.
c. $6,000 greater in 1971.
d. $6,000 less in 1971.
e. None of the above.

10. On December 20, 1971 Howard Company purchased 300 shares of Charl Company stock at $10 each. On February 27, 1972 Howard received 300 rights entitling it to purchase at $12 per share one additional share of Charl for each 10 shares then held. On that date Charl stock was selling ex-rights at $14.75 and the rights were selling at $.25. Using the theoretically preferable method, a sale of the rights for $.25 each would give Howard a gain of
a. $75.
b. $25.
c. $12.50.
d. $0.
e. None of the above.

11. Dile Company discounted a $2,000, 60 day, 6% note receivable of Holden Company dated April 1, 1972 at its own bank. The note was discounted on April 21, 1972 at a bank discount rate of 7%. The proceeds of the note to Dile Company would be

    a. $2,020.
    b. $2,015.71.
    c. $2,006.67.
    d. $2,004.29.
    e. None of the above.

12. The Wise Corporation purchased a new machine on October 31, 1971. A $250 down payment was made and three monthly installments of $800 each are to be made beginning on November 30, 1971. The cash price would have been $2,500. Wise paid no installation charges under the monthly payment plan but a $50 installation charge would have been incurred with a cash purchase. The amount to be capitalized as the cost of the machine during 1971 would be

    a. $2,700.
    b. $2,650.
    c. $2,550.
    d. $1,850.
    e. None of the above.

13. The Park Company's account balances at December 31, 1971 for Accounts Receivable and the related Allowance for Uncollectible Accounts are $600,000 and $800, respectively. From an aging of accounts receivable, it is estimated that $8,100 of the December 31 receivables will be uncollectible. The net realizable value of accounts receivable would be

    a. $600,000.
    b. $599,200.
    c. $592,700.
    d. $591,900.
    e. None of the above.

14. The Doll Company estimates the cost of its physical inventory at March 31, 1972 for use in an interim financial statement. The rate of markup on cost is 25%. The following account balances are available:

Inventory, March 1, 1972	$160,000
Purchases during March	86,000
Purchase returns	4,000
Sales during March	140,000

The estimate of the cost of inventory at March 31 would be

    a. $137,000.
    b. $130,000.
    c. $112,000.
    d. $102,000.
    e. None of the above.

15. On January 1, 1971 Wayne Company's outstanding 6% serial bond issue had the following maturities: July 1, 1971, $10,000; July 1, 1972, $10,000; July 1, 1973, $10,000; July 1, 1974, $10,000. The bonds were issued at a premium which was correctly calculated at $2 per $1,000 bond per year. Assuming a calendar year accounting period, bonds payable should be recorded on the books on December 31, 1971 at

    a. $30,120.
    b. $30,090.
    c. $30,000.
    d. $29,010.
    e. None of the above.

16. Assume the same facts as in item 15. If the bonds that mature on July 1, 1973 were purchased in the open market and retired on April 1, 1972 for $10,150 including accrued interest since January 1, the transaction resulted in
    a. A gain of $25.
    b. No gain or loss.
    c. A loss of $125.
    d. A loss of $150.
    e. None of the above.

Problem XIV-3: Multiple choice questions on APB Opinions 15 *through* 19 *(50-60 min.)*

Instructions

Select the best answer for each of the following items relating to Opinions of the Accounting Principles Board. In determining your answer to each item consider the information given in the preceding lettered statement of facts or data. Mark only one answer for each item. Your grade will be determined from your total of correct answers.

Items to be Answered

A. The following problems relate to APB *Opinions No. 17* and *No. 18.* Assume that all investments were purchased after October 31, 1970, that the reporting periods begin after December 31, 1971 and that any amortization of goodwill is by the straight-line method for a 40-year period. Ignore income taxes.

17. On January 1, 1972 Investor Corporation purchased for $20,000 a 15% common stock interest in Investee Corporation whose total common stock equity had a fair and a book value of $100,000. The investment is accounted for by the cost method. If Investee's net income during 1972 is $30,000 and Investor receives dividends of $5,000 from Investee, for 1972 Investor Corporation should report income from this investment of
    a. $5,000.
    b. $4,875.
    c. $4,500.
    d. $4,375.
    e. None of the above or not determinable from the above facts.

18. Assume the same facts as in item 17 except that Investor Corporation pays $50,000 for a 40% common stock interest in Investee Corporation, accounts for the investment by the equity method and received $13,333 in dividends from Investee during 1972. For 1972 Investor Corporation should report as income from this investment the single amount of
    a. $13,333.
    b. $13,083.
    c. $12,000.
    d. $11,750.
    e. None of the above or not determinable from the above facts.

19. The investment described in item 18 should be reported as a long-term investment in Investor Corporation's balance sheet at December 31, 1972 as a single amount of
   a. $63,083.
   b. $50,000.
   c. $48,667.
   d. $48,417.
   e. None of the above or not determinable from the above facts.

20. Assume that Operating Corporation purchases a 10% common stock interest in Service Corporation for $10,000 on January 1, 1972 and an additional 20% interest for $22,000 on January 1, 1973. The balance sheets of Service Corporation, which pays no dividends, follow:

	December 31, 1973	December 31, 1972	January 1, 1972
Cash................	$130,000	$110,000	$100,000
Total assets	$130,000	$110,000	$100,000
Common stock	$100,000	$100,000	$100,000
Retained earnings	30,000	10,000	-0-
Total owners' equity	$130,000	$110,000	$100,000

During 1972 Operating Corporation carries this investment under the cost method and on January 1, 1973 adopts the equity method. For 1973 Operating Corporation should report as income from this 30% investment the single amount of
   a. $9,000.
   b. $7,000.
   c. $6,000.
   d. $5,950.
   e. None of the above or not determinable from the above facts.

21. The investment described in item 20 should be reported as a long-term investment in Operating Corporation's balance sheet at December 31, 1973 as a single amount of
   a. $41,000.
   b. $39,000.
   c. $38,000.
   d. $37,900.
   e. None of the above or not determinable from the above facts.

B. The following problems relate to APB *Opinion No. 19.* Your answers pertain to data to be reported in the Statement of Changes in Financial Position of Retail Establishment for the year ended December 31, 1971. Balance sheets and income statements for 1971 and 1970 follow on page 423.

Additional information available included the following:

Although Retail Establishment will report all changes in financial position, management has adopted a format emphasizing the flow of cash.

All accounts receivable and accounts payable relate to trade merchandise. Cash discounts are not allowed to customers but a service charge is added to an account for late payment. Accounts payable are recorded net and always are paid to take all of the discount allowed. The Allowance for

Doubtful Accounts at the end of 1971 was the same as at the end of 1970; no receivables were charged against the Allowance during 1971.

The proceeds from the note payable were used to finance a new store building. Capital stock was sold to provide additional working capital.

Retail Establishment, Inc.
BALANCE SHEETS

	December 31,	
	1971	1970
Assets		
Current assets:		
Cash	$ 150,000	$100,000
Marketable securities, ...	40,000	
Accounts receivable–net	420,000	290,000
Merchandise inventory	330,000	210,000
Prepaid expenses	50,000	25,000
	990,000	625,000
Land, buildings and fixtures	565,000	300,000
Less accumulated depreciation	55,000	25,000
	510,000	275,000
	$1,500,000	$900,000
Equities		
Current liabilities:		
Accounts payable	$ 265,000	$220,000
Accrued expenses	70,000	65,000
Dividends payable	35,000	
	370,000	285,000
Note payable–due 1974	250,000	
Stockholders' equity:		
Common stock	600,000	450,000
Retained earnings	280,000	165,000
	880,000	615,000
	$1,500,000	$900,000

Retail Establishment, Inc.
INCOME STATEMENTS

	Year Ended December 31,	
	1971	1970
Net sales–including service charges	$3,200,000	$2,000,000
Cost of goods sold	2,500,000	1,600,000
Gross profit	700,000	400,000
Expenses (including income taxes)	500,000	260,000
Net income	$ 200,000	$ 140,000

22. Cash collected during 1971 from accounts receivable amounted to
    a. $3,200,000.
    b. $3,070,000.
    c. $2,920,000.
    d. $2,780,000.
    e. None of the above or not determinable from the above facts.
23. Cash payments during 1971 on accounts payable to suppliers amounted to
    a. $2,575,000.
    b. $2,500,000.
    c. $2,455,000.
    d. $2,335,000.
    e. None of the above or not determinable from the above facts.
24. Cash dividend payments during 1971 amounted to
    a. $120,000.
    b. $115,000.
    c. $85,000.
    d. $35,000.
    e. None of the above or not determinable from the above facts.
25. Cash receipts during 1971 which were not provided by operations totaled
    a. $400,000.
    b. $250,000.
    c. $150,000.
    d. $70,000.
    e. None of the above or not determinable from the above facts.
26. Cash payments for assets during 1971 which were not reflected in operations totaled
    a. $305,000.
    b. $265,000.
    c. $185,000.
    d. $40,000.
    e. None of the above or not determinable from the above facts.

C. The following problems relate to APB *Opinion No. 16.* Assume that all business combinations were initiated after October 31, 1970 and that all transactions occurred after that date.

27. Chun Corporation issued voting common stock in exchange for 90% of the outstanding voting common stock of Key Company. The combination was accounted for by the pooling-of-interests method. If Chun later issued voting common stock, which had a fair value of $100,000 and a par value of $1,000, for the remaining 10% of the Key common stock which had a stated value of $5,000; Chun Corporation's consolidated assets would increase
    a. $100,000.
    b. $5,000.
    c. $1,000.
    d. $0.
    e. None of the above or not determinable from the above facts.
28. Dan Corporation offered to exchange two shares of Dan common stock for each share of Boone Company common stock. On the initiation date Dan held 3,000 shares of Boone common and Boone held 500 shares of Dan common. In later cash transactions Dan purchased 2,000 shares of Boone

common and Boone purchased 2,500 shares of Dan common. At all times the number of common shares outstanding was 1,000,000 for Dan and 100,000 for Boone. After consummation Dan held 100,000 Boone common shares. The number of shares considered exchanged in determining whether this combination should be accounted for by the pooling-of-interests method is

    a. 190,000.
    b. 95,000.
    c. 93,500.
    d. 89,000.
    e. None of the above or not determinable from the above facts.

29. Fast Corporation paid $50,000 cash for the net assets of Agge Company, which consisted of the following:

	Book Value	Fair Value
Current assets	$10,000	$14,000
Plant and equipment	40,000	55,000
Liabilities assumed	(10,000)	(9,000)
	$40,000	$60,000

The plant and equipment acquired in this business combination should be recorded at

    a. $55,000.
    b. $50,000.
    c. $45,833.
    d. $40,000.
    e. None of the above or not determinable from the above facts.

D. The following problems relate to APB *Opinion No. 15.* Assume that all securities were issued after May 31, 1969.

30. The net proceeds from an issue of 1,000, ten-year, $1,000, 5% subordinated junior convertible debenture bonds were $960,000 after deducting underwriting fees of $50,000. Other issue costs were $20,000. Each debenture is convertible into 20 shares of common stock until the maturity date. The yield rate for determining whether these debentures are common stock equivalents at issuance is

    a. 5.32%.
    b. 5.21%.
    c. 5%.
    d. 4.95%.
    e. None of the above or not determinable from the above facts.

31. A warrant may be exercised to purchase two shares of common stock by paying $100 cash or by tendering a $100 face value debenture of the issuer. Market prices are $45 per common share, $80 per debenture and $12 per warrant. This warrant has an effective exercise price per share of obtainable common stock of

    a. $50.
    b. $45.
    c. $40.
    d. $12.
    e. None of the above or not determinable from the above facts.

32. Warrants exercisable at $20 each to obtain 10,000 shares of common stock were outstanding during a period when the average market price of the common stock was $25 and the ending market price was $24. Application of the treasury stock method for the assumed exercise of these warrants in computing fully diluted earnings per share will increase the weighted average number of outstanding common shares by

    a. 10,000.
    b. 8,333.
    c. 8,000.
    d. 1,667.
    e. None of the above or not determinable from the above facts.

33. Five thousand shares of $100 par value Series E Preferred Stock were issued at par in a business combination. Registration and issue costs totaled $10,000. Each Series E share is convertible into one share of common stock for 10 years and is entitled to a cumulative annual dividend of $5 for 3 years and $3 thereafter. The yield rate for determining whether the Series E shares are common stock equivalents at issuance is

    a. 5.1%.
    b. 5%.
    d. 3.06%.
    d. 3%.
    e. None of the above or not determinable from the above facts.

Problem XIV-4: Multiple choice questions on a variety of financial problems (40-50 min.)

Instructions

Select the best answer for each of the following items which relate to a variety of financial accounting problems. Mark only one answer for each item. Your grade will be determined from your total of correct answers.

Items to be Answered

1. During 1970 Larry Company, which uses the allowance method of accounting for uncollectible accounts, had charges to Doubtful Accounts Expense of $80,000 and wrote off as uncollectible accounts receivable of $55,000. These transactions decreased working capital by

    a. $80,000.
    b. $55,000.
    c. $25,000.
    d. $0.
    e. None of the above.

2. Lay Corporation, which has a calendar year accounting period, purchased a new machine for $10,000 on April 1, 1965. At that time Lay expected to use the machine for nine years and then sell it for $1,000. The machine was sold for $6,000 on September 30, 1970. Assuming straight-line depreciation, no depreciation in the year of acquisition, and a full year of depreciation in the year of retirement, the gain to be recognized at the time of sale would be

    a. $1,000.
    b. $500.
    c. $445.
    d. $0.
    e. None of the above.

3. An old machine with a book value of $8,000 was traded in on a new machine. The new machine, which had a list price of $90,000, was purchased for $68,000 cash plus the old machine even though the old machine had a market value of $18,000 at the time that it was traded in. If the theoretically preferable method of accounting for trade-ins is used, the cost of the new machine would be

    a. $90,000.
    b. $86,000.
    c. $76,000.
    d. $68,000.
    e. None of the above.

4. Assume the same facts as in item 3. If the income tax method of accounting for trade-ins is used, the purchaser would record a

    a. $16,000 gain.
    b. $4,000 gain.
    c. No gain or loss.
    d. $10,000 loss.
    e. None of the above.

5. The Vandiver Corporation provides an incentive compensation plan under which its president receives a bonus equal to 10% of the Corporation's income in excess of $100,000 before income tax but after the bonus. If income before income tax and bonus is $320,000 and the effective tax rate is 40%, the amount of the bonus would be

    a. $32,000.
    b. $30,000.
    c. $22,000.
    d. $20,000.
    e. None of the above.

6. Donna Corporation had 900,000 common shares outstanding on January 1, issued 600,000 shares on May 1 and had income applicable to common stock of $2,600,000 for the year ending December 31, 1970. Earnings per share of common stock for 1970 would be

    a. $2.89.
    b. $2.00.
    c. $1.80.
    d. $1.73.
    e. None of the above.

7. On July 1, 1971, an interest payment date, $10,000 of Cap Company bonds were converted into 200 shares of Cap Company common stock each having a par value of $40 and a market value of $55. There is $400 unamortized discount on the bonds. Under the method using book value Cap would record

    a. A $1,400 gain.
    b. A $1,000 gain.
    c. No gain or loss.
    d. A $1,600 loss.
    e. None of the above.

8. The directors of Roof Corporation, whose $80 par value common stock is currently selling at $100 per share, have decided to issue a stock dividend. Roof has an authorization for 400,000 shares of common, has issued 220,000 shares of which 20,000 shares are now held as treasury stock, and desires to capitalize $1,600,000 of the Retained Earnings account balance. To accomplish this, the directors should declare a stock dividend of

    a. 10%.
    b. 5%.
    c. 4%.
    d. 2%.
    e. None of the above.

9. The total of the partners' capital accounts was $105,000 before recognition of partnership goodwill in preparation for the withdrawal of a partner whose profit and loss sharing ratio is 1/5. He was paid $37,000 by the firm in final settlement for his interest. The remaining partners' capital accounts excluding their share of the goodwill totaled $80,000 after his withdrawal. The total agreed upon goodwill of the firm was

    a. $125,000.
    b. $80,000.
    c. $70,000.
    d. $60,000.
    e. None of the above.

10. On June 30, 1971, when the Perry Company's stock was selling at $40 per share, its capital accounts were as follows:

Capital stock (par value $25; 50,000 shares issued)	$1,250,000
Premium on capital stock	600,000
Retained earnings	3,550,000

If a 100% stock dividend were declared and the par value per share remained at $25, Capital Stock would be

    a. $3,250,000.
    b. $2,500,000.
    c. $1,250,000.
    d. $625,000.
    e. None of the above.

11. On January 1, 1965 Steven Company issued the following 6% serial bonds:

Maturity Date	Face Amount
July 1, 1970	$10,000
July 1, 1971	10,000
July 1, 1972	10,000
July 1, 1973	10,000

The bonds were issued at a premium which was correctly calculated at $2 per $1,000 bond per year. During 1969 the bond transactions decreased net working capital by

    a. $12,480.
    b. $12,100.
    c. $2,400.
    d. $2,320.
    e. None of the above.

12. Assume the same facts as in item 11. The interest expense for calendar year 1970 would be
   a. $2,180.
   b. $2,170.
   c. $2,100.
   d. $2,030.
   e. None of the above.

13. Four separate carriers have written fire insurance policies totaling $160,000 on a single property valued at $200,000. The fraction of a partial loss of $40,000 that will be collectible from a carrier whose $60,000 policy contains a 90% coinsurance clause would be
   a. 9/10.
   b. 4/5.
   c. 2/3.
   d. 1/5.
   e. None of the above.

14. On June 1, 1971 Miles Company purchased 100 shares of Zeno Corporation stock at $45 per share. Brokerage fees amounted to $26. A $3 dividend on Zeno stock had been declared on May 25, 1971 to be paid on June 18, 1971 to holders of record on June 8, 1971. On June 30, 1971 the balance in the Investment in Zeno Corporation account would be
   a. $4,526.
   b. $4,500.
   c. $4,226.
   d. $4,200.
   e. None of the above.

15. Hillside Corporation has 80,000 shares of $50 par value common stock authorized, issued and outstanding. All 80,000 shares were issued at $55 each. Retained earnings of the Company are $160,000. If 1,000 shares of Hillside common were reacquired at $62 and the retirement (par value) method of accounting for treasury stock were used, capital stock would decrease by
   a. $62,000.
   b. $55,000.
   c. $50,000.
   d. $0.
   e. None of the above.

Problem XIV-5: Multiple choice questions on price-level accounting (40-50 min.)

Instructions

Select the best answer for each of the following items which relate to price-level accounting. Mark only one answer for each item. Your grade will be determined from your total of correct answers.

Items to be Answered

16. The valuation basis used in conventional financial statements is
   a. Market value.
   b. Original cost.
   c. Replacement cost.
   d. A mixture of costs and values.
   e. None of the above.

17. An unacceptable practice for presenting general price-level information is
   a. The inclusion of general price-level gains and losses on monetary items in the general price-level statement of income.
   b. The inclusion of extraordinary gains and losses in the general price-level statement of income.
   c. The use of charts, ratios and narrative information.
   d. The use of specific price indexes to restate inventories, plant and equipment.
   e. None of the above.

18. When general price-level balance sheets are prepared, they should be presented in terms of
   a. The general purchasing power of the dollar at the latest balance sheet date.
   b. The general purchasing power of the dollar in the base period.
   c. The average general purchasing power of the dollar for the latest fiscal period.
   d. The general purchasing power of the dollar at the time the financial statements are issued.
   e. None of the above.

19. The restatement of historical-dollar financial statements to reflect general price-level changes results in presenting assets at
   a. Lower of cost or market values.
   b. Current appraisal values.
   c. Costs adjusted for purchasing power changes.
   d. Current replacement cost.
   e. None of the above.

20. During a period of deflation an entity would have the greatest gain in general purchasing power by holding
   a. Cash.
   b. Plant and equipment.
   c. Accounts payable.
   d. Mortgages payable.
   e. None of the above.

21. When preparing general price-level financial statements, it would not be appropriate to use
   a. Cost or market, whichever is lower, in the valuation of inventories.
   b. Replacement cost in the valuation of plant assets.
   c. The historical cost basis in reporting income tax expense.
   d. The actual amounts payable in reporting liabilities on the balance sheet.
   e. Any of the above.

22. For comparison purposes general price-level financial statements of earlier periods should be restated to the general purchasing power dollars of
   a. The beginning of the base period.
   b. An average for the current period.
   c. The beginning of the current period.
   d. The end of the current period.
   e. None of the above.

23. In preparing price-level financial statements, monetary items consist of
   a. Cash items plus all receivables with a fixed maturity date.
   b. Cash, other assets expected to be converted into cash and current liabilities.

c. Assets and liabilities whose amounts are fixed by contract or otherwise in terms of dollars regardless of price-level changes.
d. Assets and liabilities which are classified as current on the balance sheet.
e. None of the above.

24. In preparing price-level financial statements a nonmonetary item would be
a. Accounts payable in cash.
b. Long-term bonds payable.
c. Accounts receivable.
d. Allowance for uncollectible accounts.
e. None of the above.

25. Gains and losses on nonmonetary assets usually are reported in historical-dollar financial statements when the items are sold. Gains and losses on the sale of nonmonetary assets should be reported in general price-level financial statements
a. In the same period, but the amount will probably differ.
b. In the same period and the same amount.
c. Over the life of the nonmonetary asset.
d. Partly over the life of the nonmonetary asset and the remainder when the asset is sold.
e. None of the above.

26. If land were purchased in 1961 for $100,000 when the general price-level index was 100 and sold at the end of 1970 for $160,000 when the index was 170, the general price-level statement of income for 1970 would show
a. A general price-level gain of $70,000 and a loss on sale of land of $10,000.
b. A gain on sale of land of $60,000.
c. A general price-level loss of $10,000.
d. A loss on sale of land of $10,000.
e. None of the above.

27. If land were purchased at a cost of $20,000 in January 1964 when the general price-level index was 120 and sold in December 1970 when the index was 150, the selling price that would result in no gain or loss would be
a. $30,000.
b. $24,000.
c. $20,000.
d. $16,000.
e. None of the above.

28. If the base year is 1958 (when the price index = 100) and land is purchased for $50,000 in 1964 when the general price index is 108.5, the cost of the land restated to 1958 general purchasing power (rounded to the nearest whole dollar) would be
a. $54,250.
b. $50,000.
c. $46,083.
d. $45,750.
e. None of the above.

29. Assume the same facts as in item 28. The cost of the land restated to December 31, 1970 general purchasing power when the price index was 119.2 (rounded to the nearest whole dollar) would be

    a. $59,600.
    b. $54,931.
    c. $46,083.
    d. $45,512.
    e. None of the above.

The following information is applicable to items 30 through 33:

Equipment purchased for $120,000 on January 1, Year 1 when the price index was 100, was sold on December 31, Year 3 at a price of $85,000. The equipment originally was expected to last six years with no salvage value and was depreciated on a straight-line basis. The price index at the end of Year 1 was 125, at Year 2 was 150 and at Year 3 was 175.

30. The general price-level financial statements prepared at the end of the Year 1 would include
    a. Equipment of $150,000, accumulated depreciation of $25,000 and a gain of $30,000.
    b. Equipment of $150,000, accumulated depreciation of $25,000 and no gain of loss.
    c. Equipment of $150,000, accumulated depreciation of $20,000 and a gain of $30,000.
    d. Equipment of $120,000, accumulated depreciation of $20,000 and a gain of $30,000.
    e. None of the above.

31. In general price-level comparative financial statements prepared at the end of Year 2, the Year 1 financial statements should show equipment (net of accumulated depreciation) at
    a. $150,000.
    b. $125,000.
    c. $100,000.
    d. $80,000.
    e. None of the above.

32. The general price-level financial statements prepared at the end of Year 2 should include depreciation expense of
    a. $35,000.
    b. $30,000.
    c. $25,000.
    d. $20,000.
    e. None of the above.

33. The general price-level income statement prepared at the end of Year 3 should include
    a. A gain of $35,000.
    b. A gain of $25,000.
    c. No gain or loss.
    d. A loss of $5,000.
    e. None of the above.

Problem XIV-6: Multiple choice questions on statement of changes in financial position, business combinations, and compound interest (40-50 min.)

Instructions

Select the best answer choice for each of the following items which relate to a variety of financial accounting problems. In determining your answer to each item consider the information given in the preceding lettered statement of facts or data. Mark only one answer for each item. Your grade will be determined from your total of correct answers.

Items to be Answered

A. The following are statements of the Leathers Company:

Leathers Company
BALANCE SHEET
January 1, 1970

Assets

Current assets	$35,000
Buildings and equipment	48,000
Accumulated depreciation—buildings and equipment	(15,000)
Patents	5,000
	$73,000

Equities

Current liabilities	$ 9,000
Capital stock	27,000
Retained earnings	37,000
	$73,000

Leathers Company
STATEMENT OF SOURCE AND APPLICATION
OF FUNDS (ALL FINANCIAL RESOURCES)
For 1970

Working capital, January 1, 1970		$26,000
Funds provided:		
Operations:		
Net income	$24,000	
Gain on sale—buildings	(4,000)	
Depreciation—buildings and equipment	10,000	
Amortization—patents	1,000	31,000
Issue of capital stock		13,000
Sale of buildings		7,000
		$77,000
Funds applied:		
Dividends	$12,000	
Purchase of land	14,000	
Purchase of buildings and equipment	30,000	56,000
Working capital, December 31, 1970		$21,000

Total assets on the Balance Sheet at December 31, 1970 are $105,000. Accumulated depreciation on the building sold was $6,000.

1. When the building was sold, the Buildings and Equipment account received a credit of
   a. $17,000.
   b. $13,000.
   c. $10,000.
   d. $9,000.
   e. None of the above or not determinable from the above facts.

2. The book value of the buildings and equipment at December 31, 1970 was
   a. $65,000.
   b. $59,000.
   c. $53,000.
   d. $40,000.
   e. None of the above or not determinable from the above facts.
3. The current liabilities at December 31, 1970 were
   a. $31,000.
   b. $21,000.
   c. $19,000.
   d. $16,000.
   e. None of the above or not determinable from the above facts.
4. The balance in the Retained Earnings account at December 31, 1970 was
   a. $53,000.
   b. $49,000.
   c. $42,000.
   d. $38,000.
   e. None of the above or not determinable from the above facts.
5. Capital stock (plus capital in excess of par or stated value) at December 31, 1970 was
   a. $40,000.
   b. $37,000.
   c. $27,000.
   d. $14,000.
   e. None of the above or not determinable from the above facts.

B. The following balance sheets as of the current date are for Parent Company and its subsidiary:

Assets	*Parent*	*Consolidated*
Current assets	$218,000	$363,000
Plant	93,000	161,000
Investment in subsidiary	145,000	–
Goodwill	–	(7,000)
	$456,000	$517,000
Equities		
Current liabilities	$ 83,000	$150,000
Minority interest	–	29,200
Capital stock	320,000	320,000
Retained earnings	53,000	17,800
	$456,000	$517,000

Additional information: Parent uses the cost (legal-basis) method of accounting for its investment in 80% of the capital stock of the subsidiary.

6. The stockholders' equity of the subsidiary at the time Parent purchased its interest was
   a. $190,000.
   b. $172,500.
   c. $159,000.
   d. $152,000.
   e. None of the above or not determinable from the above facts.

7. The balance in the Capital Stock account of the subsidiary at the time Parent purchased its interest was

    a. $150,000.

    b. $125,000.

    c. $100,000.

    d. $75,000.

    e. None of the above or not determinable from the above facts.

8. The current stockholders' equity of the subsidiary is

    a. $173,000.

    b. $159,000.

    c. $152,000.

    d. $146,000.

    e. None of the above or not determinable from the above facts.

9. The current balance in the Retained Earnings account of the subsidiary is

    a. $152,000.

    b. $150,000.

    c. $146,000.

    d. $70,800.

    e. None of the above or not determinable from the above facts.

10. The current working capital of the subsidiary is

    a. $145,000.

    b. $125,000.

    c. $78,000.

    d. $67,000.

    e. None of the above or not determinable from the above facts.

C. The following symbols relate to compound interest formulas:

$_nP_i$ = The present value of an annuity of n payments of $1 each at interest rate i per period.

$_nP_i$ = The present value of $1 for n periods at interest rate i per period.

$_nA_i$ = The future value of an annuity of n payments of $1 each at interest rate i per period.

$_na_i$ = The future value of $1 for n periods at interest rate i per period.

R = A periodic cash payment (or receipt).

11. If one wishes to earn interest at an annual rate of 6% compounded quarterly on an investment that promises to pay the lump sum of $1,000 at the end of 6 years, the formula that could be used to compute the amount that should be paid now is

    a. $1,000($_{24}A_{.015}$).

    b. $1,000($_{24}a_{.015}$).

    c. $1,000($_{24}P_{.015}$).

    d. $1,000($_{24}p_{.015}$).

    e. None of the above.

12. If one wishes to earn interest at the annual rate of 4% compounded semiannually on an investment contract that promises to pay $1,000 at the end of 20 years along with semiannual interest payments of $25 (computed at an annual interest rate of 5% on the maturity amount), the formula that could be used to compute the amount that should be paid now is

    a. $1,000($_{20}P_{.04}$) + $50($_{20}P_{.04}$).

    b. $1,000($_{40}P_{.02}$) + $25($_{40}P_{.02}$).

    c. $1,000($_{20}P_{.05}$) + $50($_{20}P_{.05}$).

    d. $1,000($_{40}P_{.025}$) + $25($_{40}P_{.025}$).

    e. None of the above.

13. On May 1, 1971 one wishes to know the amount of the equal payments that must be made semiannually beginning on November 1, 1971 to have a fund of $10,000 at the end of 20 years. If one is certain that the fund will earn interest at the annual rate of 6% compounded semiannually, a formula that could be used to compute the periodic payment is

    a. $\$10,000 = R(_{40}A_{.03})$.
    b. $\$10,000 = R(_{20}A_{.06})$.
    c. $\$10,000 = R(_{40}P_{.03})$.
    d. $\$10,000 = R(_{20}P_{.06})$.
    e. None of the above.

14. On May 1, 1971 a new car was purchased on a 4-year installment contract which required payments of $100 now and $100 on the first day of each month with the last payment due on April 1, 1975. If the annual interest rate is 6% compounded monthly, the formula that could be used to compute the apparent cash price for the car is

    a. $\$1,200(_4P_{.06})$.
    b. $\$100(_{47}P_{.005}) + \$100$.
    c. $\$100(_{48}P_{.005})$.
    d. $\$100(_{47}P_{.005}) + \$100$.
    e. None of the above.

D. The Aim Company, a farm corporation, produced the following in its first year of operations:

	Selling Price Per Bushel
9,000 bushels of wheat	$2.40
6,000 bushels of oats	1.40

During the year it sold two thirds of the grain produced and collected three fourths of the selling price on the grain sold: the balance is to be collected in equal amounts during each of the two following years.

Additional data for the first year:

Wealth at beginning of year 1	$100,000
Wealth at end of year 1	115,000
Depreciation on productive plant and equipment	3,000
Other production costs (cash)	4,500
Miscellaneous administrative costs (cash)	3,600
Grain storage costs	–0–
Selling and delivery costs (incurred and paid at the time of sale)–per bushel	.10
Additional stockholder investments during year 1	–0–
Dividends paid to stockholders during year 1	10,000
Income taxes	–0–

The Aim Company is enthusiastic about the accountant's concept of matching costs and revenues; it wishes to carry the idea to the extreme and to match with revenues not only all direct costs but also all indirect costs such as those for administration.

15. If revenues were recognized when production is complete (i.e., inventory is carried at net selling price), income computed in accordance with the Company's matching objective for the first year would be
   a. $21,600.
   b. $17,900.
   c. $17,400.
   d. $7,400.
   e. None of the above.

16. If revenue were recognized on the sales basis, income computed in accordance with the Company's matching objective for the first year would be
   a. $10,400.
   b. $9,900.
   c. $9,400.
   d. $7,400.
   e. None of the above.

17. If revenue were recognized on the cash-collection basis, income computed in accordance with the Company's matching objective for the first year would be
   a. $8,700.
   b. $6,300.
   c. $4,400.
   d. $2,900.
   e. None of the above.

18. Recently the Company's president was introduced to a noted British economist who convinced him that the accountant's accrual approach to measuring income in fact was merely a partial accrual and that full accrual would require consideration of changes in "wealth" which was defined as "the present value of expected net future receipts." Following this it was suggested that a full accrual income for a period would be determined to be the amount that could be spent during a period while leaving wealth unchanged. Income measured in this way for the first year would be
   a. $30,000.
   b. $25,000.
   c. $20,000.
   d. $15,000.
   e. None of the above.

Problem XIV-7: Multiple choice questions on budgeting, manufacturing, compound interest, and breakeven analysis (40-50 min.)

Instructions

Select the best answer choice for each of the following items which relate to a variety of managerial accounting problems. In determining your answer to each item consider the information given in the preceding lettered statement of facts. Mark only one answer for each item. Your grade will be determined from your total of correct answers.

Items to be Answered

A. The Zel Company, a wholesaler, budgeted the following sales for the indicated months:

	June 1971	*July 1971*	*August 1971*
Sales on account	$1,500,000	$1,600,000	$1,700,000
Cash sales	200,000	210,000	220,000
Total sales	$1,700,000	$1,810,000	$1,920,000

All merchandise is marked up to sell at its invoice cost plus 25%. Merchandise inventories at the beginning of each month are at 30% of that month's projected cost of goods sold.

16. The cost of goods sold for the month of June 1971 is anticipated to be
  a. $1,530,000.
  b. $1,402,500.
  c. $1,275,000.
  d. $1,190,000.
  e. None of the above.

17. Merchandise purchases for July 1971 are anticipated to be
  a. $1,605,500.
  b. $1,474,400.
  c. $1,448,000.
  d. $1,382,250.
  e. None of the above.

B. The following annual flexible budget has been prepared for use in making decisions relating to product X.

	100,000 Units	*150,000 Units*	*200,000 Units*
Sales volume	$800,000	$1,200,000	$1,600,000
Manufacturing costs:			
Variable	300,000	450,000	600,000
Fixed	200,000	200,000	200,000
	500,000	650,000	800,000
Selling and other expenses:			
Variable	200,000	300,000	400,000
Fixed	160,000	160,000	160,000
	360,000	460,000	560,000
Income (or loss)	$(60,000)	$ 90,000	$ 240,000

The 200,000 unit budget has been adopted and will be used for allocating fixed manufacturing costs to units of product X; at the end of the first six months the following information is available:

	Units
Production completed	120,000
Sales	60,000

All fixed costs are budgeted and incurred uniformly throughout the year and all costs incurred coincide with the budget.

Over- and under-applied fixed manufacturing costs are deferred until year-end. Annual sales have the following seasonal pattern:

	Portion of Annual Sales
First quarter	10%
Second quarter	20
Third quarter	30
Fourth quarter	40
	100%

18. The amount of fixed factory costs applied to product during the first six months under absorption costing would be
   a. Overapplied by $20,000.
   b. Equal to the fixed costs incurred.
   c. Underapplied by $40,000.
   d. Underapplied by $80,000.
   e. None of the above.

19. Reported net income (or loss) for the first six months under absorption costing would be
   a. $160,000.
   b. $80,000.
   c. $40,000.
   d. ($40,000).
   e. None of the above.

20. Reported net income (or loss) for the first six months under direct costing would be
   a. $144,000.
   b. $72,000.
   c. $0.
   d. ($36,000).
   e. None of the above.

21. Assuming that 90,000 units of product X were sold during the first six months and that this is to be used as a basis, the revised budget estimate for the total number of units to be sold during this year would be
   a. 360,000.
   b. 240,000.
   c. 200,000.
   d. 120,000.
   e. None of the above.

C. The following inventory data relate to the Shirley Company:

	Inventories	
	Ending	Beginning
Finished goods	$95,000	$110,000
Work in process	80,000	70,000
Direct materials	95,000	90,000

Costs Incurred During the Period

Cost of goods available for sale	$684,000
Total manufacturing costs	654,000
Factory overhead	167,000
Direct materials used	193,000

22. Direct materials purchased during the year were
  a. $213,000.
  b. $198,000.
  c. $193,000.
  d. $188,000.
  e. None of the above or not determinable from the above facts.
23. Direct labor costs incurred during the period were
  a. $250,000.
  b. $234,000.
  c. $230,000.
  d. $224,000.
  e. None of the above or not determinable from the above facts.
24. The cost of goods sold during the period was
  a. $614,000.
  b. $604,000.
  c. $594,000.
  d. $589,000.
  e. None of the above or not determinable from the above facts.

D. Madisons, Inc. has decided to acquire a new piece of equipment. It may do so by an outright cash purchase at $25,000 or by a leasing alternative of $6,000 per year for the life of the machine. Other relevant information follows:

Purchase price due at time of purchase	$25,000
Estimated useful life	5 years
Estimated salvage value if purchased	$ 3,000
Annual cost of maintenance contract to be acquired with either lease or purchase	$ 500

The full purchase price of $25,000 could be borrowed from the bank at 10% annual interest and could be repaid in one payment at the end of the fifth year. Additional information:

Assume a 40% income tax rate and use of the straight-line method of depreciation.
The yearly lease rental and maintenance contract fees would be paid at the beginning of each year.
The minimum desired rate of return on investment is 10%.
All cash flows, unless otherwise stated, are assumed to occur at the end of the year.

Selected present value factors for a 10% return are given below:

Year	Present Value of $1 Received at End of Year
0	1.000
1	.909
2	.826
3	.751
4	.683
5	.621

25. The present value of the purchase price of the machine is
   a. $25,000.
   b. $22,725.
   c. $22,500.
   d. $2,500.
   e. None of the above.
26. Under the purchase alternative the present value of the estimated salvage value is
   a. $3,000.
   b. $2,049.
   c. $1,863.
   d. $0.
   e. None of the above.
27. Under the purchase alternative the annual cash inflow (tax reduction) related to depreciation is
   a. $5,000.
   b. $4,400.
   c. $2,640.
   d. $1,760.
   e. None of the above.
28. Under the purchase alternative the annual after-tax cash outflow for interest and maintenance would be
   a. $3,000.
   b. $2,500.
   c. $1,800.
   d. $1,200.
   e. None of the above.
29. If salvage value is not ignored, the before-tax interest rate implicit in the lease contract is
   a. 20% or more.
   b. More than 10% but less than 20%.
   c. Precisely 10%.
   d. Less than 10%.
   e. Not determinable from the above facts.

E. Carey Company sold 100,000 units of its product at $20 per unit. Variable costs are $14 per unit (manufacturing costs of $11 and selling costs of $3). Fixed costs are incurred uniformly throughout the year and amount to $792,000 (manufacturing costs of $500,000 and selling costs of $292,000). There are no beginning or ending inventories.

30. The breakeven point for this product is
   a. $3,640,000 or 182,000 units.
   b. $2,600,000 or 130,000 units.
   c. $1,800,000 or 90,000 units.
   d. $1,760,000 or 88,000 units.
   e. None of the above.
31. The number of units that must be sold to earn a net income of $60,000 for the year before income taxes would be
   a. 142,000.
   b. 132,000.
   c. 100,000.
   d. 88,000.
   e. None of the above.

32. If the income tax rate is 40%, the number of units that must be sold to earn an after-tax income of $90,000 would be
   a. 169,500.
   b. 157,000.
   c. 144,500.
   d. 104,777.
   e. None of the above.

33. If labor costs are 50% of variable costs and 20% of fixed costs, a 10% increase in wages and salaries would increase the number of units required to break even (in fraction form) to
   a. 807,840/5.3.
   b. 831,600/5.78.
   c. 807,840/14.7.
   d. 831,600/14.28.
   e. None of the above.

Problem XIV-8: Multiple choice questions on partnerships, retail inventory, price-volume analysis, and business combinations (50-60 min.)

Instructions

Select the best answer choice for each of the following items which relate to a variety of financial accounting problems. In determining your answer to each item consider the information given in the lettered statement of facts preceding each group of items. Unless you are told otherwise you should assume that each item is independent of the preceding item(s) in the group. Select only one answer for each item. Your grade will be determined from your total of correct answers.

Items to be Answered

A. The following balance sheet is for the partnership of Able, Boyer and Cain:

Cash	$ 20,000	Liabilities	$ 50,000
Other assets	180,000	Able, Capital (40%)	37,000
		Boyer, Capital (40%)	65,000
		Cain, Capital (20%)	48,000
	$200,000		$200,000

Figures shown parenthetically reflect agreed profit and loss sharing percentages.

1. If the assets are fairly valued on the above balance sheet and the partnership wishes to admit Day as a new 1/6 partner without recording goodwill or bonus, Day should contribute cash or other assets of
   a. $40,000.
   b. $36,000.
   c. $33,333.
   d. $30,000.

2. If assets on the initial balance sheet are fairly valued, Able and Boyer consent and Day pays Cain $51,000 for his interest; the revised capital balances of the partners would be
   a. Able,$38,500; Boyer, $66,500; Day, $51,000.
   b. Able, $38,500; Boyer, $66,500; Day, $48,000.
   c. Able, $37,000; Boyer, $65,000; Day, $51,000.
   d. Able, $37,000; Boyer, $65,000; Day, $48,000.
3. If the firm, as shown on the original balance sheet, is dissolved and liquidated by selling assets in installments, the first sale of noncash assets having a book value of $90,000 realizes $50,000 and all cash available after settlement with creditors is distributed; the respective partners would receive (to the nearest dollar)
   a. Able, $8,000; Boyer, $8,000; Cain, $4,000.
   b. Able, $6,667; Boyer, $6,667; Cain, $6,666.
   c. Able, $0; Boyer, $13,333; Cain, $6,667.
   d. Able, $0; Boyer, $3,000; Cain, $17,000.
4. If the facts are as in item 3 above except that $3,000 cash is to be withheld, the respective partners would then receive (to the nearest dollar)
   a. Able, $6,800; Boyer, $6,800; Cain, $3,400.
   b. Able, $5,667; Boyer, $5,667; Cain, $5,666.
   c. Able, $0; Boyer, $11,333; Cain, $5,667.
   d. Able, $0; Boyer, $1,000; Cain, $16,000.
5. If each partner properly received some cash in the distribution after the second sale, the cash to be distributed amounts to $12,000 from the third sale and unsold assets with an $8,000 book value remain; ignoring items 3 and 4 above, the respective partners would receive
   a. Able, $4,800; Boyer, $4,800; Cain, $2,400.
   b. Able, $4,000; Boyer, $4,000; Cain, $4,000.
   c. Able, 37/150 of $12,000; Boyer, 65/150 of $12,000; Cain, 48/150 of $12,000.
   d. Able, $0; Boyer, $8,000; Cain, $4,000.

B. The following data concerning the retail inventory method are taken from the financial records of the Bandit Company.

	Cost	Retail
Beginning inventory	$18,600	$ 30,000
Purchases	91,000	154,000
Freight in	1,400	–
Net markups	–	1,000
Net markdowns	–	1,740
Sales	–	156,760

6. The ending inventory at retail should be
   a. $28,240.
   b. $27,980.
   c. $27,240.
   d. $26,500.
7. If the ending inventory is to be valued at approximately the lower of cost or market, the calculation of the cost to retail ratio should be based on goods available for sale at (1) cost and (2) retail respectively of

  a. $111,000 and $186,740.
  b. $111,000 and $185,000.
  c. $111,000 and $182,260.
  d. $109,600 and $184,000.

8. If the ending inventory for the current period at cost amounts to $15,900, it appears that the rate of mark-on for the current period as compared to that for the preceding period was

  a. The same.
  b. Higher than before.
  c. Lower than before.
  d. Indeterminate.

9. If the foregoing figures are verified and a count of the ending inventory reveals that merchandise actually on hand amounts to $25,000 at retail, ignoring tax consequences the business has

  a. Realized a windfall gain of approximately $1,500.
  b. Sustained a loss in terms of cost of approximately $900.
  c. Sustained a loss in terms of cost of approximately $1,500.
  d. No gain or loss as there is close coincidence of the inventories.

10. If the LIFO inventory method were used in conjunction with the data, the ending inventory at cost would be

  a. $16,430.
  b. $16,060.
  c. $15,980.
  d. $15,900.

11. Assuming that the LIFO inventory method were used in conjunction with the data and that the inventory at retail had increased during the period, then the computation of retail in the cost to retail ratio would

  a. Exclude both markups and markdowns and include beginning inventory.
  b. Include markups and exclude both markdowns and beginning inventory.
  c. Include both markups and markdowns and exclude beginning inventory.
  d. Exclude markups and include both markdowns and beginning inventory.

C. The following gross margin data are taken from the financial records of the Green Company:

	Last Period	This Period
Sales	$300,000	$296,400
Cost of goods sold	200,000	203,300
Gross margin	$100,000	$ 93,100

12. If it is known that volume declined 5% from the preceding period, then it is evident that selling prices

  a. Increased 7%.
  b. Increased 4%.
  c. Increased 3.8%.
  d. Decreased 3.6%.

13. If it is known that volume declined 5% from the preceding period, then it is evident that cost prices
   a. Increased 7%.
   b. Increased 6.5%.
   c. Increased 1.65%.
   d. Decreased 3.6%.

14. Suppose volume increased 1.65% from the preceding period, then it is evident that cost prices
   a. Did not change.
   b. Declined 3.6%.
   c. Declined 5%.
   d. Declined 7%.

15. If the change in sales is partially accounted for by a 4% increase in selling prices, the amount of change in gross margin due to this single factor would be
   a. $15,600.
   b. $12,000.
   c. $11,400.
   d. $6,900.

16. If the change in cost of goods sold is partially accounted for by a 7% increase in cost prices, the amount of change in gross margin due to this single factor would be
   a. $14,000.
   b. $13,300.
   c. $6,900.
   d. $3,600.

D. The summarized balance sheets of Sweets Candy Company and Honey Wrapper Company as of December 31, 1968 are as follows:

(a)

Sweets Candy Company
BALANCE SHEET
December 31, 1968

Assets	$600,000
Liabilities	$150,000
Capital stock	300,000
Retained earnings	150,000
Total equities	$600,000

(b)

Honey Wrapper Company
BALANCE SHEET
December 31, 1968

Assets	$400,000
Liabilities	$100,000
Capital stock	250,000
Retained earnings	50,000
Total equities	$400,000

17. If Sweets Candy Company acquired a 90% interest in Honey Wrapper Company on December 31, 1968 for $290,000 and the cost (or legal basis) method of accounting for the investment was used, the amount of the debit to Investment in Stock of Honey Wrapper Company would have been
    a. $360,000.
    b. $300,000.
    c. $290,000.
    d. $270,000.

18. If Sweets Candy Company acquired an 80% interest in Honey Wrapper Company on December 31, 1968 for $210,000 and the equity (or accrual) method of accounting for the investment was used, the amount of the debit to Investment in Stock of Honey Wrapper Company would have been
    a. $320,000.
    b. $240,000.
    c. $210,000.
    d. $200,000.

19. If Sweets Candy Company acquired a 90% interest in Honey Wrapper Company on December 31, 1968 for $270,000 and during 1969 Honey Wrapper Company had net income of $22,000 and paid a cash dividend of $7,000, applying the cost method would give a debit balance in the Investment in Stock of Honey Wrapper Company account at the end of 1969 of
    a. $285,000.
    b. $283,500.
    c. $276,300.
    d. $270,000.

20. If Sweets Candy Company acquired a 90% interest in Honey Wrapper Company on December 31, 1968 for $270,000 and during 1969 Honey Wrapper Company had net income of $30,000 and paid a cash dividend of $15,000, applying the equity method would give a debit balance in the Investment in Stock of Honey Wrapper Company account at the end of 1969 of
    a. $285,000.
    b. $283,500.
    c. $276,300.
    d. $270,000.

SPECIFIC APPROACH

Problem XIV-1

1. In working with a series of errors, determine whether each error affects either profits or net working capital. Organize the results by setting up a schedule with one column headed, "Amount Overstated," and the other, "Amount Understated."

2. Although the questions on percentage of completion versus completed contract method are not difficult, they must be read carefully. Know what the question is before you attempt an answer.

3. Earnings per share problems test a candidate's knowledge of APB *Opinion No. 15*. Options and warrants should be treated as if they had been exercised, and primary earnings per share data are computed by use of the "treasury stock" method as described in APBAP Vol. 1, Sect. 2011.36:

> earnings per share data are computed as if the options and warrants were exercised at the beginning of the period ... and as if the funds obtained thereby were used to purchase common stock at the average market price during the period.

The difference between the number of shares which would be issued by exercise of the stock options and the number of shares which could be purchased with the proceeds at average market price is added to the outstanding common shares in computing primary earnings per share for the period.

In computing fully diluted earnings per share, one uses the same approach if dilution results from outstanding options and warrants, however:

> in order to reflect maximum potential dilution, the market price at the close of the period reported upon should be used to determine the number of shares which would be assumed to be repurchased (under the treasury stock method) if such market price is higher than the average price used in computing primary earnings per share. (APBAP Vol. 1, Sect. 2011.42.)

Where the terms of a convertible security make it substantially equivalent to common stock, it is treated as a common stock equivalent and is recognized for computations of earnings per share—ordinary or extraordinary.

Problem XIV-2

Although the eight ratios are quite simple, they are occasionally given in an unusual form. The other questions are remarkably elementary and would be most welcome to candidates sitting for the examination.

Problem XIV-3

This problem emphasizes the necessity of being familiar with APB Opinions. It tests a candidate's knowledge of five of them—15 through 19. Quotations are taken from various Opinions as indicated.

A. APB *Opinions 17* and *18*

Under the cost method, earnings since date of acquisition are recognized as income when distributed. However, "dividends received in excess of earnings subsequent to the date of investment are considered a return of investment and are recorded as reductions of cost of the investment." (APBAP Vol. 1, Sect. 5131.06a.)

Under the equity method, adjustments to the investment account of the investor are "similar to those made in preparing consolidated statements, including adjustments to eliminate intercompany gains and losses and to amortize goodwill."(APBAP Vol. 1,Sect. 5131.06b.)

B. APB *Opinion 19*

In calculating cash payments on accounts payable, determine the amount of purchases first.

C. APB *Opinion 16* (See APBAP Vol. 1, Sect. 1091.47.)

1. The number of shares exchanged therefore excludes those shares of the combining company (1) acquired before and held by the issuing corporation and its subsidiaries at the date the plan of combination is initiated, . . . (2) acquired by the issuing corporation and its subsidiaries after the date the plan of combination is initiated other than by issuing its own voting common stock . . .

2. An investment in stock of the issuing corporation must be expressed as an equivalent number of shares of the investor combining company because the measure of percent of shares exchanged is in terms of shares of stock of the investor company.

3. When a group of assets is acquired by purchase, "a portion of the total cost is then assigned to each individual asset acquired on the basis of its fair value." (APBAP Vol. 1, Sect. 1091.68.)

D. APB *Opinion 15*

1. Cash yield to the holder is the relationship of cash interest or cash dividend received per year to total cost. "A convertible security should be considered as a common stock equivalent at the time of issuance if, based on its market price, it has a cash yield of less than 66 2/3% of the then current bank prime interest rate. For any convertible security which has a change in its cash interest rate or cash dividend rate scheduled within the first five years after issuance, the lowest scheduled rate during such five years should be used in determining the cash yield of the security at issuance." (APBAP Vol. 1, Sect. 2011.33.)

2. The exercise price is the amount that must be paid for a share of common stock upon exercise of a warrant. Where alternative routes to exercise the warrant are available, computation should be based on the most advantageous to the holder of the warrant.

3. In the application of the treasury stock method for the assumed exercise of warrants in computing fully diluted earnings per share, the market price at the end of the period is used *if* it is higher than the average market price for the period. Otherwise, the average is used. The increase in the number of outstanding shares is the difference between the number of shares that would be issued by exercise of the warrants and the number of shares that could be purchased with the theoretical proceeds at the proper price.

Problem XIV-4

Except for two of the fifteen questions, each is on a different subject. Because expanded supporting computations accompany the solutions, no specific approach will be attempted for this problem.

Problem XIV-5

All questions relate to price-level accounting. If you feel insecure, you should review the subject of price-level accounting, usually found in an intermediate accounting book. APB *Accounting Statement No. 3* is very helpful.

Price-level accounting procedures are designed to overcome the objection that accounting combines dollars which are dissimilar in purchasing power as if they were homogeneous.

The basis of price-level accounting is the differentiation between monetary and nonmonetary items. Where the amount of an item does not change with a change in price levels, it is a monetary item—cash, receivables, contracted liabilities. No matter what happens to the price level, these dollar amounts are fixed. There is no need to convert monetary items since they are already expressed in the current dollars they will produce or require. Balances of nonmonetary items must be adjusted to reflect changes in price levels since the item was recorded. If a nonmonetary item is sold, gain or loss is expressed in end-of-period dollars.

To adjust amounts for price-level changes, divide by the price level in the base year, or in the year from which the amount is to be converted, and multiply by the price level for the period to which conversion is desired.

Problem XIV-6

A. Statement of Changes in Financial Position

The problem tests a condidate's ability to interpret a completed statement of changes in financial position and related data. Journal entries or T accounts are very helpful to solve for unknown elements.

B. Business Combinations

Whether or not one approves of the terminology, negative goodwill is shown on the consolidated balance sheet and should influence your choice of answer for question 6.

Although it is possible to determine total stockholders' equity of the subsidiary, sufficient information is not furnished to determine composition of that equity.

Keep in mind the 80% ownership.

C. Compound Interest Formulas

In each case, two issues must be decided before making your answer selection. Ask yourself, "Am I looking for a future value or a present value?" and "Does it involve one payment or a series of payments (an annuity)?"

In these formulas, interest (i) is always expressed per each interest period (n). Thus, given a 6% rate compounded semiannually, i equals .03 and n equals 2 per year.

Problem XIV-7

A. Sales Budgets

Whenever you are given a percentage by which merchandise is marked up, establish whether that percentage is based on cost (as it is in this problem) or on selling price.

B. Flexible Budgets

Review absorption versus direct costing in the General Approach to Topic IV, if you feel insecure.

C. Manufacturing

A basic knowledge of manufacturing accounting and terminology is all that is required for this section, but even basic terms have different interpretations. For example, the problem gives an amount for "Total manufacturing costs." Usually that term means additions to factory costs during the current period and is the sum of raw material used, direct labor, and overhead. The Institute, in its answer to question 23, includes the beginning raw material inventory, interpreting "total manufacturing costs" as total manufacturing costs to be accounted for.

D. Compound Interest

Determine whether you are working with a present or future value and whether it is with one amount or a series of amounts (an annuity). Some of the questions do not involve compound interest concepts, so do not be mislead.

E. Breakeven Analysis

Recall that the breakeven point is that volume where total revenue equals the sum of fixed and variable costs.

Problem XIV-8

A. Partnerships

In partnership admission situations, the crucial point is, "How is the interest of the incoming partner being acquired—by putting assets into the partnership or by purchasing an existing interest from a partner?"

In partnership dissolution, always distribute all possible losses before distributing any cash, by assuming that all non-cash assets will realize nothing. Cash withheld is treated as additional loss. As soon as each partner receives some cash, additional distributions are made in the profit and loss sharing ratio.

B. Retail Inventory

1. As conventionally applied, retail inventory method attempts to approximate cost or market, whichever is lower inventory valuation. In determining the relationship of cost and selling price of goods available for sale, net markdowns are ignored to produce a lower cost-to-retail percentage and, therefore, a lower cost valuation for the inventory.

2. The rate of mark-on is the complement of the cost percentage.

3. When applying the LIFO concept to the retail inventory method, there are several differences in the procedure:

    a. Both markdowns and markups are used to determine the cost-to-retail percentage.

    b. The beginning inventory is excluded in determining the cost-to-retail percentage, which is intended to reflect the current relationship between cost and retail prices.

    c. If the ending inventory at retail is equal to or less than the beginning inventory, the relationship existing in the beginning inventory governs, since you are using a LIFO approach.

C. Price-Volume Analysis

For each case establish the amount of the base for the current period, considering only the volume change. The amount of increase or decrease related to the base yields the price percentage change.

D. Business Combinations

APB *Opinion 16* states that in a purchase, the Investment account is debited for the cost. Whether the cost or equity method is used thereafter does not alter the initial recording.

Under the cost method, the balance in the Investment account is not affected by subsidiary's operations. Under the equity method, the account increases for the parent's portion of subsidiary's undistributed earnings since date of acquisition.

Review Problems: A Complete Examination in Accounting Practice

GENERAL APPROACH

This topic contains a photographic reproduction of the May 1973 examination in Accounting Practice. Use this examination as a trial run. Each part should be attempted in one lonely sitting of 4½ hours. Such experience should provide an enlightening self-test of proficiency. Here is a description of the problems:

Part I

1. Multiple-choice questions on financial accounting (40-50 min.)
2. Statement of changes in financial position (40-50 min.)
3. Worksheet for consolidated financial statements (50-60 min.)
4. Corporate and individual income taxation (40-50 min.)
5. Multiple-choice questions on quantitative methods (50-60 min.)
6. Multiple-choice questions on managerial accounting (50-60 min.)

Part II

1. Multiple-choice questions on income taxation of individuals (40-50 min.)
2. Budget of cash receipts and disbursements for various city funds (40-50 min.)
3. Correction of errors (30-40 min.)
4. Comparison of methods of contractor accounting (50-60 min.)
5. Job-order costing (60-70 min.)

Uniform Certified Public Accountant Examination

(Prepared by the Board of Examiners of the American Institute of Certified Public Accountants
and adopted by the examining boards of all states, territories, and the District of Columbia.)

EXAMINATION IN ACCOUNTING PRACTICE–PART I

May 9, 1973; 1:30 to 6:00 P.M.

NOTE TO CANDIDATES: Suggested time allotments are as follows:

	Estimated Minutes	
	Minimum	*Maximum*
Group I (All required):		
No. 1	40	50
No. 2	40	50
No. 3	50	60
No. 4	40	50
Total for Group I	170	210
Group II (One required)	50	60
Total	220	270

INSTRUCTIONS TO CANDIDATES

1. You must arrange the papers in numerical order of the problems. If more than one page is required for a solution, number the pages in sequence for that problem with the lead schedule first, followed by supporting computations. For instance, if three pages are used for Problem No. 2, you would show Problem 2, Page 1 of 3, Page 2 of 3 and Page 3 of 3.
The printed answer sheet provided for the objective-type items should be considered to be Page 1.

2. **Enclose all scratch sheets.** Failure to enclose scratch sheets may result in loss of grading points. Scratch sheets need not have page numbers, but you should show the problem number and place them immediately following the problem to which they relate.

3. Fourteen-column sheets should not be folded until all sheets, both wide and narrow, are placed in the proper sequence and fastened together at the top left corner. All fourteen-column sheets should then be wrapped around the back of the papers.

4. A CPA is continually confronted with the necessity of expressing his opinions and conclusions in written reports in clear, unequivocal language. Although the primary purpose of the examination is to test the candidate's knowledge and application of the subject matter, the ability to organize and present such knowledge in acceptable written language will be considered by the examiners.

DISREGARD OF THESE INSTRUCTIONS MAY BE CONSIDERED AS INDICATING INEFFICIENCY IN ACCOUNTING WORK.

(OVER)

Uniform Certified Public Accountant Examination

Number 1 (Estimated time –– 40 to 50 minutes)

Instructions

Select the best answer for each of the following items which relate to **a variety of financial accounting problems**. Use a soft pencil, preferably No. 2, to blacken the appropriate space on the separate printed answer sheet to indicate your answer. Mark only one answer for each item. Your grade will be determined from your total of correct answers.

The following is an example of the manner in which the answer sheet should be marked:

Item

95. Gross billings for merchandise sold by Baker Company to its customers last year amounted to $5,260,000; sales returns and allowances were $160,000. Net sales last year for Baker Company were

a. $5,260,000.
b. $5,200,000.
c. $5,100,000.
d. $5,000,000.

Answer Sheet

95. a. :::::::::: b. :::::::::: c. ▬▬▬ d. ::::::::::

Items to be Answered

1. Goldstein Cereals, Inc., distributes coupons to consumers which may be presented (on or before a stated expiration date) to grocers for discounts on certain cereals. The grocers are reimbursed when they send the coupons to Goldstein. In the Company's experience 30% of such coupons are redeemed, and on the average one month elapses between the date a grocer receives a coupon from the buyer and the date Goldstein receives it. On May 1, 1972, Goldstein issued coupons with a total value of $10,000 and an expiration date to the buyer of December 31, 1972. As of December 31, 1972, Goldstein had disbursed $2,500 to grocers for these coupons. The December 31, 1972, balance sheet should include a liability for unredeemed coupons of

a. $0.
b. $375.
c. $500.
d. $2,250.

2. Ecol Corporation issued voting preferred stock with a fair value of $1,000,000 in exchange for all of the outstanding common stock of Ogee Service Company. Ogee has tangible net assets with a book value of $500,000 and a fair value of $600,000. In addition, Ecol Corporation issued stock valued at $100,000 to an investment banker as a "finder's fee" for arranging the combination. As a result of this combination Ecol Corporation should record an increase in net assets of

a. $500,000.
b. $700,000.
c. $600,000.
d. $1,100,000.

3. During 1972 Hoffman Company had a net income of $50,000 (no extraordinary items) and 50,000 shares of common stock and 10,000 shares of preferred stock outstanding. Hoffman declared and paid dividends of $.50 per share to common and $6.00 per share to preferred. Although the preferred stock is convertible into common stock on a share-for-share basis, it is not classified as a common stock equivalent. For 1972 Hoffman Company should report fully diluted earnings (loss) per share of

a. $.83 1/3.
b. $1.00.
c. $ (.20).
d. $.50.

4. On April 15, 1972, a fire destroyed the entire merchandise inventory of John Anderson's retail store. The following data are available:

Sales, January 1 through April 15	$72,000
Inventory, January 1	10,000
Purchases, January 1 through April 15	70,000
Markup on cost	20%

The amount of the loss is estimated to be

a. $24,000.
b. $20,000.
c. $22,400.
d. $8,000.

5. The gross profit of Adelate Company for 1972 is $56,000, cost of goods manufactured is $300,000, the beginning inventories of goods in process and finished goods are $18,000 and $25,000, respectively, and the ending inventories of goods in process and finished goods are $28,000 and $30,000, respectively. The sales of Adelate Company for 1972 must have been

a. $341,000.
b. $346,000.
c. $356,000.
d. $351,000.

6. The business combination of Jax Company – the issuing company – and the Bell Corporation was consummated on March 14, 1973. At the initiation date, Jax held 1,000 shares of Bell. If the combination were accounted for as a pooling of interests, the 1,000 shares of Bell held by Jax would be accounted for as

(continued)

Accounting Practice – Part I

a. Retired stock.
b. 1,000 shares of treasury stock.
c. (1,000 ÷ the exchange rate) shares of treasury stock.
d. (1,000 x the exchange rate) shares of treasury stock.

7. The partnership of Wayne and Ellen was formed on February 28, 1973. At that date the following assets were contributed:

	Wayne	Ellen
Cash	$25,000	$ 35,000
Merchandise	–	55,000
Building	–	100,000
Furniture and equipment	15,000	–

The building is subject to a mortgage loan of $30,000, which is to be assumed by the partnership. The partnership agreement provides that Wayne and Ellen share profits or losses 25% and 75%, respectively. Ellen's capital account at February 28, 1973, would be
a. $190,000.
b. $160,000.
c. $172,500.
d. $150,000.

8. Based on the same facts as described in item 7, if the partnership agreement provides that the partners initially should have an equal interest in partnership capital with no contribution of intangible assets, Wayne's capital account at February 28, 1973, would be
a. $100,000.
b. $115,000.
c. $200,000.
d. $230,000.

9. Jones sold land to Smith for $200,000 cash and a noninterest-bearing note with a face amount of $800,000. The fair value of the land at the date of sale was $900,000. Jones should value the note receivable at
a. $900,000.
b. $800,000.
c. $700,000.
d. $1,000,000.

10. On April 30, 1973, White sold land with a book value of $600,000 to Black for its fair value of $800,000. Black gave White a 12%, $800,000 note secured only by the land. At the date of sale, Black was in a very poor financial position and its continuation as a going concern was very questionable. White should
a. Use the cost recovery method of accounting.
b. Record the note at its discounted value.
c. Record a $200,000 gain on the sale of the land.
d. Fully reserve the note.

11. On April 1, 1972, Austin Corporation sold equipment costing $1,000,000 with accumulated depreciation of $250,000 to its wholly owned subsidiary, Cooper Company, for $900,000. Austin was depreciating the equipment on the straight-line method over 20 years with no salvage value, which Cooper continued. In consolidation at March 31, 1973, the cost and accumulated depreciation, respectively, are
a. $1,000,000 and $300,000.
b. $900,000 and $50,000.
c. $900,000 and $60,000.
d. $750,000 and $50,000.

12. On June 30, 1972, the Ingalls Corporation sold equipment for $420,000 which had a net book value of $400,000 and a remaining life of 10 years. That same day the equipment was leased back at $1,000 per month for 5 years with no option to renew the lease or repurchase the equipment. Ingalls' rent expense for this equipment for the six months ended December 31, 1972, would be
a. $5,000.
b. $4,000.
c. $6,000.
d. $ (14,000).

13. The auditor's report covering the December 31, 1971, financial statements of Wald Corporation was qualified due to a legal suit pending against Wald. The suit was settled on June 30, 1972, and Wald was required to make payments of $40,000 per month for 20 months beginning January 1, 1973. The discounted present value of the future payments at June 30, 1972, and December 31, 1972, was $790,000 and $792,000, respectively. The charge against revenues for the year ended December 31, 1972, resulting from the settlement of the legal suit was
a. $792,000.
b. $800,000.
c. $0.
d. $790,000.

14. Sanitate Company issued 200 7% bonds for $200,000. Each $1,000 bond carries two stock warrants. Each warrant grants an option to purchase one share of $85 par value common stock at $110 per share before December 31, 1973. At the date of the bond issue Sanitate's common stock is selling for $100 per share and the warrants sold for $10 each. The credit for the warrants that Sanitate should record at the date of issue is
a. $3,636.
b. $0.
c. $2,000.
d. $4,000.

15. Based on the same facts as described in item 14, if 95% of the warrants are exercised prior to December 31, 1973, the total "capital in excess of par" created by the sale of the related common stock would be
a. $10,880.
b. $9,500.
c. $3,800.
d. $13,300.

(OVER)

Uniform Certified Public Accountant Examination

Number 2 (Estimated time –– 40 to 50 minutes)

Your firm has been engaged to examine the financial statements of Lanning Corporation for the year ended December 31, 1972. Under your supervision your assistant has prepared the following comparative balance sheet at December 31, 1972 and 1971, and the income statement for the year ended December 31, 1972.

Lanning Corporation
BALANCE SHEET
December 31, 1972
With Comparative Figures for 1971

Assets	1972	1971
Current assets:		
Cash	$ 326,500	$ 231,000
Accounts receivable, net	621,000	614,000
Inventories	1,373,000	1,293,000
Prepaid expenses	160,000	175,000
Total current assets	2,480,500	2,313,000
Investment in and advances to 35% owned corporation	940,000	625,000
Fixed assets:		
Land	54,200	54,200
Buildings	758,000	758,000
Machinery and equipment	1,584,000	1,304,000
Allowance for depreciation	(513,000)	(816,000)
Total fixed assets	1,883,200	1,300,200
Deferred research and development costs	–	150,000
	$5,303,700	$4,388,200

Liabilities and Owners' Equity		
Current liabilities:		
Notes payable, bank	$ 200,000	$ 250,000
Accounts payable	501,800	498,000
Accrued liabilities	187,500	271,000
Current portion of long-term debt	70,000	50,000
Income taxes payable	10,000	26,000
Total current liabilities	969,300	1,095,000
Long-term liabilities:		
6½% serial debentures payable	900,000	950,000
8% secured note payable	380,000	–
Deferred income taxes	119,000	167,000
Total long-term liabilities	1,399,000	1,117,000
Owners' equity:		
Preferred stock	500,000	
Common stock	1,621,000	1,621,000
Retained earnings	949,400	555,200
Treasury stock, common, at cost	(135,000)	–
Total owners' equity	2,935,400	2,176,200
	$5,303,700	$4,388,200

Lanning Corporation
INCOME STATEMENT
For the Year Ended December 31, 1972

Sales		$5,300,000
Cost of goods sold		(3,600,000)
Gross profit on sales		1,700,000
Selling, general, and administrative expenses		(563,000)
Operating income		1,137,000
Other income (expense):		
Interest expense	$(112,000)	
Equity in the earnings of 35% owned corporation	75,000	(37,000)
Net income before income taxes and extraordinary items		1,100,000
Income taxes:		
Current	(480,000)	
Deferred	(48,000)	(528,000)
Net income before extraordinary items		572,000
Extraordinary items:		
Gain on sale of equipment, less income taxes of $184,800 ($208,800 current less $24,000 deferred credit)	200,200	
Write-off of deferred research and development costs less applicable deferred income tax of $72,000	(78,000)	122,200
Net income		$ 694,200

The following additional information has been extracted from your audit work papers:

1. During January 1972 Lanning decided to change its product mix. To accomplish this, new machinery and equipment costing $1,000,000 was purchased on February 15, 1972. The vendor supplying the machinery and equipment was paid as follows:

  a. Cash payment of $100,000.
  b. Issuance of 5,000 shares of $100 par value preferred stock with a fair value of $500,000.
  c. Issuance of a $400,000, 8% note secured by the machinery and equipment and payable in 20 equal annual installments plus interest on February 15 of each year until paid in full.

2. The new machinery and equipment replaced dissimilar machinery and equipment which had an original cost of $720,000, accumulated depreciation at February 15, 1972, of $504,000, and a related deferred tax liability of $24,000. The old machinery and equipment was sold for cash on December 14, 1972. No depreciation was recorded from February 15, 1972, until the date of sale.

(continued)

4

Accounting Practice – Part I

3. Lanning wrote off $150,000 of deferred research and development costs. The extraordinary charge for this write-off is net of a related $72,000 deferred tax liability.

4. Various other transactions follow:

a. Depreciation expense for the year was $201,000.
b. The Company paid cash dividends of $300,000.
c. The Company advanced $240,000 to the corporation of which it owns 35%.

Required:

Prepare a statement of changes in financial position based on additions to and deductions from working capital to appear in the 1972 annual report of Lanning Corporation.

Number 3 (Estimated time -- 50 to 60 minutes)

On June 30, 1972, Linskey, Inc., purchased 100% of the outstanding common stock of Cresswell Corporation for $3,605,000 cash and Linskey's common stock valued at $4,100,000. At the date of purchase the book and fair values of Cresswell's assets and liabilities were as follows:

	Book Value	Fair Value
Cash	$ 160,000	$ 160,000
Accounts receivable, net	910,000	910,000
Inventory	860,000	1,025,186
Furniture, fixtures, and machinery	3,000,000	2,550,000
Building	9,000,000	7,250,000
Accumulated depreciation	(5,450,000)	—
Intangible assets, net	150,000	220,000
	$8,630,000	
Accounts payable	$ 580,000	580,000
Note payable	500,000	500,000
5% mortgage note payable	4,000,000	3,710,186
Common stock	2,900,000	—
Retained earnings	650,000	—
	$8,630,000	

By the year end, December 31, 1972, the net balance of Cresswell's accounts receivable at June 30, 1972, had been collected; the inventory on hand at June 30, 1972, had been charged to cost of goods sold; the accounts payable at June 30, 1972, had been paid; and the $500,000 note had been paid.

As of June 30, 1972, Cresswell's furniture, fixtures, and machinery and building had an estimated remaining life of eight and ten years, respectively. All intangible assets had an estimated remaining life of twenty years. All depreciation and amortization is to be computed using the straight-line method.

As of June 30, 1972, the 5% mortgage note payable had eight equal annual payments remaining with the next payment due June 30, 1973. The fair value of the note was based on a 7% rate.

Prior to June 30, 1972, there were no intercompany transactions between Linskey and Cresswell; however, during the last six months of 1972 the following intercompany transactions occurred:

1. Linskey sold $400,000 of merchandise to Cresswell. The cost of the merchandise to Linskey was $360,000. Of this merchandise, $75,000 remained on hand at December 31, 1972.

2. On December 29, 1972, Cresswell purchased, in the market, $300,000 of Linskey's 7½% bonds payable for $312,500, including $22,500 interest receivable. Linskey had issued $1,000,000 of these 20-year 7½% bonds payable on January 1, 1965, for $960,000.

3. Many of the management functions of the two companies have been consolidated since . the merger. Linskey charges Cresswell a $30,000 per month management fee.

4. At December 31, 1972, Cresswell owes Linskey two months' management fees and $18,000 for merchandise purchases.

Required:

Complete the enclosed printed worksheet for the preparation of a consolidated balance sheet and income statement for Linskey, Inc., and its subsidiary, Cresswell Corporation, for the year ended December 31, 1972. Provide computations in good form where appropriate to support entries.

Linskey's profit and loss figures are for the twelve-month period while Cresswell's are for the last six months. You may assume that both companies made all the adjusting entries required for separate financial statements unless an obvious discrepancy exists. **Income taxes should not be considered in your solution.** Round all computations to the nearest dollar.

(OVER)

Number 4 (Estimated time —— 40 to 50 minutes)

The office manager of Home Cookery Restaurant, Inc., has requested your assistance in calculating the 1972 federal taxable income for the corporation and the joint 1972 adjusted gross income of its two stockholders, Paul Roden and his wife, Sarah. The office manager has gathered all the necessary information and has begun calculating the corporation's taxable income. His preliminary work shows corporate net income of $45,800 which you have found to be correct. However, the office manager is uncertain how to handle certain items relating to the incorporation and transactions between Mr. and Mrs. Roden and the corporation. Your investigation has revealed the following background on the incorporation, items which the office manager did not know how to handle and did not include in his preliminary calculation of the corporation's income, and other supplementary information which also was not considered in the office manager's calculations.

Background on the Incorporation

In 1965 Mr. Roden opened and operated the Home Cookery Restaurant as a sole proprietorship. Effective December 31, 1971, Mr. Roden legally transferred a 50% interest in the assets and liabilities of the restaurant (sole proprietorship) to Mrs. Roden. A gift tax return was appropriately filed and no gift tax was due. The Rodens incorporated the restaurant effective January 1, 1972, and immediately transferred all of its assets and liabilities to the corporation in exchange for 50% of the corporate stock for Mr. Roden and 50% for his wife. Following is the December 31, 1971, tax basis balance sheet of the restaurant. Where the fair market value (FMV) of assets is different from the tax basis, it is shown parenthetically.

Assets

Cash		$ 1,500
Accounts receivable	$46,000	
Less allowance for bad debts	5,500	40,500
Inventory		15,000
Land (FMV, $32,000)		27,000
Equipment (FMV, $18,000)	23,000	
Less accumulated depreciation	7,000	16,000
Building (FMV, $48,000)	35,000	
Less accumulated depreciation	11,000	24,000
Total assets		$124,000

Liabilities and Capital

Trade accounts payable		$ 45,000
Mortgage payable on land and building		22,000
Total liabilities		67,000
Capital		57,000
Total liabilities and capital		$124,000

Both before and after incorporation the restaurant operated on the accrual basis and used a calendar year. The corporation accounts for bad debts by the reserve method which was the method used by the proprietorship. The restaurant is open seven days per week and both Paul and Sarah worked there full time in 1972. Paul is president of the corporation; Sarah is secretary-treasurer.

Items in Question by the Office Manager

1. **Payment to officer under wage continuation plan, $400:** The wage continuation plan provides for the payment of 50% of an employee's wages during a temporary absence from work due to illness. The plan covers all full-time employees. Sarah was away from work for 28 days, during which time she was hospitalized with pneumonia. During this period she received $100 per week. Her annual salary for 1972 would have been $10,400, excluding fringe benefits.

2. **Compensation of officer, $30,000:** Effective January 2, 1972, Paul contracted in writing with the corporation for a salary of $30,000, $20,000 of which is paid annually, and $10,000 of which is to be paid annually upon his retirement. His rights to the deferred portion are forfeitable and there are no funding arrangements.

3. **Reimbursed expenses, $3,000:** Paul accounts to the corporation for his entertainment expenses in the same manner as he was reimbursed $3,000. He paid out $3,750 for entertainment expenses on behalf of the corporation. The corporation would have reimbursed him for the additional $750 if he had bothered to make the claim.

4. **Cost of food, $3,400:** Paul and Sarah both eat their meals in the restaurant since they are required to be on duty during the meal periods. The cost of the food they consumed at work during 1972 was $3,400; the retail value was $6,000.

5. **Group term life insurance, $990:** The corporation is beneficiary of a $75,000 group term life insurance policy on Paul. The premium for the first $50,000 was $660, and the premium on the additional $25,000 was $330.

6. **Ordinary life insurance, $2,500:** Sarah is the owner and beneficiary of an ordinary life policy on Paul. Of the $2,500 annual premium, $1,100 represented an increase in the cash surrender value of the policy. Payment of the premium by the corporation was in the nature of additional compensation.

7. **Health and accident insurance, $550:** The premium paid is for both Sarah and Paul. All full-time employees are covered. Sarah was reimbursed a total of $1,800 for medical expenses relating to her illness.

8. **Sale of auto, $4,000:** On May 1, 1972, the corporation purchased an auto for $5,000 cash and immediately sold it to Paul for $4,000 cash.

9. **Rental of summer cottage, $2,100:** Paul and Sarah own a summer cottage which was rented by the corporation for the six-month period, April 1 to September 30. They received rent of $350 per month. The fair rental value of the cottage was $250 per month. The corporation

(continued)
6

used the cottage one and one-half months for entertaining. The Rodens used the cottage for four and one-half months for personal reasons. The other half of the year the house was vacant.

10. Distribution of freezer, $600: On December 29, the corporation distributed to Sarah a two-year-old freezer with a book value of $600. She assumed the applicable liability of $725. The original cost was $880, accumulated depreciation $280, and the fair market value on the date of distribution was $800.

11. Loan receivable – stockholder, $5,700: On July 1, 1972, Paul borrowed $5,700 from the corporation. On December 31, the corporation forgave the indebtedness.

12. Purchase of typewriter, $425: In addition to working in the restaurant, Sarah has been a part-time, self-employed typist. Sarah actively engaged in soliciting bona fide typing business during 1972 but generated no income. As a result, on December 29, 1972, she sold her business typewriter to the corporation. It was purchased in 1969 at a cost of $375; depreciation for 1972 was $25; accumulated depreciation to the date of sale was $225. The corporation purchased the typewriter for $425, its fair market value.

13. Collections on accounts receivable, $37,000; payments on accounts payable, $45,000: These amounts relate to the assets and liabilities transferred to the corporation from the sole proprietorship.

Supplementary Information

- Of the accounts receivable contributed to the corporation, $3,700 have been determined to be worthless at December 31, 1972.
- No depreciation has been recorded for 1972. The equipment and building transferred to the corporation had estimated useful lives from the date of transfer of 8 years and 16 years, respectively. Straight-line depreciation is to be used. **Ignore salvage value.**
- The restaurant occupies 70% of the building. The remaining 30% is an apartment where the Rodens live rent free for their own convenience because of their working hours. The fair market value of renting the apartment would be $2,400 per year.
- Mr. Roden had an unused net operating loss carryover from his proprietorship of $8,000 at January 1, 1972.

Required:

a. Beginning with the preliminary net income of $45,800, prepare a schedule calculating the 1972 taxable income of Home Cookery Restaurant, Inc. **Reasonableness of compensation is not an issue.**

b. Prepare a schedule calculating the joint adjusted gross income of Mr. and Mrs. Roden for the calendar year 1972. The foregoing information contains all of the Rodens' 1972 tax transactions. **Disregard the dividend exclusion and depreciation and rental expenses on the summer cottage**.

(OVER)

Uniform Certified Public Accountant Examination

GROUP II

(Estimated time — 50 to 60 minutes)

Solve only one of the two problems in this group. If both are solved, only the first will be considered.

Number 5

Instructions

Select the best answer for each of the following items which relate to the **application of quantitative methods to accounting problems.** In determining your answer to each item consider the information given in the preceding lettered statement of facts or data. Use a soft pencil, preferably No. 2, to blacken the appropriate space on the separate printed answer sheet to indicate your answer. Mark only one answer for each item. Your grade will be determined from your total of correct answers.

Items to be Answered

A.   As the accounting consultant for Leslie Company you have compiled data on the day-to-day demand rate from Leslie's customers for Product A and the lead time to receive Product A from its supplier. The data are summarized in the following probability tables:

Demand for Product A

Unit Demand per Day	Probability of Occurrence
0	.45
1	.15
2	.30
3	.10
	1.00

Lead Time for Product A

Lead Time in Days	Probability of Occurrence
1	.40
2	.35
3	.25
	1.00

Leslie is able to deliver Product A to its customers the same day that Product A is received from its supplier. All units of Product A demanded but not available, due to a stock-out, are back ordered and are filled immediately when a new shipment arrives.

16.   The probability of the demand for Product A being nine units during a three-day lead time for delivery from the supplier is
   a.   .00025.
   b.   .10.
   c.   .025.
   d.   .25.

17.   If Leslie reorders 10 units of Product A when its inventory level is 10 units, the number of days during a 360-day year that Leslie will experience a stock-out of Product A is
   a.   0.75 days.
   b.   36 days.
   c.   10 days.
   d.   0 days.

18.   Leslie has developed an inventory model based on the probability tables and desires a solution for minimizing total annual inventory costs. Included in inventory costs are the costs of holding Product A, ordering and receiving Product A, and incurring stock-outs of Product A. The solution would state:
   a.   At what inventory level to reorder and how many units to reorder.
   b.   Either at what inventory level to reorder or how many units to reorder.
   c.   How many units to reorder but not at what inventory level to reorder.
   d.   At what inventory level to reorder but not how many units to reorder.

B.   The Martin Corporation, which operates seven days a week, orders Product B from the Whiting Company each morning. Product B, which arrives soon after the order is placed, spoils if it is not sold at the end of the day.

The president of Martin has been using his executive judgment to determine how much of Product B to order each morning. You, as Martin's controller, have noticed that a number of costly forecasting errors have been made by the president and wish to show him that the use of a more sophisticated method of determining the order quantity of Product B would save money for the Company. As part of the preparation for your presentation of the use of various forecasting techniques, you have compiled the following data regarding the past eleven days of orders of and demand for Product B.

	X	Y	Z	Y–Z
		Number of Units Ordered	Demand in Units	Number of Units Spoiled (Short)
January 1, 1973	21	16	5
January 2, 1973	19	18	1
January 3, 1973	17	21	(4)
January 4, 1973	19	22	(3)
January 5, 1973	23	20	3
January 6, 1973	23	20	3
January 7, 1973	22	21	1
January 8, 1973	19	22	(3)
January 9, 1973	20	22	(2)
January 10, 1973	21	20	1
January 11, 1973	20	18	2
Total	224	220	4

(continued)
8

Accounting Practice – Part I

In answering each of the following items round all calculations to the next highest whole number.

19. Using the least squares time regression technique for forecasting and based on the data for the first eleven days of January, the number of units that Martin will order on January 16, 1973, is
    a. 23.
    b. 20.
    c. 21.
    d. 22.

20. Had Martin's president based his January 2, 1973, order on the exponential smoothing technique of forecasting using an alpha of 0.2 and a base of 21 units, the number of units ordered on January 2 would have been
    a. 20.
    b. 23.
    c. 19.
    d. 22.

21. After your presentation, the president favors the use of the exponential smoothing technique of forecasting, but he points out that during each month there is a single day in which demand will increase to 40 or 50 units and he desires to minimize the effect of this occurrence on the forecast. Martin should
    a. Use the exponential smoothing technique with a large alpha factor.
    b. Use the exponential smoothing technique with a small alpha factor.
    c. Use the least squares time regression technique rather than the exponential smoothing technique.
    d. Use a moving average technique rather than the exponential smoothing technique.

22. The president mentions that he expects demand to jump to approximately 35 units per day and stay at that level. He desires to use the exponential smoothing technique of forecasting but wants it to respond as quickly as possible to this expected increase. Martin should
    a. Use a moving average technique rather than the exponential smoothing technique.
    b. Use the exponential smoothing technique with a large alpha factor.
    c. Use the exponential smoothing technique with a small alpha factor.
    d. Use the least squares time regression technique rather than the exponential smoothing technique.

C. The Ball Company manufactures three types of lamps which are labeled A, B, and C. Each lamp is processed in two departments – I and II. Total available man-hours per day for departments I and II are 400 and 600, respectively. No additional labor is available. Time requirements and profit per unit for each lamp type is as follows:

	A	B	C
Man-hours required in department I	2	3	1
Man-hours required in department II	4	2	3
Profit per unit (Sales price less all variable costs)	$5	$4	$3

The Company has assigned you as the accounting member of its profit planning committee to determine the numbers of types of A, B, and C lamps that it should produce in order to maximize its total profit from the sale of lamps. The following questions relate to a linear programming model that your group has developed.

23. The coefficients of the objective function would be
    a. 4, 2, 3.
    b. 2, 3, 1.
    c. 5, 4, 3.
    d. 400, 600.

24. The constraints in the model would be
    a. 2, 3, 1.
    b. 5, 4, 3.
    c. 4, 2, 3.
    d. 400, 600.

25. The constraint imposed by the available man-hours in department I could be expressed as
    a. $4X_1 + 2X_2 + 3X_3 \leqslant 400$.
    b. $4X_1 + 2X_2 + 3X_3 \geqslant 400$.
    c. $2X_1 + 3X_2 + 1X_3 \leqslant 400$.
    d. $2X_1 + 3X_2 + 1X_3 \geqslant 400$.

26. The most types of lamps that would be included in the optimal solution would be
    a. 2.
    b. 1.
    c. 3.
    d. 0.

(OVER)
9

D.   Akron, Inc., owns 80% of the capital stock of Benson Co. and 70% of the capital stock of Cashin, Inc. Benson Co. owns 15% of the capital stock of Cashin, Inc. Cashin, Inc., in turn, owns 25% of the capital stock of Akron, Inc. These ownership interrelationships are illustrated in the following diagram:

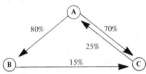

Net income before adjusting for interests in intercompany net income for each corporation follows:

Akron, Inc.	$190,000
Benson Co.	$170,000
Cashin, Inc.	$230,000

The following notations relate to items 27 through 30. **Ignore all income tax considerations.**

A_e = Akron's consolidated net income; i.e., its net income plus its share of the consolidated net incomes of Benson and Cashin.

B_e = Benson's consolidated net income; i.e., its net income plus its share of the consolidated net income of Cashin.

C_e = Cashin's consolidated net income; i.e., its net income plus its share of the consolidated income of Akron.

27.   The equation, in a set of simultaneous equations, which computes A_e is
   a. $A_e = .75\,(190,000 + .8B_e + .7C_e)$.
   b. $A_e = 190,000 + .8B_e + .7C_e$.
   c. $A_e = .75(190,000) + .8(170,000) + .7(230,000)$.
   d. $A_e = .75\,(190,000) + .8B_e + .7C_e$.

28.   The equation, in a set of simultaneous equations, which computes B_e is
   a. $B_e = 170,000 + .15C_e - .75A_e$.
   b. $B_e = 170,000 + .15C_e$.
   c. $B_e = .2\,(170,000) + .15\,(230,000)$.
   d. $B_e = .2\,(170,000) + .15C_e$.

29.   Cashin's minority interest in consolidated net income is
   a.   .15 (230,000).
   b. $230,000 + .25A_e$.
   c. $.15\,(230,000) + .25A_e$.
   d. $.15C_e$.

30.   Benson's minority interest in consolidated net income is
   a. $34,316.
   b. $25,500.
   c. $45,755.
   d. $30,675.

(continued)
10

Number 6

Instructions

Select the best answer for each of the following items which relate to a **variety of managerial accounting problems.** In determining your answer to each item consider the information given in the preceding lettered statement of facts or data. Use a soft pencil, preferably No. 2, to blacken the appropriate space on the separate printed answer sheet to indicate your answer. Mark only one answer for each item. Your grade will be determined from your total of correct answers.

Items to be Answered

A.   Amex Company is considering the introduction of a new product which will be manufactured in an existing plant; however, new equipment costing $150,000 with a useful life of five years (no salvage value) will be necessary. The space in the existing plant to be used for the new product is currently used for warehousing. When the new product takes over the warehouse space, on which the actual depreciation is $20,000, Amex Company will rent warehouse space at an annual cost of $25,000. An accounting study produces the following estimates of incremental revenue and expense on an average annual basis:

Sales	$500,000
Cost of merchandise sold (excluding depreciation)	385,000
Depreciation of equipment (straight-line)	30,000
Marketing expense	10,000

The Company requires an accounting rate of return of 11% (after income taxes) on average investment proposals. The effective income tax rate is 46%. **Ignore the time value of money.**

31.   The average annual incremental costs for the first five years (including income taxes) which must be considered in evaluating this decision are
   a. $459,500.
   b. $470,300.
   c. $473,000.
   d. $475,700.

32.   The minimum annual net income needed to meet the Company's requirement for this investment is
   a. $16,500.
   b. $8,250.
   c. $9,900.
   d. $6,600.

33.   The estimated annual residual income (after allowing for return on investment in new equipment) resulting from introduction of the new product is
   a. $18,750.
   b. $21,450.
   c. $22,545.
   d. $17,100.

Accounting Practice – Part I

34. The estimated incremental cash flow during the third year is
   a. $77,000.
   b. $57,000.
   c. $54,300.
   d. $79,700.

B. The following information is available for Keller Corporation's new product line:

Selling price per unit	$ 15
Variable manufacturing costs per unit of production	8
Total annual fixed manufacturing costs	25,000
Variable administrative costs per unit of production	3
Total annual fixed selling and administrative expenses	15,000

There was no inventory at the beginning of the year. During the year 12,500 units were produced and 10,000 units were sold.

35. The ending inventory, assuming Keller uses direct costing, would be
   a. $25,000.
   b. $32,500.
   c. $27,500.
   d. $20,000.

36. The ending inventory, assuming Keller uses absorption costing, would be
   a. $32,500.
   b. $27,500.
   c. $20,000.
   d. $25,000.

37. The total variable costs charged to expense for the year, assuming Keller uses direct costing, would be
   a. $110,000.
   b. $100,000.
   c. $117,500.
   d. $80,000.

38. The total fixed costs charged against the current year's operations, assuming Keller uses absorption costing, is
   a. $35,000.
   b. $40,000.
   c. $25,000.
   d. $15,000.

C. The Butrico Manufacturing Corporation uses a standard-cost system which records raw materials at actual cost, records materials-price variance at the time that raw materials are issued to work in process, and prorates all variances at year end. Variances associated with direct materials are prorated based on the direct-material balances in the appropriate accounts, and variances associated with direct labor and manufacturing overhead are prorated based on the direct-labor balances in the appropriate accounts.

The following information is available for Butrico for the year ended December 31, 1972:

Raw-materials inventory at December 31, 1972	$ 65,000
Finished-goods inventory at December 31, 1972:	
Direct material	87,000
Direct labor	130,500
Applied manufacturing overhead	104,400
Cost of goods sold for the year ended December 31, 1972:	
Direct material	348,000
Direct labor	739,500
Applied manufacturing overhead	591,600
Direct-material price variance (unfavorable)	10,000
Direct-material usage variance (favorable)	15,000
Direct-labor rate variance (unfavorable)	20,000
Direct-labor efficiency variance (favorable)	5,000
Manufacturing overhead incurred	690,000

There were no beginning inventories and no ending work-in-process inventory. Manufacturing overhead is applied at 80% of standard direct labor.

39. The amount of direct-material price variance to be prorated to finished-goods inventory at December 31, 1972, is a
   a. $1,740 debit.
   b. $2,000 debit.
   c. $2,610 credit.
   d. $3,000 credit.

40. The total amount of direct material in the finished-goods inventory at December 31, 1972, after all variances have been prorated is
   a. $86,130.
   b. $87,870.
   c. $88,000.
   d. $86,000.

41. The total amount of direct labor in the finished-goods inventory at December 31, 1972, after all variances have been prorated is
   a. $134,250.
   b. $131,850.
   c. $132,750.
   d. $126,750.

42. The total cost of goods sold for the year ended December 31, 1972, after all variances have been prorated is
   a. $1,682,750.
   b. $1,691,250.
   c. $1,683,270.
   d. $1,693,850.

Uniform Certified Public Accountant Examination

D. Tomlinson Retail seeks your assistance to develop cash and other budget information for May, June, and July 1973. At April 30, 1973, the Company had cash of $5,500, accounts receivable of $437,000, inventories of $309,400, and accounts payable of $133,055.

The budget is to be based on the following assumptions:

I. *Sales*

a. Each month's sales are billed on the last day of the month.

b. Customers are allowed a 3% discount if payment is made within ten days after the billing date. Receivables are booked gross.

c. Sixty percent of the billings are collected within the discount period, 25% are collected by the end of the month, 9% are collected by the end of the second month, and 6% prove uncollectible.

II. *Purchases*

a. Fifty-four percent of all purchases of material and selling, general, and administrative expenses are paid in the month purchased and the remainder in the following month.

b. Each month's units of ending inventory is equal to 130% of the next month's units of sales.

c. The cost of each unit of inventory is $20.

d. Selling, general, and administrative expenses, of which $2,000 is depreciation, are equal to 15% of the current month's sales.

Actual and projected sales are as follows:

1973	Dollars	Units
March	$354,000	11,800
April	363,000	12,100
May	357,000	11,900
June	342,000	11,400
July	360,000	12,000
August	366,000	12,200

43. Budgeted cash disbursements during the month of June 1973 are
   a. $292,900.
   b. $287,379.
   c. $294,900.
   d. $285,379.

44. Budgeted cash collections during the month of May 1973 are
   a. $333,876.
   b. $355,116.
   c. $340,410.
   d. $355,656.

45. The budgeted number of units of inventory to be purchased during July 1973 is
   a. 15,860.
   b. 12,260.
   c. 12,000.
   d. 15,600.

(END)

12

Uniform Certified Public Accountant Examination

(Prepared by the Board of Examiners of the American Institute of Certified Public Accountants
and adopted by the examining boards of all states, territories, and the District of Columbia.)

EXAMINATION IN ACCOUNTING PRACTICE–PART II

May 10, 1973; 1:30 to 6:00 P.M.

NOTE TO CANDIDATES: Suggested time allotments are as follows:

		Estimated Minutes	
All questions are required:		*Minimum*	*Maximum*
No. 1		40	50
No. 2		40	50
No. 3		30	40
No. 4		50	60
No. 5		60	70
Total		220	270

INSTRUCTIONS TO CANDIDATES

1. You must arrange the papers in numerical order of the problems. If more than one page is required for a solution, number the pages in sequence for the problem with the lead schedule first, followed by supporting computations. For instance, if two pages are used for Problem No. 3, you would show Problem 3, Page 1 of 2 and Page 2 of 2.
The printed answer sheet provided for the objective-type items should be considered to be Page 1.

2. **Enclose all scratch sheets.** Failure to enclose scratch sheets may result in loss of grading points. Scratch sheets need not have page numbers, but you should show the problem number and place them immediately following the problem to which they relate.

3. Fourteen-column sheets should not be folded until all sheets, both wide and narrow, are placed in the proper sequence and fastened together at the top left corner. All fourteen-column sheets should then be wrapped around the back of the papers.

4. A CPA is continually confronted with the necessity of expressing his opinions and conclusions in written reports in clear, unequivocal language. Although the primary purpose of the examination is to test the candidate's knowledge and application of the subject matter, the ability to organize and present such knowledge in acceptable written language will be considered by the examiners.

DISREGARD OF THESE INSTRUCTIONS MAY BE CONSIDERED AS INDICATING INEFFICIENCY IN ACCOUNTING WORK.

(OVER)

Uniform Certified Public Accountant Examination

Number 1 (Estimated time -- 40 to 50 minutes)

Instructions

Select the best answer for each of the following items which relate to the **federal income taxation of individuals**. Use a soft pencil, preferably No. 2, to blacken the appropriate space on the separate printed answer sheet to indicate your answer. The answers should be selected in accordance with the **current Internal Revenue Code and Tax Regulations**. Mark only one answer for each item. Your grade will be determined from your total of correct answers.

The following is an example of the manner in which the answer sheet should be marked:

Item

95. John Doe is 25 years old, unmarried, has good sight, and did not contribute to the support of any other person in 1972. He is entitled to a deduction for personal exemption for 1972 of

a. $1,800.
b. $1,200.
c. $750.
d. $0.
e. None of the above.

Answer Sheet

95. a. :::::::: b. ::::::: c. ▬▬ d. ::::::: e. :::::::

Items to be Answered

1. On July 1, 1972, Al Zabel traded in a machine used in his business with an adjusted basis of $4,000 for another machine by paying $8,000 cash. The new machine has a ten-year useful life and an estimated salvage value of $1,000. Mr. Zabel uses straight-line depreciation and elects first-year bonus depreciation but **not** Asset Depreciation Range (ADR). The total depreciation that he may claim on his 1972 separate return is

a. $2,450.
b. $2,070.
c. $2,950.
d. $3,500.
e. None of the above.

2. During the calendar year 1972 all medical expenses for Max Kreighton (h) and his wife (w) were as follows:

Basic medicare portion of FICA tax withheld (w)	$ 54
Basic medicare portion of self employment tax (h)	54
Supplementary voluntary medicare (h)	48
Hospitalization insurance for Mrs. Kreighton's mother who is totally supported by Max but has interest income of $900	226
Policy that guarantees $100 per week for a maximum of 100 weeks in the event of hospitalization as a result of illness (h)	$160

Mr. and Mrs. Kreighton file a joint return for 1972; they have adjusted gross income of $8,000 and elect to itemize deductions. What amount may be deducted as medical expense in computing their taxable income?

a. $137.
b. $78.
c. $24.
d. $0.
e. None of the above.

3. Ken Lamper owns a one-third interest and is an active partner in a partnership of architects which has five full-time employees. All of the partners plus employees with more than three years of service are covered in a self-employed pension plan. Part-time employees do not qualify. Mr. Lamper's distributive share of partnership income is $30,000, and he elects the standard deduction in computing his 1972 taxable income. The maximum pension plan contribution he may deduct on his own behalf is

a. $3,000.
b. $2,500.
c. $1,250.
d. $833 (nearest dollar).
e. None of the above.

4. Paul Charles, a cash basis taxpayer, owns an apartment house. In computing net rental income for 1972, the following information is ascertained:

An analysis of the 1972 bank deposit slips shows rents received in the amount of $15,000.

In December 1972, Mr. Charles received a $600 negotiable noninterest-bearing promissory note dated December 1, 1972, as rent for the months of December 1972 and January 1973 (fair market value $550).

Pursuant to instructions from Mr. Charles a past-due rent check of $175 was given to the building superintendent on December 29, 1972. He mailed it to the rental office on the 30th, it was received on January 2, and deposited on January 3, 1973.

The lease of the tenant in Apt. 4A expired on December 31, 1972, and the tenant left improvements valued at $500. The improvements were not in lieu of any rent required to have been paid.

In computing his 1972 taxable income, Mr. Charles will report gross rents of

a. $16,275.
b. $16,225.
c. $15,725.
d. $15,500.
e. None of the above.

(continued)

Accounting Practice – Part II

5. Jack Norman and his wife were divorced on April 1, 1972. Pursuant to the divorce decree he is required to make alimony payments of $125 per month beginning April 15 until such time as the death or remarriage of his former wife, plus child-support payments of $50 per month. The decree also requires him to pay $15,000 in 1972 as a lump-sum property settlement. During 1972 Mr. Norman made all of the payments he was legally obligated to make. In addition he voluntarily paid a $1,000 medical bill of his former wife. His former wife had not remarried as of December 31, 1972. Mr. Norman itemizes his deductions for 1972. He may claim an alimony deduction of
   a. $17,575.
   b. $16,575.
   c. $1,575.
   d. $1,125.
   e. None of the above.

6. On January 1, 1969, Ira Ostire, who is not a dealer, purchased ten $1,000 5% bonds of the state of California for $10,400 (maturity date, January 1, 1989). Interest is payable January 1 and July 1 each year. On December 31, 1972, he sold four of the bonds at a total price of $4,386 exclusive of interest. In computing Mr. Ostire's 1972 taxable income, the receipt of interest on the bonds and the sale of the bonds will increase his adjusted gross income by
   a. $629.
   b. $129.
   c. $113.
   d. $0.
   e. None of the above.

7. In 1972, Stan Dempsey, age 73, had wages of $4,000 and interest income of $2,100. During the previous 20 years his salary was never less than $5,000 per annum. His wife, age 68, has had no earned income in any of the 30 years of their marriage. Because Mr. Dempsey worked in a noncovered occupation, he receives no social security benefits. Mr. and Mrs. Dempsey file a joint return for 1972 and elect to utilize the joint retirement income credit. The maximum amount of retirement income to be used in the computation is
   a. $2,100.
   b. $2,286.
   c. $1,524.
   d. $0, since neither qualifies.
   e. None of the above.

8. Bob Yablow, a cash basis taxpayer, died on December 20, 1971. During 1972, his son John, as beneficiary, received the following amounts. The rights to these amounts had been distributed to John prior to their receipt by him.

Proceeds due decedent on uncollected installment obligation (father's gross-profit percentage, 25%) from sale of securities held over two years, not as a dealer	$5,000
Proceeds from December 2, 1971, sale of family jewelry acquired prior to 1960 (father's cost basis, $2,500)	$3,000
Gift from father's employer paid following his death (payment actually represented father's normal holiday bonus which he would have received had he lived)	4,000

In the computation of his 1972 taxable income, John Yablow would reflect the above amounts as
   a. Long-term capital gain of $8,000; ordinary income of $4,000.
   b. Long-term capital gain of $8,000.
   c. Long-term capital gain of $1,750; ordinary income of $4,000.
   d. Long-term capital gain of $1,750.
   e. None of the above.

9. On February 16, 1971, Fred Samson purchased 100 shares of Oscar Corp. at $40 per share. On July 28, 1972, he sold the 100 shares at $25 per share. On August 10, 1972, his wife purchased 50 shares of Oscar Corp. at $30 per share. These are the only capital asset transactions by the Samsons during 1972. In computing his 1972 taxable income, Fred may deduct from his ordinary income of $15,000 a capital loss in the amount of
   a. $1,000.
   b. $750.
   c. $1,500.
   d. $375.
   e. None of the above.

10. Charles Wilson and his wife furnished over half of the total support during 1972 of the following individuals:

Daughter, age 22, who was married on December 20, 1972, has no gross income of her own, and for 1972 files a taxable joint return with her husband
Son, age 17, with gross income of $2,500
Wife's brother, age 27, a full-time student with gross income of $1,200
Their neighbor's son, age 15, who has lived with them since May 1972 (while his parents are in Europe) and has no gross income.

Mr. and Mrs. Wilson file a joint return for 1972. The number of dependency exemptions they may claim is
   a. Four.
   b. Three.
   c. Two.
   d. One.
   e. None of the above.

(OVER)

3

11. On January 20, 1972, Tom Ferry, age 55, sold his residence for $30,000. The house had been purchased in 1953 at a cost of $22,000. In order to make it salable it had been painted in December 1971 at a cost of $500 which was paid in December. On March 12, 1972, Mr. Ferry purchased a two-family house for $55,000. The rental portion is 50%, the remainder being used as a personal residence. For 1972, Mr. Ferry will include a long-term capital gain on the sale of his residence of
- a. $8,000.
- b. $2,500.
- c. $2,000.
- d. $0.
- e. None of the above.

12. Soft Cream sells franchises to independent operators. In 1972 it sold a franchise to Edward Trent, charging an initial fee of $20,000 and a monthly fee of 2% of sales. Soft Cream retains the right to control such matters as employee and management training, quality control and promotion, and the purchase of ingredients. Mr. Trent's 1972 sales amounted to $200,000. From the transactions with Trent, Soft Cream, an accrual basis taxpayer, would include in its computation of 1972 taxable income
- a. Long-term capital gain of $24,000.
- b. Long-term capital gain of $20,000, ordinary income of $4,000.
- c. Long-term capital gain of $4,000, ordinary income of $20,000.
- d. Ordinary income of $24,000.
- e. None of the above.

13. On March 12, 1972, Al Baldwin's automobile was completely destroyed in a collision due to his unintentional negligent driving. The car, which originally cost $3,500 and had a fair market value of $2,700 immediately before the accident, was worthless afterwards. Mr. Baldwin had $250 deductible collision insurance and on June 14, 1972, he received a $2,450 check from the insurance company. He used the proceeds to purchase a car for $2,000 and to pay a $450 auto rental bill representing the cost of weekend rentals during the time he was without a car. Mr. Baldwin itemizes his deductions. The amount of casualty loss he may claim in computing his 1972 taxable income is
- a. $250.
- b. $600.
- c. $150.
- d. $950.
- e. None of the above.

14. In 1972, Warren Potter had a salary of $30,000 and no other income; however, his capital losses carried over from previous years were as follows:

Long-term capital loss carryover from 1969	$(240)
Long-term capital loss carryover from 1971	(1,360)
Short-term capital loss carryover from 1971	(580)

Mr. Potter is single. After deducting all possible carryovers in his 1972 return, his carryover to 1973 would be a
- a. Long-term capital loss of $1,000.
- b. Long-term capital loss of $760.
- c. Long-term capital loss of $600, short-term capital loss of $580.
- d. Short-term capital loss of $500.
- e. None of the above.

Number 2 (Estimated time —— 40 to 50 minutes)

The Cobleskill City Council passed a resolution requiring a yearly cash budget by fund for the City beginning with its fiscal year ending September 30, 1973. The City's financial director has prepared a list of expected cash receipts and disbursements, but he is having difficulty subdividing them by fund. The list follows:

Cash receipts

Taxes:

General property	$ 685,000
School	421,000
Franchise	223,000
	1,329,000
Licenses and permits:	
Business licenses	41,000
Automobile inspection permits	24,000
Building permits	18,000
	83,000
Intergovernmental revenue:	
Sales tax	1,012,000
Federal grants	128,000
State motor vehicle tax	83,500
State gasoline tax	52,000
State alcoholic beverage licenses	16,000
	1,291,500

(continued)
4

Accounting Practice – Part II

Charges for services:	
Sanitation fees	$ 121,000
Sewer connection fees	71,000
Library revenues	13,000
Park revenues	2,500
	207,500

Bond issues:	
Civic center	347,000
General obligation	200,000
Sewer	153,000
Library	120,000
	820,000

Other:	
Proceeds from the sale of investments	312,000
Sewer assessments	50,000
Rental revenue	48,000
Interest revenue	15,000
	425,000
	$4,156,000

Cash disbursements

General government	$ 671,000
Public safety	516,000
Schools	458,000
Sanitation	131,000
Library	28,000
Rental property	17,500
Parks	17,000
	1,838,500

Debt service:	
General obligation bonds	618,000
Street construction bonds	327,000
School bonds	119,000
Sewage disposal plant bonds	37,200
	1,101,200

Investments	358,000
State portion of sales tax	860,200

Capital expenditures:	
Sewer construction (assessed area)	114,100
Civic center construction	73,000
Library construction	36,000
	223,100
	$4,381,000

The financial director provides you with the following additional information:

1. A bond issue was authorized in 1972 for the construction of a civic center. The debt is to be paid from future civic center revenues and general property taxes.

2. A bond issue was authorized in 1972 for additions to the library. The debt is to be paid from general property taxes.

3. General obligation bonds are paid from general property taxes collected by the general fund.

4. Ten percent (10%) of the total annual school taxes represents an individually voted tax for payment of bonds the proceeds of which were used for school construction.

5. In 1970, a wealthy citizen donated rental property to the City. Net income from the property is to be used to assist in operating the library. The net cash increase attributable to the property is transferred to the library on September 30 of each year.

6. All sales taxes are collected by the City; the state receives 85% of these taxes. The state's portion is remitted at the end of each month.

7. Payment of the street construction bonds is to be made from assessments previously collected from the respective property owners. The proceeds from the assessments were invested and the principal of $312,000 will earn $15,000 interest during the coming year.

8. In 1972, a special assessment in the amount of $203,000 was made on certain property owners for sewer construction. During fiscal 1973, $50,000 of this assessment is expected to be collected. The remainder of the sewer cost is to be paid from a $153,000 bond issue to be sold in fiscal 1973. Future special-assessment collections will be used to pay principal and interest on the bonds.

9. All sewer and sanitation services are provided by a separate enterprise fund.

10. The federal grant is for fiscal 1973 school operations.

11. The proceeds remaining at the end of the year from the sale of civic center and library bonds are to be invested.

Required:

Prepare a budget of cash receipts and disbursements by fund for the year ending September 30, 1973. All interfund transfers of cash are to be included.

(OVER)

Uniform Certified Public Accountant Examination

Number 3 (Estimated time —— 30 to 40 minutes)

Your client has entered into a business combination with Jackson Company. You have been asked to examine the financial statements of Jackson so that consolidated financial statements for the years ended December 31, 1972 and 1971, can be issued for the combined companies.

The following information regarding Jackson is available:

1. Jackson started operations on January 1, 1971, and has had a December 31 year end for 1971 and 1972.

2. On January 1, 1971, Jackson leased a building for ten years at $3,500 per month. On that date Jackson put down a $2,000 deposit and paid the first and last months' rent. The total $9,000 was charged to rent expense.

3. On January 1, 1971, Jackson paid $1,440 of the premium on a three-year fire and casualty insurance policy. The policy requires additional annual premium payments of $1,080 on January 1, 1972 and 1973. Jackson has been expensing the premiums as they were paid.

4. On June 30, 1971, Jackson paid $57,000 to have special electrical wiring placed in the building leased January 1, 1971. The wiring has an estimated useful life of 20 years and no salvage value. Since the wiring could not be removed by Jackson at the end of the lease, it was charged to rent expense.

5. On January 1, 1972, Jackson sold equipment for $471,600 which cost $500,000 and had accumulated depreciation of $50,000. Equipment was credited for the selling price. On that same date, the equipment which had been sold was leased back for a rental of $2,200 per month for three years. Jackson has no option to repurchase the equipment or renew the lease.

6. On May 31, 1972, Jackson filed its first franchise tax return. The tax, which was based on the Company's capital structure as of April 30, 1972, amounted to $2,800. It covers the period from January 1, 1971 to April 30, 1973. The entire amount was expensed when paid.

7. Jackson has never written off uncollectible accounts receivable nor provided an allowance for bad debts. At December 31, 1971, no specific receivables were considered uncollectible; however, Jackson's management estimates that 5% of all receivables will prove uncollectible. At December 31, 1972, $23,500 of specific receivables (none from commission sales) were known to be uncollectible, of which $21,000 were receivable at December 31, 1971. At December 31, 1971 and 1972, accounts receivable were $400,000 and $435,000, respectively.

8. Jackson pays its salesmen a 3% commission when the cash is collected for a sale. The commission is expensed when paid. At December 31, 1971 and 1972, accounts receivable relating to commission sales amounted to $350,000 and $380,000, respectively (5% are estimated to be uncollectible). Commissions actually paid during 1972 on 1971 sales were $10,000.

9. Jackson purchased $3,130 of goods F.O.B. shipping point. The goods were not included in the December 31, 1971, physical-inventory count because they were in transit at that date. Jackson had recorded the transaction in the December 1971 purchase journal.

10. Jackson recorded an invoice in January 1973 for $2,860 of goods purchased in December. The goods were on hand and were included in the December 31, 1972, physical-inventory count.

11. On January 1, 1971, Jackson paid $35,000 for a franchise from another company which would give Jackson the exclusive right to sell certain products. The franchise expires on January 1, 2011. The cost was charged as an extraordinary item in 1971.

12. On December 31, 1971, goods having a selling price of $6,432 and a cost value of $4,311 were shipped to a customer by Jackson, F.O.B. shipping point. The goods were not included in the December 31, 1971, physical inventory; the sale was recorded in January 1972.

Required:

Prepare a working paper showing the computation of the effects of the above errors upon Jackson's income for 1971 and 1972 and upon Jackson's balance sheet as of December 31, 1972. The worksheet analysis should be presented in the same order as the facts are given with corresponding numbers 2 through 12. (Formal journal entries or financial statements are not required.) Amortization and depreciation are to be calculated by the straight-line method. **Ignore income and deferred tax considerations.** Use the following columnar headings for your working paper.

Explanation	Income 1971 Dr.	Cr.	Income 1972 Dr.	Cr.	Balance-Sheet Corrections at December 31, 1972 Amount Dr.	Cr.	Account

Number 4 (Estimated time —— 50 to 60 minutes)

The Board of Directors of DeWitt Construction Company is meeting to choose between the completed-contract method and the percentage-of-completion method of accounting for

(continued)

6

Accounting Practice – Part II

long-term contracts for reporting in the Company's financial statements. You have been engaged to assist DeWitt's controller in the preparation of a presentation to be given at the Board meeting. The controller provides you with the following information:

1. DeWitt commenced doing business on January 1, 1972.

2. Construction activities for the year ended December 31, 1972:

Project	Total Contract Price	Billings Through December 31, 1972	Cash Collections Through December 31, 1972
A	$ 520,000	$ 350,000	$ 310,000
B	670,000	210,000	210,000
C	475,000	475,000	395,000
D	200,000	70,000	50,000
E	460,000	400,000	400,000
	$2,325,000	$1,505,000	$1,365,000

Project	Contract Costs Incurred Through December 31, 1972	Estimated Additional Costs to Complete Contracts
A	$ 424,000	$106,000
B	126,000	504,000
C	315,000	–
D	112,750	92,250
E	370,000	30,000
	$1,347,750	$732,250

3. All contracts are with different customers.

4. Any work remaining to be done on the contracts is expected to be completed in 1973.

Required:

a. Prepare a schedule by project computing the amount of revenue and income (or loss) before selling, general, and administrative expenses for the year ended December 31, 1972, that would be reported under:

1. The completed-contract method.

2. The percentage-of-completion method (based upon estimated costs).

b. Following is a balance sheet which compares balances resulting from the use of the two methods of accounting for long-term contracts. For each numbered blank space on the statement, supply the correct balance [indicating dr. (cr.) as appropriate] next to the corresponding number on your answer sheet. Do not recopy the statement. **Disregard income taxes.**

DeWitt Construction Company
BALANCE SHEET
December 31, 1972

Assets	Completed-Contract Method	Percentage-of-Completion Method
Cash	$ xxxx	$ xxxx
Accounts receivable:		
Due on contracts	(1)	(5)
Cost of uncompleted contracts in excess of billings	(2)	–
Costs and estimated earnings in excess of billings on uncompleted contracts	–	(6)
Property, plant, and equipment, net	xxxx	xxxx
Other assets	xxxx	xxxx
	$ xxxx	$ xxxx

Liabilities and Stockholders' Equity		
Accounts payable and accrued liabilities	$ xxxx	$ xxxx
Billings on uncompleted contracts in excess of costs	(3)	–
Billings in excess of costs and estimated earnings	–	(7)
Estimated losses on uncompleted contracts	(4)	–
Notes payable	xxxx	xxxx
Common stock	xxxx	xxxx
Retained earnings	xxxx	xxxx
	$ xxxx	$ xxxx

(OVER)

Uniform Certified Public Accountant Examination

Number 5 (Estimated time — — 60 to 70 minutes)

The Custer Manufacturing Corporation, which uses a job-order-cost system, produces various plastic parts for the aircraft industry. On October 9, 1972, production was started on job number 487 for 100 front bubbles (windshields) for commercial helicopters.

Production of the bubbles begins in the **Fabricating Department** where sheets of plastic (purchased as raw material) are melted down and poured into molds. The molds are then placed in a special temperature and humidity room to harden the plastic. The hardened plastic bubbles are then removed from the molds and hand-worked to remove imperfections.

After fabrication the bubbles are transferred to the **Testing Department** where each bubble must meet rigid specifications. Bubbles which fail the tests are scrapped and there is no salvage value.

Bubbles passing the tests are transferred to the **Assembly Department** where they are inserted into metal frames. The frames, purchased from vendors, require no work prior to installing the bubbles.

The assembled unit is then transferred to the **Shipping Department** for crating and shipment. Crating material is relatively expensive and most of the work is done by hand.

The following information concerning job number 487 is available as of December 31, 1972 (the information is correct as stated):

1. Direct materials charged to the job:
    (a) 1,000 sq. ft. of plastic at $12.75 per sq. ft. was charged to the **Fabricating Department**. This amount was to meet all plastic material requirements of the job assuming no spoilage.
    (b) 74 metal frames at $408.52 each were charged to the **Assembly Department**.
    (c) Packing material for 40 units at $75 per unit was charged to the **Shipping Department**.

2. Direct-labor charges through December 31, 1972, were as follows:

	Total	Per Unit
Fabricating Department	$1,424	$16
Testing Department	444	6
Assembly Department	612	12
Shipping Department	256	8
	$2,736	

3. Differences between actual and applied manufacturing overhead for the year ended December 31, 1972, were immaterial. Manufacturing overhead is charged to the four production departments by various allocation methods, all of which you approve.

Manufacturing overhead charged to the **Fabricating Department** is allocated to jobs based on heat-room hours; the other production departments allocate manufacturing overhead to jobs on the basis of direct-labor dollars charged to each job within the department. The following reflects the manufacturing overhead rates for the year ended December 31, 1972:

	Rate Per Unit
Fabricating Department	$.45 per hour
Testing Department	.68 per direct-labor dollar
Assembly Department	.38 per direct-labor dollar
Shipping Department	.25 per direct-labor dollar

4. Job number 487 used 855 heat-room hours during the year ended December 31, 1972.

5. Following is the physical inventory for job number 487 as of December 31, 1972:

Fabricating Department:
(1) 50 sq. ft. of plastic sheet.
(2) 8 hardened bubbles, 1/4 complete as to direct labor.
(3) 4 complete bubbles.
Testing Department:
(1) 15 bubbles which failed testing when 2/5 of testing was complete. No others failed.
(2) 7 bubbles complete as to testing.
Assembly Department:
(1) 13 frames with no direct labor.
(2) 15 bubbles and frames, 1/3 complete as to direct labor.
(3) 3 complete bubbles and frames.
Shipping Department:
(1) 9 complete units, 2/3 complete as to packing material, 1/3 complete as to direct labor.
(2) 10 complete units; 100% complete as to packing material; 50% complete as to direct labor.
(3) 1 unit complete for shipping was dropped off the loading docks. There is no salvage.
(4) 23 units have been shipped prior to December 31, 1972.

(continued)
8

(5) There was no inventory of packing materials in the shipping department at December 31, 1972.

6. Following is a schedule of equivalent units in production by department for job number 487 as of December 31, 1972:

Custer Manufacturing Corporation
SCHEDULE OF EQUIVALENT UNITS IN PRODUCTION FOR JOB NUMBER 487
December 31, 1972

| | Fabricating Department | | | |
| | Plastic | Bubbles (units) | | |
	(Sq. ft.)	Materials	Labor	Overhead
Transferred in from raw materials	1,000	–	–	–
Production to date	(950)	95	89	95
Transferred out to other departments	–	(83)	(83)	(83)
Spoilage	–	–	–	–
Balance at December 31, 1972	50	12	6	12

| | Testing Department (units) | | |
| | | Bubbles | |
	Transferred in	Labor	Overhead
Transferred in from other departments	83	–	–
Production to date	–	74	74
Transferred out to other departments	(61)	(61)	(61)
Spoilage	(15)	(6)	(6)
Balance at December 31, 1972	7	7	7

| | Assembly Department (units) | | | |
	Transferred in	Frames	Labor	Over-head
Transferred in from raw materials	–	74	–	–
Transferred in from other departments	61	–	–	–
Production to date	–	–	51	51
Transferred out to other departments	(43)	(43)	(43)	(43)
Balance at December 31, 1972	18	31	8	8

| | Shipping Department (units) | | | |
	Transferred in	Packing Material	Labor	Over-head
Transferred in from raw materials	–	40	–	–
Transferred in from other departments	43	–	–	–
Production to date	–	–	32	32
Shipped	(23)	(23)	(23)	(23)
Spoilage	(1)	(1)	(1)	(1)
Balance at December 31, 1972	19	16	8	8

Required:

Prepare a schedule for job number 487 of ending inventory costs for (1) raw materials by department, (2) work in process by department, and (3) cost of goods shipped. All spoilage costs are charged to cost of goods shipped.

Section 2

CPA Examination
in
Accounting Theory
(Theory of Accounts)

SECTION 2

CPA Examination
In Accounting Theory
(Theory of Accounts)

GENERAL APPROACH

The subjects covered in both Theory and Practice sections of the CPA examination intertwine and overlap. Although this book has grouped Theory and Practice separately, simultaneous preparation for both sections is a productive approach. Moreover, the General Approaches to Practice contain summaries of much accounting theory. For example, see the section, Basic Concepts and Accounting Principles, in Topic I and the section, Product Costs and Income Measurement, in Topic IV.

Program for Study

Adequate accounting knowledge and effective writing skill are the keys to success on the CPA Theory section. The Theory examination usually is composed of five or six essay questions and one or two sets of multiple-choice questions. The essay questions fall into two general categories: (a) those that require a discussion of an accounting principle and its supporting logic and (b) those that present a concrete situation and require a discussion of the related accounting principles. Questions covering the difference between accounting and income tax treatments of given data appear occasionally. The multiple-choice questions supply a comprehensive test of a candidate's knowledge of accounting theory.

The Theory section always contains a question or two based upon pronouncements of the Accounting Principles Board and its successor body, the

476

Financial Accounting Standards Board (FASB). Questions also may be based on controversial topics in *The Journal of Accountancy* and other leading accounting journals such as *The Accounting Review*. Because the first draft of the examination is usually composed from 13 to 16 months in advance of the actual examination dates, the probability is small that late-breaking issues will get coverage. On the other hand, journal issues for the twelve months preceding the first drafting dates probably deserve closer study than usual.

A candidate would be foolhardy to neglect Volume 1 of *APB Accounting Principles*. In particular, he should concentrate on Sections 1021-1029, which deal with basic concepts and accounting principles. Moveover, he should keep abreast of the pronouncements of the FASB.

Remember that the examination is graded by the AICPA. In discussing controversial matters, the candidate should always recognize, even if he does not accept, the AICPA position. Minority views that are published in AICPA publications often provide reasoning which, together with the majority views, yield sufficient and balanced treatment of many issues in accounting theory.

Many candidates prefer to use their old texts as a basis for review. This method has merit as long as current editions are used and as long as there is not sole reliance on such texts. Under no circumstances should a candidate ignore APB or FASB literature.

For a 70-page survey of accounting theory, see the latest edition of Herbert E. Miller and George C. Mead (editors), *CPA Review Manual* (Prentice-Hall). For a book-length probing of all sides of accounting theory, see the latest edition of Eldon S. Hendriksen, *Accounting Theory* (Richard D. Irwin).

Candidates should recognize the importance of good writing ability. Faulty writing may measure the point difference between success and failure. Practice-writing of answers to CPA Theory questions helps sharpen writing skill and crystallizes accounting thinking.

Nature of the Theory Examination

Essay Questions

Theory and Auditing questions call mostly for essay answers. This requirement, which stresses reasoning and discussion, may be an unusual experience to many candidates. After all, candidates are accustomed to the accounting tests that they have had in school. and it seems safe to say that the vast bulk of such test questions are either objective or problem-solving in nature. In other words, the accounting major has had some experience with taking tests on accounting problems. He is less likely to have had much experience with essay questions in accounting.

Successful answers to essay questions involve knowledge of the subject and skillful communication. Both are essential ingredients of a convincing answer.

Crisp, direct, concise English will improve an answer, but it will not replace knowledge of subject matter. Say what you mean, and mean what you say.

The knack of writing successful answers to essay questions entails the following characteristics (also discussed in *Information for CPA Candidates*):

Organization: The requirements of the question should provide the broad framework for formulating an answer. Within the requirements, the candidate's main ideas should be fully stated and followed by explanatory comments and ideas of secondary importance. Short paragraphs and short sentences enhance clarity and help emphasize important ideas.

Relevance: Stick to the subject. Avoid rambling and self-contradictions. Quantity and quality of pertinent ideas, not quantity of words, are desired. In discussing both sides of a question, indicate clearly that you are doing so; otherwise, the grader will think that one part of your answer contradicts another part.

Length: Try to prepare a comprehensive, complete, yet concise answer. Brevity is dangerous, because some important points are likely to be omitted. At the same time, unnecessary repetition may lengthen an answer but still may omit as much as the brief answer omits.

Emphasis: Always reveal your perspective by stressing the important, substantive points in an answer. That is, all items that might be included in an answer for credit are not given equal weight. Therefore, concentrate on the main elements at which the question is aimed.

Reasons: The grader is interested in your own ideas and understanding. Consequently, the citing of texts or authorities is of no interest to graders. He wants to "know why the conclusions were reached—in other words, the reasons for the authoritative opinions."

Types of Questions

Theory questions generally are aimed at getting a statement of an accounting principle or rule and then an explanation, justification, or criticism of the rule. The American Accounting Association Committee on the CPA Examination points out (*Accounting Review,* XXXVII, No. 2, p. 324):

> There is a useful differentiation which should be made between the types of questions which characterize the Theory and Practice sections—namely, those questions which stress the *doing* as contrasted with those questions which stress the *reasoning* underlying the particular methods of doing....
> ... This basic characteristic [reasoning] may be subdivided into its various specific aspects as follows: (a) The nature of the accounting concept under consideration; (b) The objective to be achieved by the application of such concept; (c) The reasons why the application of such concept achieves the objective desired; (d) The conditions under which the application of such concept is appropriate or inappropriate; (e) An appraisal of criticisms levelled against such concept; (f) Alternative methods available for achieving the same objective and the conditions under which they are applicable, together with recognition of the preferred method; (g) The effect or impact of the

application of such concept or concepts on the financial statements, considered in part or as a whole; (h) An appreciation of the limitations of the significance of such concepts and the limitations which they impose on the use of such data; (i) Application of the concept in short problems requiring precise understanding of the nature of the concept.

Pitfalls to Avoid

1. Needless repetition of facts given in a question. Facts in a question should be restated only when it is necessary in shaping an answer.

2. Unsupported conclusions. It is dangerous for candidates to make dogmatic statements, to take things for granted, to assume that procedures are carried on because they "always have been done that way," to assume that graders will read meanings and reasoning into candidate's conclusions, to avoid offering supporting reasons because such reasons are "obvious."

3. Failure to answer all parts of a question.

    (a) Ignoring of a specific subdivision of a question.

    (b) Answering a request for a full discussion by offering a partial discussion only.

Too often, a candidate is heavily "balance-sheet oriented"; that is, he will consider the impact of the procedure in question on the balance sheet only, ignoring completely the impact on the income statement.

4. Failure to use simple, descriptive language. Graders are experienced and sophisticated. Avoid foreign phrases, long or stilted words, and ambiguous or fuzzy words and phrases (for example, "true profit," "conservative," "set aside.")

Points are lost because of double meanings and meaningless statements. Do not use the same words in a definition as the term being defined (for example, "indirect costs are costs which are indirect").

5. Failure to be practical, to use common sense. Practical considerations, where important, should be included in an answer. For example, a strong argument against the "net price" method of handling cash discounts is that unit cost computations become more awkward and complicated. An AICPA tabulation of 100 answers to a question on "net price" versus "gross price" treatments of cash discounts revealed that only six out of the hundred gave this argument as a portion of their answer.

On the other hand, many candidates are too heavily "income-tax oriented." You should be able to recognize the difference between accounting theory and tax accounting practice, but do not base your answers on income-tax regulations. Such an approach often raises doubt as to a candidate's possession of well-balanced ability in areas other than income taxes.

A candidate should know the many sides of accounting issues. He should also introduce cost-benefit consequences if they are of major importance. For example, the cost and value of information is an important factor in deciding whether one accounting alternative is preferable to another. A cost-benefit analysis is a central way to ponder the acceptance or rejection of historical cost, when compared to some version of fair value. The most desirable accounting alternative would depend on the costs of each possible set of information in light of perceived benefits.

Topical Analysis of Accounting Theory

These Theory questions have all been collected from the examinations most recently available up to the moment that this book went to press. They have been classified to dovetail with the topical arrangement used throughout the book.

The relative frequency of various types of subject matter in this sample of Theory examinations is not at all similar to that found on the Practice examinations. Questions on basic concepts dominate. Questions on cost accounting have started to appear more frequently. Questions on income taxes do not appear often.

A breakdown of the theory questions by topic follows. The number of questions reflect the relative importance of the topic in recent examinations. Of course, some of these questions might justifiably be classified elsewhere. For example, Questions 4 and 5 might be viewed as belonging in Topic VIII rather than Topic I.

	In Topic	*Questions*	*Relative Importance*
I	Fundamentals of accounting theory	1-11	30%
II	Source and application of funds	12	3
IV	Cost accounting	13-16	11
VI	Quantitative methods	17	3
VII	Investments	18	3
VIII	Long-term assets	19-21	8
IX	Liabilities	22-23	6
X	Stockholders' equity	24-28	11
XI	Business combinations	29	3
XIII	Income taxes	30-31	6
XIV	Miscellaneous objective questions	32-37	16
		37	100%

Recent examinations have contained seven questions each, all required. The time allowance for each question is almost always 25-30 minutes. Therefore, the time allowance is not repeated hereafter for each question except when the allowance is not 25-30 minutes.

1. Accounting entity

The concept of the accounting entity often is considered to be the most fundamental of accounting concepts, one that pervades all of accounting.

Required:

  a. 1. What is an accounting entity? Explain.
  2. Explain why the accounting entity concept is so fundamental that it pervades all of accounting.
  b. For each of the following indicate whether the accounting concept of entity is applicable; discuss and give illustrations.
  1. A unit created by or under law.
  2. The product-line segment of an enterprise.
  3. A combination of legal units and/or product-line segments.
  4. All of the activities of an owner or a group of owners.
  5. An industry.
  6. The economy of the United States.

2. General accounting theory

The following four statements have been taken directly or with some modification from the accounting literature. All of them either are taken out of context, involve circular reasoning and/or contain one or more fallacies, half-truths, erroneous comments, conclusions or inconsistencies (internally or with generally accepted principles or practices).

Statement 1
Accounting is a service activity. Its function is to provide quantitative financial information which is intended to be useful in making economic decisions about and for economic entities. Thus the accounting function might be viewed primarily as being a tool or device for providing quantitative financial information to management to facilitate decision making.

Statement 2
Financial statements that were developed in accordance with generally accepted accounting principles, which apply the conservatism convention, can be free from bias (or can give a presentation that is fair with respect to continuing and prospective stockholders as well as to retiring stockholders).

Statement 3
When a company changes from the Lifo to the Fifo method of determining the cost of ending inventories and this change results in a $1 million increase both in income after taxes and in income taxes for the year of change, the increase would stem from the elimination of Lifo reserves established in prior years.

Statement 4
If the value of an enterprise were to be determined by the method which computes the sum of the present values of the marginal (or incremental)

expected net receipts of individual tangible and intangible assets, the resulting valuation would tend to be less than if the value of the entire enterprise had been determined in another way, such as by computing the present value of total expected net receipts for the entire enterprise (i.e., the resulting valuation of parts would sum to an amount that was less than that for the whole). This would be true even if the same pattern of interest or discount rates was used for both valuations.

Required:

Evaluate each of the above numbered statements on a separate appropriately numbered answer sheet (or sheets) as follows:

a. List the fallacies, half-truths, circular reasoning, erroneous comments or conclusions and/or inconsistencies; and
b. Explain by what authority and/or on what basis each item listed in "a" above can be considered to be fallacious, circular, inconsistent, a half-truth or an erroneous comment or conclusion. If the statement or a portion of it is merely out of context, indicate the context(s) in which the statement would be correct.

3. Objectives of accounting

In the recent past the accounting profession has shown substantial interest in delineating the objectives and principles of accounting. An example of this is Statement of the Accounting Principles Board No. 4, *Basic Concepts and Accounting Principles Underlying Financial Statements of Business Enterprises,* that (1) discusses the nature of financial accounting, the environmental forces that influence it, and the potential and limitations of financial accounting in providing useful information, (2) sets forth the objectives of financial ac-accounting and financial statements and (3) presents a description of present generally accepted accounting principles.

Required:

a. What is the basic purpose of financial accounting and financial statements? Discuss.
b. Identify and discuss (1) each of the general and (2) each of the qualitative objectives of financial accounting and financial statements.

4. Cost amortization

Kwik-Bild Corporation sells and erects shell houses. These are frame struc-tures that are completely finished on the outside but are unfinished on the inside except for flooring, partition studding and ceiling joists. Shell houses are sold chiefly to customers who are handy with tools and who have time to do the interior wiring, plumbing, wall completion and finishing and other work necessary to make the shell houses livable dwellings.

Kwik-Bild buys shell houses from a manufacturer in unassembled packages consisting of all lumber, roofing, doors, windows and similar materials necessary to complete a shell house. Upon commencing operations in a new area, Kwik-Bild buys or leases land as a site for its local warehouse, field office and display houses. Sample display houses are erected at a total cost of from $3,000 to $7,000 including the cost of the unassembled packages. The chief element of cost of the display houses is the unassembled packages, since erection is a short low-cost operation. Old sample models are torn down or altered into new models every three to seven years. Sample display houses have little salvage value because dismantling and moving costs amount to nearly as much as the cost of an unassembled package.

Required:

a. A choice must be made between (1) expensing the costs of sample display houses in the period in which the expenditure is made and (2) spreading the costs over more than one period. Discuss the advantages of each method.

b. Would it be preferable to amortize the cost of display houses on the basis of (1) the passage of time or (2) the number of shell houses sold? Explain.

5. Depreciation

Depreciation continues to be one of the most controversial, difficult and important problem areas in accounting.

Required:

a. 1. Explain the conventional accounting concept of depreciation account-
      ing; and
   2. Discuss its conceptual merit with respect to
      (a) the value of the asset,
      (b) the charge(s) to expense and
      (c) the discretion of management in selecting the method.
b. 1. Explain the factors that should be considered when applying the
      conventional concept of depreciation to the determination of how the
      value of a newly acquired computer system should be assigned to
      expense for financial reporting purposes. (Income tax considerations
      should be ignored.)
   2. What depreciation methods might be used for the computer system?

6. Cash and price-level changes

Although cash generally is regarded as the simplest of all assets to account for, certain complexities can arise for both domestic and multinational companies.

Required:

a. What are the normal components of cash?

b. Under what circumstances, if any, do valuation problems arise in connection with cash?

c. Unrealized and/or realized gains or losses can arise in connection with cash. Excluding consideration of price-level changes, indicate the nature of such gains or losses and the context in which they can arise in relation to cash.

d. 1. How might it be maintained that a gain or a loss is incurred by holding constant balance of cash through a period of price-level change?

    2. Identify and give a justification for the typical accounting treatment accorded these gains or losses.

7. Realization and franchises

Southern Fried Shrimp sells franchises to independent operators throughout the Southeastern part of the United States. The contract with the franchisee includes the following provisions:

The franchisee is charged an initial fee of $25,000. Of this amount $5,000 is payable when the agreement is signed and a $4,000 noninterest bearing note is payable at the end of each of the five subsequent years.

All of the initial franchise fee collected by Southern Fried Shrimp is to be refunded and the remaining obligation canceled if, for any reason, the franchisee fails to open his franchise.

In return for the initial franchise fee Southern Fried Shrimp agrees to (1) assist the franchisee in selecting the location for his business, (2) negotiate the lease for the land, (3) obtain financing and assist with building design, (4) supervise construction, (5) establish accounting and tax records and (6) provide expert advice over a five-year period relating to such matters as employee and management training, quality control and promotion.

In addition to the initial franchise fee the franchisee is required to pay to Southern Fried Shrimp a monthly fee of 2% of sales for menu planning, recipe innovations and the privilege of purchasing ingredients from Southern Fried Shrimp at or below prevailing market rpices.

Management of Southern Fried Shrimp estimates that the value of the services rendered to the franchisee at the time the contract is signed amounts to at least $5,000. All franchisees to date have opened their locations at the scheduled time and none has defaulted on any of the notes receivable.

The credit ratings of all franchisees would entitle them to borrow at the current interest rate of 10%. The present value of an ordinary annuity of five annual receipts of $4,000 each discounted at 10% is $15,163.

Required:

a. Discuss the alternatives that Southern Fried Shrimp might use to account for the initial franchise fee, evaluate each by applying generally accepted accounting principles to this situation and give illustrative entries for each alternative.

b. Given the nature of Southern Fried Shrimp's agreement with its franchisees, when should revenue be recognized? Discuss the question of revenue recognition for both the initial franchise fee and the additional monthly fee of 2% of sales and give illustrative entries for both types of revenue.

c., Assuming that Southern Fried Shrimp sells some franchises for $35,000 which includes a charge of $10,000 for the rental of equipment for its useful life of ten years, that $15,000 of the fee is payable immediately and the balance on noninterest bearing notes at $4,000 per year, that no portion of the $10,000 rental payment is refundable in case the franchisee goes out of business and that title to the equipment remains with the franchisor; what would be the preferable method of accounting for the rental portion of the initial franchise fee? Explain.

8. Revenue realization and trading stamps

Bonanza Trading Stamps, Inc. was formed early this year to sell trading stamps throughout the Southwest to retailers who distribute the stamps gratuitously to their customers. Books for accumulating the stamps and catalogs illustrating the merchandise for which the stamps may be exchanged are given free to retailers for distribution to stamp recipients. Centers with inventories of merchandise premiums have been established for redemption of the stamps. Retailers may not return unused stamps to Bonanza.

The following schedule expresses Bonanza's expectations as to percentages of a normal month's activity which will be attained. For this purpose, a "normal month's activity" is defined as the level of operations expected when expansion of activities ceases or tapers off to a stable rate. The company expects that this level will be attained in the third year and that sales of stamps will average $2,000,000 per month throughout the third year.

Month	Actual Stamp Sales Percent	Merchandise Premium Purchases Percent	Stamp Redemptions Percent
6th	30%	40%	10%
12th	60	60	45
18th	80	80	70
24th	90	90	80
30th	100	100	95

Bonanza plans to adopt an annual closing date at the end of each 12 months of operations.

Required:

a. Discuss the factors to be considered in determining when revenue should be recognized in measuring the income of a business enterprise.

b. Discuss the accounting alternatives that should be considered by Bonanza Trading Stamps, Inc. for the recognition of its revenues and related expenses.

c. For each accounting alternative discussed in "b." above, give balance sheet accounts that should be used and indicate how each should be classified.

9. Cash versus accrual basis

Mr. Erik, owner of Erik's Retail Hardware, states that he computes income on a cash basis. At the end of each year he takes a physical inventory and computes the cost of all merchandise on hand. To this he adds the ending balance of accounts receivable because he considers this to be a part of inventory on the cash basis. Using this logic he deducts from this total the ending balance of accounts payable for merchandise to arrive at what he calls inventory (net).

The following information has been taken from his cash basis income statements for the years indicated:

	1971	1970	1969
Cash received	$173,000	$164,000	$150,000
Cost of goods sold:			
Inventory (net), January 1	8,000	11,000	3,000
Total purchases	109,000	102,000	95,000
Goods available for sale	117,000	113,000	98,000
Inventory (net), December 31	1,000	8,000	11,000
Cost of goods sold	116,000	105,000	87,000
Gross margin	$ 57,000	$ 59,000	$ 63,000

Additional information is as follows for the years indicated:

	1971	1970	1969
Cash sales	$151,000	$147,000	$141,000
Credit sales	24,000	18,000	14,000
Accounts receivable, December 31	8,000	6,000	5,000
Accounts payable for merchandise, December 31	33,000	20,000	13,000

Required:

a. Without reference to the specific situation described above, discuss the various cash basis concepts of revenue and income and indicate the conceptual merits of each.

b. 1. Is the gross margin for Erik's Retail Hardware being computed on a cash basis? Evaluate and explain the approach used with illustrative computations of the cash-basis gross margin for 1970.

2. Explain why the gross margin for Erik's Retail Hardware shows a decrease while sales and cash receipts are increasing.

10. General knowledge of AICPA literature

Select the best answer for each of the following items which relate to Opinions of the Accounting Principles Board.

21. A statement of changes in financial position typically would not disclose the effects of
   a. Capital stock issued to acquire productive facilities.
   b. Stock dividends declared.
   c. Cash dividends declared but not yet paid.
   d. A purchase and immediate retirement of treasury stock.

22. A basic objective of the statement of changes in financial position is to
   a. Supplant the income statement and balance sheet.
   b. Disclose changes during the period in all asset and all liability accounts.
   c. Disclose the change in working capital during the period.
   d. Provide essential information for financial statement users in making economic decisions.

23. When measuring the present value of future rentals to be capitalized as part of the purchase price in a lease that is to be accounted for as a purchase, identifiable payments to cover taxes, insurance and maintenance should be
   a. Included with the future rentals to be capitalized.
   b. Excluded from future rentals to be capitalized.
   c. Capitalized but at a different discount rate and recorded in a different account than future rental payments.
   d. Capitalized but at a different discount rate and for a relevant period that tends to be different than for the future rental payments.

24. Material gains resulting from sale-and-lease-back transactions usually should be accounted for
   a. As an ordinary gain of the period of the transaction.
   b. As an extraordinary gain of the period of the transaction.
   c. By amortizing the gain over the life of the lease.
   d. By crediting the gain to the cost of the related property.

25. Under the financing method of accounting for leases the excess of aggregate rentals over the cost of leased property should be recognized as revenue of the lessor
   a. In increasing amounts during the term of the lease.
   b. In constant amounts during the term of the lease.

 c. In decreasing amounts during the term of the lease.

 d. After the cost of leased property has been fully recovered through rentals.

26. In accounting for a lease the account(s) that should appear on the balance sheet of a lessor if he used the financing method but not if he used the operating method would be the

 a. Investment in Leased Property account.

 b. Investment in Leased Property and Estimated Residual Value accounts.

 c. Contracts Receivable for Equipment Rentals and Investment in Leased Property accounts.

 d. Contracts Receivable for Equipment Rentals and Estimated Residual Value accounts.

27. Shares of treasury stock delivered to effect a business combination that is properly accounted for by the pooling-of-interests method should be accounted for as being

 a. A reissue of treasury shares.

 b. A reissue of treasury shares at fair market value.

 c. Retired and then newly issued.

 d. Retired and then newly issued at fair market value.

28. When a parent company applies the pooling-of-interests method of accounting to a business combination effected at midyear, the income statement for the year

 a. Must be consolidated and should report the parent's income for the whole year and the subsidiary's income earned since the combination.

 b. Must be consolidated and report income for both parent and subsidiary for the entire year with footnotes as to certain income statement items of the separate companies for the first half of the year.

 c. May be unconsolidated and should report the parent's income for the whole year and the dividends received from the subsidiary since the combination.

 d. May be unconsolidated and should report the parent's income for the whole year and the dividends received from the subsidiary since the combination.

29. For a closely-held corporation the declaration of a 15% stock dividend should be accounted for by

 a. Capitalizing retained earnings equal to the par value of shares issued.

 b. Capitalizing retained earnings equal to the fair market value of the shares issued.

 c. Capitalizing an arbitrary amount of retained earnings.

 d. Only a memorandum entry in the capital accounts.

30. Immediate recognition, spreading and averaging are three techniques which affect the annual pension cost provision through the

   a. Recognition of actuarial gains and losses.
   b. Determination of the normal cost.
   c. Amortization of past service cost.
   d. Funding of the plan.

31. In accounting for a pension plan any difference between the pension cost charged to expense and the payments into the fund should be reported as

   a. An offset to the liability for past service cost.
   b. Accrued or prepaid pension cost.
   c. An operating expense in this period.
   d. An accrued actuarial liability.

32. Classification as an extraordinary item on the income statement would be most appropriate for the

   a. Unused portion of a capital loss to be carried forward.
   b. Substantial write-off of obsolete inventories.
   c. Sale of investments not acquired for resale.
   d. Amortization of past service costs of a pension plan.

33. If long-term investments of a manufacturing company are sold at a gain of $80,000 and this transaction increased income taxes by $20,000, the income statement for the period would disclose these effects as

   a. Operating income of $80,000 and an increase in income tax expense of $20,000.
   b. Operating income net of applicable taxes, $60,000.
   c. A prior period adjustment net of applicable taxes, $60,000.
   d. An extraordinary item net of applicable taxes, $60,000.

34. In the preparation of financial statements the accounts of a wholly owned subsidiary which exists primarily for the purpose of leasing property to the parent company should be

   a. Included in consolidated statements.
   b. Excluded from consolidated statements because inclusion would destroy interfirm comparability.
   c. Disclosed by the equity method of accounting for investments.
   d. Ignored if the parent company capitalizes the related leaseholds.

35. The installment method of recognizing revenue is not acceptable for financial reporting if

   a. The collectibility of the sales price is reasonably assured.
   b. The installment period is less than 12 months.
   c. The method is applied to only a portion of the total.
   d. Collection expenses can be reasonably predicted.

36. When the realization of the tax effects of a loss carryforward is assured beyond any reasonable doubt, recognition of tax benefits in the loss year requires

   a. The establishing of a deferred credit equal to future tax reductions.

    b. The establishing of a deferred charge to future tax expense.

    c. The establishing of a receivable from the taxing authority.

    d. Only a footnote to the financial statements.

37. In accounting for individual deferred compensation contracts on the accrual basis, cumulative charges to expense during the period of active employment should approximate

    a. The present value of future services to be performed.

    b. The estimated present value of future payments.

    c. The total amount of payments reasonably estimated to be made.

    d. An estimated percentage of the employee's cumulative earnings.

38. Proceeds from an issue of debt securities having stock purchase warrants should not be allocated between the debt and equity features when

    a. The market value of the warrants is not readily available.

    b. Exercise of the warrants within the next few fiscal periods seems remote.

    c. The allocation would result in a discount on the debt security.

    d. The debt securities must be surrendered to exercise the warrants.

39. Convertible debentures that are common stock equivalents are not considered in computing primary earnings per share if the

    a. Convertible debentures failed to meet the common stock equivalency test at the date of issuance.

    b. Convertible debentures failed to meet the common stock equivalency test for any year since the date of issuance.

    c. Inclusion decreases the loss per share.

    d. Inclusion dilutes earnings per share.

40. In computing earnings per share, options and warrants to acquire common stock are

    a. Always classified as common stock equivalents.

    b. Classified as common stock equivalents only if they have a dilutive effect.

    c. Considered only when computing fully diluted earnings per share.

    d. Treated in the same manner as senior securities.

11. Accounting changes

Accounting Principles Board Opinion Number 20 is concerned with accounting changes.

Required:

    a. Define, discuss and illustrate each of the following in such a way that one can be distinguished from the other:

    1. An accounting change.

    2. A correction of an error in previously issued financial statements.

b. Discuss the justification for a change in accounting principle.

c. Discuss the reporting (as required by Accounting Principles Board Opinion Number 20) of a change from the LIFO method to another method of inventory pricing.

12. Source and application of funds

The following statement was prepared by the Corporation's accountant:

The E. R. Roycie Corporation
STATEMENT OF SOURCE AND APPLICATION
OF FUNDS
For the Year Ended September 30, 1972

Source of funds:

Net income	$ 52,000
Depreciation and depletion	59,000
Increase in long-term debt	178,000
Common stock issued under employee option plans	5,000
Changes in current receivables and inventories, less current liabilities (excluding current maturities of long-term debt)	3,000
	$297,000

Application of funds:

Cash dividends	$ 33,000
Expenditures for property, plant, and equipment	202,000
Investments and other uses	9,000
Change in cash	53,000
	$297,000

The following additional information is available on the E. R. Roycie Corporation for the year ended September 30, 1972:

1. The balance sheet of Roycie Corporation distinguishes between current and noncurrent assets and liabilities.

2.

Depreciation expense	$ 58,000
Depletion expense	1,000
	$ 59,000

3.

Increase in long-term debt	$600,000
Retirement of debt	422,000
Net increase	$178,000

4. The Corporation received $5,000 in cash from its employees on its employee stock option plans, and wage and salary expense attributable to the option plans was an additional $22,000.

5.

Expenditures for property, plant, and equipment	$212,000
Proceeds from retirements of property, plant, and equipment	10,000
Net expenditures	$202,000

6. A stock dividend of 10,000 shares of Roycie Corporation common stock was distributed to common stockholders on April 1, 1972, when the per-share market price was $6 and par value was $1.

7. On July 1, 1972, when its market price was $5 per share, 16,000 shares of Roycie Corporation common stock were issued in exchange for 4,000 shares of preferred stock.

Required:

a. In general, what are the objectives of a statement of the type shown above for the Roycie Corporation? Explain.

b. Identify the weaknesses in the form and format of the Roycie Corporation's Statement of Source and Application of Funds without reference to the additional information.

c. For each of the seven items of additional information for the Statement of Source and Application of Funds, indicate the preferable treatment and explain why the suggested treatment is preferable.

13. Product costing (35-40 min.)

The Jonesville Company manufactures capacitors used in radios, television sets, and rockets. Some orders are filled from inventory, while others are for capacitors that are specially made to customer specification as to size, lead wires, voltage, and tolerance.

When manufacturing a custom order, the Jonesville Company intentionally produces more capacitors than are ordered by the customer. These extra capacitors are carried at no value in the Jonesville Company inventory since all costs of the job are charged to cost of goods sold at the time that the order is shipped. The extras are kept (1) to replace any capacitors that may be returned as rejects that currently constitute 20% of all units sold and (2) to fill any subsequent orders from the customer for additional units of the same item. Since there is no market for the unused custom manufactured capacitors, any that remain in inventory for two years are destroyed.

Jonesville warrants the replacement of defective capacitors returned by the purchaser. Often three to six months elapse between delivery of the order and receipt of the defectives.

Jonesville predicts that its production capacity is adequate so that no sales would be lost in future periods even though it did not have the extras on hand to cover subsequent orders of custom manufactured capacitors.

Required:

a. What are the conceptual merits of Jonesville carrying the custom manufactured extras held for replacement of defectives at:
   1. No value? Explain.
   2. Marginal or incremental cost? Explain.
   3. Full cost? Explain.

b. What are the conceptual merits of Jonesville carrying the custom manufactured extras held for subsequent sale at:
  1. No value? Explain.
  2. Marginal or incremental cost? Explain.
  3. Full cost? Explain.

c. What disclosure, if any, should Jonesville make for its obligation to replace defective capacitors? Explain

14. Variable budgets

Department A is one of 15 departments in the plant and is involved in the production of all of the six products manufactured. The department is highly mechanized and as a result its output is measured in direct machine hours. Variable (flexible) budgets are utilized throughout the factory in planning and controlling costs, but here the focus is upon the application of variable budgets only in Department A. The following data covering a time span of approximately six months were taken from the various budgets, accounting records and performance reports (only representative items and amounts are utilized here):

On March 15, 1971 the following variable budget was approved for the department; it will be used throughout the 1972 fiscal year which begins July 1, 1971. This variable budget was developed through the cooperative efforts of the department manager, his supervisor and certain staff members from the budget department.

1972 Variable Budget – Department A

Controllable Costs	Fixed Amount Per Month	Variable Rate Per Direct Machine Hour
Employee salaries	$ 9,000	$.07
Indirect wages	18,000	.09
Indirect materials		.03
Other costs	6,000	.03
	$33,000	$.19

On May 5, 1971 the annual sales plan and the production budget were completed. In order to continue preparation of the annual profit plan (which was detailed by month) the production budget was translated to planned activity for each of the factory departments. The planned activity for Department A was:

	For the 12 months ending June 30, 1972				
	Year	July	Aug.	Sept.	etc.
Planned output in direct machine hours	325,000	22,000	25,000	29,000	249,000

On August 31, 1971 the manager of Department A was informed that his planned output for September had been revised to 34,000 direct machine hours. He expressed some doubt as to whether this volume could be attained.

At the end of September 1971 the accounting records provided the following actual data for the month for the department:

Actual output in direct machine hours	$33,000
Actual controllable costs incurred:	
Employee salaries	$ 9,300
Indirect wages	20,500
Indirect materials	2,850
Other costs	7,510
	$40,160

Required:

The requirements relate primarily to the potential uses of the variable budget for the period March through September 1971.

a. What activity base is utilized as a measure of volume in the budget for this department? How should one determine the range of the activity base to which the variable rates per direct machine hour are relevant? Explain.

b. The high-low point method was utilized in developing this variable budget. Using indirect wage costs as an example, illustrate and explain how this method would be applied in determining the fixed and variable components of indirect wage costs for this department. Assume that the high-low budget values for indirect wages are $19,400 at 20,000 direct machine hours and $20,100 at 30,000 direct machine hours.

c. Explain and illustrate how the variable budget should be utilized:

    1. In budgeting costs when the annual sales plan and production budget are completed (about May 5, 1971 or shortly thereafter).

    2. In budgeting a cost revision based upon a revised production budget (about August 31, 1971 or shortly thereafter).

    3. In preparing a cost performance report for September 1971.

15. Miscellaneous managerial questions (25-30 min.)

Select the best answer for each of the following items relating to a variety of managerial accounting problems.

    19. Conversion cost is equal to the total of

        a. Direct labor and raw materials.

        b. Direct labor and factory overhead.

        c. Indirect labor and factory overhead.

        d. Factory overhead and raw materials.

20. A capital-budgeting technique that explicitly incorporates an estimated interest rate into its basic computations is the
   a. Accounting book-value method.
   b. Payback method.
   c. Net present-value method.
   d. Average rate-of-return method.

21. The payback method measures
   a. How quickly investment dollars may be recovered.
   b. The cash flow from an investment.
   c. The economic life of an investment.
   d. The profitability of an investment.

22. Given actual amounts of a semivariable cost for various levels of output, the method that will give the most precise measure of the fixed and variable components is
   a. The use of Bayesian statistics.
   b. Linear programming.
   c. The scattergram approach.
   d. The least squares method.

23. A company employing very tight (high) standards in a standard-cost system should expect that
   a. No incentive bonus will be paid.
   b. Most variances will be unfavorable.
   c. Employees will be strongly motivated to attain the standards.
   d. Costs will be controlled better than if lower standards were used.

24. Standard costing will produce the same financial statement results as actual or conventional costing when standard-cost variances are distributed to
   a. Cost of goods sold.
   b. An income or expense account.
   c. Cost of goods sold and inventory.
   d. A balance-sheet account.

25. A spending variance for variable overhead based on direct labor hours is the difference between actual variable overhead cost and variable overhead cost that should have been incurred for the actual hours worked and results from
   a. Price and quantity differences for overhead costs.
   b. Price differences for overhead costs.
   c. Quantity differences for overhead costs.
   d. Differences caused by variations in production volume.

26. The cost-volume-profit analysis underlying the conventional breakeven chart does not assume that
   a. Prices will remain fixed.
   b. Production will equal sales.
   c. Some costs vary inversely with volume.
   d. Costs are linear and continuous over the relevant range.

27. The primary difference between a fixed budget and a variable (flexible) budget is that a fixed budget
   a. Includes only fixed costs, while a variable budget includes only variable costs.
   b. Is concerned only with future acquisitions of fixed assets, while a variable budget is concerned with expenses which vary with sales.
   c. Cannot be changed after the period begins, while a variable budget can be changed after the period begins.
   d. Is a plan for a single level of sales (or other measure of activity), while a variable budget consists of several plans, one for each of several levels of sales (or other measure of activity).

28. The term "relevant range" as used in cost accounting means the range
   a. Over which costs may fluctuate.
   b. Over which cost relationships are valid.
   c. Of probable production.
   d. Over which relevant costs are incurred.

29. The method of accounting for joint-product costs that will produce the same gross-profit rate for all products is the
   a. Relative sales-value method.
   b. Physical-measure method.
   c. Actual-costing method.
   d. Services-received method.

30. The concept of "management by exception" refers to management's
   a. Consideration of only those items which vary materially from plans.
   b. Consideration of only rare events.
   c. Consideration of items selected at random.
   d. Lack of a predetermined plan.

31. Under a job-order system of cost accounting, the dollar amount of the entry involved in the transfer of inventory from work-in-process to finished goods is the sum of the costs charged to all jobs
   a. Started in process during the period.
   b. In process during the period.
   c. Completed and sold during the period.
   d. Completed during the period.

32. If over- or underapplied overhead is interpreted as an error in allocating actual costs against the production of the year, this suggests that the over- or underapplied overhead of this year should be
   a. Carried forward in the overhead control account from year to year.
   b. Eliminated by changing the predetermined overhead rate in subsequent years.
   c. Apportioned among the work-in-process inventory, the finished goods inventory, and the cost of goods sold.
   d. Treated as a special gain or loss occurring during the year.

33. The budget variance for fixed factory overhead for the normal-volume, practical-capacity, and expected-activity levels would be the
    a. Same except for normal volume.
    b. Same except for practical capacity.
    c. Same except for expected activity.
    d. Same for all three activity levels.

34. When the firm prepares its budget in terms of the expected-activity level of operations, the volume variance theoretically should be disposed of as a
    a. Loss due to idle capacity.
    b. Revision of the overhead rate based on actual activity.
    c. Deferred charge to future periods.
    d. Charge to cost of goods sold.

35. The budget for a given cost during a given period was $80,000. The actual cost for the period was $72,000. Considering these facts, it can be said that the plant manager has done a better than expected job in controlling the cost if
    a. The cost is variable and actual production was 90% of budgeted production.
    b. The cost is variable and actual production equaled budgeted production.
    c. The cost is variable and actual production was 80% of budgeted production.
    d. The cost is a discretionary fixed cost and actual production equaled budgeted production.

36. The variable factory overhead rate under the normal-volume, practical-capacity, and expected-activity levels would be the
    a. Same except for normal volume.
    b. Same except for practical capacity.
    c. Same except for expected activity.
    d. Same for all three activity levels.

16. Inventory control

Inventories usually are an important asset for both manufacturing and merchandising firms. A proper balance of inventory quantities is desirable from several standpoints. Maintaining such a balance is dependent upon a number of factors including ordering at the proper time and in the correct lot size. Serious penalties may attend both overstocking and stockout situations.

Required:

a. In connection with inventory ordering and control, certain terms are basic. Explain the meaning of each of the following:

      1. Economic order quantity.
      2. Reorder point.
      3. Lead time.
      4. Safety stock.
  b. 1. What are the costs of carrying inventories? Explain.
     2. How does overstocking add to the cost of carrying inventories?
  c. 1. What are the consequences of maintaining minimal or inadequate inventory levels?
     2. What are the difficulties of measuring precisely the costs associated with understocking?
  d. Discuss the propriety of including carrying costs (of normal inventory, overstocking and understocking) in the inventory cost:
     1. For external reporting.
     2. For internal decision making.

17. Quantitative methods

Select the best answer for each of the following items relating to the application of quantitative techniques to managerial accounting problems.

19. If a company wishes to establish a factory overhead budget system in which estimated costs can be derived directly from estimates of activity levels, it should prepare a
  a. Capital budget.
  b. Cash budget.
  c. Discretionary budget.
  d. Fixed budget.
  e. Flexible budget.

20. A company has a problem in which the treasurer complains about an excessive investment in inventories. At the same time the purchasing agent states that large inventory balances are necessary to take advantage of supplier discounts, and the production manager complains that production often is delayed by inventory shortages. The quantitative technique most relevant to this situation is
  a. Economic order quantity models.
  b. Linear programming.
  c. Payback analysis.
  d. Probability analysis.
  e. Statistical quality control.

21. A client has been plagued with excessive numbers of defective units of standard machine parts that are purchased from vendors on a regular basis. The most relevant quantitative technique for designing a formal inspection system for incoming parts is

    a. Cost-volume-profit analysis.
    b. Queuing analysis.
    c. Standard cost variance analysis.
    d. Statistical quality control.
    e. Time series or trend regression analysis.

22. A company is considering the purchase of a new conveyor belt system that is to be used for carrying parts and subassemblies from building to building within its plant complex. It is expected that the system will have a useful life of at least ten years and that it will substantially reduce labor and waiting-time costs. If the company's average cost of capital is about 15% and if some evaluation must be made of cost-benefit relationships, including the effects of interest, to determine the desirability of the purchase, the most relevant quantitative technique for evaluating the investment is
    a. Cost-volume-profit analysis.
    b. Payback analysis.
    c. Present value (or time-adjusted rate of return) analysis.
    d. Program evaluation review technique (PERT).
    e. Time series or trend regression analysis.

23. If a company wishes to forecast sales for the approaching budget year based upon the sales data for prior years that are contained in the general ledger and supporting schedules, the most relevant quantitative technique is
    a. Cost-volume-profit analysis.
    b. Economic order quantity models.
    c. Queuing analysis.
    d. Sensitivity analysis.
    e. Time series or trend regression analysis.

24. A production department in a manufacturing company does machining on two categories of parts each of which requires work from three machines. If the time and capacity restrictions on the machines are stringent, a relevant quantitative technique that permits machine-usage on the most profitable basis is
    a. Linear programming.
    b. Queuing analysis.
    c. Sensitivity analysis.
    d. Statistical quality control.
    e. Time series or trend regression analysis.

25. A company is giving consideration to the opening of a self-service gasoline station on a busy thoroughfare that carries a large volume of commuting traffic. There is concern as to the number of traffic and service lanes that should be constructed. If it is necessary to estimate traffic flows and customer waiting time as a basis for estimating the costs of providing a limited number of service facilities, the most directly relevant quantitative technique is
    a. Cost-volume-profit analysis.
    b. Payback analysis.

    c. Queuing analysis.

    d. Sensitivity analysis.

    e. Time series or trend regression analysis.

26. The president of a company that manufactures several different products finds that its gross margin on sales has been decreasing. The production manager complains that some products are charged with too much fixed overhead and the sales department is criticized for pushing the less profitable products. Inquiry discloses that neither the contribution margin nor the most profitable volume is known for any product. A relevant quantitative technique for finding the most profitable operating levels is

    a. Correlation analysis.

    b. Cost-volume-profit analysis.

    c. Program evaluation review technique (PERT).

    d. Statistical quality control.

    e. Time series or trend regression analysis.

27. A large appliance manufacturer has warehouses at many locations across the country. Each warehouse (1) has a limited capacity but services predictable demand and (2) is supplied by one or more regional factories that also have limited capacities. The marketing manager asserts that the firm cannot both minimize freight costs and keep the warehouses adequately supplied because of the complex freight rate structures. The relevant quantitative technique most generally applicable in this situation is

    a. Cost-volume-profit analysis.

    b. Linear programming.

    c. Program evaluation review technique (PERT).

    d. Queuing analysis.

    e. Sensitivity analysis.

28. A firm wishes to predict the demand for some of its consumer products. In the past the sales volume of these products has increased or decreased (with a lag) with increases and decreases in disposable income as reported in the Federal Reserve Bulletin. The firm does not know how closely sales and disposable income are related or how much of the sales demand is caused by extraneous (nonincome) factors. The relevant quantitative technique that should be applied to measure the degree of these relationships is

    a. Correlation analysis.

    b. Cost-volume-profit analysis.

    c. Game theory analysis.

    d. Linear programming.

    e. Program evaluation review technique (PERT).

29. Financial statements of a number of companies are to be analyzed for potential growth by use of a model which considers the rates of change in assets, owners' equity and income. The most relevant quantitative technique to be used in developing such a model is

    a. Correlation analysis.

    b. Differential calculus.

    c. Integral calculus

    d. Program evaluation review technique (PERT).

    e. Statistical sampling.

30. Top management of a company wishes to evaluate investment proposals of semiautonomous divisions by comparing estimates of future revenues and costs. For products with which the company or division has had little or no experience, the revenue and cost estimates are made by different personnel under varying circumstances. The most relevant quantitative technique is

    a. Linear programming.

    b. Probability analysis.

    c. Program evaluation review technique (PERT).

    d. Queuing analysis.

    e. Time series or trend regression analysis.

31. A company controls its production costs by comparing its actual monthly production costs with the expected levels. Any significant deviations from expected levels are investigated and evaluated as a basis for corrective actions. The quantitative technique that most probably is being used is

    a. Correlation analysis.

    b. Differential calculus.

    c. Risk analysis.

    d. Standard cost variance analysis.

    e. Time series or trend regression analysis.

32. A company wishes to estimate the value of its inventory by dividing the inventory into several classes and then randomly selecting several items from each class. The relevant quantitative technique is

    a. Cross-sectional analysis.

    b. Monte Carlo simulation method.

    c. Random sampling.

    d. Risk analysis.

    e. Stratified random sampling.

33. A firm wishes to compare the effects of using a new labor-saving machine with present direct labor methods. These comparisons will be made over a wide variety of operations on several typical days. The demands placed upon each operation as well as the sequence of individual operations can be described by probability distributions. The most relevant quantitative technique is

    a. Cost-volume-profit analysis.

    b. Monte Carlo simulation method.

    c. Program evaluation review technique (PERT).

    d. Statistical sampling.

    e. Time series or trend regression analysis.

34. If a firm wishes to assess the effect of changing the contribution margin

of product Z upon its optimum product mix and profitability, the most relevant quantitative technique is
  a. Correlation analysis.
  b. Cost-volume-profit analysis.
  c. Queuing analysis.
  d. Sensitivity analysis.
  e. Time series or trend regression analysis.

35. If a firm is considering the use of learning curve analysis in the determination of labor cost standards for a new product, it should be advised that this technique generally is most relevant to situations in which the production time per unit decreases as additional units are produced and the unit cost
  a. Decreases.
  b. Does not change.
  c. Increases or decreases in an unpredictable manner.
  d. Increases slightly.
  e. Increases substantially.

36. A company is controlling a complex project by determining the activities that must take place and the relationship between these activities. Attention then is focused upon those activities that have the greatest influence on the project's estimated completion date. The quantitative technique most relevant to this situation is
  a. Cost-volume-profit analysis.
  b. Parametric programming.
  c. Program evaluation review technique (PERT).
  d. Queuing analysis.
  e. Statistical sampling.

18. Investments in equity securities (15-20 min.)

Part a. Business entities often make investments by purchasing equity securities of other business entities.

Required:

Under what circumstances in current generally accepted practice should equity investments be reported in balance sheets:

1. At cost? Explain.
2. At current market value? Explain.

Part b. The Viquinn Company, a manufacturing company, has invested in equity securities of many different corporations. The Company buys and sells the securities in small blocks strictly for dividend revenue and appreciation.

Although Viquinn's total investment in equity securities is large, the amount invested in each security is small in terms both of the total of its investments and of the market for the security. All securities are traded regularly on one or more organized exchanges.

Viquinn's Board of Directors is attempting to determine whether to report its investment in these securities at (1) cost or (2) current market value.

Required:

What are the conceptual merits of the Viquinn Company reporting its investment in equity securities:

1. At cost? Explain.
2. At current market value? Explain.

19. Trade-in of machinery

Lexton Corporation acquired a new machine by trading in an old machine and paying $24,000 in cash. The old machine originally cost $40,000 and has accumulated depreciation at the date of exchange of $30,000. The new machine could have been purchased outright for $50,000 cash.

This transaction could be recorded by either of the two following methods:

Method 1	Debit	Credit
Machinery	$50,000	
Accumulated depreciation	30,000	
Gain on disposal of fixed assets		$16,000
Cash		24,000
Machinery		40,000

Method 2	Debit	Credit
Machinery	34,000	
Accumulated depreciation	30,000	
Cash		24,000
Machinery		40,000

Required:

a. Identify and discuss the reasons for recording the above transaction using Method 1.

b. Identify and discuss the reasons for recording the above transaction using Method 2.

c. Using the theoretically preferable method, give the entry to record the above transaction if the new machine had a nominal list price of $52,000, was commonly selling for $50,000 cash, and Lexton Corporation were allowed $28,000 for its old machine. Explain.

20. Goodwill and other intangible assets

Accounting practitioners, accounting authors and the courts have proposed various solutions to the problems of accounting in terms of historical cost for goodwill and similar intangibles.

Required:

a. In comparing the problems of accounting for goodwill and similar intangible assets to those for other plant assets:
1. What problems are similar? Explain.
2. What problems are different? Explain.
b. 1. What are the possible accounting treatments subsequent to the date of acquisition for the cost of goodwill and similar intangible assets? Explain.
2. Which of these treatments are preferable? Explain.

21. Intangible assets (patents)

On June 30, 1970, your client, The Vandiver Corporation, was granted two patents covering plastic cartons that it has been producing and marketing profitably for the past three years. One patent covers the manufacturing process and the other covers the related products.

Vandiver executives tell you that these patents represent the most significant breakthrough in the industry in the past 30 years. The products have been marketed under the registered trademarks Safetainer, Duratainer and Sealrite. Licenses under the patents have already been granted by your client to other manufacturers in the United States and abroad and are producing substantial royalties.

On July 1, Vandiver commenced patent infringement actions against several companies whose names you recognize as those of substantial and prominent competitors. Vandiver's management is optimistic that these suits will result in a permanent injunction against the manufacture and sale of the infringing products and collection of damages for loss of profits caused by the alleged infringement.

The financial vice-president has suggested that the patents be recorded at the discounted value of expected net royalty receipts.

Required:

a. What is an intangible asset? Explain.
b. 1. What is the meaning of "discounted value of expected net receipts"? Explain.
2. How would such a value be calculated for net royalty receipts?
c. What basis of valuation for Vandiver's patents would be generally accepted in accounting? Give supporting reasons for this basis.
d. 1. Assuming no practical problems of implementation and ignoring generally accepted accounting principles, what is the preferable basis of evaluation for patents? Explain.

2. What would be the preferable theoretical basis of amortization? Explain.

e. What recognition, if any, should be made of the infringement litigation in the financial statements for the year ending September 30, 1970? Discuss.

22. Imputed interest on notes

Business transactions often involve the exchange of property, goods, or services for notes or similar instruments that may stipulate no interest rate or an interest rate that varies from prevailing rates.

Required:

a. When a note is exchanged for property, goods, or services, what value should be placed upon the note:
    1. If it bears interest at a reasonable rate and is issued in a bargained transaction entered into at arm's length? Explain.
    2. If it bears no interest and/or is not issued in a bargained transaction entered into at arm's length? Explain.

b. If the recorded value of a note differs from the face value:
    1. How should the difference be accounted for? Explain.
    2. How should this difference be presented in the financial statements? Explain.

23. Bonds payable

On January 1, 1971 Guadagno Corporation issued for $1,106,775 its 20-year, 8% bonds which have a maturity value of $1,000,000 and pay interest semi-annually on January 1 and July 1. Bond issue costs were not material in amount. The following are three presentations of the long-term liability section of the balance sheet that might be used for these bonds at the issue date:

1. Bonds payable (maturing January 1, 1991) $1,000,000
    Unamortized premium on bonds payable 106,775
       Total bond liability $1,106,775

2. Bonds payable—principal (face value $1,000,000, maturing
    January 1, 1991)... $ 252,572*
    Bonds payable—interest (semiannual payment $40,000) 854,203**
       $1,106,775

3. Bonds payable—principal (maturing January 1, 1991) $1,000,000
    Bonds payable—interest ($40,000 per period for 40 periods) 1,600,000
       Total bond liability $2,600,000

*The present value of $1,000,000 due at the end of 40 (six-month) periods at the yield rate of 3½% per period.

**The present value of $40,000 per period for 40 (six-month) periods at the yield rate of 3½% per period.

Required:

a. Discuss the conceptual merit(s) of each of the date-of-issue balance sheet presentations shown above for these bonds.

b. Explain why investors would pay $1,106,775 for bonds which have a maturity value of only $1,000,000.

c. Assuming that a discount rate is needed to compute the carrying value of the obligations arising from a bond issue at any date during the life of the bonds, discuss the conceptual merit(s) of using for this purpose:

1. The coupon or nominal rate.
2. The effective or yield rate at date of issue.

d. If the obligations arising from these bonds are to be carried at their present value computed by means of the current market rate of interest, how would the bond valuation at dates subsequent to the date of issue be affected by an increase or a decrease in the market rate of interest?

24. Reserve for self-insurance

You discover an account entitled "Reserve for Self-Insurance" in the ledger of a new client.

Required:

a. 1. Explain the meaning of the term "self-insurance."
   2. Under what circumstances might an enterprise choose to follow a policy of "self-insurance" on its plant assets?

b. 1. Indicate two alternative approaches to establishing the "Reserve for Self-Insurance."
   2. Give the journal entries to be made under each approach (a) prior to and (b) when a loss occurs.
   3. Give the balance sheet classification of the "reserve" under each approach.

c. For each of the alternatives given in "b.1." above:
   1. Indicate the circumstances under which the approach might be used.
   2. Evaluate the theoretical propriety of the approach.

25. Convertible debt

The equityholders of a business entity usually are considered to include both creditors and owners. These two classes of equityholders have some characteristics in common, and sometimes it is difficult to make a clear cut distinction between them. Examples of this problem include (1) convertible debt and (2) debt issued with stock purchase warrants. While both examples represent debts of a corporation, there is a question as to whether there is an ownership interest in each case which requires accounting recognition.

Required:

a. Identify:
1. Convertible debt.
2. Debt issued with stock purchase warrants.
b. With respect to convertible debt and debt issued with stock purchase warrants discuss:
1. The similarities.
2. The differences.
c. 1. What are the alternative accounting treatments for the proceeds from convertible debt? Explain.
2. Which treatment is preferable? Explain.
d. 1. What are the alternative accounting treatments for the proceeds from debt issued with stock purchase warrants? Explain.
2. Which treatment is preferable? Explain.

26. Common stock equivalents

APB *Opinion No. 15* discusses the concept of common stock equivalents and prescribes the reporting of primary earnings per share and fully diluted earnings per share.

Required:

a. Discuss the reasons why securities other than common stock may be considered common stock equivalents for the computation of primary earnings per share.
b. Define the term "senior security" and explain how senior securities which are not convertible enter into the determination of earnings per share data.
c. Explain how convertible securities are determined to be common stock equivalents and how those convertible senior securities which are not considered to be common stock equivalents enter into the determination of earnings per share data.
d. Explain the treasury stock method as it applies to options and warrants in computing primary earnings per share data.

27. Secret reserves and watered stock

Part a. It has been said that the use of the LIFO inventory method during an extended period of rising prices and the expensing of all human resource costs are among the accepted accounting practices which help create "secret reserves."

Required:

1. What is a "secret reserve"? How can "secret reserves" be created or enlarged?

2. What is the basis for saying that the two specific practices cited above tend to create "secret reserves"?

3. Is it possible to create a "secret reserve" in connection with accounting for a liability? If so, explain or give an example.

4. What are the objections to the creation of "secret reserves"?

Part b. It has also been said that "watered stock" is the opposite of a "secret reserve."

Required:

1. What is "watered stock"?

2. Describe the general circumstances in which "watered stock" can arise.

3. What steps can be taken to eliminate "water" from a capital structure?

28. Stock options

Part a. Stock options are widely used as a form of compensation for corporate executives.

Required:

1. Identify five methods that have been proposed for determining the value of executive stock options.

2. Discuss the conceptual merits of each of these proposed methods.

Part b. On January 1, 1970, as an incentive to greater performance in their duties, Recycling Corporation adopted a qualified stock option plan to grant corporate executives nontransferable stock options to 500,000 shares of its unissued $1.00 par value common stock. The options were granted on May 1, 1970 at $25 per share, the market price on that date. All of the options were exercisable one year later and for four years thereafter providing that the grantee was employed by the Corporation at the date of exercise.

The market price of this stock was $40 per share on May 1, 1971. All options were exercised before December 31, 1971 at times when the market price varied between $40 and $50 per share.

Required:

1. What information on this option plan should be presented in the financial statements of Recycling Corporation at (a) December 31, 1970 and (b) December 31, 1971? Explain why this is acceptable.

2. It has been said that the exercise of such a stock option would dilute the equity of existing stockholders in the Corporation.

   (a) How could this happen? Discuss.

   (b) What condition could prevent a dilution of existing equities from taking place in this transaction? Discuss.

29. Consolidations

On October 1, 1969, the Arba Company acquired a 90% interest in the common stock of Braginetz Company on the open market for $750,000; the book value was $712,500 at that date. Since the excess could not be attributed to the undervaluation of any specific assets, Arba reported $37,500 of consolidated goodwill on its consolidated balance sheet at September 30, 1970. During fiscal 1971 it was decided that the Braginetz goodwill should be amortized in equal amounts over ten years beginning with fiscal 1971.

On October 1, 1970, Arba purchased new equipment for $14,500 from Braginetz. The equipment cost Braginetz $9,000 and had an estimated life of 10 years as of October 1, 1970. Arba uses the sum-of-the-years-digits depreciation method for both financial and income tax reporting.

During fiscal 1972, Arba had merchandise sales to Braginetz of $100,000; the merchandise was priced at 25% above Arba's cost. Braginetz still owes Arba $17,500 on open account and has 20% of this merchandise in inventory at September 30, 1972.

On August 1, 1972, Braginetz borrowed $30,000 from Arba by issuing twelve, $2,500, 9%, 90-day notes. Arba discounted four of the notes at its bank on August 31 at 6%.

Required:

a. What are criteria which could influence Arba in its decision to include or exclude Braginetz as a subsidiary in consolidated financial statements? Explain.

b. For each of the following items give the elimination entry (including explanation) that should be made on the workpapers for the preparation of the indicated consolidated statement(s) at September 30, 1972.

1. For the consolidated goodwill—to prepare all consolidated statements.
2. For the equipment:
   (a) To prepare only a consolidated balance sheet.
   (b) To prepare all consolidated statements.
3. For the intercompany merchandise transactions—to prepare all consolidated statements.
4. For the note transactions—to prepare only a consolidated balance sheet.

30. Income tax reform

The Tax Reform Act of 1969 significantly changed the federal income tax treatment of transactions involving the disposal of capital assets held for more than six months. These changes include:

Increasing the alternative tax rate applicable to capital gains.

Designating long-term capital gains as potential "tax-preference income."

Limiting the amount of a long-term capital loss deductible by noncorporate taxpayers to 50% of the loss.

Required:

a. Discuss the arguments (1) for and (2) against taxing long-term capital gains at rates lower than those imposed upon ordinary income.

b. Give the arguments for levying a special tax upon "tax-preference income."

c. Why should only 50% of a long-term capital loss be deductible by noncorporate taxpayers? In your answer discuss any other limitations upon the deduction of such a loss and the reasons for such limitations, if any.

31. Income taxes and accounting principles

Although the general requirements of the Internal Revenue Code indicate that a taxpayer is to use the same accounting method for computing taxable income that he uses in keeping his books, there are significant differences both in concept and principle between accounting for federal income taxes and for financial reporting.

Required:

a. Compare and contrast the doctrine of constructive receipt of income tax accounting with the concept(s) of revenue recognition for financial reporting purposes.

b. Through the application of income tax allocation, financial accounting seeks to reconcile the differences between tax accounting and financial accounting. What are the underlying reasons for:

　　1. Interperiod income tax allocation? Explain.

　　2. Intraperiod income tax allocation? Explain.

c. Compare and contrast the accounting treatment of an involuntary conversion (1) in the determination of taxable income and (2) in the determination of income for financial reporting.

32. Miscellaneous

Select the best answer for each of the following items relating to a variety of financial accounting concepts.

1. The practice of raising cash from trade receivables prior to their maturity dates is widespread. A term which is not associated with this practice is

    a. Hypothecation.

    b. Factoring.

    c. Defalcation.

    d. Pledging.

2. The basis for classifying assets as current or noncurrent is the period of time normally elapsed from the time the accounting entity expends cash to the time it converts

    a. Inventory back into cash, or 12 months, whichever is shorter.

    b. Receivables back into cash, or 12 months, whichever is longer.

    c. Tangible fixed assets back into cash, or 12 months, whichever is longer.

    d. Inventory back into cash, or 12 months, whichever is longer.

3. Stock warrants outstanding should be classified as

    a. Liabilities.

    b. Reductions of capital contributed in excess of par value.

    c. Capital stock.

    d. Additions to contributed capital.

4. Gross (profit) margin variation analysis may be used to determine the amount of variation in the

    a. Sales and cost of goods sold, accounted for by changes in sales price and physical volume.

    b. Operating expenses, caused by a change in the physical sales volume.

    c. Physical sales volume, caused by a change in sales price.

    d. Cost of goods sold, accounted for by a change in sales price.

5. A reserve for possible future losses on inventory should be established to

    a. Match current revenues with applicable costs.

    b. Reduce fluctuations in net income in order to lend stability to the company.

    c. Charge operations in periods of rising prices for the losses which may otherwise be absorbed in periods of falling prices.

    d. Inform stockholders that a portion of retained earnings should be set aside from amounts available for dividends because of such a contingency.

6. The acquisition cost of a heavily used raw material changes frequently. The book value of the inventory of this material at year-end will be the same if perpetual records are kept as it would be under a periodic inventory method only if the book value is computed under the

    a. Weighted-average method.

    b. First-in, first-out method.

    c. Last-in, first-out method.

    d. Base-stock method.

7. An improvement made to a machine increased its fair-market value and its production capacity by 25% without extending the machine's useful life. The cost of the improvement should be

    a. Expensed.

    b. Debited to accumulated depreciation.

    c. Capitalized in the machine account.

    d. Allocated between accumulated depreciation and the machine account.

  8. On January 15, 1963, a corporation was granted a patent on a product. On January 2, 1972, to protect its patent, the corporation purchased a patent on a competing product that originally was issued on January 10, 1968. Because of its unique plant, the corporation does not feel the competing patent can be used in producing a product. The cost of the competing patent should be

    a. Amortized over a maximum period of 17 years.

    b. Amortized over a maximum period of 13 years.

    c. Amortized over a maximum period of 8 years.

    d. Expensed in 1972.

  9. The past service cost of a pension plan should be

    a. Charged to retained earnings as a cost related to the past.

    b. Amortized over a specified period of years.

    c. Taken into consideration by providing only interest thereon currently when vested benefits have increased during the period and exceed the sum of the pension fund and the net pension liability which has not changed from the previous period.

    d. Included in the annual pension-cost provision to the extent of only interest on the unfunded portion as a minimum or up to 10% of the past service cost as a maximum.

  10. Income tax allocation procedures are not appropriate when

    a. An extraordinary loss will cause the amount of income tax expense to be less than the tax on ordinary net income.

    b. An extraordinary gain will cause the amount of income tax expense to be greater than the tax on ordinary net income.

    c. Differences between net income for tax purposes and financial reporting occur because tax laws and financial accounting principles do not concur on the items to be recognized as revenue and expense.

    d. Differences between net income for tax purposes and financial reporting occur because, even though financial accounting principles and tax laws concur on the items to be recognized as revenues and expenses, they do not concur on the timing of the recognition.

  11. The term "revenue recognition" conventionally refers to

    a. The process of identifying transactions to be recorded as revenue in an accounting period.

    b. The process of measuring and relating revenue and expenses of an enterprise for an accounting period.

    c. The earning process which gives rise to revenue realization.

    d. The process of identifying those transactions that result in an inflow of assets from customers.

12. The installment method of recognizing revenue
a. Should be used only in cases where there is no reasonable basis for estimating the collectibility of receivables.
b. Is not a generally accepted accounting principle under any circumstances.
c. Should be used for book purposes only if it is used for tax purposes.
d. Is an acceptable alternative accounting principle for a firm which makes installment sales.

13. In computing the loss per share of common stock, cumulative preferred dividends not earned should be
a. Deducted from the loss for the year.
b. Added to the loss for the year.
c. Deducted from income in the year paid.
d. Added to income in the year paid.

14. The occurence which most likely would have no effect on 1972 net income (assuming that all involved are material) is the
a. Sale in 1972 of an office building contributed by a stockholder in 1960.
b. Collection in 1972 of a receivable from a customer whose account was written off in 1965.
c. Settlement based on litigation in 1972 of previously unrecognized damages from a serious accident that occurred in 1970.
d. Worthlessness determined in 1972 of stock purchased on a speculative basis in 1969.

15. Which one of the following types of losses is excluded from the determination of current-period net income?
a. Material losses resulting from transactions in the company's own bonds payable.
b. Material losses resulting from unusual sales of assets not acquired for resale.
c. Material losses resulting from the write-off of intangibles.
d. Material losses resulting from adjustments specifically related to operations of prior years.

16. If four separate carriers have written fire insurance policies totaling $60,000 on a single property with a cash value at $100,000, what fraction of a loss of $20,000 would be collectible from a carrier whose $30,000 policy contains a 90% co-insurance clause.
a. 60/90.
b. 30/90.
c. 30/60.
d. 20/100.

17. In the conversion of the trial balance of a foreign branch to domestic currency, the average rate of exchange for the current year should be applied to

a. Sales.
b. Notes payable.
c. Home office current.
d. Accumulated depreciation.

18. For purposes of adjusting financial statements for changes in the general level of prices, monetary items consist of
   a. Assets and liabilities whose amounts are fixed by contract or otherwise in terms of dollars regardless of price-level changes.
   b. Assets and liabilities which are classified as current on the balance sheet.
   c. Cash items plus all receivables with a fixed maturity date.
   d. Cash, other assets expected to be converted into cash, and current liabilities.

33. Miscellaneous

Select the best answer.

1. The account, Equity in Assigned Accounts Receivable, should be classified as
   a. An asset.
   b. A contra-asset.
   c. A liability.
   d. A contra-liability.

2. If a company converted a short-term note payable into a long-term note payable, this transaction would
   a. Decrease only working capital.
   b. Decrease both working capital and the current ratio.
   c. Increase only working capital.
   d. Increase both working capital and the current ratio.

3. If an industrial firm uses the absorption costing method for assigning cost to its inventories and the units-of-production method for computing depreciation on its only plant asset, factory machinery, the credit to accumulated depreciation from period to period during the life of the asset will
   a. Be constant.
   b. Vary with unit sales.
   c. Vary with sales revenue.
   d. Vary with production.

4. The calculation of the number of times bond interest is earned involves dividing
   a. Net income by annual bond interest expense.
   b. Net income plus income taxes by annual bond interest expense.
   c. Net income plus income taxes and bond interest expense by annual bond interest expense.
   d. Sinking fund earnings by annual bond interest expense.

5. The dating of retained earnings is associated with
   a. Earnings accumulated by a subsidiary corporation subsequent to the date of acquisition.
   b. Earnings accumulated by a foreign subsidiary subsequent to the date of a currency devaluation.
   c. The date directors met and declared the corporation was over-capitalized.
   d. Earnings accumulated subsequent to the date of a quasi-reorganization.

6. If a company classifies its expenses as cost of goods sold, employee salaries and benefits, depreciation, taxes, purchased services, and other expenses, the classification basis used is by
   a. Area of responsibility.
   b. Object of expenditure.
   c. Services received.
   d. Function performed.

7. Price index numbers generally are used in connection with the
   a. LIFO retail inventory method.
   b. Annuity method of calculating depreciation.
   c. Amortization of premium or discount of serial bond issues.
   d. Calculation of past service costs of pension plans.

8. A general description of the depreciation methods applicable to major classes of depreciable assets
   a. Is not a current practice in financial reporting.
   b. Is not essential to a fair presentation of financial position.
   c. Is needed in financial reporting when company policy differs from income tax policy.
   d. Should be included in corporate financial statements or notes thereto.

9. Assume that a manufacturing corporation has (1) good quality control, (2) a one-year operating cycle, (3) a relatively stable pattern of annual sales and (4) a continuing policy of guaranteeing new products against defects for three years that has resulted in material but rather stable warranty repair and replacement costs. Any liability for the warranty
   a. Should be reported as long-term.
   b. Should be reported as current.
   c. Should be reported as part current and part long-term.
   d. Need not be disclosed.

10. The ratio of total cash, trade receivables and marketable securities to current liabilities is
    a. The acid test ratio.
    b. The current ratio.
    c. Significant if the result is 2 to 1 or better.
    d. Meaningless.

11. Companies A and B begin 1972 with identical account balances and their revenues and expenses for 1972 are identical in amount except that Company A has a higher ratio of cash to noncash expenses. If the cash balances of both

Companies increase as a result of operations (no financing or dividends), the ending cash balance of Company A as compared to Company B will be

    a. Higher.

    b. The same.

    c. Lower.

    d. Indeterminate from the information given.

  12. Conventionally accountants measure income

    a. By applying a value-added concept.

    b. By using a transactions approach.

    c. As a change in the value of owners' equity.

    d. As a change in the purchasing power of owners' equity.

  13. Expenses related to effecting a business combination accounted for by the pooling-of-interests method should be

    a. Deducted in determining the net income of the resulting combined corporation for the period in which the expenses are incurred.

    b. Capitalized and amortized over a discretionary period elected by management.

    c. Charged to Retained Earnings when incurred.

    d. Treated as a prior period adjustment.

  14. Two companies which have merged or combined in 1971 in accordance with pooling-of-interests accounting are contemplating the preparation of statements at year-end 1972. It has been proposed to present 1970 statements also on a comparative basis.

    a. The 1970 statements must remain as they were prepared originally.

    b. The 1970 statements must be restated so as to reflect what the results would have been had the merger occurred then or earlier.

    c. The 1970 statements must be dropped from consideration as it is not possible to prepare statements to reflect a relationship which did not in fact exist in 1970.

    d. The 1971 statements must be so prepared as not to reflect the combination.

  15. Meredith Company and Kyle Company were combined in a purchase transaction. Meredith was able to acquire Kyle at a bargain price. The sum of the market or appraised values of identifiable assets acquired less the fair value of liabilities assumed exceeded the cost to Meredith. After revaluing noncurrent assets to zero there was still some "negative goodwill." Proper accounting treatment by Meredith is to report the amount as

    a. An extraordinary item.

    b. Part of current income in the year of combination.

    c. A deferred credit and amortize it.

    d. Paid-in capital.

  16. On the consolidated balance sheet of a parent and its only subsidiary two different types of goodwill may be reflected: (1) ordinary goodwill and (2) goodwill from consolidation. The second type

a. Should be combined with the first type and both should be eliminated.

b. Reflects the fact that the subsidiary was acquired at a price in excess of the fair value of its identifiable net assets.

c. Reflects the fact that the subsidiary already had goodwill on its books.

d. Reflects the fact that the subsidiary was acquired at a bargain price.

17. An accountant who recommends the adjustment of financial statements for price-level changes should not support his recommendation by stating that

a. Purchasing power gains or losses should be recognized.

b. Historical dollars are not comparable to present-day dollars.

c. The conversion of asset costs to a common-dollar basis is a useful extension of the original cost basis of asset valuation.

d. Assets should be valued at their replacement cost.

18. A company sold property at a price which exceeded book value and then leased back the property for ten years. The gain resulting from the sale should be recognized

a. Over the term of the lease.

b. At the end of the ten-year period or termination of the lease, whichever is earlier.

c. In the year of the sale.

d. As a prior period adjustment.

34. Miscellaneous

Select the best answer for each of the following items which relate to a variety of financial accounting concepts.

1. If business conditions are stable, a decline in the number of days' sales outstanding from one year to the next (based upon a company's accounts receivable at year-end) might indicate

a. A stiffening of the company's credit policies.

b. That the second year's sales were made at lower prices than the first year's sales.

c. That a longer discount period and a more distant due date were extended to customers in the second year.

d. A significant decrease in the volume of sales of the second year.

2. In pricing inventories at the lower of cost or market a method of determining cost that cannot be used for both financial and federal income tax reporting is

a. FIFO.

b. LIFO.

c. Weighted average.

d. Specific identification.

3. The use of a Discounts Lost account implies that recorded cost of a purchased inventory item is its

    a. Invoice price.

    b. Invoice price plus the purchase discount lost.

    c. Invoice price less the purchase discount taken.

    d. Invoice price less the purchase discount allowable whether or not taken.

4. The primary basis of accounting for inventories is cost. A departure from the cost basis of pricing the inventory is required only when there is evidence that when the goods are sold in the ordinary course of business their

    a. Selling price will be less than their replacement cost.

    b. Utility will be less than their cost.

    c. Replacement cost will be more than their net realizable value.

    d. Replacement cost will be less than their cost.

5. In those rare instances where appraisal increments in the value of plant and equipment have been recorded, depreciation on the appraisal increments should be

    a. Ignored because the increments have not been paid for and should not be matched with revenue.

    b. Charged to retained earnings.

    c. Charged to expense.

    d. Charged to an appropriation of retained earnings.

6. The consistency standard of reporting requires that

    a. Expenses be reported as charges against the period in which they are incurred.

    b. The effect of changes in accounting upon income be properly disclosed.

    c. Extraordinary gains and losses should not appear on the income statement.

    d. Accounting procedures be adopted which give a consistent rate of return.

7. If losses and prior period adjustments are ignored, an exception to the general rule that costs should be charged to expense in the period incurred is

    a. Depreciation charges on equipment used in the construction of a new building for the company's own use.

    b. Factory overhead costs on a product manufactured and sold during the accounting period.

    c. Idle manufacturing capacity costs when a plant is closed unexpectedly due to a strike.

    d. The cost of abnormal shrinkage and scrap incurred in the manufacture of a product included in ending inventory.

8. If bonds are issued initially at a discount and the straight-line method of amortization is used for the discount, interest expense in the earlier years will be

    a. Greater than if the compound interest method were used.

    b. The same as if the compound interest method were used.

    c. Less than if the compound interest method were used.

    d. Less than the amount of the interest payments.

9. The current section of a balance sheet should never include
   a. A receivable from a customer not collectible for over one year.
   b. Deferred income taxes resulting from interperiod income tax allocation.
   c. Goodwill arising in a business combination accounted for as a purchase.
   d. Premium paid on a bond investment.
10. Plant assets may properly include
    a. Deposits on machinery not yet received.
    b. Idle equipment awaiting sale.
    c. Property held for investment purposes.
    d. Land held for possible use as a future plant site.
11. An item that is not a contingent liability is
    a. Notes receivable discounted.
    b. Accommodation endorsements on customer notes.
    c. Additional compensation that may be payable on a dispute now being arbitrated.
    d. Estimated claims under a service warranty on new products sold.
12. When the fiscal year of the taxpayer is different from that of the taxing authority, the amount of the taxpayer's monthly accrual of property taxes should be based upon
    a. The taxpayer's fiscal year.
    b. The taxing authority's fiscal year.
    c. A 12-month period beginning with the assessment date.
    d. A 12-month period beginning with the lien date.
13. Cash dividends are usually declared on one date, payable on a subsequent date to stockholders of record on some intermediate date. Conceptually the investor-stockholder has realized revenue from the dividend on the date
    a. The dividend is declared.
    b. Of record.
    c. The corporation mails the dividend check.
    d. The stockholder receives the dividend check.
14. The outstanding common stock of Mevlas, Inc. is owned 85% by the Airam Company and 15% by Nime, Inc. On Airam Company's consolidated statements Nime, Inc. should be considered
    a. An investor.
    b. An unconsolidated subsidiary.
    c. An affiliate.
    d. A minority interest.
15. In the preparation of consolidated financial statements, intercompany items for which eliminations will not be made are
    a. Purchases and sales where the parent employs the equity method.
    b. Receivables and payables where the parent employs the cost method.
    c. Dividends received and paid where the parent employs the equity method.

d. Dividends receivable and payable where the parent employs the equity method.

16. The account(s) in a foreign subsidiary's trial balance that should not be translated to domestic currency in terms of the current rate of exchange would be
   a. Sales.
   b. Intercompany accounts payable incurred during the year.
   c. Long-term liabilities incurred several years ago.
   d. Long-term receivables obtained several years ago.

17. Tree Company acquired 80% of the outstanding stock of Limb Company, a foreign company. In preparing consolidated statements the paid-in capital of Limb Company should be translated into dollars at the
   a. Exchange rate effective when Limb Company was organized.
   b. Current exchange rate.
   c. Average exchange rate for the period Tree Company has held the Limb Company stock.
   d. Exchange rate effective at the date Tree Company purchased the Limb Company stock.

18. The concept of the accounting entity is applicable
   a. Only to the legal aspects of business organizations.
   b. Only to the economic aspects of business organizations.
   c. Only to business organizations.
   d. Wherever accounting is involved.

19. Each year a company has been investing an increasingly greater amount in machinery. Since there are a large number of small items with relatively similar useful lives, the company has been applying the straight-line depreciation method at a uniform rate to the machinery as a group. The ratio of this group's total accumulated depreciation to the total cost of the machinery has been steadily increasing and now stands at .75 to 1. The most likely explanation of this increasing ratio is that the
   a. Estimated average life of the machinery is greater than the actual average useful life.
   b. Estimated average life of the machinery is equal to the actual average useful life.
   c. Estimated average life of the machinery is less than the actual average useful life.
   d. Company has been retiring fully depreciated machinery that should have remained in service.

20. Other things being equal, income computed by the direct costing method will exceed that computed by an absorption cost method if
   a. Units produced exceed units sold.
   b. Units sold exceed units produced.
   c. Fixed manufacturing costs increase.
   d. Variable manufacturing costs increase.

35. Miscellaneous

Select the best answer choice for each of the following items which relate to a variety of issues in financial accounting.

1. Property under construction to be sold and leased back for operating use under a leasing arrangement which in substance is a purchase should be reported on a classified balance sheet under the caption
   a. Long-term investments.
   b. Deferred charges.
   c. Property, plant and equipment.
   d. Short-term investments.
2. During the current year a court decided that employees at the Hart Company's plant which closed down two years ago were entitled either to severance pay or to added pension benefits if transferred to other Company operations. The amounts involved are material and afford an example for the current year of
   a. A prior period adjustment of retained earnings.
   b. An extraordinary item on the income statement.
   c. A contingent liability.
   d. A casualty loss on the income statement.
3. When presenting pension plan costs on an income statement, past and current service costs
   a. Must be shown separately in computing operating income.
   b. May be either combined or shown separately.
   c. Must be separated so that past service costs can be treated as a prior period adjustment.
   d. Both should not be included on the income statement for a single year.
4. If goodwill arising from the consolidation appears among the assets on the consolidated balance sheet of a parent company and its only subsidiary, this indicates that the subsidiary
   a. Was acquired at a price that was less than the underlying book value of its tangible assets.
   b. Was accounted for as a pooling of interests.
   c. Already had goodwill on its books.
   d. Was acquired at a price in excess of the underlying book value of its tangible assets.
5. If preferred stock has a liquidation preference in excess of its par value,
   a. Earnings per share calculations will be different than if there had been no such preference.
   b. Retained earnings equal to the amount of the preference should be appropriated.
   c. Dividends on that stock should not be allowed to be in arrears.

d. The fact should be prominently disclosed in the equity section of the balance sheet.

6. A company sold property at a price which exceeded book value and then leased back the property for ten years. The gain resulting from the sale should be recognized

a. In the year of sale.

b. At the end of the ten-year period or termination of the lease, whichever is earlier.

c. Over the term of the lease.

d. As a prior period adjustment.

7. A transaction which would appear as an application of funds on a conventional funds statement using the all financial resources concept, but not on a statement using the traditional working capital concept would be the

a. Acquisition of property, plant and equipment for cash.

b. Reacquisition of bonds issued by the reporting entity.

c. Acquisition of property, plant and equipment with an issue of common stock.

d. Declaration and payment of dividends.

8. The accounting for a quasi-reorganization usually includes a

a. Write-up of assets and write-down of retained earnings.

b. Write-down of both assets and retained earnings.

c. Write-down of assets and elimination of a deficit.

d. Write-up of assets and elimination of a deficit.

9. Most methods of pricing inventories are in accord with generally accepted accounting principles and generally are permissible for income tax purposes. Two methods that do not fall into this category are

a. Base stock and LIFO.

b. Direct costing and LIFO.

c. Direct costing and base stock.

d. Weighted average and direct costing.

10. An account which would be classified as a current liability is

a. Dividends payable in stock.

b. Accounts payable—debit balances.

c. Reserve for possible losses on purchase commitments.

d. Excess of replacement cost over LIFO cost of basic inventory temporarily liquidated.

11. Cole Manufacturing Corporation issued bonds with a maturity amount of $200,000 and a maturity ten years from date of issue. If the bonds were issued at a premium, this indicates that

a. The yield (effective or market) rate of interest exceeded the nominal (coupon) rate.

b. The nominal rate of interest exceeded the yield rate.

c. The yield and nominal rates coincided.

d. No necessary relationship exists between the two rates.

12. On April 15, 1971 the Rest-More Corporation accepted delivery of merchandise which it purchased on account. As of April 30 the Corporation had not recorded the transaction or included the merchandise in its inventory. The effect of this on its balance sheet for April 30, 1971 would be

    a. Assets and owners' equity were overstated but liabilities were not affected.

    b. Owners' equity was the only item affected by the omission.

    c. Assets and liabilities were understated but owners' equity was not affected.

    d. Assets and owners' equity were understated but liabilities were not affected.

13. Companies that carry no insurance against insurable casualty losses sometimes use an account called "reserve for self-insurance." In preparing a balance sheet this account preferably would appear as a

    a. Liability.

    b. Part of retained earnings.

    c. Deduction from the Cash Surrender Value of Insurance account.

    d. Deferred credit.

14. The debit for a sales tax properly levied and paid on the purchase of machinery preferably would be a charge to

    a. The machinery account.

    b. A separate deferred charge account.

    c. Miscellaneous tax expense (which includes all taxes other than those on income).

    d. Accumulated depreciation—machinery.

15. Goodwill should be written off

    a. As soon as possible against retained earnings.

    b. As soon as possible as an extraordinary item.

    c. By systematic charges against retained earnings over the period benefited, but not more than 40 years.

    d. By systematic charges to expense over the period benefited, but not more than 40 years.

16. Assuming that the ideal measure of short-term receivables in the balance sheet is the discounted value of the cash to be received in the future, failure to follow this practice usually does not make the balance sheet misleading because

    a. Most short-term receivables are not interest bearing.

    b. The allowance for uncollectible accounts includes a discount element.

    c. The amount of the discount is not material.

    d. Most receivables can be sold to a bank or factor.

17. Interperiod tax allocation would not be required when

    a. Research and development costs are written off in the year of the expenditure for tax purposes but capitalized for accounting purposes.

    b. Statutory (or percentage) depletion exceeds cost depletion for the period.

    c. Accelerated depreciation is used for tax purposes and the straight-line method is used for accounting purposes.

    d. Different methods of revenue recognition are used for tax purposes and accounting purposes.

18. The installment method of recognizing revenue

    a. Should be used only in cases where there is no reasonable basis for estimating the collectibility of receivables.

    b. Is not a generally accepted accounting principle under any circumstances.

    c. Should be used for book purposes only if it is used for tax purposes.

    d. Is an acceptable alternative accounting principle for a firm which makes installment sales.

19. A major difference between a statement of source and application of working capital and a cash-flow statement likely would be in the treatment of

    a. Dividends declared and paid.

    b. Sales of noninventory assets for cash at a loss.

    c. Payment of long-term debt.

    d. A change during the period in the accounts payable balance.

20. Where financial statements for a single year are being presented (without comparative statements), a prior period adjustment recognized in the current year ordinarily would

    a. Be shown as an adjustment of the balance of retained earnings at the start of the current year.

    b. Affect net income before extraordinary items of the current year.

    c. Be shown as an extraordinary item on the current year's income statement.

    d. Be included in an all-inclusive income statement.

36. Miscellaneous

Select the best answer choice for each of the following items which relate to a variety of issues in accounting theory.

1. A restriction of retained earnings is most likely to be required by the

    a. Exhaustion of potential benefits of the investment credit.

    b. Purchase of treasury stock.

    c. Payment of last maturing series of a serial bond issue.

    d. Amortization of past service costs related to a pension plan.

2. A feature common to both stock split-ups and stock dividends is

    a. A reduction in total capital of a corporation.

    b. A transfer from earned capital to paid-in capital.

    c. A reduction in book value per share.

    d. Inclusion in a conventional statement of source and application of funds.

3. Marketable securities held to finance future construction of additional plants should be classified on a balance sheet as
 a. Current assets.
 b. Property, plant and equipment.
 c. Intangible assets.
 d. Investments and funds.

4. The APB (Accounting Principles Board) has been functioning for more than a decade. The best statement as to its current position with respect to generally accepted accounting principles is that
 a. Accounting Research Bulletins (issued by its predecessor) remain in effect if not specifically modified or rescinded.
 b. Accounting Research Bulletins are no longer in effect.
 c. Compliance with its pronouncements has become mandatory.
 d. It has rendered Opinions covering all of the generally accepted accounting principles.

5. Accounting for a governmental unit tends to be somewhat different from that for a business, but accounting for a business is most like accounting for
 a. A special revenue fund.
 b. A special assessment fund.
 c. An enterprise fund (utility fund).
 d. A capital projects fund (bond fund).

6. An example of an item the entire amount of which is usually an incremental cost is
 a. Manufacturing overhead.
 b. Direct cost.
 c. Conversion cost.
 d. Period cost.

7. Calculation of the amount of the equal periodic payments which would be equivalent to a year 0 outlay of $1,000 is most readily effected by reference to a table which shows the
 a. Amount of 1.
 b. Present value of 1.
 c. Amount of an annuity of 1.
 d. Present value of an annuity of 1.

8. The principal disadvantage of using the percentage-of-completion method of recognizing revenue from long-term contracts is that it
 a. Is unacceptable for income tax purposes.
 b. May require that interperiod tax allocation procedures be used.
 c. Gives results based upon estimates which may be subject to considerable uncertainty.
 d. Is likely to assign a small amount of revenue to a period during which much revenue was actually earned.

9. For income statement purposes depreciation is a variable expense if the depreciation method used for book purposes is

    a. Units-of-production.

    b. Straight line.

    c. Sum-of-years-digits.

    d. Declining balance.

10. When permanent improvements constructed by a governmental unit are to benefit and to be paid for largely by taxpayers in the immediate area, the receipts and expenditures related to the project should be accounted for in

    a. A special revenue fund.

    b. A special assessment fund.

    c. An intragovernmental service fund (working capital fund).

    d. The general fixed assets group.

11. When a portion of inventories has been pledged as security on a loan,

    a. The value of the portion pledged should be subtracted from the debt.

    b. An equal amount of retained earnings should be appropriated.

    c. The fact should be disclosed but the amount of current assets should not be affected.

    d. The cost of the pledged inventories should be transferred from current assets to noncurrent assets.

12. A contingent liability

    a. Has a most probable value of zero but may require a payment if a given future event occurs.

    b. Definitely exists as a liability but its amount and/or due date is indeterminate.

    c. Is commonly associated with operating loss carry-forwards.

    d. Is not disclosed in the financial statements.

13. Property, plant and equipment should be reported as valued at cost less accumulated depreciation on a balance sheet dated December 31, 1970 unless

    a. Some obsolescence is known to have occurred.

    b. An appraisal made during 1970 disclosed a higher value.

    c. The amount of insurance carried on the property is well in excess of its book value.

    d. Some of the property still on hand was written down in 1966 pursuant to a quasi-reorganization.

14. The valuation of inventories on a prime cost basis

    a. Would achieve the same results as direct costing.

    b. Would exclude all overhead from reported inventory costs.

    c. Is always achieved when standard costing is adopted.

    d. Is always achieved when the LIFO flow assumption is adopted.

15. An example of an item which is not an element of working capital is

    a. Accrued interest on notes receivable.

    b. Treasury stock.

    c. Goods in process.

    d. Temporary investments.

16. The test of marketability must be met before securities owned can be properly classified as
   a. Debentures.
   b. Treasury stock.
   c. Long-term investments.
   d. Current assets.
17. An example of an item which is not a liability is
   a. Dividends payable in stock.
   b. Advances from customers on contracts.
   c. Accrued estimated warranty costs.
   d. The portion of long-term debt due within one year.
18. Convertible subordinated debentures
   a. Have priority over other indebtedness.
   b. Are usually secured by a first or second mortgage.
   c. Pay interest only in the event earnings are sufficient to cover the interest.
   d. Can be exchanged for other securities.
19. The practice of realizing cash from trade receivables prior to their maturity dates is widespread. A term which is not associated with this practice is
   a. Hypothecation.
   b. Factoring.
   c. Defalcation.
   d. Pledging.
20. If, in consolidated financial statements, a domestic subsidiary meets the criteria for inclusion as a consolidated subsidiary but is not consolidated, the investment in the subsidiary should be reported
   a. Under the equity method.
   b. At cost.
   c. Either at cost or under the equity method.
   d. At market value.

37. Fund accounting and management accounting

Select the best answer choice for each of the following items which relate in Part A to fund accounting and in Part B to various managerial accounting problems.
Part A

21. When used in fund accounting, the term "fund" usually refers to
   a. A sum of money designated for a special purpose.
   b. A liability to other governmental units.
   c. The equity of a municipality in its own assets.
   d. A fiscal and accounting entity having a set of self-balancing accounts.

22. Depreciation on the fixed assets of a municipality should be recorded as an expense in the
    a. Enterprise (utility) fund.
    b. General fund.
    c. Special assessment fund.
    d. Special revenue fund.
23. In municipal accounting the accrual basis is recommended for
    a. Only agency, debt service (sinking), enterprise (utility), general and special revenue funds.
    b. Only capital projects (bond), enterprise (utility), intragovernmental service (working capital), special assessment and trust (endowment) funds.
    c. Only enterprise (utility), general and intragovernmental service (working capital) funds.
    d. None of the funds.
24. Fixed and current assets are not accounted for in the same fund, with the exception of the
    a. General fund.
    b. Intragovernmental service (working capital) fund.
    c. Special assessment fund.
    d. Special revenue fund.
25. The balance sheet in the financial report of a municipality may be prepared
    a. On a consolidated basis after eliminating the effects of interfund transactions.
    b. On a combined basis showing the assets and equities of each fund with a total column indicating the aggregate balance for each identical account in all of the funds.
    c. On a combined basis showing the assets and equities of each fund, but without a total column indicating the aggregate balance for each identical account in all of the funds.
    d. For each fund on a separate page but never presenting all funds together on the same page.
26. The presence of an Expenditures Chargeable to Reserve for Encumbrances account in a city's general fund trial balance indicates that the ordinance governing the lapsing of appropriations provides that encumbrances outstanding at the end of the fiscal year
    a. Lapse.
    b. Lapse, but outstanding purchase orders are honored out of a special contingency fund.
    c. Lapse, but a new appropriation is made to cover them in a subsequent year.
    d. Do not lapse.

27. The budget which relates input of resources to output of services is the
  a. Line-item budget.
  b. Object-of-expenditure budget.
  c. Performance budget.
  d. Resource budget.

28. The activities of a street improvement project which is being financed by requiring each owner of property facing the street to pay a proportionate share of the total cost should be accounted for in the
  a. Capital projects (bond) fund.
  b. General fund.
  c. Special assessment fund.
  d. Special revenue fund.

Part B

29. The major assumption as to cost and revenue behavior underlying conventional cost-volume-profit calculations is the
  a. Constancy of fixed costs.
  b. Variability of unit prices and efficiency.
  c. Curvilinearity of relationships.
  d. Linearity of relationships.

30. The accounting area in which the only objective of depreciation accounting relates to the effect of depreciation charges upon tax payments is
  a. Capital budgeting.
  b. Cost-volume-profit analysis.
  c. Income determination.
  d. Responsibility accounting.

31. A basic cost accounting method in which the fixed overhead cost is added to inventory is
  a. Absorption (or full) costing.
  b. Direct costing.
  c. Job-order costing.
  d. Process costing.

32. The type of spoilage which should not affect the recorded cost of inventories is
  a. Abnormal spoilage.
  b. Normal spoilage.
  c. Seasonal spoilage.
  d. Standard spoilage.

33. A device for making interim reports better predictors of annual outcomes is
  a. Responsibility reporting.
  b. Seasonalized assignment of fixed costs.

c. Seasonal assignment of variable costs.

d. Consolidated reporting.

34. The product cost determined in a conventional standard cost accounting system is a

a. Direct cost.

b. Fixed cost.

c. Joint cost.

d. Expected cost.

35. Of most relevance in deciding how or which costs should be assigned to a responsibility center is the degree of

a. Avoidability.

b. Causality.

c. Controllability.

d. Variability.

36. Of most relevance in deciding how indirect costs should be assigned to product is the degree of

a. Avoidability.

b. Causality.

c. Controllability.

d. Linearity.

37. The measure of employee attitude toward objectives which is most relevant in participative budgeting is the level of

a. Absorption.

b. Appreciation.

c. Arbitrariness.

d. Aspiration.

38. Of little or no relevance in evaluating the performance of an activity would be

a. Flexible budgets for mixed costs.

b. Fixed budgets for mixed costs.

c. The difference between planned and actual results.

d. The planning and control of future activities.

39. Measuring the net income of an enterprise segment

a. Avoids arbitrary cost allocations.

b. Involves consideration of more than the controllable and traceable items.

c. Is identical to measuring its activity (traceable items only).

d. Is identical to measuring the performance of its manager.

40. The most useful information derived from a breakeven chart is the

a. Amount of sales revenue needed to cover enterprise fixed costs.

b. Amount of sales revenue needed to cover enterprise variable costs.

c. Relationship between revenues and costs at various levels of activity.

d. Volume or output level at which the enterprise breaks even.

Section 3

CPA Examination
in
Auditing

CPA Examination
in Auditing

GENERAL APPROACH

CPA questions in Auditing, probably more than any other part of the examination, require a demonstration of practical "know-how" and a familiarity with the day-to-day routines and problems that public accountants encounter. Nevertheless, plenty of everyday experience is not the key to preparation; instead, as in the other sections of the examination, a solid "academic" overview is needed.

Although the academic perspective is paramount, incisive use of experience can be especially useful in preparing for Auditing. Junior accountants tend to get mired in the detail of one or two phases of an over-all audit program. They often lack the perspective needed to deal successfully with the auditing examination because of either the pressure of their daily work or the lack of individual interest and initiative in grasping the relationship of the junior's contribution to the audit program as a whole.

Scope

The Auditing examination emphasizes questions on generally accepted auditing standards and procedures. Questions on internal control have become more frequent in recent examinations. Of course, the candidate must demonstrate his knowledge of accepted accounting principles as well. Major areas covered include the following (for an elaboration, see *Information for CPA Candidates*, Purpose and Scope section.)

1. *Generally accepted auditing standards.* Ten standards codified in three divisions: (a) general, (b) field work, and (c) reporting. Questions may require interpretations of the meaning of the standards, but they are more likely to require applications of the standards to specific circumstances.

2. *Internal accounting control.* Various controls, deficiencies in controls, impact upon audit procedures, detection of fraud, questionnaires, knowledge of flow charting.

3. *Automatic data processing and computers.* Level of understanding demanded for audit purposes. Testing shall be progressively more extensive until candidates must demonstrate (a) a basic knowledge of at least one computer system; (b) ability to design, analyze, and flowchart a system; (c) knowledge of at least one computer language sufficient to program, debug, and test a simple problem; and (d) an understanding of control procedures and modifications of auditing methods in a computer setting.

4. *Audit programs and procedures.* The term *procedure* refers to a question about detailed activities of members of the audit staff, while the term *program* has broader scope and deals with the general technique of auditing.

    (a) Questions may describe an existing accounting situation and ask for a general plan of attack.

    (b) Questions may state a procedure and ask the reason for its use.

    (c) Questions may describe an existing accounting situation and then require a tailored, specific audit program for a particular account. Emphasis is the understanding of the objectives of the audit procedures, and not on the procedures themselves.

5. *Auditing evidence.* The significance of various evidence obtained by observation, inquiry, examination, confirmations, reconciliations, analyses, comparisons, and the like. Knowledge of types of information contained in documents such as insurance policies, contracts, leases, indentures, and so forth.

6. *Auditing theory.* Knowledge of the logic and doctrines that explain the nature of auditing. Areas include the attest function, nature and purpose of audit evidence, doctrine of due care, and concepts of independence, integrity, and personal responsibility.

7. *Auditor's report.* Covered in each CPA examination. Drafting of short-form report, qualifications to reports, adverse opinions, denial of opinion, disclosure. Evaluation of an auditor's report. Responsibilities for unaudited financial statements.

8. *Professional responsibility.* Questions based on the profession's rules of professional conduct. Professional relations with clients and other CPAs. The topic of legal responsibility appears in the Business Law section.

9. *Constructive service suggestions.* Recognizing need for modifications of systems, realignment of personnel duties, and miscellaneous management and tax services.

10. *Statistical sampling in auditing.* These will appear from time to time as may be justified by current professional development in this area.

534 CPA Examination in Auditing

Preparation

Once again, the candidate should study carefully *Information for CPA Candidates* at the outset of his review. The chapter on "Auditing" in Miller and Mead's *CPA Review Manual* is highly recommended for a summary review. The *Statement on Auditing Standards* is easily the most important AICPA publication; it is a codification of all Statements on Auditing Procedure through No. 54. *Case Studies on Auditing Procedures* and on *Internal Control* are other AICPA publications that may be helpful. *Information for CPA Candidates* says (p. 27): "Also appearing frequently are questions based on *Statements of Responsibilities in Tax Practice.* ... and on *Statements on Management Advisory Services.*"

Information for CPA Candidates emphasizes that "nearly every" Auditing section tests the following: (a) audit programs or procedures, (b) internal control, (c) auditor's report, (d) automatic data processing and computers, and (e) statistical sampling. The emphasis is on the objectives rather than a mere listing of procedures or mechancial reproduction of memorized auditing standards.

The candidate without auditing experience has an imposing task of preparation. A careful analysis of AICPA *Case Studies* is probably the nearest approximation to actual auditing experience. Understanding the relationship between internal control and auditing procedures is particularly important.

Techniques of Answers

Most Auditing questions may be answered effectively if the following points are kept in mind:

1. Use outline form and short sentences, particularly for audit programs, procedures, and reporting decisions. Number or letter headings; follow with explanations; indent and identify subheadings. This facilitates grading and helps the candidate in obtaining well-organized and complete answers. A word of caution: the outline should be in the form of *complete* sentences.

2. The techniques for answering essay questions apply to both Theory and Auditing questions. These techniques were summarized previously in the General Approach to Theory. Of special importance is the need to be specific.

3. Know the facts of the question and relate the facts to the requirements. Where audit programs are required, the necessary facts include type and size of business and degree of internal control.

4. Take time to visualize the format and content of the answer before writing anything. Use time limits indicated for each question as a guide in judging the reasonableness of approach. Time estimates are tied to the amount of analysis and writing needed for a satisfactory answer.

5. When a question asks for types, classifications, or categories, the answer should contain a listing which is mutually exclusive and nonrepetitive.

6. Use precise audit terms. *Information for CPA Candidates* states (p. 39):

> Words such as analyze, confirm, compare, foot, inspect, reconcile, trace, and vouch have precise meanings which no one with an appropriate command of the vocabulary can mistake. On the other hand, words such as verify or check do not have a precise meaning as far as audit procedures are concerned, and they should be avoided unless you intend to deal in generalities.

7. As mentioned earlier, many questions may ask for an audit program for a particular account in a specific situation. This minimizes the chances of the memory experts who offer general audit programs by rote; in turn, it maximizes the chances of the candidate who has seasoned judgment and general knowledge of business operations and accounting processes. However, memorized general audit programs, intelligently used, may be extremely helpful as a checklist—as a starting point in the formulation of an appropriate, tailored audit program.

Pitfalls to Avoid

Common shortcomings of answers include the following:

1. *Poor audit programs.* (a) An answer is deficient when it offers indiscriminate listing of too many or of irrelevant audit procedures where the question requires a careful selection among them. (b) Some candidates lack flexibility and over-all business knowledge. This handicap is evident where questions deal with audit programs for various businesses, such as jewelry stores, shoe stores, and bus companies. These questions require some imagination, a grasp of the limitations of audit procedures, and a recognition of some of the auditor's available sources of evidence beyond the accounting records.

2. *Conflicting statements.* If the candidate discusses an alternate line of argument, he should label it as such. Otherwise, one part of his answer may be inconsistent with the other.

3. *Repetition.* Careful illustrations used in answers often clarify the candidate's meaning. One example is enough for each general point cited.

4. *Generalized answers.* Failure to deal with the facts and requirements of a question is a common mistake. The "spray" or "shot-gun" answer, which includes all bundles of trivia that may be remotely connected with a question, merely demonstrates the candidate's absence of judgment and ability with respect to the specific question.

5. *Sense of proportion.* The candidate must show perspective—the ability to see the whole, to break the whole into its major and minor parts, to identify the important elements. Answers are inadequate when they devote the bulk of attention to the unimportant or the obvious in questions based on a special situation.

6. *Reasons for conclusions.* Conclusions may be guessed. Therefore, reasons in support of conclusions carry more weight. The correct conclusion without convincing reasoning is inadequate treatment.

7. *Failure to follow through an idea.* If the candidate is in doubt as to whether a part of an answer is self-explanatory, he should explain further. Follow-through is important. Half-answers and indefinite statements are insufficient. Do not say "it is not material," "true income," or "it is inconsistent" without fortifying such statements with an explanation of how they are applicable to a given question.

8. *Oversimplification of an outline form of answer.* Use a few sentences to explain ideas.

Generally Accepted Auditing Standards

The ten generally accepted auditing standards are broad criteria for performing the audit function. There are three general standards: (a) possession of adequate technical training and proficiency, (b) independence in mental attitude and (c) exercise of due professional care. There are three standards of field work: (a) adequate plans and supervision, (b) evaluation of internal control and (c) acquisition of sufficient evidence through inspection, observation, inquiries, and confirmations. There are four standards of reporting: (a) explicit citing of whether financial statements are in conformity with generally accepted accounting principles, (b) explicit citing of whether principles have been consistently applied, (c) adequate disclosure in financial statements and (d) expression of some type of professional opinion regarding the financial statements.

The general standards emphasize the desired personal characteristics of the CPA as a professional individual. The remaining standards pertain to the conduct and output of the audit.

Professional Conduct

Professional ethics are constantly evolving. Consequently, a candidate should examine recent issues of *The Journal of Accountancy* to keep abreast. Moreover, the code was restated in 1972. Be sure to obtain the AICPA *Restatement of the Code of Professional Ethics* as your basic reference.

The code is basically an elaboration of the three general auditing standards. The code has five major sections that aim at assuring the professional stature of accounting. Some highlights of these sections are:

1. *Independence, integrity and objectivity.* Avoid situations that would impair the credibility of independence in the minds of the public, particularly (a) certain financial relationships with clients and (b) relationships in which a CPA is virtually part of management or an employee under management's control.

2. *Competence and technical standards.* Opinion must be based on proficient work performed by qualified personnel, and conform with both generally accepted auditing standards and generally accepted accounting principles. Departures from these standards and principles must be disclosed and justified. Must not vouch for the achievability of any forecasted financial statements.

3. *Responsibilities to clients.* Must not breach confidential information without the consent of the client except in narrowly specified circumstances (for example, compliance with a validly issued subpoena). No contingent fees permitted (for example, where fee is dependent on the attainment of a specified result).

4. *Responsibilities to colleagues.* Must not encroach on the practice of another public accountant. Must not offer employment to an employee of another public accountant without first informing such accountant; this rule is not applicable if the employee applies for employment on his own initiative.

As you know, the code is stated in generalities that are subject to varying interpretations. The AICPA has issued some interpretations that elaborate on the proper conduct of the CPA.

The AICPA has also issued some advisory opinions on the responsibility of CPAs in tax practice. Some major recommendations include the idea that a CPA can sign a tax return as a preparer if his review gives him a knowledge similar to that which he would have possessed had he prepared the return. Moreover, the confidential relationship prohibits the CPA from informing anyone of an erroneous tax return. However, if a CPA is preparing a current year's tax return for a client who has not taken corrective action on a material error in a return of a previous year, the CPA should consider withdrawing from the tax engagement.

The Code of Professional Ethics is totally applicable to management services, except for those rules solely applicable to the expression of an opinion on financial statements. The boundaries of management services that are permissible for CPAs should be determined by the CPA, based on his evaluation of his technical competence. The role of the CPA should be that of an advisor, not a decision maker. To be independent, the CPA should not be involved in the final decision-making process.

Phases of a Normal Audit

The normal audit contains three major phases that will now be discussed briefly: evaluation of internal control, accumulation of evidence, formulation of an audit report.

1. *Evaluation of internal control.* Thorough evaluation of the internal control system is needed to decide on the type, quality, and quantity of audit evidence that should be accumulated. The two most widely used methods of getting a description of the internal control system are by questionnaires or by flow-charting.

The following ten general characteristics form a checklist that may be used as a starting point for judging the effectiveness of internal control:

Reliable personnel	Document control
Separation of powers	Bonding, vacations, and rotation of duties
Supervision	Independent check and reconciliation
Fixing of responsibility	Physical safeguards
Routine and automatic checks	Economic feasibility of any system

2. *Accumulation of evidence.* The next phase of the audit entails the accumulation of evidence through tests of transactions and direct tests of account balances. These tests are conducted to assure that the internal control system is functioning as specified and that the financial reports are fairly stated.

To choose appropriate tests in a particular situation, the auditor must pinpoint the basic objectives of each audit area, the kind of audit evidence available, and the specific factors that determine which evidence should be accumulated.

If the objectives of each audit area are thoroughly understood, an audit program can be tailored for specific needs. Miller and Mead's *CPA Review Manual* enumerates the following basic objectives as a useful framework for the candidate to develop audit programs:

1. Existence.
   a. The transactions and amounts that are included in the records are valid.
   b. The transactions and amounts that should be included in the records are actually recorded.
2. Ownership of assets.
   a. The recorded assets are owned.
   b. The owned assets are recorded.
3. Valuation. The recorded transactions and subsidiary account balances are stated at the correct dollar amount.

4. Classification. The recorded transactions and subsidiary account balances are properly classified.

5. Cut-off. The transactions are recorded in the proper period.

6. Mechanical accuracy. The footings, extensions, and transfers of information are correct.

7. Overall reasonableness. The balance in the account being considered appears to be reasonably correct.

8. Disclosure. The account being verified is properly disclosed on the financial statements.

These basic objectives apply to each item listed below. Special features or objectives are mentioned concerning each of these eight items:

Cash—Accuracy of amount available for unrestricted managerial use. Internal control is especially important here.

Receivables—Existence, classification, pledged or assigned accounts, collectibility, adequacy of allowance for bad debts.

Inventories—Physical existence, accurate count, proper pricing and its relation to cost of sales, clerical accuracy.

Investments—Establish ownership, cost, purpose, location, classification, valuation.

Fixed Assets—Existence and ownership, analysis of current additions and disposals, consistency and adequacy of depreciation methods, comparison of depreciation provisions with trade practices and internal revenue agent's reports.

Liabilities—Neither overstatement nor understatement nor *omissions* of any liabilities, disclosure of liens upon assets, complete footnotes where necessary.

Ownership Equities—Determine history and classification of each subdivision; trace authority for any changes in accounts during year.

Revenue and Expenses—Many items of revenue and expense are proved when related assets and liabilities are verified. The only additional verification needed for most items is usually accomplished via comparison with related data of prior years. Amortization, depreciation, and repairs frequently get special attention.

The kinds of audit evidence include all information gathered by physical examination, confirmation, documentation, inquiries of client, checks on mechanical accuracy, comparisons of relationships, and reviews of subsequent events.

Factors regarding what evidence should be accumulated include the nature of the client, his organization, the scope of the engagement, the system of internal control, and materiality. The auditor may vary the evidence by changing (a) his audit procedures, (b) the extent of the application of an audit procedure, and (c) the timing of the procedure.

3. *Formulation of audit report.* The audit report informs the reader of the financial statements about the work and findings of the audit. The candidate should be familiar with the variety of possible reports. The work of the auditor is commonly covered in a scope paragraph in the standard unqualified report; his findings appear in the opinion paragraph.

The qualified report may result from a limitation of scope of the audit, or departures from generally accepted accounting principles, or violations of consistency. Therefore, a report may be qualified as to *either* scope or opinion or both. However, this report may be used only when the auditor believes that the financial statements are still fairly presented. If the exceptions are significant, an adverse opinion or disclaimer must be issued.

An adverse opinion is rendered when exceptions are material enough to justify an opinion that the financial statements are not fairly presented. The difference between an adverse opinion and a qualified opinion is attributable to the materiality of the exceptions.

A disclaimer of an opinion is used only when the auditor lacks knowledge about whether the financial statements are fairly presented. A disclaimer may arise from inadequate auditing procedures or from unusual uncertainties regarding a matter that materially affects the financial statements.

The difference between a disclaimer and a qualified opinion is attributable to the materiality of either the scope limitation or the unusual uncertainty. The difference between a disclaimer and an adverse opinion is attributable to the extent of the auditor's knowledge. Disclaimers arise from the absence of knowledge, whereas adverse opinions arise from the presence of knowledge about the unfairness of the financial statements.

Topical Analysis of Auditing

For the convenience of the reader, these questions are loosely divided among five general topical headings. However, the questions are becoming increasingly general and more difficult to classify because they cover a number of topics in sub-parts. For example, questions on internal control may also cover computer applications. Questions on sampling, which are now included in every CPA examination, may be part of a larger multiple-choice question covering internal control, or audit opinions, or auditing standards. The safest way to assure preparation is to study the areas covered under "Scope" earlier in this General Approach. In any event, the Auditing Examination is becoming less and less concerned with the ability to prepare detailed step-by-step audit programs and more and more concerned with a candidate having a well-balanced grasp of the auditor's general function and responsibilities:

Topics	Questions	Percentage
Auditing standards and professional responsibility	1-7	23.4
Auditor's reports and opinions	8-14	23.3
Internal control	15-19	16.7
Audit evidence, procedures, and programs	20-26	23.3
Statistical sampling	27-30	13.3
	30	100.0

Recent examinations have contained seven questions each, all required. The time allowance for each question has been 25-30 minutes; therefore the time allowance is not repeated hereafter for each question.

REFERENCES

In addition to the references mentioned earlier in this section, the following textbooks are available:

Holmes, Arthur W., and Wayne S. Overmyer, *Basic Auditing Principles,* 4th Ed. (Homewood, Illinois: Richard D. Irwin, Inc., 1972).
Meigs, Walter B., E. John Larsen, and Robert F. Meigs, *Principles of Auditing,* 5th ed. (Homewood, Illinois: Richard D. Irwin, Inc., 1973).
Porter, Thomas, and John C. Burton, *Auditing: A Conceptual Approach* (Belmont, California: Wasdworth Publishing Co., 1971).
Stettler, Howard F., *Systems Based Independent Audits,* 2nd Ed. (Englewood Cliffs, N.J.: Prentice-Hall, Inc. 1974).
Willingham, John J., and D. R. Carmichael, *Auditing Concepts and Methods* (New York: McGraw-Hill Book Company, 1971).

1. Nature of audit

The following three statements are representative of attitudes and opinions sometimes encountered by CPAs in their professional practices:

1. Today's audit consists of test checking. This is dangerous because test checking depends upon the auditor's judgment, which may be defective. An audit can be relied upon only if every transaction is verified.
2. An audit by a CPA is essentially negative and contributes to neither the gross national product nor the general well-being of society. The auditor does not create; he merely checks what someone else has done.
3. It is important to read the footnotes to financial statements, even though they often are presented in technical language and are incomprehensible. The auditor may reduce his exposure to third-party liability by stating something in

the footnotes that contradicts completely what he has presented in the balance sheet or income statement.

Required:

Evaluate each of the statements and indicate:

a. Areas of agreement with the statement, if any.

b. Areas of misconception, incompleteness or fallacious reasoning included in the statement, if any.

Complete your discussion of each statement (both parts a and b) before going on to the next statement.

2. Auditing standards and opinions

Select the best answer choice for each of the following items relating to auditing standards and the auditor's opinion on financial statements.

1. A CPA will issue an adverse auditor's opinion if
   a. The scope of his examination is limited by the client.
   b. His exception to the fairness of presentation is so material that an "except for" opinion is not justified.
   c. He did not perform sufficient auditing procedures to form an opinion on the financial statements taken as a whole.
   d. Such major uncertainties exist concerning the company's future that a "subject to" opinion is not justified.

2. An auditor will express an "except for" opinion if
   a. The client refuses to provide for a probable federal income tax deficiency that is material.
   b. The degree of uncertainty associated with the client company's future makes a "subject to" opinion inappropriate.
   c. He did not perform procedures sufficient to form an opinion on the consistency of application of generally accepted accounting principles.
   d. He is basing his opinion in part upon work done by another auditor.

3. John Greenbaum, CPA, provides bookkeeping services to Santa Fe Products Co. He also is a director of Santa Fe and performs limited auditing procedures in connection with his preparation of Santa Fe's financial statements. Greenbaum's report accompanying these financial statements should include a
   a. Detailed description of the limited auditing procedures performed.
   b. Complete description of the relationships with Santa Fe that imperil Greenbaum's independence.
   c. Disclaimer of opinion and statement that financial statements are unaudited on each page of the financial statements.

d. Qualified opinion because of his lack of independence together with such assurance as his limited auditing procedures can provide.

4. It was impracticable for a CPA to observe the physical inventory that his client conducted on the balance-sheet date. The CPA satisfied himself as to inventory quantities by other procedures. These procedures included making some physical counts of the inventory a week later and applying appropriate tests to intervening transactions. In his report on the financial statements the CPA

a. Must disclose the modification of the scope of his examination and express a qualified opinion.

b. Must disclose the modification of the scope of his examination, but may express an unqualified opinion.

c. May omit reference to any modification of the scope of his examination and express an unqualified opinion.

d. May omit reference to modification of the scope of his examination only if he describes the circumstances in an explanatory paragraph or his opinion paragraph.

5. In connection with his examination of the financial statements of Sacramento Co., a CPA is unable to form an opinion as to the proper statement of several accounts. A piecemeal opinion may be appropriate if

a. The accounts in question are immaterial in terms of Sacramento's financial position and results of operations.

b. The failure to form an opinion is the result of restrictions imposed by the client.

c. The piecemeal opinion is accompanied by a qualified opinion on the financial statements taken as a whole.

d. In the auditor's judgment, the piecemeal opinion will serve a useful purpose.

6. For purposes of expressing a piecemeal opinion, the threshold of materiality ordinarily is

a. Higher (i.e., larger amounts are immaterial) because the auditor is not expressing an overall opinion on financial position and the results of operations.

b. Lower (i.e., smaller amounts are material) because the individual items stand alone, thus affording a smaller base.

c. Unchanged from the threshold that the auditor would use in expressing an overall opinion on financial position and the results of operation.

d. Not applicable because piecemeal opinions may be used only for accounts that are subject to fairly exact quantification.

7. In forming his opinion upon the consolidated financial statements of Juno Corp., a CPA relies upon another auditor's examination of the financial statements of Hera, Inc., a wholly owned subsidiary whose operations constitute 30% of Juno's consolidated total. Hera's auditor expresses an unqualified opinion on that company's financial statements.

The CPA examining Juno Corp. may be expected to express an unqualified opinion but refer to the report by the other auditor if

a. He concludes, based upon a review of the other auditor's professional standing and qualifications, that he is willing to assume the same responsibility as though he had performed the audit of Hera's financial statements himself.

b. He is satisfied with the audit scope for the subsidiary, based upon his review of the audit program, but his inquiries disclose that the other auditor is not independent or lacks professional standing.

c. He is satisfied with the other auditor's professional standing but concludes, based upon a review of the audit program, that the audit scope for the examination of Hera's financial statements was inadequate.

d. He is satisfied with the other auditor's professional reputation and audit scope but is unwilling to assume responsibility for the other auditor's work to the same extent as though he had performed the work himself.

8. If a principal auditor decides that he will refer in his report to the examination of another auditor, he is required to disclose the

a. Name of the other auditor.

b. Nature of his inquiry into the other auditor's professional standing and extent of his review of the other auditor's work.

c. Portion of the financial statements examined by the other auditor.

d. Reasons why he is unwilling to assume responsibility for the other auditor's work.

9. A CPA, conducting his first examination of the financial statements of Apollo Corporation, is considering the propriety of reducing his work by consulting with the predecessor auditor and reviewing the predecessor's working papers. This procedure is

a. Acceptable.

b. Required if the new auditor is to render an unqualified opinion.

c. Acceptable only if the CPA refers in his report to his reliance upon the predecessor auditor's work.

d. Unacceptable because the CPA should bring an independent viewpoint to a new engagement.

10. The statement that best expresses the auditor's responsibility with respect to events occurring between the balance-sheet date and the end of his examination is that

a. The auditor has no responsibility for events occurring in the subsequent period unless these events affect transactions recorded on or before the balance-sheet date.

b. The auditor's responsibility is to determine that a proper cutoff has been made and that transactions recorded on or before the balance-sheet date actually occurred.

    c. The auditor is fully responsible for events occurring in the subsequent period and should extend all detailed procedures through the last day of field work.

    d. The auditor is responsible for determining that a proper cutoff has been made and performing a general review of events occurring in the subsequent period.

11. An auditor's unqualified short-form report

    a. Implies only that items disclosed in the financial statements and footnotes are properly presented and takes no position on the adequacy of disclosure.

    b. Implies that disclosure is adequate in the financial statements and footnotes.

    c. Explicitly states that disclosure is adequate in the financial statements and footnotes.

    d. Explicitly states that all material items have been disclosed in conformity with generally accepted accounting principles.

12. On August 15, 1972, a CPA completed field work on an examination of the financial statements of the Cheyenne Corporation for the year ended June 30, 1972. On September 1, 1972, before issuance of the CPA's report on the financial statements, an event occurred that the CPA and Cheyenne agree should be incorporated by footnote in the financial statements for the year ended June 30, 1972. The CPA has not otherwise reviewed events subsequent to the completion of field work. The CPA's report should be dated:

    a. September 1.

    b. June 30, except for the footnote, which should be dated September 1.

    c. August 15.

    d. August 15, except for footnote, which should be dated September 1.

For items 13 to 18 assume that a CPA is expressing an opinion on Azalea Company's financial statements for the year ended September 30, 1972, that he completed field work on October 21, 1972, and that he now is preparing his opinion to accompany the financial statements. In each item a "subsequent event" is described. This event either was disclosed to the CPA in connection with his review of subsequent events or after the completion of field work. You are to indicate in each case the required financial-statement disclosure of this event. Each of the six cases is independent of the other five and is to be considered separately. Your answer choice for each item 13 to 18 should be selected from the following responses:

    a. No financial-statement disclosure necessary.

    b. Disclosure in a footnote to the financial statements.

    c. Adjustment to the financial statements for the year ended September 30, 1972.

    d. Disclosure by means of supplemental, pro forma financial data.

13. A large account receivable from Taylor Industries (material to financial-statement presentation) was considered fully collectible at September 30, 1972. Taylor suffered a plant explosion on October 25, 1972. Since Taylor was uninsured, it is unlikely that the account will be paid.

14. The Tax Court ruled in favor of the Company on October 25, 1972. Litigation involved deductions claimed on the 1969 and 1970 tax returns. Azalea had provided in Accrued Taxes Payable for the full amount of the potential disallowances. The Internal Revenue Service will not appeal the Tax Court's ruling.

15. Based on a directors' resolution on October 5, 1972, Azalea's common stock was split 3-for-1 on October 10, 1972. Azalea's earnings per share have been computed based upon common shares outstanding at September 30, 1972.

16. Azalea's manufacturing division, whose assets constituted 75% of Azalea's total assets at September 30, 1972, was sold on November 1, 1972. The new owner assumed the bonded indebtedness associated with this property.

17. On October 15, 1972, a major investment adviser issued a pessimistic report on Azalea's long-term prospects. The market price for Azalea's common stock subsequently declined by 50%.

18. At its October 5, 1971, meeting, Azalea's Board of Directors voted to double the advertising budget for the coming year and authorized a change in advertising agencies.

3. Professional conduct

Select the best answer choice for each of the following items which relate to a CPA's standards of professional conduct and responsibility.

1. A CPA should reject a management advisory services engagement if
   a. It would require him to make management decisions for an audit client.
   b. His recommendations are to be subject to review by the client.
   c. He audits the financial statements of a subsidiary of the prospective client.
   d. The proposed engagement is not accounting-related.

2. Printers, Inc., an audit client of James Frank, CPA, is contemplating the installation of an electornic data processing system. It would be inconsistent with Frank's independence as the auditor of Printers' financial statements for him to
   a. Recommend accounting controls to be exercised over the computer.
   b. Recommend particular hardware and software packages to be used in the new computer center.
   c. Prepare a study of the feasibility of computer installation.
   d. Supervise operation of Printers' computer center on a part-time basis.

3. The CPA should not undertake an engagement if his fee is to be based upon

    a. The findings of a tax authority.

    b. A percentage of audited net income.

    c. Per diem rates plus expenses.

    d. Rates set by a city ordinance.

4. The CPA ethically could

    a. Perform an examination for a financially distressed client at less than his customary fees.

    b. Advertise only as to his expertise in preparing income tax returns.

    c. Base his audit fee on a percentage of the proceeds of his client's stock issue.

    d. Own preferred stock in a corporation which is an audit client.

5. The CPA should not

    a. Disclose that he is a CPA in a situation wanted advertisement.

    b. Describe himself as a tax expert or management consulting specialist.

    c. Apply for a position with another firm without informing his present employer.

    d. Advise clients and professional contacts of the opening of a new office.

6. If a CPA is not independent, his auditor's report should include a

    a. Qualified opinion.

    b. Description of the reasons for his lack of independence.

    c. Description of the auditing procedures followed.

    d. Disclaimer of opinion.

7. With respect to examination of the financial statements of the Third National Bank, a CPA's appearance of independence ordinarily would not be impaired by his

    a. Obtaining a large loan for working capital purposes.

    b. Serving on the committee which approves the bank's loans.

    c. Utilizing the bank's time-sharing computer service.

    d. Owning a few inherited shares of Third National common stock.

8. Mercury Company, an audit client of Eric Jones, CPA, is considering acquiring Hermes, Inc. Jones' independence as Mercury's auditor would be impaired if he were to

    a. Perform on behalf of Mercury a special examination of the financial affairs of Hermes.

    b. Render an opinion as to each party's compliance with financial covenants of the merger agreement.

    c. Arrange through mutual acquaintances the initial meeting between representatives of Mercury and Hermes.

    d. Negotiate the terms of the acquisition on behalf of Mercury.

9. Maria Laboratories and the Mini-Salve Company were combined on February 1, 1971 in a transaction which was properly accounted for as a pooling of interests. In footnotes to the combined financial statements for the year ended April 30, 1971, the revenue, extraordinary items and net income for each of the separate companies should

     a. Be disclosed for the year ended April 30, 1971.

     b. Be disclosed for the nine months ended January 31, 1971.

     c. Be disclosed for the three months ended April 30, 1971.

     d. Not be disclosed for any period.

10. A principal purpose of a letter of representation from management is to

     a. Serve as an introduction to company personnel and an authorization to examine the records.

     b. Discharge the auditor from legal liability for his examination.

     c. Confirm in writing management's approval of limitations on the scope of the audit.

     d. Remind management of its primary responsibility for financial statements.

11. At his client's request a CPA has performed only such procedures as he considers necessary to form an opinion as to cash on hand and in banks as of April 30, 1971. He may issue a piecemeal opinion as to these balances only if

     a. The piecemeal opinion is accompanied by an adverse opinion with respect to the financial statements taken as a whole.

     b. This opinion does not overshadow or appear to contradict his disclaimer of opinion as to the financial statements taken as a whole.

     c. Cash on hand and in banks is immaterial in terms of the client's financial position as of April 30, 1971.

     d. Assets other than cash on hand and in banks are immaterial to the client's financial position as of April 30, 1971.

12. King Distribution Company has used accounting principles which are not generally accepted. King's management suggests that the CPA prepare financial statements on plain paper without an accompanying opinion for management's delivery to the bank. The CPA's response to King's suggestion should be to

     a. Refuse the request unless a disclaimer of opinion is included.

     b. Agree to the request provided he may discuss the statements with bank officials.

     c. Refuse the request unless a qualified or adverse opinion is included.

     d. Agree to the request only if a disclaimer is included and each page of the statements is marked "Unaudited."

13. The CPA would issue an adverse auditor's opinion instead of a qualified opinion if

     a. His exception to the fairness of presentation was so material that a qualified opinion was not justified.

     b. He prepared the financial statements from the client's records without performing an audit.

     c. The client limited the scope of his examination.

     d. He did not confirm receivables or observe the taking of the physical inventory.

14. An example of an event occurring in the period of the auditor's field

work subsequent to the end of the year being audited which normally would not require disclosure in the financial statements or auditor's report would be

    a. Decreased sales volume resulting from a general business recession.

    b. Serious damage to the company's plant from a widespread flood.

    c. Issuance of a widely-advertised capital stock issue with restrictive covenants.

    d. Settlement of a large liability for considerably less than the amount recorded.

15. The essence of a CPA's independence is

    a. Avoiding significant financial interest in the client.

    b. Maintaining a mental attitude of impartiality.

    c. Performing the examination from the viewpoint of the stockholders.

    d. Being sure no relatives or personal friends are employed by the client.

16. If another auditor's examination of a subsidiary company's financial statements results in an unqualified opinion, the auditor of the parent company may express an unqualified opinion on the fairness of the consolidated statements provided that, as a minimum, he

    a. Assumes responsibility for the proper performance of the work done by the subsidiary's auditor.

    b. Reviews the working papers of the subsidiary's auditor.

    c. Satisfies himself as to the independence and professional reputation of the subsidiary's auditor.

    d. Performs his own examination of the subsidiary's financial statements.

17. The CPA who regularly examines Viola Corporation's financial statements has been asked to prepare pro forma income statements for the next five years. If the statements are to be based upon the Corporation's operating assumptions and are for internal use only, the CPA should

    a. Reject the engagement because the statements are to be based upon assumptions.

    b. Reject the engagement because the statements are for internal use.

    c. Accept the engagement provided full disclosure is made of the assumptions used and the extent of the CPA's responsibility.

    d. Accept the engagement provided Viola certifies in writing that the statements are for internal use only.

18. A CPA rendered an unqualified opinion on the financial statements of Beemster Company for the year ended December 31, 1970. Beemster is now preparing to issue common stock. The prospectus for the common stock issue includes year-end statements and auditor's opinion together with unaudited financial statements for the three months ended March 31, 1971. The CPA has performed only a limited review of Beemster's financial statements for the three months ended March 31, 1971. Nothing came to his attention in this review which would indicate that the March 31 statements were not fairly presented.

The underwriters of the common stock issue have requested that the CPA

furnish them with a comfort letter giving as much assurance as possible relative to the March 31 financial statements. His response to this request should be to
   a. Give negative assurance as to the March 31 financial statements but disclaim an opinion on the statements.
   b. Furnish to the underwriters a piecemeal opinion covering only the first three months of 1971.
   c. Furnish to the underwriters an opinion that the March 31 statements were fairly presented subject to year-end audit adjustments.
   d. Inform the underwriters that no comfort letter is possible without an audit of the financial statements for the three months ended March 31, 1971.

19. Subsequent to rendering an unqualified report on the financial statements of Rosenberg Company for the year ended December 31, 1970, a CPA learns that property taxes for the year 1970 have been significantly under-accrued. This resulted from the Company's disregard of a taxing authority ruling that was made prior to completion of the CPA's examination but was not brought to his attention. Upon learning of the ruling the CPA's immediate responsibility is
   a. Advisory only since he did not learn of the ruling until after completion of his examination.
   b. To make certain that the 1970 income statement is restated when the December 31, 1971 financial statements are prepared.
   c. To immediately issue a disclaimer of opinion relative to the 1970 financial statements.
   d. To ascertain that immediate steps are taken to inform all parties to whom this information would be important.

20. On February 23, 1971 a CPA completed his examination of the financial statements of Emory Corporation for the year ended December 31, 1970 and issued an unqualified opinion. In March Emory's controller prepared the federal income tax return and asked the CPA to perform sufficient work so that he could sign the preparer's declaration. While the CPA was reviewing the return, he noted that a deduction had been claimed which had not been considered in determining the federal income tax liability shown in the financial statements. His research indicates that the deduction is justified. Under these circumstances the CPA
   a. May sign the preparer's declaration on the federal income tax return.
   b. May sign the preparer's declaration but should explain the circumstances in a note attached to the return.
   c. Should not sign the preparer's declaration because the tax liability conflicts with the audited financial statements.
   d. Should never sign the preparer's declaration, regardless of this situation, because he did not prepare the return.

4.Miscellaneous topics

1. Generally the auditor's opinion on financial statements should be dated to coincide with the
   a. Balance sheet date.
   b. Completion of all important audit procedures.
   c. Closing of the client's books.
   d. Transmittal of the report to the client.

2. In the income statement for a partnership the provision for federal income taxes should be
   a. Omitted.
   b. Based upon prevailing partnership rates.
   c. Based upon the taxes paid by the partners.
   d. Based upon the effective tax rate of each partner applied to his share of the net income.

3. The CPA's reporting responsibilities are not met by attaching an explanation of the circumstances and a disclaimer of opinion to financial statements if the CPA
   a. Believes that the financial statements are false or misleading.
   b. Has neither confirmed receivables nor observed the taking of the physical inventory.
   c. Is uncertain about the outcome of a material contingency.
   d. Has not performed sufficient auditing procedures to express an opinion.

4. An auditor is justified in omitting from his report on financial statements a reference to the consistent application of accounting principles only if
   a. This is his initial examination and the financial statements for previous years were examined by another competent independent auditor.
   b. The client company is newly organized and this is its first reporting period.
   c. He performed a similar examination during the previous year and is satisfied that accounting principles have been consistently applied.
   d. This is his initial examination and the financial statements were not previously audited.

5. A CPA completed his initial examination of the financial statements of Alisa Kay Cosmetics and formed an opinion that accounting principles had been consistently observed in the current year as compared to the preceding year. Alisa Kay's controller requests that the CPA attach comparative income statements for five years to his report but not extend his examination to the previous years. Under these circumstances the CPA should
   a. Attach the statements as requested because his opinion as to consistency is required to extent only to the preceding year.

b. Attach the statements to his report and delete the reference to consistency.

c. Attach the statements if he is allowed to form and express an opinion as to consistency throughout the five-year period.

d. Refuse under any circumstances to attach comparative statements to his report because this is his initial examination.

6. A CPA is completing an examination of the financial statements of the Proshek Trucking Company. The Company had been depreciating its trucks over an eight-year period but determined that a more realistic life is ten years and based this year's depreciation provision upon that life. The change and the effects of the change have been adequately disclosed in a note to the financial statements. If the CPA agrees that the change in estimated life was properly made, he should

a. Omit mention of the change in his report because it results from changed conditions, is not a change in accounting principles and has been properly disclosed.

b. Recognize this change as one that involves a choice between two generally accepted principles of accounting and qualify his report as to consistency.

c. Render an unqualified opinion provided that comparative income statements for prior years are restated based upon the ten-year life.

d. Insist that comparative income statements for prior years be restated and render an opinion qualified as to consistency.

7. A CPA was engaged to examine the consolidated financial statements of the Kauffman Tool Company and its Canadian subsidiary. He arranged for a reputable firm of Canadian chartered accountants to conduct the examination of the Canadian subsidiary's financial statements. The CPA reviewed both the audit program and the working papers prepared by the Canadian firm and is willing to accept full responsibility for the performance of the examination of the subsidiary's financial statements. The Canadian chartered accountants expressed an unqualified opinion on the subsidiary's financial statements and the CPA has no exceptions on the parent's statements or the procedures used to prepare the consolidated statements. Under these circumstances, the CPA's report on the consolidated statements

a. Should include a piecemeal opinion covering the parent's statements and a qualified opinion as to the Canadian subsidiary.

b. Need make no reference to the chartered accountants' examination.

c. Must include a reference to the chartered accountants' examination in the scope paragraph or a middle paragraph together with an unqualified opinion paragraph.

d. Must include a qualification of the opinion paragraph stating that the CPA's unqualified opinion is based in part upon the chartered accountants' examination.

8. Gregory George, a candidate for the state legislature, is preparing personal financial statements for submission to the electorate. Mr. George's statement of assets and liabilities should be prepared on the

    a. Cost basis.

    b. Basis of cost adjusted for general price-level changes.

    c. Lower of cost or estimated value basis.

    d. Bases of both cost and estimated value.

9. A CPA is examining the financial statements of the Knodle Corporation for the year ended June 30, 1971. Approximately 95% of the assets of the Knodle Corporation consist of investments in the stocks of subsidiary companies. None of these stocks are actively traded. The CPA has satisfied himself that investments are properly stated at cost and that equity in the underlying assets of the subsidiaries, which is to be shown in a footnote, has been properly computed based upon the unaudited financial statements of the subsidiaries. Under these circumstances the CPA's report on the financial statements of the Knodle Corporation should include

    a. An unqualified opinion.

    b. A qualified opinion.

    c. An adverse opinion.

    d. A disclaimer of opinion.

10. In an examination of a manufacturing company's financial statements the direct verification of an income statement account is least likely to result from the auditor's examination of

    a. Accounts receivable.

    b. Plant, property and equipment.

    c. Cash.

    d. Long-term investments.

11. Kiting most likely would be detected by

    a. Tracing the amounts of daily deposits from the cash receipts journal to bank statements.

    b. Confirming accounts receivable by direct communication with debtors.

    c. Preparing a four-column proof of cash.

    d. Preparing a schedule of interbank transfers.

12. Maria Nolan, CPA, in examining the financial statements of the Quinn Helicopter Corporation for the year ended September 30, 1971, found a material amount of receivables from the federal government. The governmental agencies replied neither to the first nor second confirmation requests nor to a third request made by telephone. Miss Nolan satisfied herself as to the proper statement of these receivables by means of other auditing procedures. The auditor's report on Quinn's September 30, 1971 financial statements requires

    a. Neither a comment on the use of other procedures nor an opinion qualification.

    b. Both a scope qualification and an opinion qualification.

   c. No reference to the use of other auditing procedures but does require
      an opinion qualification.
   d. A description of the limitation on the scope and the other auditing
      procedures used but does not require an opinion qualification.
   13. The auditor is most likely to learn of the pledging of accounts receivable
from
   a. An analysis of the Accounts Receivable account.
   b. An analysis of the Sales account.
   c. An analysis of the Interest Expense account.
   d. Direct confirmation with debtors.
   14. In connection with his examination of the Beke Supply Company for the
year ended August 31, 1971 Derek Lowe, CPA, has mailed accounts receivable
confirmations to three groups as follows:

Group Number	Type of Customer	Type of Confirmation
1	Wholesale	Positive
2	Current retail	Negative
3	Past-due retail	Positive

The confirmation responses from each group vary from 10% to 90%. The most
likely response percentages are

   a. Group 1 90%, Group 2 50%, Group 3 10%.
   b. Group 1 90%, Group 2 20%, Group 3 50%.
   c. Group 1 50%, Group 2 90%, Group 3 10%.
   d. Group 1 10%, Group 2 50%, Group 3 90%.
   15. On November 4, 1971, two months after completing field work and
rendering an unqualified opinion as to the financial statements of Lambert
Collieries for the year ended June 30, 1971, a CPA learns of four situations
concerning this client which were not previously known to him. The CPA is
required to determine that appropriate disclosure is made to persons relying
upon the audited financial statements for the year ended June 30, 1971 in the
situation of the
   a. Flooding of one of Lambert's two mines on October 15, 1971. This
      mine was acquired in 1967.
   b. Discovery on October 25, 1971 of a defect in the title to the other
      mine, also acquired in 1967.
   c. Settlement on November 3, 1971 of a damage suit against Lambert at
      an amount significantly lower than that reported in the audited balance
      sheet.
   d. Decline in coal prices by $2 per ton on October 1, 1971. Net income
      for the coming year is expected to decrease 50% as a result.

16. The general group of the generally accepted auditing standards includes a requirement that
    a. The auditor maintain an independent mental attitude.
    b. The audit be conducted in conformity with generally accepted accounting principles.
    c. Assistants, if any, be properly supervised.
    d. There be a proper study and evaluation of internal control.

17. In forming his opinion on the financial statements of Kille Corporation a CPA must decide whether an accounting treatment proposed by Kille has substantial authoritative support. The CPA is most likely to accept a source as constituting substantial authoritative support if it is
    a. A pronouncement by an industry regulatory authority.
    b. An accounting research study published by the AICPA.
    c. A speech or article by the managing partner of a national CPA firm.
    d. An AICPA industry audit guide.

18. A client has proposed an accounting treatment. The situation is not reviewed in the usual primary sources of substantial authoritative support. In this case the most authoritative support available is
    a. Research studies of authoritative professional societies.
    b. Accounting textbooks and reference books.
    c. Predominant practice within the industry or business in general.
    d. The company's treatment of similar transactions in prior years.

5. Professional ethics

The following cases relate to the CPA's management of his accounting practice.

Case 1

Tom Jencks, CPA, conducts a public accounting practice. In 1970 Mr. Jencks and Harold Swann, a non-CPA, organized Electro-Data Corporation to specialize in computerized bookkeeping services. Mr. Jencks and Mr. Swann each supplied 50% of Electro-Data's capital, and each holds 50% of the capital stock. Mr. Swann is the salaried general manager of Electro-Data. Mr. Jencks is affiliated with the Corporation only as a stockholder; he receives no salary and does not participate in day-to-day management. However, he has transferred all of his bookkeeping accounts to the Corporation and recommends its services whenever possible.

Required:

Organizing your presentation around Mr. Jencks' involvement with Electro-Data Corporation, discuss the propriety of:

a. A CPA's participation in an enterprise offering computerized bookkeeping services.

b. The use of advertising by an enterprise in which a CPA holds an interest.

c. A CPA's transfer of bookkeeping accounts to a service company.

d. A CPA's recommendation of a particular bookkeeping service company.

Case 2

Judd Hanlon, CPA, was engaged to prepare the federal income tax return for the Guild Corporation for the year ended December 31, 1971. This is Mr. Hanlon's first engagement of any kind for the Guild Corporation.

In preparing the 1971 return, Mr. Hanlon finds an error on the 1970 return. The 1970 depreciation deduction was overstated significantly—accumulated depreciation brought forward from 1969 to 1970 was understated, and thus the 1970 base for declining balance depreciation was overstated.

Mr. Hanlon reported the error to Guild's controller, the officer responsible for tax returns. The controller stated: "Let the revenue agent find the error." He further instructed Mr. Hanlon to carry forward the material overstatement of the depreciable base to the 1971 depreciation computation. The controller noted that this error also had been made in the financial records for 1970 and 1971 and offered to furnish Mr. Hanlon with a letter assuming full responsibility for this treatment.

Required:

a. Evaluate Mr. Hanlon's handling of this situation.

b. Discuss the additional action that Mr. Hanlon should now undertake.

Case 3

Fred Browning, CPA, has examined the financial statements of the Grimm Company for several years. Grimm's president now has asked Mr. Browning to install an inventory control system for the Company.

Required:

Discuss the factors that Mr. Browning should consider in determining whether to accept this engagement.

6. Income taxes and ethics

In connection with his examination of the financial statements of the Thames Corporation a CPA is reviewing the Federal Income Taxes Payable account.

Required:

a. 1. Discuss reasons why the CPA should review federal income tax returns for prior years and the reports of internal revenue agents.

2. What information will these reviews provide? (Do not discuss specific tax return items.)

b. With the approval of its Board of Directors, the Thames Corporation made a sizable payment for advertising during the year being audited. The Corporation deducted the full amount in its federal income tax return. The controller acknowledges that this deduction probably will be disallowed because it relates to political matters. He has not provided for this disallowance in his federal income tax provision and refuses to do so because he fears that this will cause the revenue agent to believe that the deduction is not valid. What is the CPA's responsibility in this situation? Explain.

7. Income tax returns (20-25 min.)

As part of his relationship with his client, a CPA often is asked to prepare or review the client's federal income tax return.

Required:

a. In each of the following independent cases:
   1. State the CPA's obligation, if any, with respect to signing the preparer's declaration on the federal income tax return.
   2. Explain or justify the position taken.

Case 1
The tax return of Rogers, Inc. was prepared by the Company controller, a recognized expert in the field of taxation. The president of Rogers asks the independent CPA to review the return and sign the preparer's declaration.

Case 2
The CPA prepares the client's tax return, signs the preparer's declaration and forwards the return to the client for signature. The client requests that the CPA prepare a revised return and sign the preparer's declaration; the revision involves certain changes which are unacceptable to the CPA.

Case 3
At his wife's request, the CPA prepares the tax return for his brother-in-law. The only compensation received for this engagement is reimbursement for secretarial typing services.

b. In the course of the preparation of a client's federal income tax return, it is discovered that certain data which must be included in the tax return are not available. These data can be estimated to complete the return.
   1. Explain and illustrate the circumstances under which the CPA may prepare federal tax returns involving the use of estimates.

2. Discuss the CPA's responsibilities with respect to the manner of presentation and disclosure of estimates which are used in a tax return that he prepares.

8. Audit reports and opinions

Select the best answer for each of the following items relating to financial statements and the auditor's report.

1. An auditor's opinion exception arising from a limitation on the scope of his examination should be explained in

   a. A footnote to the financial statements.
   b. The auditor's report.
   c. Both a footnote to the financial statements and the auditor's report.
   d. Both the financial statements (immediately after the caption of the item or items which could not be verified) and the auditor's report.

2. An auditor need make no reference in his report to limitations on the scope of his audit if he

   a. Finds it impracticable to confirm receivables but satisfies himself by other procedures.
   b. Does not audit the financial statements of an unaudited subsidiary that represents 75% of the parent's total assets.
   c. Omits confirmation of receivables at the client's request but satisfies himself by other procedures.
   d. Does not observe the opening inventory and is unable to satisfy himself by other procedures.

3. Footnotes to financial statements should not be used to

   a. Describe the nature and effect of a change in accounting principles.
   b. Identify substantial differences between book and tax income.
   c. Correct an improper financial statement presentation.
   d. Indicate bases for valuing assets.

4. Assuming that none of the following have been disclosed in the financial statements, the most appropriate item for footnote disclosure is the

   a. Collection of all receivables subsequent to year-end.
   b. Revision of employees' pension plan.
   c. Retirement of president of company and election of new president.
   d. Material decrease in the advertising budget for the coming year and its anticipated effect upon income.

5. An exception in the auditor's report because of the lack of consistent application of generally accepted accounting principles most likely would be required in the event of

   a. A change in the rate of provision for uncollectible accounts based upon collection experience.

    b. The original adoption of a pension plan for employees.

    c. Inclusion of a previously unconsolidated subsidiary in consolidated financial statements.

    d. The revision of pension plan actuarial assumptions based upon experience.

6. A CPA is completing his examination of the financial statements of the Juneau Service Company for the year ended April 30, 1972. During the year Juneau's employees were granted an additional week's vacation, and this had a material effect upon vacation pay expense for the year and the accrued liability for vacation pay at April 30, 1972. In the opinion of the CPA, this occurrence and its effects have been adequately disclosed in a footnote to the financial statements. In his auditor's report, the CPA normally will

    a. Omit any mention of this occurrence and its effects.

    b. Refer to the footnote in his opinion paragraph but express an unqualified opinion.

    c. Refer to the footnote and express an opinion that is qualified as to consistency.

    d. Insist that comparative income statements for prior years be restated or express an opinion that is qualified as to consistency.

7. While assisting Phoenix Co. in the preparation of unaudited financial statements, James Jackson, CPA, noted that Phoenix had increased property, plant and equipment to reflect a recent property appraisal. In this circumstance Mr. Jackson's reporting responsibility is met by

    a. Issuing the statements on plain paper without reference to the CPA.

    b. Advising Phoenix's management of the deviation from generally accepted accounting principles.

    c. Describing the deviation from generally accepted accounting principles in his disclaimer of opinion.

    d. Stating in his disclaimer of opinion that Phoenix's financial statements are unaudited.

8. The primary responsibility for the adequacy of disclosure in the financial statements and footnotes rests with the

    a. Partner assigned to the engagement.

    b. Auditor in charge of field work.

    c. Staffman who drafts the statements and footnotes.

    d. Client.

9. The use of an adverse opinion generally indicates

    a. Uncertainty with respect to an item that is so material that the auditor cannot form an opinion on the fairness of presentation of the financial statements as a whole.

    b. Uncertainty with respect to an item that is material but not so material that the auditor cannot form an opinion on the fairness of the financial statements as a whole.

c. A violation of generally accepted accounting principles that has a material effect upon the fairness of presentation of the financial statements, but is not so material that a qualified opinion is unjustified.

d. A violation of generally accepted accounting principles that is so material that a qualified opinion is not justified.

10. The use of a disclaimer of opinion might indicate that the auditor
   a. Is so uncertain with respect to an item that he cannot form an opinion on the fairness of presentation of the financial statements as a whole.
   b. Is uncertain with respect to an item that is material but not so material that he cannot form an opinion on the fairness of presentation of the financial statements as a whole.
   c. Has observed a violation of generally accepted accounting principles that has a material effect upon the fairness of presentation of financial statements, but is not so material that a qualified report is unjustified.
   d. Has observed a violation of generally accepted accounting principles that is so material that a qualified opinion is not justified.

11. An auditor's "subject to" report is a type of
   a. Disclaimer of opinion.
   b. Qualified opinion.
   c. Adverse opinion.
   d. Standard opinion.

Items 12 to 18 apply to an examination by Leo Gonzales, CPA, of the financial statements of Lectronic Leasing Company for the year ended December 31, 1971. A cash advance to Computer Credit Corporation is material to the presentation of Lectronic's financial position. Computer Credit's unaudited financial statements show negative working capital, negative stockholders' equity and losses in each of the five preceding years. Mr. Gonzales has suggested an allowance for the uncollectibility of the advance to Computer Credit.

All of the capital stock of both Lectronic and Computer Credit is owned by Paul McRae and his family. Mr. McRae adamantly refuses to consider an allowance for uncollectibility. He insists that Computer Credit eventually will be profitable and be able to repay the advance. Mr. McRae proposes the following footnote to Lectronic's statements:

Footnote to Financial Statements

At December 31, 1971 the Company had advanced $500,000 to Computer Credit Corporation. We obtained written confirmation of this debt from Computer Credit Corporation and reviewed unaudited financial statements of Computer Credit Corporation. Computer Credit Corporation is not in a position to repay this advance at this time, but the Company has informed us that it is optimistic as to the future of Computer Credit Corporation. Computer Credit Corporation's capital stock is wholly owned by Lectronic Leasing Company's common shareholders.

Several of the following items state assumptions about this situation. Unless otherwise stated, each assumption is independent of the others and applies only to that particular item.

12. With respect to Lectronic's advance to Computer Credit, Mr. Gonzales
   a. Needs no disclosure in his auditor's report because the common ownership of the two companies has been adequately disclosed.
   b. Needs no disclosure in his auditor's report because the auditor is not expected to be an expert appraiser of property values.
   c. Should be concerned in formulating his auditor's opinion primarily with the issue of collectibility from Lectronic's viewpoint.
   d. Should be concerned in formulating his auditor's opinion primarily with the consolidated financial position of the two companies.

13. A deficiency in the given footnote is that it
   a. Does not identify the auditor.
   b. Is worded as a representation of the auditor.
   c. Does not state the auditor's conclusion or opinion.
   d. Includes the client's representation as to collectibility.

14. Assume that Mr. Gonzales concludes, based upon appropriate audit procedures, that the advance to Computer Credit will not be repaid. His report will include
   a. A "subject to" qualification or disclaimer of opinion.
   b. An "except for" qualification or adverse opinion.
   c. A "subject to" qualification or adverse opinion.
   d. An "except for" qualification or adverse opinion.

15. Assume that Mr. Gonzales concludes, based upon appropriate audit procedures, that Mr. McRae's optimism concerning Computer Credit can neither be substantiated nor disproved and that the matter is so uncertain that he cannot form an opinion concerning the advance. His report will include
   a. A "subject to" qualification or disclaimer of opinion.
   b. An "except for" qualification or disclaimer of opinion.
   c. A "subject to" qualification or adverse opinion.
   d. An "except for" qualification or adverse opinion.

16. Assume that Mr. Gonzales introduces the opinion paragraph of his report as follows: "With the explanation given in Footnote 1, in our opinion the aforementioned financial statements present fairly . . ." This is
   a. An unqualified opinion.
   b. A "subject to" opinion.
   c. An "except for" opinion.
   d. An improper type of reporting.

17. Assume that Mr. Gonzales introduces the opinion paragraph of his auditor's report as follows: "Because of the uncertainty with respect to the collectibility of the advance referred to in Footnote 1, we are unable to express an opinion . . ." This is
   a. A disclaimer.

b. Negative assurance.

c. An adverse opinion.

d. An improper type of reporting.

18. Assume that subsequent to the completion of field work (but prior to issuance of Mr. Gonzales' report) Mr. McRae and his family sell all of their stock in Computer Credit and the new owners repay the advance from Lectronic. Mr. Gonzales' opinion as to Lectronic's 1971 financial statements will be

   a. Unaffected because the sale of Computer Credit stock occurred subsequent to the audit date.

   b. Unaffected because the sale of Computer Credit stock occurred subsequent to the completion of field work.

   c. Qualified unless the repayment of the advance is recorded by Lectronic as a December 31 transaction.

   d. Unqualified because the issue of collectibility is now settled.

9. Piecemeal opinions

Dale Goodman, CPA, is examining the financial statements of the Madison Company for the year ended March 31, 1972. At Madison's request, the confirmation of accounts receivable and observation of the physical inventory are omitted from this examination. Since he cannot express any opinion as to receivables and inventory, Mr. Goodman omits all normal auditing procedures related to those accounts. Receivables and inventory account for 60% of total assets.

Mr. Goodman decides to express a piecemeal opinion and proposes the following report:

To: The Board of Directors
    Madison Company

We have examined the balance sheet of Madison Company as of March 31, 1972 and the related statements of income and retained earnings and changes in financial position for the year then ended. Our examination was made in accordance with generally accepted auditing standards, and accordingly included such tests of the accounting records and such other procedures as we considered necessary in the circumstances, except that we did not communicate with debtors to confirm accounts receivable balances or observe and test the methods used in the determination of inventory quantities.

With the exception of accounts receivable and inventories, our examination indicated that all other accounts were maintained, and the aforementioned financial statements were prepared, in accordance with generally accepted accounting principles applied on a basis consistent with that of the preceding year. However, because of the materiality of accounts receivable and inventories, we are unable to express an independent accountant's opinion as to the fairness of presentation of the accompanying financial statements taken as a whole.

                                                              Dale Goodman, CPA

April 26, 1972

Required:

a. Without reference to the specific situation described above, answer the following questions relating to piecemeal opinions in general.

1. How does a piecemeal opinion differ from a qualified opinion?
2. Why does the expression of a piecemeal opinion with respect to specific items require a more extensive examination of such items than would ordinarily be required if the auditor were expressing an opinion on the financial statements taken as a whole?
3. Why is it important that a piecemeal opinion be carefully worded?

b. Discuss whether Mr. Goodman is justified in expressing a piecemeal opinion in the specific situation where Madison Company has limited the scope of his examination.

c. Without prejudice to your answer for part b, assume that a piecemeal opinion is justified. List deficiencies in the form and content of Mr. Goodman's proposed report.

10. Engagement and representation letters

The major written understandings between a CPA and his client, in connection with an examination of financial statements, are the engagement (arrangements) letter and the client's representation letters.

Required:

a. 1. What are the objectives of the engagement (arrangements) letter?
2. Who should prepare and sign the engagement letter?
3. When should the engagement letter be sent?
4. Why should the engagement letter be renewed periodically?

b. 1. What are the objectives of the client's representation letters?
2. Who should prepare and sign the client's representation letters?
3. When should the client's representation letters be obtained?
4. Why should the client's representation letters be prepared for each examination?

c. A CPA's responsibilities for providing accounting services sometimes involve his association with unaudited financial statements. Discuss the need in this circumstance for:

1. An engagement letter.
2. Client's representation letters.

11. Substantial authoritative support

A CPA's report on financial statements includes his opinion as to whether the statements are presented in accordance with generally accepted accounting principles. In evaluating the general acceptability of an accounting principle, the CPA must determine whether the principle has substantial authoritative support.

Required:

a. Describe the procedure that a CPA should follow in forming an opinion as to whether he should accept an accounting principle proposed by a client for use in preparing the current year's financial statements. Assume that the principle has been consistently applied.

b. Cite primary sources and authorities which a CPA might consult in determining whether an accounting principle has substantial authoritative support. (A source is primary if it is sufficient evidence by itself to constitute substantial authoritative support.)

c. Cite secondary sources and authorities which the CPA might consult in determining whether an accounting principle has substantial authoritative support. (A source is secondary if it must be combined with one or more other secondary sources to constitute substantial authoritative support.)

12. Materiality

The concept of materiality is important to the CPA in his examination of financial statements and expression of opinion upon these statements.

Required:

Discuss the following:

a. How are materiality (and immateriality) related to the proper presentation of financial statements?

b. In what ways will considerations of materiality affect the CPA in
   1. Developing his audit program?
   2. Performance of his auditing procedures?

c. What factors and measures should the CPA consider in assessing the materiality of an exception to financial statement presentation?

d. How will the materiality of a CPA's exceptions to financial statements influence the type of opinion he expresses? (The relationship of materiality to *each type* of auditor's opinion should be considered in your answer.)

13. Disclosure and auditor's opinion

You are completing an examination of the financial statements of The Hilty Manufacturing Corporation for the year ended February 28, 1971. Hilty's financial statements have not been examined previously. The controller of Hilty has given you the following draft of proposed footnotes to the financial statements:

The Hilty Manufacturing Corporation
NOTES TO FINANCIAL STATEMENTS
Year Ended February 28, 1971

Note 1. Because we were not engaged as auditors until after February 28, 1970, we were unable to observe the taking of the beginning physical inventory. We satisfied ourselves as to the balance of physical inventory at February 28, 1970 by alternative procedures.

Note 2. With the approval of the Commissioner of Internal Revenue, the Company changed its method of accounting for inventories from the first-in first-out method to the last-in first-out method on March 1, 1970. In the opinion of the Company the effects of this change on the pricing of inventories and cost of goods manufactured were not material in the current year but are expected to be material in future years.

Note 3. The investment property was recorded at cost until December 1970 when it was written up to its appraisal value. The Company plans to sell the property in 1971, and an independent real estate agent in the area has indicated that the appraisal price can be realized. Pending completion of the sale the amount of the expected gain on the sale has been recorded in a deferred credit account.

Note 4. The stock dividend described in our May 24, 1970 letter to stockholders has been recorded as a 105 for 100 stock split-up. Accordingly, there were no changes in the stockholders' equity account balances from this transaction.

Note 5. For many years the Company has maintained a pension plan for certain of its employees. Prior to the current year pension expense was recognized as payments were made to retired employees. There was no change in the plan in the current year, but upon the recommendation of its auditor, the Company provided $64,000, based upon an actuarial estimate, for pensions to be paid in the future to current employees.

Required:

For each Note 1 to 5 discuss:

a. The note's adequacy and needed revisions, if any, of the financial statements or the note.

b. The necessary disclosure in or opinion modification of the auditor's report. (For this requirement assume the revisions suggested in part "a," if any, have been made.)

Complete your discussion of each note (both parts "a" and "b") before beginning discussion of the next one.

14. Disclosure

Lancaster Electronics produces electronic components for sale to manufacturers of radios, television sets and phonographic systems. In connection with his examination of Lancaster's financial statements for the year ended December 31, 1970 Don Olds, CPA, completed field work two weeks ago. Mr. Olds now is evaluating the significance of the following items prior to preparing his auditor's report. Except as noted none of these items have been disclosed in the financial statements or footnotes.

Item 1
Recently Lancaster interrupted its policy of paying cash dividends quarterly to its stockholder. Dividends were paid regularly through 1969, discontinued for all of 1970 in order to finance equipment for the Company's new plant and resumed in the first quarter of 1971. In the annual report dividend policy is to be discussed in the president's letter to stockholders.

Item 2
A ten-year loan agreement, which the Company entered into three years ago, provides that dividend payments may not exceed net income earned after taxes subsequent to the date of the agreement. The balance of retained earnings at the date of the loan agreement was $298,000. From that date through December 31, 1970 net income after taxes has totaled $360,000 and cash dividends have totaled $130,000. Based upon these data the staff auditor assigned to this review concluded that there was no retained earnings restriction at December 31, 1970.

Item 3
The Company's new manufacturing plant building, which cost $600,000 and has an estimated life of 25 years, is leased from the Sixth National Bank at an annual rental of $100,000. The Company is obligated to pay property taxes, insurance and maintenance. At the conclusion of its ten-year noncancelable lease, the Company has the option of purchasing the property for $1. In Lancaster's income statement the rental payment is reported on a separate line.

Item 4
A major electronics firm has introduced a line of products that will compete directly with Lancaster's primary line, now being produced in the specially designed new plant. Because of manufacturing innovations, the competitor's line will be of comparable quality but priced 50% below Lancaster's line. The competitor announced its new line during the week following completion of field

work. Mr. Olds read the announcement in the newspaper and discussed the situation by telephone with Lancaster executives. Lancaster will meet the lower prices which are high enough to cover variable manufacturing and selling expenses but will permit recovery of only a portion of fixed costs.

Required:

For each item 1 to 4 discuss:

a. Any additional disclosure in the financial statements and footnotes that the CPA should recommend to his client.

b. The effect of this situation on the CPA's report upon Lancaster's financial statements. For this requirement assume that the client did not make the additional disclosure recommended in part "a."

Complete your discussion of each item (both parts "a" and "b") before beginning discussion of the next item. The effects of each item on the financial statements and the CPA's report should be evaluated independently of the other items. The cumulative effects of the four items should not be considered.

15. Internal control of church collections

You have been asked by the board of trustees of a local church to review its accounting procedures. As a part of this review you have prepared the following comments relating to the collections made at weekly services and record-keeping for members' pledges and contributions:

The church's board of trustees has delegated responsibility for financial management and audit of the financial records to the finance committee. This group prepares the annual budget and approves major disbursements but is not involved in collections or record-keeping. No audit has been considered necessary in recent years because the same trusted employee has kept church records and served as financial secretary for 15 years.

The collection at the weekly service is taken by a team of ushers. The head usher counts the collection in the church office following each service. He then places the collection and a notation of the amount counted in the church safe. Next morning the financial secretary opens the safe and recounts the collection. He withholds about $100 to meet cash expenditures during the coming week and deposits the remainder of the collection intact. In order to facilitate the deposit, members who contribute by check are asked to draw their checks to "cash."

At the request a few members are furnished prenumbered predated envelopes in which to insert their weekly contributions. The head usher removes the cash from the envelopes to be counted with the loose cash included in the collection and discards the envelopes. No record is maintained of issuance or return of the envelopes, and the envelope system is not encouraged.

Each member is asked to prepare a contribution pledge card annually. The pledge is regarded as a moral commitment by the member to contribute a stated weekly amount. Based upon the amounts shown on the pledge cards, the financial secretary furnishes a letter to requesting members to support the tax deductibility of their contributions.

Required:

Describe the weaknesses and recommend improvements in procedures for
a. Collections made at weekly services.
b. Record-keeping for members' pledges and contributions. Organize your answer sheets as follows:

Weakness	Recommended Improvement

16. Special study of internal control

The financial statements of the Tiber Company have never been audited by an independent CPA. Recently Tiber's management asked Anthony Burns, CPA, to conduct a special study of Tiber's internal control; this study will not include an examination of Tiber's financial statements. Following completion of his special study, Mr. Burns plans to prepare a report that is consistent with the requirements of Statement on Auditing procedure No. 49, "Reports on Internal Control."

Required:

a. Describe the inherent limitations that should be recognized in considering the potential effectiveness of any system of internal control.
b. Explain and contrast the review of internal control that Mr. Burns might make as part of an examination of financial statements with his special study of Tiber's internal control, covering each of the following:
   1. Objectives of review or study.
   2. Scope of review or study.
   3. Nature and content of reports.

Organize your answer for part b. as follows:

Examination of Financial Statements	Special Study
1. Objective	1. Objective
2. Scope	2. Scope
3. Report	3. Report

c. In connection with a loan application, Tiber plans to submit the CPA's report on his special study of internal control, together with its latest unaudited financial statements, to the Fourth National Bank.

Discuss the propriety of this use of the CPA's report on internal control.

17. Internal control of direct labor

In connection with his examination of the financial statements of the Olympia Manufacturing Company, a CPA is reviewing procedures for accumulating direct labor hours. He learns that all production is by job order and that all employees are paid hourly wages, with time-and-one-half for overtime hours.

Olympia's direct labor hour input process for payroll and job-cost determination is summarized in the following flow-chart:

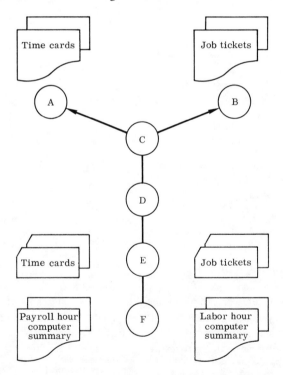

Steps A and C are performed in timekeeping, step B in the factory operating departments, step D in payroll audit and control, step E in data preparation (keypunch), and step F in computer operations.

Required:

For each input processing step A through F:
a. List the possible errors or discrepancies that may occur.

b. Cite the corresponding control procedure that should be in effect for each error or discrepancy.

Note: Your discussion of Olympia's procedures should be limited to the input process for direct labor hours, as shown in steps A through F in the flowchart. **Do not discuss** personnel procedures for hiring, promotion, termination, and pay rate authorization. **In step F do not discuss** equipment, computer program, and general computer operational controls.

Organize your answer for each input-processing step as follows:

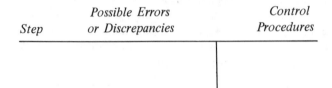

Step	Possible Errors or Discrepancies	Control Procedures

18. Internal control and computers

The Lakesedge Utility District is installing an electronic data processing system. The CPA who conducts the annual examination of the Utility District's financial statements has been asked to recommend controls for the new system.

Required:

Discuss recommended controls over:
a. Program documentation.
b. Program testing.
c. EDP hardware.
d. Tape files and software.

19. Internal control, computers

George Beemster, CPA, is examining the financial statements of the Louisville Sales Corporation, which recently installed an off-line electronic computer. The following comments have been extracted from Mr. Beemster's notes on computer operations and the processing and control of shipping notices and customer invoices:

To minimize inconvenience Louisville converted without change its existing data processing system, which utilized tabulating equipment. The computer company supervised the conversion and has provided training to all computer department employees (except key punch operators) in systems, design, operations and programming.

Each computer run is assigned to a specific employee, who is responsible for making program changes, running the program and answering questions. This procedure has the advantage of eliminating the need for records of computer operations because each employee is responsible for his own computer runs.

At least one computer department employee remains in the computer room during office hours, and only computer department employees have keys to the computer room.

System documentation consists of those materials furnished by the computer company—a set of record formats and program listings. These and the tape library are kept in a corner of the computer department.

The Company considered the desirability of programmed controls but decided to retain the manual controls from its existing system.

Company products are shipped directly from public warehouses which forward shipping notices to general accounting. There a billing clerk enters the price of the item and accounts for the numerical sequence of shipping notices from each warehouse. The billing clerk also prepares daily adding machine tapes ("control tapes") of the units shipped and the unit prices.

Shipping notices and control tapes are forwarded to the computer department for key punching and processing. Extensions are made on the computer. Output consists of invoices (in six copies) and a daily sales register. The daily sales register shows the aggregate totals of units shipped and unit prices which the computer operator compares to the control tapes.

All copies of the invoice are returned to the billing clerk. The clerk mails three copies to the customer, forwards one copy to the warehouse, maintains one copy in a numerical file and retains one copy in an open invoice file that serves as a detail accounts receivable records.

Required:

Describe weaknesses in internal control over information and data flows and the procedures for processing shipping notices and customer invoices and recommend improvements in these controls and processing procedures. Organize your answer sheets as follows:

Weakness	Recommended Improvement

20. Audit procedures

Items 19 to 27 apply to a CPA's examination of the financial statements of the Mia Sal Corporation for the year ended December 31, 1971. An auditing procedure is described in each item and four potential errors or questionable practices are listed as answer choices. You are to choose the error or questionable practice that has the best chance of being detected by the **specific** auditing procedure given.

19. The CPA observes the count of marketable securities on December 31, 1971. He records the serial number of each security and checks the serial number and number of shares (or principal amount) to company records.
    a. The treasurer misappropriated interest receipts by clipping coupons from company-owned bonds and redeeming them in his own name.
    b. The treasurer borrowed securities on May 15, 1971 to use as collateral for a personal loan. He repaid the loan and replaced the securities on December 2, 1971.
    c. The treasurer misappropriated and sold securities on April 4, 1971. He speculated successfully with the proceeds and replaced the misappropriated securities on December 29, 1971.
    d. The no-par stock of Sure-Shot Mines split 2 for 1 on November 19, 1971. The stock certificate for the additional shares was received directly by the treasurer who made no record of the receipt and misappropriated the shares.

20. The CPA reviews transactions in the repairs and maintenance account for the year and examines supporting documents on a test basis.
    a. Certain necessary maintenance was not performed during the year because of a shortage of workmen.
    b. The cost of erecting a roof over the storage yard was considered to be maintenance.
    c. The annual painting of the Company's delivery trucks was capitalized.
    d. Materials issue slips were not prepared for some of the maintenance supplies used.

21. Accompanied by the production manager, the CPA tours Mia Sal's plant.
    a. Depreciation expense was recognized in 1971 for a machine which was fully depreciated.
    b. Overhead has been underapplied.
    c. Necessary plant maintenance was not performed during the year.
    d. Insurance coverage on the plant has been allowed to lapse.

22. The CPA reconciles the trial balance total of the accounts receivable subsidiary ledger to the general ledger control account.
    a. A December 21 check from L. T. Lawrence was posted in error to the account of L. D. Lauritz.

b. The Jacob Macomber account is uncollectible and should be written off.

c. An invoice sent to Gerald Garfinkle was improperly computed. (The sales entry and entries in the accounts receivable subsidiary ledger are made from duplicates of this invoice.)

d. One of the opening balances in the accounts receivable subsidiary ledger was improperly carried forward from the previous accounting period.

23. The CPA confirms a representative sample of open accounts receivable as of December 31, 1971 and investigates respondents' exceptions and comments.

a. One of the cashiers has been covering a personal embezzlement by lapping.

b. One of the sales clerks has not been preparing charge slips for credit sales to his family and friends.

c. The EDP control clerk has been removing all sales invoices applicable to his account from the data file prior to processing.

d. The credit manager has misappropriated remittances from customers whose accounts have been written off.

24. The CPA examines all unrecorded invoices on hand as of February 29, 1972, the last day of field work.

a. Accounts payable are overstated at December 31, 1971.

b. Accounts payable are understated at December 31, 1971.

c. Operating expenses are overstated for the 12 months ended December 31, 1971.

d. Operating expenses are overstated for the two months ended February 29, 1972.

25. The CPA analyzes the accrued interest payable account for the year, recomputes the amounts of payments and beginning and ending balances and reconciles to the interest expense account.

a. Interest revenue of $52 on a note receivable was credited against miscellaneous expense.

b. A provision of the Company's loan agreement was violated. Common dividends are prohibited if income available for interest and dividends is not three times interest requirements.

c. Interest paid on an open account was charged to the raw material purchases account.

d. A note payable had not been recorded. Interest of $150 on the note was properly paid and charged to the interest expense account.

26. The CPA reviews the 1971 prepaid insurance ledger and balances the total to the general ledger account.

a. Mia Sal's excess liability coverage, which expired December 31, 1970, was not renewed in 1971.

b. A premium refund for a three-year policy expiring in 1972 was credited to the account and not amortized.

c. Mia Sal has not recognized the probable loss associated with a damage suit that is only partially covered by insurance.

d. An insurer improperly computed the amount of a premium paid by Mia Sal.

27. The CPA compares 1971 revenues and expenses with the prior year and investigates all changes exceeding 10%.

a. The cashier began lapping accounts receivable in 1971.

b. Because of worsening economic conditions, the 1971 provision for uncollectible accounts was inadequate.

c. Mia Sal changed its capitalization policy for small tools in 1971.

d. An increase in property tax rates has not been recognized in Mia Sal's 1971 accrual.

Items 28 to 36 apply to a CPA's examination of Pyzi Manufacturing's financial statements for the year ended December 31, 1971.

28. The concept of materiality will be least important to the CPA in determining the

a. Scope of his audit of specific accounts.

b. Specific transactions which should be reviewed.

c. Effects of audit exceptions upon his opinion.

d. Effects of his direct financial interest in Pyzi upon his independence.

29. The CPA reviews Pyzi's payroll procedures. An example of an internal control weakness is to assign to a department supervisor the responsibility for

a. Distributing payroll checks to subordinate employees.

b. Reviewing and approving time reports for subordinates.

c. Interviewing applicants for subordinate positions prior to hiring by the personnel department.

d. Initiating requests for salary adjustments for subordinate employees.

30. In connection with his review of key ratios, the CPA notes that Pyzi had accounts receivable equal to 30 days' sales at December 31, 1970 and 45 days' sales at December 31, 1971. Assuming that there had been no changes in economic conditions, clientele or sales mix, this change most likely would indicate

a. A steady increase in sales in 1971.

b. An easing of credit policies in 1971.

c. A decrease in accounts receivable relative to sales in 1971.

d. A steady decrease in sales in 1971.

31. The CPA learns that collections of accounts receivable during the first ten days of January were entered as debits to cash and credits to accounts receivable as of December 31. The effect generally will be to

a. Leave both working capital and the current ratio unchanged at December 31,

b. Overstate both working capital and the current ratio at December 31.

c. Overstate working capital with no effect on the current ratio at December 31.

d. Overstate the current ratio with no effect on working capital at December 31.

32. The CPA tests sales transactions. One step is tracing a sample of sales invoice to debits in the accounts receivable subsidiary ledger. Based upon this step, he will form an opinion as to whether
    a. Each sales invoice represents a bona fide sale.
    b. All sales have been recorded.
    c. All debit entries in the accounts receivable subsidiary ledger are properly supported by sales invoices.
    d. Recorded sales invoices have been properly posted to customer accounts.

33. In connection with his review of plant additions, the CPA ordinarily would take exception to the capitalization of the cost of the
    a. Major reconditioning of a recently acquired second-hand lift truck.
    b. Machine operator's wages during a period of testing and adjusting new machinery.
    c. Room partitions installed at the request of a new long-term lessee in Pyzi's office building.
    d. Maintenance of an unused stand-by plant.

34. The CPA's examination normally would not include
    a. Determining that dividend declarations have been in compliance with debt agreements.
    b. Tracing the authorization of the dividend from the directors' minutes.
    c. Detail checking from the dividend payment list to the capital stock records.
    d. Reviewing the bank reconciliation for the imprest dividend account.

35. Pyzi wishes to conduct its physical inventory on a sampling basis. Many items will not be counted. The CPA will accept the sampling method only if the client's inventory controls are highly effective and
    a. Pyzi is willing accept a scope qualification in the auditor's report.
    b. Pyzi is willing to accept an opinion qualification in the auditor's report.
    c. The sampling plan has statistical validity.
    d. Over 75% of the dollar value of the inventory is counted.

36. As part of his examination the CPA obtains a letter of representation from Pyzi's management. A major purpose of a letter of representation is to provide
    a. A reminder to management of its primary responsibility for financial statements.
    b. Management's approval for the scope of the examination.
    c. Authorization to examine all records and company documents.
    d. An introduction to company employees, customers, suppliers and other interested parties.

21. Audit procedures

Part a. In a properly planned examination of financial statements, the auditor coordinates his reviews of specific balance-sheet and income-statement accounts.

Required:

Why should the auditor coordinate his examinations of balance-sheet accounts and income-statement accounts? Discuss and illustrate by examples.

Part b. A properly designed audit program enables the auditor to determine conditions or establish relationships in more than one way.

Required:

Cite various procedures that the auditor employs that might lead to detection of each of the following two conditions:

1. Inadequate allowance for doubtful accounts receivable.
2. Unrecorded retirements of property, plant, and equipment.

22. Physical inventory

In connection with his examination of the financial statements of Knutson Products Co., an assembler of home appliances, for the year ended May 31, 1972, Ray Abel, CPA, is reviewing with Knutson's controller the plans for a physical inventory at the Company warehouse on May 31, 1972. **Note:** in answering the two parts of this question do not discuss procedures for the physical inventory of work in process, inventory pricing or other audit steps not directly related to the physical inventory taking.

Part a. Finished appliances, unassembled parts and supplies are stored in the warehouse, which is attached to Knutson's assembly plant. The plant will operate during the count. On May 30, the warehouse will deliver to the plant the estimated quantities of unassembled parts and supplies required for May 31 production, but there may be emergency requisitions on May 31. During the count the warehouse will continue to receive parts and supplies and to ship finished appliances. However, appliances completed on May 31 will be held in the plant until after the physical inventory.

Required:

What procedures should the Company establish to insure that the inventory count includes all items that should be included and that nothing is counted twice?

Part b. Warehouse employees will join with accounting department employees in counting the inventory. The inventory-takers will use a tag system.

Required:

What instructions should the Company give to the inventory takers?

23. Cutoff test

In connection with his examination of the financial statements of Houston Wholesalers, Inc. for the year ended June 30, 1971, a CPA performs several cutoff tests.

Required:

a. 1. What is a cutoff test?
   2. Why must the cutoff tests be performed for both the beginning and the end of the audit period?
b. The CPA wishes to test Houston's sales cutoff at June 30, 1971. Describe the steps that he should include in this test.
c. The CPA obtains a July 10, 1971 bank statement directly from the bank. Explain how he will use this cutoff bank statement:
   1. In his review of the June 30, 1971 bank reconciliation.
   2. To obtain other audit information.

24. Computer tapes

Roger Peters, CPA, has examined the financial statements of the Solt Manufacturing Company for several years and is making preliminary plans for the audit for the year ended June 30, 1972. During this examination Mr. Peters plans to use a set of generalized computer audit programs. Solt's EDP manager has agreed to prepare special tapes of data from Company records for the CPA's use with the generalized programs.

The following information is applicable to Mr. Peters' examination of Solt's accounts payable and related procedures:

1. The formats of pertinent tapes are on page 578.
2. The following monthly runs are prepared:
   a. Cash disbursements by check number.
   b. Outstanding payables.
   c. Purchase journals arranged (1) by account charged and (2) by vendor.
3. Vouchers and supporting invoices, receiving reports and purchase order copies are filed by vendor code. Purchase orders and checks are filed numerically.

Master File–Vendor Name

Vendor Code | Rec Type | Space | Blank | Vendor Name | Blank | Card Code 100

Master File–Vendor Address

Vendor Code | Rec Type | Space | Blank | Address–Line 1 | Address–Line 2 | Address–Line 3 | Blank | Card Code 120

Transaction File–Expense Detail

Vendor Code | Rec Type | Blank | Batch | Voucher Number | Voucher Date | Vendor Code | Invoice Date | Due Date | Invoice Number | Purchase Order Number | Debit Account | Prod Type | Product Code | Blank | Amount | Quantity | Card Code 160

Transaction File–Payment Detail

Vendor Code | Rec Type | Blank | Batch | Voucher Number | Voucher Date | Vendor Code | Invoice Date | Due Date | Invoice Number | Purchase Order Number | Check Number | Check Date | Blank | Amount | Blank | Card Code 170

4. Company records are maintained on magnetic tapes. All tapes are stored in a restricted area within the computer room. A grandfather-father-son policy is followed for retaining and safeguarding tape files.

Required:

  a. Explain the grandfather-father-son policy. Describe how files could be reconstructed when this policy is used.
  b. Discuss whether Company policies for retaining and safeguarding the tape files provide adequate protection against losses of data.
  c. Describe the controls that the CPA should maintain over:
    1. Preparing the special tape.
    2. Processing the special tape with the generalized computer audit programs.
  d. Prepare a schedule for the EDP manager outlining the data that should be included on the special tape for the CPA's examination of accounts payable and related procedures. This schedule should show the:
    1. Client tape from which the item should be extracted.
    2. Name of the item of data.

25. Audit procedures, equipment

In connection with a recurring examination of the financial statements of the Louis Manufacturing Company for the year ended December 31, 1969, you have been assigned the audit of the Manufacturing Equipment, Manufacturing Equipment—Accumulated Depreciation and Repairs to Manufacturing Equipment accounts. Your review of Louis's policies and procedures has disclosed the following pertinent information:

1. The Manufacturing Equipment account includes the net invoice price plus related freight and installation costs for all of the equipment in Louis' manufacturing plant.

2. The Manufacturing Equipment and Accumulated Depreciation accounts are supported by a subsidiary ledger which shows the cost and accumulated depreciation for each piece of equipment.

3. An annual budget for capital expenditures of $1,000 or more is prepared by the budget committee and approved by the board of directors. Capital expenditures over $1,000 which are not included in this budget must be approved by the board of directors and variations of 20% or more must be explained to the board. Approval by the supervisor of production is required for capital expenditures under $1,000.

4. Company employees handle installation, removal, repair and rebuilding of the machinery. Work orders are prepared for these activities and are subject to the same budgetary control as other expenditures. Work orders are not required for external expenditures.

Required:

a. Cite the major objectives of your audit of the Manufacturing Equipment, Manufacturing Equipment—Accumulated Depreciation and Repairs of Manufacturing Equipment accounts. Do not include in this listing the auditing procedures designed to accomplish these objectives.

b. Prepare the portion of your audit program applicable to the review of 1969 additions to the Manufacturing Equipment account.

26. Audit working papers

An important part of every examination of financial statements is the preparation of audit working papers.

Required:

a. Discuss the relationship of audit working papers to each of the standards of field work.

b. You are instructing an inexperienced staffman on his first auditing assignment. He is to examine an account. An analysis of the account has been prepared by the client for inclusion in the audit working papers. Prepare a list of the comments, commentaries and notations that the staffman should make or have made on the account analysis to provide an adequate working paper as evidence of his examination. (Do not include a description of auditing procedures applicable to the account.)

27. Statistical sampling

The use of statistical sampling techniques in an examination of financial statements does not eliminate judgmental decisions.

Required:

a. Identify and explain four areas where judgment may be exercised by a CPA in planning a statistical sampling test.

b. Assume that a CPA's sample shows an unacceptable error rate. Describe the various actions that he may take based upon this finding.

c. A nonstratified sample of 80 accounts payable vouchers is to be selected from a population of 3,200. The vouchers are numbered consecutively from 1 to 3,200 and are listed, 40 to a page, in the voucher register. Describe three different techniques for selecting a random sample of vouchers for review.

28. Miscellaneous and sampling

Items 19 to 24 relate to internal control and the review of internal control that the CPA conducts in connection with his examination of financial statements.

19. Of the following, the best statement of the CPA's primary objective in reviewing internal control is that the review is intended to provide
   a. Reasonable protection against client fraud and defalcations by client employees.
   b. A basis for reliance on the system and determining the scope of other auditing procedures.
   c. A basis for constructive suggestions to the client for improving his accounting system.
   d. A method for safeguarding assets, checking the accuracy and reliability of accounting data, promoting operational efficiency, and encouraging adherence to prescribed managerial policies.

20. A company holds bearer bonds as a short-term investment. Custody of these bonds and submission of coupons for interest payments normally is the responsibility of the
   a. Treasury function.
   b. Legal counsel.
   c. General-accounting function.
   d. Internal-audit function.

21. Operating control of the check-signing machine normally should be the responsibility of the
   a. General-accounting function.
   b. Treasury function.
   c. Legal counsel.
   d. Internal-audit function.

22. Matching the supplier's invoice, the purchase order, and the receiving report normally should be the responsibility of the
   a. Warehouse-receiving function.
   b. Purchasing function.
   c. General-accounting function
   d. Treasury function.

23. A CPA learns that his client has paid a vendor twice for the same shipment, once based upon the original invoice and once based upon the monthly statement. A control procedure that should have prevented this duplicate payment is
   a. Attachment of the receiving report to the disbursement support.
   b. Prenumbering of disbursements vouchers.

   c. Use of a limit or reasonableness test.

   d. Prenumbering of receiving reports.

24. A computer programmer has written a program for updating perpetual-inventory records. Responsibility for initial testing (debugging) of the program should be assigned to the

   a. EDP-department control group.

   b. Internal-audit control group.

   c. Programmer.

   d. Machine operator.

Items 25 to 31 relate to the auditing procedures that a CPA performs in connection with his examination of financial statements. Each item is independent and should be considered separately.

25. On December 31, 1971, a company erroneously prepared an account-payable voucher (Dr. Cash, Cr. Accounts Payable) for a transfer of funds between banks. A check for the transfer was drawn January 3, 1972. This error resulted in overstatements of cash and accounts payable at December 31, 1971.

Of the following procedures, the **least** effective in disclosing this error is review of the

   a. December 31, 1971 bank reconciliations for the two banks.

   b. December 1971 check register.

   c. Support for accounts payable at December 31, 1971.

   d. Schedule of interbank transfers.

26. A CPA obtains a January 10 cut-off bank statement for his client directly from the bank. Very few of the outstanding checks listed on his client's December 31 bank reconciliation cleared during the cut-off period. A probable cause for this is that the client

   a. Is engaged in kiting.

   b. Is engaged in lapping.

   c. Transmitted the checks to the payees after year end.

   d. Has overstated its year-end bank balance.

27. A CPA observes his client's physical-inventory count on December 31, 1971. There are eight inventory-taking teams, and a tag system is used. The CPA's observation normally may be expected to result in detection of which of the following inventory errors:

   a. The inventory-takers forget to count all of the items in one room of the warehouse.

   b. An error is made in the count of one inventory item.

   c. Some of the items included in the inventory had been received on consignment.

   d. The inventory omits items on consignment to wholesalers.

28. Only one of the following four statements, which compare confirmation of accounts payable with suppliers and confirmation of accounts receivable with debtors, is true. The true statement is that

a. Confirmation of accounts payable with suppliers is a more widely accepted auditing procedure than is confirmation of accounts receivable with debtors.
b. Statistical-sampling techniques are more widely accepted in the confirmation of accounts payable than in the confirmation of accounts receivable.
c. As compared to the confirmation of accounts payable, the confirmation of accounts receivable will tend to emphasize accounts with zero balances at balance-sheet date.
d. It is less likely that the confirmation request sent to the supplier will show the amount owed him than that the request sent to the debtor will show the amount due from him.

29. Of the following, the most common argument against the use of negative accounts-receivable confirmations is that
a. The cost-per-response is excessively high.
b. Statistical-sampling techniques cannot be applied to selection of the sample.
c. Recipients are more likely to feel that the confirmation is a request for payment.
d. The implicit assumption that no response indicates agreement with the balance may not be warranted.

30. Braginetz Corporation acts as its own registrar and transfer agent and has assigned these responsibilities to the Company secretary. The CPA primarily will rely upon his
a. Confirmation of shares outstanding at year-end with the Company secretary.
b. Review of the corporate minutes for data as to shares outstanding.
c. Confirmation of the number of shares outstanding at year-end with the appropriate state official.
d. Inspection of the stock book at year-end and accounting for all certificate numbers.

31. As part of his search for unrecorded liabilities, a CPA examined invoices and accounts-payable vouchers. In general this examination may be limited to
a. Unpaid accounts-payable vouchers and unvouchered invoices on hand at the balance-sheet date.
b. Accounts-payable vouchers prepared during the subsequent period and unvouchered invoices received through the last day of field work whose dollar values exceed reasonable amounts.
c. Invoices received through the last day of field work (whether or not accounts-payable vouchers have been prepared) but must include all invoices of any amount received during this period.
d. A reasonable period following the balance-sheet date, normally the same period used for the cut-off bank statement.

Items 32 to 36 apply to an examination by Lee Melinda, CPA, of the financial statements of Summit Appliance Repair Co. for the year ended June 30, 1972. Summit has a large fleet of identically stocked repair trucks. It establishes the total quantities of materials and supplies stored on the delivery trucks at year-end by physically inventorying a random sample of trucks.

Mr. Melinda is evaluating the statistical validity of Summit's 1972 sample. He knows that there were 74 trucks in the 1971 required sample. Assumptions about the size, variability, specified precision (confidence interval), and specified reliability (confidence level) for the 1972 sample are given in each of the following five items. You are to indicate in each case the effect upon the size of the 1972 sample as compared to the 1971 sample. Each of the five cases is independent of the other four and is to be considered separately. Your answer choice for each item 32 to 36 should be selected from the following responses:

    a. Larger than the 1971 sample size.
    b. Equal to the 1971 sample size.
    c. Smaller than the 1971 sample size.
    d. Of a size that is indeterminate based upon the assumptions as given.

32. Summit has the same number of trucks in 1972, but supplies are replenished more often, meaning that there is less variability in the quantity of supplies stored on each truck. The specified precision and specified reliability remain the same. Under these assumptions the required sample size for 1972 should be _____.

33. Summit has the same number of trucks supplies are replenished less often (greater variability); Summit specifies the same precision but decides to change the specified reliability from 95% to 90%. Under these assumptions, the required sample size for 1972 should be _____ .

34. Summit has more trucks in 1972. Variability and specified reliability remain the same, but with Melinda's concurrence Summit decides upon a wider specified precision. Under these assumptions the required sample size for 1972 should be _____ .

35. The number of trucks and variability remain the same, but with Melinda's concurrence Summit decides upon a wider specified precision and a specified reliability of 90% rather than 95%. Under these assumptions the required sample size for 1972 should be _____ .

36. The number of trucks increases, as does the variability of quantities stored on each truck. The specified reliability remains the same, but the specified precision is narrowed. Under these assumptions the required sample size for 1972 should be _____ .

29. Auditing procedures and statistical techniques

21. Negative accounts receivable confirmations would be most appropriate in confirming the balances of

a. Large over-due accounts.
b. Small accounts which have been written off.
c. Customers whose large balances represent many small purchases.
d. Accounts due from governmental subdivisions.

22. The auditing procedure which would be of least assistance in detecting the lapping of accounts receivable is
   a. Comparison of the aging schedule of the accounts at the end of this year to that of a year ago.
   b. Tracing payment dates shown on confirmation returns to the accounts receivable records.
   c. Tracing individually listed checks from the duplicate deposit slip to the accounts receivable records.
   d. Examination of the dates of checks included in one day's deposit.

23. With respect to proceedings of the meetings of the board of directors of a client corporation, the normal auditing procedure is to
   a. Obtain from the company secretary a minutes representation letter which summarizes actions pertinent to the financial statements.
   b. Discuss proceedings of the board with its chairman or his designated representative.
   c. Review the minutes of all meetings.
   d. Obtain tapes or written transcripts of all meetings or attend all meetings.

24. The cashier of Baker Company covered a shortage in his cash working fund with cash obtained on December 31 from a local bank by cashing an unrecorded check drawn on the Company's New York Bank. The auditor would discover this manipulation by
   a. Preparing independent bank reconciliations as of December 31.
   b. Counting the cash working fund at the close of business on December 31.
   c. Investigating items returned with the bank cut-off statements.
   d. Confirming the December 31 bank balances.

25. A CPA is examining the financial statements of a small telephone company and wishes to test whether customers are being billed. One procedure that he might use is to
   a. Check a sample of listings in the telephone directory to the billing control.
   b. Trace a sample of postings from the billing control to the subsidiary accounts receivable ledger.
   c. Balance the subsidiary accounts receivable ledger to the general ledger control account.
   d. Confirm a representative number of accounts receivable.

26. Lowe Co. stores a portion of its finished goods inventory in a reputable public warehouse. Certain customers have been authorized to make withdrawals

at will from the public warehouse, which informs Lowe Co. daily of the withdrawals and balances on hand. In connection with his examination of the financial statements of Lowe Co. for the year ended February 28, 1971, the CPA generally will rely most upon his

    a. Examination of the report from the public warehouse for February 28, 1971.

    b. Direct confirmation of the balances stored as of February 28, 1971.

    c. Observation of the physical inventory on February 28, 1971.

    d. Observation of a daily physical inventory sometime during the year ended February 28, 1971.

27. A covenant in Zero Company's indenture for an outstanding 1961 issue of mortgage bonds requires the maintenance at all times of a current ratio in excess of 2 to 1. The indenture also provides that should any covenant be violated, the bond trustee has the option of requiring immediate payment of the principal due.

A CPA is engaged in his initial examination of financial statements of Zero Company for the year ended December 31, 1970. He notes that the current ratio has not met indenture requirements since 1965 and is 1.7 at December 31, 1970. The bond trustee has been furnished financial statements yearly and has not questioned the failure to comply with the covenant; in response to a standard confirmation letter the trustee indicated that to the best of his knowledge there has been no covenant violations to December 31, 1970. Under the circumstances the CPA should

    a. Rely upon the bond trustee's confirmation and require no classification or further inquiry.

    b. Require reclassification of the bonds payable as a current liability.

    c. Request that the management representation letter explicitly refer to the noncompliance with the covenant and management's expectation that the trustee will take no action.

    d. Request that Zero Company obtain a waiver of the requirement from the bond trustee.

28. In an examination of financial statements a CPA generally will find stratified sampling techniques to be most applicable to

    a. Recomputing net wage and salary payments to employees.

    b. Tracing hours worked from the payroll summary bank to the individual time cards.

    c. Confirming accounts receivable for residential customers at a large electric utility.

    d. Reviewing supporting documentation for additions to plant and equipment.

29. A CPA's client maintains perpetual inventory records. In the past all inventory items have been counted on a cycle basis at least once during the year and physical inventory differences have been minor. Now, the client wishes to

minimize costs of conducting the physical inventory by changing to a sampling method in which many inventory items will not be counted during a given year. For purposes of expressing an opinion on his client's financial statements the CPA will accept the sampling method only if

    a. The sampling method has statistical validity.

    b. A stratified sampling plan is used.

    c. The client is willing to accept an opinion qualification in the auditor's report.

    d. The client is willing to accept a scope qualification in the auditor's report.

30. In an examination of financial statements a CPA would not find use of statistical sampling techniques to be generally applicable if

    a. The population of items were large.

    b. Absolute precision of measurement were required.

    c. None of the items were individually significant.

    d. The population were not normally distributed.

31. The frequency distribution of employee years of service for Henry Enterprises is right skewed (i.e., it is not symmetrical). If a CPA wishes to describe the years of service of the typical Henry employee in a special report, the measure of central tendency that he should use is the

    a. Standard deviation.

    b. Arithmetic mean.

    c. Mode.

    d. Median.

32. Annual data for ten years are to be summarized in an auditor's special report. The geometric mean should be used in determining the annual experience for the past ten years for the

    a. Income for a year.

    b. Percentage gain or loss in market value of securities during a year.

    c. Percentage of bad debt losses to sales for a year.

    d. End-of-year current ratio.

33. A CPA's client cannot recall the name of the mathematical technique for solving resource allocation problems by maximizing or minimizing a function subject to one or more constraints which he heard described at a recent management seminar. This technique is

    a. Decision tree analysis.

    b. Least-squares analysis.

    c. Linear programming.

    d. Attribute sampling.

34. A CPA has been asked by his client, a department store, to assist in determining the effects on customer service of eliminating a clerk in one department. The probability of a customer's arriving for service is the same at all moments in time regardless of what had happened in previous moments. If the

CPA analyzes this queueing (waiting-line) problem mathematically, the frequency distribution generally used would be the

    a. Cauchy.

    b. Bamma.

    c. Beta.

    d. Poisson.

    35. In connection with his examination of the financial statements of Juicy Melons, Inc. a CPA is testing the effectiveness of the Company's inspection system for purchases from melon growers. For one lot of 2,000, Company inspectors found the bad melon rate to be 4%. If the CPA wishes to sample from this lot with confidence level of 90% and a precision (confidence interval) of ±2%, the required sample size is 230. If the precision is changed to ±1% and other specifications remain the same, the required sample size is

    a. 684.

    b. 251.

    c. 209.

    d. 63. In determining your answers to items 36 to 40 consider the information given in the following statement of facts.

    A CPA's client is considering the adoption of statistical sampling techniques. Accordingly he has asked the CPA to discuss these techniques at a meeting of client employees. In connection with this presentation the CPA prepared the following table which shows the comparative characteristics of two populations and the samples to be drawn from each. [For example, in Case 1 the variability of population 1 is smaller than that of population 2 whereas the populations are of equal size and the samples to be drawn from them have equal specified precisions (confidence intervals) and specified reliabilities (confidence levels).]

| | Population 1 Relative to Population 2 | | Sample from Population 1 Relative to Sample from Population 2 | |
	Size	*Variability*	*Specified Precision*	*Specified Reliability*
Case 1	Equal	Smaller	Equal	Equal
Case 2	Smaller	Equal	Equal	Higher
Case 3	Equal	Equal	Wider	Equal
Case 4	Larger	Equal	Narrower	Equal
Case 5	Equal	Greater	Equal	Higher

    Using the table and the technique of unrestricted random sampling with replacement, meeting participants are to be asked to determine the relative required sample sizes to be drawn from the two populations. Each of the five cases is independent of the other four and is to be considered separately.

    36. The required sample size from population 1 in case 1 is

    a. Larger than the required sample size from population 2.

    b. Equal to the required sample size from population 2.

c. Smaller than the required sample size from population 2.
d. Indeterminate relative to the required sample size from population 2.
37. The required sample size from population 1 in case 2 is
   a. Larger than the required sample size from population 2.
   b. Equal to the required sample size from population 2.
   c. Smaller than the required sample size from population 2.
   d. Indeterminate relative to the required sample size from population 2.
38. The required sample size from population 1 in case 3 is
   a. Larger than the required sample size from population 2.
   b. Equal to the required sample size from population 2.
   c. Smaller than the required sample size from population 2.
   d. Indeterminate relative to the required sample size from population 2.
39. The required sample size from population 1 in case 4 is
   a. Larger than the required sample size from population 2.
   b. Equal to the required sample size from population 2.
   c. Smaller than the required sample size from population 2.
   d. Indeterminate relative to the required sample size from population 2.
40. The required sample size from population 1 in case 5 is
   a. Larger than the required sample size from population 2.
   b. Equal to the required sample size from population 2.
   c. Smaller than the required sample size from population 2.
   d. Indeterminate relative to the required sample size from population 2.

30. Internal control and statistical sampling

19. From the standpoint of good procedural control, distributing payroll checks to employees is best handled by the
   a. Treasury department.
   b. Personnel department.
   d. Payroll accounting section.
   e. Departmental supervisors.
20. To minimize the opportunity for fraud, unclaimed salary checks should be
   a. Deposited in a special bank account.
   b. Kept in the payroll department.
   c. Left with the employee's supervisor.
   d. Held for the employee in the personnel department.
21. A responsibility that should be assigned to a specific employee and not shared jointly is that of
   a. Access to the company's safe deposit box.
   b. Placing orders and maintaining relationships with a prime supplier.
   c. Attempting to collect a particular delinquent account.
   d. Custodianship of the cash working fund.

22. For control purposes the quantities of materials ordered may be omitted from the copy of the purchase order which is

    a. Forwarded to the accounting department.

    b. Retained in the purchasing department's files.

    c. Returned to the requisitioner.

    d. Forwarded to the receiving department.

23. Freije Refrigeration Co. has an inventory of raw materials and parts consisting of thousands of different items which are of small value individually but significant in total. A fundamental control requirement of Freije's inventory system is that

    a. Perpetual inventory records be maintained for all inventory items.

    b. The taking of physical inventories be conducted on a cycle basis rather than at year-end.

    c. The storekeeping function not be combined with the production and inventory record-keeping functions.

    d. Materials requisitions be approved by an officer of the Company.

24. The sales department bookkeeper has been crediting house-acocunt sales to her brother-in-law, an outside salesman. Commissions are paid on outside sales but not on house-account sales. This might have been prevented by requiring that

    a. Sales order forms be prenumbered and accounted for by the sales department bookkeeper.

    b. Sales commission statements be supported by sales order forms and approved by the sales manager.

    c. Aggregate sales entries be prepared by the general accounting department.

    d. Disbursement vouchers for sales commissions be reviewed by the internal audit department and checked to sales commission statements.

Items 25 to 29 apply to an examination of the financial statements of Lorantas Educational Machines Co. which is being conducted by John Wilson, CPA.

25. In connection with his review of charges to the plant maintenance account Mr. Wilson is undecided as to whether to use probability sampling or judgment sampling. As compared to probability sampling, judgment sampling has the primary disadvantage of

    a. Providing no known method for making statistical inferences about the population solely from the results of the sample.

    b. Not allowing the auditor to select those accounts which he believes should be selected.

    c. Requiring that a complete list of all the population elements be compiled.

    d. Not permitting the auditor to know which types of items will be included in the sample before the actual selection is made.

26. Mr. Wilson believes that the error occurrence rate of expensing capital items is 2%, which will have an immaterial effect upon the financial statements. The maximum acceptable occurrence rate is 3%. Under these circumstances Mr. Wilson should select a plan of
a. Discovery sampling.
b. Attribute sampling.
c. Variable sampling.
d. Stratified sampling.

27. Mr. Wilson reviewed a random sample of 40 maintenance job orders and determined in each the dollar amount of capital items improperly expensed. He wishes to estimate this amount for the population (all maintenance job orders) with a 95% level of confidence. The 95% refers to the probability that the true population value will fall within the limits thus established for
a. Only this sample.
b. All samples selected from this population.
c. All samples of this size selected from this population.
d. All samples of this size selected from any population.

28. Mr. Wilson has estimated with 95% confidence that the total dollar amount of capital items improperly expensed is $43,200±$9,216. If he reduces the interval estimate from ± $9,216 to ± $4,608 without sampling further, his confidence level changes from 95% to
a. 99.3%.
b. 90%.
c. 68%.
d. 47.5%.

29. Lorantas had two billing clerks during the year. Snow worked three months and White worked nine months. Mr. Wilson wishes to use discovery sampling to test clerical accuracy during the tenure of each clerk. If the quantity of bills per month is constant and the same specified reliability and maximum tolerable occurrence rate is specified for each population, the ratio of the sample drawn from White's bills to the sample drawn from Snow's bills would be
a. More than 3:1.
b. 3:1.
c. More than 1:1 but less than 3:1.
d. 1:1.

Items 30 to 33 apply to an examination of the Rasmussen Art Supply Co. which is being conducted by Gerald Murray, CPA. Mr. Murray plans to select sufficient inventory items for test counts and pricing tests so that he can make a rough estimate of total inventory cost.

30. The size of Mr. Murray's statistical sample is influenced by the degree of variability of the cost of the items being sampled. The standard deviation, a basic measure of variation, is the

    a. Average of the absolute differences between the individual values and their mean.

    b. Square root of the average of the absolute differences between the individual values and their mean.

    c. Average of the squared differences between the individual values and their mean.

    d. Square root of the average of the squares of the differences between the individual values and their mean.

31. The greater the variability in the cost of the items being sampled (as measured by population standard deviation) the

    a. Greater the usefulness of a table of random numbers in selecting a sample.

    b. Larger the sample size required to make reliable statements with a given precision.

    c. Greater should be the level of confidence required when establishing the estimate.

    d. More likely that an interval estimate made from sample data will be correct.

32. Mr. Murray does not know the standard deviation of the cost of the items in Rasmussen's inventory. He can assume that the standard deviation computed from his sample is an adequate estimate of the population standard deviation if the sample

    a. Is randomly selected, regardless of the number of items in the sample.

    b. Is randomly selected and contains at least 30 items.

    c. Contains at least 30 items, even if not randomly selected.

    d. Either is randomly selected or contains at least 30 items.

33. Mr. Murray decides to use stratified sampling. The basic reason for using stratified sampling rather than unrestricted random sampling is to

    a. Reduce as much as possible the degree of variability in the overall population.

    b. Give every element in the population an equal chance of being included in the sample.

    c. Allow the person selecting the sample to use his own judgment in deciding which elements should be included in the sample.

    d. Reduce the required sample size from a nonhomogeneous population.

34. Balmes Company asks its CPA's assistance in estimating the proportion of its active 30-day charge account customers who also have an active install-ment credit account. The CPA takes an unrestricted random sample of 100 accounts from the 6,000 active 30-day charge accounts. Of the accounts selected ten also have active installment credit accounts. If the CPA decides to estimate with 95% confidence, the estimate is that

a. At most 10% of the active 30-day charge account customers also have active installment credit accounts.

b. At least 10% of the active 30-day charge account customers also have active installment credit account.

c. Between 7% and 13% of the active 30-day charge account customers also have active installment credit accounts.

d. Between 4% and 16% of the active 30-day charge account customers also have active installment credit accounts.

35. Popper Company asks its CPA's assistance in estimating the average gross value of the 5,000 invoices processed during June 1971. The CPA estimates the population standard deviation to be $8. If he wishes to achieve a precision of ± $2 with a 95% level of confidence, he should draw an unrestricted random sample of

a. 404 elements.

b. 101 elements.

c. 96 elements.

d. 62 elements.

36. In connection with his examination of the financial statements of the Patricia Roberts Corporation a CPA is making a rough estimate of the total value of an inventory of 2,000 items. His estimate of the total, based upon the mean of the unrestricted random sample, will be within the desired precision limits of - $18,000 provided that the difference between the sample mean and the true population mean is not more than

a. $36.

b. $18.

c. $9.

d. $4.50.

Section 4

CPA Examination
in
Business (Commercial) Law

CPA Examination
in Business (Commercial) Law

GENERAL APPROACH

The Business Law section tests a candidate's knowledge of textbook coverage of legal problems inherent in business activities, including audit activities. The scope of the examination is increasingly broad, so candidates cannot hope to become thoroughly familiar with all possible topics. Although cramming for examinations is usually frowned on by educators, we recommend concentrated study of Business Law during the three or four weeks immediately preceding the CPA examination. The Business Law section emphasizes knowledge of facts, and retention of such material is short-lived.

All questions on Business Law have the general aims of seeing whether candidates recognize the type of legal problem that exist, the applicable legal principles or rules, and the implications of the principles in a particular situation. Obviously, acquaintance with the meaning of various legal terms is essential.

If the pattern of recent examinations persists, the candidate may expect eight main questions, including three objective questions containing 30 true-false questions each. The grade for the objective questions is computed by subtracting a penalty for incorrect answers from the correct ones; omitted answers are not subtracted.

The essay questions usually contain a few sub-parts. The general tips on writing essay answers are applicable to the Business Law section. Among the more important are:

1. Without straddling the issue, the candidate should sometimes recognize

and state the principles of law that might point toward alternate conclusions. At the same time, stipulate why the chosen conclusion is superior.

2. If a question contains several parts, be certain to read the entire question before attempting to answer any part. In this way, the answers may be thought out in better perspective, then tailored to avoid excessive repetition.

3. Use legal terms correctly or avoid their use completely.

4. Make a decision when one is required. Include your reasoning, together with any special assumptions that you feel are needed.

Candidates are expected to base their answers on the Uniform Commercial Code and other uniform acts where pertinent. Where the uniforms acts do not apply, the Law questions generally try to test knowledge of majority rules. However, where minority rules are covered by the textbooks, knowledge of both majority and minority rules is expected.

The following topics, listed alphabetically, will appear on future CPA examinations (for elaboration see the section, Purpose and Scope, in *Information for CPA Candidates*):

> Accountant's legal responsibility
> Antitrust
> Bankruptcy
> Commercial paper
> Contracts
> Federal securities regulation
> Forms of business organizations
> Insurance
> Property
> Regulation of employer-employee relationships
> Sales
> Secured transactions
> Suretyship
> Wills and estates and trusts

As you can see, the coverage is so broad that some gambling on preparation is necessary. Questions that have appeared infrequently might deserve scant attention; wills, estates, trusts, personal property, real property, and mortgages belong in the infrequent category. The AICPA has explicitly designated questions on antitrust laws, federal securities regulation, and employer-employee regulations as the newer topics to be covered.

Moreover, as indicated by the topical headings that follow, agency law may be covered even though it is not explicitly listed in *Information for CPA Candidates*. Furthermore, the ability to recognize and define legal problems might be considered a separate topic.

Topical Analysis of Business Law

For the convenience of the reader, these questions have been divided into the following twelve topical headings. The number of questions under each topic reflects the relative importance of that topic in recent examinations. However, there is overlap among topics, and the preceding comments about coverage should be considered before making hasty predictions.

Topic	Question	Relative Importance
Accountant's legal responsibility	1-3	10%
Antitrust	4	3
Bankruptcy	5	3
Commercial paper	6-7	6
Contracts	8-12	17
Forms of business organization	13-17	17
Insurance	18-19	7
Property	20	3
Secured transactions	21-23	10
Suretyship	24-25	7
Agency	26-28	10
Identification of legal problems	29-30	7
	30	100%

The time allowance for each question is usually 20-25 minutes; a few questions are allowed 25-30 minutes. Therefore, a time budget of 25 minutes per question is appropriate.

REFERENCES

Frascona, Joseph, *CPA Law Review,* 4th Ed. (Homewood, Illinois: Richard D. Irwin, Inc., 1972).

Lakin, Leonard, and Howard J. Berger, *CPA Law Examination Review* (St. Paul, Minnesota: West Publishing Co., 1972).

Miller, Herbert E., and George C. Mead, editors, *CPA Review Manual,* 4th Ed. (Englewood Cliffs, N.J.: Prentice-Hall, Inc., 1972), pp. 603-722.

Wyatt, John W., and Madie B. Wyatt, *Business Law,* 4th Ed. (New York: McGraw-Hill Book Company, 1971).

1. Accountant's legal responsibility

Part a. Risk Capital Limited, a Delaware corporation, was considering the purchase of a substantial amount of the treasury stock held by Florida Sunshine Corporation, a closely held corporation. Initial discussions with the Florida Sunshine Corporation began late in 1969.

Wilson and Wyatt, Florida Sunshine's accountants, regularly prepared quarterly and annual unaudited financial statements. The most recently prepared financial statements were for the year ended September 30, 1970.

On November 15, 1970 after protracted negotiations, Risk Capital agreed to purchase 100,000 shares of no par, Class A Capital Stock of Florida Sunshine at $12.50 per share. However, Risk Capital insisted upon audited statements for calendar year 1970. The contract specifically provided:

> Risk Capital shall have the right to rescind the purchase of said stock if the audited financial statements of Florida Sunshine for calendar year 1970 show a material adverse change in the financial condition of the Corporation.

The audited financial statements furnished to Florida Sunshine by Wilson and Wyatt showed no such material adverse change. Risk Capital relied upon the audited statements and purchased the treasury stock of Florida Sunshine. It was subsequently discovered that, as of the balance sheet date, the audited statements were incorrect and that in fact there had been a material adverse change in the financial condition of the Corporation. Florida Sunshine is insolvent and Risk Capital will lose virtually its entire investment.

Risk Capital seeks recovery against Wilson and Wyatt.

Required:

1. Discuss each of the theories of liability that Risk Capital will probably assert as its basis for recovery.

2. Assuming that only ordinary negligence is proven, will Risk Capital prevail? State "yes" or "no" and explain.

Part b. Wells and White, the accountants for the Allie Corporation, provided various professional services for Allie over 15 years under annual retainer agreements. The services included tax return preparation, special cost analyses and the preparation of the Corporation's audited and unaudited financial statements.

The relationship had been quite harmonious until the retirement of Roberts, the president and founder of Allie Corporation. His successor, Strong, was a very aggressive, expansion-oriented individual who lacked the competence and personal attraction of his predecessor. Two years after Roberts' retirement the unbroken record of increases in annual earnings was in jeopardy.

Strong realized that a decrease in earnings would have an unfavorable impact on his image and on his plans to merge with a well known conglomerate. He called Wells, the senior partner of Wells and White, and demanded that the method of computing and reporting the current year's earnings be changed in a way that would preserve the upward trend in earnings.

Although the proposed method would be within the realm of generally accepted accounting principles, Wells subsequently told Strong that, in the exercise of its professional judgment, the firm could not agree to such a change. Strong promptly dismissed the firm and refused to pay the final billing of $1,750 for services rendered to the date of dismissal under its agreement with Wells and White.

Wells and White have brought suit against Allie Corporation for the $1,750. Allie Corporation responded by denying liability on the ground that the firm's refusal to cooperate constituted a breach of contract which precluded recovery. Allie also counterclaimed by demanding the return of all audit working papers, correspondence and duplicate tax returns and supporting explanations pertaining to Allie Corporation.

Required:

1. Is the Wells and White account receivable valid and enforceable against the Allie Corporation? State "yes" or "no" and explain.

2. Will Allie Corporation prevail on its counterclaim demanding return of the audit working papers, correspondence and tax returns? State "yes" or "no" and explain.

Part c. Continuing the situation described in Part "b" above: Strong was unable to find other accountants who approved of the proposed change in the method of computing and reporting earnings, so he abandoned this demand and then engaged new accountants, Bar & Cross. Income continued to decrease in the next two quarters and Strong became convinced that the cause of this must be due to defalcations by some dishonest employee. Therefore, he engaged Bar & Cross to make a special study to discover the guilty person. After several months of intensive work Bar & Cross were able to discover minor defalcations of $950. Of this amount, $600 was stolen during the last two years while Wells and White were Allie Corporation's accountants. Allie Corporation sues Wells and White for the loss.

Required:

Will Allie Corporation recover the loss from Wells and White? State "yes" or "no" and explain.

2. Accountant's legal responsibility

Part a. The CPA firm of Winston & Mall was engaged by the Fast Cargo Company, a retailer, to examine its financial statements for the year ended August 31, 1971. It followed generally accepted auditing standards and examined transactions on a test basis. A sample of 100 disbursements was used to test vouchers payable, cash disbursements and receiving and purchasing procedures. An investigation of the sample disclosed several instances where purchases had been recorded and paid for without the required receiving report being included in the file of supporting documents. This was properly noted in the working papers by Martin, the junior who did the sampling. Mall, the partner in charge, called these facts to the attention of Harris, Fast Cargo's chief accountant, who told him to not worry about it, that he would make certain that these receiving reports were properly included in the voucher file. Mall accepted this and did nothing further to investigate or follow-up on this situation.

Harris was engaged in a fraudulent scheme whereby he diverted the merchandise to a private warehouse where he leased space and sent the invoices to Fast Cargo for payment. The scheme was discovered later by a special investigation and a preliminary estimate indicates that the loss to Fast Cargo will be in excess of $20,000.

Required:

1. What is the liability, if any, of Winston & Mall in this situation? Discuss.
2. What additional steps, if any, should have been taken by Mall? Explain.

Part b. Barton and Co. have been engaged to examine the financial statements for Mirror Manufacturing Corporation for the year ended September 30, 1971. Mirror Manufacturing needed additional cash to continue its operations. To raise funds it agreed to sell its common stock investment in a subsidiary. The buyers insisted upon having the proceeds placed in escrow because of the possibility of a major contingent tax liability. Carter, president of Mirror, explained this to Barton, the partner in charge of the Mirror audit. He indicated that he wished to show the proceeds from the sale of the subsidiary as an unrestricted current account receivable. He stated that in his opinion the government's claim was groundless and that he needed an "uncluttered" balance sheet and a "clean" auditor's opinion to obtain additional working capital. Barton acquiesced in this request. The government's claim proved to be valid and, pursuant to the agreement with the buyers, the purchase price of the subsidiary was reduced to $450,000. This, coupled with other adverse developments, caused Mirror to become insolvent with assets to cover only some of its liabilities. Barton and Co. is being sued by several of Mirror's creditors who loaned money in reliance upon the financial statements upon which it rendered an unqualified opinion.

Required:

What is the liability, if any, of Barton and Co. to the creditors of Mirror Manufacturing? Explain.

Part c. In conducting the examination of the financial statements of the Farber Corporation for the year ended September 30, 1971, Harper, a CPA, discovered that Nance, the president who was also one of the principal stockholders, had borrowed substantial amounts of money from the Corporation. He indicated that he owned 51% of the Corporation, that the money would be promptly repaid and that the financial statements were being prepared for internal use only. He requested that these loans not be accounted for separately in the financial statements, but be included in the other current accounts receivable. Harper acquiesced in this request. Nance was correct as to his stock ownership and the fact that the financial statements were for internal use only. However, he subsequently became insolvent and was unable to repay the loans.

Required:

What is Harper's liability? Explain.

3. Accountants' legal responsibility and federal securities regulation

Each of the lettered statements of facts below is followed by numbered sentences that state legal conclusions relating to those facts. You are to determine whether each legal conclusion is true or false according to the general principles of accountants' legal responsibility and federal securities regulation.

A. James Sack, a partner in the firm of Walters, Jones, & Sack, CPAs, prepared tax returns for Ominus, a closely held family corporation. The Corporation's books were kept by a family member. While preparing the tax returns, Sack realized that the books and records were poorly kept and contained several inaccuracies. However, he relied upon them and based his tax computations exclusively upon them. As a result, Sack erroneously included in taxable income some items which did not actually represent income. The errors subsequently were discovered, but, by that time, it was too late to file an amended return or claim for refund to recover the excess taxes paid.

31. James Sack was negligent in preparing the tax return.
32. The Internal Revenue Service would be unable to subpoena Walters, Jones, & Sack's working papers because they are privileged communications.
33. Walters, Jones, & Sack will be liable for the excess amount of taxes paid by Ominus.
34. Only Sack, and not the CPA firm, would be liable under the circumstances described.
35. Sack's firm could defend successfully a suit brought by Ominus to recover the excess amount of tax by establishing the contributory negligence of Ominus.
36. The fact that Sack had not been informed of the inadequacy of the records totally exonerates him from liability.
37. Sack has committed a fraud.
38. If Sack had joined Ominus in willfully attempting to evade tax, he would be guilty of a felony.

B. The partnership, Winslow, Wilson, & Carr, CPAs, prepared the income tax returns for Charles Bosphor for several years. The staff accountant who prepared Bosphor's tax return for 1970 properly elected to report certain income as an installment sale.

The next year a new staff man was assigned to the task of preparing Bosphor's return. He inadvertently failed to include the installment income for 1971. An audit of the return by the Internal Revenue Service revealed the error, and additional tax and interest were assessed.

39. Winslow, Wilson, & Carr were negligent in the preparation of the tax return in question.
40. Winslow, Wilson, & Carr will be liable for the tax assessed.
41. Winslow, Wilson & Carr will be liable for the interest assessed.
42. It was Charles Bosphor's responsibility to check the returns and inform Winslow, Wilson, & Carr of the error.
43. Good accounting practice would dictate that a new man on an engagement review his predecessor's work for the past several years.

C. Fred Watson, a partner of Watson, Weller, & Welsh, CPAs, does the accounting work for Micro Manufacturing, Inc. Micro is closely held and does not require audited financial statements. Watson delivered Micro's most recent set of financial statements to Mason, Micro's President. The financial statements were accompanied by a covering letter clearly indicating that the statements were unaudited and that no opinion was expressed on them. However, each financial statement was not labeled unaudited. Mason used the financial statements to borrow money from Prospero. Mason did not show Prospero the firm's covering letter.

44. If the financial statements had been clearly labeled unaudited, Watson or his firm could not be held liable for misrepresentations contained therein.
45. Mason, Micros president, has acted fraudulently.
46. At a minimum, the CPA firm should have clearly labeled each page of the financial statements unaudited.

D. Kenneth Chance, a senior accountant with the partnership of South, Wall, Evers, & Co., CPAs, resigned after several years with the firm. During his employment, he had examined the financial statements of Zelex Corporation and became a close friend of the controller and the financial vice-president of Zelex.

After establishing his own firm, Chance actively solicited the business of Zelex, even though the South firm had been engaged to perform the current year's audit. During the audit, Zelex dismissed the South firm alleging that Chance's replacement was personally obnoxious, performed his work in a slipshod manner, and was dating one of the Company's female bookkeepers. Zelex demands the return of all of its books and records and the firm's working papers.

47. Zelex could dismiss the South firm without liability solely upon the personality conflict that arose with respect to Chance's replacement.
48. If Chance's replacement were negligent in performing his work, Zelex could terminate the relationship and recover damages.
49. Zelex has the right to the return of its books and records.
50. The South firm must turn over its working papers to Zelex.
51. If none of Zelex's allegations are true, Zelex will be liable for breach of contract.

E. Xavier, Francis, & Paul are a growing medium-sized partnership of CPAs located in the midwest. One of the firm's major clients is considering offering its stock to the public. This will be the firm's first client to go public.

52. The firm should thoroughly familiarize itself with the Securities Act of 1933, the Securities Exchange Act of 1934 and Regulation S-X.
53. If the client is unincorporated, the Securities Act of 1933 will *not* apply.
54. If the client is going to be listed on an organized exchange, the Securities Exchange Act of 1934 will *not* apply.
55. The Securities Act of 1933 imposes an additional potential liability on firms such as Xavier, Francis, & Paul.
56. So long as the company engages in exclusively intrastate business, the federal securities laws will *not* apply.

F. The partnership of Maxwell, Plumb, & Fisk, CPAs, has been engaged by Vitrolic Partners, their largest client, to examine the financial statements in connection with the offering of 2,000 limited-partnership interests in Vitrolic to the public at $5,000 per subscription.

57. Maxwell, Plumb, & Fisk may disclaim any liability under the federal securities acts by an unambiguous, bold-faced disclaimer of liability on their work.
58. If the Securities Act of 1933 applies, Maxwell, Plumb, & Fisk have responsibility only for the financial statements as of the close of the fiscal year in question.
59. The dollar amount in question is sufficiently small so as to provide an exemption from the Securities Act of 1933.
60. The Securities Exchange Act of 1934 will apply to Vitrolic.

4. Antitrust law

Each of the lettered statements of facts below is followed by numbered sentences that state legal conclusions relating to those facts. You are to determine whether each legal conclusion is true or false according to the general principles of antitrust law.

A. The presidents of three competing manufacturing corporations engaged in interstate commerce decided to eliminate what they called "senseless price cutting" in the tri-state area in which they compete. Each agreed that prices should be determined on the basis of fairness to the public and to his company. To implement their verbal agreement, the three presidents have established a four-month rotating price-leadership arrangement. Each company has served four months of each year as the designated price leader. The price leader has set the minimum price for all competing products sold by the three companies. Each president has agreed that his company would abide strictly by the prices set by the price leader.

You are the CPA for one of these companies.

61. The government can bring criminal action against the presidents of the three companies.
62. The government can seek injunctive relief prohibiting the continuation of the agreement.
63. Private individuals who suffer damages as a result of the agreement can recover treble damages.
64. Any party suing the presidents of the three corporations would rely primarily on the Sherman Act.
65. If one of the corporations refused to abide by the agreement, the others could obtain damages for breach of contract.
66. If the corporations can show that "senseless price cutting" did exist in fact, they will not have violated antitrust law.
67. If the corporations can show that the minimum prices established by the price leader were always fair to the public, the corporations will not have violated antitrust law.
68. If there is a violation of antitrust law, the government validly can seize any of the corporations' goods that are shipped in interstate commerce pursuant to the agreement.
69. The corporations will not have violated antitrust law if the value of goods shipped in interstate commerce is less than $50,000 each year.
70. There is no violation of antitrust law if the prices established under the agreement are uniformly beneath the prices charged prior to its implementation.

B. The following problems arose during the examination of the financial statements of Northup, Inc. Northup, a large manufacturer of industrial products, is attempting to acquire a controlling block of shares of Jackson, Inc., a competing manufacturer. Jackson's market share is about 40% in the section of the United States in which Northup and Jackson compete. Northup's share of this market is about 35%. Four other firms compete for the remaining 25%.

Northup is also considering the purchase of Keller Corporation, one of its major customers (Keller's average annual purchases from Northup have been about $12,000,000), to assure itself of an outlet for a substantial quantity of its products. Northup intends to have Keller continue as a subsidiary. Keller also purchases substantial dollar volumes (usually around $5,000,000 per year) from Northup's competitors.

Some time ago, independent of its present acquisition activities, Northup stopped dealing with Lambert, one of its distributors. Lambert and Northup had entered into a distributorship agreement giving either party the right to terminate on at least 90 days prior written notice. Northup had given such notice. Lambert has nevertheless instituted a treble damage suit under the antitrust laws against Northup. Lambert alleges that it will lose a substantial capital investment made in connection with this distributorship.

Northup, Jackson, Keller, and Lambert are all in interstate commerce.

71. Northup would avoid an antitrust action by purchasing the assets rather than the stock of Jackson.

72. One of Northup's risks is the threat of injunction prior to the delivery of the Jackson shares.

73. Assuming that the acquisition of Jackson is completed without antitrust attack, the Department of Justice is thereafter precluded from instituting suit to divest the acquisition.

74. If the Jackson acquisition were attacked as anti-competitive, a possible defense would be available to Northup if Jackson were in bankruptcy and there were no other prospective purchaser of the Jackson shares.

75. If Northup abandoned the acquisition of Jackson it would *not* be illegal *per se* for Northup and Jackson to agree to allocate customers and for each to refrain from soliciting customers of the other.

76. The acquisition of Jackson would violate the anti-merger section of the Clayton Act if the merger merely tended to create, though it did not in fact yet create, a monopoly, absent any unique facts.

77. The acquisition of Keller would be illegal if Northup intended Keller to purchase only from Northup to the exclusion of Northup's competitors.

78. The acquisition of Keller is totally without legal justification; hence, the intent of Northup is totally irrelevant.

79. Northup's termination of the distributorship agreement with Lambert constitutes an illegal refusal to deal with or to boycott in violation of the antitrust law.

C. Cranston, Inc., a manufacturer of various electrical products, sells some of its goods to over 20 retailers in a five-state area. It has been selling to Allen, a retailer in this area, at lower prices than it charges other retailers in the area. This low price was made in good faith to meet equally low prices legally offered by competing manufacturers as evidenced by the competing manufacturers' sales invoices. Cranston has also been selling goods at reduced prices to Barry, another retailer within the area. The prices to Barry reflect savings to Cranston in the cost of manufacture and delivery accruing from Barry's purchases in large quantities. Two other retailers in the area, Coleman and Dixon, are being sold to at prices lower than Cranston sells outside the area.

Cranston and its retailers are engaged in interstate commerce. Each of Cranston's product lines contains only goods of like grade and quality. Cranston holds a substantial share (50%) of the market in the five-state area, but only has a small (4%) share of the national market. All of Cranston's retailers compete with one another. Each retailer buys substantial quantities (between $1,000,000 to $2,000,000 per year) of each of Cranston's products.

80. The sales to Allen violate the antitrust laws against price discrimination.
81. The sales to Barry violate the antitrust laws against price discrimination.
82. Cranston's competing manufacturers would have an antitrust action against Cranston.
83. Cranston could agree with Branston, a competing manufacturer, to sell to various retailers at certain specified prices so long as Cranston's prices were above its direct variable costs attributable to goods sold.
84. If Cranston's sales were attacked by its competitors as discriminatory, a valid defense would be to prove that the effect of such discrimination did not substantially lessen competition.
85. Cranston could legally adopt a merchandising plan to pay for or furnish services to all its customers in the five-state area on proportionally equal terms.
86. Cranston would violate antitrust law if it were to license certain of its unique products to retailers on condition that they purchase from Cranston all their major requirements of Cranston's other products.

D. Four corporations are the largest manufacturers in their industry. Their combined share of the market has constituted over 90 percent each year for many years. As members of a trade association, certain officers of these corporations meet periodically to discuss topics of mutual interest. Matters discussed include engineering design, production methods, product costs, product pricing, merchandising policy, and inventory levels. The representatives also usually see each other after the association meetings for cocktails where they discuss these and other business matters. These representatives have maintained prices in accordance with an informal oral agreement terminable at will by any company wishing to withdraw. However, they have never reduced their agreement to a written document or memorandum. The four corporations compete with each other in interstate commerce. The states in which these corporations do business have typical "fair trade" laws.

87. The members of the trade association validly may appoint the trade association as their representative to allocate manufacturing quotas.
88. An arrangement relating to price fixing would be illegal *per se* if the government merely proved the existence of the oral agreement.
89. The distributors of the four corporations legally could enter into price maintenance agreements among themselves to prescribe the minimum prices at which they would resell the products bearing the brand name, trademark, or trade name of any of the four corporations.
90. The retailers of the four corporations legally could enter into price maintenance agreements among themselves to prescribe the minimum prices at which they would resell the products bearing the brand name, trademark, or trade name of any of the four corporations.

5. Bankruptcy (20-25 min.)

During the examination of the financial statements of Delta Corporation, you note that as of September 30, 1972:

Current liabilities exceed current assets.
Total assets substantially exceed total liabilities.
Cash position is poor and current payables are considerably in arrears.
Trade and secured creditors are pressing for payment and several lawsuits have been commenced against Delta.

Further investigation reveals the following:

On August 31, 1972, Delta made a $1,000 payment to Oliveros on a $20,000 mortgage indebtedness over one year in arrears. The fair-market value of the mortgaged property is $35,000.
On September 20, 1972, a trade creditor, Miller, obtained a judgment against Delta which under applicable law constitutes a lien on Delta's real property.
On September 22, 1972, Delta paid a substantial amount to Helms, a supplier, on an account over one year old.
On September 27, 1972, Delta executed and delivered a financing statement to Honea, a vendor, from whom Delta had purchased some new machinery six months earlier. Honea duly filed and perfected the financing statement.

Required:

1. As of September 30, 1972, did any of the above transactions legally constitute acts of bankruptcy? Explain.

2. As of September 30, 1972, could the creditors of Delta file an involuntary petition in bankruptcy against Delta if a sufficient number of them having a sufficient amount of claims decide to do so? Explain.

3. Independent of your answers to parts 1 and 2, assume the same facts set out above except that Delta's total liabilities exceed total assets and that on October 2, 1972, Delta filed a voluntary petition in bankruptcy, and a Trustee has been appointed.

    a. What are the rights, if any, of the Trustee against each of the creditors involved in the four transactions stated in the problem? Explain.

    b. What are the general requirements for creditors to be entitled to vote on and participate in a bankruptcy proceeding? Explain for each of the four creditors involved whether he meets these requirements. Why?

6. Commercial paper

Each of the lettered statements of facts below is followed by numbered sentences that state legal conclusions relating to those facts. You are to determine whether each legal conclusion is true or false according to *Articles 3 and 4 of the Uniform Commercial Code (Commercial Paper and Bank Deposits and Collections).*

A. On April 1, 1971, Howard Norton purchased $10,000 of merchandise from Mark Kerr to whom he executed and delivered the following instrument:

April 1, 1971

In consideration of merchandise sold and delivered to me this date, I promise to pay to the order of Mark Kerr the sum of ten thousand dollars ($10,000.00) on November 1, 1971 together with interest at the rate of 6% per annum from the date hereof. In the event that this instrument is referred to an attorney for collection, I will pay a reasonable attorney's fee.

/S/ Howard Norton

31. The provision for an attorney's fee makes this instrument nonnegotiable.

32. The instrument must state the consideration received to be negotiable.

33. If this instrument were written in pencil, it would not be negotiable.

34. If this instrument had stated that it was subject to the terms of an agreement between the parties, it would not be negotiable.

35. This instrument is bearer paper.

B. Harold Sullivan executed and delivered to Paul Wilson a $500 negotiable note payable to bearer. Wilson indorsed it: "Pay to the order of Frank Ford /s/ Paul Wilson."

    36. Ford may negotiate the instrument by delivery alone because it was originally bearer paper.

    37. Wilson's indorsement is a special, unqualified and nonrestrictive indorsement.

    38. If Wilson had indorsed the instrument in blank, it would be legal for Ford to write above Wilson's indorsement: "Pay to the order of Frank Ford."

    39. If Ford had indorsed the instrument "For collection only /s/ Frank Ford," this would be a restrictive indorsement that would prevent further transfer or negotiation.

    40. If Ford endorsed the instrument "Pay to the order of John Duncan $200 /s/ Frank Ford" and delivered it to Duncan, an effective negotiation would be effected.

C. Gavin Lee delivered a $50 check to Donald Fox. Fox wrongfully raised the amount to $250 using spaces which Lee negligently had left blank. Then Fox indorsed and delivered the check to Coppola who took it for value, in good faith and without notice of the alteration. In due course the check was presented for payment to Lee's bank which paid it in good faith and in accordance with reasonable commercial standards. Lee protested when the bank charged his account for $250.

    41. The bank may not charge Lee's account for any amount because the unauthorized material alteration discharges Lee from all liability.

    42. The bank may charge Lee's account for only $50.

    43. The bank may charge Lee's account for $250.

    44. If Lee had stopped payment on the check, Coppola could have recovered only $50 from Lee.

    45. If Coppola was not a holder in due course, he could not recover any amount from Lee.

D. A bookkeeper prepared the payroll for the several hundred employees of Allied Corporation and included five fictitious names for nonexistent employees. Morton, treasurer of the Corporation, signed these five checks drawn on the Valley Bank. The bookkeeper indorsed the fictitious names on the five checks and deposited them in her account in the Richmond Bank. Later she withdrew all of the money and absconded. The Richmond Bank collected the money from the Valley Bank which charged the Corporation's account.

    46. The five checks drawn to fictitious names are order paper.

    47. The bookkeeper's endorsement in the name of a fictitious payee is an effective indorsement.

48. The bookkeeper's indorsement in the name of the fictitious payee is a forgery.
49. Allied Corporation can recover from the Richmond Bank.
50. Allied Corporation can recover from the Valley Bank.

E. Atlas purchased merchandise from White and upon delivery it issued in exchange a promissory note payable to the order of White and indorsed by Cole. At maturity White presented the note for payment; Atlas failed to pay and White gave Cole due notice of dishonor. In White's action against Cole on his indorsement, Cole defended on the grounds that he received no consideration for the indorsement, that he indorsed the instrument solely for the purpose of lending his name to Atlas and that these facts were known to White.

51. Notice of the accommodation character of Cole's indorsement was given because it was not in the chain of title.
52. Judgment in the action would be for Cole.
53. If Cole had signed the instrument as a co-maker and White had brought an action against him without first attempting to collect from Atlas, Cole would have a valid defense.
54. In the event that Cole pays the note at maturity he may recover the full amount from Atlas.
55. If Atlas pays the note at maturity, he may recover against Cole.

F. Percy is the holder of a demand note bearing the indorsemt of Carl Ladd, the payee.

56. To charge the maker the note must be presented for payment.
57. To charge the indorser the note must first be presented to the maker for payment.
58. Presentment may be made personally, by mail (effective when received) or through a clearing house.
59. Ladd, the payee of the note, may be a holder in due course.
60. If Ladd indorsed the note "Collection guaranteed /s/ Carl Ladd," his liability would be primary.

7. Negotiable instruments

Part a. Frank Thornton, a professional golfer, was employed as a coach by Lakeside Golf Association, Inc., a membership corporation which owned and operated a country club and golf course. By proper vote Thornton was authorized to buy golf clubs costing $5,000 on the Association's credit and to issue a note in the Association's name. Thornton contracted to buy the clubs from Professional Golf Shop for $5,000. Upon delivery of the clubs Thornton wrote out, signed and delivered the following note:

January 15, 1972

Three months after date we promise to pay to the order of Professional Golf Shop the sum of five thousand dollars. Value received.

Lakeside Golf Association, Inc.

/s/ Frank Thornton

The note was duly negotiated by Professional Golf Shop to Leonard who is a holder in due course. The note is now due and has been presented by Leonard for payment to Lakeside Golf Association, Inc. and to Frank Thornton.

Required:

1. Is Thornton personally liable on the note? State "yes" or "no" and discuss.
2. Is Lakeside Golf Association, Inc. liable on the note? State "yes" or "no" and discuss.

Part b. On July 9, 1971 Donnell, hard pressed for cash, borrowed $2,000 from Munro in exchange for his promissory note for $2,000 plus 12% interest payable on January 9, 1972 to the order of Munro. The statutory legal rate of interest for this transaction was 8%. In August 1971 Munro indorsed the note in blank and sold and delivered it to Gaylord for $2,000 cash. On January 3, 1972 Gaylord sold and delivered the note without indorsement to Tucker for $2,100 cash. Tucker failed to present the note for payment on January 9, 1972, and on March 1, 1972 he indorsed the note in blank "without recourse" and sold and delivered it to Dunfee for $1,950 cash. Neither Gaylord, Tucker nor Dunfee had any knowledge of the transaction in which the note originated.

Required:

1. Was Tucker a holder in due course? State "yes" or "no" and discuss.
2. Is Dunfee entitled to the rights of a holder in due course? State "yes" or "no" and discuss.
3. Is Donnell liable to Dunfee? State "yes" or "no" and discuss.
4. Is Gaylord liable to Dunfee? State "yes" or "no" and discuss.
5. Is Tucker liable to Dunfee? State "yes" or "no" and discuss.

Part c. Robert Little mailed his $180 check drawn upon the Last National Bank to Wilfred, his creditor. An employee of Wilfred stole the check from Wilfred's office, indorsed Wilfred's name on it and delivered it to Sam's Grocery Store for $30 in groceries and $150 in cash. Sam indorsed the check "for deposit" and deposited it in his account with Valley National Bank which collected it from Last National Bank and credited the $180 to Sam's account. Last National Bank charged Little's account.

Required:

Assume that yesterday Wilfred complained to Little that he had not received the check and that Wilfred and Little then discovered what had happened to it.

Discuss separately the rights and liabilities of each of the following with respect to the check:
1. Little.
2. Last National Bank.
3. Valley National Bank.
4. Sam.
5. Wilfred.

8. Contracts

You are the in-charge accountant on the examination of the financial statements of the Kell Manufacturing Corporation. After gathering information concerning accounts-receivable and payable confirmation exceptions, your assistant seeks your guidance in clearing the following exceptions:

A. A $6,000 positive account-receivable confirmation request was returned by Beck Company stating that no balance is due to Kell.

Investigation has revealed the following background information.

Kell received a telephone order from Beck offering to purchase 1,000 bike sprockets at $6 per sprocket. The sprockets were an odd size, were to be manufactured specifically for Beck, and could not be sold to other customers in the ordinary course of business. Kell changed its production molds to accommodate the odd size and started production, Kell then received a phone call from Beck canceling the order because the order which Beck had received requiring the special sprockets had fallen through.

Kell, insisting that the contract was valid and that Beck was obligated to take and to pay for the odd size sprockets, sent Beck an invoice for the purchase price of the 1,000 sprockets. Beck's purchasing agent returned the sale invoice with a note that the contract of sale was oral and that Beck has no obligation to pay.

Required:

Is Beck liable on the oral contract? Explain.

B. A $26,000 positive account-receivable confirmation request was returned by Thompson Bike Company with the comment that the balance due Kell was overstated by $5,000.

Investigation revealed the following information regarding the $5,000 in question. Kell received a written order from Thompson for immediate shipment of 2,000 size #2 bike chains at $2.50 each. The order specified that the chains were to be shipped by rail, FOB Kell's shipping dock. Kell promptly packed the chains and shipped them according to Thompson's requirements.

The day following shipment, Kell sent Thompson an acknowledgment of the order. The acknowledgment was received by Thompson two days later.

Unfortunately, the goods were delayed several days in transit due to flooding which destroyed a bridge along the delivery route. As a result of the delay, Thompson ordered identical bike chains from a competing manufacturer and wired Kell to cancel the order.

Kell contends that Thompson is liable for the purchase price of the chains. Thompson claims that there was no contract since acceptance by Kell by prompt delivery or notice had not been received within a reasonable time.

Required:

Is Thompson liable to Kell for the bike chains ordered? Explain.

C. A negative-confirmation request regarding a past-due $300 receivable was returned by Fincher Construction Co. with the comment that the bill had been paid in full.

Investigation revealed that Kell had sold Fincher, at auction, some old typewriters and other miscellaneous office equipment. The contract of sale contained no warranties and provided in clear, bold, and specific terms that the buyer accept the goods "with all faults." Several months after Fincher received the items from Kell, several of the typewriters repeatedly broke down, and repairs costing $300 were required to put the typewriters into proper working order. When paying Kell's invoices, Fincher deducted the $300 repair charge.

Required:

Is Fincher entitled to deduct the $300 repair charge from the sale price? Explain.

D. An account-payable confirmation request received from one of Kell's major vendors, Rosser Corp., reflects an invoice which Kell has not recorded. Your assistant has discovered that Kell sent Rosser an order for 3,000 gears to be shipped by rail, FOB Rosser's place of business. The goods were received by Kell, but inspection revealed that the gears were badly pitted and did not conform to Kell's specifications. Kell promptly notified Rosser that it refused to accept the shipment and that it was holding the gears for Rosser's disposal. The day after Rosser received notification of the refusal, a fire in Kell's warehouse further damaged the gears. Rosser notified Kell that it must pay the agreed contract price for the gears; or, at least pay for the damage caused by the fire. Neither party had insurance on the gears destroyed by the fire.

Required:

Does Kell have any liability to Rosser? Explain.

9. Contracts

During the course of your examination of the financial statements of Grand Fashions, Inc., a retail dress merchant, you learned of the following transactions with wholesale dress merchants:

Transaction 1

The Corporation telephoned Stevens Company and ordered from Stevens' catalog 50 Junior Model dresses in assorted sizes for a total price of $300. The next day the Corporation received a written confirmation of the order from Stevens with a request that it sign and return the duplicate of the confirmation, which it did not do. A month later the Corporation sought to avoid the contract claiming that it was not liable since it did not sign the confirmation order.

Transaction 2

The Corporation placed a telephone order with Scott Company for ten dozen dresses for $1,000. The next day the Corporation received, inspected and accepted five dozen of the dresses. The Corporation refused to accept the balance when tendered and sought to return the other five dozen dresses claiming that it was not obligated.

Transaction 3

The Corporation purchased 25 dozen all-silk dresses from Lawrence Company after examining a sample dress make of all-silk that Lawrence Company submitted. The written confirmation received by the Corporation contained the words "as per sample submitted to the company." Upon delivery, inspection and testing the Corporation determined that the dresses were 65% silk and 35% dacron and immediately informed Lawrence Company that it wanted to return the dresses for full credit. Lawrence Company insisted that the Corporation take the dresses less a 25% discount, but the Corporation refused to do so.

Transaction 4

The Corporation executed a written contract with Roberts Company to purchase a miscellaneous collection of dresses for $5,000. A week before the agreed shipment date, Roberts called the Corporation and said "We cannot deliver at $5,000; unless you agree to pay $6,000, we will cancel the order." After considerable discussion the Corporation agreed to pay $6,000 if Roberts would ship as agreed in the contract. After the goods had been delivered and accepted by the Corporation, it refused to pay $6,000 insisting that it is legally obligated to pay only $5,000.

Required:

Discuss separately the validity of the contentions made by Grand Fashions, Inc. with respect to each of the four transactions.

10. Contracts

Part a. During the examination of the financial statements of the Williams Watch Company the following problem was discovered.

On January 16, 1971 Crane, one of Williams' salesmen, called upon Parke, the vice president of purchasing for Carter Department Stores. He showed Parke the new line of mod watches with large, bright-colored faces. Parke ordered 150 watches costing from $5 to $20 with a total cost of $1,475. Delivery was to be made not later than March 15, 1971. Crane wrote the orders in his order book as Parke orally indicated the quantity of each watch he desired. Neither party signed anything.

Crane promptly submitted the Carter order to the sales department. The next day the order was recorded and a memorandum was sent to Carter Department Stores in care of Parke. The memorandum described the transaction indicating the number and prices of the watches purchased and was signed by S. A. Williams, vice president of marketing; however, the total price and delivery terms were excluded erroneously.

Parke received the memo on Janury 20. He read it and placed it in his goods on order file. On the 20th of February the market for mod watches collapsed and fair market value of the watches dropped to approximately $700. Parke promptly notified Williams Watch by phone that Carter Stores was not interested in the mod watches and would refuse delivery. Williams Watch filed suit for damages against Carter.

Required:

Will Williams Watch prevail in its suit against Carter Department Stores? State "yes" or "no" and discuss the relevant legal implications of the above facts.

Part b. In examining the accounts receivable of the Mercury Publishing Company the following problem was discovered.

During the months of November and December 1970 Famous Music Shops, Inc. ordered and was shipped sheet music and music books having a total invoice price of $565.29. The amount of Famous Music's indebtedness to Mercury has not been disputed.

Investigation revealed that on March 1, 1971, exasperated with the number and frequency of Mercury's written demands for settlement of the account, Famous Music sent Mercury a large number of the previously purchased book and a check for $255.04. The total price of the returned books on Famous Music's original invoice was $310.25, so that this amount plus the check equaled the amount owed. There was not dispute as to this point.

Famous Music's letter to Mercury included a list of the books being returned and stated that the credit for the return plus the enclosed check for the balance constituted payment of the account in full. The following was written on the face of the check: "Complete and final settlement of our account payable."

The letter and check reached Mercury in due course. Mercury cashed the check, but declined to accept the books for credit. On March 7, 1971 Mercury wrote Famous Music as follows: "We are not crediting your account with these books, but are holding them subject to your disposal."

On March 15, 1971 Famous replied reaffirming its position as indicated in its letter of March 1.

Famous claimed that there was a general custom throughout the United States permitting the return of such books. Mercury denied that such a custom existed. Mercury's counsel submitted a memorandum stating that there was authority supporting both sides of the proposition and that in fact there was a bona fide dispute as to whether such a custom existed.. The attorney's memorandum concluded that "this issue can only be determined by litigation."

Famous Music has refused to accept the returned books or to pay any more on the account.

Required:

1. What are the legal problems and implications of the above facts? Discuss.
2. Is the Mercury account receivable valid and enforceable against Famous? State "yes" or "no" and explain.

11. Contracts

Part a. In the course of an examination of the financial statements of the Lilliputian Shop, a retailer, it was learned that a lawsuit was being brought against the Company by Jack and Jill Creations, Inc. Further investigation disclosed the following:

Jack and Jill Creations, Inc., a children's clothing manufacturer, entered into a written contract that was complete in all its terms for the sale of 1,000 boy and girl sailor suits to the Lilliputian Shop at $10 each. Five days later they orally agreed that the written agreement be changed to double the quantity to 2,000 suits and to reduce the price to $9 each. When the time for delivery came, Jack and Jill had been unable to manufacture the extra 1,000 suits and offered to deliver 1,000 suits at $10 each. Lilliputian refused to accept delivery.

Required:

What legal problems are suggested by these facts? Discuss.

Part b. In the course of an examination of the financial statements of Harrison and Company you find that a claim has been made against the Company by Roth Corporation. Your examination of the purchase order file reveals copies of the following letters and telegrams.

Roth in New York and Harrison in California are dealers in equipment used in garment factories. On October 1 Harrison sent and Roth received the following telegram:

> Enter my order for 10 Model 104 sewing machines at $110; two weeks delivery; 30 days net cash.
>
> /s/ Harrison

On the same day, without replying, Roth shipped Harrison the ten machines which arrived at Harrison's place of business on October 13. But on October 3, Harrison had changed his mind and telegraphed Roth "Cancel my order of October 1. /s/ Harrison."

When Roth received Harrison's telegram, he immediately wrote Harrison a letter explaining that the goods had been shipped. Harrison refused to accept the machines, claiming he had no contract with Roth.

Required:

    1. What legal problems are suggested by these facts? Discuss.

    2. How should this transaction be reflected in the financial statements of Harrison? Discuss.

12. Contract and sales law

Each of the lettered statements of facts below is followed by numbered sentences that state legal conclusions relating to those facts. You are to determine whether each legal conclusion is true or false according to the *Uniform Commercial Code and the general principles of contract and sales law.*

A. Masten was the tenant of a first floor store in an office building in a large metropolitan city where he sold newspapers, tobacco, fruit, candy and soft drinks. Winslow acquired the property including the store and his agent negotiated with Masten for continuation of his lease to the store. A lease for three years was signed. It contained a provision that the lessee, Masten, should "use the premises only for the sale of newspapers, fruit, candy, soda water, etc.," with the further stipulation that "it is expressly understood that the tenant is not allowed to sell tobacco in any form under penalty of instant termination of this lease." Masten signed the lease after having it read to him by two persons, one of whom was his daughter.

Masten claims that in the course of his dealings with Winslow's agent it was agreed that he should have the exclusive right to sell soft drinks in the building in consideration of his promises to not sell tobacco and to pay an increased rent and for entering into the lease agreement. No such stipulation was included in the lease. Shortly after it was signed Winslow rented the adjoining store in the same building to a drug company under a lease which contained no restriction on the use of the premises for selling soda water and soft drinks. Masten alleged that this was in violation of his lease with Winslow and claimed that the sale of these beverages by the drug company had greatly reduced his receipts and profits.

        1. Winslow should rely upon the parol evidence rule in his defense to Masten's claim.

2. If Masten could show that he had been defrauded by Winslow's agent, he would prevail.
3. Masten could correctly contend that he entered into an independent oral contract for the exclusive right to sell soda.
4. If the oral promise had been made after the execution of the lease, the parol evidence rule would still apply.
5. Masten's legal position is substantially strengthened by the express written prohibition against his selling tobacco.
6. Generally, the courts would hold that the formal lease agreement entered into by the parties constituted the entire contract between the parties.
7. Under the stated facts, Winslow probably will prevail.

B. Harris was negotiating to sell his department store to Lowe. Early in January 1971 Harris gave Lowe financial information that indicated a steady growth in both sales volume and income and that income for the preceding year was $240,000. The negotiations continued until April 30, 1971 when Lowe signed a contract with Harris to buy the department store and made a down payment of $25,000. Later, upon examination of the accounts of the department store, Lowe discovered that between January and April sales volume and income had declined materially. Harris knew these facts at the time the contract was made.

8. The Statute of Frauds could be used by Lowe as the basis for a claim against Harris.
9. Most courts would resort to the concept of *caveat emptor* (buyer beware) in deciding this dispute.
10. Harris could contend correctly that nondisclosure by itself does not constitute fraud.
11. Lowe will prevail in a suit against Harris for fraud.
12. If Harris had not known of the decline in sales and income at the time the contract of sale was signed, Lowe's best remedy would have been to seek a rescission of the contract based upon innocent misrepresentation.

C. Mayer, a lumber dealer located in the Pacific Northwest, delivered the following message to the Union Telegraph Company for transmission to Allen, a barrel maker:

Allen
Modesto, California
  Will sell 20M barrel stave sets delivered at your warehouse. Four twenty per set. Net cash. July shipment. Answer quick.
                                                              Mayer

The message as delivered to Allen omitted the word "twenty" in the price. Allen immediately sent the following telegram:

Mayer
    Accept your telegraphic offer on the barrel stave sets. Could also use some barrel tops and bottoms.
                                                                    Allen

13. There was no offer because Mayer did not intend to sell the staves at $4 per set.
14. If Allen were aware of the mistake in the price quoted in the telegram, he could not enforce the contract at a price of $4 per set.
15. Mayer will prevail in a suit against Allen becuase there was no written contract and the Statute of Frauds applies.
16. Mayer is not bound by the erroneous offer because the mistake was made by Union Telegraph.
17. A contract between Mayer and Allen at a price of $4 per set was made upon Allen's telegraphing his acceptance.
18. Neither party is obligated to perform because there was a mutual mistake of fact.
19. Assuming that a contract was made at a price of $4 per set, Mayer can recover the difference from Union Telegraph if it was negligent in transmitting Mayer's message.

D. The Grande Mining Company sold all of its assets to the Stoddard Mining Company for cash. Under the terms of the contract Stoddard assumed all of the debts of Grande. Stoddard integrated the Grande assets into its operations. It worked several of the Grande mines for two years and continued to pay both its creditors and those of Grande. Stoddard has begun to default on payments to its creditors including some of Grande's.

20. Grande has no liability to its former creditors.
21. The Grande creditors were creditor beneficiaries of the promise by Stoddard to assume the debts of Grande.
22. By accepting the payments over the first two years the creditors of Grande impliedly released Grande from the debts.
23. The consent of the creditors is required for Grande to delegate the payment of its debts to Stoddard.
24. The creditors could recover against either Grande or Stoddard, but not both.
25. If Grande pays its former creditors, it will be entitled to reimbursement from Stoddard.

E. James Scrib & Son, book publishers, and Studio Book Shop entered into a two-year contract under which Studio agreed to buy from Scrib each month books having a net invoice price of not less than $200. Scrib agreed to extend credit for one month on open account and gave Studio the right to return up to 50% of its book purchases provided that the books were returned within three months of receipt and that returns did not reduce net purchases for the month to less than the $200 minimum.

During the first year Studio encountered financial difficulties and became three months past due in payments on its account which then had a balance of $826. Biltmore, the owner of Studio, negotiated a change in the terms of the contract under which he promised to pay the $826 within two weeks if he were permitted to have (1) a two-month period of open-account credit, (2) the right to return 70% of book purchases and (3) the $200 minimum for net purchases reduced to $100. Scrib agreed orally to these changes in order to obtain the $826 payment and upon its receipt Scrib immediately repudiated the changes and indicated it would sell to Studio only on the terms of the original contract.

26. No consideration was required for the agreement modifying the original contract to be binding.
27. If consideration were required, the payment within two weeks of the $826 would constitute consideration.
28. The modification of the contract will be invalid unless the Statute of Frauds is satisfied.
29. If the modification had been in writing and signed by Scrib, it would have been binding upon him.
30. Studio is no longer bound by the original contract.

13. Corporations and dividends

Part a. While examining the financial statements of a corporation, questions may arise regarding the right of a stockholder to share in the earnings of the corporation and the related role, duties, and obligations of the board of directors in declaring and paying dividends.

Required:

1. When does a dividend vest in a stockholder? Discuss.
2. How large a dividend may a corporation legally declare? Discuss.
3. What is a director's liability in the event of an illegal dividend? Discuss.

Part b. The Kramer Corporation, a closely held company, has 1,000,000 shares of common stock outstanding. The balance of retained earnings and cash accounts are presently $3,000,000 and $4,000,000, respectively. These amounts appear to be in excess of Kramer's historic business needs, having been accumulated during an unusually profitable period which is unlikely to recur. The Kramer Board of Directors recently decided to retain all of the Corporation's earnings for investment in projects which do not appear destined to increase, or even maintain, the Corporation's rate of return on capital. The Board of Directors indicated that it intended to withhold the payment of dividends indefinitely to finance the planned expansion. The Board of Directors has approved the payment of higher salaries and additional bonuses to several officers (who are also directors) as an incentive to administer the expansion program. The prices of Kramer's products are also to be reduced in an effort to expand sales.

A minority stockholder of Kramer, Mr. Moffat, is dissatisfied with the new dividend policy and suspects that the planned expansion program will not be in the best interests of the Corporation. Moffat and Kramer's management have a record of open hostility. You have been retained by Moffat as his accountant to aid his attorney in the determination of the relevant facts for a possible suit.

Required:

1. Can Moffat accompanied by his attorney and accountant inspect the books and records of Kramer in this connection? State "yes" or "no" and explain. What are the Corporation's rights in this connection?

2. Can Moffat compel the payment of a cash dividend by Kramer? State "yes" or "no" and explain.

3. Discuss the legal means by which Moffat may proceed to redress his grievances.

14. Corporations

Part a. Dobbins, Eckert and Nash formed the DEN Corporation to conduct their automobile business. The stock was issued in equal numbers of shares to each of them. At the time of incorporation, the three stockholders entered into an agreement which included a provision that the Corporation's stock could not be sold to an outsider unless it were first offered to the Corporation at the same price and on the same terms and conditions.

Required:

1. Are the terms of the stockholders' agreement relating to the sale of the Corporation's stock valid? State "yes" or "no" and explain.

2. Assume that the restrictions on the sale of the Corporation's stock are valid and that in violation of the stockholders' agreement Eckert sold his stock to Jordan who purchased the stock in good faith and without notice of the stockholders' agreement. Eckert's stock certificate made no reference to the agreement. In such a case may the Corporation or Dobbins and Nash void the sale by Eckert to Jordan? State "yes" or "no" and explain.

Part b. Eastern Phosphate Company was incorporated to "exploit phosphate resources and to deal in all manner of phosphate products." In recent years Eastern's business has been on the decline and the board of directors decided to terminate its phosphate business and to enter the real estate development business. To carry out this plan the directors voted to sell all of the Corporation's operating assets which would not be needed in the real estate business and to invest the proceeds in undeveloped land.

Required:

1. Assume that Lake, an Eastern stockholder, learns of the directors' plans and that he and other Eastern stockholders violently disagree with them. What rights, if any, do Lake and other dissenting stockholders have? Explain.

2. Assume that Eastern proceeds with the directors' plan and sells its operating assets. Then Eastern's irate stockholders replace the entire board of directors with new members who seek to set aside the sale of assets. Will the new directors succeed? State "yes" or "no" and explain.

3. Assume that as a result of implementing the plans of the old board of directors, Eastern suffers heavy losses. What rights, if any, do the stockholders of Eastern have against the members of the old board? Explain.

15. Partnership

Taylor, Polk, and Buchanan are partners doing business as Famous Autographs. Their partnership agreement provides that they are to continue their partnership for ten years, that all partners are to be active in the management and that Taylor is to act as sales manager while Polk and Buchanan are to purchase autographs for the Firm. Taylor and Polk each contributed $20,000 to the Firm and Buchanan contributed $10,000. The partnership agreement is silent as to how profits and losses are to be shared. During the next three years the Firm incurred losses of $8,000, $12,000 and $15,000 respectively, and conditions in the industry were such that the Firm could not continue except at a loss. Taylor, a well-to-do businessman, asked the other partners to dissolve the Firm at the end of the fourth year but Polk and Buchanan, although personally insolvent, were optimistic about the future and refused to do so.

Required:

a. How should the first year's income be divided? Discuss.

b. Does Taylor have a right to have the partnership dissolved at the end of the fourth year? If so, how must he proceed? Discuss.

c. What is the Firm's liability, if any, on a contract that was made by Taylor in violation of the partnership agreement for the purchase of an autograph from Skinner? Discuss.

d. Discuss the legal effect on the partnership of Polk's assignment of his interest in the partnership to Barron.

e. Assume the Firm failed at the end of the fourth year. For what portion of the Firm's debts, that remained after the Firm's assets were applied to Firm debts, would Taylor be personally liable to Firm creditors? Discuss.

f. Would your answer to part e above be the same under all of the facts stated in the problem except that a certificate of limited partnership had been duly filed and published designating Polk and Buchanan as general partners and Taylor as a limited partner? State "yes" or "no" and discuss.

16. Partnerships

Each of the lettered statements of facts below is followed by numbered sentences that state legal conclusions relating to those facts. You are to determine whether each legal conclusion is true or false according to the *Uniform Partnership and Limited Partnership Acts.*

A. Peters, Long, and Tyler formed a general merchandising partnership. Cash capital contributions were $50,000 from Peters, and $25,000 each from Long and Tyler. The partnership agreement provides that the partners are to share profits and losses in proportion to capital contribution balances and that the partnership is to have a duration of ten years.

61. This is a limited partnership.
62. If the partnership makes a profit of $100,000 during its first year of operations, Peters is entitled to $50,000.
63. If the partnership agreement were silent on the subject of the division of profits the answer to item 62 would be different.
64. If a judgment is entered against the partnership, each of the partners would be personally liable for the full amount thereof, and the judgment creditor could proceed to collect from any one of them.
65. In item 64, the judgment creditor must first exhaust the assets of the partnership before he can proceed against the individual assets of the partners.
66. If Tyler should die, the partnership would be dissolved as a matter of law.
67. Any one of the partners may retire from the business at any time and dissolve the partnership without liability.

B. The partners of the partnership described in part "A" decided to admit Kramer as a partner if he would make a capital contribution of $25,000 and Kramer agreed to this. At the time of Kramer's admission the partnership agreement was amended to provide that no partner shall make any contract for the firm involving more than $50,000 without the express consent of all other partners.

68. Kramer's admission required the dissolution of the old partnership and the formation of a new partnership.

69. Kramer would be liable personally for obligations of the partnership incurred prior to his admission.

70. If Kramer is liable for partnership obligations incurred prior to his admission to the firm, such obligations could be collected out of both his partnership and personal assets.

71. If Kramer as a partner on behalf of the firm and in the normal course of business signs a contract obligating the firm to buy $150,000 worth of merchandise without first obtaining the consent of all of his partners, the firm may disaffirm the contract.

72. The answer to item 71 would be different if the party with whom Kramer contracted was aware of the limitation on Kramer's authority contained in the partnership agreement.

73. If Kramer made the contract described in item 71, he would be liable to his partners for any loss suffered as a result.

74. If Kramer made the contract described in item 71 for his own account, he would have breached his fiduciary obligations to his partners.

75. In item 74 Kramer would be liable to his partners for any profit he made on the contract.

C. Assume that Tyler, one of the partners in the partnership described in parts "A" and "B," has died.

76. Tyler's death terminates the partnership.

77. Tyler's estate would not be liable to third persons for partnership business transactions conducted prior to his death.

78. If after Tyler's death the surviving partners enter into a new contract with Smith, an old customer of the firm who had no actual notice of Tyler's death, Tyler's estate could be liable to Smith as a partner.

79. If a proper notice of dissolution were published prior to the making of the contract described in item 78 and Smith had not extended credit to the partnership prior to Tyler's death, Tyler's estate would not be liable to Smith.

80. If the surviving partners decide to continue the business as a new partnership, creditors of the old partnership also are creditors of the new partnership.

81. If the surviving partners continue the business and fail to settle accounts with Tyler's estate, the estate may have the value of Tyler's interest determined as of the date of his death and may recover this amount from the new partnership.

D. Crocker, Baxter, and Morton are partners in a grocery store. While Baxter and Morton were on vacation and could not be reached, Crocker decided (1) to sell the assets and goodwill of the business to Peterson at a price that Crocker felt was in excess of value and (2) to submit a claim against the partnership to arbitration.

82. Crocker has no authority to dispose of the partnership's assets and goodwill.
83. Crocker has authority to submit the claim to arbitration.
84. Although Crocker had no authority from his partners to dispose of the assets and goodwill or to submit the claim to arbitration, Crocker's acts have bound the partnership.
85. If Crocker had contacted his partners to ask for their concurrence prior to selling the business and submitting the claim to arbitration and Baxter agreed with Crocker but Morton did not, Crocker would have had authority to bind the partnership.

E. Cooper and Jordan have conducted a brokerage business as a partnership for some years. Recently they decided to admit Yancy as a limited partner and to conduct the business in the future as a limited partnership. Accordingly Cooper, Jordan and Yancy executed a limited partnership agreement and as required by law they duly filed an appropriate certificate which recited that Cooper and Jordan were the general partners and that Yancy was the limited partner. The agreement provided for an equal division of profits.

86. As a limited partner Yancy must contribute cash or property to the partnership.
87. Yancy would not be liable personally to creditors of the firm.
88. If Yancy actively participated in the management of the business, he still would not be liable personally to creditors of the firm.
89. Without any contrary provision in the agreement, Yancy validly could assign his interest to another and his assignee would have an absolute right to be substituted for Yancy as a limited partner.
90. Cooper validly can be a limited and general partner at the same time.

17. Partnership and trust law

Each of the lettered statements of facts below is followed by numbered sentences that state legal conclusions relating to those facts. You are to determine whether each legal conclusion is true or false according to the general principles of partnership and trust law.

A. You have been engaged to examine the financial statements of the Apex Manufacturing Company. Your examination revealed that the Company is owned equally by Gerald Peters, George Jackson, and Donald Wells, evidenced by 1,000 shares of no-par stock held by each. However, your examination further disclosed that the owners have never filed incorporation papers in any jurisdiction. All three owners are actively engaged in the conduct of the business. The Company borrowed $10,000 from William Wells, Donald's brother, secured by a corporate note signed by "Donald Wells, President." All three owners signed individually as sureties on the note.

1. Since the owners of Apex intended to create a corporation, they could assert successfully the *de facto* corporation doctrine in defending suits by the Company's creditors against them personally.
2. Apex Manufacturing Company is *not* a *de jure* corporation.
3. The attorney general of the state in which Apex maintains its home office can obtain a court order prohibiting the Company from doing business as a corporation.
4. William Wells would be able to proceed successfully against the individuals even if a *de jure* corporation were created.
5. Taking the facts as stated, the owners could establish that they created a valid limited partnership.
6. In fact, the three owners are operating as a general partnership with each having personal liability for the Company's debts.

B. Charles Jones, Franklin Jones, Harry Small, and Robert Wax are general partners in Jones & Son, General Contractors. Each partner contributed $25,000 in capital. In addition, Wax loaned the partnership $50,000. Profits and losses are shared equally. Liabilities to outside creditors exceed partnership assets by $50,000. The partnership is in the process of dissolution and liquidation.

7. Wax has a right to repayment of his loan prior to the distribution of any assets to the firm's creditors.
8. The partnership's resulting deficit will be shared equally after repayment of Wax's loan.
9. By operation of law, partnership dissolution occurs when the partnership or an individual partner is bankrupt.
10. Assuming Wax was a *bona fide* limited partner (instead of a general partner), he would not have any personal liability for partnership debts.
11. Again, assuming that Wax is a *bona fide* limited partner, his loan will rank equally with other similar outside creditors' loans according to limited partnership law.
12. A limited partnership cannot be created validly unless the parties have complied with the jurisdiction's limited partnership law.

C. You are examining the financial statements of the general partnership of Walter Lamb, Martin Fox, and Henry Farr. Your examination of the signed partnership agreement reveals that the agreement contains only the following provisions:

> The partnership was created on January 3, 1972.
>
> The purpose of the partnership was to assemble and sell lamps.
>
> Messrs. Lamb and Fox were to contribute $10,000 each, and Mr. Farr was to contribute $20,000 to partnership capital.
>
> Mr. Lamb was to devote full-time, while Messrs. Fox and Farr were to devote half-time to the operation of the partnership. Partnership profit before any allocation to partners is $30,000.

13. Farr is entitled to interest on the extra $10,000 of capital he contributed.
14. Lamb has the right to a reasonable salary because he devoted more time to the firm's business than either Fox or Farr.
15. Profits and losses are to be shared according to the partners' respective capital contributions.
16. The partnership, not the individual partners, owns the firm's business assets.
17. The partners have equal rights in the management of the partnership business.
18. A partner may assign his partnership interest to an outsider without the consent of the other partners.
19. The partnership is terminable at will by any partner without incurring liability to the other partners.
20. Each partner owes a fiduciary duty to the partnership.

    D. Accountant Smathers is Trustee of a testamentary trust established by Parker's will. The corpus of the trust consists of "blue chip" securities and a large office building subject to a mortgage. The will provides that trust income is to be paid to Parker's wife during her lifetime, that the Trust will terminate on her death, and that the corpus is then to be distributed to the Brookdale School for Boys.

21. If Smathers receives a cash dividend on one of the Trust securities, he may not use it to purchase additional securities for the trust corpus without compensating Parker's wife.
22. If Smathers receives a 5% stock dividend, he should distribute it to Mrs. Parker.
23. The cost of insurance on the office building should be deducted by Smathers from the income paid to Mrs. Parker.
24. Monthly principal payments to amortize the mortgage are deducted from Mrs. Parker's income.
25. Proceeds from the fire insurance on the office building would be a part of the corpus.
26. The cost of exercising stock warrants is chargeable to trust income.

27. The Brookdale School is the residuary beneficiary of the trust created under Parker's will.
28. The beneficiaries of the trust have an equitable interest in the trust income and corpus.
29. The beneficiaries of the trust would have standing in court to proceed against the trustee for waste of the corpus.
30. If Mrs. Parker and the Brookdale School agree to terminate the trust and divide the corpus, Smathers would have to comply with their wishes.

18. Insurance

You have been assigned to review the insurance coverage as of June 30, 1972, of Foley & Co., a partnership. As part of your work you inspect the correspondence file with Foley's insurance agent. The file reveals that Foley has filed a number of claims with Adams Insurance which remain unpaid. You extracted the following facts from the correspondence file regarding each unpaid claim.

A. Foley dispatched an order on November 11, 1971, to Western Computer Co. accompanied by its check in full payment for 1,000 computer components to be shipped by boat, FAS Vessel at Western's home port. The parts were labeled, packed, crated, and picked up for delivery to the pier. On the way to the pier, the truck caught fire and the goods were completely destroyed. Foley sent a claim to Adams for recovery under its blanket insurance policy which covers "all goods in Foley's possession, owned by it, or to which it had any legally recognized insurable interest."
Adams denies liability on the policy, claiming:
    a. The risk of loss had not passed to Foley.
    b. Foley did not have any legally recognized insurable interest.

Required:

Is Adams correct in either of its contentions? Explain.

B. Foley carries $200,000 of life insurance on each of its partners to fund the "buy out" clause of the partnership agreement.
One of the partners, Flack, retired at age 70 during the year ended June 30, 1971, and was duly paid for his partnership interest by the partnership. The partnership continued to pay the premiums on Flack's life insurance until his death in October 1971.
Adams denies any liability on the policy, claiming:
    a. In his application for life insurance in 1964, Flack misrepresented the state of his health by neglecting to mention that he had had a severe coronary in 1960.

b. The partnership has no insurable interest in the life of Flack after his retirement.

Required:

Can Foley collect the $200,000 life insurance covering Flack? Explain.

C. During January 1972, Cragsmoore, one of Foley's employees, negligently dropped a lighted cigar on some packing material which caught fire and totally destroyed the warehouse and the goods stored therein. The warehouse and contents were covered by a $2 million fire insurance policy which contains a 90% co-insurance clause. The loss was subsequently appraised at $2.5 million.

Foley seeks to recover for the loss. Adams denies any and all liability; or, in the alternative, claims that it is not obligated to pay the full $2 million.

Required:

What can Foley recover? Explain.

19. Insurance

Part a. In connection with the examination of the financial statements of G. F. Riggs, Inc. for the year ended September 30, 1971 a question arose regarding a claim to the proceeds of an insurance policy on the life of John Maxwell, one of G. F. Riggs' employees. An investigation revealed the following:

G. F. Riggs installs and repairs industrial and home heating systems. On August 11, 1968 John Maxwell was hired by the Corporation as superintendent and chief estimator. He was to devote his entire time to his assigned duties which were "superintending, estimating, soliciting, etc.," and "to put forth his best efforts at all times with a view to aiding in the management and progress of G. F. Riggs, Inc. in every way." For his services Maxwell was to receive a salary of $28,500 per year plus a 5% commission on all sales which resulted from his individual efforts. Furthermore, Maxwell was granted a nontransferable option to buy 500 shares of G. F. Riggs common stock at $20 a share. The Corporation had a right of first refusal to purchase Maxwell's shares in the event that Maxwell, his estate or heirs sought to sell the shares to anyone other than existing shareholders. Maxwell exercised the option on May 2, 1970 and owned 500 shares of the 40,000 shares outstanding.

In applying for the job Maxwell had lied about his age, indicating that he was three years younger than he actually was. Shortly after the hiring G. F. Riggs purchased a life insurance policy with a face amount of $100,000 on Maxwell's life and indicated in the application that his age was 42 years (instead of 45). Maxwell consented in writing to the Corporation's insuring him, took the physical examination and signed the application.

Maxwell committed suicide on September 15, 1971. The insurer has denied liability because (1) G. F. Riggs had no insurable interest in the life of Maxwell at the time the insurance was taken out, (2) there was a material misrepresentation of the insured's age and (3) the suicide voids the policy.

Required:

Should an account receivable be established by G. F. Riggs, Inc. for the face (or some other) amount of the insurance policy on the life of Maxwell? Explain.

Part b. Skidmore Trucking Company decided to expand its operations into the warehousing field. After examining several available properties it decided to purchase a carbarn for $100,000 from a local bus company and to convert it into a warehouse. The standard real estate purchase contract was signed by the parties. The contract obligated Skidmore to pay the seller on an apportioned basis for the prepaid premiums on the existing fire insurance policy ($100,000 extended coverage). The policy expired two years and one month from the closing date.

At the closing the seller duly assigned the fire insurance policy to Skidmore in return for the payment of the apportioned amount of the prepaid premiums; but Barton W. Broxbury, the attorney for Skidmore, failed to notify the insurance company of the change in ownership.

Skidmore took possession of the premises and after extensive renovation began to use the building as a warehouse. Soon afterward one of Skidmore's employees negligently dropped a lighted cigarette into a trash basket and started a fire which totally destroyed the building.

Required:

What are the legal problems and implications of these facts? Discuss.

20. Real Property

Each of the lettered statements of facts below is followed by numbered sentences that state legal conclusions relating to those facts. You are to determine whether each legal conclusion is true or false according to the *general principles of real property law.*

A. Brown wished to raise some additional capital for his manufacturing business. Ames, his accountant, suggested that he mortgage his estate, Longacre. Brown then did this, receiving a $10,000 loan from Central Bank and giving his mortgage bond in that amount. Brown neglected to advise either Ames or the Bank that he previously had mortgaged Longacre to Collins who failed to record the mortgage. The Bank promptly recorded its mortgage. In anticipation of his son Henry's wedding to Helen Smith, Brown deeded Longacre as a wedding gift to Henry Brown and Helen Smith. Henry and Helen recorded the deed and were married.

61. Collins' mortgage is prior in time and would take priority over that of the Bank.
62. Henry and Helen's deed would not be subject to the lien of Collins' mortgage.
63. Henry and Helen's deed would not be subject to the lien of the Bank's mortgage.
64. If the deed to Henry and Helen stated that it was subject to the Bank's mortgage, Henry and Helen would be called upon personally to pay any deficiency on foreclosure by the Bank.
65. If Henry and Helen had assumed the Bank mortgage, the answer to item 64 would be different.
66. On foreclosure Brown could be called upon to pay the Bank any deficiency.
67. The deed to Henry and Helen created a tenancy by the entirety.
68. If Henry and Helen were married at the time they received the deed, the answer to item 67 would be different.
69. Either Henry or Helen may dispose of his or her interest in Longacre without the consent of the other.
70. If Henry and Helen were tenants by the entirety in Longacre and Helen dies first, Henry automatically becomes the owner of the entire estate even if Helen's will provides otherwise.

B. The Western Lumber Company owns a large tract of timberland. Unknown to Western, Skidmore has enclosed part of Western's tract with a fence, built a cabin upon it and plans to farm the land commercially. The applicable prescription period under local law is 15 years. Skidmore mistakenly believes that the land in question is part of the adjacent tract which he owns.

71. At the end of the prescription period, Skidmore will obtain title by adverse possession against Western.
72. If Skidmore should die before the end of the prescription period, his heirs must hold adversely against Western for an additional 15 years in order to acquire title by adverse possession.
73. If Skidmore merely occupies the land in question, but acknowledges that it is owned by Western, he cannot acquire title by adverse possession against Western.

C. Parker contracts to purchase Greenacre from Archer as a site for his factory. Prior to closing, Parker discovers that there are liens for unpaid taxes against the property, that the property is subject to an easement of right of way and that the property is zoned for residential use. The contract of sale does not mention any of the foregoing.

74. Parker may decline to close the sale unless Archer pays and discharges the tax liens.
75. Parker must accept title subject to the easement of right of way.
76. Parker must accept title subject to the zoning restriction on the property.
77. If Parker accepts title without knowledge of the above facts and receives a full warranty deed from Archer, upon learning the facts he would have grounds for an action against Archer because of defects in the title.
78. If Parker took a quitclaim deed from Archer, the answer to item 77 would be the same.

D. Church and Jasper, CPAs, wish to relocate their offices. The lease on their present offices is for five years with three years to run and it contains a survival clause which provides that the tenant's liability shall survive the landlord's termination of the lease for a breach by the tenant. Their landlord is not agreeable to canceling the lease which also prohibits a sublease without the landlord's consent. Church and Jasper have a financially responsible and respectable prospective subtenant but have reason to believe that the landlord will not consent to a sublease.

79. If Church and Jasper sublease the premises without the landlord's consent, they will breach their lease and entitle the landlord to terminate the lease.
80. If the landlord terminates the lease under the circumstances described in item 79, Church and Jasper would not be liable to the landlord for any deficiency in rent for the balance of the term of their lease.
81. Regardless of the prohibition against subletting in their lease, Church and Jasper may assign their lease to a third party without breaching the lease.
82. Assuming that Church and Jasper are free to assign their lease, they will not be liable to the landlord under the lease for the performance of all of their obligations as tenants.
83. If the landlord consents to a subletting, the mere giving of such consent will relieve Church and Jasper of any further obligations under the lease.
84. If the landlord consents to a subletting, he may collect the rent due under the lease directly from the subtenant.
85. If Church and Jasper assign their lease, the landlord may not collect the rent due directly from the assignee.

E. Assume Church and Jasper have decided to remain in their present quarters until their lease expires on June 1. On May 15 they entered into a two-year lease for new office space with Bolt Realty Corporation to commence

June 1. On May 25 Church and Jasper discover that the occupant of their new space, whose lease expires on May 31, has not vacated and does not plan to do so until June 15.

86. If the lease is silent on the point, Bolt Realty will not be liable to Church and Jasper for damages if Bolt is unsuccessful in evicting the old tenant before June 1.

87. If Bolt Realty takes no action against the old tenant and does not deliver possession on June 1, Church and Jasper are free to terminate the lease without liability to Bolt.

88. If Bolt Realty neglected to sign the lease but Church and Jasper had signed it, it would be enforceable against Bolt.

89. If Church and Jasper retain their old offices until June 15, their old landlord may elect to hold them as holdover tenants for an additional year.

90. In the circumstances described in item 89, the old landlord may evict Church and Jasper.

21. Secured transactions

Each of the lettered statements of facts below is followed by numbered sentences that state legal conclusions relating to those facts. You are to determine whether each legal conclusion is true or false according to *Article 9 of the Uniform Commercial Code (Secured Transactions).*

A. Sullivan leased a commercial printing press to Hanes under a written agreement providing for 60 monthly payments of $250. The agreement further provided that after the last lease payment is made, title to the press will vest in Hanes without a further bill of sale.

31. The arrangement between Sullivan and Hanes is a secured transaction under the Uniform Commercial Code.

32. If the arrangement between the parties is a secured transaction, then the lease agreement must be signed by both parties to be effective as a security agreement.

33. The lease agreement may be filed as a financing statement if it complies with the requirements set forth for a financing statement in Article 9 of the Uniform Commercial Code.

34. If a financing statement is filed, it must be signed by the secured party and the debtor.

35. A financing statement must state a maturity date to be valid.

B. Fast Loans, Inc., a small loan company, loaned $600 to Morton to purchase a television set for his home. The security agreement between the parties provided that pending repayment of the loan the Company is to have a security interest in the television set as well as in all other consumer goods thereafter owned by Morton. Three months later Morton brought a refrigerator for cash for his home. Thereafter Morton defaulted on the loan and the Company seeks to seize the refrigerator which it claims is subject to its security agreement.

36. The Company has no security interest in the refrigerator.
37. If Morton acquired the refrigerator thirty days after the Company made the loan, the Company's security interest would attach to the refrigerator.
38. The clause in the security agreement which provides for a security interest in the refrigerator is called an after-acquired property clause.
39. The Company has a purchase-money security interest in the television set.
40. A financing statement must be filed by the Company to perfect its security interest in the television set.

C. Fillmore borrowed $25,000 from City Bank under a written security agreement which provided that the bank was to have, as security for the loan, "a security interest in all of the tangible assets of the debtor." A creditor of Fillmore later contended that the security agreement was void and ineffective because of the description of the collateral.

41. The creditor was not correct in contending that the security agreement was void and ineffective.
42. A security agreement may be signed by the parties one month before the loan is made.
43. The description of the collateral in this security agreement would include Fillmore's accounts receivable.
44. The description "accounts receivable" in a security agreement would not be legally sufficient.
45. A copy of a financing statement filed in a public office may be obtained by anyone upon payment of the statutory fee.

D. Grant, a radio dealer, borrowed $15,000 from Newton Bank and entered into a written agreement which gave the bank a security interest in all of the radios that Grant had in inventory plus any that were acquired later. On the date of the loan the bank filed a proper financing statement. Subsequently Grant borrowed $2,000 from State Bank to purchase 100 new radios. State Bank immediately filed a proper financing statement covering its security interest in the new radios before allowing Grant to take possession of them. When Grant defaulted on both loans, State Bank attempted to seize the 100 new radios but Newton Bank claimed that its security interest prevailed because State Bank had not notified Newton Bank of its security interest before allowing Grant to take possession.

46. Newton Bank was correct in claiming that its security interest prevailed.
47. State Bank has a purchase-money security interest in inventory collateral.
48. A purchase-money security interest in inventory collateral will automatically have priority over a conflicting security interest in the same collateral.
49. If the purchase-money security interest is perfected at the time the debtor receives possession of the collateral or within ten days thereafter, a purchase-money security interest in collateral other than inventory has priority over a conflicting security interest in the same collateral.
50. The Uniform Commercial Code defines when a default occurs.

E. Alexander manufactures and sells television sets. To secure a $100,000 loan Alexander gave Jackson Finance Company a security interest in all of his equipment and inventory including all television sets and raw materials on his premises. Alexander defaulted in the repayment of the loan at a time when he had very few manufactured television sets but a considerable amount of raw material including cabinets, tubes and wiring. To reduce Alexander's indebtedness Jackson Finance Company, using good business judgment, decided (1) to have the raw materials made up into television sets and sell them and (2) to lease the repossessed equipment.

51. Jackson Finance Company has no legal right to complete the manufacturing of the television sets.
52. Jackson Finance Company may lease the repossessed equipment if doing so is commercially reasonable.
53. Disposition of the collateral may be by public or private proceedings.
54. If the disposition is commercially reasonable, the collateral may be disposed of as a unit or in parcels and at any time and place and on any terms.
55. Jackson Finance Company may buy the collateral at any public or private sale.

F. Briarcliff Bank made a $3,000,000 loan to Holly Building Corporation and took a real estate mortgage on Holly Corporation's 21-story office building. One year later Holly Corporation borrowed $200,000 from Central Bank to help it finance the purchase and installation of speed elevators and machinery in the building. Holly Corporation gave Central Bank a chattel mortgage on the elevators and accessory machinery after they were installed and Central Bank immediately filed a financing statement. When Holly Corporation failed to pay Central Bank on its loan, that bank sought a court order to remove the elevators pursuant to the terms of its chattel mortgage. Briarcliff Bank resisted this order contending that its (Briarcliff Bank's) consent to the Central Bank's security interest had not been obtained at the time of installation of the elevators and also that Briarcliff Bank had not disclaimed its interest in the installed elevators.

56. The Briarcliff Bank was not correct in its contentions.
57. The elevators and accessory machinery are classified as goods under the Uniform Commercial Code.
58. If Central Bank's security interest in the elevators and accessory machinery attached before they became fixtures, Central Bank would have priority over Briarcliff Bank's interest in the real estate.
59. Any person may request the filing officer to issue his certificate showing whether there is on file any presently effective financing statement naming Central Bank as secured party and Holly Building Corporation as debtor.
60. Under the Uniform Commercial Code, Central Bank must comply with the request of any person for a verification of Holly Corporation's indebtedness to Central Bank.

22. Secured transactions

Part a. An examination of the financial statements of Bardlow, Inc., disclosed that Bardlow had purchased a plant site from Charles Swinton for cash. Because he was in serious financial difficulty, Swinton sold the property for $69,500 about $5,000 less than its fair-market value. A cursory check by Bardlow's attorneys of Swinton's title did not disclose that Security State Bank held a duly recorded $25,000 first mortgage on property. Swinton did not mention the mortgage at any time during the negotiations. At the closing, Bardlow received a warranty deed with full covenants.

Swinton intended to continue to make the mortgage payments, but additional financial setbacks made this impossible. Swinton later fled the jurisdiction. The mortgage payments are three months in arrears.

Required:

1. How should the transaction be handled on Bardlow's balance sheet? Explain.
2. What rights and/or liabilities does Bardlow have as to (a) Security State Bank, (b) Swinton, and (c) Bardlow's attorneys?

Part b. In September 1971, Ahab Warehousing, Inc., a client of yours, sold its entire business to William Snodgrass. By the terms of the sale, Ahab received a large cash payment and Snodgrass' notes for $120,000, payable in installments over the next two years. The notes were secured by the rental income from space in a warehouse that was sold to Snodgrass and leased on a long-term basis to a local shipper. Also, Snodgrass assumed Ahab's original first mortgage on the warehouse.

The local shipper was duly notified of the sale of the warehouse, the assignment of the lease to Snodgrass, and of Ahab's security interest in the rents. The deed on the warehouse was properly recorded, the assumption agreement and the security agreement regarding the rents being duly recited therein. No other recordation was made by either Ahab or Snodgrass.

Less than a year after purchasing Ahab's business, Snodgrass filed a voluntary petition in bankruptcy. He had borrowed heavily from lending institutions, relatives, and friends. Most of the lenders are general (unsecured) creditors.

Snodgrass' general creditors are attempting to recover two items from Ahab: (1) the portion of the cash attributable to the accounts receivable which were part of the assets of the business sold to Snodgrass by Ahab and (2) the rents which Ahab has been collecting on the leased warehouse space since Snodgrass defaulted on the notes owed to Ahab.

The holder of the first mortgage assumed by Snodgrass has notified Ahab that it intends to hold Ahab to its original promise to pay the mortgage.

Required:

From Ahab's position, what are the legal implications of the actions of the general creditors and the mortgage holder? Explain.

23. Secured transactions

Part a. Davis Hardware, Inc., a wholesale distributor of hardware products, needed $100,000 of additional working capital. It made arrangements to borrow this amount from the State Bank. The parties signed a loan agreement which provided that the Bank would lend Davis $100,000 secured by a security interest in "Davis' present and future inventory and accounts receivable and the proceeds thereof." The parties also signed a financing statement containing the same description of the collateral. The Bank then filed the financing statement in the appropriate public office. One week later the Bank loaned Davis the $100,000. One year later Davis defaulted in the repayment of the loan and the Bank attempted to enforce its security interest. Davis contended that the security agreement was unenforceable because (1) the loan was not made on the day that the security agreement was signed; (2) the Bank could not acquire a security interest in future inventory and future accounts receivable and (3) the description of the collateral in the security agreement and the financing statement was legally insufficient.

Required

Discuss the legal validity of each of Davis' defenses.

Part b. In the course of an examination of the financial statements of

National Finance Company for the year ended September 30, 1971 the auditors learned that the Company has just taken possession of certain heavy industrial equipment from Nevins Manufacturing Company, a debtor in default, which previously borrowed $80,000 from National secured by a security interest in that collateral.

Required:

1. Can National sell the collateral at a private sale? State "yes" or "no" and explain.

2. Can National retain the collateral in satisfaction of the secured obligation under any circumstances? State "yes" or "no" and explain.

3. Can Nevins redeem the collateral under any circumstances? State "yes" or "no" and explain.

24. Suretyship

During the course of your examination of the financial statements for the year ended March 31, 1971 for Finest Fashions, Inc., a company with a dozen retail stores specializing in the sale of exclusive maxi coats and dresses, you learned of a claim of $50,000 asserted against the Company by Fancy Fabrics. Upon investigation you learned that the Company purchased most of its merchandise from Terry Knitting Mills, a large manufacturer. Several months ago when Terry was in financial difficulty and could no longer purchase raw materials from Fancy Fabrics on credit, Terry asked the Company and Grand Gowns, Inc. to sign as co-sureties its purchase order to Fancy Fabrics for raw materials costing $50,000. Both companies did so on the same day that Terry signed the purchase order. When Terry did not pay on the due date, Fancy Fabrics did not notify either surety. However, 15 days later the Company received a demand for payment of the entire purchase price of $50,000 from Fancy Fabrics. The Company has refused to pay contending that its contract as surety was unenforceable because (1) it did not recieve any consideration, (2) it received no notice of default and (3) its maximum liability, if any, is $25,000.

Required:

a. Discuss the validity of each defense asserted by your client, Finest Fashions, Inc.

b. If Finest Fashions pays $50,000 to Fancy Fabrics, what would be its rights against Grand Gowns? Explain.

c. If Finest Fashions pays $50,000 to Fancy Fabrics, what would be its rights against Terry? Explain.

d. If Fancy Fabrics extended Terry's time for payment for another six months without Finest Fashions' consent what would be the legal effect on the Company's obligation? Explain.

25. Surety and bankruptcy

Each of the lettered statements of facts below is followed by numbered sentences that state legal conclusions relating to those facts. You are to determine whether each legal conclusion is true or false according to suretyship and bankruptcy law.

A. Clifford sued Hatfield as surety for Buckley on a $200,000 contract. Hatfield advised Care, his accountant, that no notice had been given or demand made upon him, Hatfield, prior to the commencement of the action.

- 61. Hatfield was legally entitled to notice of Buckley's default before commencement of the action.
- 62. Clifford was not legally required to demand payment from Hatfield before commencement of the action.
- 63. Clifford can recover in a suit against Hatfield without first proceeding against Buckley.
- 64. Hatfield's liability is secondary.
- 65. In the absence of special statute an oral surety contract is valid and enforceable.

B. Agor, a clock dealer, placed an order for 100 grandfather clocks costing $20,000 with Chimes, Inc. The latter requested a surety to protect itself from loss. Hayes and Tilden signed the contract as sureties without receiving any consideration.

- 66. The suretyship relation arises by operation of law.
- 67. Hayes and Tilden are not liable as sureties since they received no consideration.
- 68. If Hayes and Tilden are liable, each is liable to the creditor for the full amount of the debt.
- 69. If a cosurety pays the full amount of the debt, he has a right to contribution from his cosurety.
- 70. A suretyship relation may be created by the parties after the principal's obligation arises.

C. Hoover contracted with the Mills Corporation to construct a movie theater according to stated plans and specifications. A performance bond was obtained from the Troy Insurance Company to protect Hoover from loss in the event of breach of contract by the Mills Corporation. The bond specified that no modifications would be made to the plans and specifications without the consent of Troy.

- 71. Troy is not a surety.

72. If a material modification was made in the plans and specifications without Troy's consent, Troy would be discharged.
73. Troy can avoid liability to Hoover if it can prove that its performance bond was obtained through the fraud of Mills.
74. Troy can avoid liability to Hoover if Mills obtains a discharge in bankruptcy.
75. If Troy holds collateral pledged to it by Mills, Hoover has the right to have the collateral used to satisfy the principal debt after default.

D. An accountant is often confronted with problems relating to bankruptcy proceedings. The following items relate to pertinent points of law with which he should be familiar.

76. Insolvency in the bankruptcy sense is a financial status in which the aggregate fair value of the assets of an entity is not sufficient to pay outstanding liabilities.
77. A preference in bankruptcy prefers one creditor over the others.
78. A preference in bankruptcy will not result from the present transfer of property as security for a prior debt.
79. Acts of Bankruptcy include concealing, mutilating or falsifying books of account in contemplation of bankruptcy.
80. An involuntary petition in bankruptcy must state that one or more acts of bankruptcy were committed within the three months preceding the date of filing.
81. The Federal Bankruptcy Act specifically grants the Federal District Courts exclusive original jurisdiction over bankruptcy proceedings.
82. The filing of a voluntary petition in bankruptcy does not automatically operate as an adjudication or determination that the petitioner is bankrupt.
83. An involuntary petition in bankruptcy may be filed only if the debtor has committed an act of bankruptcy.
84. An involuntary petition in bankruptcy must be filed by at least three creditors if the debtor has 12 or more creditors.
85. The federal Bankruptcy Act considers a partnership as an entity separate from the partners.
86. Federal, state and local taxes are discharged by bankruptcy.
87. Insolvency in the bankruptcy sense is the same as insolvency in the equity sense.
88. A trustee in bankruptcy proceeding is usually elected by the creditors.
89. A priority in a bankruptcy proceeding is given for administration costs including accountants' and attorneys' fees.
90. A referee in a bankruptcy proceeding is elected by a majority of the creditors having provable claims.

26. Agency law

Each of the lettered statements of facts below is followed by numbered sentences that state legal conclusions relating to those facts. You are to determine whether each legal conclusion is true or false according to the *Uniform Commercial Code and the general principles of agency law.*

A. Fowler, an adult, knew that Youngblood, 19 years old, was very knowledgeable about automobiles. Fowler orally authorized Youngblood to buy him a second-hand automobile from Best Auto Deals, Inc. for a price not to exceed $400.

1. The appointment of Youngblood as agent is void because it was not in writing.
2. The appointment of Youngblood as agent is void because of his infancy.
3. Fowler and Youngblood may each disaffirm the agency relationship because of Youngblood's infancy.
4. Fowler may not disaffirm any contract made with Best by Youngblood on his behalf by asserting Youngblood's infancy.
5. Best may disaffirm the contract made with Fowler, through Youngblood, by asserting Youngblood's infancy.

B. Riche, a well-known millionaire, hired Ball to buy an autograph of President George Washington from Carey, an autograph dealer. Riche instructed Ball to purchase the autograph in Ball's name from Carey at a price not to exceed $5,000. Ball entered into such a contract for $4,500 in his own name. Before the contract was performed Carey discovered Riche's identity and refused to perform hoping to obtain a higher price from Riche.

6. Riche may enforce the contract made by Ball and Carey even though his name does not appear in the contract.
7. Carey may disaffirm the contract with Ball provided he does so immediately after discovering Riche's identity.
8. After Riche's identity becomes known to Carey, Ball's liability on the contract terminates.
9. Ball's apparent authority usually will be greater if he acts for an undisclosed principal rather than a disclosed principal.
10. Although Riche is an undisclosed principal, he will be liable for any torts committed by Ball within the scope of his employment.

C. Phineas, the owner of The Greatest Circus hired Drake as his general manager. Drake, without Phineas' authorization, made certain fraudulent misrepresentations to induce the Magnificent Tumblers to enter into a contract with Phineas.

    11. Phineas may disaffirm the contract.
    12. Phineas will be liable for fraud if Drake was acting within the scope of his authority.
    13. If Drake is liable to the Magnificent Tumblers for fraud, he is entitled to indemnification from Phineas even though he knew he was committing fraud if he acted within the scope of his employment.
    14. If Phineas pays any damages to the Magnificent Tumblers for Drake's fraud, he may recover such damages from Drake in a separate action.
    15. The Magnificent Tumblers may rescind the contract with Phineas.

D. Ego, a famous movie producer, employed Glibb as his agent under a written two-year agreement to sign contracts in Ego's name with actors and actresses for a new movie. Ego died suddenly one year later. Neither Glibb nor third parties who dealt with him have knowledge of Ego's death.

    16. Ego's estate is liable on contracts made by Glibb before Ego's death.
    17. Glibb will be personally liable for contracts made by him after Ego's death.
    18. Glibb's authority to act as Ego's agent continues until he receives actual or constructive notice of Ego's death.
    19. In all cases the death of a principal will terminate an agency relationship.
    20. Ego's estate will be liable to Glibb for the remaining year of the employment contract.

E. Stanton hired Pinter to collect payments due on installment sales by making door-to-door collections. Stanton discharged Pinter when he discovered that Pinter was selling competing lines of merchandise to Stanton's customers. After the dismissal, Pinter (1) collected $150 from Dalton, a customer from whom Pinter had made collections in the past and who did not have notice of Pinter's dismissal and (2) assaulted Gavin, another customer, from whom he tried unsuccessfully to make a collection and who also did not have notice of Pinter's dismissal.

    21. Stanton's rights against Pinter are limited to discharging Pinter and recovering the $150 that Pinter collected from Dalton.
    22. Dalton's payment to Pinter discharges Dalton's $150 indebtedness to Stanton.
    23. Gavin may recover against Stanton for Pinter's assault.
    24. Pinter had apparent authority to collect from Dalton after his dismissal.
    25. If Pinter were an independent contractor, he would still be an agent of Stanton.

F. Opel, a poultry dealer, represented himself as Farmer Jones' agent and agreed to sell all of Jones' old hens to Bennett. Jones, who was present during this conversation, remained silent although he had not authorized Opel to act as his agent. Later Jones refused to perform and Bennett sued Jones.

    26. Opel had actual authority to sell the hens.

    27. Opel had apparent authority to sell the hens.

    28. The stated facts create an agency by estoppel.

    29. Agency by estoppel is imposed by law rather than created by the mutual consent of the parties.

    30. Jones can ratify the contract within a reasonable time and enforce it against Bennett if he chooses to do so.

27. Agency

Part a. In the course of your examination of the financial statements of Prince Realty Corporation for the year ended March 31, 1971 you learned of the following: Prince orally employed Baker, 20 years old, to manage an apartment house that it owned. Prince Realty instructed Baker not to contract for any repair work without its prior approval. Prince Realty also instructed Baker to collect in person the monthly rent from the 100 tenants. Contrary to these instructions Baker contracted with Trinity Plumbing Company to repair some plumbing for $200 and a bill for the services rendered has been submitted to Prince Realty for payment. In addition, Corbin, a tenant, asserted a claim against Prince Realty alleging that he was assaulted by Baker who was attempting to collect past due rent. Although Baker was discharged after managing the apartment for three months, he collected the rent for the fourth month on all apartments and absconded. After learning this Prince Realty has billed the tenants for the fourth month's rent.

Required:

    1. Is Prince Realty liable to Trinity Plumbing? State "yes" or "no" and discuss.

    2. Is Prince Realty liable to Corbin? State "yes" or "no" and discuss.

    3. Can Prince Realty recover from the tenants for the fourth month's rent? State "yes" or "no" and discuss.

Part b. In the course of your examination of the financial statements of Higgins Electronics, Inc. for the year ended March 31, 1971 you learned of a claim for $75,000 that James Ladd had made against the Company. Your investigation disclosed that the Company wanted to purchase some valuable used electronic equipment from Ladd, a competitor. The Company hired Lemmon to make the purchase in his name and instructed him not to disclose that he was acting for the Company. Lemmon signed a contract in his own name to purchase the equipment from Ladd for $75,000 with delivery and payment to be made 30 days later. Before the payment date the Company learned of a major technological breakthrough in electronic equipment and decided to buy new equipment which incorporated the discovery. Lemmon was instructed immediately to neither pay nor accept delivery of the used equipment. When Ladd learned subsequently that the Company was Lemmon's principal he sued the Company for breach of contract. The Company defended contending that it was not liable to Ladd because (1) Ladd intended to contract with Lemmon only and (2) recovery was barred because Ladd discovered the identity of the Company after the contract was executed.

Required:

1. Discuss the validity of each defense asserted by your client, Higgins Electronics, Inc.
2. Discuss the extent of Lemmon's liability to Ladd.

28. Agency

On October 1 Great Puppet Shows, Inc. hired Mandrake as its new purchasing agent. The Company knew that Puppetland Corp. was interested in selling certain stage scenery and props but it believed that it could purchase the property for less money if it did not disclose its identity. Therefore, it instructed Mandrake to drive over to Puppetland's office the next day and negotiate for the purchase of the property in his own name without disclosing the Company's identity. Mandrake was authorized to spend up to $5,000.

On October 2 Mandrake negotiated and signed a contract with Puppetland for the purchase of the property for $4,500 and for delivery and payment on October 15.

After signing the contract Mandrake began to drive back to the Company office. On the way he stopped at a bar for a few drinks which he knew was in violation of a Company policy which prohibited drinking of alcoholic beverages during working hours. After becoming intoxicated he left the bar and began driving to the office. Enroute he negligently struck and killed a pedestrian. Upon learning these facts the Company immediately discharged Mandrake who then advised Puppetland that when he signed the contract in his own name he was really doing so for his former employer's benefit and that he wanted nothing more to do with the contract.

Required:

a. Does Puppetland have the right to enforce the contract against the Company? State "yes" or "no" and discuss.

b. Does Puppetland have the right to enforce the contract against Mandrake? State "yes" or "no" and discuss.

c. Does the Company have the right to enforce the contract against Puppetland? State "yes" or "no" and discuss.

d. Does the pedestrian's estate have a right to recover against Mandrake and Great Puppet? State "yes" or "no" and discuss.

e. Does the Company have a right to recover against Mandrake if it incurs any liability to the pedestrian's estate? State "yes" or "no" and discuss.

29. Identification of legal problems

Part a. On April 1, 1971 Howard, a dealer in mining stocks, sold Hayley 10,000 shares of Alaska Uranium Ltd. at $1 per share knowingly misrepresenting that the Corporation had proven uranium deposits in its Alaska tract. Hayley paid for the stock on April 1, 1971 and on April 15, 1971, on the advice of friends, he had the Corporation investigated and found that it never had any prospects of uranium but that it had just discovered a copper vein on the tract and was putting it into production. On February 1, 1972 Hayley received a check from the Corporation for its one cent per share dividend and deposited it. One month later Hayley regretted his purchase and commenced legal action against Howard and Alaska Uranium Ltd.

Required:

What legal problems are suggested by these facts? Discuss.

Part b. General Drug Corporation was interested in the promotion in the state legislature of a certain bill designed to prohibit misrepresentations describing brand name drugs as superior to those described generically where the chemical composition and quality are identical. It agreed to pay Jennings Duval, an attorney, $7,500 for his services in drawing the proposed legislation, producing its introduction in the legislature and making an argument for its passage before the legislative committee to which it would be referred. Duval rendered these services and submitted his bill for payment which was unpaid at the end of the accounting period.

Required:

1. What legal problems are suggested by these facts? Discuss.
2. How should this transaction be reflected in the financial statements of General Drug Corporation?

Part c. On July 9, 1971 Benjamin Wade, president of American Philatelic Corporation, with the approval of the board of directors, engaged Nikal, a certified public accountant, to conduct a special interim review of the Corporation's financial statements for the nine months ended September 30, 1971 and to render his report on November 30, 1971 for inclusion in the prospectus to be issued in conjunction with an issuance of common stock. No definite sum for the engagement was agreed upon. Nikal proceeded at reasonable speed, but on November 10 he complained to Wade that the Corporation's staff was so inefficient and uncooperative that it might be impossible to meet the deadline. Wade said "Don't worry. I'll fix that." Nikal went on with his work, but the staff of the Corporation showed no improvement. Despite Nikal's reasonable efforts, the report was not ready until December 12. Wade, acting on behalf of the Corporation, refused to accept the report or pay for the accounting services since delivery of the report by November 30 was a condition of the contract and now it did not serve its intended purpose.

Required:

1. What legal problems are suggested by these facts? Discuss.

2. How should this transaction be reflected in the financial statements of American Philatelic Corporation at December 31, 1971?

Part d. Cobb and Claire, an accounting firm operating nationally over a long period of years with branch offices in all major cities and coverage of all major industrial areas in the United States, acquired the entire practice and goodwill of Wingfield and Lavender, another accounting firm operating nationally and with branch offices in all major cities. The price was to be paid in ten annual installments. The agreement provided that the five major partners of Wingfield and Lavender, both individually and as members of the accounting firm, were not to engage in practice anywhere in the United States for three years.

Required:

What legal problems are suggested by these facts? Discuss.

30. Identification of legal problems

Part a. Ultrasound, Inc., a closely held sound systems manufacturer, decided to offer its stock to the general public, and entered into an underwriting contract in which the investment banking firm of Fairweather, Reed and Wilson agreed to market the shares.

Fairweather later repudiated the contract when it discovered Ultrasound's "true" financial picture. Fairweather claimed that it had been induced to sign the contract by a misrepresentation as to the Corporation's income for the current period.

The facts disclosed that Fairweather had been given unaudited, condensed income statements prepared by Ultrasound's internal accountants showing income of $6 million for the first 9 months and $11 million for the entire year ending December 31, 1971. Thus Fairweather was led to believe that the remarkable increase in the last quarter's income was due to the enthusiastic consumer acceptance of Ultrasound's new line of sound systems.

More complete information that became available later revealed that Ultrasound's fourth quarter income had been only $800,000 and that the $4.2 million difference was due to a write-up of the finished goods inventory to selling price that had not been disclosed in the condensed statements. Upon discovering this, Fairweather promptly repudiated the underwriting agreement.

Required:

What legal problems are suggested by these facts? Explain.

Part b. Charles Worthington, the founding and senior partner of a successful and respected CPA firm, was a highly competent practitioner who always emphasized high professional standards. One of the policies of the Firm was that all reports by members or staff be submitted to Worthington for review.

Recently, Arthur Craft, a junior partner in the Firm, received a phone call from Herbert Flack, a close personal friend. Flack informed Craft that he, his family and some friends were planning to create a corporation to engage in various land development ventures; that various members of the family are presently in a partnership (Flack Ventures) which holds some land and other assets; and that the partnership would contribute all of its assets to the new corporation, and the corporation would assume the liabilities of the partnership.

Flack asked Craft to prepare a balance sheet of the partnership that he could show to members of his family, who were in the partnership, and friends to determine whether they might have an interest in joining in the formation and financing of the new corporation. Flack said he had the partnership general ledger in front of him and proceeded to read to Craft the names of the accounts and their balances at the end of the latest month. Craft took the notes he made during the telephone conversation with Flack, classified and organized the data into a conventional balance sheet and had his secretary type the balance sheet and an accompanying letter on Firm stationery. He did not consult Worthington on this matter or submit his work to him for review.

The transmittal letter stated: "We have reviewed the books and records of Flack Ventures, a partnership, and have prepared the attached balance sheet at March 31, 1972. We did not perform an examination in conformity with generally accepted auditing standards, and therefore do not express an opinion on the accompanying balance sheet." The balance sheet was prominently marked "unaudited." Craft signed the letter and instructed his secretary to sent it to Flack.

Required:

What legal problems are suggested by these facts? Explain.

Part c. Cragsmore & Company, a medium sized partnership of CPAs, was engaged by Marlowe Manufacturing, Inc., a closely held corporation, to examine its financial statements for the year ended December 31, 1971.

Prior to preparing the auditor's report William Cragsmore, a partner, and Fred Willmore, a staff senior, reviewed the disclosures necessary in the footnotes to the financial statements. One footnote involved the terms, costs and obligations of a lease between Marlowe and Acme Leasing Company.

Fred Willmore suggested that the footnote disclose the following: "The Acme Leasing Company is owned by persons who have a 35% interest in the capital stock and who are officers of Marlowe Manufacturing, Inc."

On Cragsmore's recommendation, this was revised by substituting "minority shareholders" for "persons who have a 35% interest in the capital stock and who are officers."

The auditor's report and financial statements were forwarded to Marlowe Manufacturing for review. The officer-shareholders of Marlowe who also owned Acme Leasing objected to the revised wording and insisted that the footnote be changed to describe the relationship between Acme and Marlowe as merely one of affiliation. Cragsmore acceded to this request.

The auditor's report was issued on this basis with an unqualified opinion. But the working papers included the drafts that showed the changes in the wording of the footnote.

Subsequent to delivery of the auditor's report, Marlowe suffered a substantial uninsured fire loss and has been forced into bankruptcy. The failure of Marlowe to carry any fire insurance coverage was not noted in the financial statements.

Required:

What legal problems are suggested by these facts for Cragsmore & Company? Discuss.